Handbook of Research on the Efficacy of Training Programs and Systems in Medical Education

Ruth Gotian
Weill Cornell Medicine, USA

Yoon Kang
Weill Cornell Medicine, USA

Joseph Safdieh
Weill Cornell Medicine, USA

A volume in the Advances in Medical Education, Research, and Ethics (AMERE) Book Series

Published in the United States of America by
IGI Global
Medical Information Science Reference (an imprint of IGI Global)
701 E. Chocolate Avenue
Hershey PA, USA 17033
Tel: 717-533-8845
Fax: 717-533-8661
E-mail: cust@igi-global.com
Web site: http://www.igi-global.com

Library of Congress Cataloging-in-Publication Data

Names: Gotian, Ruth, 1970- editor. | Kang, Yoon, 1969- editor. | Safdieh,
  Joseph E., editor.
Title: Handbook of research on the efficacy of training programs and
  systems in medical education / Ruth Gotian, Yoon Kang, Joseph Safdieh,
  editors.
Description: Hershey, PA : Medical Information Science Reference, [2020] |
  Includes bibliographical references and index. | Summary: "This book
  focuses on key considerations in medical curriculum and content delivery
  and features new methods of knowledge and skill transfer"--Provided by
  publisher"-- Provided by publisher.
Identifiers: LCCN 2019030802 (print) | LCCN 2019030803 (ebook) | ISBN
  9781799814689 (hardcover) | ISBN 9781799814696 (ebook)
Subjects: MESH: Education, Medical | Curriculum | United States
Classification: LCC R737 (print) | LCC R737 (ebook) | NLM W 18 | DDC
  610.71/1--dc23
LC record available at https://lccn.loc.gov/2019030802
LC ebook record available at https://lccn.loc.gov/2019030803

This book is published in the IGI Global book series Advances in Medical Education, Research, and Ethics (AMERE) (ISSN: 2475-6601; eISSN: 2475-661X)

British Cataloguing in Publication Data
A Cataloguing in Publication record for this book is available from the British Library.

For electronic access to this publication, please contact: eresources@igi-global.com.

Advances in Medical Education, Research, and Ethics (AMERE) Book Series

ISSN:2475-6601
EISSN:2475-661X

MISSION

Humans are living longer now than ever as a result of advances in the medical field. Having the tools available to train knowledgeable and ethical future generations of doctors and medical researchers is essential to continuing to advance our understanding of the human body and develop new ways of treating and curing sickness and disease.

The **Advances in Medical Education, Research, and Ethics (AMERE)** book series highlights publications pertaining to advancements in pedagogical practice for developing future healthcare professionals, research methods, and advancements in the medical field, as well as moral behavior and practice of healthcare professionals, students, and researchers. Featuring research-based book publications that are highly relevant to the healthcare community, this series is ideally designed for library inclusion at medical universities and research institutions as well as personal use by medical professionals, researchers, and upper-level students entering the field.

COVERAGE

- Clinical Research
- Conflicts of Interest
- Ethics in Medicine
- Healthcare Pedagogy
- Medical Curricula
- Medical Simulation
- Patient Data
- Professional Development
- Research Methods
- Scientific Misconduct

IGI Global is currently accepting manuscripts for publication within this series. To submit a proposal for a volume in this series, please contact our Acquisition Editors at Acquisitions@igi-global.com or visit: http://www.igi-global.com/publish/.

The Advances in Medical Education, Research, and Ethics (AMERE) Book Series (ISSN 2475-6601) is published by IGI Global, 701 E. Chocolate Avenue, Hershey, PA 17033-1240, USA, www.igi-global.com. This series is composed of titles available for purchase individually; each title is edited to be contextually exclusive from any other title within the series. For pricing and ordering information please visit http://www.igi-global.com/book-series/advances-medical-education-research-ethics/132365. Postmaster: Send all address changes to above address. © © 2020 IGI Global. All rights, including translation in other languages reserved by the publisher. No part of this series may be reproduced or used in any form or by any means – graphics, electronic, or mechanical, including photocopying, recording, taping, or information and retrieval systems – without written permission from the publisher, except for non commercial, educational use, including classroom teaching purposes. The views expressed in this series are those of the authors, but not necessarily of IGI Global.

Titles in this Series

For a list of additional titles in this series, please
https://www.igi-global.com/book-series/advances-medical-education-research-ethics/132365

Gender Equity in the Medical Profession
Maria Irene Bellini (Belfast Health and Social Care Trust, UK) and Vassilios E. Papalois (Imperial College London, UK)
Medical Information Science Reference • © 2020 • 339pp • H/C (ISBN: 9781522595991) • US $265.00

Preparing Physicians to Lead in the 21st Century
Valerie Anne Storey (University of Central Florida, USA) and Thomas Edward Beeman (University of Pennsylvania Health System, USA)
Medical Information Science Reference • © 2019 • 245pp • H/C (ISBN: 9781522575764) • US $245.00

Optimizing Medical Education With Instructional Technology
Erdem Demiroz (Trakya University, Turkey) and Steven D. Waldman (University of Missouri – Kansas City School of Medicine, USA)
Medical Information Science Reference • © 2019 • 291pp • H/C (ISBN: 9781522562894) • US $215.00

Exploring the Pressures of Medical Education From a Mental Health and Wellness Perspective
Christina Ramirez Smith (University of the Bahamas, Bahamas)
Medical Information Science Reference • © 2018 • 349pp • H/C (ISBN: 9781522528111) • US $225.00

Impact of Medical Errors and Malpractice on Health Economics, Quality, and Patient Safety
Marina Riga (Health Economist-Researcher, Greece)
Medical Information Science Reference • © 2017 • 334pp • H/C (ISBN: 9781522523376) • US $200.00

Advancing Medical Education Through Strategic Instructional Design
Jill Stefaniak (Old Dominion University, USA)
Medical Information Science Reference • © 2017 • 349pp • H/C (ISBN: 9781522520986) • US $205.00

Organizational Culture and Ethics in Modern Medicine
Anna Rosiek (Nicolaus Copernicus University in Toruń, Collegium Medicum in Bydgoszcz, Poland) and Krzysztof Leksowski (Nicolaus Copernicus University in Toruń, Collegium Medicum in Bydgoszcz, Poland)
Medical Information Science Reference • © 2016 • 448pp • H/C (ISBN: 9781466696587) • US $225.00

701 East Chocolate Avenue, Hershey, PA 17033, USA
Tel: 717-533-8845 x100 • Fax: 717-533-8661
E-Mail: cust@igi-global.com • www.igi-global.com

List of Contributors

Table of Contents

Section 5
Technology in Medical Education

Section 6
Student Voices

Detailed Table of Contents

Section 1
Administrative Processes: Accreditation and Admissions

Accreditation is a driving force in higher education that faces continually increasing scrutiny resulting from demands of the public. People want to be assured their doctors are well-trained and can care for them, their engineers are well-schooled and can design safe structures, and their lawyers have been well-educated to protect their interests. This chapter explores the history and importance of accreditation in medical education, provides guidelines and a timeline for accreditation, and looks at the effort required for success. The chapter also includes a glimpse at the process and the institutional commitment necessary to demonstrate and document a quality learning environment to the accrediting bodies.

Chapter 2

This chapter includes in-depth information on the medical school application process in the United States (US), the various admissions criteria and selection processes, and the range of interview and assessment modalities used to evaluate applicant competencies. It also provides information about the various pathways aspiring physicians may take to seek admission to medical school. In these sections, evidence is provided highlighting the work that has been done to better understand these areas. The chapter concludes with the important perspectives of an admissions committee chair and a pre-health advisor to further elucidate this complex process.

Chapter 3

Jan L. Reichard-Brown, Susquehanna University, USA
Lolita A. Wood-Hill, Yeshiva University, USA
Ellen M. Watts, Fordham University, USA

Undergraduate students from disadvantaged backgrounds can find the adjustment to college academics and other collegiate expectations confusing and disconcerting. They must learn to understand and navigate what has been referred to as the Hidden Curriculum: the ideas, norms, and expectations that are not overtly stated, but which the student must implicitly understand. These students don't even know what they don't know when they arrive on campus. This chapter focuses on aspects of the undergraduate hidden curriculum, particularly as they affect the career of the pre-medical student and the student's potential for becoming a competitive applicant to medical school. Several illustrative case studies are presented and analyzed in light of what is referred to as the Bachelors Hidden Curriculum (BHC). The chapter closes with a discussion of approaches that pre-medical advisors and student mentors may take to try to mitigate the impact of the BHC on these worthy students.

Section 2
Evolving Curricular Programming

Chapter 4

M. Renee Prater, The Edward Via College of Osteopathic Medicine, USA

Each generation is defined not solely by the date of their birth, but also for their beliefs, their priorities, and their motivations. Many factors play heavily into the development of each generation's collective identify, including parenting styles, significant political and current events, changing gender roles, and other formative experiences. These factors significantly and uniquely influence how each generation lives, learns, and interacts with others (Gerhardt, 2016). While most medical educators today are baby boomers, the majority of medical students are millennial and generation Z individuals, who communicate, learn, and interact very differently than their instructors. As a result, effective medical educators are challenged to update their methods of instruction to best suit these newer generations of learners for better assimilation, clinical application, and long-term retention of material, to maintain delivery of high-quality healthcare in the country for future generations (Desy et al., 2017; Waljee, 2018).

Chapter 5

Aaron L. Burshtein, Donald and Barbara Zucker School of Medicine at Hofstra/Northwell, USA
Joshua G. Burshtein, Donald and Barbara Zucker School of Medicine at Hofstra/Northwell, USA
Peter A. Gold, Donald and Barbara Zucker School of Medicine at Hofstra/Northwell, USA
Luke Garbarino, Donald and Barbara Zucker School of Medicine at Hofstra/Northwell, USA
David E. Elkowitz, Donald and Barbara Zucker School of Medicine at Hofstra/Northwell, USA

Medical education has undergone an evolution from passive, lecture-based learning environments to curricula that accentuate an active and dynamic system. Stemming from technological innovation, a greater amount of responsibility has been placed on students during clerkships and residency. In addition, a shift in USMLE assessment focuses on interpretation and application as compared to the former memorization-heavy approach. Therefore, learning has been modified to prepare students for the future medical landscape. Through the use of Team-Based, Problem-Based, and/or Case-Based Learning, medical students are taught to understand content rather than memorize it. The authors elucidate the rationale behind active learning and present a guide for medical educators to adopt this style of learning in every part of the undergraduate medical school training process.

Chapter 6

Susan Ely, California Health Sciences University College of Osteopathic Medicine, USA
Joanne H. Greenawald, Virginia Tech Carilion School of Medicine, USA
Richard C. Vari, Virginia Tech Carilion School of Medicine, USA

An account of 21st century problem-based learning (PBL) in preclinical medical education is provided through a detailed explanation of the overall process, a description of PBL case construction, and a brief consideration of related activities, including case wrap-up sessions and facilitator debriefing meetings. Composition of student PBL groups, the role of the faculty facilitator, and PBL decorum are also explored in this chapter. The implementation of PBL in a new medical school curriculum by rational design is compared to the introduction of PBL into an existing medical school curriculum by retrofit. Advantages and challenges of PBL are enumerated; a brief comparison of PBL with team-based learning (TBL) is also included.

Chapter 7

I. Michael Leitman, Icahn School of Medicine at Mount Sinai, USA
Brian Nickerson, Icahn School of Medicine at Mount Sinai, USA

Formal training in leadership development has become increasingly popular among physicians. There is a growing interest to provide this educational content to medical students and residents so that they will have these skills upon the start of their clinical or academic medical practice. It is possible to provide the proper management skills to medical trainees so they will have the opportunity to utilize and master these competences during their education. This chapter provides an overview of the available content and the literature to support the integration of this curriculum into formal undergraduate and graduate medical education. This chapter provides a template for the development of a longitudinal experience and the necessary proficiencies to allow trainees to develop as effective clinical leaders.

Chapter 8

Arthur L. Frank, Drexel University, USA

This chapter considers the role and value of the study of the humanities in medical education. Most authors on this subject believe the study of the humanities results in a better physician. However, few papers document this almost universally accepted idea. This chapter cites the available literature on the subject and also considers how the study of the humanities has become more common in countries beyond the United States. The study of the humanities is thought to improve physician communication and to influence ethical behaviors, ultimately improving patient care.

    Robin Arnsperger Selzer, University of Cincinnati, USA
    Rohan Srivastava, University of Cincinnati, USA
    Alexis Huckleberry, Vanderbilt University, USA

Medical education emphasizes cross-cultural training programs to meet the needs of diverse patients and understand social determinants of health as root causes leading to healthcare disparities. The question remains about how to best accomplish this in the curriculum. Students in pursuit of medical education need intercultural training early to examine implicit biases, treat the patient not just the disease, and become patient advocates before they practice. This chapter addresses critical issues related to the human side of healthcare. The Intercultural Development Inventory® (IDI®) and accompanying reflection prompts were administered to 40 pre-med students. Findings revealed students overestimated their intercultural understanding and 97.5% had monocultural mindsets. Six themes demonstrated how the IDI® can be used to develop critically reflective future healthcare providers: Reframing Reactions, Lack of Exposure to Other Cultures, Lack of Cultural Self-Awareness, Bi-cultural Identity and Fitting In, Healthcare Connections, and Diversity and University Opportunities.

    Vinita C. Kiluk, University of South Florida Morsani College of Medicine, USA
    Alina R. Zhu, University of South Florida Morsani College of Medicine, USA
    Antoinette C. Spoto-Cannons, University of South Florida Morsani College of Medicine, USA
    Dawn M. Schocken, University of South Florida Morsani College of Medicine, USA
    Deborah J. DeWaay, University of South Florida Morsani College of Medicine, USA

Across the nation, many medical schools have begun to include short courses during key transition points in the curriculum to help prepare students to succeed in the new area where they will be learning. This chapter introduces the reader to these "transition courses" that were not a part of medical education 20 years ago. These courses utilize combinations of high- and low-fidelity simulation, standardized patients, small group sessions, team-based learning and didactics. The authors explore four key transition areas that have seen an influx of these short courses: Orientation to Medical School, Return to Clerkship, Orientation to Clerkship, and Capstone or Boot camp. Each of these four courses is examined in content and relevance in preparing the medical student for the transition in their academic career.

    Andrea A. Anderson, The George Washington School of Medicine and Health Sciences, USA
    Yolanda C. Haywood, The George Washington School of Medicine and Health Sciences, USA
    Juliet Lee, The George Washington School of Medicine and Health Sciences, USA
    Claudia U. Ranniger, The George Washington School of Medicine and Health Sciences, USA
    Grace E. Henry, The George Washington School of Medicine and Health Sciences, USA

Transitions in medical school are a recognized point of stress for learners. Overall, stress is a known aspect of any period of transition, where the unknown looms large and new skills need to be acquired to achieve mastery of the next step. As the medical needs of the population grow, medical schools are admitting larger and more diverse classes. These students will undergo several major points of transition in their undergraduate medical education careers including the period of matriculation to the first year and the transition from the preclinical years into the clinical years. The George Washington School of Medicine has developed a longitudinal approach including two specific programs to support students during these recognized points of academic transition. The Prematriculation Program (PMP) and the Foundations of Clinical Practice course address the specific needs of these stages. The authors contend that an intentional approach to support students at periods of known academic risk is a beneficial aid to student success.

Chapter 12
    Emanuele Fino, Aston Medical School, UK
    Bishoy Hanna-Khalil, Aston Medical School, UK

Assessment in medical education has changed dramatically over the last two decades. The current, global call for medical practitioners has encouraged medical schools to open their doors and expand their curricula, generating an increasing demand for guidance with regards to the assurance and improvement of the quality of training programs and systems. This chapter provides the reader with an overview of psychometric post-examination analysis. The authors' view is that these are strategic educational assets that can help medical educators to understand and evidence the extent to which assessment data and their interpretation reflect the achievement of learning objectives, and the validity of assessment methods implemented in medical education programs.

Section 3
Models of Academic Support: Advising and Mentoring

Chapter 13
    Dawn Dillman, Oregon Health and Science University, USA
    Shoshana Zeisman-Pereyo, Oregon Health and Science University, USA

This chapter examines learning support models in undergraduate medical education. LCME requires robust system of student support for certification. Learning specialists with degrees in education are frequently in charge of leading student support systems. This may include tutoring programs, United States Medical Licensing Exam (USMLE), and other standardized exam preparation. Visibility and accessibility are key to the success of any support program. LCME also mandates both academic and career advising. Advising, mentoring, and coaching are often thought of as interchangeable terms. However, they each have unique implications and their applicability to medical education is explored. Learning communities are frequently used to enhance the delivery of the advising system. Specific examples are given.

Section 4
Professional Identity and Career Development Across the Continuum

Chapter 14

Stephanie Chervin, University of Michigan, USA
Mariella Mecozzi, University of Michigan, USA
David Brawn, University of Michigan, USA

The premedical baccalaureate period is critical to shaping a high-achieving, diverse, and service-oriented medical school applicant pool. The focus on achieving superior academic performance in premedical coursework captures the attention of most premedical students, but equal attention must be paid to developing the personal qualities and experiences that will form the foundation of their future capacity to understand and communicate with patients. Premedical students are best served to major in a field for authentic intellectual reasons regardless of the field's immediate connection to the health care field. There is a growing trend for applicants to have a gap year or more between the undergraduate period and medical school. The authors discuss the role of letters of evaluation and the premedical committee in the application process. The authors have more than 40 years of combined experience in premedical academic and career advising at a large, research-focused public institution.

Chapter 15

Amber J. Heck, TCU and UNTHSC School of Medicine, USA
Courtney E. Cross, TCU and UNTHSC School of Medicine, USA
Veronica Y. Tatum, TCU and UNTHSC School of Medicine, USA

Medical educators have long debated how to address one pivotal question: Which students will succeed in medical school? Traditionally, the approach to guaranteeing success in undergraduate medical education focused heavily on a rigorous admissions process. While student selection processes have evolved over time, so have the multiple categories of interventions to prepare students for success in medical school. These interventions are most often aimed at enhancing either academic or emotional preparedness in future or current students and are perhaps best described as early medical education readiness interventions. This chapter organizes these programs into the three overarching categories of preadmissions, prematriculation, and postmatriculation interventions, and will discuss the history and current landscape of each of these categories in detail. Further, the authors make recommendations for medical school administrators and directors of such programs to consider when designing their institutional approach to early medical education readiness interventions.

Chapter 16

Sophia Chen, Rutgers New Jersey Medical School, USA
Christin Traba, Rutgers New Jersey Medical School, USA
Sangeeta Lamba, Rutgers New Jersey Medical School, USA
Maria Soto-Greene, Rutgers New Jersey Medical School, USA

This chapter reviews the steps for professional and career development of medical students. While the two overlap, there are distinct differences in preparation of students for lifelong professional vs. career development. Professional development involves professional/social identity as well as professional competence. Authors describe curricular implementation to help students achieve professional competence, including specific tools to form professional/social identities and recognize unconscious biases, essential for personal growth, psychological health, and successful careers of future physicians. In parallel to professional development, career specific advising must start in Year 1 of medical school as well. This chapter delineates the differences in academic vs. career advising, advising versus counseling, and a stepwise approach by medical school year to help guide students to their ultimate career path exploring career specialties to choosing one and ultimately preparing for residency.

Chapter 17

Medical residents have a growing responsibility to educate their fellow residents and serve as the primary teachers for medical students; however, many residents have reported lacking the skills needed to be effective teachers. Clinical educator tracks (CET) were designed to provide a more intense and diverse opportunity for residents to receive training in areas of learning theory, teaching, evaluation and assessment, curriculum design, research, and leadership. This chapter highlights promising practices in established CET programs in the United States and spotlights one CET program in Louisiana as an example. Based on a review of the literature, CET programs have the following promising practices in common: a commitment to teaching and learning, continuous improvement through program design and evaluation, and a focus on leadership and mentoring. The authors elaborate on the CET program at LSU Health Center and discuss future trends in CET programming.

Chapter 18

The changing landscape of medical practice, the explosion of medical knowledge, and the introduction of new technologies and teaching methods have impelled a re-examination of the various roles of the medical educator. This chapter examines each of those roles -- content expert, competency expert, role model, teacher of critical thinking, promoter of life-long learning, patient educator -- from both a historical and modern perspective. The overall requirements for faculty development are described and, for each of the educator's roles, specific faculty development suggestions are put forth to meet the evolving needs of modern medical educators.

Continuing professional development is a critical responsibility within the complex role of today's physician. This chapter provides an overview of continuing professional development for physicians. The authors propose self-determination theory (SDT) as a foundational framework for discussing physician continuing professional development. They also address a variety of motivating factors for physicians being involved in continuing professional development. These factors include regulatory requirements, continued competence, career planning, and their own commitment to learn. Lastly, the authors include a discussion of various continuing professional development formats and the benefits of each, as well as challenges and barriers to effective continuing education.

Section 5
Technology in Medical Education

This chapter analyzes the role played by technology in undergraduate medical education (UME) using two perspectives: how technology is used as a tool to facilitate teaching and how medical students are taught to use technology in the clinical setting. For each perspective, a survey of literature, published from 2009 to 2019, was conducted to understand the current state. Authors critically examine the current state and describe and analyze issues with it. Recommendations are made for improving the blending of medical education, technology, pedagogy, and clinical practice. The narrative in this chapter is at the intersection of digital technology, educational theories, and medical settings (educational and practice).

Chapter 21

This chapter presents an assessment of the rapidly evolving state of health-related technology and its developing impact on health care, medical education, patient care, and care delivery. This is collectively referred to as the digital health movement in medicine. This chapter provides a broader understanding of how digital health is changing not only the practice of medicine, but the consumer market that pertains to health care and medicine at large. The authors discuss the current state of digital health in medicine, the challenges of conventionally assessing digital health-related competencies, and the relative difficulty of adapting contemporary medical education to include digital health modalities into traditional undergraduate medical education. This chapter also showcases three unique case studies of early-adopting medical institutions that have created digital health learning opportunities for their undergraduate medical student population.

Chapter 22

The Liaison Committee on Medical Education (LCME) requires that medical schools track compliance and continuous quality improvement (CQI) efforts across a broad range of LCME standards. However, LCME does not state what form these tracking efforts should take, or how medical schools should represent this information to the Committee or internally. This chapter provides an overview of the Keck School of Medicine of the University of Southern California's (KSOM) new approach to CQI tracking using an online dashboard. The project resulted in an online platform that represents the CQI project progress across a range of elements, maintains visual consistency across a range of data sources and file types, and is easily accessible by relevant stakeholders. This innovation from KSOM illustrates how a web-based platform supports CQI efforts, and how this design can be translated to other contexts. The design presented in this chapter provides guidelines for the development and innovation of CQI tracking initiatives at other schools.

Chapter 23

Surgical education has been compressed by integrated residency programs and restrictions on the number of hours surgical residents are allowed to work. Instilling basic technical skills as early as the first year of medical school can help maximize preparedness for surgical rotation and residency. This overview includes a detailed description of low, medium, and high-fidelity simulation-based training techniques and recommends introduction of surgical simulation early in the medical school curriculum. A personal vignette highlights this recommendation.

Section 6
Student Voices

Chapter 24

This reflection chapter is from the perspective of the first-year medical student: teetering the line between the naïveté of embarking into an ambiguous future and the wisdom developing in the midst of self discovery. From the early moments of dissecting in the anatomy lab to making decisions about which content to study further during spare time, the first year of medical school sets the stage for collecting signs and symptoms into a diagnosis and a plan. This lens extends into steps for self-reflection: outline values and current needs (akin to taking your own history); reflect on interests and skills (identifying signs); consider the roles of a physician in society (coming up with a differential for who you might become); identify opportunities for the future (crafting an action plan); seek out connections with other students, trainees, and physicians (assembling a team). In this way, students can be encouraged to take a moment to center themselves in the way they will for the patients under their care to make sense of it all.

The author describes his journey of learning in medicine from childhood through graduation from medical school. The author describes how each of his mentors played a specific role at crucial points in his development. His parents and a high school professor inspired him to pursue medicine as a career. Academic, clinical, and research mentors assisted in the author's preparation for medical school. Finally, medical school faculty and staff at Weill Cornell Medicine enriched his medical school experience, guided his choice of psychiatry as a specialty, and encouraged him to think about the structure of his future career. The author gratefully emphasizes the importance of all of his mentors' efforts and resolves to serve a similar mentorship role for the next generation of physicians.

Chapter 26

The most influential assignment of the author's career was the first assignment in his first undergraduate class: take a picture and describe it in a thousand words. From there, the author found a way to spend each semester of college writing about the photo essays by Robert Frank and Brassai, exploring surrealistic works by Jorge Luis Borges and Federico Garcia Lorca, or pursing artistic musings. Given the author's enthusiasm for creative pursuits, his standing as an MD/PhD student may come as a surprise. However, creative courses served as outlets from his medical school prerequisite-heavy course load. The author craved their self-guided and exploratory approach. This craving grew to incorporate an interest in research. What follows is the tortuous route that led the author to join an MD/PhD program.

Chapter 27

Finding meaning in this age of the burnout epidemic has become the latest obsession in clinical medicine. Many choose introspection, mindfulness, or mental health treatments to refuel their moral reserves, but research may also help to serve that goal. In this chapter, the author writes about his journey as an immigrant to the United States at 16, navigating the educational system to eventually attend Oxford and Harvard on full scholarships, and finding meaning through research.

Foreword

It is my great pleasure to have been invited by the editors to write the Forward for this book *Handbook of Research on the Efficacy Training Programs and Systems in Medical Education,* as I wind down from the formal administrative duties in my forty-year career as a general internist, medical educator, and senior medical education administrator at Weill Cornell Medical College (WCM). I contribute this Forward to publicly introduce this exciting new compendium of writings on a number of topical subjects reflective of and critical to the field of medical education, and also, in part, to reflect on the unique context of this book from the privileged view I have had of the fascinating world of medical education during my career. Although there are many excellent books covering aspects of medical school education and administration, this book is unique in its longitudinal perspective, covering important milestones from pipeline programs and admissions, to curricular administration and transition courses. It also includes a focus on the professional identity formation of a physician, a core principle of the landmark 2010 report from the Carnegie Foundation for the Advancement of Teaching (Cooke et al., 2010). This book is intended to serve a wide range of audiences, from potential medical student applicants to medical school faculty and administrators who plan to incorporate some aspect of medical education into their careers. Its purpose is to introduce the reader to the excitement, processes and procedures, innovation, challenges, and future promise that the field of medical education presents to all who engage in its activities.

First a bit of background to frame the context of this book. In spite of its critical importance to the training of future physicians and scientists, the many component parts of the field of medical education are unfamiliar territory to many people. As a field, the wide scope and the many domains within medical education are most visible to those who directly engage in it: medical student applicants, medical students who journey through the programs to graduate, the faculty, staff, and administrators of medical schools, and to physicians in academic health care settings. However, even for those who complete medical school, the challenges, processes, and competition for medical schools to succeed in programmatic development, excellent student outcomes, innovation, educational scholarship, learner assessment, and learner appreciation within each area of medical education are not explicitly apparent. This book introduces a discussion of many of these important aspects, which, while not usually described in one resource, critically underlie the strengths of the medical education experience.

Of course, a critical component of medical education programs are the medical students themselves. This book uniquely provides the student perspective, navigating through the complexities of the admissions process and how to approach medical school once accepted.

The reader can enjoy direct student contributions describing and reflecting on their journey in medical education, and also learn about the highly selective nature of the applicant pool to medical school, the preparation that is expected of medical student applicants, and the importance of recruiting diverse student bodies to medical schools to achieve both individual medical school missions and to train a work force that is fully equipped to take on the broad challenges of culturally competent patient care and ethical research and education in the future. In addition, included in this book is the complex and important topic of supporting medical students through the educational program in order to reach their career aspirations. The book explores the importance of mentoring and presenting an enriched learning environment, integrated with the science curriculum, along with mandatory offerings in culture and the humanities as elements that allow students to thrive in their training and serve as healthy contributors to the future of medicine. Included are both MD and MD-PhD student stories written by actual students about the bumpy road to medical school, filled with twists, turns and hidden corners. They are very authentic and transparent in their stories and give appropriate recognition to the importance of their support system and mentors.

When I joined Cornell Medical University Medical College (now WCM) as a newly minted internist in 1980, I knew that I wanted medical education to be a major part of my career aspirations. It was important to me to help educate those who came after me, and I was intrigued with the learning process of becoming a doctor. How do you package learning material best and convey it to the learner effectively? How do you get trainees to learn better and faster and acquire expertise? How do you measure different educational outcomes, student skill performance, or even determine how to weigh the wide variety of curricular offerings in medical schools across the nation? At that time, finding experts to mentor me in that career choice were few and far between. I had to look outside of my medical college, to national organizations such as the Society of General Internal Medicine and the Association for American Medical Colleges to develop my knowledge base, skill set, and understanding of innovative programmatic and scholarly activities. Essentially, I had to learn how to become an effective medical educator and administrator. Thus, an ongoing challenge is producing the next generation of high level medical educators. This book discusses the challenges in grooming and developing skilled medical educator faculty, fully cognizant of the existing and considerable evidence that merely being a content expert in your medical or scientific field does not mean you can teach that content well to learners. This book discusses this important challenge that faces every medical school today.

Since the days of my early professional development, medical education has finally been recognized and voiced as a major mission of a medical college, along with clinical care and medical research. The lag in that recognition will seem counterintuitive to most lay people until one understands that, from an institutional perspective, medical education, unlike clinical care and medical research, does not provide medical schools with a revenue stream such as patient care reimbursement monies and research grant monies. Some will find it interesting to know that the vast majority of medical school faculty members are not directly paid to teach medical students—it is considered a duty of their faculty appointment. Because of this, through the 1980's and 1990's, with the slumping of National Institutes of Health and other grant funding sources, the pressures on faculty to sustain their professional compensation through research and clinical patient care competed with the uncompensated time spent teaching medical students. This led to faculty concentrating on clinical care and research, often at the expense of their teaching duties. In addition, medical schools in the US and Canada must be accredited by the Liaison Committee on Medical Education (LCME), which is charged with developing the procedural and programmatic standards with which medical schools must comply. The time it takes to develop and implement the processes and systems for compliance also takes up considerable valuable faculty time. Only recently have medical schools realized the importance of providing sufficient incentives for faculty to devote their time and careers to the heavy teaching loads and program coordinating and leadership activities required to produce physicians. This book provides insight into the demands of the accreditation process, its impact on medical education, and the tensions inherent in supporting the careers of medical educators today.

And then there is the competition to build and implement innovative medical educational curriculum, sufficient to maintain a competitive edge for the school to attract the best and brightest medical student applicants. A number of significant writings over time and periodically since 1910, and especially in the 1990's and in this century (Flexner, 1910) have provided the basis for the content, format, and scope of curricular and extracurricular adjunctive activities of the program leading to the MD degree. In conjunction with accreditation standards, these writings have shaped modern educational programs today, including faculty-student interactions, faculty incentives, and academic promotion activities. This book explores the challenges and competition faced by schools to incorporate modern learning theories, develop activated learning formats, create innovative curricula, apply new educational technologies, and critically analyze the outcomes of educational programs. The chapter on psychometric evaluation of assessments is expertly written and covers the topic extremely well.

Finally, the contributors to this book are an inclusive, geographically and culturally diverse group of experts in their domains of medical education who write from their observations, personal experience, and current attention to the standards, policies and procedures that pertain to their area of expertise. To identify authors for this book, the editors used their extensive and divergent networks ranging from pre-health advisors, education deans, medical educator and student networks, with the specific goal of obtaining as many diverse authors as possible, with diversity defined as gender, ethnicity, geography and type of institution (private or public). There are 69 authors (42 women, 27 men, and 6 from groups underrepresented in medicine) contributing to this outstanding work with 39 institutions represented from across the country. The student authors provide expert descriptions of their personal experiences in medical education, and the faculty contributors represent the range of domains that are most active in the field at this time. The combination of the authors' perspectives provides a unique 360-degree insight into the many different aspects of medical education. It simultaneously provides both an impressive overview of topics but also delves into sufficient detail to provide the reader with deeper understanding. The editors aimed to identify best practices and modernize the continued national dialogue about major challenges and opportunities that exist for medical schools to this very day. I believe that they have succeeded in achieving their goal.

So now it is time for the reader to sit back and enjoy, explore, and learn about the complicated world of medical education from a wide variety of perspectives and expertise. This journey will provide deep insight into the challenges, issues and future promise for the training of our health care professionals. It is hoped that it will also excite, encourage, and inform those who find themselves interested in medical education, and serve as a resource for all who engage in this noble venture.

Respectfully submitted:

Carol L. Storey-Johnson
Weill Cornell Medicine, USA

REFERENCES

Boyer, E. L. (1990). Scholarship Reconsidered: Priorities of the Professoriate. The Carnegie Foundation for the Advancement of Teaching. San Francisco, CA: Jossey-Bass.

Cooke, M., Irby, D. M., & O'Brien, B. C. (2010). Educating Physicians: A Call for Reform of Medical School and Residency, The Carnegie Foundation for the Advancement of Teaching. San Francisco, CA: Jossey-Bass.

Curry, L., & Wergin, J. F. (1993). Educating Professionals. San Francisco, CA: Jossey-Bass.

Flexner, A. (1910). *Medical Education in the United States and Canada: A Report to The Carnegie Foundation for the Advancement of Teaching*. Boston, MA: The Merrymount Press.

Preface

Having worked together within the same institution for 15 years, we recognized that we each held knowledge and experience in unique sectors of the intricate mosaic that comprises the medical education mission. The cornerstone of the mission are the students, faculty, administration, the education program itself, and both internal and external processes and dynamics in the modern world of biomedical science and healthcare delivery. Multiple energetic conversations before and after meetings fueled the germ of the idea for us to combine our collective knowledge and network in order to form this comprehensive book on medical education. Together, we planned on tackling the multi-dimensional world of medical education, finding core denominators and themes to produce a book, which could be used as a personal and institutional reference and faculty development tool.

Together, we have nearly 60 years of combined experience in medical education. We recognized that while we had overlapping expertise, we each held a passion for a different element of medical education. As three academic deans at Weill Cornell Medicine, we recognized that we were in a unique position to leverage our excitement, experience and broad network to produce a book on medical education.

Medicine and science is an ever-expanding field, with each generation required to acquire a wider and deeper breadth of knowledge and skills. Current expansions in knowledge and technology dictate that we cannot continue to educate in the same manner we've been doing for decades. Students today represent even more diverse upbringings, backgrounds, and expectations and interface with technology at the earliest levels of their social and educational experience. As medical educators, we must learn to understand our students fully, enhance their learning and use all of the tools at our disposal, including, and especially, those mediums we weren't trained with during our own education.

Technology and team learning play an integral part in medical education today in everything from flipped classrooms to evaluations. Measuring the quality of our work is pivotal as is ensuring the development and wellbeing of our faculty and students. Multiple programs continue to develop in order to meet these critical functions.

This book is a manual of sorts to help readers navigate dilemmas, new opportunities and hidden meanings. It is designed to open our minds to perspectives and ideas, which might broaden our own. We are all perpetually learning and this is another opportunity in life for all of us to learn together and independently.

When conceiving this book, we aimed at having authors as diverse as the tapestry of the medical profession. We specifically cast a wide net in order to find the experts and thought leaders in various aspects of the field. In order to obtain a diverse author pool, one of our first unanimous decisions was to find authors who represented the gender, ethnicity, geography and type of institutions that participate in medical education. We feel we have reached our goal. Our 27 chapters, written by 69 collective authors represent 39 institutions in both the United States and Europe. Perspectives of state, private, Ivy League and independent organizations are expressed. In total, 61% of the authors are female and we estimate 9% are underrepresented minorities. The diversity of our authors and institutions provide rich and varied perspectives, which we feel strengthens the collective narrative and provides a more robust overview of our field.

Our initial goal was to have an edited book with 10-12 chapters, based on themes we are faced with in our professional roles. These include topics we are often asked to present in public forums, spend significant parts of our days working on, as well as major challenges and opportunities our faculty often have questions, issues or concerns about. Early on in our process, it became apparent that more chapters were warranted as there was so much more to delve into. Even with 27 chapters, medical education is so far reaching and evolving that despite best efforts, it could never be all-inclusive.

In short, we put together a book we wished we had as a reference when we were starting our journey as educators and as we took on additional responsibilities. We asked the authors to be authentic in their voice and they rose to the occasion. They wrote about achievements, challenges, mistakes that were made and opportunities lost and gained. The nuances and unspoken expectations were highlighted with as much emphasis as written guidelines. The authors wrote with gratitude to their mentors, the professionals who came before them, and the generation who will follow in their footsteps. Mentors opened doors and created opportunities for many of our authors. Hearing their stories was encouraging, uplifting and a reminder to all of us to lift others up as we move up our own career ladder.

Overview of Subject Matter

In the United States, 176 medical schools (141 MD and 35 DO), 400 teaching hospitals as well as its more than 173,000 faculty members, 89,000 medical students and 129,000 resident trainees encompass the field of medical education. This field is a $25.9 billion industry and it is steadily increasing. While there are journals devoted to medical education, little has been written in a comprehensive manner about the various facets of medical education including its programs, training, preparation and administrative models. The content of medical education knowledge transfer is compounded as medical breakthroughs impacting treatment and disease are discovered at an increasingly rapid pace. While much of knowledge transfer remains unchanged through the generations, there are unique hallmarks to this generation's learning, ranging from the impact of technology on learning formats to the use of standardized patients and virtual reality in the classroom.

This book on medical education is comprehensive and provides a 360-degree view of medical education, specifically undergraduate medical education, also known as 'medical school' and the preparatory training both before and during medical school. It will take the reader on a journey of a student as they prepare and go through medical school to become a novice practitioner and medical professional as well as a lifelong learner. The evolving landscape the faculty must traverse is dissected and examined. Those who teach are constantly learning to find new ways to deliver meaningful information in effective and efficient formats.

Key considerations in medical curriculum and content delivery, such as lectures, blended learning and simulations are the foundation of this book. It also examines new methods of knowledge and skill transfer and solidification, including team based learning and standardized patients. The road to diversifying the physician pool is explored complete with preparatory programs and the challenges of hidden curriculums, the unspoken rules and nuances students are meant to know. The book features major and high profile issues in medical education as well as emerging topics.

This book provides a comprehensive and transparent look into the professional identity development of physicians and the components parts of this process. The journey is long and involves hundreds of people to develop every single physician. Little has been researched on the impact of many of the content delivery methods, programs and systems. Our hope is that this book will start a national dialogue that will lead to further investigation into the process and impact of the training programs and systems provided in medical education. As we study markers of success in physicians and scientists (RG), oversee quality control and education within medical education (YK) and training of physicians (JS), the content of this book will help us further our collective research which may eventually lead to the altering and optimization of how physicians are trained.

Audience

Our goal with this book is that it will serve as an important resource for educators and learning practitioners working within medical education, a number that is steadily on the rise. With a national call for additional physicians, more medical schools are opening their doors. This book will serve as a vital resource to new and established medical educators, those who are looking to build something new as well as those who are looking to reimagine their standard way of practice. This book will serve as a history and benchmark for those working within the field and will influence how learning is facilitated.

Overview of the Content

The 27 chapters are broken up into six main categories, which provide the underpinnings to the complex and intricate nuances that make up the field of undergraduate medical education.

The first theme is Administrative Processes: Accreditation and Admissions. Chapter 1 discusses accreditation with an eye toward the high level impact and role that the accreditation processes and requirements can play in shaping the medical education mission.

Chapters 2 and 3 discuss the various facets of admissions from the preparation in the undergraduate years through the actual application to medical school. Issues of hidden curriculum, cost and unspoken nuances are elucidated.

The second, and our largest, theme is Evolving Curricular Programming. Chapters 4-12 discuss the medical school curriculum and the assessment of mastery of new knowledge. Medical school encompasses both a basic science and a clinical curriculum, which is taught in both lecture, and small group formats with experiential learning to underscore the application of acquired knowledge. Chapters 4 and 5 explore how to teach the newest generation of medical students and fully engage them in the learning material. Chapter 6 considers the pros and cons of problem-based learning, a tool that's been utilized in medical education for the last quarter-century.

Medical education in this century goes far beyond teaching clinical and basic science. Today management skills are introduced into the curriculum, as discussed in Chapter 7 and humanities, Chapter 8, are becoming more commonplace.

Impacting the human side of healthcare is revealed in Chapter 9 while opportunities for transition courses are revealed in Chapters 10 and 11. Medical education is taught at an extremely rapid pace and keeping up newly acquired knowledge requires extensive assessments, which are discussed in chapter 12.

Models of Academic Support, Advising and Mentoring is the next theme. The myriad avenues to support and advise students academically, socially and mentally are reviewed in Chapter 13. As the journey to medical school is increasingly competitive and the sheer vastness of information medical students need to learn at unprecedented paces require all those who oversee medical students to be open to and advocates of student wellbeing in its many forms. Advising and mentoring students today, who have so much information at their fingertips, requires more contemporary approaches. With student burnout on the rise, processes and procedures must be in place to support students when they need it most.

The fourth theme of the book is the Professional Identity and Career Development Across the Continuum, discussed in Chapters 14-19. The sheer fund of knowledge coupled with the changing landscape of both the physician workforce and the students, requires us to continually develop our faculty and students alike. Preparation for medical school from the premedical years through medical school is discussed in Chapters 14-16. A unique opportunity for residency training, specifically the clinical educator is explored in Chapter 17. Chapters 18 and 19 identify key approaches to this critical topic of continuous education and development for our colleagues and the next generation of physicians.

One of the biggest changes in medical education in recent years is the use of technology in teaching and learning. The latest generation of physicians has embraced technological advancements. As such, the fifth theme of our book is Technology in Medical Education. Chapters 20-23 explore the uses of technology in medical education and how it has evolved over time and potential uses for the future. The chapters explain how the use of technology has evolved as a teaching and learning tool and how to use dashboards as a source of continuous quality improvement. Finally, simulation used as a tool for practice and reinforcement of knowledge is described in Chapter 23.

This book was written and peer-reviewed by education professionals and edited by three academic deans. We felt the voices of students were vital to give this book the authentic viewpoint that was required. Medical and MD-PhD students at different segments of their training look back and forward in Chapters 24 through 27 and share, most genuinely, what they learned about the process and themselves while identifying mentors who helped shape the course of their lives.

This book offers an inside look at the full spectrum of medical education from the early college years and all through medical school. It provides an overview of everything from advising and preparation for different types of students, evolving curriculum, teaching methods, assessments, technological resources and accreditation. We put this book together with the thought that it will be a resource for those entering the field and seasoned professionals. By combining our areas of expertise and network, we were able to offer a comprehensive book on medical education.

The process was enjoyable and a learning opportunity for all of us. We really enjoyed working together and learning about each other in the process. We hope you derive as much pleasure in delving into thought-provoking perspectives and content as we have in the process of collaborating and editing to produce it.

Enjoy!

Ruth Gotian
Weill Cornell Medicine, USA

Yoon Kang
Weill Cornell Medicine, USA

Joseph Safdieh
Weill Cornell Medicine, USA

Acknowledgment

We would like to acknowledge our dean, Dr. Augustine M.K. Choi, who has fostered a culture of mentorship, wellbeing, and a diverse medical center community. His visionary leadership has enhanced the academic and interpersonal climate at our institution and his commitment to the needs of medical students and the power of inclusion inspired us as we considered the scope and authorship of this book. We would also like to acknowledge the authors of the chapters, who have also ably served as peer reviewers of other chapters.

Ruth Gotian would like to thank her friends, colleagues and co-editors Drs. Yoon Kang and Joe Safdieh for being so dedicated to our collective vision and doing their part to hold us all accountable. Working with you has been a journey of a lifetime and I am enriched because of our work together. Ruth is grateful to Drs. Hugh Hemmings and Kane Pryor for their support and valuable tips along the way. A special and enormous thank you to Amnon, Benjamin, Jonathan and Ethan "Eitan" Gotian, for their steadfast support and encouragement; today and always.

Yoon Kang would also like to thank her co-editors for their wise and thoughtful engagement in this work. She also thanks Dean Choi for his clear dedication to the success of the education mission and Carol Storey-Johnson for her longstanding friendship and exemplary role modeling. Yoon is also very grateful to her family, particularly to her daughter Alexis, as an endless source of the support, patience, and joy that fuel all of her passions and pursuits.

Joe Safdieh would like to thank his chairperson, Dr. Matthew Fink, who has created a culture of educational achievement in the Weill Cornell Department of Neurology. Joe also offers a huge thanks to his spouse Nathan, and amazing children, Lori and Eddie who have served as sources of support and inspiration.

Finally, we would like to thank our world class medical students, to whom we dedicate this book.

Section 1

Administrative Processes: Accreditation and Admissions

Chapter 1
US Medical School Accreditation:
Approach and Process

Bonnie M. Granat

SUNY Downstate College of Medicine, USA

ABSTRACT

Accreditation is a driving force in higher education that faces continually increasing scrutiny resulting from demands of the public. People want to be assured their doctors are well-trained and can care for them, their engineers are well-schooled and can design safe structures, and their lawyers have been well-educated to protect their interests. This chapter explores the history and importance of accreditation in medical education, provides guidelines and a timeline for accreditation, and looks at the effort required for success. The chapter also includes a glimpse at the process and the institutional commitment necessary to demonstrate and document a quality learning environment to the accrediting bodies.

ACCREDITATION: A HISTORY

Accreditation is a driving force in higher education, which faces continually increasing scrutiny from demands of the public. People want to be assured that their doctors are well trained and can care for them, that their engineers are well schooled and can design safe structures, and that their lawyers have been well educated to protect their interests (Eaton, 2015).

The standards put forth by the accrediting bodies are designed to guide schools to provide quality education and help institutions keep pace with societal needs (Hegji, 2017). It is safe to say that educational administrators always have accreditation standards in mind as they consider curricula, policy, and procedural changes. The author has often been asked about the origins of organizations that accredit schools, so this chapter presents some history.

Not surprisingly, the structures of U.S. colleges and universities have their roots in England and Scotland. Schools like Oxford University and Cambridge University served as models for our academic organizations with one significant difference; our colonial colleges were granted the power to award

DOI: 10.4018/978-1-7998-1468-9.ch001

degrees. In England, this authority was awarded and centralized by the Privy Council, a formal advisory board to the Monarch (Seldon,1962; Hegji, 2017).

In the early years of United States' independence, the autonomy to grant degrees resulted in colleges and universities that came and went rather quickly and had widely varying requirements for admissions and graduation. In terms of stability, many institutions were ill-equipped to manage financial strains, competition, internal stresses, natural disasters, and unfavorable locations. As a result, over 80% of educational institutions founded before the Civil War were no longer in existence by the early 1900's (Seldon, 1962; Hegji,2017).

The lack of cohesion amongst admissions and graduation requirements created challenges for higher education on all fronts. Some colleges were more like high schools, and it was difficult to evaluate what constituted adequate learning to be awarded a degree. Recognizing the need for some level of congruency but at the same time not wanting governmental restrictions, colleges and universities began to devise their own system of policing themselves. In some cases, existing organizations took on the charge and served as starters for new groups who would establish guidelines (Seldon, 1962).

Early institutions, such as The New England Association (1885) which was formed by a group of schoolmasters of secondary schools, the Middle States Association (formed in 1887), Southern Association (formed in 1895 by Vanderbilt University), and the North Central Association (formed in 1895 in the Midwest), pushed for clarity of mission and purpose in higher education (Thelin, 2011). Shortly thereafter, the Northwest Association of Secondary and Higher Schools (the predecessor of the two organizations that now serve that region) was formed in 1917, and the Western Association was founded in 1923 (Harcleroad & Eaton, 2005). Initially, the main focus of these organizations was on accreditation of secondary schools and establishment of uniform college entrance requirements. (Harcleroad & Eaton, 2005)

In considering this historical information, one may be inclined to believe that America's rocky start in higher education must have been different in medical education, but it was not. In fact, the history of medical schools runs in complete parallel with the past of the nation's colleges and universities (Seldon, 1962).

Establishment of Accreditation Guidelines

The two organizations that led the charge to develop standards in allopathic medicine were the American Medical Association (AMA), founded in 1845, and the Association of American Medical Colleges (AAMC), founded in 1876. However, medical schools sprouted up so quickly that there were concerns about the whole enterprise. By 1880, there were 100 medical schools, by 1890 there were 133. By the late nineteenth century, 161 allopathic medical schools were educating medical students, and the first osteopathic medical school was established shortly thereafter in 1892 (Cook, 2006; Ludmerer,1996). By 1898, a number of osteopathic colleges had been established. However, there was a lack of standardization in the admission and graduation requirements of these schools as well. With deficits in medical training recognized early on, some standards were proffered. But it wasn't until 1910 when Abraham Flexner wrote his influential report, which included a conceptual model of how modern medical education should be conducted, that things began to change.

A disciple of John Dewey (my personal education hero), Abraham Flexner, was recruited by a group of men who called themselves the Hopkins Circle, named by William Welch, the Dean at Johns Hopkins University. Flexner, a teacher and rather well-known expert on educational practices, was the only non-physician in the group. The group tasked Flexner to evaluate the quality of the 155 medical schools in the United States and Canada. In Flexner's view, only 31 of the schools he visited were worthy of remaining in operation (1910). The actions of state medical licensing boards to deny recognition to poor schools eventually sealed their fate (Duffy, 2011).

Flexner made several general recommendations – most notable was the expansion of both the laboratory component in the first two years and the practical hospital experiences in the third and fourth years. Flexner subscribed to the Dewey's philosophy of learning by doing (1900), and espoused that medical schools should operate such that "students no longer merely watch, listen, and memorize, but be actively involved in the learning of medicine". In addition, he encouraged experience with dissection, the actual looking at the body, while students are in medical school (Duffy, 2011).

Flexner also emphasized, "scientific inquiry and discovery, not past traditions and practice, should point the way to the future in both medicine and medical education (1910)." Many of the tenants of Flexner's academic model of American medical education are still significant and present in today's medical pedagogy. Flexner's report transformed the nature and process of medical education and became the basis for both allopathic and osteopathic accreditation processes (Duffy, 2011; Cook, 2006).

From their inception, the AMA and AAMC kept themselves separate with the AMA representing physicians' professional interests and AAMC focusing on medical education, but the entry of the United States into World War II spurred an alliance. Just two and a half months after the bombing at Pearl Harbor, the two groups hurriedly convened (Kessebaum, 1992; AMA History, 2019; About AAMC, 2019; LCME, 2019). The national crisis created by the entry of the United States into the war was going to impact the field of medicine, and the groups had two concerns. First, they discussed protecting medical students from the Selective Service Act: and second, they evaluated schools to see if they could meet demands the war put on them for shorter, accelerated medical training (Kessebaum, 1992; AMA, History 2019; AAMC, 2019; LCME, 2019).

To accomplish their goals, these two organizations created the Liaison Committee on Medical Education (LCME). The LCME charge was immediately evident: to create standards for medical education. From the very beginning, the LCME recognized the gravity of their responsibility (Kessebaum, 1992). Since 1942, the LCME has provided guidelines and support for medical education and has ensured high educational standards through rigorous accreditation (Kessebaum, 1992).

Osteopathic educators and leaders also quickly recognized that the attainment and maintenance of high educational standards was essential. By 1902, the American Osteopathic Association provided machinery for the inspection and approval of osteopathic colleges. This commitment to ensure cohesion existed in many forms throughout the history of osteopathic medical education. Osteopathic schools developed their own accrediting body, the Commission on Osteopathic College Accreditation (COCA), which closely parallels the LCME (Gevitz, 2019).

Eventually, regional and national accreditors were established across the United States in the late nineteenth century. Federal recognition of accrediting agencies was initiated in 1952, shortly after the passage of the Veterans' Readjustment Assistance Act (the GI Bill), to assess higher education quality and link it to determining which institutions would qualify to receive federal aid. However, rather than creating its own system of quality assurance, the federal government opted to rely on existing accrediting agencies (Hegji, 2017).

Today, there are three main types of accrediting agencies operating in the United States. Seven regional accreditors serve degree-granting colleges and universities in specific regions of the country. In addition, there are 10 recognized national accreditors, four small faith-related accreditors, and the federal government recognizes 17 specialized accreditors that cover institutions with only one type of program (e.g., a law or medicine) (Hegji, 2017). In February 2004, the American Osteopathic Association Commission on Osteopathic College Accreditation (COCA) was formed, and it is now the sole accrediting body for colleges of osteopathic medicine (Gevitz, 2019).

Although the LCME, a specialized accreditor, is recognized by the U.S. Department of Education (ED) as an accrediting agency for medical educational *programs*, the LCME is not recognized as an *institutional* accrediting agency. It therefore lacks standing to accredit stand-alone medical schools as institutions of higher education. As a result, institutional accreditation, which is granted by regional accrediting agencies and is required to qualify for federal financial assistance programs authorized under Title IV of the Higher Education Act, is also required for schools accredited by the LCME (IAMC, 2019).

Purpose of Accreditation in Higher Education

The U.S. Department of Education describes the practice of accreditation as "a means of conducting nongovernmental, peer evaluation of educational institutions and programs" and lists the following as some of the purposes of accreditation (Hegji, 2017; U.S. Department of Education, 2019):

- Assuring quality: Accreditation is the primary means by which colleges, universities, and programs assure quality to students and the public.
    - Create a culture of continuous improvement of academic quality at colleges and universities and stimulate a general raising of standards among educational institutions.
    - Involve the faculty and staff comprehensively in institutional evaluation and planning.
    - Establish criteria for professional certification and licensure.
- Providing access to federal and state funds: Accreditation is required for access to federal funds such as student aid and other federal programs. Federal student aid funds are available to students only if the institution or program they are attending is accredited by (an ED-recognized) accrediting organization. State funds to institutions and students are generally contingent on accredited status.
- Engendering private sector confidence: Accreditation status of an institution or program is important to employers when evaluating credentials of job applicants and when deciding whether to provide aid support for current employees seeking additional education. Private individuals and foundations look for evidence of accreditation when making decisions about private giving.
- Ease of transfer (of credits): Accreditation is important to students for smooth transfer of courses and programs among colleges and universities. Receiving institutions have confidence in accepting credits from other accredited schools.

Accreditation by LCME

LCME describes its purpose:

By judging the compliance of medical education programs with nationally accepted standards of educational quality, the LCME serves the interests of the general public and of the medical students enrolled in those programs. (The Functions and Structure of a Medical School - LCME, 2018)

Steps Involved in LCME Accreditation

Accreditation of medical schools in the United States consists of on-site peer reviews directed by the LCME. Reviews for accreditation are currently on an eight-year cycle and schools begin preparation two years prior to the visit. The process is comprised of the following steps (The Functions and Structure of a Medical School - LCME, 2018):

1. Completion of the Data Collection Instrument (DCI) that contains the school's response to meeting 12 standards (listed below) and 93 elements, the Independent Student Analysis (ISA), and compilation of supporting documents including the AAMC Graduate Questionnaire Report.
2. Analysis of the material listed above and other information sources, synthesized into an institutional Self-study Summary Report.
3. Review by the LCME of the self-study material.
4. Visit by an ad hoc survey team and preparation of the survey team report for review by the LCME.
5. Action on accreditation by the LCME

Description of Components

Data Collection Instrument

The LCME Data Collection Instrument (DCI) details the standards and specific data within each standard needed as part of an accreditation submission. For a full accreditation submission, there are 12 standards, and within those standards 93 specific elements. There are questions in the DCI that are linked to each of the elements. The LCME recommends that each portion of the DCI be completed by those most knowledgeable about the topics. A template for this document is available (LCME DCI for Full Accreditation Surveys, 2019)

Self-study Summary Report

The Self-study Summary Report is created during the self-study process. A medical school is required to conduct a self-study, bringing together representatives of the administration, faculty, students, and other stakeholders, to collect and evaluate data about the medical school and the programs it offers, identify strengths and challenges, and develop strategies to maintain strengths and address challenges. This report is informed by and includes the data gathered from the DCI and the Independent Student Analysis (ISA) (LCME Student Prep in Accreditation, 2019).

Graduation Questionnaire

The Medical School Graduation Questionnaire (GQ) is a national questionnaire administered by the AAMC. The GQ includes questions related to, pre-clinical, clinical, and elective experiences, general medical education and readiness for residency, student services, experiences of mistreatment, financial aid and indebtedness, career intentions and finally, strengths of the medical school and areas that need

Figure 1.
* Additional supporting documents such as meeting minutes should be made available for the visit, but not submitted

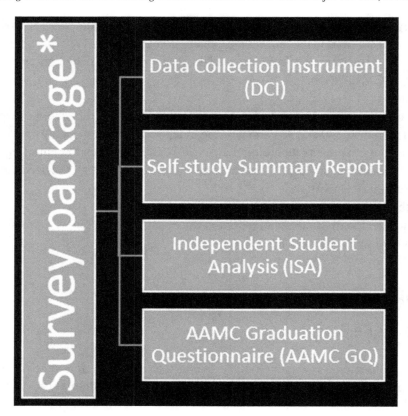

improvement. On all of these topics, comparisons to an All Schools Summary are provided, enabling each institution to evaluate their school compared to others. (LCME GQ, 2019)

Independent Student Analysis (ISA)

The Independent Student Analysis (ISA) is an independent review of relevant topics, such as the quality of the medical education program, the learning environment, and the adequacy of the institution's resources. A student group, designated by the dean, gathers data by surveying the entire student body. It is that data which informs the ISA (LCME Student Prep in Accreditation, 2019).

LCME Accreditation Standards

Schools are required to meet 12 standards consisting of 93 data elements. These 12 standards span the entire mission of the medical school and cover the following topics (LCME, 2019)

Standard 1: Mission, Planning, Organization and Integrity
Standard 2: Leadership and Administration
Standard 3: Academic and Learning Environments

Standard 4: Faculty Preparation, Productivity, Preparation, and Policies
Standard 5: Educational Resources and Infrastructure
Standard 6: Competencies, Curricular Objectives, and Curricular Design
Standard 7: Curricular Content
Standard 8: Curricular Management, Evaluation, and Enhancement
Standard 9: Teaching Supervision, Assessment, and Student and Patient Safety
Standard 10: Medical Student Selection, Assignment, and Progress
Standard 11: Medical Student Academic Support, Career Advising, and Educational Records
Standard 12: Medical Student Health Services, Personal Counseling, and Financial Aid Services

Details of the 12 standards and 93 data elements can be found at https://lcme.org/publications/ (The Functions and Structure of a Medical School - LCME, 2018)

LCME Accreditation Actions and Follow-up

When considering the accreditation status of a medical education program leading to the MD degree, the LCME may at any time take any of the following actions (Rules of Procedure LCME, 2018):

- Grant an accreditation status (accredited; accredited, preliminary status; accredited, provisional status).
- Continue an accreditation status, with or without specifying the term of accreditation.
- Continue an accreditation status, with a shortened accreditation term.
- Continue accreditation but place the program on warning.
- Continue accreditation but place the program on probation.
- Deny accreditation.
- Withdraw accreditation.

The LCME may also require one or more follow-up activities and/or completion of status reports if it determines that the program has unsatisfactory performance in one or more elements, is not in compliance with all accreditation standards, or if the LCME has identified areas that require monitoring where the final outcome could result in noncompliance with one or more accreditation standards or unsatisfactory performance in one or more elements (Rules of Procedure LCME, 2018).

Accreditation by COCA

COCA describes its purpose (Commission on Osteopathic College Accreditation Handbook, 2015):

By assessing the compliance of osteopathic medical education programs based on the nationally accepted standards of the COCA, we serve the interests of the public and of the students enrolled in our Colleges of Osteopathic Medicine.

Steps Involved in COCA Accreditation

Osteopathic medical schools are accredited by a separate, but parallel accrediting body. Accreditation of osteopathic medical schools in the United States consists of on-site peer reviews directed by the COCA.

Reviews for accreditation are currently on a ten-year cycle (for those schools that are accredited with "Exceptional Outcome" (Accreditation of Colleges of Osteopathic Medicine, 2019).

and schools begin preparation one and one half to two years prior to the visit. The process is comprised of the following steps, which mirrors those of LCME (Commission on Osteopathic College Accreditation Handbook, 2015):

1.   The on-site visit process begins with the site visit schedule, which guides the schedule of the data gathering process.
2.   The institution conducts a self-study.
3.   The COCA will conduct its own review of the COM self-study prior to the meeting where the COM's full or provisional site visit will be reviewed.
4.   The school is visited by the COCA team.
5.   The COCA makes decisions about the COM accreditation status.

COCA Accreditation Standards

Osteopathic schools are required to meet 12 standards, which are quite similar to those of LCME. Differences are largely in presentation of standards. For example, COCA Standard 6: Curriculum, subsumes LCME Standard 5 (Educational Resources and Infrastructure), Standard 6 (Competencies, Curricular Objectives and Curricular Design) and Standard 7 (Curricular Content). In addition, guidelines are included for the practice of Osteopathic Manipulative Medicine (Accreditation of Colleges of Osteopathic Medicine, 2019).

Standard 1: Mission and Governance
Standard 2: Leadership and Administration
Standard 3: Finances
Standard 4: Facilities
Standard 5: Learning Environment
Standard 6: Curriculum
Standard 7: Faculty and Staff
Standard 8: Scholarly Activity
Standard 9: Students
Standard 10: Graduate Medical Education (GME)
Standard 11: Program and Student Assessment and Outcomes
Standard 12: Institutional Accreditation

COCA Accreditation Actions

When considering the accreditation status of an osteopathic medical education program leading to a DO degree, the COCA may take any of the following actions (Accreditation of Colleges of Osteopathic Medicine, 2019).

Accreditation with Exceptional Outcome: Accreditation granted for 10 years.

- Accreditation: Accreditation granted for 7 years.
- Accreditation with Heightened Monitoring: Accreditation granted for 4 years.
- Accreditation with Warning: Accreditation granted for 2 years.
- Accreditation with Probation: Accreditation granted for 1 year.
- Withdrawal of Accreditation.

Other Accreditation Processes

New Medical Schools

Both the LCME and COCA offer additional guidelines for new medical schools, which lead to initial accreditation. These reviews are coordinated between the school and the accreditor and take place before the opening of the new school (Commission on Osteopathic College Accreditation Handbook, 2018; LCME, 2019).

Figure 2. General Timeline for Accreditation Preparation
LCME Renewal of Recognition by the U.S. Department of Education Timeline (LCME, 2019).

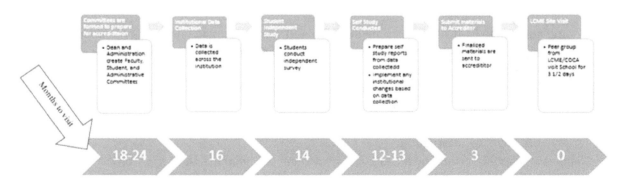

Schools Requiring Follow-Up Review

Depending upon the decision of the accreditation status after the review, a follow-up report or visit may be required (Commission on Osteopathic College Accreditation Handbook, 2018; LCME, 2019).

Substantive Change

Another occasion for an off-cycle review by LCME or COCA is when the school makes a substantive change. These are changes, which rise to the level of review, such as a change in location, a change in educational mission, a change in the length of the degree program, acquisition of another institution, development of a new program or the creation of a branch campus (Commission on Osteopathic College Accreditation Handbook, 2018; LCME, 2019).

Annual Reports

LCME accredited schools are required to submit an annual report, which provides quantitative data such as faculty count, graduating students, and class size to the LCME secretariat. The LCME secretariat makes comparisons from year-to-year against preset measures and will contact the school for additional data and the rationale for significant differences (Commission on Osteopathic College Accreditation Handbook, 2018; LCME, 2019).

Preliminary Accreditation - New Medical Schools

Both the LCME and COCA offer additional guidelines for new medical schools, which lead to initial accreditation. These reviews are coordinated between the school and the accreditor and take place before the opening of the new school.

The self-study process involves an institutional self-analysis based upon the standards. For new and developing medical schools, the process involves a 3 step review which take place (1) prior to the admission of a charter class (2) during implementation of the pre-clerkship, but prior to the beginning of clinical (clerkship) training, and (3) near the conclusion of clinical training, but prior to graduation of the charter class leading to full accreditation.

The general steps in the process for schools seeking preliminary accreditation are as follows:

1. Completion Data Collection Instrument (DCI) and compilation of supporting documents
2. Self-study task force within the new school analyses DCI, prepares the Planning Self-study report and submitted them to LCME
3. LCME reviews the DCI and Planning Self-study to determine the school's readiness for a survey visit and preliminary accreditation
4. If the survey visit is awarded, the medical school is permitted to update the DCI and Planning self-study with any new information
5. The new school is visited by an ad hoc survey team and prepares the survey report for review by the LCME
6. Action on preliminary accreditation by the LCME (Guide to the Planning Self-study for Preliminary Accreditation: LCME, 2019)

There are similar processes in place for accreditation by COCA (COM-accreditation-standards, 2018)

Accreditation: A Value-Added Proposition

Martha Casazza (2018) describes accreditation as a "value-added proposition," noting that it can and should go beyond simple accountability. The institution should analyze the data to examine its current position and to critically inform future practice. While striving to meet standards, the organization would be well served to recognize the potential of the process to positively impact its internal effectiveness.

A recent qualitative study was conducted via interviews and focus groups in Canada, regarding the impact of accreditation on medical school processes. Of those contacted, 82% contributed to the study. The following nine positive influences were noted by the respondents (Blouin D, Tekian A, Kamin C, Harris IB., 2017):

Governance

Participants appreciated oversight, both from accreditors and within the school. Organizational charts, committees and councils were delineated during the process and communication lines improved (Boulin et al., 2017)..

Data collection and analysis

Participants felt accreditation encouraged implementation and refinement of data gathering processes, sometimes resulting in the hiring of personnel and the acquisition of new hardware and/or software (Boulin et al., 2017).

Monitoring Systems

Participants noted that the process of accreditation encouraged implementation and refinement of centralized monitoring systems, such as calendaring and curriculum mapping (Boulin et al., 2017).

Documentation

Participants reported that accreditation encouraged the documentation of policies, procedures and processes, which formalizing the flow of information.

Creation and revision of policies and procedures

Participants felt the process of accreditation encouraged the creation of policies, procedures and processes and moved protocols to more formal status (Boulin et al., 2017).

CQI

Accreditation activities highlighted the need for Continuous Quality Improvement and development of internal program reviews. Some reported additional personnel hired to take on oversight of CQI. At the very least changes were formally implemented. A section of this chapter is devoted to Continuous Quality Improvement (Boulin et al., 2017).

Engagement

Schools reported that accreditation engaged staff and faculty, by including them in the process and discussing common goals for the school.

Academic accountability

Participants been reported that schools learned that they needed to prioritize academic work and to compensate faculty for their efforts (Boulin et al., 2017).

Curriculum reforms

Accreditation certainly motivates curricular reform and changes to curriculum management. Schools reported new efforts made toward curriculum mapping, attention to learning objectives and learning modalities. Further, respondents reported that accreditation helped the school garner resources from their institution to produce curricular reforms (Boulin et al., 2017).

Accreditation: Critiques

The very nature of the positive processes identified above seems to indicate that they are inextricable parts of a quality education. Still, critiques also emerged (Blouin D, Tekian A, Kamin C, Harris IB., 2017)

Four perceived negative consequences of accreditation were identified by this research (Boulin et al., 2017) and three others were noted by Kelchen (2017), in an article entitled, "Higher education accreditation and the federal government. Elevate the Debate." All seven are listed below:

Costly

Participants noted both the financial and human resource demands and called the process distracting. Accreditation too burdensome. A survey in 2015, indicated that regional accreditation can cost colleges as much as $300,000 (Vanderbilt University 2015). That is in addition to the program accreditation (LCME or COCA) which is estimated to cost approximately $300,000 as well (quoted in AFMC Senior Administrators Committee. *Personal communication* with *D. Boulin, April 4, 2016)*

Takes A Toll On Faculty

Several described the process of accreditation as stressful and stated that it had a negative impact on morale (Boulin et al., 2017).

Thwarts Innovation

Respondents reported that accreditation had the potential to thwart innovation by requiring adherence to rules or standards (Boulin et al., 2017).

Potential negative impact on school reputation - Concerns were voiced about the possible negative impact that citations would have on the school's reputation, impeding the ability to fundraise and recruit students (Boulin et al., 2017)

Quid Pro Quo

Comments were made regarding the community of commissioners and reviewers. The concern is that a quid pro quo may exist where I review your institution and you review mine (Kelchen, 2017).

Static Accreditation Relationships

There are no choices for who provides accreditation. Medical schools are accredited by LCME and the regional accreditation is based upon the school's location. There is no flexibility (Kelchen, 2017).

Finance Versus Student Learning

Finally, there is the concern that too much focus is on finance and too little is on student learning – something difficult to quantify (Kelchen, 2017).

Accreditation Changes Over Time

Throughout the years, the LCME kept pace with the changes in educational demands. The committee evaluated an increasingly broad range of areas beyond curriculum details, such as admissions standards, institutional organization, and administration, associated hospitals, physical facilities, faculty, class size, tuition, fees, scholarship support, transfer criteria for admission or transfer of students, remote campuses and due process, diversity and quality improvement (Eaglen, 2017). By 1957, LCME adopted *Functions and Structure of a Modern Medical School* as its compendium of accreditation standards. Variations of that document have existed since its inception and are still in place today (Eaglen, 2017).

A few changes of the updates that took place over the years are notable. Beginning in 2002, the LCME shifted from prose formatted standards to a numbered list of standards. The goal of this change was to reduce subjectivity, increase objectivity, and reduce redundancy. (Eaglen, 2017). The LCME was successful in this endeavor, but an uptick in severe action decisions (SAD) was noted. An LCME severe action decision (SAD) is one that grants a medical education program an unspecified or shortened term of accreditation, places the program on warning or probation status, or withdraws the program's accreditation, while a non-severe action decision (N-SAD) is one that continues accreditation without a severe action decision (Hunt, Migdal, Waechter, & Barzansky, 2015).

Research by Hunt, co-secretary for LCME and senior director of accreditation services, AAMC, et al. (2016) offers some insight into the connection between the change in 2002 and the increase in negative outcomes for schools. Before the reformatting of standards, team findings were not tied to standards, and issues at schools were difficult to identify and track. Without specific standards, reports were less precise, used broad, general statements and were more open to interpretation by the LCME as it reviewed the survey team's report. Also, the clarity of expectations, noted in the new standards, made teams more able to identify deficiencies. Further, clarification of standards enabled improved team training.

The next significant change took place after a long revision effort completed in 2015 when the LCME issued modified standards. The revised standards are a reformatted and distilled version of the preexisting 132 standards, streamlined down to 12 and delineated by 93 elements. There were also notable changes in the language used to express each element. Importantly, the prescriptive language of "should" and "must" was replaced with simple declarative sentences. Making it clear that the standards were expectations. This means that *all standards must be met* (Eaglen, 2017). With that in mind, two elements that have generated attention in in the recent literature, *3.3 Diversity/Pipeline Programs and Partnerships* and *1.1 Continuous Quality Improvement*, will be considered here. Element 3.3 is listed below:

3.3 Diversity/Pipeline Programs and Partnerships

A medical school has effective policies and practices in place, and engages in ongoing, systematic, and focused recruitment and retention activities, to achieve mission-appropriate diversity outcomes among its students, faculty, senior administrative staff, and other relevant members of its academic community. These activities include the use of programs and/or partnerships aimed at achieving diversity among qualified applicants for medical school admission and the evaluation of program and partnership outcomes (The Functions and Structure of a Medical School - LCME, 2018)

It is imperative that medical schools consider the necessity to care for our increasingly diverse population and both recruit and train their students accordingly (Verdonk & Janczukowicz, 2018; Boaatright,et al, 2018). The benefits of diversity among physicians have been well articulated. Research indicates that minority physicians are more likely to practice in communities with higher minority populations. (Bollinger, 2003; Current Trends in Medical Education. AAMC diversity facts and figures, 2016). Further, studies indicate that patients are more likely to choose physicians of their own race or identity, perhaps because physicians who share patient's race or identity may be more culturally sensitive to their needs. (Nivet, 2010, Sanchez, et al., 2015; Sanchez et al. 2016; Yu et al, 2013; Analysis in Brief - Data and Analysis – AAMC, 2016)

Although medical schools began initial diversity efforts in the mid-1960s to keep pace with the larger social justice movement of that time, beginning in the 1990s academic research began to reveal many more benefits of being educated in diverse environments. Social and cognitive advantages were identified, such as engaging in new and innovative ways to problem solve, personal growth, increased purpose in life, recognition of racism and increased volunteerism. It began to be evident that diversity in education does not only benefit the common good, it is an indicator of quality education (Boatright et al., 2018).

In 2009, the Liaison Committee on Medical Education (LCME) strengthened diversity requirements for accreditation. Specifically, the committee went beyond its previous recommendation that medical schools "*should* have policies and practices ensuring the gender, racial, cultural, and economic diversity of its students (IS-16)" to all medical schools "*must*" have such policies and practices in place. From medical schools "*should* develop programs or partnerships aimed at broadening diversity among qualified broadening diversity among qualified applicants for medical school admission" (MS-8), to medical schools "*must*" have such programs or partnerships in place. Failure to do so began to lead to citations.

Further, schools were encouraged to recruit and develop faculty with diversity in mind. Standard FA-1(2009) called for the "recruitment and development of a medical school's faculty should take into account its mission, the diversity of its student body and the population that its serves body, and the population that its serves." Supreme Court decisions, input from both the AAMC and a broad-based advisory group focused on diversity informed the change of standards IS-16 and MS-8. Failure to comply with the new standards could lead to citations, and affect accreditation status (Boatright et al., 2018; AAMC Faculty Diversity in U.S. Medical Schools: Progress and Gaps Coexist, 2019).

A study by Boatright et al.(2018) in the Journal of the American Medical Association looked at the impact of diversity requirements put in place in 2009 by the Liaison Commission on Medical Education. According to a study, after 2009 the overall trend of declining enrollment of nonwhite students reversed. The standards put in place in 2009 did not set numerical goals, nor did they require medical schools to do so. The LCME required schools to have a "mission-appropriate" diversity policy with the goal of admitting qualified candidates from groups not historically well represented in medical schools and to document that they had ongoing recruitment efforts. Schools were also encouraged to define diversity broadly, including (but not limited to) sex, race, ethnicity and socioeconomic status.

Because accreditation reviews are generally every eight years, the research evaluated statistics in 2002 and again in 2017, to compare the period before and after the 2009 standards were put in place. Historically black medical schools and those in Puerto Rico were excluded from the analysis, and data were compared for 120 medical schools.

The changes were as follows:

In 2002, 49 percent of newly enrolled students were women, 6.8 percent were black, 5.4 percent were Hispanic and 20.8 percent were Asian.

In 2017, 50.4 percent of new students were women, 7.3 percent were black, 8.9 percent were Hispanic and 24.6 percent were Asian.

The researchers acknowledged that many medical schools may have had diversity initiatives regardless of what the accreditor required, but the authors found that the accreditor's requirements along with the motivating obligation to report results, led to increased activity.

The accreditor's actions appear to have had a positive (but modest) impact on the diversity of medical school admissions, and the study noted that in the eight years prior to the enactment of the standards in 2009, the enrollment share of women and black students had actually *dropped* each year. Boatright concluded, "The standards do make a difference," and have led to meaningful change, asserting, "It is a tool that diversity advocates didn't have before to implement diversity programs (2018)."

Despite increases in representation of Black, Hispanic, Native American, lesbian, gay, bisexual, and transgender physicians, certain groups remain underrepresented in the field of medicine. As of this writing, underrepresented minorities and women comprise a disproportionately small percentage of physicians compared to the general population (Yu et al, 2013; Analysis in Brief - Data and Analysis – AAMC, 2016).

Continuous Quality Improvement (CQI)

Perhaps the element generating the most attention in academic literature and in MEPs is 1.1 Strategic Planning and Continuous Quality Improvement. Schools are working to implement programmatic goals and effective monitoring before their eight-year review. Element 1.1 is listed below:

1.1 Strategic Planning and Continuous Quality Improvement

A medical school engages in ongoing strategic planning and continuous quality improvement processes that establish its short and long-term programmatic goals, result in the achievement of measurable outcomes that are used to improve educational program quality, and ensure effective monitoring of the medical education program's compliance with accreditation standards (The Functions and Structure of a Medical School - LCME, 2018)

History and Intentions of Continuous Quality Improvement (CQI)

Accreditation reviews at intervals (for LCME 8 years), while serving as incentives for change, were deemed not optimal at ensuring continuous evaluation and improvement activities. To mitigate this short-coming, LCME accredited schools are required to submit an annual report. The LCME secretariat then serves to make comparisons from year-to-year for various benchmarks, such as faculty count, graduating students, and class size. But the concern of many is that these basic data analytics do not go far enough and recognizing a need to monitor outcomes, and make progressive adjustments, the LCME has now incorporated the requirement of Continuous Quality Improvement into Standard 1.1.

Philosophy of CQI

In a book entitled Accreditation on the Edge, Sylvia Manning offered her rationale to mandate continuous quality improvement. "There is no standing still: an institution is either improving or declining (Manning, 2018)." Likely, there is truth in this. Quality is sustained only by keeping up with current needs, regardless of whether changes are necessary in admissions, content, technology, philosophy, pedagogy, physical space, staffing, enrollment, financial stability or the many other essentials of a complex organization such as a medical school.

William Edwards Deming is widely acknowledged as a leading management thinker; he is considered by many to be the master of continual improvement of quality. Deming became known for his pioneering work in Japan in 1950, where he taught top managers and engineers the methods for improving how they worked and learned together. He focused on both internal and external operations considering interactions between departments and with suppliers and customers. Deming was a visionary, whose belief in continual improvement led to a set of transformational theories and teachings that changed the way we think about quality, management, and leadership. His work is the basis for what is now known as Continuous Quality Improvement (Deming-the-man, 2019)

Continuous quality improvement (CQI) is used in organizations as a strategy to bring about continuous development of processes. It is a systematic approach which can be incremental, and bring change over time, or dramatic for immediate changes. All processes are continually reviewed in terms of their efficiency, effectiveness, and flexibility. While the overall goal of CQI programs is universal, there are a variety of ways to conduct CQI studies. including the popular Plan-Do-Study-Act (PDSA) mode. The Plan-Do-Study-Act (PDSA) cycle is shorthand for testing a change — by planning it, trying it, observing the results, and acting on what is learned (Deming, 1986). The process of continuous quality improvement programs in medical education can be implemented by identifying problems, implementing and monitoring corrective action and studying its effectiveness.

In considering quality improvement as a component of accreditation, one can take a cue from Peter Ewell's (2009) two assessment lenses or paradigms (Casazza, 2018), the "Improvement Paradigm" and the "Accountability Paradigm." This comparison is very useful and as it highlights the functional duality of accreditation. The former is underscored by its emphasis on formative assessment that is internally focused with an ethos of engagement. The latter is summative and framed by its judgmental nature that is externally focused with an ethos of compliance.

The two paradigms, "Improvement Paradigm" and "Accountability Paradigm" can be employed to value aspects of the accreditation process.

Using Ewell's model of two paradigms as a lens for accreditation underscores the opportunity to gather data for two purposes. Effective CQI activities can support educational quality improvement and ensure a good accreditation outcome. In fact, perhaps the real strength of accreditation for medical education is its potential to encourage a culture of continuous quality improvement. (Blouin & Tekian, 2018). Applying these two conceptual models, the addition of CQI to the accreditation standards seems like a worthwhile enhancement.

Although direct linkages between accreditation and quality education are difficult to establish (Blouin & Tekian, 2018) research by van Zanten, Boulet and Greaves (2012b) supports the value of accreditation as a mechanism for quality assurance and improvement. In the study, international accreditation experts were asked to rate 150 standards widely used in medical school accreditations. The experts were provided with a 3-point scale with 1 indicating, *Not important* (the standard is not useful for determining quality), 2 indicating *Important, but not essential* (the standard is somewhat useful for determining quality, but not required) and 3 indicating *Essential* (the standard is very useful for determining quality and is required). The findings of their study indicated that the respondents found that of the majority of the 150 compiled standards, were at least important in determining quality of educational experiences, with fourteen standards deemed essential by all participants (van Zanten, Boulet and Greaves, 2012b).

Table 1. (Ewell, 2009)

aspect	Improvement Paradigm	Accountability Paradigm
Focus	Institution-centered	External mandate
Intent	Formative: to use the resulting information to enhance teaching and learning.	Summative: to demonstrate compliance to accreditors
Data	Gathered and judged directly by faculty and administrators	Gathered, mostly by faculty and administrators, and judged by external evaluators according to external measures
Ethos	Seeking continuous improvement and a culture of evidence	Compliance
Communication	Multiple means of communication are used to disseminate assessment results to a variety of internal constituents	Relies on transparent public reporting
Results applied	To guide action through multiple feedback loops	To assure external stakeholders of the effectiveness of the institution

Critiques of CQI

Many have called the LCME requirement of CQI as "formative accreditation" (Stratton, 2019; Barzansky, 2015). This seems an apt description as we see parallels to the formative student assessment processes. However, familiarity with the rather well established student assessment world does not preclude CQI from critics.

Stratton's article, *Legitimizing Continuous Quality Improvement (CQI): Navigating Rationality in Undergraduate Medical Education*, looks at both the positive and negative impressions of CQI. In Stratton's view CQI reflects, "an effort to quantify, monitor, and manipulate educational outcomes and processes (2019)." The result, notes Stratton, is voluminous educational documentation, reporting, and review, using benchmarks that may or may not reflect actual learning. These requirements, some fear, are shaping what we do and how and what we teach in Medical Education. All of this effort to quantify, keep track and analyze often generates additional curricular overhead, as schools create accreditation and CQI offices.

In a recent article in the NY Times, "The Misguided Drive to Measure 'Learning Outcomes,'" Molly Worthen (2018) writes about some common concerns regarding institutional focus on documenting learning outcomes, maximizing efficiency and meeting external requirements. Trying to reduce learning to a list of skills, says Wortham, undervalues what students should be getting from higher education.

There is pressure to ensure that students graduate with skills and to prove it with data, but this may ignore the needs of underprepared students, who don't do well. Wortham (2018) also criticizes the high cost of assessment processes, which in her view yield meager results. She suggests thoughtful consideration of reigning in what has become an assessment "industry." Wortham (2018) points out, as does Stratton (2019), that this increased effort requires additional staffing and can lead to increases in the cost of higher education.

Worthen acknowledges that having conversations about what is and is not working for students is always a good idea, but she remains troubled about how much of this time spent on things like CQI really goes toward improving opportunities for actual learning.

LCME Standards March 2014 effective July 1, 2015.

How to Develop CQI Processes

Two articles that offer valuable recommendations on how to successfully implement CQI are "Continuous quality improvement in an accreditation system for undergraduate medical education: Benefits and challenges (Stratton, 2019)", and "Legitimizing Continuous Quality Improvement (CQI): Navigating Rationality in Undergraduate Medical Education (Barzansky, et al., 2018)"

Consider the following when developing a process for Continuous Quality Improvement:

- Focused Processes (Barzansky et al.,2019)
  - information should be directly linked to standards to ensure compliance.
  - schools should review *selected* standards periodically.
- Feasible Processes (Barzansky et al.,2019; Stratton, 2019)
  - internal data collection instruments which are used for other purposes should be adapted for CQI.
  - CQI benchmarks should be based upon LCME standards.

- ○ Data should be shared when possible, with multiple accrediting agencies
- ○ CQI should not be a duplication of effort.
- Buy-in from leadership (Barzansky et al.,2019; Stratton, 2019)
  - ○ Help leaders to understand that CQI is not merely for accreditation – which is important, but it can benefit students and faculty for research, facilities, funding, etc.
  - ○ Since CQI is ongoing the process requires continued availability of support personnel and necessary resources to maintain data collection and interpretation
- Centralized coordination but… (Stratton, 2019)
  - ○ Do not remove the process to a remote office, disassociated from the faculty
  - ○ Include CQI training in faculty development
  - ○ Perform CQI "with" faculty not "on" faculty
- Share results and accountability (Stratton, 2019)
  - ○ Report results of CQI to faculty
    - ▪ Use dashboards
    - ▪ Share outcomes
  - ○ Work from a stance of "we should" rather than "you must"
    - ▪ Empowers individuals to have creative control
- Scrutinize measures and outcomes (Stratton, 2019)
  - ○ Ensure that there is a healthy degree of critical review of outcomes
  - ○ Don't be too quick to accept responsibility for student successes and reluctant to take responsibility for student failures
  - ○ Share metrics with stakeholders

Severe Action Decisions – How to Avoid Them

An article published in 2016, The Variables That Lead to Severe Action Decisions (SADs) by the Liaison Committee on Medical Education, Hunt, et al. provide useful cautionary advice to schools preparing for accreditation. The study, published in 2016, looked at data from 2004-2012. Although the standards have been updated, and there has been effort on the part of LCME to better prepare schools through webinars and consultations, the findings, are still relevant. First, the study found that SADs were associated with the total number of areas of noncompliance. Multiple areas of noncompliance were more likely to lead to Severe Action.

Programs that received a SAD were more likely to be noncompliant in multiple elements during the accreditation cycle. Second, chronic noncompliance, defined as noncompliance in two consecutive full surveys, led to SAD. It should be noted that the US Department of Education requires that accredited schools who are noncompliant must make changes and document their modifications within two years of receiving a citation. The third situation likely to generate a severe action decision is when a school provides insufficient or unclear responses in the DCI. Schools should take advantage of the resources available from the secretariat's office to ensure a successful completion of the DCI. Lastly, elements 8.1 and 8.7 were the most likely to lead to SAD. These standards, listed and described below, deserve additional attention from Medical Education Programs (MEPs) (Hunt et al., 2016).

Curricular Management

A medical school has in place an institutional body (e.g., a faculty committee) that oversees the medical education program as a whole and has responsibility for the overall design, management, integration, evaluation, and enhancement of a coherent and coordinated medical curriculum (The Functions and Structure of a Medical School - LCME, 2018)

Curricular integration now serves as a hallmark of quality medical education. The LCME appropriately points to the need for central oversight. Successful integration and coordination requires a central authority to ensure a cohesive and comprehensive curriculum without gaps and redundancies. The dynamic nature of the field of medicine and the requisite teaching necessitates continual review and updating.

Comparability of Education/Assessment

A medical school ensures that the medical curriculum includes comparable educational experiences and equivalent methods of assessment across all locations within a given course and clerkship to ensure that all medical students achieve the same medical education program objectives (The Functions and Structure of a Medical School - LCME, 2018).

As medical schools expand to accommodate increasing numbers of students, new UME institutions and clerkship sites are established. LCME element 8.7 ensures that students have comparable opportunities regardless of the setting in which they are educated, within the institution.

Frequently Cited Elements

Below is a complete list of the elements that the LCME reports are frequently cited.

Student Role in Accreditation

Students play a vital role in the accreditation process. One or more students should be appointed by the dean to be members of the Self-Study Task Force, the team that includes faculty, administrators and other stakeholders. More importantly, a student leadership team – usually with representatives from each academic year, creates the Independent Student Analysis (ISA). This process begins with the creation of a survey; which the student leadership team sends to all members of all registered classes. The LCME provides guidelines for the data which should be surveyed by the student team. In summary, their evaluation should appraise the accessibility of the dean and faculty, quality of the curriculum, workload, required courses and clerkships, student assessment processes, student support and health services, the learning environment, and resources visit (LCME Student Participation in Accreditation, 2019).

Independent Student Analysis (ISA)

The student leadership team analyzes the outcomes from the survey and creates the Independent Student Analysis ISA. The student group also should review the school-specific results of the most recently administered AAMC Medical School Graduation Questionnaire (which the school should provide to the student group). This data could be used in the final ISA report. The ISA also must contain a quantitative summary of the survey results. Since findings from the ISA will be included in the institution's Self-study

significant predictor of SAD	Variable	Summary Description
1 √	**Insufficient Response to DCI**	
2 √	**Chronic Noncompliance**	
3 √	**Total Noncompliances**	
	9.8	Formative and summative assessment
	6.2 & 8.6	Required clinical experiences and monitoring
4 √	**8.1**	**Curriculum management**
	1.4	Affiliation agreements
5 √	**8.7**	**Comparability across instructional sites**
	9.5	Narrative feedback
	12.1	Student educational debt
	8.3	Systematic review and revision of the curriculum (now combined in 8.3)
	11.2	Career counseling
	9.1	Resident preparation
	5.4	Sufficient buildings and equipment
	3.3	Student diversity (now combined with faculty diversity in 3.3)
	9.7	Midcourse feedback
	8.2	Educational program objectives
	12.5	Health care providers' involvement
	3.6	Student mistreatment
	9.2	Faculty appointments
	8.3	Monitoring curriculum content (now combined in 8.3)
	5.11	Study and lounge space and secure storage
	3.3	Faculty diversity (now combined with student diversity in 3.3)

Report, the student's process should be completed early on the accreditation timeline, approximately 10 months before the survey visit (LCME Student Participation in Accreditation, 2019).

Representatives During Survey Visit

An additional role students play in an institutions accreditation is during the survey visit. A number of students will meet with survey team members and provide information to compliment and flesh out data that has been sent to the survey team. These students serve as the face of the school and their input is highly regarded by the visiting survey team (LCME Student Participation in Accreditation, 2019).

Input into the Graduate Questionnaire

Student input plays a crucial role in the accreditation process via the GQ. As previously mentioned, input from the Graduate Questionnaire becomes part of the DCI and is reflected in the Self-study Summary Report (AAMC Graduate Questionnaire (GQ), 2019)

Student Role in COCA Accreditation

The Commission on Osteopathic College Accreditation (COCA) closely parallels the LCME. Element 11.4: Student Survey: requires that a COM must cooperate with the administration of the COCA prepared student survey of accreditation items as part of the comprehensive accreditation process. (Commission on osteopathic college accreditation of colleges of osteopathic medicine: COM accreditation standards and procedures, 2019).

Format of a Typical Accreditation Visit

At least three months before the survey visit, the members of the survey team receive all of the information that the program collected and analyzed in its self-study process.

The survey team reviews that information and develops a preliminary assessment of the program before arriving at the medical school for the survey visit. The visit begins late on a Sunday afternoon and typically ends mid-day on Wednesday. This process may be extended if there are additional campuses.

GRADUATE MEDICAL EDUCATION ACCREDITATION

ACGME (Accreditation Council for Graduate Medical Education) describes its purpose:

The Mission of the ACGME is to improve health care and population health by assessing and advancing the quality of resident physicians' education through accreditation.

Through accreditation, innovations, and initiatives, the ACGME strives to ensure that residents and fellows train in educational environments that support patient safety, resident and fellow education, and physician well-being." (ACGME Residents-and-Fellows/Welcome, 2019)

The ACGME is a private nonprofit organization, established in 1981 (Maniar et al., 2018), which accredits post-medical doctorate training programs. At its inception, the ACGME sought to ensure the adequacy of learning opportunities and to standardize the structure and organization of residency programs and subspecialty fellowships. As time went by it became clear that the ACGME should also monitor educational outcomes and evaluate residency programs to assure adequate opportunities for residents to develop into competent patient care providers and professionals.

In 1999, the ACGME established six core competencies and shifted their emphasis from process-oriented to outcomes oriented (ACGME 2013, A Brief History). The core competencies, Patient Care, Medical Knowledge, Practice-based Learning and Improvement, Interpersonal Communication Skills, Medical Professionalism, and Systems-based Practice, became the domains of expertise used by GME programs to evaluate their residents in training (Nasca, Philibert, Brigham, & Flynn, 2012)

By 2009, each competency was further delineated by milestones, which residents are required to master at key stages of their medical training. At the same time, the **Next Accreditation System** (NAS) was in development and was implemented in phases between 2012 and 2014. The goals of this ACGME initiative were, to enhance the ability of the peer-review system to prepare physicians for practice, move toward accreditation on the basis of educational outcomes, to reduce the burden associated with accreditation, to help poor programs to improve, and to encourage rather than discourage innovation (Nasca, Philibert, Brigham, & Flynn, 2012)

CLINICAL LEARNING ENVIRONMENT REVIEW (CLER)

Beginning in 2013, the Next Accreditation System (NAS) moved the ACGME from a snapshot review to a model of continuous assessment, much like the CQI now in place for undergraduate medical education. This long-term evaluation was designed to track resident progress by the achievement of observable milestones at developmental levels that target the six competencies.

The ACGME has responded to this need by implementing the CLER (Clinical Learning Environment Review Program) a key component of the Next Accreditation System. CLER was designed to enhance quality of care and safety in teaching hospitals. In 2012, the ACGME established CLER and began to provide formative, constructive feedback to teaching hospitals, medical centers and other clinical settings. CLER is conducted via site visits with visiting teams focusing on the following six areas important to resident training and patient care;

1. Engagement of residents in patient safety
2. Engagement of residents in quality improvement including reducing health disparities
3. Enhancing practice for care transitions
4. Promoting appropriate resident supervision
5. Duty hour oversight and fatigue management
6. Enhancing professionalism in the learning environment (Nasca, Philibert, Brigham, & Flynn, 2012; Wagner et al., 2016):

CLER Site Visit

The CLER site visits take place on short-notice visits (no fewer than 10 days' notice) and the Sponsoring Institution's designated institutional official (DIO) is the primary contact. The CLER Representatives will visit one participating site per Sponsoring Institution. Site visitors may elect to go to more than one location at that site, especially if there are ambulatory clinical or specialty facilities within walking distance.

The ACGME accreditation includes scheduled site visits every 10 years, an annual review of submitted residency performance outcome data, and periodic CLER site visits (approximately every 24 months) to maintain accreditation (ACGME Clinical Learning Environment Review (CLER), 2019)

AOA JOINS ACGME

In 2014, the American Osteopathic Association (AOA), the American Association of Colleges of Osteopathic Medicine, and the Accreditation Council for Graduate Medical Education (ACGME) agreed to establish a new, single accreditation system for graduate medical education in the United States. The ACGME will now serve as the accreditor for both allopathic and osteopathic residency and internship programs. The 5-year transition period, from July 1, 2015, through June 30, 2020, was put in place to give AOA training programs time to apply for and receive ACGME accreditation (Buser et al., 2018; Brennan, N., Cole, L., Campea, M, 2014). By 2020, all residency programs in the U.S. will be accredited by the Accreditation Council for Graduate Medical Education (ACGME) (AOA The American Osteopathic Association Supports Revised ACGME Common Program Requirement, 2017; AMA Single accreditation system for graduate medical education: What to know, 2016).

REGIONAL ACCREDITATION

As previously mentioned, there are multiple regional and national accreditors, which accredit institutions overall, not just individual programs (as the LCME does). Institutional accreditation is required for Title IV federal financial assistance and *must* be in place for successful LCME accreditation. Below, the categories of standards for the Middle States Commission on Higher Education (MSCHE) are listed as a representative sample of regional accreditation areas of review (Revised Standards MSCHE, 2018):

Standard I: Mission and Goals. Standard II Ethics and Integrity Ethics
Standard III: Design and Delivery of the Student Learning Experience
Standard IV: Support of the Student Experience
Standard V: Educational Effectiveness
Standard VI: Planning, Resources, and Institutional Improvement
Standard VII: Governance, Leadership and Administration

Accreditation Review Activities for MSCHE are on an eight-year cycle and also include a self-study evaluation and on-site evaluation visit. In addition, the commission requires a Mid-Point Peer Review (MPPR) in the fourth year following the self-study evaluation and on-site evaluation visit (Revised Standards MSCHE, 2018).

Generally, the work done for the LCME accreditation will be adequate to meet most of the requirements of a school's regional accreditor. However, regional accreditation may take place on a different schedule, and requires participation of the entire institution. Further, preparation for the regional accreditation must be done in accordance with the regional guidelines.

In contrast to the LCME, the COCA has the authority to provide both programmatic and institutional accreditation. COCA accredits free-standing colleges of osteopathic medicine where no other educational program is offered (institutional accreditation) and serves as the federal Title IV gatekeeper for those institutions. This distinction means that stand alone osteopathic medical schools do not need additional regional accreditation (AOA Staff, 2018).

U.S. ED RECOGNIZES LCME AND COCA

The LCME is recognized by the U.S. ED as the reliable authority for the accreditation of medical education programs leading to the M.D. degree. To maintain this recognition, every five years the LCME is reviewed by U.S. ED, specifically by National Advisory Committee on Institutional Quality and Integrity (NACIQI). The most recent review of the LCME occurred during the May 2018 NACIQI meeting. In August 2018, the LCME was granted renewed recognition to the for the next five-year period (LCME Renewal of Recognition by the U.S. Department of Education, 2019).

Likewise, the COCA is federally recognized by the U.S. ED and has been granted authority for accreditation since 1952. In August 2018, the U.S. ED granted AOA's COCA renewed recognition as an *institutional and programmatic* accrediting agency for a period of three years. (AOA Staff, 2018).

FINAL THOUGHTS

Accreditation is a critically important endeavor for any medical school. It is a process for evaluating and recognizing good education. It is essential for a school's survival. Simply put, a school without accreditation will cease to exist (Davis, 2018). Accreditation requires concerted and organized effort from the entire institution, including the faculty, administrators, students and community (Barzansky et al.,2019; Stratton, 2019). Critics note the expense of the accreditation process, in dollars, effort, and stress. Moreover, some critics see accreditation guidelines as restrictive. However, many are happy to have the accreditation review process as a trigger for continuous quality improvement. Clearly, improvements in policies, procedures, and curriculum frequently result from the guidelines of accreditation standards and it is widely accepted that accreditation drives positive change (Blouin et al., 2017).

REFERENCES

AAMC Faculty Diversity in U.S. Medical Schools. Progress and Gaps Coexist (2019) Retrieved from https://www.aamc.org/data/aib/474174/december2016facultydiversityinu.s.medicalschoolsprogressandgaps.html

AboutA. A. M. C. (2019). Retrieved from https://www.aamc.org/about/

Accreditation Council for Graduate Medical Education. (2019). Retrieved from https://www.acgme.org/Residents-and-Fellows/Welcome

ACGME Clinical Learning Environment Review (CLER). (2019). Retrieved from https://www.acgme.org/What-We-Do/Initiatives/Clinical-Learning-Environment-Review-CLER

AMA Single accreditation system for graduate medical education: What to know (2016). Retrieved from https://www.ama-assn.org/residents-students/match/single-accreditation-system-graduate-medical-education-what-know

Analysis in Brief - Data and Analysis - AAMC. Retrieved from https://www.aamc.org/data/aib/474174/december2016facultydiversityinu.s.medicalschoolsprogressandgaps.html

AOA The American Osteopathic Association Supports Revised ACGME Common Program Requirements. Retrieved from https://osteopathic.org/2017/03/10/the-american-osteopathic-association-supports-revised-acgme-common-program-requirements/

Barzansky, B. (2019, May 8). Survey Prep Workshop to prepare schools for their upcoming full survey visit. Presented at the 2019 annual LCME Secretariat Workshop, Washington, DC.

Barzansky, B., Hunt, D., Moineau, G., Ahn, D., Lai, C.-W., Humphrey, H., & Peterson, L. (2015). Continuous quality improvement in an accreditation system for undergraduate medical education: Benefits and challenges. *Medical Teacher, 37*(11), 1032–1038. doi:10.3109/0142159X.2015.1031735 PMID:25897708

Blouin, D., Tekian, A., Kamin, C., & Harris, I. B. (2017). The impact of accreditation on medical schools' processes. *Medical Education, 52*(2), 182–191. doi:10.1111/medu.13461 PMID:29044652

Boatright, D. H., Samuels, E. A., Cramer, L., Cross, J., Desai, M., Latimore, D., & Gross, C. P. (2018). Association Between the Liaison Committee on Medical Education's Diversity Standards and Changes in Percentage of Medical Student Sex, Race, and Ethnicity. *Journal of the American Medical Association, 320*(21), 2267. doi:10.1001/jama.2018.13705 PMID:30512090

Bollinger, L. C. (2003). The Need for Diversity in Higher Education. *Academic Medicine, 78*(5), 431–436. doi:10.1097/00001888-200305000-00002 PMID:12742776

Brennan, N., Cole, L., & Campea, M. (2014) *Allopathic and osteopathic medical communities commit to a single graduate medical education accreditation system.* Retrieved from http://www.acgme.org/portals/0/pdfs/nasca-community/singleaccreditationrelease2-26.pdf

Buser, B. R., Swartwout, J. E., Biszewski, M., & Lischka, T. (2018). Single accreditation system update: A year of progress. *The Journal of the American Osteopathic Association, 118*(4), 264–268. doi:10.7556/jaoa.2018.051 PMID:29582061

Casazza, M. (2018). Accreditation: A value-added proposition. *NADE Digest, 9*(2), 3–7.

Commission on Osteopathic College Accreditation Handbook. (2018). Retrieved from https://osteopathic.org/wp-content/uploads/2018/02/coca-handbook.pdf

Commission on osteopathic college accreditation of colleges of osteopathic medicine: COM accreditation standards and procedures. (2019). Retrieved from https://osteopathic.org/wp-content/uploads/2018/02/com-continuing-accreditation-standards.pdf

Cooke, M., Irby, D. M., Sullivan, W., & Ludmerer, K. M. (2006). American Medical Education 100 Years after the Flexner Report. *The New England Journal of Medicine, 355*(13), 1339–1344. doi:10.1056/NEJMra055445 PMID:17005951

Current Trends in Medical Education. Retrieved from http://www.aamcdiversityfactsandfigures2016.org/report-section/section-3/

Davis, D. (2018). The medical school without walls: Reflections on the future of medical education. *Medical Teacher Volume, 40*(10), 1004–1009. doi:10.1080/0142159X.2018.1507263 PMID:30259766

Deming, W. E. (1986). *Out of the crisis.* Cambridge, MA: Massachusetts Institute of Technology, Center for Advanced Engineering Study.

Deming-the-man. (2019). Retrieved from https://deming.org/deming/deming-the-man The W. Edwards Deming Institute

Dewey, J. (1900). *The child and the curriculum; The school and society*. Chicago, IL: University of Chicago Press.

Duffy, T. P. (2011). The Flexner Report – 100 years later. *The Yale Journal of Biology and Medicine, 84*(3), 269–276. PMID:21966046

Eaglen, R. H. (2017). *Academic quality and public accountability in academic medicine: the 75-year history of the Lcme*. Washington, DC: Association of American Medical Colleges.

Eaton, J. S. (2015). *An overview of U.S. accreditation*. Washington, DC: CHEA.

Ewell, P. T. (2009, November). Assessment, accountability, and improvement: Revisiting the tension (NILOA Occasional Paper No. 1). Urbana, IL: University of Illinois and Indiana University, National Institute of Learning Outcomes Assessment. Retrieved from http://www.learningoutcomeassessment. org/documents/PeterEwell_005.pdfGarun

Flexner, A. (1910). *Medical education in the United States and Canada*. Washington, DC: Science and Health Publications.

Functions and structure of a medical school – LCME Standards. (2018). Retrieved from http://lcme. org/publications/

Gevitz, N. (2019). *The DOs: osteopathic medicine in America*. Baltimore, MD: Johns Hopkins University Press.

Graduate QuestionnaireA. A. M. C. (GQ) Retrieved from https://www.aamc.org/data/gq/

Guide to the Planning Self-study for Preliminary Accreditation. LCME. (2019, May). Retrieved August 16, 2019, from https://lcme.org/publications/

Harcleroad, F. F., & Eaton, J. S. (2005). The hidden hand: External constituencies and their impact. In P. G. Altbach, R. O. Berdahl, & P. J. Gumport (Eds.), *American higher education in the twenty-first century: social, political, and economic challenges* (p. 263). Baltimore, Md.: JHU Press.

Hegji, A. (2017). *An overview of accreditation of higher education in the United States*. Congressional Research Report (CRS) Report R43826, Washington, DC.

HistoryA. M. A. (2019). Retrieved from https://www.ama-assn.org/about/ama-history/ama-history

Hunt, D., Migdal, M., Waechter, D., & Barzansky, B. (2015). *Expanding the LCME Severe Action Decisions Analysis to Gauge the Effect of the 2002 Accreditation Standards Reformatting. Expanding the LCME Severe Action Decisions Analysis to Gauge the Effect of the 2002 Accreditation Standards Reformatting*. Washington, DC: AAMC.

Hunt, D., Migdal, M., Waechter, D. M., Barzansky, B., & Sabalis, R. F. (2016). The Variables That Lead to Severe Action Decisions by the Liaison Committee on Medical Education. *Academic Medicine, 91*(1), 87–93. doi:10.1097/ACM.0000000000000874 PMID:26287918

Kassebaum, D. K. (1992). Origin of the LCME, the AAMC– AMA partnership for accreditation. *Academic Medicine, 67*(2), 85–87. doi:10.1097/00001888-199202000-00005 PMID:1547000

Kelchen, R. (September, 2017). Higher education accreditation and the federal government. Elevate the Debate. Washington, D.C.: Urban Institute.

LCME DCI for Full Accreditation Surveys. (2019). Retrieved from https://lcme.org/publications/

LCME Renewal of Recognition by the U.S. Department of Education (LCME). (2019). Retrieved from http://lcme.org/doe-renewal-recognition/

LCME Renewal of Recognition by the U.S. Department of Education Timeline (LCME). (2019). Retrieved from http://lcme.org/accreditation-preparation/schools/2020-21-academic-year/2020-21-full-survey-visit-preparation/#Timeline

Liaison Committee on Medical Education (LCME). (2019). Retrieved from https://www.aamc.org/members/osr/committees/48814/reports_lcme.html

Liaison Committee on Medical Education (LCME). (2019). Retrieved from http://lcme.org/accreditation-preparation/schools/2020-21-academic-year/2020-21-full-survey-visit-preparation/

Ludmerer, K. M. (1996). *Learning to heal: The development of American medical education Paperback.* Baltimore, MD: Johns Hopkins University Press.

Maniar, K. P., Arva, N., Blanco, L. Z. Jr, Mao, Q., Morency, E. G., Rodriguez, R., ... Nayar, R. (2019). Accreditation Council for Graduate Medical Education (ACGME) Self-Study for Pathology: One Institutions Experience and Lessons Learned. *Archives of Pathology & Laboratory Medicine, 143*(10), 1271–1277. doi:10.5858/arpa.2018-0467-RA PMID:31017451

Manning, S. (2018). Quality assurance and quality improvement. In *Accreditation on the Edge: Challenging quality assurance in higher* (pp. 13–30). Baltimore, MD: JOHNS HOPKINS UNIV Press.

Nasca, T. J., Philibert, I., Brigham, T., & Flynn, T. C. (2012). The Next GME Accreditation System—Rationale and Benefits. *The New England Journal of Medicine, 366*(11), 1051–1056. doi:10.1056/NEJMsr1200117 PMID:22356262

Nivet, M. A. (2010). Minorities in academic medicine: Review of the literature. *Journal of Vascular Surgery, 51*(4), S53–S58. doi:10.1016/j.jvs.2009.09.064 PMID:20036099

Rules of procedure LCME. (2018). Retrieved from http://lcme.org/publications/

Sánchez, J. P., Poll-Hunter, N., Stern, N., Garcia, A. N., & Brewster, C. (2016). Balancing Two Cultures: American Indian/Alaska Native Medical Students' Perceptions of Academic Medicine Careers. *Journal of Community Health, 41*(4), 871–880. doi:10.100710900-016-0166-x PMID:26896055

Sánchez, N. F., Rankin, S., Callahan, E., Ng, H., Holaday, L., Mcintosh, K., ... Sánchez, J. P. (2015). LGBT Trainee and Health Professional Perspectives on Academic Careers—Facilitators and Challenges. *LGBT Health, 2*(4), 346–356. doi:10.1089/lgbt.2015.0024 PMID:26788776

Selden, W. K. (1962). The history and role of accrediting in higher education. *Journal of the American Medical Association, 181*(7), 613–615. doi:10.1001/jama.1962.03050330043009 PMID:13910406

Staff A. O. A. (2018). *The DO.* Retrieved from https://thedo.osteopathic.org/2018/08/coca-receives-usde-renewal-as-recognized-accrediting-agency

Standards for accreditation and requirements of affiliation MSCHE. (2019). Retrieved from https://www.msche.org/standards/

Standards, Publications, & Notification Forms: LCME. (n.d.). Retrieved from https://lcme.org/publications/

Stratton, T. D. (2019). Legitimizing Continuous Quality Improvement (CQI): Navigating Rationality in Undergraduate Medical Education. *Journal of General Internal Medicine, 34*(5), 758–761. doi:10.100711606-019-04875-1 PMID:30788765

Student ParticipationL. C. M. E. in Accreditation. (2019). Retrieved from http://lcme.org/accreditation-preparation/students/#Student-Participation-in-Accreditation

The History and Application of the LCME's Diversity Standards. Retrieved from https://www.aamc.org/download/279018/data/brazanskyslides.pdf

Thelin, J. R. (2011). *A history of American higher education.* Baltimore, MD: Johns Hopkins University Press.

U.S. Department of Education. (2019). *Accreditation in the United States.* Retrieved from http://www2.ed.gov/admins/finaid/accred/accreditation.html#Overview

Vanderbilt University. (2015). *The Cost of Federal Regulatory Compliance in Higher Education: A Multi-Institutional Study.* Nashville, TN: Vanderbilt University.

Verdonk, P., & Janczukowicz, J. (2018). Editorial: Diversity in Medical Education. *MedEdPublish, 7*(1). doi:10.15694/mep.2018.000001.1

Wagner, R., Patow, C., Newton, R., Casey, B. R., Koh, N. J., & Weiss, K. B. (2016). The Overview of the CLER Program: CLER National Report of Findings 2016. *Journal of Graduate Medical Education, 8*(2Suppl 1), 11–13. doi:10.4300/1949-8349.8.2s1.11 PMID:27252798

Worthen, M. (2018). The misguided drive to measure 'learning outcomes.' The New York Times Sunday Review. Retrieved from https://www.nytimes.com/2018/02/23/opinion/sunday/colleges-measure-learning- outcomes.htm

Yu, P. T., Parsa, P. V., Hassanein, O., Rogers, S. O., & Chang, D. C. (2013). Minorities struggle to advance in academic medicine: A 12-y review of diversity at the highest levels of Americas teaching institutions. *The Journal of Surgical Research, 182*(2), 212–218. doi:10.1016/j.jss.2012.06.049 PMID:23582226

Zanten, M. V., Boulet, J. R., & Greaves, I. (2012). The importance of medical education accreditation standards. *Medical Teacher, 34*(2), 136–145. doi:10.3109/0142159X.2012.643261 PMID:22288991

Chapter 2
Admission to US Medical Schools:
From Application to Selection

Leila E. Harrison
https://orcid.org/0000-0002-6804-075X
Washington State University Elson S. Floyd College of Medicine, USA

Christina J. Grabowski
https://orcid.org/0000-0003-1707-1238
University of Alabama at Birmingham School of Medicine, USA

Leila Amiri
University of Illinois College of Medicine, USA

Radha Nandagopal
https://orcid.org/0000-0002-5959-9594
Washington State University Elson S. Floyd College of Medicine, USA

Richard Sanker
Baylor University, USA

ABSTRACT

This chapter includes in-depth information on the medical school application process in the United States (US), the various admissions criteria and selection processes, and the range of interview and assessment modalities used to evaluate applicant competencies. It also provides information about the various pathways aspiring physicians may take to seek admission to medical school. In these sections, evidence is provided highlighting the work that has been done to better understand these areas. The chapter concludes with the important perspectives of an admissions committee chair and a pre-health advisor to further elucidate this complex process.

DOI: 10.4018/978-1-7998-1468-9.ch002

INTRODUCTION

Application to and selection for medical school continues to be a competitive process in the US. According to the Association of American Medical Colleges (AAMC), there were 52,777 applicants to MD degree-granting medical schools for the 2018 entering class (AAMC, 2018a), of which 41% matriculated (AAMC, 2018b). Applicants also have the option of applying to colleges of osteopathic medicine. In the same application cycle, the American Association of Colleges of Osteopathic Medicine (AACOM) reported 20,981 applications for 7,467 seats (AACOM, 2018). The application process is lengthy with applications for both MD and DO programs opening in early May, over a year prior to expected matriculation. Furthermore, the process has evolved over the years making it more important for applicants, pre-health advisors, admissions committees, and medical education faculty to be familiar with the variety of assessment modalities and applicant characteristics and experiences desired by medical schools.

The goal of this chapter is to provide an in-depth account of the full continuum of medical school admissions, including the different ways medical schools use materials in the application or from the interview to make decisions. It includes an overview of the holistic review framework adopted by many medical schools to align their admissions criteria to institution-specific missions and goals while also diversifying the physician workforce to better meet the healthcare needs of their changing patient populations. It also provides an overview and examples of programs that highlight the different pathways students can come through. The important perspectives of the admissions committee and pre-health advisor are also included. This chapter aims to demystify the admissions process while highlighting evidence-based practices for selection.

APPLICATION SERVICES

There are three different application services to apply to US medical schools: the American Medical College Application Service (AMCAS), the American Association of Colleges of Osteopathic Medicine Application Service (AACOMAS), and the Texas Medical and Dental Schools Application Service (TMDSAS). Each of these serves unique medical colleges, making it important for applicants and advisors to know their differences, deadlines, and processes. This section of the chapter provides details of each of these application services, including their differences and schools served.

As of early 2019, there were 154 MD-granting US medical schools accredited by the Liaison Committee on Medical Education (LCME, 2019). The majority of these programs utilize the centralized application service through the AAMC which is AMCAS. The application includes questions about demographics, personal and familial background, academic background, essays, and an option for including 15 activities the applicant wishes to share. There are currently 35 DO-granting US medical schools accredited by the American Osteopathic Association's Commission on Osteopathic College Accreditation (AOA, 2019), many with multiple locations. Most of these programs utilize the centralized application service AACOMAS, and the application includes similar information as AMCAS. There are nine public MD programs and one public DO program in the state of Texas, which utilize TMDSAS. TMDSAS is slightly different than AMCAS in that rather than limiting activities to only 15, TMDSAS provides sections for employment, leadership, research, healthcare, and community service, allowing applicants to submit unlimited activities for each section. These application services provide a centralized process for applicants to apply to multiple programs.

Many medical schools also require secondary applications as a way of obtaining specific information from applicants as it applies to the program, mission, and goals. These secondary applications often include essays and questions regarding additional demographic information not acquired through the central application services. Medical schools use these additional tools to better assess whether applicants are a fit for their program as well as to learn more about applicants' competencies and motivation. Applicant competencies often include non-metric information, which may not always be clear in the application process.

APPLICANT COMPETENCIES – WHAT ARE MEDICAL SCHOOLS LOOKING FOR?

When medical schools are making the difficult decisions to select future students for their programs, they do so with many factors in mind. These factors include whether the applicant is aligned with the school mission and evidence in the application that tells the school the applicant will likely be successful in the medical school curriculum, among other competencies. Through a vetting process that included an exhaustive search of the literature and review and input by several advisory panels, the medical school admissions community identified nine core personal competencies that are deemed important for entering medical students (Koenig et al., 2013). These nine competencies cover both interpersonal and intrapersonal areas and include:

- Service orientation
- Social skills
- Cultural competency
- Teamwork
- Oral communication
- Ethical responsibility to self and others
- Reliability and dependability
- Resilience and Adaptability
- Capacity for Improvement

This is not meant to be a comprehensive list, and schools will often include additional competencies that align with their mission. However, these provide a solid foundation for what medical schools are looking for in applicants. The following section provides detailed examples of some of these competencies in context of the literature to provide evidence of their potential value to medical school admissions committees.

Intra and Interpersonal Competencies

Teamwork as a competency for entering medical students can help medical school admissions committees gauge whether applicants have enough experience in and reflection about what it means to work as part of a team. In a thorough review of the literature, Rosen et al. (2018) provided insight into the impact of being able to work well in teams on healthcare outcomes. This specific interpersonal competency is defined as the ability to work collaboratively with others toward shared goals, can provide feedback, and puts the team above self (AAMC, 2019a). Rosen et al. state that the ability to work in teams can impact the quality and safety of care. As part of the competency of teamwork, and as a separate core competency, is oral communication. Communicating in teams and passing on critical information in high stress situations can impact patient health outcomes. Rosen et al. point out that communication failures can cause otherwise preventable harm to patients, which speaks to the need for future doctors to have an ability to convey and listen to information effectively in teams.

Another core competency for entering medical students identified by Koenig et al. (2013) is cultural competence, which involves appreciating multiple dimensions of diversity, interacting effectively with those of varied backgrounds, considering and seeking a multitude of perspectives, and addressing bias in oneself and others (AAMC, 2019a). This term is sometimes replaced with cultural humility. The patient population in the US is diverse with many racial, ethnic, and socioeconomic disparities, among others, in healthcare. Cultural competence is an important foundation for entering medical students. This can be further developed through their training in Undergraduate Medical Education (UME) and into Graduate Medical Education (GME); however, specifically assessing for it in admissions benefits institutions and future patient populations by allowing curricular time to be spent on skills development rather than skills acquisition. Cultural competence can help alleviate disparities and improve patient-doctor communication and satisfaction (Betancourt, Corbett, & Bondaryk, 2014). Through the application process, schools can thoughtfully learn about applicant experiences with diverse populations and seek their reflections about these experiences in essays and interviews. If schools have distinct goals and a mission to serve certain populations (e.g., rural or underserved), seeking applicants who have had relevant experiences or who come from those backgrounds may be better suited for the curriculum and aims of the program.

A final example of one of the core competencies of entering medical students is resilience. Burnout is an important concern in the practice of medicine. Lu, Dresden, McCloskey, Branzetti, and Gisondi (2015) found that among emergency physicians, nearly 60% of resident and attending physicians reported burnout. Burnout includes emotional exhaustion, perception of low accomplishment, and depersonalization (Lu et al., 2015; O'Brien, Simpkin, & Spector, 2017). These physicians indicated that high levels of burnout led to suboptimal care practices (Lu et al., 2015). Screening for resilience in entering medical students is not the final and only solution to or prevention of this issue later in UME, GME, and practice; however, O'Brien et al. (2017) argue that enhancing resilience among healthcare providers can help prevent or cope with burnout. Resilience does not rest solely with the individual; learning and practice environments can provide resources and support which help to build resilience (O'Brien et al., 2017). In reviewing applications and interviewing applicants, evidence of overcoming hardship, healthy coping skills, and demonstration and reflection of adaptability and resilience can provide insight into the underlying preparedness of incoming medical students to work through the stresses of medical education and clinical practice.

The core competencies of entering medical students are multifaceted and often difficult to assess in the admissions process. Admissions committees should be aligned with the school's mission about which competencies they believe are the most important in helping them carry out that mission. This could include adopting the core competencies already vetted (Koenig et al., 2013) and identifying unique values that align with the school mission. An example of the latter might be looking for applicants who have experiences in rural or underserved communities if the school's intent is to make an impact in those communities.

Assessing an applicant's intra and interpersonal competencies may not be a straightforward process. The personal statement in the AMCAS application as well as those in the secondary applications can provide additional insight to admissions committees about an applicant's life story and, in particular, can shed light on their communication skills, empathy, resilience, motivation, and alignment with the school mission. Admissions committees should create a defined, structured rubric for this assessment so that each applicant is being assessed on the same competences. Later in this chapter, other assessment modalities that aim at evaluating these intra and interpersonal competencies are discussed.

Science, Thinking, and Reasoning Competencies

The core competencies for entering medical students also include competencies outside of intra and interpersonal behaviors and experiences (Koenig et al., 2013). These include thinking, reasoning, and science competencies, which can be assessed through similar modalities. Schools will also often look at intellectual experience such as being engaged meaningfully in research as well as how applicants performed in science coursework. In early 2015, the Medical College Admission Test (MCAT) released a new version of the MCAT which had not previously been revised since 1991. With a shift in scoring, a fourth section was added along with some changes within the three other sections. This current version of the MCAT includes the following four sections: biological and biochemical foundations of living systems, chemical and physical foundations of biological systems, psychological, social, and biological foundations of behavior, and critical analysis and reasoning skills. The newest section - psychological, social, and biological foundations of behavior - is a helpful addition to admissions committees as it tests applicants on their understanding of how psychological, social, and biological factors influence behavior, perceptions, and well-being – all important to the practice of medicine.

The MCAT and grade point average (GPA) are often used to narrow down the applicant pool, informing who is interviewed and/or selected (Monroe, Quinn, Samuelson, Dunleavy, & Dowd, 2013). Conducting local research to determine the level at which, and if, the MCAT and GPA relate with or predict similar performance later in medical school would be beneficial as there is mixed evidence nationally about these metrics as predictors of future performance. For example, the MCAT has been found to be a predictor of performance on the United States Medical Licensing Exam (LCME) Step 2 Clinical Knowledge (Andriole & Jeffe, 2012) and is correlated with USMLE Step 1 performance (Durning et al., 2015). Another study found weak relationships between undergraduate GPA and medical school GPA and USMLE Step 1 and 2CK scores (Durning et al., 2015). Since the current version of the MCAT was only introduced in 2015 with these applicants enrolling as early as 2016, there is a paucity of published research on how these relate to the USMLE Step 1. These students would be entering third year as early as 2019; thus, evidence for the relationships with USMLE Step 2CK and CS and after are still in the future. Through its MCAT validity study, the AAMC provides some initial evidence relevant to the 2015 MCAT. Students who had higher MCAT total scores scored higher on USMLE Step 1, but there was variability in Step 1 scores for each total MCAT score (AAMC, 2019b). There was an overall 96% pass rate on the USMLE for this group (AAMC, 2019b). Evidence is consistent with the previous version of the MCAT indicating that using the MCAT and GPA together rather than either alone is a better predictor of performance in medical school in the pre-clerkship years (AAMC, 2019b).

Using local data to assess the predictability of these metrics on later performance would be fruitful to ensure they are not being overused or assessed at higher levels than necessary in admissions. The AAMC's Roadmap to Excellence: Key Concepts for Evaluating the Impact of Medical School Holistic Admissions (AAMC, 2013) is a helpful guide for evaluating admissions processes that follow the holistic review framework. Within this guide, there is feedback that evaluating outcomes alone is less meaningful than evaluating them along with student characteristics and the learning environment, which may be contributing to the student's performance (AAMC, 2013). The next section covers the holistic review framework in more detail.

ADMISSIONS SELECTION PROCESSES – HOW DO WE ASSESS APPLICANTS?

Medical schools have evolved in the way they assess applicants to their programs. Through a survey evaluating the changes in medical school admissions from 1986 to 2008, Monroe et al. (2013) found that 64% of admissions deans ranked nonacademic data as highly important in their decisions as compared to 50% in 1986. Additionally, in 1986, metrics such as cumulative and science GPA were ranked highest; in 2008, interviews and letters of recommendation were ranked higher than metrics (Monroe et al., 2013). Holistic review is a framework formally established by the AAMC to help medical schools meet their missions and includes the following goals: to identify applicants who are academically qualified to succeed in medical school, to identify applicants who have the experiences and attributes that will help them become well-rounded physicians, and to support enrolling a student body that better serves an increasingly diverse US population (Addams, Bletzinger, Sondheimer, White, & Johnson, 2010). Holistic review is as an approach that allows schools to intentionally assess applicants' readiness for medical school and alignment with the school's mission through a balanced consideration of their experience, attributes, and metrics through all stages of the admissions process (i.e., screening, interviewing, and selection; Addams, 2010). Since many medical schools in the US acknowledge utilizing holistic review as the framework for their admissions process (Urban Universities for HEALTH, 2014), it is the focus of this section.

Incorporating the balanced consideration of an applicant's experience, attributes, and metrics throughout the application process can make an impact on the earliest stages. Holistic review has been shown to increase diversity within an interview pool more than if the applicants' GPA and MCAT scores were primarily used for screening (Grabowski, 2018; Harrison, 2019). Holistic review has facilitated the enrollment of a student body with 75% African Americans (Elks et al., 2018). In another program which intentionally gave more weight to non-cognitive factors such as some of the intra and interpersonal competencies previously discussed, more students underrepresented in medicine (i.e., African American, Hispanic, and American Indian) were admitted (Ballejos, Rhyne, & Parkes, 2015). When MCAT and GPA have been highly prioritized in the selection of a matriculating class, diversity suffers (Heller et al., 2014). Diversity is not necessarily indicative of only race and ethnicity but may include many characteristics and experiences the medical school deems important in helping to meet community and population needs, depending on the mission. There are medical schools in states that function under legal prohibitions of race/ethnicity considerations; therefore, considering other factors, such as applicants hailing from disadvantaged backgrounds, can also help to produce a healthcare workforce that is culturally competent and ready to address health disparities among similar populations (Thomas & Dockter, 2019).

Coupling the holistic review process with the core competencies for entering medical schools as they relate with the school mission is an admissions process that is thoughtful and intentional. Using meritocracy instead of a holistic review presents challenges to achieving diversity in medical school classes (Razack, Hodges, Steinert, & Maguire, 2015). Razack et al. encourage that other forms of excellence also be considered. Since some of the core competencies such as the intra and interpersonal competencies are not easily assessed, developing defined rubrics and asking additional questions on the secondary applications allow schools admissions processes to strategically and equitably assess all applicants. Some ways of doing so are to utilize structured interviewing such as the Multiple Mini Interview (MMI) or situational judgment tests (SJT), which are discussed in more detail in the next section. Razack et al. caution that focusing solely on academic excellence can produce a hidden bias which favors applicants from privileged backgrounds.

Looking at past educational environments can also provide insight about an applicant's background (AAMC, 2013). Talamantes, Henderson, Fancher, and Mullan (2019) make the point that applicants who started their higher education in community colleges may provide insight about their background and access. If a medical school wants to increase the number of socioeconomically disadvantaged or first-generation students in its classes with the hopes of serving broader communities, the admissions process should be thoughtful about being accepting of community college coursework. Additionally, in a national sample, Talamantes et al. (2018) found that those who attended community college in their pathway were more likely to practice in family medicine. Furthermore, among those in family medicine residency, 32.7% African American/black and 50.8% Latino residents attended community college (Talamantes et al., 2018). These are good indicators that depending on the school mission, thoughtfully looking at applicant's past experiences, including educational experiences, may help the school meet its mission.

Holistic review provides a framework for enrolling broadly diverse classes that promote a learning environment where different experiences and perspectives are shared (Scott & Zerwic, 2015). Holistic review's impact is not meant to stop at enrolling a diverse class; it is critical that medical schools are prepared to support all students enrolled. This means that enrolling students from various life circumstances or academic access and preparedness may need unique support. The learning environment can have an impact on whether students thrive. Non-traditional students are another diverse group that may be captured through holistic review admissions practices (Harrison, 2019). Studies have shown that non-traditional students feel isolated (Goncalves & Trunk, 2014) and rate the learning environment more negatively than other students (Smith et al., 2016). Morehouse School of Medicine has implemented a successful mentoring and faculty engagement process to support their students, resulting in a 2% attrition rate when enrolling 75% African American students (Elks et al., 2018). Talamantes et al. (2019) argue that addressing structural barriers that preclude diverse students from being accepted and partnering within these communities to help foster a more diverse healthcare workforce are steps to enrolling medical school classes that better mirror the nation's population. More information on different pathways is discussed later in this chapter.

Finally, a key component of selection processes should be bias training and discussions. Additionally, the tools that are selected should be thoughtfully reviewed for evidence of bias. Both implicit and explicit bias can have an impact on the review of application materials. Thoughtful and intentional training should be provided to admissions committee members, reviewers/screeners, and interviewers on the ways in which our personal biases can influence our decisions. Capers, Clinchot, McDougle, and Greenwald (2017) found implicit white preference amongst all members of their admissions committee through the Implicit Association Test (IAT). Training about biases and ways to mitigate them in selection should be included in admissions committee training programs as well as ongoing committee discussions.

INTERVIEW AND ASSESSMENT MODALITIES – WHAT TOOLS CAN WE USE?

Medical schools use a wide variety of methods to evaluate applicant competencies in line with their institution-specific curricula and missions. In addition to using many different methods of evaluation for school-specific criteria, schools employ these methods at different stages in the application review process, ranging from application screening to final selection. In this section, some of the most common modalities for evaluation at various stages of the selection process and across multiple applicant competency areas are highlighted.

Academic Metrics

Evaluation of academic preparedness remains an important step in the holistic review process. Each institution has school-specific criteria for evaluating student preparedness to ensure students can handle the academic rigors of medical education. Admissions committees have been using academic metrics to evaluate science, thinking, and reasoning competency areas for many years. Researchers have consistently found previous grades and test scores to be good predictors of medical school grades and licensing exam scores (Kreiter & Kreiter, 2007). In addition to using GPAs and MCAT scores, admissions committees consider additional aspects of academic preparation such as rigor of coursework, trend in grades (ascending or descending), as well as academic majors, to determine whether an applicant is likely to be successful in the school's curricula. Admissions committees should evaluate the predictive value of academic metrics for their own curricula and outcomes to ensure alignment between admissions criteria and mission-driven outcomes.

As already stated, the timing and weighting of applicant data and evaluation tools vary by medical school and by stage of the admission process. This difference holds especially true for academic metrics. A 2013 survey of medical school admissions officers showed that schools more heavily use GPAs and MCAT scores in determining who to invite to submit a secondary application and to interview than they use academic metrics to determine offers of acceptance (Monroe et al., 2013). At many medical schools, once an applicant has been determined to have the academic metrics necessary to move forward in the process, more emphases are placed on non-academic competencies.

While metrics like grades and test scores may help predict basic science and standardized test performance in medical school (Andriole & Jeffe, 2012; Artino et al., 2012; Dunleavy, Kroopnick, Dowd, Searcy, & Zhao, 2013), the literature highlights some limitations to their use in predicting clinical performance (Basco, Gilbert, Chessman, & Blue, 2000; White, Dey, & Fantone, 2009) and professionalism (Cohen, 2006; Wagoner, 2006). In an effort to predict performance beyond basic sciences and standardized tests, admissions committees employ a wide variety of evaluation tools aimed at interpersonal and intrapersonal competencies. Multiple interview models and their contributions to the admissions selection process are discussed next.

Interviews

The admissions interview is the most commonly used selection modality in making acceptance decisions. In 2008, all medical schools reported using interviews in selection (Dunleavy & Whittaker, 2011). In a 2011 AAMC survey, medical school admissions officers identified interview recommendations as the most important application data used for making offers of admission (Dunleavy, Sondheimer,

Bletzinger, & Castillo-Page, 2011). Admissions officers are not the only ones who think positively of the interview process. In a systematic review of medical school selection methods, researchers found that both interviewers and interviewees view interviews in a positive light (Patterson et al., 2016). As stated earlier, while academic competencies are more closely scrutinized at the application screening stage of the admissions selection process, intrapersonal and interpersonal competencies are more heavily weighted using tools such as interviews in deciding who to offer admission (Dunleavy et al., 2011).

It is important to note that interviews provide value beyond evaluation and selection. In addition to using interviews as a means for making acceptance decisions, medical schools use interviews to add a human touch to the admissions process, to gather additional information not already reported in the application file, as well as to recruit desirable students (Albanese, Snow, Skochelak, Huggett, & Farrell, 2003; Edwards, Johnson, & Molidor, 1990). From the applicant perspective, it is an opportunity to learn about the school and culture, as well as the surrounding community.

While interview formats vary from school to school, the most common formats used in medical school admissions are the traditional one-on-one interview and the Multiple Mini Interview (MMI). Some schools use a combination of both traditional and MMI interviews to optimize the advantages of each format. The following sections highlight how schools are using these modalities and recent studies on their effectiveness.

Traditional Interviews

More than 80% of admissions officers surveyed in 2008 indicated that their medical schools used traditional one-on-one interviews in the selection process and that interviewers were comprised mostly of faculty and staff with some current student involvement (Dunleavy & Whittaker, 2011). While most medical schools use traditional interviews, schools vary in whether their interviews are structured or unstructured, what content and scoring is involved, as well as in the number and length of interviews offered, which may account for the mixed findings in the literature concerning interview reliability and validity (Patterson et al., 2016).

Structured interviews ensure that interviewers ask the same or similar questions and/or use a defined rubric for assessment. Unstructured interviews allow flexibility for the interviewer to ask and evaluate the applicant without a defined list of questions or rubric. To achieve higher reliability, the literature supports the use of more structured interview processes (Albanese et al., 2003; Edwards, Johnson & Molidor, 1990). The desire to improve the reliability of interviews has led to some innovations in medical school interviews such as the highly structured MMI process.

Multiple Mini Interviews

Multi-sampling interviewing techniques like the MMI offer more structure than traditional interviews as well as multiple assessments from different raters. Researchers at McMaster University created the MMI, a process similar to an objective structured clinical examination (OSCE), to provide a better tool than personal interviews and personal statements to assess non-cognitive attributes such as interpersonal skills and professionalism. The MMI consists of multiple short stations designed specifically to assess applicant attributes while simultaneously increasing the reliability and decreasing the bias that have been known to plague the personal interview process (Eva, Rosenfeld, Reiter, & Norman, 2004). Rather than interacting with a small number of interviewers in a traditional format, interviewees move from station to station with multiple different raters evaluating their performance in varying scenarios and activities. Interviewers, conversely, focus on a single question, activity, or scenario and observe multiple applicants. In addition to providing greater reliability, using multiple stations and/or scenarios provides schools with opportunities to rate applicants on the attributes they are most interested in evaluating in their institution-specific admissions processes. While more research is needed on the validity of the MMI tool, some studies show the MMI predicts program and licensing exam performance (Eva et al., 2009).

While the increased reliability of the MMI has been acknowledged by many admissions professionals, there remain some concerns about whether specific applicant characteristics are correlated with MMI performance. In other words, does the MMI have biases based on applicant personality or characteristics? In one study, researchers found that the personality traits of extraversion and agreeableness were associated significantly with high MMI scores (Jerant et al., 2012). In another multi-institution study, students from disadvantaged backgrounds were associated with lower MMI scores, females and older students were associated with higher MMI scores, and no association was found between applicants underrepresented in medicine (URM) and MMI scores (Jerant et al., 2015). More research is needed to better understand the possible impact of MMI scores across various applicant characteristics. Still, a systematic review of MMI research reported that interviewees and interviewers alike perceived the MMI as a fair method for selection (Pau et al., 2013).

Situational Judgment Tests

Another assessment tool that is gaining in popularity among admissions committees is the Situational Judgment Test (SJT). SJTs are used to evaluate the appropriateness of examinee responses to various scenarios or situations. These assessments have been used in the corporate environment for years. In an SJT, examinees are typically asked to evaluate the appropriateness or effectiveness of responses to various scenarios or situations. Medical schools have recently begun to use SJTs to evaluate competencies beyond academics (Lievens, 2013). As discussed previously, interview techniques that are structured are increasingly being employed by medical schools to evaluate non-cognitive attributes such as the interpersonal and intrapersonal competencies previously mentioned. Admissions professionals, however, are in search of evaluation tools that may be used at earlier stages of the application evaluation process. Interviews are costly and can only include a limited number of applicants. SJTs have the potential to be administered to large numbers of applicants and therefore, may provide more holistic data at the screening stage of the admissions process without requiring costly travel and interviewer resources.

Researchers have found SJTs to complement academic metrics to provide additional information about non-cognitive and professional attributes (Patterson et al., 2012). They have been found to have good predictive validity. While metrics like GPA and MCAT may help predict basic science and standardized test performance in medical school (Andriole & Jeffe, 2012; Artino et al., 2012; Dunleavy et al., 2013), the SJT has been shown to predict interpersonal and communication skills on the OSCE in medical school and job performance as a physician up to nine years following the SJT (Lievens, 2013). While just starting to gain popularity among medical schools, SJTs show promise for use in assessing personal competencies early in the selection process.

APPLICANT PATHWAYS

Applicant populations who are first-generation college graduates, come from low-socioeconomic backgrounds, are underrepresented minorities in medicine, and grew up in rural areas are often not the majority in their medical school classes. Even in recent years, the AAMC reports that matriculants into medical schools in the US come from affluent backgrounds and are mostly White and Asian (AAMC, 2016). This section provides information about admissions processes that consider these applicant pools and evidence of other pathways into and through medicine.

According to the US census in 2016, 47 million Americans lived in rural communities (United States Census, 2016). Extant research shows that one of the factors that strongly predicts practicing in a rural community is being from such a community (Rabinowitz, 2011). Medical schools in states with high rural communities have developed programs that are designed to recruit students from these communities into medical school and report higher placement of graduates into rural communities in their states. The programs outlined in this section all have a common model of strong recruitment, special admissions, and additional programming for the students. The Rural Medical Education Program at the University of Illinois has a broad recruitment program that includes a dual application to both the College of Medicine and the rural education program. Applicants are evaluated for potential to return to rural communities for practice. In addition to the regular MD curriculum, these students participate in a 16-week preceptorship with a rural physician (MacDowell, Glasser, & Hunsaker, 2013). Similarly, the University of Washington School of Medicine (UWSOM) has established the Targeted Rural Underserved Track (TRUST). The TRUST program includes the states of Washington, Wyoming, Alaska, Montana, and Idaho, which are among the most rural states in the US (Greer et al., 2016). Applicants are evaluated by the UWSOM via an additional application that evaluates their commitment to serve in a rural community. Accepted students experience four years of specialized extracurricular activities that provide exposure to rural medicine. This program also boasts a high placement of physicians into primary care in rural settings.

Michigan State University College of Human Medicine established the Rural Physician Program (RPP) in 1974 (Wendling, Phillips, Short, Fahey, & Mavis; 2016). A subset of students who are accepted into the medical school are interviewed for likelihood to practice in a rural setting and are selected prior to matriculation. RPP participants experience clinical rotations in rural communities in the Upper Peninsula area of northern Michigan. A 30-year data analysis revealed that participants in this program had a higher likelihood of practicing primary care and in a rural setting in comparison to the non-RPP students. The University of Kansas Medical School opened a campus in 2011 that is situated in a small town of 50,000 to attract local residents who may have an interest in serving rural communities (Cathcarte-Rake, Robinson, & Paolo, 2017). Application and admission to the program occurs in the sophomore year of college for rural students with guaranteed admission to the medical school. The institution also provides loans that cover tuition, which is forgiven if after residency the physician establishes a practice in rural Kansas. Since the program is young, there are no data regarding practice location; however, the majority of graduates pursued primary care residency tracks. These are a few examples of the many targeted admission and retention programs that are available nationally to recruit rural students into medicine. The common theme among these programs is a true understanding of the rural community and recruitment of rural students, intentional admission, and specific extracurricular activities that allow for immersion into rural healthcare settings.

Students who are first in their family to attend college are considered underrepresented in medicine (Brosnan et al., 2016). The Stanford Medial Youth Science Program (http://smysp.stanford.edu/) partners with low resourced, primarily minority-serving high schools in Northern California to expose students to science and medicine. The program boasts high success in producing students who go to college at a higher rate than the state and almost half enter graduate or medical programs (Winkleby, Ned, & Crump, 2015). The authors attribute the success of the program to an understanding of the needs of the local community, among other things. Talamantes et al. (2014) used archival data from the AAMC medical school applicant pool of 2012 to investigate the educational pathway that applicants experienced before matriculating to medical school. Their main focus was on the community college trajectory. They found that one-third of the applicants went through a community college pathway and 34% of the Latino matriculants had been through the community college track. Furthermore, their study revealed that students who started in the community college environment had a higher interest in practicing in underserved communities. This finding is useful at a variety of levels, and importantly, it provides a large pool of students who are underrepresented in medicine as a strong target for recruitment efforts.

The University of California Irvine instituted the Program in Medical Education – PRIME designed to increase medical student engagement with disadvantaged Latino communities in 2004 (Bailey & Willies-Jacobo, 2012). The program was not only successful in bringing attention and care to underserved communities, it also managed to increase the number of underrepresented students in the medical school. Admission to the program was via a supplemental application that described the candidate's interest in the PRIME. In a two-year analysis of applications, the authors found that applicants who were female, from disadvantage backgrounds, or underrepresented in medicine were more likely to indicate an interest in this specific program (Bailey & Willies-Jacobo, 2012). Bailey and Willies-Jacobo concluded that the student's connection to a familiar community was part of the reason for the interest they observed in the specific groups. Collaboration between medical schools in Arizona, Colorado, New Mexico, and Utah has resulted in a two-day pre-admissions workshop that targets American Indian/Alaskan Native (AI/AN) applicants to medical school (Ballejos et. al., 2018). The data from the 2011-2016 application cycles suggests that the number of AI/AN applicants to medical school who have attended this workshop has steadily increased over the duration of the program despite the number of students matriculating to medical school remaining stagnant. The authors intend to increase the number of states that are participating in this initiative to further the reach of the program.

In contrast to what has been presented thus far, which has primarily consisted of creating mechanisms to increase the applications of underrepresented students, the faculty at The Ohio State School of Medicine decided to review how the admissions committee functioned. Capers et al. (2017) investigated the influence of implicit bias in the admissions process. The authors discovered that the admissions committee exhibited a high level of implicit White preference in the evaluation of candidates. The participants reported that they had a better understanding of their bias and this impacted their admissions decisions in the subsequent year. In thinking back to the increase in AI/AN applications in the Ballejos et al. (2018) study, this finding supports the notion that some of the work rests with admissions committees and not solely with increasing the pipeline. Additionally, the AAMC conducted Holistic Review in Admissions workshops for several years. An analysis of the composition of the students matriculating into schools that participated in the workshop revealed an increase in four measures of diversity: percent first-generation college students, percent of black/African American and Latino/Hispanic students, and overall percent of racial diversity (Grbic, Morrison, Sondheimer, Conrad, & Milem, 2019). This provides additional support for the need for admissions committees to be intentional in the selection process.

ADMISSIONS COMMITTEE PERSPECTIVE

Faculty at US medical schools and universities come from a variety of backgrounds, usually without a shared understanding of the medical school application process or of the evolving definitions of holistic review. Thus, appropriate recruitment and training are critical to maintain a functioning and thriving Admissions Committee. If the Committee is seen as largely "too much work," junior faculty or those with significant research or clinical commitments will be discouraged from membership, though their voices are critical to the process. This section focuses on recruitment and retention techniques for faculty on the Admissions Committee, the benefits of community member participation on the committee, and the need for diverse voices on the committee.

Admissions Committees must review hundreds of applications at various stages of the review process, necessitating efficiency. Thus, committee members often define what they are looking for, and may be quick to judge an applicant. Applications with serious grammatical or even minor, but many, errors are discouraging to reviewers. Applications with incomplete or missing answers to questions (or clear discrepancies) may warrant a call to the applicant, but the volume of applications received by most medical schools is an impediment to this extra check. The applicant who tells a story of "why medicine" and articulates clearly "why *this* medical school" is likely to go much further, especially if these statements, experiences, and attributes align with the school's mission.

Given the detailed and laborious nature of application review, medical schools often struggle to recruit and retain faculty for committees such as admissions, which have a heavy, unpaid workload. Critically, faculty must be thoroughly introduced to the expectations and responsibilities of membership, including deadlines, time commitments, and ethical and conflict of interest policies. Aligning with university expectations for service and citizenship, and if possible, with promotion and tenure guidelines, can be helpful to recruiting membership. Incentive systems to encourage service, credit toward promotion, and even small rewards, such as refreshments at meetings and a committee annual dinner event, can help faculty to feel recognized and valued for their contributions to the organization.

To comply with the LCME standards (specifically Standard 10), administrative leadership's roles must be made clear to faculty, and possibilities for undue influence or coercion of committee members must be mitigated. One institution addresses these areas for potential pitfalls through communication, starting at an Admissions Committee Annual Retreat. The retreat includes all Admissions Committee members, including those from regional campuses, to allow for trust building and the development of rapport. These aspects may seem unimportant but are vital to the accomplishment of the heavy workload ahead.

As Admissions Committee members, community leaders and non-physicians offer a unique perspective on the selection of medical students and in shaping the overall admissions process. Community members and non-physicians bring a patient's perspective to the forefront and are particularly focused on the mission-alignment of candidates. While a physician faculty member may remember their own application to medical school and their own perspectives on that process, the non-physicians and community members can focus, often to a greater degree, on "Who should be the next generation of physicians from our school?"

Creating a committee environment that is inclusive of diverse voices is paramount to a well-functioning Admissions Committee and to upholding the principles of holistic review (Addams et al., 2010). The inclusion of faculty, regional campus participants, students, community leaders, and non-physician members is certainly an important first step. To be truly effective, however, the environment within Admissions Committee discussions must adhere to the principle of inclusion of all voices. Training on, and attention to, implicit and explicit biases, the practice of self-awareness of bias, and sharing the values of hearing each voice help to make inclusion the norm, rather than an afterthought (Capers et al., 2017). Members should be encouraged to speak up about what they hear in their own and others' presentations of applicants and to complete discussions "in the room." Critically, accurate timekeeping, mundane though it may seem, demonstrates to the committee that applicants who are presented receive equal time, and that particular members' opinions are not prioritized over others.

Admissions Committee service is difficult and challenging, but also highly rewarding and aligned with the mission of medical education—a major incentive for participation. Few scholarships currently exist in the area of promoting Admissions Committee effective practices; committee chairs or members may find that their own academic pursuits are enhanced when they consider scholarly approaches to maintaining a functioning group. More work is necessary to define the function, leadership, and characteristics of a well-run and appropriately focused Admissions Committee in the era of holistic review.

PRE-HEALTH ADVISOR PERSPECTIVE

The implementation of the holistic review in admissions, the new 2015 MCAT, and the expansion of the application services (AMCAS, TMDSAS, AACOMAS) have had a significant impact on the work of pre-health advisors and their respective offices. Many collegiate undergraduate premedical programs have responded and evolved to better prepare students for their future training in the medical profession and support their matriculation into medical school, which has led to a variety of approaches in pre-health advising and programming. Pre-health advisors and faculty are confronted with many logistical and programming concerns and issues in their efforts to help their students develop into competitive medical school applicants. To be competitive in the holistic review process, premedical students have to navigate a rigorous science curriculum, prepare for the MCAT, and participate in a variety of professional, scholastic and service activities throughout their undergraduate career, while advisors support their efforts through advising, special programming, committee letters.

Curricular advising has always been the cornerstone of the pre-health advisor's relationship with their students. Pre-health advisors encouraged their students to explore their curricular opportunities and seek opportunities to expand their knowledge, backgrounds and skills in the variety of academic disciplines at their institutions. Through a more robust and diverse curriculum, the students can better define their interests and aspirations, while cultivating their awareness and appreciation for culture and diversity that will aid them in their future patient interactions. Moreover, students who engage in a wide range of academic courses will certainly be better prepared for the new sections (Critical Analysis and Reasoning and Psychological, Social and Biological Foundations of Behavior) in the 2015 MCAT. Consequently, premedical academic advising is far more dynamic and requires thoughtful strategies that challenges students to work beyond the basic science requirements of medical school admissions.

To be competitive in the holistic admissions process, students have to demonstrate intelligence, professionalism, self-awareness, empathy, ethics, motivation, resilience, and the abilities to collaborate, communicate and problem-solve beyond their academic curriculum. It is beneficial for student applications if they can engage in leadership roles, community service, and research activities. To address this, some premedical advisors have to work outside of their academic advising roles and into the field of student development. Pre-health advisors have to both challenge and support their students through workshops, activities, and programs to cultivate these service-minded and scholarly attributes and abilities. Moving out of the traditional academic advising models does present many challenges, but has also led to an opportunity for creativity and meaningful engagement, both in and outside of the classroom, for the advisors. Pre-health advisors and premedical programs need to be creative, innovative, and adaptable so as to provide the experiences necessary for the students to be ready for their careers in medicine and competitive in the holistic review process.

Considering the dynamic shift in medical school admission assessment towards a more holistic review process, pre-health advisors are developing new programs and activities that cultivate the student's interpersonal and intrapersonal qualities, while also supporting and encouraging scholarly achievement. Moreover, they have to maintain their role in ensuring the students partake in the necessary curriculum to meet the requirements of each medical school, and to be ready for the MCAT. Over half of the student's undergraduate career is dedicated to completing the minimum recommended courses for medical school. In addition to the traditional curricular advising, many premedical programs sponsor a range of activities and specialized coursework that encourage and allow their students to engage in community service and professional experiences, while providing thoughtful reflection on their personal aspirations. These new programs need the partnership of healthcare providers and academic medical centers to generate professional and educational experiences and mentorship. These partnerships can take the shape of undergraduate research programs, health-related internships, clinical service activities, shadowing, and community outreach. Many pre-health programs are also involved in global health programs and sponsor medical mission trips both in and outside of the United States. It is also necessary to have a variety of medical doctors and other healthcare providers meet and engage with students on the college campus through academic coursework or student life activities. These partnerships need to be strategically developed to ensure they support the professional and personal growth of the student while not impeding the clinical work of the medical practices or the research efforts of the academic centers. Many, if not most, healthcare practices/offices and medical research centers are not orientated to engage with undergraduate students, so these partnerships do require significant planning and coordination on the part of the pre-health advisors to be successful and sustainable. Additionally, partnering with area medical schools to provide workshops, presentations, and student panels can help increase acceptance to medical school as well as informed decisions earlier in the collegiate career about whether to pursue medicine (Harrison, White, & Sanker, 2017). All of these endeavors require the advisors to be adept at balancing the students' curriculum and proactive in developing the relationships with healthcare professions. It may also be the case that these partnerships and exposure may not be possible due to limited access; thus, other opportunities such as community service may be prioritized. If medical schools can seek to understand these limitations, it can help them better understand the applicants coming through those programs.

Another outcome of the holistic review is that more non-traditional applicants are being considered for admission, which also creates some new challenges and opportunities for pre-health advisors. To address this development, advisors are more intentional in their support of non-traditional and more social-economically diverse college students, which has provided opportunities for pre-health programs to collaborate with student success and multicultural affairs offices. New curricular models and strategies are being designed and implemented as well as specialized post-baccalaureate programs to support the emerging population of these non-traditional applicants. Programs such as Minority Association of Pre-medical Students (MAPS) and Student National Medical Association (SNMA) are becoming more critical and substantial parts of many pre-health programs. To address the needs of these students, pre-health offices and advisors must work across their campuses and even the greater local, state and global communities to support the success of these students. The traditional premedical academic departments are rethinking their coursework and curricular structure to meet the emerging needs of this cohort, while working more closely with programs in their Office of Access and Learning Accommodations (OALA). Online courses and supplemental instruction are becoming far more common within science departments. All of this requires the undergraduate faculty and pre-health advisors to be adaptable and work year-round to provide the accelerated curriculum and programs to support the diverse needs of their students. To accomplish all of this, pre-health advisors need to innovate their advising programs, while incorporating technology such as the Internet into the pre-health advising systems curricular operations.

Consequently, pre-health programs are becoming vibrant centers of advising, career counseling, and student engagement. Pre-health advisors have a much broader and more significant impact on the lives of their students and their institutions. These new dimensions of engagement and mentorship do present many challenges for pre-health advisors. They and their campuses require the resources and staffing needed to provide these services and programs. More importantly, they also need the support and active participation of the medical schools and medical professionals. The medical profession is seeking a more dynamic and diverse pool of candidates; it therefore, needs to provide opportunities of engagement and partnerships with undergraduate institutions and their pre-health programs. Additional ways for pre-health advisors to engage is through the National Association of Advisors for the Health Professions (NAAHP) which has a biannual national meeting allowing pre-health advisors and professional schools to network, present their programs and research findings, and learn effective practices. This organization also has regional organizations with conferences offered in the off-years from the national conference. NAAHP offers rich resources to both pre-health advisors and new medical educators working in the admissions space. Finally, NAAHP facilitates the publication of a journal called "The Advisor" where both pre-health advisors and professional schools can submit manuscripts for publication.

A final important aspect to consider is that not all colleges/universities have pre-health advisors or pre-health centers. Many rely on science faculty to provide guidance and advising without the resources, both financial and knowledge of the application process or medical education. Medical educators and administrators should remember that not all applicants come through well-staffed pre-medical advising centers. Many applicants navigate the application process on their own. This might be especially true for rural and/or underserved institutions or non-traditional applicants. Equal access to guidance is not the reality which could further disadvantage rural and first-generation applicants, among others. Medical schools could target these under-resourced schools in their pathway programs and recruitment to provide guidance to faculty and students.

CONCLUSION

The goals of this chapter were to provide an in-depth, well-rounded coverage of many of the factors that are part of the medical school admissions process in the US, as well as to provide a review from the literature for each topic. Furthermore, the perspectives from two key areas of admissions, the admissions committee chair and the pre-health advisor, provided unique insight from those who work closely with the selection process and with the applicants themselves. The admissions process to medical school is not a simple linear process taking in only certain pieces of information. Instead, it includes a plethora of information about applicants and data of their achievements to help admissions committees make informed decisions about who to accept. Many medical schools receive thousands of applications for only a few hundred seats each cycle making this a critical process for selecting the future physician workforce to meet the ever-changing needs of our diverse communities. Each medical school has a unique process that often has the mission at its core. The ways in which they evaluate candidates and the characteristics or experiences they are looking for can vary broadly. Additionally, admissions committees must be mindful that not all applicants had equal or any access to advising when applying. Finally, medical schools must be aware of and thoughtfully provide bias training for those involved in any way in the process. Utilizing assessment tools and rubrics which are highly structured are part of helping to minimize bias in the process, however individuals involved must also be trained on the impact explicit and implicit biases can have when reviewing applications and making decisions. Building processes that are data-informed and that utilize effective practices can better optimize the time of the group making decisions and assure that processes remain aligned with schools' missions and with state and federal law.

REFERENCES

Addams, A. N., Bletzinger, R. B., Sondheimer, H. M., White, S. E., & Johnson, L. M. (2010). *Roadmap to diversity: Integrating holistic review practices into medical school admission processes*. Washington, DC: Association of American Medical Colleges.

Albanese, M. A., Snow, M. H., Skochelak, S. E., Huggett, K. N., & Farrell, P. M. (2003). Assessing personal qualities in medical school admissions. *Academic Medicine, 78*(3), 313–321. doi:10.1097/00001888-200303000-00016 PMID:12634215

American Association of Colleges of Osteopathic Medicine. (2018). *AACOMAS Applicant Pool Profile Entering Class 2018*. Retrieved from https://www.aacom.org/reports-programs-initiatives/aacom-reports/applicants

American Osteopathic Association. (2019). Osteopathic medical schools. Retrieved from https://osteopathic.org/about/affiliated-organizations/osteopathic-medical-schools/

Andriole, D. A., & Jeffe, D. B. (2012). A national cohort study of U.S. medical school students who initially failed Step 1 of the United States Licensing Examination. *Academic Medicine, 87*(4), 529–536. doi:10.1097/ACM.0b013e318248dd9c PMID:22361789

Artino, A. R. Jr, Gilliland, W. R., Waechter, D. M., Cruess, D., Calloway, M., & Durning, S. J. (2012). Does self-reported clinical experience predict performance in medical school and internship? *Medical Education, 46*(2), 172–178. doi:10.1111/j.1365-2923.2011.04080.x PMID:22239331

Association of American Medical Colleges. (2013). *Roadmap to excellence: Key concepts for evaluating the impact of medical school holistic admissions*. Retrieved from https://members.aamc.org/eweb/upload/Holistic%20Review%202013.pdf

Association of American Medical Colleges. (2016). *Diversity in medical education: Facts and figures 2016*. Retrieved from http://www.aamcdiversityfactsandfigures2016.org/

Association of American Medical Colleges. (2018a). *Table A-3: Applicants to U.S. Medical Schools by State of Legal Residence, 2009-2010 through 2018-2019*. Retrieved from https://www.aamc.org/download/321460/data/factstablea3.pdf

Association of American Medical Colleges. (2018b). *Table A-4: Matriculants to U.S. Medical Schools by State of Legal Residence, 2009-2010 through 2018-2019.* Retrieved from https://www.aamc.org/download/321462/data/factstablea4.pdf

Association of American Medical Colleges. (2019a). Core competencies for entering medical students. Retrieved from https://www.aamc.org/admissions/dataandresearch/477182/corecompetencies.html

Association of American Medical Colleges. (2019b). *Using MCAT Data in 2020 Medical Student Selection.* Retrieved from https://www.aamc.org/download/498250/data/usingmcatdatain2020medstudentselection.pdf

Bailey, J. A., & Willies-Jacobo, L. J. (2012). Are disadvantaged and underrepresented minority applicants more likely to apply to the Program in Medical Education-Health Equity? *Academic Medicine, 87*(11), 1535–1539. doi:10.1097/ACM.0b013e31826d6220 PMID:23018330

Ballejos, M. P., Olsen, P., Price-Johnson, T., Garcia, C., Parker, T., Sapién, R. E., & Romero-Leggott, V. (2018). Recruiting American Indian/Alaska Native students to medical school: A multi-institutional alliance in the U.S. Southwest. *Academic Medicine, 93*(1), 71–75. doi:10.1097/ACM.0000000000001952 PMID:29045274

Ballejos, M. P., Rhyne, R. L., & Parkes, J. (2015). Increasing the relative weight of noncognitive admission criteria improves underrepresented minority admission rates to medical school. *Teaching and Learning in Medicine, 27*(2), 155–162. doi:10.1080/10401334.2015.1011649 PMID:25893937

Basco, W. T. Jr, Gilbert, G. E., Chessman, A. W., & Blue, A. V. (2000). The ability of a medical school admission process to predict clinical performance and patient's satisfaction. *Academic Medicine, 75*(7), 743–747. doi:10.1097/00001888-200007000-00021 PMID:10926028

Betancourt, J. R., Corbett, J., & Bondaryk, M. R. (2014). Addressing disparities and achieving equity: Cultural competence, ethics, and health-care transformation. *Chest, 145*(1), 143–148. doi:10.1378/chest.13-0634 PMID:24394825

Brosnan, C., Southgate, E., Outram, S., Lempp, H., Wright, S., Saxby, T., ... Kelly, B. (2016). Experiences of students who are first in family to attend university. *Medical Education, 50*(8), 842–851. doi:10.1111/medu.12995 PMID:27402044

Capers, Q. I. V. IV, Clinchot, D., McDougle, L., & Greenwald, A. G. (2017). Implicit bias in medical school admissions. *Academic Medicine, 92*(3), 365–369. doi:10.1097/ACM.0000000000001388 PMID:27680316

Cathcart-Rake, W., Robinson, M., & Paolo, A. (2017). From infancy to adolescence: Kansas University School of Medicine- Salina: A rural medical campus story. *Academic Medicine, 92*(5), 622–627. doi:10.1097/ACM.0000000000001455 PMID:27805948

Cohen, J. J. (2006). Professionalism in medical education, an American perspective: From evidence to accountability. *Medical Education, 40*(7), 607–617. doi:10.1111/j.1365-2929.2006.02512.x PMID:16836532

Dunleavy, D., Sondheimer, H., Bletzinger, R., & Castillo-Page, L. (2011). Medical school admissions: More than grades and test scores. *Analysis in Brief, 11*(6), 1–2.

Dunleavy, D. M., Kroopnick, M. H., Dowd, K. W., Searcy, C. A., & Zhao, X. (2013). The predictive validity of the MCAT exam in relation to academic performance through medical school: A national cohort study of 2001-2004 matriculants. *Academic Medicine, 88*(5), 666–671. doi:10.1097/ACM.0b013e3182864299 PMID:23478635

Dunleavy D. M. & Whittaker, K. M. (2011). The Evolving Medical School Admissions Interview. *Analysis in Brief, 11*(7).

Durning, S. J., Dong, T., Hemmer, P. A., Gilliland, W. R., Cruess, D. F., Boulet, J. R., & Pangarao, L. N. (2015). Are commonly used premedical school or medical school measures associated with board certification? *Military Medicine, 180*(4), 18–23. doi:10.7205/MILMED-D-14-00569 PMID:25850122

Edwards, J. C., Johnson, E. K., & Molidor, J. B. (1990). The interview in the admission process. *Academic Medicine, 65*(3), 167–177. doi:10.1097/00001888-199003000-00008 PMID:2407259

Elks, M. L., Herbert-Carter, J., Smith, M., Klement, B., Knight, B. B., & Anachebe, N. F. (2018). Shifting the curve. Fostering academic success in a diverse student body. *Academic Medicine, 93*(1), 66–70. doi:10.1097/ACM.0000000000001783 PMID:28678099

Eva, K. W., Reiter, H. I., Trinh, K., Wasi, P., Rosenfeld, J., & Norman, G. R. (2009). Predictive validity of multiple mini-interview for selecting medical trainees. *Medical Education, 43*(8), 767–775. doi:10.1111/j.1365-2923.2009.03407.x PMID:19659490

Eva, K. W., Rosenfeld, J., Reiter, H. I., & Norman, G. R. (2004). An admissions OSCE: The multiple mini-interview. *Medical Education, 38*(3), 314–326. doi:10.1046/j.1365-2923.2004.01776.x PMID:14996341

Goncalves, S. A., & Trunk, D. (2014). Obstacles to success for the nontraditional student in higher education. *Psi Chi Journal of Psychological Research, 19*(4), 164–172. doi:10.24839/2164-8204.JN19.4.164

Grabowski, C. J. (2018). Impact of holistic review on student interview pool diversity. *Advances in Health Sciences Education: Theory and Practice, 23*(3), 487–498. doi:10.100710459-017-9807-9 PMID:29288323

Grbic, D., Morrison, E., Sondheimer, H. M., Conrad, S. S., & Milem, J. F. (2019). The association between a holistic review in admissions workshop and the diversity of accepted applicants and students matriculating to medical school. *Academic Medicine, 94*(3), 396–403. doi:10.1097/ACM.0000000000002446 PMID:30188373

Greer, T., Kost, A., Evans, D. V., Norris, T., Erickson, J., McCarthy, J., & Allen, S. (2016). The WWAMI Targeted Rural Underserved Track (TRUST) Program: An innovative response to rural physician workforce shortages. *Academic Medicine, 91*(1), 65–69. doi:10.1097/ACM.0000000000000807 PMID:26200575

Harrison, L. E. (2019). Using holistic review to form a diverse interview pool for selection to medical school. *Baylor University Medical Center Proceedings, 32*(2), 218–221. doi:10.1080/08998280.2019.1576575 PMID:31191132

Harrison, L. E., White, B. A., & Sanker, R. (2017). Exposing premedical students to the full continuum and practice of a physician for informed decisions: Innovative partnership between an undergraduate program and a medical school. *The Advisor,* 9-13.

Heller, C. A., Rua, S. H., Mazumdar, M., Moon, J. E., Bardes, C., & Gotto, A. M. Jr. (2014). Diversity efforts, admissions, and national rankings: Can we align priorities? *Teaching and Learning in Medicine*, *26*(3), 304–311. doi:10.1080/10401334.2014.910465 PMID:25010244

Jerant, A., Fancher, T., Fenton, J. J., Fiscella, K., Sousa, F., Franks, P., & Henderson, M. (2015). How medical school applicant race, ethnicity, and socioeconomic status relate to multiple mini-interview based admissions outcomes: Findings from one medical school. *Academic Medicine*, *90*(12), 1667–1674. doi:10.1097/ACM.0000000000000766 PMID:26017355

Jerant, A., Griffin, E., Rainwater, J., Henderson, M., Sousa, F., Bertakis, K. D., ... Franks, P. (2012). Does applicant personality influence multiple mini-interview performance and medical school acceptance offers? *Academic Medicine*, *87*(9), 1250–1259. doi:10.1097/ACM.0b013e31826102ad PMID:22836836

Koenig, T. W., Parrish, S. K., Terregino, C. A., Williams, J. P., Dunleavy, D. M., & Volsch, J. M. (2013). Core personal competencies important to entering students' success in medical school: What are they and how could they be assessed early in the admission process? *Academic Medicine*, *88*(5), 603–613. doi:10.1097/ACM.0b013e31828b3389 PMID:23524928

Kreiter, C. D., & Kreiter, Y. (2007). A validity generalization perspective on the ability of undergraduate GPA and the medical college admission test to predict important outcomes. *Teaching and Learning in Medicine*, *19*(2), 95–100. doi:10.1080/10401330701332094 PMID:17564535

Liaison Committee on Medical Education. (2019). Accredited MD programs in the United States. Retrieved from http://lcme.org/directory/accredited-u-s-programs/

Lievens, F. (2013). Adjusting medical school admission: Assessing interpersonal skills using situational judgement tests. *Medical Education*, *47*(2), 182–189. doi:10.1111/medu.12089 PMID:23323657

Lu, D. W., Dresden, S., McCloskey, C., Branzetti, J., & Gisondi, M. A. (2015). Impact of burnout on self-reported patient care among emergency physicians. *The Western Journal of Emergency Medicine*, *16*(7), 996–1001. doi:10.5811/westjem.2015.9.27945 PMID:26759643

MacDowell, M., Glasser, M., & Hunsaker, M. (2013). A decade of rural physician workforce outcomes for the Rockford Rural Medical Education (RMED) Program, University of Illinois. *Academic Medicine*, *88*(12), 1941–1947. doi:10.1097/ACM.0000000000000031 PMID:24128632

Monroe, A., Quinn, E., Samuelson, W., Dunleavy, D. M., & Dowd, K. W. (2013). An overview of the medical school admission process and use of applicant data in decision making: What has changed since the 1980s? *Academic Medicine*, *88*(5), 672–681. doi:10.1097/ACM.0b013e31828bf252 PMID:23524917

O'Brien, S. E., Simpkin, A. L., & Spector, N. D. (2017). Promoting resilience in academic medicine: Fertile ground for future work. *The Journal of Pediatrics*, *182*, 6–7. doi:10.1016/j.jpeds.2016.11.056 PMID:28007471

Patterson, F., Ashworth, V., Zibarras, L., Coan, P., Kerrin, M., & O'Neill, P. (2012). Evaluation of situational judgement tests to assess non-academic attributes in selection. *Medical Education*, *46*(9), 850–868. doi:10.1111/j.1365-2923.2012.04336.x PMID:22891906

Patterson, F., Knight, A., Dowell, J., Nicholson, S., Cousans, F., & Cleland, J. (2016). How effective are selection methods in medical education? A systematic review. *Medical Education, 50*(1), 36–60. doi:10.1111/medu.12817 PMID:26695465

Pau, A., Jeevaratnam, K., Chen, Y., Fall, A., Khoo, C., & Nadarajah, V. (2013). The Multiple Mini-Interview (MMI) for student selection in health professions training – A systematic review. *Medical Teacher, 35*(12), 1027–1041. doi:10.3109/0142159X.2013.829912 PMID:24050709

Rabinowitz, H. K. (2011). AM last page: Truths about the rural physician supply. *Academic Medicine, 86*(2), 272. doi:10.1097/ACM.0b013e31820add6c PMID:21270556

Razack, S., Hodges, B., Steinert, Y., & Maguire, M. (2015). Seeking inclusion in an exclusive process: Discourses of medical school student selection. *Medical Education, 49*(1), 36–47. doi:10.1111/medu.12547 PMID:25545572

Rosen, M. A., DiazGranados, D., Dietz, A. S., Benishek, L. E., Thompson, D., Pronovost, P. J., & Weaver, S. J. (2018). Teamwork in healthcare: Key discoveries enabling safer, high-quality care. *The American Psychologist, 73*(4), 433–450. doi:10.1037/amp0000298 PMID:29792459

Scott, L. D., & Zerwic, J. (2015). Holistic review in admissions: A strategy to diversify the nursing workforce. *Nursing Outlook, 63*(4), 488–495. doi:10.1016/j.outlook.2015.01.001 PMID:26187088

Smith, S. D., Dunham, L., Dekhtyar, M., Dinh, A., Lanken, P. N., Moynahan, K. F., ... Skochelak, S. E. (2016). Medical student perceptions of the learning environment: Learning communities are associated with a more positive learning environment in a multi-institutional medical school study. *Academic Medicine, 91*(9), 1263–1269. doi:10.1097/ACM.0000000000001214 PMID:27119332

Talamantes, E., Henderson, M. C., Fancher, T. L., & Mullan, F. (2019). Closing the gap: Making medical school admissions more equitable. *The New England Journal of Medicine, 380*(9), 803–805. doi:10.1056/NEJMp1808582 PMID:30811906

Talamantes, E., Jerant, A., Henderson, M. C., Giffin, E., Fancher, T., Grbic, D., ... Franks, P. (2018). Community college pathways to medical school and family medicine residency training. *Annals of Family Medicine, 16*(4), 302–307. doi:10.1370/afm.2270 PMID:29987077

Talamantes, E., Mangione, C. M., Gonzalez, K., Jimenez, A., Gonzalez, F., & Moreno, G. (2014). Community college pathways: Improving the U.S. physician workforce pipeline. *Academic Medicine, 89*(12), 1649–1656. doi:10.1097/ACM.0000000000000438 PMID:25076199

Thomas, B. R., & Dockter, N. (2019). Affirmative action and holistic review in medical school admissions: Where we have been and where we are going. *Academic Medicine, 94*(4), 473–476. doi:10.1097/ACM.0000000000002482 PMID:30277960

United States Census Bureau. (2016). Retrieved from https://www.census.gov/newsroom/press-releases/2016/cb16-210.html

Urban Universities for HEALTH. (2014). *Holistic admissions in the health professions. Findings from a national survey.* Retrieved from http://urbanuniversitiesforhealth.org/media/documents/holisticadmissionsinthehealthprofessions.pdf

Wagoner, N. E. (2006). Admission to medical school: Selecting applicants with the potential for professionalism. In D. T. Stern (Ed.), *Measuring Medical Professionalism* (pp. 235–263). New York: Oxford University Press.

Wendling, A. L., Phillips, J., Short, W., Fahey, C., & Mavis, B. (2016). Thirty years training rural physicians: Outcomes from the Michigan State University College of Human Medicine Rural Physician Program. *Academic Medicine, 91*(1), 113–119. doi:10.1097/ACM.0000000000000885 PMID:26332428

White, C. B., Dey, E. L., & Fantone, J. C. (2009). Analysis of factors that predict clinical performance in medical school. *Advances in Health Sciences Education: Theory and Practice, 14*(4), 455–464. doi:10.100710459-007-9088-9 PMID:18030590

Winkleby, M. A., Hed, J., & Crump, C. (2015). Tapping underserved students to reshape the biomedical workforce. *Journal of Community Medicine & Health Education, 5*(2), 340. doi:10.4172/2161-0711.1000340 PMID:26120496

KEY TERMS AND DEFINITIONS

Admissions Committee: The majority faculty body at a medical school which makes most, if not all, of the selection decisions for entrance into the program. This committee's oversight is also guided by requirements of the LCME.

Core Competencies: Interpersonal and intrapersonal competencies medical schools look for in applicants that inform selection decisions.

Holistic Review: A framework developed by the Association of American Medical Colleges that encourages the balanced consideration of an applicant's experiences, attributes, and metrics to help the school meet its mission.

Liaison Committee on Medical Education (LCME): The accrediting body for MD programs in the United States and Canada.

Multiple Mini Interviews: A structured assessment with multiple stations or scenarios used to evaluate applicants for key characteristics and competencies, much like Objective Structured Clinical Examinations.

Pre-health Advisor: In the US higher education system, the pre-health advisor helps students while at college/university as they prepare to apply to medical school. Pre-health and pre-medical advisor are often used synonymously.

Situational Judgement Test: An assessment used to measure appropriateness of examinee responses to realistic scenarios; often used to assess applicant attributes.

Chapter 3
Advising and Mentoring Disadvantaged Students Through the Medical School Admissions Process:
When Students Don't Know What They Don't Know

Jan L. Reichard-Brown
Susquehanna University, USA

Lolita A. Wood-Hill
Yeshiva University, USA

Ellen M. Watts
Fordham University, USA

ABSTRACT

Undergraduate students from disadvantaged backgrounds can find the adjustment to college academics and other collegiate expectations confusing and disconcerting. They must learn to understand and navigate what has been referred to as the Hidden Curriculum: the ideas, norms, and expectations that are not overtly stated, but which the student must implicitly understand. These students don't even know what they don't know when they arrive on campus. This chapter focuses on aspects of the undergraduate hidden curriculum, particularly as they affect the career of the pre-medical student and the student's potential for becoming a competitive applicant to medical school. Several illustrative case studies are presented and analyzed in light of what is referred to as the Bachelors Hidden Curriculum (BHC). The chapter closes with a discussion of approaches that pre-medical advisors and student mentors may take to try to mitigate the impact of the BHC on these worthy students.

DOI: 10.4018/978-1-7998-1468-9.ch003

BACKGROUND

The institutions providing undergraduate medical education seek to increase the diversity of the future physician workforce. (AAMC n.d.). To this end many medical schools disseminate programming to educate high school and college students, representing diverse populations, about medicine as a career and the pathway to that career. However, the expansion of the diversity of the future physician workforce can only be accomplished if those students are accepted to medical school and matriculate. Students finding the application process complicated and incomprehensible become at risk for entering the formal medical education process with a reduced level of confidence and less affirmation of their abilities, compared with their classmates. Disadvantaged, rural, and students from minority communities are at greatest risk regarding the application process to medical school and the completion of a medical school education. This will impact their potential for success during their undergraduate medical education. (Miller, 2014).

One, of many things, that becomes a potential roadblock to academic success and a career in medicine for these students is the Hidden Curriculum. This chapter will address the Hidden Curriculum as it pertains to becoming a competitive applicant to medical school. Understanding the Hidden curriculum and its effects will allow for better admissions decisions regarding students from disadvantaged backgrounds and hopefully increase retention rates in medical school for this population (Kusobuski et. al., 2017).

THE HIDDEN CURRICULUM IN UNDERGRADUATE BACHELORS EDUCATION

The Hidden Curriculum *includes values, intergroup relations and celebrations that enable students' socialization processes* (Kentli, 2009, p. 83). This concept of the Hidden Curriculum came to the forefront after the publication of Phillip Jackson's work, *Life in Classrooms*. Now, 50 years later, this concept embodies the attitudes, behaviors, values, and institutional expectations that students must successfully navigate to ensure satisfactory progress through the formal education curriculum (Margolis et al., 2001, Kentli, 2009; Smith, 2013). The Hidden Curriculum became the focus of a great deal of educational research since Jackson's book. Unfortunately, the Hidden Curriculum pertaining to higher education, particularly undergraduate bachelor level education, here referred to as "Bachelors Hidden Curriculum (BHC)," received much less attention in the intervening years, albeit works by White and Lowenthall (2019), Smith (2013), and Margolis et al. (2001) continue to shed light on the intricate mechanisms that affect students' ability to move forward within an educational system.

Students navigating the college experience need to master the formal curriculum as outlined on individual course syllabi and institutional requirements for graduation. In addition, they need to understand the informal curriculum encompassing co-curricular activities, student life expectations, work-study programs and financial aid. Lastly, they must acclimatize to the BHC, which includes unspoken messages and implied behaviors, necessitating the understanding of unfamiliar values and attitudes depending upon the students' background (Elliot, Baumfield, Reic, & Makara, 2016).

The BHC in most undergraduate colleges and universities is mercurial. The expected skills attitudes and values will be constantly evolving and shifting due to the influence of changing power structures within the institution and changing societal norms and issues such as gender, race, and class will continue to shape hidden curricula (Esposito, 2011).

The academic culture which evolved on most college and university campuses drew fundamentally from white, middle-class and upper middle-class norms, expectations, and values (Smith, 2013). For students who identify outside this cohort, the BHC becomes yet another body of new information they must master. First-generation college students find themselves adrift in an environment with which their support network from home has little or no experience (Chatelain, 2018). The fact that successful completion of an undergraduate BA or BS program can be correlated with the level of parental college experience (Cataldi, Bennett, & Chen, 2018), lends further support to the idea that the BHC can impact a student's potential for success. Regardless of parental education level, low-income first-generation students whose parents take a positive, active role in their child's college search and adjustment to life on campus are more likely to finish their college program. In contrast, students whose families did not make college attendance a clear goal and emphasized financial or family concerns over educational achievement were much less likely to enroll and/or finish their program (Mitchall & Jaeger, 2016). It could be argued that supportive families understood the need for their child to identify and work within the BHC, even if they did not identify it as such. Clearly the BHC will seem more obvious to white, middle-class students with college-educated parents. They will understand the need to speak up and ask questions in class, approach professionals regarding shadowing and internship experiences, and build relationships with faculty and staff outside of the classroom (Smith, 2013). Many low-income, first-generation, and students of color arrive on campus with disparate skill sets compared to students from middle-class families with college educated parents. They will find the types of expected interactions difficult and unfamiliar. Yet, successful completion of a degree program may require they attain these very skills.

Within any institution, successful navigation of the BHC will help the student attain the GPA, MCAT score, and other credentials required to become a successful applicant to medical school. Additionally, pre-medical students find nested within the BHC the subset of ideas, attitudes, values, and expectations, implicit for successful navigation of the medical school application process. Obviously, moving on to undergraduate medical education requires a highly successful bachelors education experience.

THE HIDDEN CURRICULUM IN UNDERGRADUATE MEDICAL EDUCATION

The concept of the Hidden Curriculum in Medical Education (MEHC) takes on a different meaning from the above BHC. The MEHC addresses the issues of professionalism (O'Donnell, 2014; Rabow, 2014; Cruess & Cruess, 2014) and the acculturation of medical professionals. *The Hidden Curriculum in Health Professional Education,* edited by Hafferty and O'Donnell (2014), provides a collection of essays that not only address the MECH for physicians (Taylor & Wendland, 2014; Wear, Zarconi, & Garden, 2014; Rabow, 2014), but other health professionals, including nurses (Day & Benner, 2014) and allied health professionals (Wright-Peterson & Bender, 2014). The MEHC can be explained, superficially, as the way health professions students learn to view themselves, the patients, and the other providers as professionals, while they learn to interact within the healthcare system (Andarvazh, Afshar, & Yazdani, 2017; Thistlewaite, 2014). Unfortunately, the MEHC can provide health professions students with conflicting lessons on professionalism. Students have reported that the ways in which mentors and teachers refer to patient groups and other professionals outside of the classroom or clinic can contrast sharply with formal didactic lessons on accepted attitudes and behaviors (Phillips & Clark, 2012).

The MEHC is an important component of acculturation toward becoming a professional clinician functioning within the health care system. However, before the student reaches the MEHC, they must first successfully navigate the BHC.

The BHC Interactions with Other Theories

Students from disadvantaged backgrounds often worry that one day, everyone will see that they are not as bright or as skilled as their college peers (Smith, 2013). Unfortunately, for disadvantaged students, the enigma of the medical school application process itself may reinforce their perceptions of being less able or qualified than others with whom they matriculate. Imposter Syndrome (Peteet, Montgomery, Jerren, & Weekes, 2015), is feeling as if you are somehow less able than others. Imposter Syndrome in students leads them to disengage from class discussions, avoid asking for help or questioning assumptions, and filling their time with activities that make them feel good but which do not add to any needed skill sets. They often engage in activities that connect them to like-minded students, all struggling to fit in and all on the outside of their new culture. They disconnect with their academic selves because they need a sense of belonging (Tenhouse, n.d.; Verschleden, 2017). Imposter Syndrome may be present in every aspect of the college experience, as the chasm between the majority experience and that of the disadvantaged student grows with each new experience. One could argue that the further the student travels from their familial center, the greater the risk for exacerbating the above feelings.

Similarly, the concept of cognitive bandwidth comes into play. All of us have a finite amount of brainpower or cognitive resources. Students, who have experienced economic disadvantage, discrimination, housing insecurity, and all the other ills connected to poverty, need to use more of their cognitive resources (bandwidth) for surviving and processing what is around them. Consequently, even as very young children they have had less mental and cognitive resources to devote to learning and growing (Verschelden, 2017). These students struggle academically because much of their brain power is devoted to life issues. The reduction in cognitive bandwidth can last for years. Likewise, students starting their undergraduate college career in an environment where they do not ascribe to the dominant group on campus, often need to quickly learn the underpinnings of the BHC and, more importantly, how to navigate it successfully. Consequently, the level of bandwidth available for learning new academic subject matter could be reduced. It is plausible that the BHC can magnify issues of Imposter Syndrome and cognitive bandwidth reduction. At many different stages, students can turn a corner and find unclear expectations and difficulties for which their experiences have not prepared them. The stories shared below illustrate these concepts.

THE BHC, MECH AND THE PRE-MEDICAL STUDENT

The case studies presented below and throughout the rest of the chapter represent real student interactions. The authors of this chapter collectively represent approximately 40 years of pre-health professions advising. The identifying information has been changed to protect the advisees' privacy but the situations accurately represent advisor-advisee interactions as they unfolded.

Undergraduate pre-medical advisers are tasked with helping all aspiring physicians navigate the medical school admission process (Holistic Review in Medical School Admissions, n.d.). For many pre-medical students this information is provided through advising coupled with the soft skills students learned throughout their formal education. In addition, family-based values, other opportunities, and networking with physicians plus other health care professionals provide needed information and insights into the process.

Unfortunately, under-represented, economically disadvantaged, rural and first-generation college students may not enter the medical school admissions process with equivalent levels of understanding and preparedness (Oyewole, 2001). Said students often find the route complicated and at times incomprehensible. (Chatelain, 2018). Theirs is a journey rife with nuances they cannot see, and for which they are ill prepared. Advisors too are stymied—often making assumptions about academic, social, and cultural norms which can fall outside of the experiences of their disadvantaged students (Smith, 2013).

Case Studies And Insights

BHC Disparities

Farhad is a Muslim woman, born in Bangladesh and a resident of the US since age two. Farhad attended a prestigious high school and gained admission to a reputable college. However, she cannot seem to find the right shadowing or networking experiences. She lives in an urban area and should have access to many exciting and unique experiences. However, the neighborhood she lives in is not safe after dark and she must limit her experiences to opportunities where she will be able to travel by public transportation during daylight hours. The BHC would suggest that all students will have equal access to meaningful shadowing and networking experiences. They only need to exercise initiative and perseverance to attain these opportunities.

Paola is a Latina applicant, thrilled to be offered her first interview. She shares her news with her undergraduate Pre-Medical Advisor who grew up in socioeconomic circumstances similar to Paola, and feels confident in her ability to help disadvantaged students. They spoke about many pertinent issues. When the young woman asked the advisor what to wear, the answer was a friendly and well meaning, "Wear your Sunday best." The day after Paola's interview, the dean from the medical school called and asked why the advisor sent this student in her prom dress! In retrospect, the advisor knew to coach Paola about the interview and making small talk at lunch but made incorrect assumptions concerning the applicant's understanding of professional attire. The BHC expects that Paola will know what constitutes appropriate interview attire and have the means to acquire such clothing.

George, a young man from a small, rural section of his state attends college in the same region and operates on a very tight budget. He received an interview invitation from a school in an urban area about 180 miles from his college. He figures if he drives and leaves very early in the morning, he should make the first event and can save money on lodging. He scrounges enough money to put gas in the car and pay for the tolls. The BHC assumes that George could cover his interview expenses including travel and meals on the road. While the medical school website provided driving directions, it assumed students understood rush hour driving, parking difficulties and the uncertainties of urban commuter traffic.

Within the perspective of the BHC the following explanations appear accurate. **Farhad** was unable to access meaningful clinical experiences due to her neighborhood and transportation challenges. **Paola's** wardrobe gaffe left her humiliated and feeling less qualified than her peers. **George** arrived at his interview a half hour late and soaking wet on a very rainy morning assuming there would be affordable parking close by. To many, including himself, he appeared as an unsophisticated rube that would never make it in a fast-paced urban medical school environment.

CASE STUDY ANALYSIS - BANDWIDTH AND IMPOSTER SYNDROME

Farhad, may have also experienced a bandwidth limiting environment. Her academic career and achievements occurred during the time when she acted in her role as the family's first born. The role brought with it responsibilities to translate for her non-English speaking parents, navigate social structures, and assist with raising her siblings. Her emotional resources were stretched, making her academic achievements even more laudable. One wonders how much higher she could have soared had she not been required to expend bandwidth in other areas; few from majority cultures would recognize and acknowledge her obligation to balance these competing priorities.

All three students mentioned above expressed concerns regarding their future goals which could be viewed within the context of imposter syndrome. Maria's experiences also add clarity to the discussion. **Maria** was a very bright student from an immigrant family. She matriculated at the university before her 17th birthday. As the oldest child, her parents relied on her to help translate and navigate their lives in the United States. While her grades were quite good, the emotional stress of family responsibilities, fitting in as a younger student, and navigating the BHC, left her with a great deal of anxiety, causing health concerns. In addition, her relative youth and absence from campus on weekends reinforced her feeling of incompetence and being an imposter. Maria is expected to advise her younger siblings on the path to college, but feels ill-equipped to manage it herself.

The imposter syndrome takes its toll, as the BHC pops up at any given juncture. When **Farhad** met other students, she began to feel that she did not belong in this college setting. Few "traditional" college students carry such heavy family responsibilities making it difficult for her to experience college culture outside of the classroom. When explaining her many obligations to majority students, Farhad feels discomfort in drawing attention to her non-majority experiences. Similarly, **Maria** is unprepared for the stresses that college requirements create in her already-stressful life. She is straddling two different worlds and beginning to feel as if she no longer truly belongs in either.

Paola earned her interview spot, but was embarrassed by her social gaffe. Does she belong in the medical professional world, she wondered. One is tempted to smile at the nature of Paola's misstep. It should be noted that the medical school dean contacted the advisor about the mistake. Thus, it was not as minor as it may seem to the casual observer.

Commuter students present more circumstances which slam up against the BHC, imposter Syndrome and the idea of cognitive bandwidth. **Wendy** lived at home about 25 miles from a rural college campus. With no public transportation, she needed to drive every day. Since she attended a residential rural college, cancellation of class or special events rarely occurred. She participated in a limited amount of activities held in the late afternoon or early evening. Inclement weather could be an issue and, at times, her father forbade her from traveling due to snow storms or flooding events. She relied on the largess of her professors to excuse her absence. Her classmates, on the other hand, could be quite unforgiving when she missed project meetings because she could not get to campus. The BHC assumes that students will be available for study and tutorial sessions whenever they are be scheduled. Imposter syndrome led Wendy to believe she did not belong, because she did not have 24/7 access to resources on campus and could not accommodate her team's meeting schedule. Some of Wendy's cognitive bandwidth would be tied up with the details of the commute, helping on the farm, and time management issues that are unique for a commuter student. First-generation rural commuter students, like urban commuter students, may try to load their schedules with as many credits as possible. The extra credits represent a bargain, and the means to cut their undergraduate career timeline and subsequent financial obligations shorter by a semester or even a year. Many do not realize that the BHC expects students to be able to accurately judge their maximal capacity for study and academic success.

Cultural and Social Roadblocks- Compounded by the BHC

As stated previously, the BHC has roots in the majority experience (Smith 2013), first generation, disadvantaged, and rural students have, thus far, grown up under different cultural, academic, and social norms. Students, mentors and advisors face many additional challenges planning a successful academic program, allowing these students to become competitive medical school applicants.

COURSE SELECTION AND ACADEMIC TIMELINES

Medical school applications require strong academic achievement and students may drop a course if there is a problem during the semester; it is understood by most that this option is to be considered only in certain exceptional circumstances. Students growing up in a family environment promoting the ideals of hard work and self-reliance can find it difficult to ask for help, or embrace a course correction. Their families may consider it counterintuitive to withdraw from a course when the family culture stresses hard work, valuing completion over all else. **Maria** was a college senior when she encountered significant health issues. She was counseled to withdraw from some classes and concentrate on her health. Faculty and staff needed to convince her and her family that it was acceptable to withdraw from some classes, thereby preserving her GPA.

Likewise, students and their families may perceive that only one road exists to medical school requiring a science-intense, four-year, undergraduate career, followed by immediate matriculation. The BHC, which recognizes that balancing course loads to maintain a GPA is a reasonable strategy, strikes these students and their families as counterproductive. Consequently, well-meaning family members can offer misguided encouragement, urging students to keep pushing forward despite academic or personal struggles. Studies indicate alternating a semester with a heavy course load with one that provides an easier course load may lead to better graduation rates (Witteveen & Atewell, 2017). Withdrawing from classes can be viewed as failure through the cultural lens of the family. Even though advisors emphasize, that this strategy provides the safety net needed to preserve a GPA, it does not always satisfy the student or their family. Pre-medical students could find themselves stuck between an advisor, with whom they may not have yet built a strong relationship, and a well-meaning, supportive family urging them to carry on. It they attend a liberal arts institution they may also run into push back from those educated outside of the United States, saying things such as, "Shouldn't you be taking another science course?" "Don't take humanities." "Can't you finish in three years?"

THE BHC AND ALTERNATIVE STUDENT PRIORITIES

The interpretation of the BHC and the sense of inadequacy derived from impostor syndrome may drive students of color, first-generation, economically disadvantaged, and rural students to become over-involved in campus clubs and activities. An overcommitted student with a rigorous academic schedule may leave no room for such students to weather even minor setbacks. For example, a common cold can academically derail an entire semester for some of these students. They live under the mistaken assumption that more is better, thinking that awards and accolades will make up for a mediocre GPA. Families invest so much into getting these students to college that the students feel pressured to take advantage of every opportunity.

Disadvantaged applicants may sometimes be too invested in their activities and personal story to hear the reality of a poorly crafted application. Poor MCAT scores and a low GPA cannot be offset by the hardships of life (Aspiring Docs, n.d.). Getting students to understand that tough idea while remaining cognizant of their accomplishments is a delicate dance with which advisors struggle.

Neda had a 2.4 science GPA when she met with her advisor, ready to apply to medical school. Her last use of formal advising services occurred during her freshman year. In the interim she became heavily involved in paid research, while caring for her small child, as a single parent. Her research mentor continually told her she would make a great physician, but that statement was based solely on her research activity. Although the research advisor could access Neda's academic records, the continual encouragement did not include an assessment of her other credentials, such as her relatively low GPA. Neda's MCAT scores were similarly noncompetitive, with not enough time dedicated to preparing for this important exam. Despite a strong effort, Neda's advisor could not help her move forward. When the advisor offered an honest assessment of how competitive her application was at this time, the unwanted news put the advisor in the enemy camp. Neda eventually found a position in research, but never again tried for admittance into medical school. This scenario plays out often for disadvantaged students: mentors, wanting to be encouraging, give false hope, and often do not themselves understand why the student focuses their attention on a research project when final exams and preparing for professional school clearly requires more time than the student has allowed. Communication between the faculty mentor and the advisor's office might have helped **Neda** understand that she was not yet ready (Smith, 2013), thereby allowing her the opportunity to remediate her academic work and MCAT instead of leaving college with an unfulfilled dream.

Advisors, too, struggle to keep these issues in mind. Disadvantaged students often experience challenges with time management, the roots of which are frequently based in financial need. Many jobs on campus might pay minimum wage and offer limited hours. Off campus, the pay scale can be better, but there is a trade-off with scheduling flexibility. **Sarah** worked at a grocery store at home and continued her part-time employment at the same grocery chain a few miles from campus. She could set a schedule around classes before the semester started, however, once her schedule was fixed, changing was difficult. Attendance at mandatory events, connecting with team members for group-based projects, or even scheduling meetings with her professors became difficult when available times conflicted with her set work schedule. The BHC expects that students seeking employment will find flexible evening or weekend work, and that the hours will be limited, allowing academics to remain the priority. For disadvantaged students, reducing work hours equals losing money; when 20 to 30-hour workweeks are necessary, classes and academic performance can become a casualty.

The BHC can be especially difficult for students who are placed in situations of responsibility regarding their family structure. Family responsibilities, including caring for younger siblings or elderly family members, may preclude academic endeavors during later hours. African-American males raised by single mothers can find themselves becoming the man of the house at an early age. They become the role model, mentor, and caretaker for the younger children in their homes and within the community at large which can necessitate them needing to put aside their dreams and aspirations. The stagnation in the numbers of African-American males entering medicine is alarming (Laurencin & Murray, 2017).

The first-generation American student, like Farhad or Maria may be the only one in the family that speaks English. Problems with social security, utilities, or chronic illness, require their physical presence. This level of responsibility makes for an emotionally mature person, however, it can also invoke fear and guilt as the student tries to balance school and family obligations. These difficulties may follow students into their professional training, often derailing their careers at a point when the stakes have become even higher.

The BHC assumes students are financially savvy and that their families can demonstrate financial responsibility. Obtaining loans requires an acceptable credit rating. Many disadvantaged students, due to ethical and cultural mores may not manage their own finances and, hence, have no credit rating. They will not be able to obtain financial aid without a co-signatory.

Anna came from an extremely economically disadvantaged background. She wanted to be a physician, but since she was not quite as competitive as she would like, decided to pursue a post-bac program. As she was preparing the financial paperwork, she discovered her prohibitive credit score. Why? Her mother had taken one of the credit card applications flooding the mail of graduating college seniors and filled it out in Anna's name, then defaulted on the bill. Anna was saddled with the credit debt and the very low credit score that resulted. Anna could not attend the post-bac program and gave up her dream of becoming a physician.

Mary, another economically disadvantaged student, came to college on a scholarship. She was bright, hardworking, and graduated with an outstanding GPA. Her interests never wavered from health care. However, her family looked at the potential debt for medical school and insisted she look at a career as a Physician Assistant or Nurse Practitioner, since the programs were shorter and the annual tuition, less. Even though her advisor offered to talk with her family about medical school debt and how it could be managed, Mary would not contradict her family's wishes. She would have made an excellent physician from an under-represented group working in primary care within a small town/rural community, yet she pursued a career as a PA at her family's insistence.

One wonders how many strong candidates become lost along the way, or leave medical school because they could not balance family responsibilities while trying to pursue their personal dreams.

The BHC Assumes Access to Appropriate Experiential Learning.

The BHC assumes that an environment rich in resources is equally accessible to all. Many middle-class, pre-medical students will approach their family's health care providers, other family members, or close acquaintances, to create these opportunities. First-generation and economically disadvantaged students often feel that they do not have entre into the medical professional world. They see no pre-existing network of contacts and must approach a total stranger to ask for assistance. Here, again, we see imposter syndrome: "Why would this person want to talk to me?"

Rural students run into an additional problem; the lack of geographic density for providers. Many rural health care providers out of necessity support large practices since there are fewer providers in general. These providers may be reluctant to take on a shadowing student who could slow them down. These students may receive advice encouraging them to spend the summer in an urban area where many more opportunities exist without regard to the economic impact of that advice, assumptions made that such students have access to housing, transportation, and funding. In many cases, students hear "if you want this enough you will find a way to make it happen". Such attitudes ignore the multiple barriers such students face; no experience with healthcare professionals, managing work and volunteer hours against school obligations, understanding the importance of having significant exposure to medicine as an applicant.

The BHC and the High Numbers Game

The BHC assumes that all students are skilled at taking high-stakes tests in a computer-based testing environment. Students pour through reference materials, like the MSAR and school websites, looking at MCAT and GPA statistics. When they get their MCAT scores if there exists a disconnection between a strong GPA and a very mediocre MCAT score, disadvantaged students often see it as evidence of their personal short-comings and not a lack of experience with high-stakes computer-based testing.

In reality, the cohort of students who are under-represented in medicine, rural, first-generation, and economically underserved, most likely come from a background where students take few standardized tests. Their computer skills can be rudimentary, and they may not have the resources or the extended time needed to prepare. These students need to be reminded that they are not defined by their MCAT score, and then be given concrete advice and guidance on how to study and how to master online-standardized testing. The BHC assumes students understand how to take advantage of the many sources for test preparation materials, the logistics of practice test taking, how much time is needed to prepare, and possess the financial means to take advantage of the proffered help.

The AAMC Core Competencies- Thinking Outside the BHC

Even when students understand the nuances of the numbers, they can often feel like they do not have enough going for them. They look at the AAMC Pre-Professional Competencies (The Core Competencies for Entering Medical Students n.d.) and become overwhelmed thinking they cannot demonstrate these skills in the same fashion as some of their peers. . Students who fall into the disadvantaged cohort group need to think outside the BHC and look at their personal life experiences as demonstrations of said competencies.

When the AAMC introduced the idea of Pre-Medical Core Competencies to promote holistic review and validate experiences outside the traditional classroom setting, even the savviest student found it difficult to comprehend the value in assessing such attributes. Applying this basic premise, that life experiences forge the skills and empathy physicians need for each patient encounter, becomes a lost opportunity for the disadvantaged students. Disadvantaged students will hide their differences in core life experiences,

Table 1. Demonstration of competencies and the individual narrative

Pre-Professional Competencies	Thinking and Reasoning Competencies	Science Competencies
Service Orientation Social Skills Cultural Competence Teamwork Oral Communication Ethical Responsibility to Self and Others Reliability and Dependability Resilience and Adaptability Capacity for Improvement	Critical Thinking Quantitative Reasoning Scientific Inquiry Written Communication	Living Systems Human Behavior

ashamed to be seen as "other." They fail to recognize that a career as a medical professional requires many immeasurable skills acquired through a myriad of life experiences.

Advisors know that *Thinking and Reasoning*, and *Science* competencies can be illustrated through academic and research experiences. Students enter the process knowing that they need excellent grades and standardized test scores. Consequently, they diligently focus on academic achievement. When complicated, busy lives impact this goal, the disadvantaged students often assume they have blown it. The Pre-Professional Competencies could provide the greatest resource for students struggling with BHC to demonstrate the capabilities they honed, sometimes unknowingly, over the years. Consider more of **Farhad's** story. Her academics were solid, but on the low end of acceptable for MD programs, similarly, her standardized test scores were good, but not outstanding. Like many first generation students, she over-extended herself with activities and experiences. Her advisor suggested she focus more on her grades. The student was advised to apply after her senior year, in an attempt to "Finish strong," and "Prove you have what it takes." **Farhad** then shared specific details of her home life.

Her family of five lived in a one-bedroom apartment, and she commuted between 30 to 60 minutes by bus to campus. Her parents spoke little English, so as the oldest she assisted with most official interactions. Because they lived in a dangerous neighborhood, staying late at the library to study was not possible. She studied surrounded by family, and sometimes extended family from Bangladesh, in a one-bedroom apartment. When scheduling early courses, **Farhad** had to be sure that her commute time would allow her to arrive at campus by 8:00 A.M., Her mornings also required navigating the many people in the apartment that day.

Considering the Pre-Professional Core Competencies, what might **Farhad's** story tell an admissions committee? Certainly, her club and activities demonstrated leadership, service orientation, and social skills, as she was elected by her peers., Cultural competence becomes apparent in her seamless navigation between worlds, along with *teamwork* in the way she was able to live among so many others, as well as *ethical responsibility to self and others,* through mentoring her siblings and helping her family navigate a system in which they remained cultural strangers.

Farhad's cultural norms can be contrasted with the commonly valued experience of student/athletes. Replace her crowded home life with a life on a bus constantly travelling to track meets. She cannot stay late on campus due to her commute, but if she were an athlete, she may be required to participate in mandatory evening, weight training. Instead of her family obligations, let's make her captain of the women's track team. Each scenario illustrates valuable competencies but, within the context of the BHC, the athletic scenario probably is easier to understand and value

Rural students also may find it difficult to put their lives into the context of the Pre-Professional Core Competencies when they realize that they don't have access to the wealth of experiences available to urban and suburban students. They demonstrate *teamwork* by working on the family farm or in the family business during the summer. They could work 18-hour days to try to bring in corn, hay, or soybeans when the weather seems favorable. This commitment to their family and others in the farming community also demonstrates *ethical responsibility, reliability and dependability.* Many rural students, not just those living on a farm, live miles from the nearest grocery store, hardware store, healthcare facility, or any other suburban convenience. These students learn to problem solve, demonstrate *reliability and dependability,* and find solutions through unconventional means (often called "MacGyvering" after the TV show), which can reflect *resilience and adaptability* and *capacity for improvement.* Many times the rural students will be the first to help out when snow or flooding become issues, demonstrating a service orientation.

Medical School Application Process- Yet another example of the BHC

Applying to medical school requires applicants to undertake, for some, another set of new skills, which need to be mastered to submit a successful application. First, it assumes the student has access to a credit card and knows how to use it.

The Disadvantaged Status option provides an opportunity to describe, in 1325 characters, circumstances that adversely affected an applicant's path to medicine (Disadvantaged Status, n.d.). The very term is inaccurate and can be viewed pejoratively by the very candidates it presumes to help. Most candidates express pride in their family's accomplishments and bristle at being considered disadvantaged. First-generation college students see themselves as fortunate compared to their parents and grandparents, the proud bearers of a new standard. Since they don't understand the BHC, they determine that the term "disadvantaged" applies to someone else.

Even when these students recognize the need for help, they are often stymied by the timing needed to take advantage of programs designed to support their applications. Applying for the Fee Assistance Program (FAP) before they schedule the MCAT mandates filling out the application well in advance of scheduling a test date. The process also requires access to both of their parent's financial information regardless of the students' emancipation or marital status. Depending upon the student's cultural background, parents may be unwilling to release their financial records or be too proud to provide the documentation that their family lives in extreme need.

Students growing up in rural areas may have difficulty documenting their need status. For some applications the percentage of students eligible for a school breakfast of lunch program is used as a metric to assess if the applicants high school may have been under-resourced. School breakfast and lunch programs are often under-subscribed by rural families too proud to admit that their children go to school hungry. These children may be sent to school with empty lunch bags and boxes. Even at a very young age, the student learns to hide their family's level of need. In addition, rural students will experience increased expenses compared with some of their urban or suburban peers. They will need access to a car to get to a far-away MCAT testing site, and they most likely, must stay in a hotel the night before the exam. Expenses continue to mount when it comes time for the interview. If a rural student plans to use public transportation to travel to an interview city, they may still need to drive, sometimes for hundreds of miles, to get to an airport or train station.

The BHC of the application process assumes that students during the course of their college career engage in one-on-one interactions with their professors, advisors, and mentors, allowing those individuals to write a personalized letter evaluating their strengths and weaknesses. Disparities between the student's cultural background and that of the author can lead to letters that are less personal and not really of much help to the applicant. Students who belong to the majority group on campus may find the process of getting to know the faculty and staff much more comfortable and something for which they have been groomed. (Smith, 2013)

The BHC also comes into play with writing personal statements. The nature of the personal statement assumes the applicant is comfortable drawing attention to themselves or highlighting their achievements. Many, mainstream, American applicants are comfortable with sharing personal details in an essay and know how to highlight their achievements in an engaging fashion. Within the context of the personal statement and the interview, first generation, economically-deprived, and under-represented minority students, could be much less comfortable sharing their personal stories or touting their attributes. They spend their entire lives trying to fit in, and writing about what makes them special is beyond their experience. As these students talk with their peers, they realize they do not share the same kinds of opportunities and experiences, and may view their own experiences as underwhelming. They may feel that their lives are unremarkable. **Rachel,** a first-generation college student grew up in a rural community. While she waited for her medical school interview, the applicants were talking amongst themselves. They discussed the colleges and universities and their hometowns. Rachel realized that she was the only one in the cohort that day from a small rural community and a university that would not be considered "top tier." She reported wondering why she was even invited to interview; she was not like the other applicants, (Impostor Syndrome). The others latched onto common ground and she had nothing to contribute to the conversation. Before her official interview even started, her cognitive currency had been tied up with other issues that detracted from her ability to interview well.

THE BHC AND THE INTERVIEW

The initial joy of an interview offer can fade quickly when the student begins to understand what will be needed to make it a success. The BHC expects students will have acquired certain skill sets regardless of their background. Interview attire can become an area of difficulty, as it was for **Paola** and her prom gown. If the interview includes a social gathering, the students may be reluctant to go because "making small talk" is not a skill with which they have had much practice (**Rachel**). They may not understand that while the event is "optional," it is really in their best interests to attend. Similarly, they may not understand the interactions, which encompass a typical "American" meet and greet. Handshaking may not be part of their home culture nor direct eye contact with the person with whom you are speaking, regardless of authority or station. They might be asked to be around alcohol, and while there may be no pressure to imbibe, for some students, the presence is enough to contribute to their sense of not belonging. Some medical schools will provide students with a student host to help save money. Home stays with total strangers can be completely outside of the student's cultural norm.

Depending upon the student's home culture, it may be virtually impossible for a female student to speak-up in a male-dominated interview. Similarly, some men may find it very difficult to respond to a female interviewer in the same fashion they would respond to a male asking them questions.

Franklin was a student from a tight-knit religious community. Interacting with other religions and cultures was uncommon, as was interacting with females outside of his family. **Franklin** also had no one in his insular community who had attended college. He prepared himself for the academics of college by studying on his own utilizing the public library. Franklin had shown enormous courage, marking his own path, and exhibiting natural talent in science and math, but he had no idea what else would be required as a pre-med student. Shaking hands or interacting with female faculty and other women was uncomfortable and Franklin struggled academically his first year on campus. He also perceived he was different from his peers, many of whom came from professional families where the intersection between eclectic groups of people was commonplace. It took several years of constant collaboration with his advisor to overcome his unease with others, especially women. Additionally, learning about ethical dilemmas in medicine, such as abortion and euthanasia, presented challenges to his beliefs, Franklin felt uncomfortable engaging in such discussions. He already felt different; to voice his opinion would put a spotlight on the disconnect he felt much of the time. Franklin wisely took a gap year and worked in a multicultural healthcare center in a large urban area. He learned to be comfortable around women and other religious beliefs and cultures, and became adept at asking questions and in seeking out guidance.

He entered medical school ready for the challenges of the curriculum without the baggage of trying to blindly navigate the BHC.

Many medical schools are in urban areas. Unfortunately, the rural student can have zero experience with public transportation. **Billy** lived his entire life in a small rural town. Everywhere he and his family needed to go, they went by car. The only bus he had ever ridden was the public-school bus and services, such as Uber, had not reached his rural region. Family would drive him to the train station or airport if necessary, but once Billy arrived in the city for his interview, he needed to quickly learn about buying public transportation passes, using a rideshare app, or navigating complicated bus or train lines. Unlike his urban and suburban counterparts, he would find the process of physically getting to the interview at least as stressful as the interview itself.

The urban student visiting a more rural medical school may also run into transportation difficulties. There may be a nearby train station or airport, but depending on distance, transportation may require a pre-arranged shuttle service, something which the urban student may not consider given the transportation options in their home city. Without access to a car, interviews at some schools become very difficult.

Checking Boxes and the Successful Applicant-The Misunderstood BHC

Among upper level pre-medical students, especially, there seems to exist the idea, often perpetuated by frequently visited pre-med websites, that there is one single ideal medical school application, and if applicant just fulfills everything in that model application, most certainly they will be offered acceptance. In this situation, everyone seems to perpetuate an identical BHC. A successful applicant mentoring these students will often outline steps that lead to their personal success and encourage mirroring. This single successful applicant becomes the authority on what medical schools want. Thinking along these lines can work like quicksand to the aspiring applicant. The student becomes obsessed with amassing a pre-described set of experiences, not because they enjoy them, or they will provide valuable experiences, but because they "look good on their application." The BHC assumes all candidates can acquire such experiences. Students lose sight of the idea that they are individuals with their own unique backgrounds and experiences. .

SOLUTIONS AND RECOMMENDATIONS FOR ADVISORS AND MENTORS

Advisors and faculty must work in tandem to ensure disadvantaged students make use of tutoring and mentoring opportunities. Asking students to outline outside commitments each semester can help advisors plan realistic schedules while remaining mindful that summer school and an extra year may not be economically feasible. Summer programs away from home, even though they offer compensation and MCAT prep, may not be possible for students who struggle to make ends meet. Helping them to find positions near home, creating a library of free materials, and developing peer study programs can work.

MCAT prep, for the student who has little experience with a standardized test, is essential, but almost always financially out of reach. Advisors can reach out to MCAT prep companies and organizations that have programs in place to help economically disadvantaged students. In addition, advisors can work with their financial aid and development offices to put resources into place for these students, bearing in mind that students need practice taking the tests, not just learning content.

Helping students find appropriate support services to help their families may be the biggest help an advisor can provide for a student. **Marcel** was the eldest son of a single parent who worked as a hairdresser. Marcel was the man of the house and in charge of his younger sisters. He constantly missed classes his first semester, failing biology lab and pre-calculus. When asked, he explained that he had to travel from one section of the city to another every day and, if there was a problem, he had to stay home. It became abundantly clear that his circumstances were not going to change. Marcel began organizing his classes over two or three days a week. While it meant he was in class for long hours on those days, it gave him time to take care of his family. Marcel's grades turned around and he entered medical school, after a two-year gap that allowed him to earn money to pay for test prep and application expenses. In that time, his sister graduated from high school and could take over as the interpreter and family problem-solver. The advisor helped Marcel see that on his application, his commitment to his extended family, typical of Caribbean cultures, was truly community service.

Disadvantaged students often feel pressured to engage in "typical pre-med" experiences. Financially needy students may find volunteering opportunities in an emergency department or clinic a fiscal disaster. Finding paying jobs in healthcare can be easy if you live in a big city, but in rural areas such opportunities will be few and may be too far. Working as a waitress is not the same as treating a patient as an EMT, but the skills needed to successfully manage expectations, to organize, to remember client choices, manage demanding people, and work as part of team, are skills that transfer well to medicine. Thinking outside the box, students can take positions as pharmacy techs, scribes, home health aides, or medical assistants at homes for the disabled, all of which are paid positions providing exposure to the field. What they may fail to grasp is that community service does not have to be volunteer service. Students who need a significant part-time job to stay in school or help their families will not have the luxury of spending 10 to 20 hours a week as a volunteer. They should be encouraged to find employment in areas that could be considered community service, such as a senior center or after-school daycare program for underprivileged kids, running educational programming at a local community center, or managing a local food bank.

The BHC expects that students are college-ready the first day of classes. Many matriculating students present high-school transcripts full of AP courses, community college credits, and university coursework. Students coming from under-resourced, urban, or rural public-school districts may not have had access to this form of advanced work. In fact, some may have never even had a high school biology or chemistry class. These students will need to play academic catch-up from the very first day (Butrymowciz, 2017). Ironically, these students represent the top of their high school class and arrive at college thinking that they have a good handle managing the academic load, only to be "gob smacked" the first week of classes. College demands are unrelenting and the uninitiated can be easily overwhelmed, again exposing the student to the risks of Impostor Syndrome and reduced cognitive bandwidth. Their limited self-confidence can erode quickly, especially when compounded by the unknowns of the BHC. Identifying an advisor with personal experience as a first-generation college student can be an effective solution. Such a mentor can offer realistic advice with knowledge of both worlds. Advisors can also provide support when students need to navigate between their family values and a sometimes-conflicting worldview at school.

Advisors can be proactive and send out information to students before classes begin. **Andrew** and his brother were entering in the fall and reached out to an advisor over the summer. Understanding that the boys would be taking first semester biology, their advisor contacted more advanced students and found older versions of the biology text and the syllabus. By the time the students entered fall semester, both had reviewed the first three weeks of the syllabus and were able to stay ahead of the class throughout the semester. The advisor now routinely collects biology, chemistry, and math textbooks, with the accompanying syllabi, before the end of the school year. Having the ability to provide prep in advance made many students' transition to college more manageable and released some cognitive bandwidth to deal with other areas of the BHC.

Financial literacy and understanding the costs involved in applying to medical school, in addition to the cost of attendance, is of the utmost importance. Students need to know that they need money for the MCAT, for the application, secondary applications, travel, and deposits to hold their seats. They must also consider moving expenses and funding to hold them over until their monies become available through financial aid at their medical school. Planning for emergencies at home, at school, and unforeseen equipment costs and books, will make their transition smoother.

Students may try to earn all the money before they apply, often resulting in an application that is just too late. They miss school application deadlines or end up pushing the application back a year. Making students aware of deadlines, of needing to shift financial and time priorities as they prepare their application, and allowing for the time needed to study for the MCAT, while at the same time continuing their success in the classroom and lab, can be overwhelming. Raising these issues early in a disadvantaged student's college experience will help them to meet these challenges in a timely manner.

Ali, a first-generation Pakistani male, as a college sophomore, would not make eye contact with the female pre-medical advisor. She was a person of authority and, as a Muslim male, he should not make contact with a female who was not family. During the course of his college career, he took two classes from his advisor. Only after three years of extended contact did he feel comfortable having a conversation and looking her in the eye. He applied to medical school post-graduation and, since he was local, came by to share the good news of his acceptance. When the advisor asked if she could give him a congratulatory hug, he happily agreed. The point is that it took extensive personal contact for Ali to develop a level of comfort with behaviors the BHC implicitly expects. Advisors need to understand that making eye contact and shaking hands with strangers may require many group activities, even practicing "cocktail party skills" with peers, for some students to become comfortable. Role-playing games, videotaped mock interviews, and communicating about where to stay once they arrive on campus, are all solutions used to help disadvantaged students engage successfully with the application process.

Advisors and mentors aware of the BHC, Imposter Syndrome and lost bandwidth can work to recognize the signs of a student struggling under their weight. The result of such feelings may lead disadvantaged students to fill their time with pledging, research, and a myriad of social activities that allow them to feel better about themselves. These activities in and of themselves are not problematic. However, using these time-consuming activities to avoid feelings of academic or social inadequacy can have disastrous results. Students avoid tutors, review of exams, and talking with advisors, hoping that somehow their other activities will fill the academic void. Advisors tuned into these defense mechanisms can gently nudge students and help them develop strategies for success.

All of these actions can help students see that their individual journeys, have value. The fact that these students' experience academic success, despite having responsibilities other students do not have, serves to highlight a positive outcome that they should embrace.

CONCLUSION

Students from disadvantaged backgrounds work extremely hard to become successful medical school applicants. They understand the overt requirements needed for producing a competitive medical school application. What they don't know is what they don't know. Advisors and mentors cognizant of the concepts of BHC and MEHC, impostor syndrome, and bandwidth limitations, can positively impact the students' application process and potential outcome. The application process itself may produce a profound emotional effect on all who attempt admission to medical school. Even successful applicants might still question their suitability. Advisors and mentors working with students to mitigate the BHC and other associated issues, not only improve the application of their students, but perhaps, more importantly, help validate the students' acceptance into this new world of a medical profession and potentially increase the diversity of the medical workforce. Students entering the formal medical school curriculum with a stronger sense of self-confidence and self-worth will have more time, energy, and personal resources to put towards that training.

REFERENCES

AAMC. (n.d.) AAMC Diversity Facts and Figures. Retrieved from http://www.aamcdiversityfactsand-figures2016.org/report-section/section-2

Andarvazh, M., Afshar, L., & Yazdani, S. (2017). Hidden curriculum and analytical definition. *Journal of Medical Education*, *16*(4), 198–207.

Author name. (n.d.). Personal financial literacy among US medical students. Retrieved from www.mededpublish.org/ manuscripts/847 Not cited in text.

Butrymowciz, S. (2017). Most colleges enroll many students who are not prepared for higher education. In *The Hechinger Report*. Retrieved from https://hechingerreport.org/colleges-enroll-students-arent-prepared-higher-education/

Cataldi, E., Bennett, C., & Chen, X. (2018). First-generation students: College access, persistence and post-bachelor's outcomes. U.S. Department of Education, NCES.

Chatelain, M. (2018). We must help first-generation students master academe's "hidden curriculum." *The Chronicle of Higher Education*. Retrieved from https://www.chronicle.com/article/We-Must-Help-First-Generation/244830

Cruess, R., & Creus, S. (2014). Reframing medical education to support professional identity formation. *Academic Medicine*, *89*(11), 1446–14451. doi:10.1097/ACM.0000000000000427 PMID:25054423

Day, L., & Benner, P. (2014). The hidden curriculum in nursing education. In F. W. Hafferty, & J. F. O'Donnell (Eds.), The Hidden Curriculum in Health Professional Education (140-149). Hanover, NH: Dartmouth College Press.

Docs, A. (n.d.). *Dealing with application anxiety*. Retrieved from https://students-residents. aamc.org/applying-medical-school/article/dealing-application-anxiety

Dyrbye, L. N., Thomas, M. R., Eacker, A., Harper, W., Massie, F. S., Power, D. V., ... Shanafelt, T. D. (2007). Race, ethnicity, and medical student well-being in the United States. [Not cited in text]. *Archives of Internal Medicine, 167*(19), 2103–2109. doi:10.1001/archinte.167.19.2103 PMID:17954805

Elliot, D., Baumfield, V., Reic, K., & Makara, K. (2016). Hidden treasure: Successful international doctoral students who found and harnessed the hidden curriculum. *Oxford Review of Education, 42*(6), 733–748. doi:10.1080/03054985.2016.1229664

Esposito, J. (2011, November). Negotiating the gaze and learning the hidden curriculum: A critical race analysis of the embodiment of female students of color at predominantly white institutions. *The Journal for Critical Education Policy Studies, 9*, 143–164.

Hafferty, F., & O'Donnell, J. (Eds.). (2014). *Hidden curriculum in health professions education.* Hanover, NH: Dartmouth College Press.

Holistic Review in Medical School Admissions. (n.d.). In *Choosing a Medical Career. AAMC.* Retrieved from https://students-residents.aamc.org/choosing-medical-career/article/holistic-review-medical-school-admissions

Kentli, F. (2009). Comparison of hidden curriculum theories. *European Journal of Education Studies, 1*(2), 83–88.

Kosobuski, A. W., Whitney, A., Skildum, A., & Prunuske, A. (2017). Development of an interdisciplinary pre-matriculation program designed to promote medical students' self efficacy. *Medical Education Online, 22*(1), 1272835. doi:10.1080/10872981.2017.1272835 PMID:28178916

Laurencin, C. T., & Murray, M. (2017). An American crisis: The lack of black men in medicine. *Journal of Racial and Ethnic Health Disparities, 4*(3), 317–321. doi:10.100740615-017-0380-y PMID:28534304

Margolis, E., Soldatenko, M., Acker, S., & Gair, M. M. (2001). Peekabo hiding and outing the curriculum. In E. Margolis (Ed.), The Hidden Curriculum in Higher Education (1-20). New York, NY: Routledge.

Miller, C. (2014). Implementation of study skills programs for entering at risk medical students. *Advances in Physiology Education, 38*(3), 229–234. doi:10.1152/advan.00022.2014 PMID:25179612

Mitchall, A., & Jaeger, A. (2018). Parental influences on low-income, first generation students' motivation on the path to college. *The Journal of Higher Education, 89*(4), 582–606. doi:10.1080/00221546.2018.1437664

O'Donnell, J. (2014). Introduction: The hidden curriculum: A focus on learning and closing the gap. In F. W. Hafferty & J. F. O'Donnell (Eds.), *The Hidden Curriculum in Health Professional Education* (pp. 1–20). Hanover, NH: Dartmouth College Press.

Oyewole, S. (2001). Sustaining minorities in pre-health advising programs: Challenges and strategies for success. In B. Smedley, A. Sith, L. Colburn, & C. Evans (Eds.), *The Right Thing to Do: Enhancing Diversity in the Health Professions: Summary of the Symposium in Honor of Herbert N. Nickens M. D.* Washington DC: National Academies Press. Retrieved from https://www.ncbi. nlm.nih.gov/books/NBK223624

Peteet, J. B., Montgomery, L., Jerren, C., & Weekes, J. C. (2015). Predictors of imposter phenomenon among talented ethnic minority undergraduate students. *The Journal of Negro Education, 84*(2), 175–186. doi:10.7709/jnegroeducation.84.2.0175

Phillips, S., & Clarke, M. (2012). More than an education: The hidden curriculum, professional attitudes and career choice. *Medical Education, 46*(9), 887–893. doi:10.1111/j.1365-2923.2012.04316.x PMID:22891909

Rabow, M. W. (2014) Becoming a doctor: Learning from the hidden curriculum in medical education. In F. W. Hafferty & J. F. O'Donnell (Eds.), The Hidden Curriculum in Health Professional Education (130-139). Hanover, NH: Dartmouth College Press.

Smith, B. (2013). *Mentoring at risk students through the hidden curriculum of higher education*. Lanham, MD: Lexington Book.

Status, D. (2020). *n.p* (p. 25). AMCAS Application Guide; Retrieved from https://apps.aamc.org/amcas/guide/2020_AMCAS_applicant_guide.pdf

Taylor, J., & Wendland, C. (2014). The hidden curriculum in medicine's "culture of no culture": Health professional education. In F. W. Hafferty, & J. F. O'Donnell (Eds.), The Hidden Curriculum in Health Professional Education (53-62). Hanover, NH: Dartmouth College Press.

Tenhouse, A. (n.d.) College extracurricular activities impacts on students: Types of extracurricular activities. *8 Minute Reads*. Retrieved from https://education.stateuniversity.com/pages/1855/ College-Extracurricular-Activities.html

The Core Competencies for Entering Medical Students. (n.d.) In *Applying to Medical School, AAMC*. Retrieved from https://students-residents.aamc.org/applying-medical-school/article/core-competencies

Thistlewaite, J. (2014). Hidden among us: The language of inter- and outer-professional identity and collaboration. In F. W. Hafferty, & J. F. O'Donnell (Eds.), The Hidden Curriculum in Health Professional Education (158-168). Hanover, NH: Dartmouth College Press.

Verschelden, C. (2017). *Bandwidth recovery helping students reclaim cognitive resources lost to poverty, racism and social marginalization*. Sterling, VA: Stylus Publishing.

Wear, D., Zarconi, J., & Garden, R. (2014). Disorderly conduct: Calling out of the hidden curriculum(s) of professionalism. In F. W. Hafferty, & J. F. O'Donnell (Eds.), The Hidden Curriculum in Health Professional Education (63-75). Hanover, NH: Dartmouth College Press.

White, J., & Lowenthal, P. (2019). Academic Discourse and the Formation of an Academic Identity: Minority College Students and the Hidden Curriculum. Academic Press.

Witteveen, D., & Attwell, P. (2017). The college completion puzzle: A hidden Markov model approach. *Research in Higher Education, 58*(4), 449–467. doi:10.100711162-016-9430-2

Wright-Peterson, V., & Bender, C. (2014). Making the invisible visible: Uncovering the hidden curriculum in allied health education. In F. W. Hafferty, & J. F. O'Donnell (Eds.), The Hidden Curriculum in Health Professional Education (140-147). Hanover, NH: Dartmouth College Press.

Section 2
Evolving Curricular Programming

Chapter 4
Teaching Millennials and Generation Z:
New Opportunities in Undergraduate Medical Education

M. Renee Prater

The Edward Via College of Osteopathic Medicine, USA

ABSTRACT

Each generation is defined not solely by the date of their birth, but also for their beliefs, their priorities, and their motivations. Many factors play heavily into the development of each generation's collective identify, including parenting styles, significant political and current events, changing gender roles, and other formative experiences. These factors significantly and uniquely influence how each generation lives, learns, and interacts with others (Gerhardt, 2016). While most medical educators today are baby boomers, the majority of medical students are millennial and generation Z individuals, who communicate, learn, and interact very differently than their instructors. As a result, effective medical educators are challenged to update their methods of instruction to best suit these newer generations of learners for better assimilation, clinical application, and long-term retention of material, to maintain delivery of high-quality healthcare in the country for future generations (Desy et al., 2017; Waljee, 2018).

INTRODUCTION

The field of medicine is presently at an exciting and daunting juncture: medical research, novel diagnostics, and new drug developments are offering health care providers an ever-increasing wealth of information in the fields of disease pathophysiology, laboratory and imaging diagnosis, and treatment modalities to best care for patients. However, this wealth of information has reached a tipping point in the volume of information necessary to be a competent practicing physician. As a result, health care educators are quickly realizing that strict reliance on didactic lecture-based medical education is no longer tenable. Additionally, with generational and gender differences in learning styles, and an increasing awareness of

DOI: 10.4018/978-1-7998-1468-9.ch004

the importance of mental health and work-life balance, medical educators and their students are tasked with the job of adapting novel teaching, learning, and testing styles to maximize efficiency of information acquisition, retention, and clinical application, while being sensitive to the time and capacities of all those involved.

BACKGROUND

In recent years, the field of medical knowledge has exploded, with new, exciting and innovative advances in diagnostics and treatments becoming available on a daily basis. Recent reports in Nature Medicine report paradigm-changing advances in artificial intelligence technologies in medicine (He *et. al*, 2019), advances in stem-cell-based interventions (MacPherson & Kimmelman, 2019), greatly improved understanding of how the gut microbiome influences overall health (Poyet *et. al*, 2019), and use of big data approaches for precision health (Rose *et. al*, 2019), just to name a few. These advances have empowered health care providers with greatly improved understanding of the pathophysiology of diseases at the cellular and molecular levels, new therapeutic developments including genomic, immune, and dietary interventions, the application of precision medicine, and the microbiome. The application of this new knowledge in the healthcare setting translates into increased lifespan and better quality of life for patients. However, this abundant new knowledge also represents an ever-expanding repertoire of information that today's medical students must master to become competent and capable practicing physicians. As the vastness of medical knowledge continues to expand, undergraduate medical educators are faced with the task of deciding what information to present and to what depth to teach in undergraduate education versus what will be learned on clinical rotations, how to best present it in a manner that engages the students for long-term learning and optimal clinical application, and how to examine the students' medical knowledge to ensure public safety of their future patients.

As the preclinical medical curriculum is incrementally expanded to maximize preparation for competitive board exam (U.S. Medical Licensing Examination and Comprehensive Osteopathic Medical Licensing Examination of the U.S.) performance, medical educators must remain ever-mindful of the need to preserve the mental health and work-life balance of students, as burn-out and substance abuse in medical students are real and significant issues (Jackson, Shanafelt, Hasan, Satele, & Dyrbye, 2016). Specifically, Jackson *et al.* (2016) completed a national survey of U. S. medical students assessing alcohol abuse/dependence, burnout, depression, suicidality, quality of life and fatigue. Of the 12,500 students surveyed, 32.5% of respondents met diagnostic criteria for alcohol abuse/dependence. Students who were burned out, depressed, or reported low quality of life were more likely to abuse alcohol. In another study (dos Santos Boni *et al,* 2018), 330 Brazilian undergraduate medical students were queried regarding their level of burnout and the factors that may have contributed to these issues. Nearly 71% reported high levels of emotional exhaustion, with nearly as many reporting high cynicism and low academic efficacy. Forty-five percent reported burnout, with the highest frequency of affected students in the first year of their studies, and the incidence of burnout in medical school seemed to be associated with increasing difficulty of the curriculum.

This issue of poor work-life balance in the healthcare field extends far beyond undergraduate medical education and has been addressed in residency and in private practice realms as well. Until the late 1990's and early 2000's, the expectation of physicians and residents was to work as many hours as needed to deliver effective patient care in addition to providing ancillary services such as charting. As most healthcare workers are paid a fixed salary, not hourly, these long hours were not viewed as being beneficial to the healthcare worker, and were potentially even detrimental to the patient in cases of provider fatigue. In a 2001 study of 4,510 obstetric/gynecologic residents (Defoe, Power, Holzman, Carpentieri, & Schulkin, 2001), over 75% reported working between 61 and 100 hours per week, and 71% reported sleeping less than 3 hours per night while on call. Of all respondents, three out of four requested limits on their work hours for three main reasons: 1) fatigue, 2) need for more personal time and 3) fear of compromising quality of care. But this issue is not limited to the field of obstetrics and gynecology: an evaluation of the American Medical Association's Graduate Medical Education database in 2004 (Baldwin & Daugherty, 2004) revealed a similar trend of sleep deprivation in first and second year medical residents that was linked to higher likelihood of serious accidents or injuries, conflicts with medical staff, use or abuse of alcohol, increased consumption of medications to maintain alertness, increased rates of physical and emotional health issues, and working in an impaired condition that led to elevated rates of significant medical errors. As a result of these and many other studies, in 2002 the American Osteopathic Association (AOA) imposed an 80-hour work limit in their residencies (Zonia, LaBaere, Stommel, & Tomaszewski, 2005), and in 2003, the Accreditation Council for Graduate Medical Education (ACGME) imposed restrictions on work hours of medical staff to not exceed a maximum of 80 hours per week (Levine & Spang, 2014). However, this work-hour restriction did little to improve the quality of healthcare (Ahmed *et. al*, 2014), likely due to a combination of poor compliance with this cap/under-reporting hours or persistence of ancillary duties such as maintaining medical records/charting over and above the 80-hour work week. So work-life balance in the medical profession remains an issue that must continue to be addressed for the betterment of the health of providers and their patients.

THE GENERATIONAL DIVIDES

What factors are fueling this interest in improving work-life balance in the medical profession? Recent studies forecast an increasing physician shortage (Jackson *et. al*, 2018) that is linked to reduced job satisfaction, increased job turnover, and earlier retirement. Stratifying the physician population, women and younger physicians report increased job dissatisfaction, which could be remedied in part by reducing work hours and improving the culture in the work environment. According to 2016 United States census data, the average age of actively licensed physicians is 51 years, and 30% of all physicians are aged 60 years or older (Young *et. al*, 2017). As the "baby boomer" physician population is nearing or at retirement age the younger generations are entering the physician workforce. These younger physicians, who belong to the millennial generation and generation Z (gen Z), seem to be more acutely aware of the need for rest and personal time in order to maintain their own physical and emotional health and provide optimal care for their patients. These generations are cognizant that the medical knowledge base that is required to competently practice medicine continues to explode, and increased competition for residency positions brings with it ever-greater expectations for leadership, research/scholarly activity, and volunteerism during medical school to out-compete their peers for coveted residency positions. So, while these young future physicians are entering the profession with their eyes wide open as to the mental and physical demands of the training and the practice of medicine, they are also wise to the issue of stress, burnout, substance abuse, and mental health disorders in an overworked physician population. As a result, they seek to shift the tide of medical school, residency, and clinical practice to improve quality of life for themselves and their peers, thus ensuring quality of healthcare for their patients.

To optimize efficacy in medical education and practice, it is important to understand each generation's values and learning styles that make them distinct from other generations. A deep understanding of each generation's characteristics is essential in providing a learning environment that is conducive to their success and happiness. The four main generations who currently comprise the physician workforce today are: baby boomers, who were born between 1946 and 1964; generation X who were born between 1965 and 1976; millennials or generation Y, who were born between 1977 and 1995; and generation Z or centennials who were born after 1995 (Colby & Ortman 2014). According to Gauer and Jackson (2018), the average age of students matriculating into medical school is now 24 years (birth year approximately 1995, which is at the cusp between the millennial and gen Z generations), while the average age of full-time faculty members at U. S. medical schools is 50 years (birth year 1969) (Skarupski *et. al*, 2019). Clearly, differences in teaching and learning styles between these two populations exist and must be considered in the medical education arena. To better understand the personalities and priorities of each generation, a brief review of the typical characteristics of each generation is outlined below: what they hold as important, how they learn and process information, and how they prefer to interact with others in professional settings.

The Baby Boomer Generation

The Baby Boomer Generation, our medical educators, were born between 1946 and 1964, and currently comprise the majority of medical teaching faculty today (Skarupski *et al.*, 2019). Baby boomers are characterized by their competitiveness, self-discipline, and strong work ethic. They are competent and ambitious and are known for the quality of "living to work". They have been raised to be self-sufficient and independent, and while they respect authority, they are willing to take on the responsibility necessary to achieve their goals, and are willing to put in extra time in order to see a project to completion (Maiers, 2017). These qualities significantly impacted the way baby boomers learned in school, and as a result, influence the way they teach their students today. Additionally, they tend to be considered as idealistic, and learned best through one-way communications via lecture and required reading assignments (Romanello, 2005). Baby boomers as medical students were generally taught in a linear fashion: they were taught by lectures in courses based on a specific discipline such as anatomy, physiology, pharmacology, etc., and were required to independently "connect the dots" from one discipline to the next to improve their overall understanding of the etiopathogenesis, diagnosis, and management of disease. For example, they were expected to integrate concepts learned in anatomy and physiology together in order to understand the normal form and function of the workings of the human body in health, and then apply this knowledge to the study of diseases and their treatments (Warren, 2012). Since computer/internet technology at the time was still in its infancy, baby boomers learned using textbooks, handouts, overhead projectors, filmstrips and video recordings. They read textbooks from cover-to-cover, which provided a strong structural framework for the material but often risked the unintended result of "siloing" of information. With siloing, each subject matter is presented and learned in isolation, with little to no integration across disciplines. As a result of the lecture-based format of information delivery, coupled with the expectation to read textbooks and other required material on their own, baby boomer medical students were tasked with the responsibility to integrate the information that they were provided independently, and to relate this information across disciplines, to formulate a more complete understanding of the entirety of the disease process or its management into their overall body of knowledge.

Generation X

Generation X is known for being independent, pragmatic, and somewhat skeptical, as they were the generation of "latch-key kids" (Maiers, 2017). With the divorce rate of their parents being much higher than the prior generation, they were forced to be self-reliant at an earlier age, and entered the work force younger as well, so they possess valuable real-life experience. They tend to be resourceful, well-educated problem-solvers that are reality-driven – in other words, they need to see the application of learned material in the real world. They are more competent with technology than the baby boomers, and they tend to value freedom and balance of work and life, so their best learning style is through "real world" assignments, individual learning and case studies. Generation X were taught more in modules than in a linear fashion like their baby boomer predecessors, and were provided with a mixture of lectures and group learning activities (Romanello, 2005). Being more apt to use technology, they were less dependent on books for gleaning necessary information, and tended to not read their textbooks cover-to-cover. This generation began a transformational shift in the philosophies and practices of teaching and learning in medical education, to ease away from traditional lecture-based instruction with required reading from textbooks, towards a more interactive, flexible, and technology-based curriculum that offered greater clinical applications for students.

Generation Y or the Millennials

Generation Y or the millennials, along with gen Z, are the most racially and ethnically diverse in the nation's history (DeBard, 2004) and comprise the majority of medical students today. They exhibit very different philosophies and approaches to living and learning, and are known as the "entitled generation" or the "me generation". Although many believe that this generation is sheltered and narcissistic, perhaps in fact they are simply a bit more individualistic than prior generations (Grant, 2017). They have been recognized as being less civically and politically engaged than their baby boomer or generation X counterparts, although they are regarded as more confident, team- and service-oriented, open-minded, and more supportive of work-life balance, gay rights, and equal rights for minorities as compared to their prior generational counterparts (Gerhardt, 2016; DeMaria, 2013; DeBard, 2004). They tend to be optimistic, and have relatively short attention spans and express a need for positive, immediate feedback. They highly prioritize achievement and as such are the most competitive and highly educated generation thus far. While they have a strong sense of entitlement following adolescent sheltering by helicopter parents, they lean towards being visual learners, concerned with style over substance, and have a high expectation for use of technology and multi-media in their instruction. They are not book readers and are unlikely to purchase required books, although they may access electronic books as supplemental resources if available. They thrive with group projects and opportunities to connect with other learners through social media (Maiers, 2017).

Generation Z

Generation Z, the youngest of the generations, are the largest generation in the U.S. and will represent 40% of the population by the year 2020 (Kalkhurst, 2018). Like millennials, they are a highly racially, sexually, and culturally diverse generation who are incredibly tech savvy, and have grown up with smart phones, internet, and social media as a way of life, and as such, they are referred to as "multimodal learners" (Abrahams, 2015). In fact, it has been estimated that gen Z students regularly use up to five different screens, which occupy ten hours of gen Z's daily activities (Kalkhurst, 2018). Because of their absolute comfort level with the use of technology and multi-media, they do not need to be, nor do they prefer to be spoon-fed information. A recent survey showed that 51% of gen Z students learn by doing as compared to only 12% saying they learn through listening (Kozinsky, 2017). However, while gen Z students in general demonstrate independent learning skills and do not seem to be overwhelmed with the information overload of the internet, they seem to have very short attention spans, so frequent one-hour lectures are not conducive to optimal learning in this generation. Instead, gen Z students seem to perform best with digital resources, small bytes of information at a time, and rely on instant gratification which could be accomplished with small low-stakes formative evaluations embedded into their curriculum. Additionally, gen Z students appear to generally lack an important part of adult learning, which is critical thinking skills. Since independent learning, critical thinking and problem-solving are essential to the practice of medicine but are not strengths of this generation, instructional styles must be adjusted away from the one-way communication of information through classroom lectures, and towards problem-based learning, team-based learning, case-based learning, and flipped-classroom styles of instruction to best meet the needs of this generation of learners.

TEACHING MILLENNIALS AND GEN Z MEDICAL STUDENTS

The amount of medical knowledge needed to successfully complete preclinical education and national board exams has exploded in modern years. Burg & French (2012) estimated that the body of new medical knowledge attained over the past 50 years far exceeds the amount of medical knowledge that was attained in the 500 years before. Because of this explosion of knowledge, medical educators are tasked with the important job of distilling and presenting the necessary information to their preclinical medical students in a way that is attainable and manageable and will ensure successful completion of board exams and safe management of patients in clinical rotations. Additional attention must be given to providing support for student anxiety and burnout that could impair academic success and future patient safety. This realization requires that the vast amount of information provided to medical students be delivered in the form of student-centered, problem-based or case-based modules, rather than in a traditional teacher-centered lecture-based passive learning style. This shift in teaching styles should include more opportunities for active learning, to give assignments that develop and improve critical thinking and problem-solving skills, to schedule learning content with greater flexibility and freedom to complete assignments, to test knowledge using small formative exams that offer immediate feedback in addition to higher stakes summative exams, and to create opportunities for imaginative, group, and kinesthetic learning (Koh, Khoo, Wong, & Koh, 2008). These efforts to modify instructional styles to accommodate the depth and breadth of medical education are in part due to the way in which the newer generations learn and process large amounts of information. As a result of the way the millennial and gen Z students learn and interact in professional and social settings, a more active learning style that utilizes group learning, active learning, technology, and regular low-stakes formative feedback has been viewed as an effective means to teach in a preclinical medical setting today.

Millennials and gen Z students prioritize social relationships, and most millennials and gen Z students deeply value open and regular communication with peers as well as their instructors, and the extent to which a student engages in their learning is a strong predictor of their success (Handelsman, Briggs,

Sullivan, & Towler, 2005). Since they value communication and teamwork, sociability (talkativeness, friendliness and good nature), composure (poise, calm and control), and credibility are important qualities they seek in their peers as well as in their teaching faculty (Gerhardt, 2016). Millennials and gen Z students learn in professional social groups in the form of in-person group work, and they prefer to use technology to connect with each other and the body of medical knowledge. So they seek opportunities to interact and connect with their peers and their instructors either in person or via social media to enhance retention of the vast information that is provided to them in their preclinical education years. Millennial and gen Z students greatly value flexibility in the style of instruction as well as in their learning pace and completion of assignments (Handelsman *et al.,* 2005). They have been shown to best succeed in their undergraduate medical curricula when given independent or group learning activities that foster active learning styles and critical thinking skills. Incorporating the use of technology is key in the effective engagement of this generation of learners, who rely on up-to-date, wireless on-line information for best understanding and retention of material (Benditz *et. al*, 2018; Riley, 2018). Effective use of technology to allow medical students of these generations to thrive include those activities that expose students to active and kinesthetic learning that offer them the rationale and the relevance for attaining and retaining new knowledge, and may include laboratories, high-fidelity simulations, and standardized patient encounters.

Millennials and gen Z students in general have been shown to have shorter attention spans, and are most responsive to visual/special, auditory/musical, and kinesthetic/tactile learning modalities that do not easily fit into traditional didactic learning styles but can be utilized in creative and innovative new methods of instruction (Cameron & Pagnattaro, 2017). Given shorter attention spans, effective engagement with students in skill-building, human interactions, and academic performance is key to a successful curriculum (Handelsman *et al.,* 2005). Given the learning strategies of these generations of medical students, an interdisciplinary, active learning format, given in short bursts of information rather than more traditional hour-long lectures, appears to be most effective. When coupled with a detailed statement of goals that includes clear expectations of students and specific educational objectives, flexible progression, learner assessment and feedback and intended outcomes, as well as occasional personalized learning plans to best suit individual learning styles, millennial and gen Z students are set up for success (Desy, Reed, & Wolanskyj, 2017). Innovative methods of mentorship such as micromentoring, reverse mentoring and collaborative mentorship have shown to be effective ways that faculty can communicate with students to provide diverse perspectives for student feedback, and reduce information siloing, competition and isolation (Waljee, Chopra, & Saint, 2018). While these forms of mentoring do not typically lend themselves to assessment, opportunities to give small, low-stakes and frequent formative assessments to the learners may provide the frequent, positive feedback they crave (Desy *et al.,* 2017). Small formative tests can offer flexibility and freedom in time management and creative expression, and will be further explored below.

Today's student learners are very divergent from the baby-boomer/generation X styles of learning, who were trained using primarily didactic lecture-based learning with summative testing. This disparity in learning styles challenges today's medical educators to determine the best ways to adapt their teaching styles and their content to meet the needs of these younger generations, while still delivering quality instruction that will ensure academic and clinical success. To accomplish this transition in teaching styles to best meet the needs of medical students today, medical educators are tasked to redesign curriculum to provide a variety of active learning opportunities such as group or problem-based learning, kinesthetic learning in the form of labs, high-fidelity simulations, competency-based medical education including milestones and entrustable professional activities, flipped classrooms, and simulated patient encounters, and to offer regular formative or ungraded assessments that will provide the supportive feedback that today's students are seeking (Riley, 2018; Desy *et al.,* 2017; Hopkins *et. al*, 2018). Jenkins & Allen (2017) outlined a five-step design process for education that ensure opportunities for personal growth, conceptual understanding/critical thinking, feedback, and skill building. These five steps include: *1) identifying learning outcomes and selecting desired competencies, 2) selecting appropriate instructional strategies; 3) considering situational factors, 4) designing appropriate assessment measure, and 5) providing opportunities for evaluative feedback.* These steps, when used to redesign a medical curriculum, provide a nice framework into which innovative teaching styles that integrate active and kinesthetic learning may be incorporated, for better success of today's medical students (Jenkins & Allen, 2017). An important step that must be considered when redesigning a medical curriculum is to incorporate a strong interdisciplinary approach to teaching, which includes self-regulated learning to engage the student and improves self-efficacy to ensure meaningful learning and long-term retention of material by millennials (Palmer, 2015).

GENDER DIFFERENCES IN LEARNING STYLES

In addition to generational differences in learning styles, there are also pronounced, generally recognized differences in styles of learning between the genders. As we continue to see a rise in the proportion of female students entering medical school, effective educators must be cognizant of differences in communication and learning styles between male and female medical students in order to most effectively transmit information to students in a way that is most understandable, palatable, and memorable. Gender roles are continuing to evolve in today's society, more so today than ever before, and these evolving roles are closely related to the ways in which each gender interacts in society and in their personal and professional relationships. These gender roles, much like the generational characteristics, are tied to the influences of politics and culture. Regarding differences between male and female students, especially in their younger years, boys tend to prefer larger social groups and be more active and restless than their female counterparts in the classroom, and as a result, they may more effectively learn by active group learning activities rather than sitting and passively listening for long periods of time (Seifert & Sutton, 2009). Boys also seem to be more comfortable with speaking up in class or in group situations, which would also favor group learning assignments over passive learning styles. However, because more gregarious and extroverted students of either gender may tend to dominate conversations and group work, it is imperative that the facilitator of any group assignment be mindful of the importance of full participation of each member, and construct and administer the assignment in a way that encourages participation of each member of the group. In contrast to their male counterparts, younger female students tend to demonstrate greater academic motivation and higher achievement, although adolescent female students may be inclined to downplay their abilities to be considered more likeable by both genders (Davies, 2005; Freeman, 2004). So, close attention of facilitators to ensure full participation of all students is a key to success in the classroom.

As students leave college and enter medical school, gender differences persist and represent small but significant differences in the way females and males prefer to learn in the preclinical medical school environment. This issue of gender differences in learning styles is especially relevant as the proportion of female students matriculating into medical school continues to rise each year. In the 2016-2017 academic year, female students comprised 49.8% of the new allopathic matriculants, and 45.9% of the new osteopathic matriculants (Basha, Bauer, Modrakowski, & Baker, 2018). This represents a major shift in the demographics of medical students over these four generations. For example, in the academic year of 1965-1966, 9.3% of allopathic medical school matriculants were women, and 6.9% of graduates were women (Association of American Medical Colleges [AAMC], 2016). This percentage climbed to 38.5% female matriculants and 36% of graduates who were female in academic year 1990-1991, and then finally tipped the scales to nearly 50% female medical students in 2017. The statistics are similar in the osteopathic field, with only 18% of practicing osteopathic physicians being female in 1993, and 41% in 2018 (AAMC, 2016). This trend continues as in 2018 the enrollment for osteopathic colleges is 49% women, with 44% female graduates (American Association of Colleges of Osteopathic Medicine [AACOM], 2019), which is a huge shift from the 1968-1969 academic year, when only 4% of enrollees were female. Important differences exist in the way female and male students process information. For example, Benditz *et al.* (2018) found that female students preferred to use highlighting for required reading, and preferred internet research and small group learning, while male students tended to prioritize the use of digital books over their female counterparts. Because of apparent differences not only in generational styles of learning but also in gender preferences in methods and materials for learning, medical educators must be nimble and aware of these inclinations and adjust their teaching methodologies to maximize the ability of their students to be successful in the preclinical curriculum.

SOLUTIONS AND RECOMMENDATIONS

It is evident that learning styles of each generation have shifted dramatically from the baby boomers through generations X, Y and Z, with gender preferences also representing significant challenges in teaching style. In response, prevailing teaching methods must evolve with the generations. In response to learning styles of the newer generations, educators have begun to shift from passive to active learning styles, to encourage team-building and group learning. Group learning is a type of active learning (Bonwell & Eison, 1991) that is referred to as constructivism, which is a method of teaching in which students gain their own understanding of the topic, which is built upon their prior knowledge. This type of learning is best accomplished when students are given an assignment that promotes teamwork and use of internet or other resources to complete the assignment, rather than just listening, watching, and taking notes. The three main types of active group learning include:

1. **Student-centered learning**, which is tailored specifically to the diverse learning needs of students, and places students in the center of the learning process. More modern schools of thought in higher education believe that this style of learning resonates well with the millennial and generation Z students, who are more inclined towards team-based and individual methods of learning, which offers them more control over timing and outcomes.

2. **Problem-based learning**, in which a student or group of students are given a problem, scenario, or clinical case. The assignment includes targeted, open-ended questions to answer, and the students are expected to use available resources to independently solve the problem or the case to demonstrate their understanding of the material. In the study of medicine, problem-based or case-based learning has gained great favor in recent years, as this style of learning fosters deeper interdisciplinary understanding of the etiopathogenesis, diagnosis and management of illnesses. Using this method of instruction, students gain understanding into the anatomy and physiology of the organ system,

the pathophysiology and clinical manifestations of disease, the laboratory and imaging techniques necessary to definitely diagnose the disorder, and the pharmacologic, surgical, or osteopathic manipulative management of the disease.

3. **Experiential learning**, where students engage in active learning by demonstrating skills or engaging in "*authentic learning activities*" that could be directly applied to clinical practice. Some examples of this include anatomy, microbiology and osteopathic manipulation laboratories, as well as clinical skills laboratories, high-fidelity simulations, and standardized patient encounters (Center for Teaching Excellence, 2019).

Several different styles of teaching incorporate methods of instruction currently used in the medical education arena. A recent publication (Innova, 2015) divides teaching styles into five main categories: 1) Authority Style, 2) Delegator Style, 3) Facilitator Style, 4) Demonstrator Style and 5) Hybrid Style. Each of these styles have their merits and their challenges in preclinical medical education, so a solid understanding of how each of these teaching styles may be modified and applied to each generation is key to effective teaching and learning.

The first category, the **Authority Style**, is typically used with large class sizes, in lecture halls or auditoriums. Also commonly referred to as an "expository" method of teaching, in this style, the instructor provides a lengthy lecture or one-way communication to the audience, with little to no audience participation. Students are expected to sit and listen, take notes, and memorize key pieces of information delivered to them. While this style of instruction was popular with the baby boomers, and was an effective means to teach that generation of strict and disciplined learners, this style is not conducive to optimal learning of the millennials or gen Z students, who seek more efficient ways of using technology, group learning, and active learning. However, lectures can still be effective if they are used judiciously, and in ways that encourage active learning by the students: lectures can be video-recorded to allow students to view the information at a time that is optimal for their learning. Features such as the ability to stop and start the video recording gives the student a chance to self-pace their mastery of the material, and incorporating a series of formative or probing questions periodically throughout the video recording would reinforce that learning and encourage a more active learning style. Using multi-media tools within the video-recorded lecture can also help to keep students engaged, and give them real-life applications that would enhance learning. Examples of these tools includes audio-video clips, images, graphics, case presentations, and periodic formative assessments sprinkled throughout the lecture, using technology such as i-clickers or equivalent. Lectures can provide structure and framework to broad concepts, and when used thoughtfully and more sparingly in combination with other teaching styles, can augment millennial and gen Z learning in undergraduate medical education.

The second category, the **Delegator Style,** involves group work or lab-based learning with peer feedback. In this style of instruction, there is a delegator or a tutor who is assigned to lead the group, to encourage active participation and promote collaboration between group members, and to keep the group on task to complete the project or learning module. This method of instruction can be classified as a "constructivist" style of learning, in which students learn how to learn by receiving initial training, and then are expected to take initiative for their own learning experience. In this style, also referred to as "cooperative learning", the group leader can lead by modeling, by coaching, or by a concept called "instructional scaffolding", where instructors can enhance or encourage individual or group learning activities by offering supports for students to aid in the mastery of the assignment (Hitch & Nicola-Richmond, 2017). As students master the assignment, these supports are gradually removed. Much like installing training wheels on the bicycle of a child learning to ride, these scaffolds can aid the student in the completion of an assignment or task; examples of scaffolding include instructor modeling the task and then asking the student to replicate their actions, or to encourage the student, individually on in a group, to practice a task or assignment by working collaboratively with others, under the direction or supervision of the instructor. This style is most useful when the learning is multi-step in nature, and has gained popularity in recent years. It offers a distinct advantage to the newer generations of medical students, as this style of learning involves active learning, team work, and greater autonomy in mastery of the material. This style of instruction is increasingly being used with great success in undergraduate medical education in case-based or problem-based learning formats, as it promotes life-long learning skills, and allows students to build new knowledge on an existing foundation of previously acquired knowledge. However, the main instructor is removed from a position of authority, which may result in some groups not mastering the material correctly or in the proper depth or context that was intended by the instructor. For these reasons, this style of instruction must be used in conjunction with regular formative assessments as detailed below, to ensure proper mastery of material.

The third category, the **Facilitator Style,** employs self-learning in the classroom, where the instructor poses questions to the students. This method of instruction can also be classified as a constructivist style of learning, in which the facilitator offers an open-ended question, an issue, or a case study, and students are expected to take initiative for their own learning experience. In this method of instruction, the students are not "spoon fed" the information, which has been shown to be appealing especially to gen Z learners, and can be referred to as "discovery learning", "inquiry-based learning", or "**flipped classroom**". Instead of passively receiving information from the instructor as in the authority style, students in a flipped classroom are expected to discover the answers independently, which helps to develop deeper understanding of the material and improves critical thinking and problem-solving skills. Students are tasked to study the content independently prior to class using required reading materials, videos, or pre-recorded lectures and then completing written assignments or pre-quizzes to individually assess knowledge in a formative format. Students are then asked to interact with their group during assigned class time, to reinforce the material they studied independently, and then apply this knowledge in clinical scenarios (Frankl *et. al*, 2017). This form of instruction requires active participation, critical thinking skills and a strategy of inquiry and problem-solving in order to master the material, which are critical skills that are necessary for a successful medical career. A recent meta-analysis of this type of instruction has been shown to increase student performance in STEM (science, technology, engineering and math) education (Freeman *et. al*, 2014). It is believed that this method of instruction leads to improved retention of material, which is vital to success in a medical school curriculum. However, this style places high demand on instructor/facilitator time and interaction, which can be difficult to successfully accomplish in large class settings. Additionally, the layout of the room to encourage effective group interactions is vital to its success.

One type of facilitator-based teaching style that has been increasingly implemented in preclinical medical education in recent years is **problem-based learning (PBL)**. Developed in medical education in the late 1960s (Frenk *et. al*, 2010), the intention of PBL is to promote life-long learning, to help students develop independent learning styles and valuable critical thinking skills, to learn how to best use the literature, and to gain skills in teamwork and collaboration in the professional environment. In PBL, students are given assignments and are expected to learn by engaging in group discussions in order to integrate and clinically apply medical knowledge in an interdisciplinary and clinically relevant fashion. Typically, groups of six to ten students are randomly assigned together for a period of six to ten weeks, during which time they typically meet several times a week for two-hour sessions. During their group sessions, they are expected to practice "hypothetico-deductive reasoning", which is a type of clinical reasoning skill consisting of professional argumentation using claims with data and sufficient warrant to back up their claims (Ju, Choi, & Yoon, 2017). To support the group's progress, each group is assigned a mentor or facilitator, which places a high demand on instructor time with larger class sizes. After the six- to ten-week period, groups are reformed to encourage social and interpersonal skill building with different groups of students. A recent review of problem-based learning approaches reinforces the intent of PBL as a way to encourage deep learning of preclinical medical knowledge that can be related to prior knowledge and will be retained long-term and be applied to the students' future practice of medicine, rather than just relying on surface learning (e.g., memorizing key information to reproduce on exams, but not committing the information to long-term memory or clinical application). Many students enter into medical school having been successful in undergraduate education using rote memorization and surface learning, and are then challenged to modify their study strategies to incorporate deeper learning, critical thinking, and problem-solving. As these students enter into medical school, they are faced with a high perceived workload that further encourages surface learning/rote memorization ("memorize and dump" strategy) that may offer temporary success on exams during their preclinical education, but will prepare them poorly for the problem-solving, critical thinking, and deep understanding of the mechanisms of disease that are vital to a successful career in medicine. Additionally, that high perceived workload will more likely lead to feelings of burnout, exhaustion, and diminished interest in the subject matter, and anxiety and depression are real and significant issues in the field of medical education today, as discussed previously. In contrast, PBL is a student-centered approach to teaching that offers an opportunity for students to modify their learning style, which will benefit them throughout their career. In a PBL approach to learning, student groups are provided with a problem or case in a step-wise progression (e.g., prior medical history, then current history/physical exam/laboratory findings, etc.) without prior preparation or study. Because the student's knowledge is insufficient to fully understand the content, underlying principles, or clinical context, the group is tasked with gathering the needed information, either independently or together, after which time they re-convene to discuss and share what they have each learned, for a deeper understanding of the assigned content. PBL modules often contain scaffolding in the form of facilitators or tutors to help guide the discussion and ensure students gain the necessary information to be competent in that area of study. A big advantage of PBL learning is that it forces students to integrate information across disciplines, and to understand underlying mechanisms for a deeper approach to learning (Dolmans, Loyens, Marcq, & Gijbels, 2016). In a review of 21 programs that implemented PBL in their curriculum, 11 programs experienced higher deep learning, while six programs reported no improvement and four reported a decrease in deep learning, with little effect on surface learning (Dolmans *et al.,* 2016). Factors that may play into the success or failure of a PBL approach to medical instruction include: sufficient allotment of time to allow individual preparation as well as group discussions; the use of digitally enhanced learning modules in the form of virtual patients rather than paper-based learning modules (Sobocan, Turk, Dinevski, Holj, & Balon, 2016); access to well-trained and accessible facilitators or tutors to ensure everyone in the group is gleaning the necessary information in the module; and the type of testing that will guide students in their preparation of the required material. Competencies that appear to be positively influenced by PBL include technical, social, cognitive, managerial, research, teaching and knowledge, with social and cognitive dimensions most positively influenced by this type of instruction (Koh *et al.,* 2008).

Similar to problem-based learning, **case-based learning (CBL)** is a relatively new approach to teaching in the preclinical medical curriculum that is increasingly being adopted by medical schools nationwide and has been well received by millennial and gen Z students. In CBL, medical students are exposed to real-world clinical scenarios early in their preclinical education, and are tasked to develop learning objectives based on these clinical scenarios, to gain interdisciplinary competency of the disease in an individual or group setting (Jhala & Mathur, 2019; Waliany *et. al*, 2019). Typical cases consist of a fictitious medical record, containing prior medical history, information gathered at an initial visit (e.g., history and physical exam findings), and pertinent additional diagnostic information (e.g., laboratory, radiologic, etc.). Students are expected to use this information to develop a differential diagnosis list, suggest additional workup, and formulate an appropriate treatment plan. Ideally, facilitators are blind to the final diagnosis to minimize any bias in guiding student groups in their discovery of the necessary information.

Team-based learning (TBL) is a structured style of small group learning that is similar to problem-based learning and case-based learning but has some distinct differences. TBL is a learner-centered and instructor-directed form of learning that originated in the early twentieth century in business education, and has more recently been adopted into the medical education arena (Haidet *et. al*, 2012). Seven core design elements underlie the TBL method (Burgess, McGregor, & Mellis, 2015; Haidet *et al.*, 2012). These seven core elements are: team formation, readiness assurance (pre-group individual multiple choice assessment), immediate feedback, sequencing of in-class problem solving (e.g., individual study followed by pretest followed by group and then inter-group and then entire class discussion, followed by individually completed summative exam), the four S's: significant problem, same problem (all groups are solving the same problem simultaneously), specific choice (group has to decide on a single best answer) and simultaneous reporting (such as i-clickers or holding up color-coded cards simultaneously across all groups during the in-class discussion), incentive structure (such as summative evaluation after group and class discussions) and peer review.

In TBL, an entire class participates in small teams of approximately six students, who work together to solve authentic problems. Typically, students are expected to complete a pre-reading assignment and a competency-based exam independently before coming to class. Then the small team gathers to discuss their answers, and the rationale behind their choices. This offers opportunities for social interactions, team-building, and constructive argumentation that is generally viewed positively by millennials and gen Z students. Once all group members come to a consensus, the class reconvenes to participate in inter-group discussion and receive feedback and clarification from the facilitator/instructor about any questions or confusion that the individual teams may have experienced. So, TBL shares some important similarities to PBL in that assignments are clinically relevant, and the majority of learning is done independently and in small groups, with an emphasis on peer-to-peer mentoring and cooperation. Because these learning styles are forms of active learning, the majority of the responsibility for mastery of material is on the individual student, which promotes deeper understanding of the content; and because assignments are based on professionally relevant questions, learning is typically interdisciplinary in nature which offers positive benefits for the student as they prepare for clinical practice. With both learning styles, feedback is present from peers, from facilitators, and from the pre-read quiz that individuals complete prior to initiating the group discussion, and these forms of low-stakes, immediate confirmatory or corrective feedback are highly valued by millennials and gen Z students (Dolmans, Michaelsen, Van Merrienboer, & Van der Vleuten, 2015). The major difference between PBL and TBL is that with PBL, each group has its own facilitator which is present throughout the group discussions, whereas with TBL, a large class has one facilitator that manages all groups, and is not present during the group discussion but is present when the groups reconvene in the classroom for a review of the content.

The fourth category, the **Demonstrator Style**, shares similarities to the Authority or expository style in that there is an instructor who is teaching and leading the students in the learning process. This is a style in which scaffolding can be easily implemented to gradually build new knowledge and skills upon existing knowledge. However instead of the subject matter being delivered in a lecture format, in a demonstrator style, the instructor uses demonstrations such as multimedia presentations and class activities to teach the lesson. This style of teaching is very common in the undergraduate medical education environment through anatomy, microbiology and osteopathic manipulative medicine labs, clinical procedural skills labs, and increasingly with high-fidelity simulations.

The last category, the **Hybrid Style**, endeavors to incorporate a number of different teaching styles within the classroom, in response to the individual needs of students. This style is typically not conducive to effective teaching in large settings, but can be applied in small group settings. However, teaching styles such as TBL can be applied in a hybrid format, i.e., portions of each course can be offered in a TBL format, whereas other portions of the course can be offered in a traditional lecture style or in an independent learning style.

Formative assessments, when used appropriately, can provide a low-stakes and effective means for immediate feedback for improvement of student understanding during the learning process. These informal assessments would be followed up by summative assessments to more formally assess student mastery of the material. There are 10 useful approaches to the use of formative assessments, as outlined in a recent publication (Watanabe-Crockett, 2019). These methods are generally well-received by millennials and gen Z students, as they are low-stakes, typically ungraded assessments that open two-way communications between instructor and student, and are effective means to gauge student understanding and teaching effectiveness. These methods are detailed below.

1. **Analyzing Student Work**. Students' knowledge, attitudes and skills, as well as their strengths and weaknesses on a subject matter, can be easily gauged by evaluating their homework, tests and quizzes. These formative assessments allow for mid-course curricular adjustments to reinforce particular topics. This is an example of the immediate feedback that millennial and gen Z students prefer in their learning process.

2. **Round Robin Charts**. This strategy of formative assessment involves creation of charts that are passed from one small group to the next, to answer open-ended questions that are then discussed with the entire group. This strategy of formative assessment fosters group work, active learning, and immediate student feedback, which are all viewed positively by these younger generations.

3. **Strategic Questioning**. Posing higher order questions that require "why" or a "how" responses is an effective way to encourage critical thinking and assimilation of information, and effectively check depth of understanding of participating students. As the newer generations tend to struggle with critical thinking and higher-order problem solving, this type of questioning can be instrumental in honing these skills for their future medical practice.

4. **Three-Way Summaries**. In this strategy, students respond to questions or prompts with short answers that are 10-100 words long. Students who are able to distill their answer into a few words are more likely to understand the concept. This strategy can even be used on social media such as Twitter which may resonate well with tech-savvy younger generations.

5. **Think-Pair-Share**. This is a simple formative assessment strategy in which students write down their answer to a question posed by the instructor; then they are paired with another student to share and discuss their responses. Discussions are facilitated by the instructor. This type of formative assessment encourages active and group learning strategies, which is a high priority for millennial and gen Z learners.

6. **3-2-1 Countdown**. This strategy adeptly tests the level of relevance a student feels about a topic: students are required to respond to 3 statements: 3 things you didn't know before today's lesson; 2 things that surprised you about the topic and 1 thing you want to start doing with what you have learned. While this type of formative assessment may not have practical application in large class-rooms which is typical of most undergraduate medical schools, it may help to encourage critical thinking, and reinforce topics learned in class.

7. **Classroom Polls**. Silent polls are a fast way to gauge student understanding in a way that may be more comfortable for shy students. Additionally, use of technology such as computers or mobile devices is typically well-received by millennials and gen Z students. Because group learning activities often favor extroverted students, and occasionally the more dominant members of the group carry the responses of the entire group, formative assessments such as classroom polls allow individual work which is a highly valued type of learning by millennial and gen Z students, and also allows introverted or less confident students to participate fully and without judgment.

8. **Exit/Admit Tickets**. These are small pieces of paper/cards that students use to write short answers to questions, or to summarize main topics that were taught in class that day. Any lingering questions or gaps in knowledge the professor discovers upon review of the tickets can be addressed in the next class. Since millennials and gen Z students prefer immediate feedback and active learning, this can be an effective means to survey the level of understanding of a classroom of students. However, in large class sizes, this may result in an undue time commitment for professors to evaluate each individual student's ticket.

9. **One-Minute Papers**. These are similar to exit/admit tickets, in that they are short writings that are completed at the end of class, to answer questions about the lecture, to pose questions on confusing topics, or to give feedback.

10. **Creative Extension Projects**. Instructors can assign short one-hour to one-day projects to assess student understanding of a topic. Projects could entail creation of a poster, collage, skit, set of flashcards, or presentation to fellow students. These projects require visual learning, teamwork, style, and potential use of technology which are high priority for active, creative learning styles of millennial and gen Z students, and can reinforce higher-order thinking and long-term retention of difficult material that often plagues gen Z learners.

CONCLUSION

As generations evolve, so do the thoughts, behaviors, learning styles, and life preferences of each successive generation. As the field of medicine blossoms with knowledge, the practices of medical education must continually evolve to accommodate the effective dissemination of preclinical knowledge in an appropriate volume and an acceptable format for the present generations of medical students. The beauty of the newer generations of learners, the millennials and the gen Z students, is that their philosophies toward meaningful learning, sociability and team approaches, their yearning for interactive disease-based learning, their demand for manageable work hours that improve work-life balance, and the implementation of team-based care models will provide a superb venue for optimizing patient-focused health care that will competently and compassionately care for their patients into the next generation.

REFERENCES

Abrahams, F. (2015, July). Understanding Generation Z learning styles in order to deliver quality learning experiences. Retrieved May 8, 2019, from www.precisionindustries.com.au

Ahmed, N., Devitt, K. S., Keshet, I., Spicer, J., Imrie, K., Feldman, L., ... Rutka, J. (2014). A systematic review of the effects of resident duty hour restrictions in surgery: Impact on resident wellness, training and patient outcomes. *Annals of Surgery, 259*(6), 1041–1053. doi:10.1097/SLA.0000000000000595 PMID:24662409

American Association of Colleges of Osteopathic Medicine. (2019, May). 2018-2019 First-Year Enrollment by Gender Race-Ethnicity and Osteopathic Medical College. Retrieved May 8, 2019, from https://www.aacom.org/reports-programs-initiatives/aacom-reports/student-enrollment

Association of American Medical Colleges. (2016). Medical Students, Selected Years, 1965-2015. Retrieved May 8, 2019, from https://www.aamc.org/download/481178/data/2015table1.pdf

Association of American Medical Colleges. (2017, December). *More women than men enrolled in U. S. Medical Schools in 2017*. Retrieved May 8, 2019, from https://news.aamc.org/press-releases/article/applicant-enrollment-2017/)

Baldwin, D. C. Jr, & Daugherty, S. R. (2004). Sleep deprivation and fatigue in residency training: Results of a national survey of first- and second-year residents. *Sleep, 27*(2), 217–223. doi:10.1093leep/27.2.217 PMID:15124713

Basha, M. E., Bauer, L. J., Modrakowski, M. C., & Baker, H. H. (2018). Women in osteopathic and allopathic medical schools: An analysis of applicants, matriculants, enrollment, and chief academic officers. *The Journal of the American Osteopathic Association, 118*(5), 331–336. doi:10.7556/jaoa.2018.064 PMID:29710355

Benditz, A., Pulido, L., Renkawitz, T., Schwarz, T., Grifka J., & Weber, M. (2018). Are there gender-dependent study habits of medical students in times of the World Wide Web? *Biomed Research International,* Dec. 6, 3196869.

Bonwell, C. C., & Eison, J. A. (1991). ASHE-ERIC Higher Education Report: Vol. 1. *Active learning: creating excitement in the classroom.* Washington, DC: The George Washington University School of Education and Human Development.

Burg, G., & French, L. (2012). The age of Gutenberg is over: A consideration of medical education – past, present and future. *Der Hautarzt, 63*(S1Supplement 1), 38–44. doi:10.100700105-011-2301-z PMID:22543945

Burgess, A. W., McGregor, D. M., & Mellis, C. M. (2015). Applying established guidelines to team-based learning programs in medical schools: A systematic review. *Academic Medicine*, *89*(4), 678–688. doi:10.1097/ACM.0000000000000162 PMID:24556770

Cameron, E. A., & Pagnattaro, M. A. (2017). Beyond millennials: Engaging generation z in business law classes. *Journal of Legal Studies Education*, *34*(2), 317–324. doi:10.1111/jlse.12064

Center for Teaching Excellence, University of Waterloo. *Active Learning Activities.* (2019). Retrieved May 8, 2019, from https://uwaterloo.ca

Colby, S. L., & Ortman, J. M. (2014). The baby boom cohort in the United States: 2012 to 2060. The US Census Bureau, 1-6.

Davies, J. (2005). Expressions of gender: An analysis of pupil's gendered discourse styles in small group classroom discussions. *Discourse & Society*, *14*(2), 115–132. doi:10.1177/0957926503014002853

DeBard, R. (2004). Millennials coming to college. *New Directions for Student Services*, *106*(106), 33–45. doi:10.1002s.123

Defoe, D. M., Power, M. L., Holzman, G. B., Carpentieri, A., & Schulkin, J. (2001). Long hours and little sleep: Work schedules of residents in obstetrics and gynecology. *Obstetrics and Gynecology*, *97*(6), 1015–1018. PMID:11384712

DeMaria, A. N. (2013). Here come the millennials. *Journal of the American College of Cardiology*, *61*(15), 1654–1656. doi:10.1016/j.jacc.2013.03.009 PMID:23524049

Desy, J. R., Reed, D. A., & Wolanskyj, A. P. (2017). Milestones and millennials: A perfect pairing – competency-based medical education and the learning preferences of generation Y. *Mayo Clinic Proceedings*, *92*(2), 243–250. doi:10.1016/j.mayocp.2016.10.026 PMID:28160874

Dolmans, D., Michaelsen, L., Van Merrienboer, J. V., & Van der Vleuten, C. (2015). Should we choose between problem-based learning and team-based learning? No, combine the best of both worlds! *Medical Teacher*, *37*(4), 354–359. doi:10.3109/0142159X.2014.948828 PMID:25154342

Dolmans, D. H. J. M., Loyens, S. M. M., Marcq, H., & Gijbels, D. (2016). Deep and surface learning in problem-based learning: A review of the literature. *Advances in Health Sciences Education: Theory and Practice*, *21*(5), 1087–1112. doi:10.100710459-015-9645-6 PMID:26563722

Dos Santos Boni, R. A., Paiva, C. E., de Oliveira, M. A., Lucchetti, G., Fregnani, J. H. T. G., & Paiva, B. S. R. (2018). Burnout among medical students during the first years of undergraduate school: Prevalence and associated factors. *PLoS One*, *13*(3). doi:10.1371/journal.pone.0191746 PMID:29513668

Frankl, S., Newman, L., Burgin, S., Atasoylu, A., Fishman, L., Gooding, H., ... Schwartzstein, R. (2017). The case-based collaborative learning peer observation worksheet and compendium: An evaluation of tool for flipped classroom facilitators. *MedEdPORTAL*, *13*, 10583. doi:10.15766/mep_2374-8265.10583 PMID:30800785

Freeman, D. (2004). *Trends in educational equity of girls and women.* Washington, DC: United States Department of Education, National Center for Educational Statistics.

Freeman, S., Eddy, S. L., McDonough, M., Smith, M. K., Okoroafor, N., Jordt, H., & Wenderoth, M. P. (2014). Active learning increases student performance in science, engineering and mathematics. [PNAS]. *Proceedings of the National Academy of Sciences of the United States of America, 111*(23), 8410–8415. doi:10.1073/pnas.1319030111 PMID:24821756

Frenk, J., Chen, L., Bhutta, Z. A., Crisp, N., Evans, T., Fineberg, T., ... Kistnasamy, B. (2010). Health professionals for a new century: Transforming education to strengthen health systems in an interdependent world. *Lancet, 376*(9756), 1923–1958. doi:10.1016/S0140-6736(10)61854-5 PMID:21112623

Gauer, J. L., & Jackson, J. B. (2018). Relationships of demographic variables to USMLE physician licensing exam scores: A statistical analysis on five years of medical student data. *Advances in Medical Education and Practice, 9*, 39–44. doi:10.2147/AMEP.S152684 PMID:29391841

Gerhardt, M. W. (2016). The importance of being...social? Instructor credibility and the millennials. *Studies in Higher Education, 41*(9), 1533–1547. doi:10.1080/03075079.2014.981516

Grant, G. B. (2017). Exploring the possibility of peak individualism, humanity's existential crisis, and an emerging age of purpose. *Frontiers in Psychology, 8*, 1478. doi:10.3389/fpsyg.2017.01478 PMID:28928689

Haidet, P., Levine, R. E., Parmelee, D. X., Crow, S., Kennedy, F., Kelly, A., ... Richards, B. F. (2012). Perspective: Guidelines for reporting team-based learning activities in the medical and health sciences education literature. *Academic Medicine, 87*(3), 292–299. doi:10.1097/ACM.0b013e318244759e PMID:22373620

Handelsman, M. M., Briggs, W. L., Sullivan, N., & Towler, A. (2005). A measure of college student course engagement. *The Journal of Educational Research, 98*(3), 184–192. doi:10.3200/JOER.98.3.184-192

He, J., Baxter, S. L., Xu, J., Xu, J., Zhou, X., & Zhang, K. (2019). The practical implementation of artificial intelligence technologies in medicine. *Nature Medicine, 25*(1), 30–36. doi:10.103841591-018-0307-0 PMID:30617336

Hitch, D., & Nicola-Richmond, K. (2017). Instructional practices for evidence-based practice with pre-registration allied health students: A review of recent research and developments. *Advances in Health Sciences Education: Theory and Practice, 22*(4), 1031–1045. doi:10.100710459-016-9702-9 PMID:27469244

Hopkins, L., Hampton, B. S., Abbott, J. F., Buery-Joyner, S. D., Craig, L. B., Dalrymple, J. L., ... Page-Ramsey, S. M. (2018). To the point: Medical education, technology and the millennial learner. *American Journal of Obstetrics and Gynecology, 218*(2), 188–192. doi:10.1016/j.ajog.2017.06.001 PMID:28599897

Innova. (2015, April). *How effective are these five teaching styles?* Retrieved May 8, 2019, from https://www.innovadesigngroup.co.uk/news/how-effective-are-these-five-teaching-styles/

Jackson, E. R., Shanafelt, T. D., Hasan, O., Satele, D. V., & Dyrbye, L. N. (2016). Burnout and alcohol abuse/dependence among U.S. medical Students. *Academic Medicine, 91*(9), 1251–1256. doi:10.1097/ACM.0000000000001138 PMID:26934693

Jackson, T. N., Pearcy, C. P., Khorgami, Z., Agrawal, V., Taubman, K. E., & Truitt, M. S. (2018). The physician attrition crisis: A cross-sectional survey of the risk factors for reduced job satisfaction among US surgeons. *World Journal of Surgery, 42*(5), 1285–1292. doi:10.100700268-017-4286-y PMID:29067517

Jenkins, D. M., & Allen, S. J. (2017). Aligning instructional strategies with learning outcomes and leadership competencies. *New Directions for Student Leadership, 156*(156), 43–58. doi:10.1002/yd.20270 PMID:29156115

Jhala, M., & Mathur, J. (2019). The association between deep learning approach and case-based learning. *BMC Medical Education, 19*(1), 106. doi:10.118612909-019-1516-z PMID:30975134

Ju, H., Choi, I., & Yoon, B. Y. (2017). Do medical students generate sound arguments during small group discussions in problem-based learning? An analysis of preclinical medical students' argumentation according to a framework of hypothetico-deductive reasoning. *Korean Journal of Medical Education, 29*(2), 101–109. doi:10.3946/kjme.2017.57 PMID:28597873

Kalkhurst, D. (2018, March). *Engaging Gen Z students and learners.* Retrieved May 8, 2019, from https://www.pearsoned.com/engaging-gen-z-students/

Koh, G. C. H., Khoo, H. E., Wong, M. L., & Koh, D. (2008). The effects of problem-based learning during medical school on physician competency: A systematic review. *Canadian Medical Association Journal, 178*(1), 34–41. doi:10.1503/cmaj.070565 PMID:18166729

Kozinsky, S. (2017, July). *How Generation Z is Shaping the Change in Education.* Retrieved May 8, 2019, from https://www.forbes.com/sites/sievakozinsky/2017/07/24/how-generation-z-is-shaping-the-change-in-education/#57e1ad716520

Levine, W. N., & Spang, R. C. III. (2014). ACGME duty hour requirements: Perceptions and impact on resident training and patient care. *The Journal of the American Academy of Orthopaedic Surgeons, 22*(9), 535–544. doi:10.5435/JAAOS-22-09-535 PMID:25157035

MacPherson, A., & Kimmelman, J. (2019). Ethical development of stem-cell-based-interventions. *Nature Medicine, 25*(7), 1037–1044. doi:10.103841591-019-0511-6 PMID:31270501

Maiers, M. (2017). Our future in the hands of millennials. *Journal of the Canadian Chiropractic Association, 61*(3), 212–217. PMID:29430050

Palmer, J. S. (2015). The millennials are coming: Improving self-efficacy in law students through universal design in learning. *Cleveland State Law Review, 63*, 675–706.

Poyet, M., Groussin, M., Avila-Pacheco, J., Jiang, X., Kearny, S. M., ... Alm, E. J. (2019). A library of human gut bacterial isolates paired with longitudinal multiomics data enables mechanistic microbiome research. *Nature Medicine, 25*(9), 1442–1452. doi:10.103841591-019-0559-3 PMID:31477907

Riley, B. (2018). Using the flipped classroom with simulation-based medical education to engage millennial osteopathic medical students. *The Journal of the American Osteopathic Association, 118*(10), 673–678. doi:10.7556/jaoa.2018.147 PMID:30264142

Romanello, M. (2005). Generational diversity: Teaching and learning approaches. *Nurse Educator, 30*(5), 212–216. doi:10.1097/00006223-200509000-00009 PMID:16170263

Rose, S. M. S. F., Contrepios, K., Moneghetti, K. J., Zhou, W., Mishra, T., Mataraso, S., ... Snyder, M. P. (2019). A longitudinal big data approach for precision health. *Nature Medicine, 25*(5), 792–804. doi:10.103841591-019-0414-6 PMID:31068711

Seifert, K., & Sutton, R. (2009). *Educational Psychology.* Retrieved May 8, 2019, from https://courses.lumenlearning.com/suny-educationalpsychology/chapter/gender-differences-in-the-classroom/

Skarupski, K. A., Welch, C., Dandar, V., Mylona, E., Chatterjee, A., & Singh, M. (2019). Late-career expectations: a survey of full-time faculty members who are 55 or older at 15 U. S. medical schools. *Academic Medicine,* epub ahead of print.

Sobocan, M., Turk, N., Dinevski, D., Holj, R., & Balon, B. P. (2016). Problem-based learning in internal medicine: Virtual patients or paper-based problems? *Internal Medicine Journal, 47*(1), 99–103. doi:10.1111/imj.13304 PMID:27800653

Waliany, S., Caceres, W., Merrell, S. B., Thadaney, S., Johnstone, N., & Osterberg, L. (2019). Preclinical curriculum of prospective case-based teaching with faculty- and student-blinded approach. *BMC Medical Education, 29*(1), 31. doi:10.118612909-019-1453-x PMID:30674302

Waljee, J. F., Chopra, V., & Saint, S. (2018). Mentoring millennials. *Journal of the American Medical Association, 319*(15), 1547–1548. doi:10.1001/jama.2018.3804 PMID:29677306

Warren, L. (2012). *Generational Learning Differences: Myth of Reality?* Retrieved May 8, 2019, from https://www.microassist.com/learning-dispatch/arelearning-differences-between-generations-a-myth/)

Watanabe-Crockett, L. (2019, July). 10 Innovative Formative Assessment Examples for Teachers to Know. Retrieved May 8, 2019, from https://www.wabisabilearning.com/blog/formative-assessment-examples

Young, A., Chaudhry, H. J., Pei, X., Arnhart, K., Dugan, M., & Snyder, G. B. (2017). A census of actively licensed physicians in the United States. *Journal of Medical Regulation, 103*(2), 7–21. doi:10.30770/2572-1852-103.2.7

Zonia, S. C., LaBaere, J. R. II, Stommel, M., & Tomaszewski, D. D. (2005). Resident attitudes regarding the impact of the 80-duty-hours work standards. *The Journal of the American Osteopathic Association, 105*(7), 307–313. PMID:16157519

Chapter 5
The Evolution of Core Curriculum in Medical Schools:
From Passive to Active Learning

Aaron L. Burshtein
Donald and Barbara Zucker School of Medicine at Hofstra/Northwell, USA

Joshua G. Burshtein
Donald and Barbara Zucker School of Medicine at Hofstra/Northwell, USA

Peter A. Gold
Donald and Barbara Zucker School of Medicine at Hofstra/Northwell, USA

Luke Garbarino
Donald and Barbara Zucker School of Medicine at Hofstra/Northwell, USA

David E. Elkowitz
Donald and Barbara Zucker School of Medicine at Hofstra/Northwell, USA

ABSTRACT

Medical education has undergone an evolution from passive, lecture-based learning environments to curricula that accentuate an active and dynamic system. Stemming from technological innovation, a greater amount of responsibility has been placed on students during clerkships and residency. In addition, a shift in USMLE assessment focuses on interpretation and application as compared to the former memorization-heavy approach. Therefore, learning has been modified to prepare students for the future medical landscape. Through the use of Team-Based, Problem-Based, and/or Case-Based Learning, medical students are taught to understand content rather than memorize it. The authors elucidate the rationale behind active learning and present a guide for medical educators to adopt this style of learning in every part of the undergraduate medical school training process.

DOI: 10.4018/978-1-7998-1468-9.ch005

BACKGROUND

Why Change the Core Curriculum?

Undergraduate medical schools serve as the source for transformation of students into physicians. The purpose of a core curriculum is to integrate comprehension of physiological and pathological processes with the mindset of thinking like a physician. In recent years, medical school core curricula have been undergoing a fundamental shift, evolving from the traditional, teacher-based curriculum to a student-centered and active learning approach. The teacher-centric approach began as early as the 1760s with the apprenticeship-based curriculum model and has persisted despite various forms of curricular changes (Papa & Harasym, 1999). As of 2018, a total of 124 medical schools indicated that a curriculum change is being planned or has been implemented within the past three years (Association of American Medical Colleges [AAMC], 2018). Specifically, newly formed medical schools, as well as current schools, have or are transitioning to some semblance of a student-centered curriculum in the form of case-based learning (CBL), problem-based learning (PBL), and/or team-based learning (TBL) (AAMC, 2018; Haidet, Kubitz, & McCormack, 2014).

Modernization of the core curriculum shifts focus from reiteration of factual information to application of knowledge to novel, problem-solving settings. Advancements in medical research and technology have produced a greater volume of material that students need to use in patient care, much of which can be accessed quickly if not immediately known. The pedagogy of the progressive curriculum trains physicians for a role where they need to use readily available information to apply in a unique situation. With educators being accustomed to the traditional method of education, it is vital to ensure this transition is thorough and efficient.

Curricular changes have occurred due to several fundamental reasons. The essential driving force is due to the greater onus placed on students in patient care as well as the transformation of medical examinations for physician certification. There has been a growing responsibility placed on medical students during their clerkships and residents. Expectations for competency in a wide range of activities, including communication and procedures, have been rising; it is the responsibility of medical schools to prepare students for these roles (Raymond, Mee, King, Haist, & Winward, 2011). Student transition into medical clerkship has been studied extensively, with many reporting difficulties in time management due to the longer hours, faster pace and greater intensity (Surmon, Bialocerkowski, & Hu, 2016). A common concern expressed by students was their inability to contextualize and integrate their preclinical knowledge into a patient-centered, clinical experience. A significant barrier in the adaptation to clerkship was the nature by which preclinical assessments were carried out, emphasizing recall of facts rather than the understanding of concepts (Surmon et al., 2016). This is exemplified with the struggle to apply knowledge and skills to practice, as the learning in the preclinical years did not foster an approach for doing so (Surmon et al., 2016). Whereas traditional testing fosters rapid acquisition of information in order to be prepared for the next assessment, students benefit in the long term with a contextual approach that integrates learning within clinical frameworks (Surmon et al., 2016). Clerkship requires learning through patient encounters and occurs at a faster pace compared to the preclinical curriculum where learning is completed via lectures and textbooks. The nature of learning is autonomous and longitudinal, requiring reflection to identify knowledge gaps and an impetus to fill in those gaps through research. It is therefore imperative that assessment in the preclinical years models the behaviors and aligns with the methodology of learning in graduate medical education.

The curricular evolution also stems from the need to adapt to current medical practices and assessments. In order to have a proper means of student evaluation in the expanding healthcare environment, the United States Medical Licensing Examination (USMLE) underwent a transformation in 2009, updating its format to ensure practice readiness while testing the "ability to obtain, interpret, and apply scientific and clinical information" (Haist, Katsufrakis, & Dillon, 2013). Whereas the prior USMLE experienced the unintended consequence of students focusing on short-term, "binge and purge" memorization, there was a need to reflect the reality of patient care where basic sciences serve as a long-term foundation to patient care (Haist et al., 2013). In addition, analysis completed by The National Board of Medical Examiners demonstrated a lack of practice readiness in communication skills, information retrieval, evaluation, and integration (Haist et al., 2013). The new methods of assessment alter the focus from straightforward knowledge to the proficiency with which students can use and apply information (Cohen, 2013). The premise that *assessment drives learning* encourages undergraduate medical curricula to shift to a dynamic pedagogy of education and alter their approach to foster the development of critical thinking.

As a result of medical advancements and societal changes, this chapter will further detail the curricular changes that are occurring, how they are implemented, and why they are important for shaping the next generation of physicians.

THE THEORY BEHIND ACTIVE LEARNING

A curriculum of active learning that engages students rests on the day to day activities that embody a learning process designed to build a cohesive network of comprehension. The result is molding students to develop sophistication in the approach to learning where there is an understanding of the interrelationships of fundamentals within a greater collective, so called *conceptual knowledge*, while concurrently gathering *factual knowledge* through textbooks and lectures. It is the interplay between these two factors that allows both recall and application to occur at the greatest potential (Jacoby, Wahlheim, & Coane, 2010). Take a traditional lecture for example, where students will engage the lecturer with the goal of seizing the exact phrasing expressed by the professor. In this case, they fall to the misconception that knowing the material is equated to repeating the words through which they learned it. True mastery of the lecture lies with the mastery of the *ideas* on which the lecture is based (Brown, 2014). To start off, an example where an idea is learned compared to factual memorization is the following: bilateral pitting edema in the lower extremities is a consequence of right heart failure, and one of the mechanisms behind it lies with the hydrostatic forces of the blood pooling in the venous system. Ascites due to liver failure also has a relationship to fluid forces, where the low protein levels in the blood lower the oncotic pressure. There are two basic methods to learn this topic. The first is simple memorization that right heart failure presents with bilateral lower extremity pitting edema and liver failure presents with ascites. The second is comprehension of the relationship between hydrostatic and oncotic forces as well as the flow of blood in the body, and subsequently applying these concepts to the pathological disease states. The latter option allows the student to have a broader base of knowledge such that these concepts can be adapted to a new disease that may affect fluid or protein imbalances.

When active learning is at the core of a curriculum, it is essential to have a means by which to ensure that learning has occurred, for teaching a concept is not the same as absorbing it. In the curricular process of active learning, there is an adaptation of Bloom's Taxonomy, the so-called "pyramid of learning," where the development of one skill serves as a foundation for a more advanced one (Bloom, 1956).

In order to enable students to reach the highest level, a curriculum must both foster the qualities and consistently develop them. One of the primary methodologies of an active, student-centered curriculum rests on the principle of making learning more durable. When students place more effort into a problem, coupled with the struggle of mentally retrieving the necessary information, learning becomes deeper and the concept more ingrained (Jacoby, 1978). Accomplishing this level of comprehension requires several components in a curriculum. First, students are tasked to gain a basic level of knowledge through pre-reading and research prior to the class session. Second, an appropriate question needs to be posed by either the student or faculty in order to garner a higher-order answer. The question is the driving force for learning and becomes a tool by which higher-order thinking is used to transition into critical thinking. The process of a student generating their own question uncovers the depth of their comprehension and induces a well-rounded integration of prior knowledge into a new concept. This process builds from the notion - to discover what you do not know requires that you understand what you know.

Instead of being presented a mass load of information to drill over and over, students are placed in a position where delayed recall is required, which has been shown to solidify memory. This type of balance is contained in each portion of the curriculum, pre-readings, research for cases or problems, lab pre-work, and clinical exposure. Breaking apart the bulk of information on a certain topic allows for periods of forgetfulness to set in, which subsequently requires more effort to retrieve that specific information. Research also shows that interleaving various issues creates a stronger power of discrimination and comprehension, although it may seem longer and ineffective (Kornell & Bjork, 2008a). This methodology rests on the creation of *desirable difficulties*, which are short-term impediments that allow for greater acquisition of knowledge (Brown, 2014). Although they elicit greater effort, decrease the pace of learning, and impart an uncomfortable feeling onto students, these challenges will compensate with stronger, more refined learning (Bjork & Bjork, 1992). Desirable difficulties "trigger encoding and retrieval processes that support learning, comprehension, and remembering" (Bjork & Bjork, 2009). It is of great importance to recognize at this point that if the student is not exposed to the background information necessary for response to these difficulties, they transition from desirable to undesirable and become an impediment to learning. A product of this practice is the capability of identifying differences between topics and subtopics. An example of such is in a question positing why the clinical presentation of pulmonary hypertension is different from an Atrioventricular block. For this question, both may present with dyspnea, but it is essential to know the additional characteristics that would have a patient be diagnosed with one versus the other. These include other components of a physical examination (edema, heart sounds), changes on a Wiggers Diagram and Pressure-Volume Loop, and appearance on ECG. It also poses a question for what information is actually necessary to diagnose one condition versus the other. The onus is placed on the student to establish a response to these difficulties. It therefore generates a greater will to respond to more challenging inquiries because they are taught that learning needs to be a struggle where their mistakes are not failures, but rather lessons in the greater scheme of comprehension. When allowed space and time to struggle with a problem, students are faced with anxiety and go through a disruption of the learning process, but in this case, it will result in much better outcomes due to the heavy investment (Austin & Croziet, 2012).

Interleaved learning is complementary to spaced repetition, and the added effort enables stronger understanding (Cepeda, Pashler, Vul, Wixted, & Rohrer, 2006). Spaced learning, which is practicing in periods that are spaced out over time, could be explained as a desirable difficulty. It forces a process of consolidation where new information is incorporated into long-term memory and the neural connections strengthen to connect to prior knowledge. It also permits students to experience critical evaluation of a topic that is analogous to the real-world presentations, where the problem is unpredictable rather than following a step-by-step pattern. With this type of involvement, the transfer of learning is enhanced, which is the application of your knowledge to a new situation. An active learning curriculum is therefore structured to empower these processes: doing research for a case, followed by subsequent discussion of the case, then experiencing a related topic in lab, as well as an additional component in supplementary lectures. If not for this process, students are given a block of information at one time, be it in a lecture or lab session, and never see it again until the examination. With interleaved and spaced learning, multiple subtopics are learned side by side, piece by piece throughout a week or two, facilitating a rounded exploration of the content and pushing students to develop a pattern of analysis that more closely resembles a real-world clinical scenario.

A central premise in a student-centered core curriculum requires the student to attempt the solution to a question prior to being offered the answer, which is defined as *generation*. This act prevents students from memorizing a given solution in addition to identifying gaps in their understanding of the given material (Jacoby, 1978; Slamecka & Graf, 1978). It further ensures that the student is able to apply knowledge from prework, forcing effortful recall, and thus serves to verify acquisition of information. Generation is used, for example, in a lab session where a faculty member questions which arteries should be clamped during a hysterectomy be prevent bleeding, or how a patient with an endometrial leiomyoma would present clinically. This form of questioning drives a student to not only know the factual information, but to subsequently apply it to a new scenario. The student is required to put the facts into their own words to develop a cohesive and higher-level answer, which is a practice termed *elaboration*. It moves away from mechanical repetition, which by itself does not lead to long-term retention (Tulving, 1966), to where new material is given meaning and connected to what is already known. Learning takes place to a significantly greater degree when an effort was made and a wrong answer was supplied as opposed to if no attempt was made (Jacoby, 1978). It is at the point when a student generates an answer and places a concept into their own words that they become invested in the answer, outlining their understanding of the concept and uncovering the gaps that were present. The process by which connections are created is the higher-order nature of thinking and is a necessary ingredient for critical thinking, where variables constantly change and new information is presented.

Active learning is best facilitated when a curriculum implements sessions around student-centered, team-based interactions. Allowing student-to-student collaboration builds long-term skills such as communication, leadership, and accountability. In contrast, an impediment to effective learning in a lecture-based curriculum is that the more advanced an educator becomes in a topic, the harder it becomes to teach it. This may result in student confusion after a lecture despite hearing it from an expert on the topic. The method of presentation may also inhibit the educator from adapting to the students and teaching the topic in a way that best enables the class to learn. As individuals become further removed from the initial struggle to solve a problem, the steps necessary to obtain the solution become encapsulated within mental models (Brown, 2014). When students engage with other students to study the material, they understand which small steps are needed in order to attain complete comprehension (Mazur, 2009). In this setting, students are the driving force of both the methodology of learning as well as the information needed to acquire. They become more engaged with the material because they are the ones who possess control rather than passively reading a textbook or listening to someone else deliver the content (Crumly, Dietz, & D'Angelo, 2014). In addition, each small group is different, permitting an ever-changing environment that requires constant adaptation to new group members. Building skills necessary in real-world settings, such as applying different learning strategies and using discussion as an assessment to identify knowledge gaps (Crumly et al., 2014), enables students to have deeper and more meaningful experiences in the classroom.

Despite the substantial movement of educational institutions to adopt student-directed learning, it is not plausible to expect students to espouse all of the aforementioned strategies on their own. Although the mechanism behind durable learning requires more self-direction by students, many of the strategies are not employed by students at all. Even under circumstances when students are aware of the effective strategies, encouragement is not enough. Analogous to learning a sport or instrument, students need to be guided by an educator who understands the process and can identify where additional practice is needed (Kornell & Bjork, 2008b). As such, there needs to be a system in place that guides students with the proper learning objectives and techniques. A curriculum that contains objective measures is able to disseminate the illusion of mastery and compare a student's stage of learning with the expectation of the medical community.

At the center of active learning is the theory that *assessment drives learning*, where posing a question imposes retrieval practices and alleviates the impression of proficiency. In this type of curriculum, a means by which to continually assess what a student knows and identify what is still unclear is highlighted by *calibration* (Brown, 2014). When learning any new information, it is common to fall to a misconception that one sufficiently understands a concept. To enhance a student's realistic assessment of comprehension, a curriculum can incorporate components that reinforce a persistent nature of calibration. This can be achieved with the use of an objective tool to accurately assess what you know and do not know. When implementing calibration practice quizzes, such as weekly essays or multiple-choice questions, it is vital that students ensure they answer the questions explicitly, for it is common that they may look at a question and think they know the answer, when in reality they would be unable to compose a coherent solution. An additional mechanism of calibration is a model created by Eric Mazur, *peer instruction*, where students are required to learn material prior to class via assigned pre-reading (Brown, 2014). The subsequent session is composed of higher-level, conceptual questions that necessitates students apply the ideas from the pre-reading. Imbedded in this practice is the creation of a desirable difficulty that the students need to overcome, such that through this process the students employ the underlying concepts of the lecture material (Brown, 2014). As a means of self-reflection, the student can identify if there was an issue with the process of reaching understanding or if there was a gap in specific details. The educator is able to ascertain how well the students are comprehending the material and adjust the session to focus on areas that need to be elaborated upon. The instructor is amendable to student questions and provides a means by which more extensive understanding can be achieved, rather than being a static lecture where material is presented to students for the first time. A curriculum where there is a dynamic between educators and students results in a greater engagement as well as an active means of evaluation for how well an educator is able to convey a concept.

To assess student comprehension properly, essays are an instrument to complement the active learning curriculum. In a medical licensing system designed with multiple choice questions, it may be unclear why essay exams can be effective. A core curriculum with appropriate testing can provide deeper learning – writing essays instead of choosing from multiple choice options forces the student to overcome obstacles of recalling memories and engage in higher-order thinking instead of passive reception of the already written answer choices (Brown, 2014). When testing requires the generation of a thought-out answer, students go through a process where they interpret the question contents and select specific information to effectively answer that question. As a form of active learning, they need to work through a difficulty in order to solve a question, utilizing discriminatory skills to consolidate their thoughts into a thorough explanation. An example of an essay-style question could be a clinical vignette about two elderly male patients who present with a similar complaint, trouble with urination, but one appears cachexic and has lost 10 lbs. recently. The question could ask what tests you would do diagnose the patients, and what you would expect to see in those tests. To further elucidate this point, consider the setting of a multiple-choice exam where a student selects a multiple-choice question with a specific reasoning behind the answer choice. In the case when the student's reasoning is incorrect, but the correct answer was chosen, the student will develop a false sense of proficiency in the topic. There is no space for learning to occur and in subsequent situations that require understanding of the topic, the student will not have the foundation to choose the correct answer. On the other hand, in an essay-based examination, the student will still write the correct answer, but here there is a space for the explanation to be written out, which can now be used as a springboard for learning to occur.

In order for students to continually develop the skills in an active learning environment, there needs to be a fundamental consistency imbedded in the process. The premise that assessment drives learning can be highlighted through an example of when the system is not consistent. In a curriculum where there are weekly essays, which are not counted towards a grade, students are meant to complete the essays as a means of testing themselves for knowledge of material and ability to apply that material to questions. If the assessments that count toward the grade utilize a multiple-choice method, it would be conceivable that students would not place effort into the weekly essays because the practice is not the same as the test. Therefore, the benefit of the continual testing through weekly essays is diminished and students miss out on opportunities to gain deeper understanding of content. The logic behind using a weekly testing scheme needs to be the same as the logic for using an end-of-course assessment. When this type of consistency is present, students are able to use the weekly assessments as a model for the end-of-course assessment, working on skills such as generation, elaboration, spaced repetition, etc., in order to identify strengths and weaknesses as a means to prepare for the final examination.

Complementary to a curriculum that accentuates a pedagogy centered around learning in an engaging and thought-provoking setting, providing students with an opportunity for clinical experience allows for real-world application. It is at this juncture that students need to merge their current medical knowledge into a coherent, patient-centered encounter where there is no pre-determined outcome such as with an examination. When students are given tasks to complete, whether it is an office or hospital setting, they become part of the treatment process of a patient and therefore are invested in ensuring that accurate care is delivered. Tasks may include obtaining elements of a history of present illness, medical history, and performing a preliminary physical examination. Individuals who use these experiences to extract lessons and strategies from their encounters become more successful learners as they are able to apply these in future settings (Brown, 2014). There will never be two situations that are exactly the same; however, as a student it is vital to develop habits to extract concepts from larger circumstances and incorporate them into a developing mental structure (Brown, 2014). When faced with a specific case, even if a physician has seen the same disease for 10 years, applying critical thinking can prevent a misdiagnosis, catch an atypical presentation, or treat a patient more effectively than before. This type of learning can be exercised continuously within a medical curriculum in a practice known as *reflection*.

Students work on optimizing their habits by reflecting on their progress to develop stronger learning. After a small or large group session, a faculty member can lead student reflection inquiring as to what went well within the session or what could have been done better to improve (Brown, 2014). A step back to view the larger picture assesses daily performance where students are given the opportunity to amend their practices and become more efficient and well-rounded learners. Consistency in the reflective process lays a foundation and is necessary for maximal learning at each stage in medical education, be it at the level of undergraduate training or the level of residency training. Without proper reflections, a student who is underperforming may never realize the reason for their faults. Individuals rarely receive negative feedback because it is not a common practice in education, and it is unpleasant for someone to deliver this type of news. However, it is a fundamental component of an active learning curriculum as it forces an introspective approach to uncover the smallest components of an action. Through both self-reflection and group reflections, students are able to speak to strengths and weaknesses of a recently completed session, advocating for self-improvement as well as highlighting group progress. Active learning rests on the idea of student engagement, which is consistently reinforced through reflection, and encompasses the step-by-step actions that develop into a dynamic and compelling learning process.

THE APPLICATION OF THE THEORY

Successful learning is a combination of understanding facts and applying them into novel situations. In order for students to succeed in the rapidly changing medical environment, medical education models/curriculums must adopt a pedagogy of promoting critical thinking rather than fact acquisition.

But there is no way to predict the future – teach a student one fact yet another is encountered in the workplace. The student faces confusion how to respond. An example of this phenomenon can be appreciated from the traditional clerkship setting in the past. Students followed the attending physician to a patient room and were questioned about the patient's condition, medications, side effects, comorbidities, and on and on. Had the student not known the answer, the student took a trip across the hospital to the library, found a book that dealt with the disease in question, and spent hours drilling the information. Upon return to the floors, the physician is already gone and so are the learning opportunities that came with rounding. If the student is lucky, the student will be able to see that patient the next day, but one cannot leave medical education to luck. With the exponential growth of technology all of those books are available in your pocket and that fact the student missed is retrieved within seconds. All of that time that was lost is now put to use in a more productive and efficient patient encounter. The attending physician, knowing the student can look up any fact, now posits a high-level question that cannot be answered with one memorized fact. The student cannot respond to the problem without the proper tools to figure out a solution.

Understanding how to learn is crucial to provide the highest level of patient care. The learning model of traditional lectures trains students to receive information from a prepared presentation and reiterate first-order knowledge for the purpose of achieving basic understanding and relationships of topics. Most traditional curricula involve use of the systems-based approach to learning medicine. This strategy involves a lecture setting in which students are taught one organ system at a time, including the anatomy and physiology (Dubin, 2016). An example is when students are learning about the Reproductive system in classroom sessions, they have complementary anatomy sessions that cover the pelvic and reproductive organs. Systems-based learning has shown to provide a quality education and is currently used in most medical schools (Dubin, 2016). However, the lecture style curriculum offers less engagement with students and poor integration of content (Papa & Harasym, 1999).

Active Learning offers an alternative to the traditional model - it combines first-order facts with higher-order integration. Active Learning describes a general method and strategy for teaching and learning in the classroom or lecture hall, as it seeks to shift the focus from the teacher to the learner (Fornari &

Poznanski, 2017). The majority of medical schools have been implementing active learning, and as of 2012-2013, 116 out of 136 medical schools reported enhanced use of active/engaged learning formats (AAMC, 2013). As opposed to traditional curricular structure, adapting to Active Learning will have the benefits of learners creating their own study program, acquiring skills for problem-solving, gaining motivation and confidence in their thoughts and answers, learning from peers how to engage in higher-order discussions, and practicing inter-personal professional skills such as communication, negotiation, and peer assessment of performance. Active Learning takes place through the context of application of knowledge to cases or problems that are clinically relevant or tailored for a specific context (Fornari & Poznanski, 2017). Learners are also able to relate new information with their own interests, deepening the connection between the material and their own curiosities. Learners are consistently relating their knowledge to novel patient situations, simulating the methodology of patient treatment as a physician, as well as within the interprofessional team, from the very beginning of their undergraduate medical education.

There are numerous strategies to apply Active Learning in undergraduate medical education. In the traditional or lecture model, active learning can be implemented by moving away from PowerPoints in the lecture sessions and making the sessions around higher order questions and application-based activities. An example is for the instructor to ask students in an immunology session about the relation-ship between leukemias and lymphomas and in what circumstances each would arise. This technique is known as Brainstorming, and its purpose is to have students engaged and using their brain (Fornari & Poznanski, 2017). Another activity that student may perform is Think-Pair-Share, where students are told to discuss a differential diagnosis for several minutes with a neighbor for a patient with an enlarged lymph node and then answer to the instructor. This strategy emphasizes student thought and makes the sessions value added.

Furthermore, because classroom time devoted to learning content becomes limited, the flipped class-room model calls for delivery of content to students prior to class and to free up time for exercises that stimulate higher-order questioning (Fornari & Poznanski, 2017). This model is most effective with high level understanding of the knowledge prior to the active learning sessions that is later applied to exercises, which revise, challenge, and enrich the learners' comprehension and thought-processes. Learners arrive to classes with a sense of what they do not understand as well as what they do, which allows them to give greater attention to areas where improvement is needed (Fornari & Poznanski, 2017). These aspects of the flipped classroom can be broken down into three components that are essential for excellent delivery and acquisition of knowledge, 1) pre-class delivery, 2) student-centered active learning, and 3) assess-ment of student learning (Fornari & Poznanski, 2017). Each component cannot be mastered without the other, as active learning can only take place with prior knowledge comprehension, and assessment can only occur with a command of higher-order information that is attained through active learning. In addi-tion, due to the growing volume of information, teachers are having difficulty covering a comprehensive level of content within tight time constraints of a lecture. In the flipped classroom model, students take advantage of technology that provides access to this information prior to class, are able to self-pace their learning, and utilize methods of content delivery that suit their style of learning, including video lectures, web-based modules, and/or textbooks.

Team-Based Learning

Team-Based Learning (TBL) provides another aspect of Active Learning that necessitates higher-order objectives and deliberations. TBL is a teaching method that incorporates multiple small groups into a large group setting (Haidet et al., 2014). This system has been implemented in postsecondary and professional education for the past 20 years, demonstrating positive outcomes in areas of knowledge acquisition, preparedness, participation and engagement, better communication processes, and team performance (Haidet et al., 2014; Thompson, Schneider, Haidet, Perkowski, & Richards, 2007). A TBL curriculum offers "a special form of collaborative learning using a specific sequence of individual work, group work, and immediate feedback to create a motivational framework in which students increasingly hold each other accountable for coming to class prepared and contributing to discussion" (Sibley & Spirdinoff, n.d.). Its purpose is to transform the learning environment from one where the instructor directly conveys certain knowledge to the learner, which encourages rote memorization and recall, to one that promotes active learning through the application of knowledge.

TBL learning strategies are implemented in three distinct phases, including a period for peer feedback. Phase I, or the Preparatory Phase, begins with students studying the learning objectives of the TBL module prior to the class through the use of textbooks, review chapters, passages, and/or lecture videos (Sibley & Spirdinoff, n.d.; Thompson et al, 2007). Learners must be considerate of the resources they use, as they should not be too complex, and time spent should not be too onerous (Fornari & Poznanski, 2017). During Phase II, or the Readiness Assurance Phase, students are administered readiness assurance tests to determine their level of preparation from Phase I. These tests are taken individually and in groups to foster peer-to-peer teaching and communication (Fornari & Poznanski, 2017; Thompson et al., 2007). Phase III, or the Application Exercise Phase, requires groups of students to use the foundational knowledge they studied in the Preparatory Phase to answer higher-order, application problems (Fornari & Poznanski, 2017; Thompson et al., 2007). Students are required to hold discussions with group members to dissect the situations and present and defend their answers. Additionally, groups membership is held consistent for the duration of the course, providing an opportunity to build cohesion for the further enhancement of learning. Application exercise questions can be administered in various formats, including multiple choice and short answer; however, they must adhere to the "4 Ss" of TBL, including 1) teams working on *Significant* problems, 2) teams working on the *Same* problem at any given time, 3) teams making a *Specific* choice, and 4) teams revealing the choices *Simultaneously* (Fornari & Poznanski, 2017). These specifications provide important guidelines to ensure each group may benefit from the problem-solving activities without the input of other groups' ideas.

The final phase of TBL is the peer evaluation period, a fundamental component to facilitate immediate feedback for continuous self-improvement. Peer evaluation trains students to think like physicians, who are constantly involved in life-long learning through effective feedback (Fornari & Poznanski, 2017). Quality feedback enables students to reflect on their experiences to enhance their beneficial qualities and adjust their deficiencies. Learning through self-improvement triggers students to frequently evaluate their knowledge and seek ways to develop.

A part of self-improvement occurs through instructor feedback. In the TBL curriculum, instructors are vital to facilitate student learning in the small groups. The facilitators role includes important aspects, such as active listening, proper time management, providing notice if the group strays off topic, and providing individualized feedback for constant student improvement, to maintain direction and assure completion of the goals for the session. The TBL strategies offer an enhanced education model for the acquisition, discussion, and application of knowledge to novel situations for deeper understanding of the content, while offering an opportunity to train communication and deliberation skills for the professional physician environment.

Problem-Based and Case-Based Learning

Similar to the team-based approach, Problem-Based Learning (PBL) and Case-Based Learning (CBL) are additional curricular aspects that foster active learning. In a PBL format, small groups discuss information introduced and identified through meaningful problems or cases (Loyens, Magda, & Rikers, 2008). The cases are revealed over time; for example, the first day, the group receives the first couple of pages with the chief complaint, history, etc. and the group can come up with a differential diagnosis. From this part of the case, the group develops learning objectives from a very wide differential and subsequently researches them. The group then meets the next day to get more of the case revealed, develop a narrower differential diagnosis, and generate new learning objectives to research. This same pattern continues until the entirety of the case is covered and ideal learning objectives, created by the faculty, are given to the learners.

Through this process the learners explore various issues, using their intrigue to guide discussion, while the facilitator may stimulate conversation, but plays a minimal role (Srinivasan, Wilkes, Stevenson, Nguyen, & Slavin, 2007; Dolmans, Michaelsen, Van Merriënboer, & Van Der Vleuten, 2014). The problem discussion takes place prior to learners receiving other curricular information for that topic, and therefore prioritizes prior knowledge to aid in solving the issues (Loyens et a., 2008). The learners are tasked with trying to explain the problems that they encounter, and in the process discover what they already know, what they do not know yet, and/or which questions still need to be answered through learning objectives (Dolmans, Grave, Wolfhagen, & Van Der Vleuten, 2005). Following the sessions, the learners research and study their gaps in knowledge to come to a more complete understanding of the material. The subsequent group meetings are used to discuss the material and synthesize what each learner has understood about the topics and generate additional learning objectives (Dolmans et al., 2014). Throughout this process, learners are able to actively engage with clinical situations, often realistic patient problems, and drive their own learning. Problem-based learning exemplifies learner problem solving, independent learning, and teamwork to handle each issue presented in the case (Srinivasan et al., 2007).

PBL has several specific goals for learners, including to 1) construct an extensive knowledge base, 2) develop applicable problem-solving skills, 3) cultivate self-directed learning skills, 4) become effective collaborators, and 5) become intrinsically motivated to learn (Barrows & Kelson, 1995). Fostering a broad understanding of the clinical sciences involves a time intensive effort to improve, and it necessitates applying information to a wide-range of problem situations to create "flexible knowledge" (Barrows & Kelson, 1995). A self-directed approach is vital to the success of learners in a PBL curriculum, as they are required to use their curiosity for information to drive understanding of the material. Self-directed learning (SDL) is defined as "the preparedness of a student to engage in learning activities defined by him- or herself, rather than by a teacher" (Schmidt, 2000). This is a crucial foundation that applies to learners' autonomous learning within the PBL curriculum. Students need to assess their learning issues/problems that are developed from the cases and independently are able to determine aspects that need to be researched in the literature for a complete understanding. Learning in a lecture-based undergraduate medical curriculum places SDL as a secondary objective to the information being taught. In contrast, the very nature of a PBL curriculum prioritizes the personal autonomy of learners to determine the level of their own self-directed scholarship.

Furthermore, PBL inherently cultivates collaboration between learners through initial discussion of the problems and during subsequent session deliberations. Yet, learners must develop these skills to effectively convey information to peers and identify strengths and weaknesses within the group dynamic. Lastly, intrinsic motivation to learn occurs throughout a PBL curriculum when learners are inspired by their own interests, intrigue, and challenges (Barrows & Kelson, 1995). It has been shown that in-depth PBL problems that allow for dissection of the material provide learners with an opportunity to be more engaged and involved in the learning process (Gijselaers & Schmidt, 1990). To encourage this aspect of scholarship, each PBL problem must have value for the learners, such as an engaging and relatable problem to a physician's role or when the education is connected to personal meaning to learners, such as social or patient issues in society. Problems that relate to clinical scenarios and realistic situations can increase learner impetus to acquire a high level of information. In turn, the greater depth of research and education learners accomplish has shown to lead to higher achievement both within the PBL sessions and in the greater course context (Dolmans et al., 2005). Studies have shown that PBL style learning is effective in improving learner and faculty satisfaction without a difference in multiple choice test scores when compared to traditional lecture-based curriculum (Distlehorst, Dawson, Robbs, & Barrows, 2005). Through the implementation of these goals, the PBL curriculum provides a framework to develop personal skills and concurrently train for the clinical environment of being a physician.

However, the PBL curricular format has several limitations. Due to its format of student-drive inquiry, it may be seen as an inefficient use of time, creating frustrations for time-pressured learners, and may lead to tangential or inaccurate conclusions (Srinivasan et al., 2007). PBL curriculums generally have cases that span a longer time, and difficulty may arise since different groups may develop very different learning objectives until the case is revealed at the end. Additionally, learners may not be able to apply the information presented in the case scenarios to clinical cases in the event that the case scenarios are not adequately written. This puts a large burden on the case to be a source of information and an applicatory tool. Additionally, the facilitator's knowledge is argued to be wasted as they do not participate in the active discussion of learners in the initial analyzation of the case scenarios and during the second group meeting. Nonetheless, due to the circumstance that facilitators cannot act as content experts, learners are stimulated to rely on their own knowledge instead of predicating their discussion on the facilitator.

Case-Based Learning (CBL) is another curricular reform taking place in undergraduate medical education that comprises a student-centered model. CBL involves the discussion of a clinical case in small groups with advanced preparation guiding the discussion (Srinivasan et al., 2007). In this type of program, the case for the week is revealed all at once. This is a way for the curriculum to ensure that everyone is learning the same content during the same week or time period. It maintains a focused approach to the case and allows learners to explore their curiosities in an efficient manner. Furthermore, during the case analysis sessions, learners do not generate differential diagnoses but have a specified "goal" for the case and create learning objectives from the case to cover the "goal." In subsequent sessions, the groups discuss the information that they have acquired from researching their learning objectives. An example of a CBL session about angina pectoris would be for students to read a case centered around an older patient presenting with intermittent chest pain. The case has a goal of understanding the pathophysiology of angina pectoris and the process of atherosclerotic plaque formation in arteries. The case will include a medical history, symptoms, lab values, and pharmacology and procedures to provide a treatment. Students stop periodically throughout the case to decide which information is important to research and use clinical reasoning to discuss what is occurring to the patient. In subsequent sessions during the week, students would discuss what they learned about angina, atherosclerotic plaque formation, treatments, lab values seen in angina, etc.

Learners in the Case-Based model are tasked with identifying, discussing, and answering the issues presented in the case while remaining in the framework of the learning objectives (Srinivasan et al., 2007). Learning objectives form the guideline that learners follow so that they are able to apply information to higher order questions. This method is predicated on the learners' determination to study appropriate material to the best of their ability and subsequently discuss it in future sessions. Any remaining gaps in knowledge are filled through discussion with peers and faculty following the sessions. CBL sessions have a more structured approach than PBL sessions, and facilitators may offer incorrect information that learners discuss. Variations of the CBL format exist where the facilitator does not offer correct information and let the learners figure out what they know and don't know, encouraging curiosity and confidence in their knowledge.

CBL cases are a source of generating inquiry and learning how to apply the information to authentic, realistic clinical situations. By exposing learners to clinical scenarios early, they are able to form diagnoses and management plans for the majority of diseases and understand underlying mechanisms and effects on patients (Thistlethwaite et al., 2012). An additional benefit is that learners are able to confront issues surrounding the whole patient rather than approach diseases and treatment through separate, unconnected processes (Carrero et al., 2009). Cases convey a human perspective to the disease and can foster a deeper understanding of clinical effects as well as a long-term impact on patient lives. Disease or scientific process in cases are therefore accompanied by their contexts, background, and future implications that provide this additional dimension (Allchin, 2013). Consequently, learners are able to quickly adjust to the clinical environment, and they can utilize and build upon their foundations during clinical rotations in the undergraduate medical setting as well as during residency.

In both PBL and CBL, learners are driven to answer higher-order problems with the first-order information they have acquired. Both PBL and CBL consist of small groups, utilize cases, and generate learning objectives to drive learning. Differences between PBL and CBL arise in how these cases are used to develop learning objectives. Whereas PBL cases are revealed over time and learning objectives are made from differential diagnoses, which are narrowed down as the case progresses, CBL cases are given in their entirety. Learners evaluate the case to generate learning objectives and extract the science that pertains to a "goal" for the case. Similar to TBL, these problems can be application based through realistic cases, and can have various formats including multiple choice or short answers. The largest benefit that learners receive in the PBL and CBL learning environment is that the curricula create cognitive conflicts within each individual that lead to fundamental conceptual changes. Employing their knowledge, learners debate, argue, and adjust their frameworks to come to a more complete understanding. PBL and CBL curricula have the potential to develop critical thinking skills that are beyond the conventional conceptual framework of knowledge and drive the exploration of medicine to innovative heights.

A common theme of all active learning strategies (TBL, PBL, CBL) is being able to apply information by answering higher-order questions. This application is the cornerstone of this curricular reform because questioning is the driving force of thinking (Paul & Elder, 2008). Specialized learning platforms can enable students to cultivate the attributes of learning factual information to subsequently apply the concepts in a clinical setting. Medical education must incorporate interactive and stimulating instruction such that future physicians will develop into self-sufficient and innovative thinkers.

Socratic Questioning

Discussions facilitated through Socratic questioning in any educator-learner environment, whether in traditional or student-centered settings, enrich student experience for better learning. Socratic questioning, also referred to as Socratic dialogue, is a teaching method that engages students in a discussion of the content, instead of a traditional format where the educator speaks at students (Fornari & Poznanski, 2017). It is an organized technique of assessing and applying knowledge through interactive, adaptive, and directed questioning of learners. The instructor that leads the Socratic questioning asks questions in a systematic and disciplined manner (Fornari & Poznanski, 2017). Examples of questioning to guide Socratic dialogue are to ask students in a cardiology session to describe coronary circulation, to differentiate between left and right coronary dominance, to explain the distribution of arterial supply from the coronary arteries to different regions of the myocardium, then to correlate abnormal ECG patterns with location of myocardial infarction. Higher order questions can also be asked such as which region and layers of the heart would be affected with a left LAD blockage or asking a student to explain why a patient would experience cardiac tapenade 3-10 days after a myocardial infarction. These questions and subsequent discussions provide an opportunity to assess students, provide clarification of misunderstood information, and apply this information to clinical examples (Fornari & Poznanski, 2017).

Through Socratic dialogue, the instructor may determine if students acquired first-order knowledge from prior assignments. Depending on student comprehension, the instructor can ask additional questions to delve deeper into the subject matter and stimulate new ideas to connect various topics. Such discussion provides an opportunity to clarify misunderstandings that students may have acquired from preparatory assignments. Additionally, this dialogue may distinguish what a student or instructor does and does not know about a particular topic, which stimulates curiosity and growth for students as future physicians (Fornari & Poznanski, 2017). Furthermore, students are able to connect their knowledge to clinical paradigms during Socratic questioning sessions. The instructor may ask deeper, integrated questions about how the topic of discussion connects to patients and diseases, cultivating relevance to subjects that may otherwise seem disconnected from patient care.

The methods of Socratic questioning are critical for active learning to be integrated into patient care when students become physicians. Our prior scenario at the beginning of this section described a student during rotations who did not know a certain fact and missed a crucial opportunity to practice his clinical skills. This was emblematic of traditional clinical medical education and occurred because the student was unable to adapt his knowledge to a new situation. Instead of looking up specific facts, modern-age students must learn to apply constantly evolving information to patient encounters. Socratic questioning stimulates critical thinking and autonomous learning, both of which can be implemented regardless of the scientific facts and clinical advancements that occur in medicine (Fornari & Poznanski, 2017). Lastly, Socratic questioning is a tool that can be used by learners in their future medical practice. The questioning method can be employed during assessment of patients, for example. It can be used to delve into a patient's history, problem solve in areas of complexity, and/or diagnose an underlying pathology causing disease (Fornari & Poznanski, 2017). Additionally, learners may use Socratic questioning to self-direct and improve one's own autonomous leaning. Since the Socratic method leads to thinking that is more contemplative and introspective, physicians will be able to more effectively solve complex issues in an intense medical environment.

Developing Active Learning within a curriculum is crucial to train undergraduate medical students for their future professions. However, difficulty arises for traditional-based medical schools to implement student-centered curricula. There are several factors that may prevent schools from this transition, including the financial resources, the recruitment of faculty, and the training of faculty. For a medical school to have small-group sessions, as in PBL or CBL, the architecture of the school must be retrofitted to contain smaller-sized classrooms. Also, recruitment of faculty is required due to the large class sizes. As of 2018-2019, the average class size of medical schools in the United States is 143 students (AAMC, 2019). Each small-group must have a faculty member present and this may pose an issue to medical schools.

Finally, a major issue confronted when transitioning to this type of a curriculum is that teachers or facilitators do not know how to teach in the Active Learning environment (Fornari & Poznanski, 2017; Graffam, 2007). Resources must be allocated to train faculty to be facilitators of small-groups, not presenters of content material. Teachers in undergraduate medical education follow the methodology in which they were taught since they largely lack the training for active learning. Without training, most faculty are simply acting as information-imparting instructors (Graffam, 2007). This understanding of the role of the teacher is simplistic and implies that to be an effective instructor, one only needs to have an excellent understanding of the material (Fang, 1996). In order to change the way teaching is done, instructors must understand the purpose of active learning and how to implement components in the medical education. Once this is accomplished, educators, now armed with an active learning modality, can impart the goals onto the learners and transform them from passive to active learners (Fornari & Poznanski, 2017). The learners' understanding of active learning, how it is applied, and how to accomplish it in active learning classes is of paramount importance for successful application of the curriculum. Student-centered curricula are very labor intensive and medicals schools must have the resources to implement these changes.

CONCLUSION

Undergraduate medical education has been undergoing a curricular transformation from a traditional approach to a student-centered pedagogy that prioritizes active learning. This type of curriculum includes tools necessary for active learning, such as making learning more durable and using questions as the basis for acquisition of knowledge. The curriculum is predicated on the dedication of learners to work as peer instructors, in addition to consistent interaction with faculty, to acquire knowledge more effectively and efficiently. Student-based curricula, through TBL, PBL, and/or CBL, encourage the application of learned information to novel scenarios, which fosters deeper knowledge and cultivates higher-level connections. The fundamental adaptation of the medical school core curriculum reflects the evolution of the physician's role in medicine.

REFERENCES

Allchin, D. (2013). Problem- and Case-Based Learning in Science: An Introduction to Distinctions, Values, and Outcomes. *CBE Life Sciences Education*, *12*(3), 364–372. doi:10.1187/cbe.12-11-0190 PMID:24006385

Association of American Medical Colleges. (2013). Curriculum Changes in US Medical Schools: Types of Change in 2012-2013. Retrieved from https://www.aamc.org/initiatives/cir/427196/27.html

Association of American Medical Colleges. (2018). [Chart] Curriculum Changes in US Medical Schools: Types of Change in 2017-2018. Retrieved from https://www.aamc.org/initiatives/cir/427196/27.html

Association of American Medical Colleges. (2019). U.S. Medical School Applications and Matriculants by School, State of Legal Residence, and Sex, 2018-2019. Retrieved from https://www.aamc.org/data/facts/applicantmatriculant/

Autin, F., & Croizet, J. (2012). Reframing Metacognitive Interpretation of Difficulty of Anagram Task. *Journal of Experimental Psychology*, 610–618. doi:10.1037/a0027478 PMID:22390266

Barrows, H. S., & Kelson, A. C. (1995). Problem-based learning in secondary education and the problem-based learning institute. *Springfield, IL. Problem-Based Learning Institute*, *1*(1), 1–5.

Bjork, R. A., & Bjork, E. L. (1992). A new theory of disuse and an old theory of stimulus fluctuation. In A. F. Healy, S. M. Kosslyn, & R. M. Shiffrin (Eds.), *From learning processes to cognitive processes: Essays in honor of William E. Estes* (Vol. 2, pp. 35–67). Hillsdale, NJ: Erlbaum.

Bjork, R. A., Bjork, E. L., & Pomerantz, J. R. (2009). Making things hard on yourself, but in a good way: Creating desirable difficulties to enhance learning. In M. A. Gernsbacher, R. W. Pew, & L. M. Hough (Eds.), *Psychology and the real world: Essays illustrating fundamental contributions to society* (pp. 56–64). New York, NY: Worth.

Bloom, B. S. (1956). *Taxonomy of Educational Objectives, Handbook I: The Cognitive Domain*. New York: David McKay Co.

Brown, P. C. (2014). *Make It Stick: The Science of Successful Learning*. Cambridge, MA: The Belknap Press of Harvard University Press. doi:10.4159/9780674419377

Carrero, E., Gomar, C., Penzo, W., Fábregas, N., Valero, R., & Sánchez-Etayo, G. (2009). Teaching basic life support algorithms by either multimedia presentations or case based discussion equally improves the level of cognitive skills of undergraduate medical students. *Medical Teacher*, *31*(5), e189–e195. doi:10.1080/01421590802512896 PMID:19241215

Cepeda, N. J., Pashler, H., Vul, E., Wixted, J. T., & Rohrer, D. (2006). Distributed practice in verbal recall tasks: A review and quantitative synthesis. *Psychological Bulletin*, *132*(3), 354–380. doi:10.1037/0033-2909.132.3.354 PMID:16719566

Cohen, J. J. (2013). Will Changes in the MCAT and USMLE Ensure That Future Physicians Have What It Takes? *Journal of the American Medical Association*, *310*(21), 2253. doi:10.1001/jama.2013.283389 PMID:24302085

Crumly, C., Dietz, P., & DAngelo, S. (2014). *Pedagogies for student-centered learning: Online and on-ground*. Minneapolis, MN: Fortress Press.

Distlehorst, L. H., Dawson, E., Robbs, R. S., & Barrows, H. S. (2005). Problem-Based Learning Outcomes: The Glass Half-Full. *Academic Medicine*, *80*(3), 294–299. doi:10.1097/00001888-200503000-00020 PMID:15734816

Dolmans, D., Michaelsen, L., Van Merriënboer, J., & Van Der Vleuten, C. (2014). Should we choose between problem-based learning and team-based learning? No, combine the best of both worlds! *Medical Teacher, 37*(4), 354–359. doi:10.3109/0142159X.2014.948828 PMID:25154342

Dolmans, D. H., Grave, W. D., Wolfhagen, I. H., & Cees, P. (2005). Problem-based learning: Future challenges for educational practice and research. *Medical Education, 39*(7), 732–741. doi:10.1111/j.1365-2929.2005.02205.x PMID:15960794

Dubin, B. (2016). Innovative Curriculum Prepares Medical Students for a Lifetime of Learning and Patient Care. *Missouri Medicine, 113*(3), 170–173. PMID:27443039

Fang, Z. (1996). A review of research on teacher beliefs and practices. *Educational Research, 38*(1), 47–65. doi:10.1080/0013188960380104

Fornari, A., & Poznanski, A. (2015). *How-to guide for active learning.* Huntington, WV: International Association of Medical Science Educators.

Gijselaers, W. H., & Schmidt, H. G. (1990). Development and evaluation of a causal model of PBL. *Innovation in Medical Education. An Evaluation of Its Present Status.,* 95-113.

Graffam, B. (2007). Active learning in medical education: Strategies for beginning implementation. *Medical Teacher, 29*(1), 38–42. doi:10.1080/01421590601176398 PMID:17538832

Haidet, P., Kubitz, K., & McCormack, W. T. (2014). Analysis of the Team-Based Learning Literature: TBL Comes of Age. *Journal on Excellence in College Teaching, 25*(3-4), 303–333.

Haist, S. A., Katsufrakis, P. J., & Dillon, G. F. (2013). The Evolution of the United States Medical Licensing Examination (USMLE). *Journal of the American Medical Association, 310*(21), 2245. doi:10.1001/jama.2013.282328 PMID:24302081

Jacoby, L. L. (1978). On interpreting the effects of repetition: Solving a problem versus remembering a solution. *Journal of Verbal Learning and Verbal Behavior, 17*(6), 649–667. doi:10.1016/S0022-5371(78)90393-6

Jacoby, L. L., Wahlheim, C. N., & Coane, J. H. (2010). Test-enhanced learning of natural concepts: Effects on recognition memory, classification, and metacognition. *Journal of Experimental Psychology. Learning, Memory, and Cognition, 36*(6), 1441–1451. doi:10.1037/a0020636 PMID:20804279

Kornell, N., & Bjork, R. A. (2008a). Learning Concepts and Categories. *Psychological Science, 19*(6), 585–592. doi:10.1111/j.1467-9280.2008.02127.x PMID:18578849

Kornell, N., & Bjork, R. A. (2008b). Optimising self-regulated study: The benefits—and costs—of dropping flashcards. *Memory (Hove, England), 16*(2), 125–136. doi:10.1080/09658210701763899 PMID:18286417

Loyens, S. M., Magda, J., & Rikers, R. M. (2008). Self-Directed Learning in Problem-Based Learning and its Relationships with Self-Regulated Learning. *Educational Psychology Review, 20*(4), 411–427. doi:10.100710648-008-9082-7

Mazur, E. (2009, Nov. 12). Confessions of a Converted Lecturer: Eric Mazur. Retrieved from https://www.youtube.com/watch?v=WwslBPj8GgI

Papa, F. J., & Harasym, P. H. (1999). Medical curriculum reform in North America, 1765 to the present. *Academic Medicine*, *74*(2), 154–164. doi:10.1097/00001888-199902000-00015 PMID:10065057

Paul, R., & Elder, L. (2008). Critical thinking: The art of Socratic questioning, part III. *Journal of Developmental Education*, *31*(3), 34–35.

Raymond, M. R., Mee, J., King, A., Haist, S. A., & Winward, M. L. (2011). What New Residents Do During Their Initial Months of Training. *Academic Medicine*, *86*, S59–S62. doi:10.1097/ACM.0b013e31822a70ff PMID:21955771

Schmidt, H. (2000). Assumptions underlying self-directed learning may be false. *Medical Education*, *34*(4), 243–245. doi:10.1046/j.1365-2923.2000.0656a.x PMID:10733717

SibleyJ.SpirdinoffS. (n.d.). What is PBL? Retrieved from http://www.teambasedlearning.org/

Slamecka, N. J., & Graf, P. (1978). The generation effect: Delineation of a phenomenon. *Journal of Experimental Psychology. Human Learning and Memory*, *4*(6), 592–604. doi:10.1037/0278-7393.4.6.592

Srinivasan, M., Wilkes, M., Stevenson, F., Nguyen, T., & Slavin, S. (2007). Comparing Problem-Based Learning with Case-Based Learning: Effects of a Major Curricular Shift at Two Institutions. *Academic Medicine*, *82*(1), 74–82. doi:10.1097/01.ACM.0000249963.93776.aa PMID:17198294

Surmon, L., Bialocerkowski, A., & Hu, W. (2016). Perceptions of preparedness for the first medical clerkship: A systematic review and synthesis. *BMC Medical Education*, *16*(1), 89. doi:10.118612909-016-0615-3 PMID:26968816

Thistlethwaite, J. E., Davies, D., Ekeocha, S., Kidd, J. M., Macdougall, C., Matthews, P., ... Clay, D. (2012). The effectiveness of case-based learning in health professional education. A BEME systematic review: BEME Guide No. 23. *Medical Teacher*, *34*(6), e421–e444. doi:10.3109/0142159X.2012.680939 PMID:22578051

Thompson, B. M., Schneider, V. F., Haidet, P., Perkowski, L. C., & Richards, B. F. (2007). Factors Influencing Implementation of Team-Based Learning in Health Sciences Education. *Academic Medicine*, *82*(Suppl), S53–S56. doi:10.1097/ACM.0b013e3181405f15 PMID:17895691

Tulving, E. (1966). Subjective organization and effects of repetition in multi-trial free-recall learning. *Journal of Verbal Learning and Verbal Behavior*, *5*(2), 193–197. doi:10.1016/S0022-5371(66)80016-6

Chapter 6
21st Century Problem-Based Learning:
A Medical Education Asset by Rational Design or Retrofit

Susan Ely
California Health Sciences University College of Osteopathic Medicine, USA

Joanne H. Greenawald
Virginia Tech Carilion School of Medicine, USA

Richard C. Vari
Virginia Tech Carilion School of Medicine, USA

ABSTRACT

An account of 21st century problem-based learning (PBL) in preclinical medical education is provided through a detailed explanation of the overall process, a description of PBL case construction, and a brief consideration of related activities, including case wrap-up sessions and facilitator debriefing meetings. Composition of student PBL groups, the role of the faculty facilitator, and PBL decorum are also explored in this chapter. The implementation of PBL in a new medical school curriculum by rational design is compared to the introduction of PBL into an existing medical school curriculum by retrofit. Advantages and challenges of PBL are enumerated; a brief comparison of PBL with team-based learning (TBL) is also included.

INTRODUCTION

As new medical schools continue to emerge in the United States, some will consider adopting problem-based learning (PBL) as a curriculum delivery modality in the first two years of undergraduate medical education. This decision will be in part or *in toto* as a rational design process. In contrast, retrofitting of PBL into existing undergraduate medical curricula is also under consideration or an on-going process

DOI: 10.4018/978-1-7998-1468-9.ch006

at some U.S. medical schools. This rise in curricular PBL integration is in response to the requirement that medical schools undertake regular, broad curriculum reviews of content and delivery methods as part of continuous quality improvements. This integration aims to meet accreditation agency mandates for the provision of self-directed learning opportunities to enhance metacognition in adult learners by implementing active learning in a small group format.

The goal of this chapter is to explore the andragogy of PBL, providing a detailed account of the process as a curricular delivery method in undergraduate medical education. This chapter is not intended to provide data on student outcomes that can be directly ascribed to a PBL curriculum. Instead, the collective experience of the authors will be used to highlight considerations specific to the implementation and utilization of PBL in either a rational design or a retrofit scenario. Chapter objectives are intended to provide the following:

- **Historical Background:** An outline of PBL in undergraduate medical education with an emphasis on its use in the 21ˢᵗ century
- **PBL Process Overview:** A description of the method of active, student-directed content acquisition
- **Analysis:** PBL implementation by rational design vs. retrofit
- **Outline of Perceived Advantages of PBL:** Advantages to undergraduate medical education and a delineation of challenges
- **Comparison of PBL to Team-Based Learning (TBL):** Briefly comparing two active learning modalities used in undergraduate medical education

HISTORICAL PERSPECTIVE: PROBLEM-BASED LEARNING IN 20ᵀᴴ and 21ˢᵀ CENTURY MEDICAL EDUCATION

PBL emerged in the second half of the 20ᵗʰ century at McMaster University School of Medicine in Hamilton, Ontario, Canada as a way to revitalize undergraduate medical education (Barrows, 1994; Gallagher, 1997; Norman & Schmidt, 1992). Although the philosophy informing PBL has remained recognizable since its inception, the pre-Internet era comprised a more challenging time in which to implement this self-directed instructional format. The advent of the Internet and the ever-expanding availability of online learning resources have greatly enhanced the feasibility of self-directed student learning in PBL and other curricular contexts (Pluta, Richards, & Mutnick, 2013).

By the early 21ˢᵗ century, a majority of U.S. allopathic medical schools were incorporating PBL, in varying degrees, into their preclinical curricula (Kinkade, 2005). As the second decade of the 21ˢᵗ century ends, new U.S. medical schools are creating preclinical PBL curricula by rational design (e.g., Carle Illinois College of Medicine). Other institutions are revising their educational strategies to incorporate PBL (e.g., California Northstate University College of Medicine).

PBL OVERVIEW

At its inception, PBL in undergraduate medical education had a well-defined structure (Barrows, 1986; Taylor & Miflin, 2008). Many early practitioners attempted to retain it in its "pure" form (Nendaz & Tekian, 1999). The original intent of PBL was to provide a richer, expanded motivation for learning by structuring content in a clinical setting. Over time, the development of clinical reasoning skills would be fostered in the learner while enhancing skills used in self-directed learning (Barrows, 1986). In its more recent interpretation, features of the original format are retained. Institutions are, however, likely to modify aspects of PBL to better integrate the process into their curricula. The following describes a version of PBL preclinical curriculum delivery based on three U.S. medical schools that comprise the authors' past and present institutions.

Outline of the Overall PBL Process

PBL centers around an extensive clinical case for students to work on in small groups over the course of one week. Ideally, the PBL group will meet in a small room where students are seated around one table and facing one another. As they progress through the case, the students will discuss topics that they feel warrant further clarification. As they engage in peer teaching, one student in each group, the "Researcher" for the week, may use a computer to provide instant elucidation of well-circumscribed topics. Over the course of the week, students will collectively and individually identify areas in which they have knowledge gaps. They will do research to learn more about those areas that represent deficiencies in understanding. In addition, they will present what they have learned to the group and critically evaluate the resources used to construct their presentations.

The weekly PBL schedule usually comprises a two-hour session on Monday and two-to-three-hour sessions on Wednesday and Friday. This is a collective activity that requires the full engagement of all participants. Therefore, attendance is mandatory. A trained faculty facilitator is also present during the entire group meeting. As delineated below, the facilitator must refrain from teaching, answering direct questions about the case, or delivering content. Ideally, there may be an additional wrap-up session on Friday. During this time, the patient described in the case, as well as the patient's physician (who is often one of the authors of the case), meet the entire cohort of students. All PBL groups will come together for the concluding session. Students will be able to address case questions to both the patient and physician.

Day 1

On Day 1 (Monday), the case will be projected on a large screen in the PBL room. One student, acting as the "Leader" for the week, will oversee progression through the case. The students will take turns slowly reading aloud through the first day of the case, defining terms as necessary, responding to prompts in the case as described below, and evaluating lab results, imaging results, and other visual exhibits from the case. As the group progresses through the case, one student, the "Scribe" for the week, will use a whiteboard to list hypotheses or differential diagnoses designated by the group. The Scribe will also list potential learning objectives identified by the group as they evaluate gaps in their knowledge.

As described later, cases are constructed with specific ending points on Day 1 and Day 2. This keeps groups synchronized as they move through the case. At the end of the first session, the Leader will preside as the group selects which learning objectives become topics for individual student presentations on Day 2. Depending on the PBL program and whether the group is in preclinical year 1 or year 2, either all or about half of the students in the group will prepare presentations for the next session.

Day 2

When the group reconvenes on Day 2 (Wednesday), the session will begin with individual student presentations lasting 10 to 12 minutes. These somewhat formal presentations will require students to stand as they address the group. Presentations may employ any format deemed effective by the student, including PowerPoint, concept maps on a whiteboard, or interactive games/quizzes. Presentations will be archived for later use as study materials. Ideally, each speaker will end her/his presentation with an annotated reference list in which the speaker critically evaluates their resources. The speaker will attempt to answer questions elicited by group members after viewing the presentation. The speaker will also be able to ask colleagues, including the Researcher, for help in answering questions. Students should be prepared to provide constructive feedback on the presentations.

After the presentations on student-identified learning objectives, the group will resume reading aloud through the case. At the conclusion of Day 2, students will have a much clearer understanding of clinical diagnoses appropriate to the case. Students should also have a good basis for revising their list of student-identified learning objectives. Once the student learning objective list is revised, the Leader can reveal the official case learning objectives to the group. These learning objectives, devised by the case author(s) and other faculty members, may constitute testable content derived from the case. If necessary, the group will decide how to combine case learning objectives to ensure complete coverage. If students are presenting once per week, those who did not present on Day 2 will divide the remaining learning objectives for presentation on Day 3 (Friday). By the second semester of weekly PBL sessions, students will be very adept at anticipating the case learning objectives. It may be necessary to remind students that researching their own learning objectives is a valuable part of the process, even when the topic does not comprise a faculty-generated learning objective.

Day 3

Day 3 (Friday) session will begin with the remaining student presentations. At the conclusion of Day 3, the Leader will initiate a discussion about the week's successes and areas for improvement in subsequent sessions.

All facilitators and students will be required to attend the Day 3 case wrap-up session if these are available. Students will wear professional dress and white coats because they will be meeting a patient.

Oral delivery of a formal presentation in a subjective/objective/assessment/plan (SOAP) format should be required from second-year students during Day 2 and Day 3. This presentation will reinforce a sense of student advancement between the first and second preclinical years in PBL. It will also provide beneficial practice as students enter the clinical portion of their education. Students will take turns doing this over the course of multiple weeks of PBL. This should be considered a formal situation; students will be asked to stand when presenting the patient.

Ideally, students will present the patient from memory. However, at the beginning of the year, students may need to use notes. Physician-written patient presentation guidelines should be issued to students and facilitators at the beginning of the second year. Students may find this process difficult. It should be emphasized that this is an opportunity for students to practice a necessary skill. Therefore, it is best to consider all patient presentation feedback to be formative.

In a program with both physician (Doctor of Medicine, MD and/or Doctor of Osteopathic Medicine, DO) and Doctor of Philosophy (PhD) PBL facilitators, it may be necessary to offer training to nonphysician facilitators for providing feedback on student patient presentations. The ultimate future audience for a patient presentation will be an attending physician, although all attending physicians will have individual requirements for patient presentations. Nevertheless, the practice itself is valuable regardless of differences in facilitator experience and/or the expectations of future attending physicians.

Assessment

Assessment of PBL content and participation can be accomplished in several ways. In the experience of these authors in a curriculum with weekly PBL sessions for the entire academic year, participation assessment includes midcourse/midblock formative feedback in a 20-to-30-minute session between facilitator and individual group members. Students should be invited to fill out the assessment rubric prior to the session and compare this to the facilitator's completed rubric. PBL participation will be assessed on a pass/fail basis. In the rare event that a student is in danger of not passing the participation portion of PBL, it is incumbent upon the facilitator to notify the student in writing during the midcourse/midblock formative assessment. The same procedure will be followed for the final participation assessment.

Contemporary medical students desire frequent feedback. PBL encourages informal peer-to-peer and facilitator-to-student feedback after every student presentation and at the end of each week. This allows students to participate in continuous improvement throughout the course/block.

Content in PBL cases will be assessed during a final summative exam. This may take the form of a purpose-built exam that resembles a PBL case, or targeted questions based on case learning objectives and included in the comprehensive end-of-course/end-of-block exam. This assessment strategy has worked well in the experience of these authors. Because PBL is an intensive undertaking for both participating students and faculty, small summative assessments during a course/block may not be feasible or ideal.

A peer evaluation component should be built into PBL. For example, students may be asked to name a "most valuable PBL colleague" at the end of each course. Once a semester or year, the top 10% of the class with the greatest number of votes can be recognized. This honor might be worthy of mention in the medical student performance evaluation (MSPE) to support students' application to residency programs. Students will also be required to provide constructive feedback on one or more peers. The feedback should focus on positive aspects of their PBL contributions, as well as areas for improvement. Similarly, faculty-issued letters of distinction can be used to confer kudos to exceptional PBL participants.

STRUCTURE OF THE PBL LEARNING CASE

The PBL content flows from the clinical case for the week. The case usually has a direct or indirect connection to other curricular components during that week. Because of this connection it is beneficial to find ways in which the case can be written so that an obvious overlap in subject matter is not immediately apparent. For example, during a musculoskeletal system course, the case patient may present with a condition (e.g., an eating disorder in a young female gymnast) that leads her to switch to a team sport (soccer). While playing soccer, however, she sustains an injury that uncovers osteosarcoma.

Printed Version of the Case for Faculty Facilitators

The following is a detailed description of the case provided to faculty facilitators in a very specific printed format. This section also illustrates the overall structure of a PBL case. Subsequently, there will be a briefer account on the students' version of the case.

Cases begin with a cover page bearing a generic title (e.g., course number, week 4, 2019). The patient's invented name appears on the title page along with a color photo of an age- and race-appropriate surrogate patient. The actual name and photograph of the patient may be used with their written permission. The picture can show the patient's face or, in the case of the female patient above, it can show a photo of an adolescent girl doing gymnastics and another photo of the girl playing soccer. The footer of the document indicates the course number and week, the name of the patient, and page numbers. A copyright notice may be placed in the footer. Case authors are not identified on the cover of the case because students may use what they know about the specialty area of the author(s) to conjecture about case content. Instead, authors are listed at the end of the case. This information is not revealed until the case concludes on Day 3.

Printed versions of the case are distributed only to faculty facilitators. Cases are constructed as Word documents, finished in a PDF format, and printed on one side of the page. There are two columns per page; information in the right column assists the facilitator if they are not a case content expert. The material in the right column is a facilitator guide and should not be shared with students. This material can include definitions, information about differential diagnoses, drug facts, basic science information, possible student answers to prompts in the case, and tips on how long to let students struggle with a concept before asking whether the problem might be too big for them to solve during the session. To keep track of which material belongs on which side of the page, it is convenient to use black typeface for the student version (left side of the page) and provide facilitator notes in a second color (right side of the page).

Cases are often written from the point of view of a third- or fourth-year medical student or a resident. This allows the case to include dialogue with the patient, and between various care providers (e.g., medical student and chief resident). The goal is to bring the case close to the experience level of the students so they can readily imagine themselves as part of the case. Cases can progress over long periods of time (including jumping ahead a few years) so that the third-year medical student revisits the same patient during his/her residency training. In fact, cases do not need to progress linearly in time. It is possible to write a compelling case that begins in the present, jumps into the past, and returns to the present or future. Day 3 of the case is often written as an epilogue, serving to conclude the case while tying up loose ends. Long-term outcomes may be included in the epilogue.

As students progress through the case, they encounter a series of prompts in bold italics. In the printed faculty facilitator version of the case, the text of the case and the prompts would be in black typeface on the left side of the page. The prompts are meant to elicit discussion within the group. Prompts can range from very simple items (*What is the chief complaint?* or *What is the patient's BMI?*) to more involved questions (*What is on your differential diagnoses list at this point? Justify your answer.*). Prompts may also relate to images or lab results in the case. For example, while playing soccer the female athlete in the previous example suffered a nondisplaced fracture of the distal tibia. However, the X-ray also shows unusual bone formation at the site of the fracture. Ideally, students would recognize that the bone appeared abnormal. For beginning students, it is useful to include a normal X-ray for comparison. The prompt to the students may be: *Describe what you see on the X-ray.* The facilitator's information in the right column of the printed case would indicate that there is a nondisplaced fracture of the distal tibia. It may also include a differential diagnoses list for focal bone abnormalities in a child of this age.

As students progress through this part of the case, the facilitator should note the extent to which the students recognize an abnormality and which items were included on their differential list. The facilitator would not, however, point out the abnormality or provide additional items for the differential diagnoses list. More complicated basic science or clinical prompts can be included as the case progresses. Prompts may relate to more general concepts like the appropriate composition of the healthcare team for a given situation (for example, a 14-year-old patient with an amputation secondary to osteosarcoma who now presents with what appears to be a serious infection). The prompt may also ask what needs to be said to the patient and her family regarding her prognosis.

Under the direction of the Leader, students should spend time discussing every prompt. Otherwise, the faculty facilitator must remind the group that all prompts require full discussion until an answer emerges or the group concludes that the prompt becomes a learning objective. For straightforward prompts, the Researcher may address the issue. Well-written prompts with minimal directives are crucial to the successful flow of the case. These prompts serve as a guide to aspects of the case that may require students' attention. As students become more familiar with PBL, they will realize that some prompts assist in the development of learning objectives.

A PBL case is sequentially revealed to students in a realistic order. The overall sequence in which information is presented should reflect and reinforce what students are being taught in their clinical/medical skills course. This will, however, depend on what is going on in the case (for example, a scheduled office visit may include a different set of encounters and procedures as compared to an acute patient in the emergency department). When clinically appropriate, the case should appear in a structured format, including chief complaint (in the patient's own words), history of present illness, past medical history, family history, social history, review of systems, and physical exam. The repetition of this format provides practice in organizing and presenting patient information. At this point, a prompt may ask students to identify labs or imaging studies to be ordered, including a requirement that all choices be justified. On the right side of the page, the facilitator can see what the case author(s) suggest as appropriate labs/imaging and their justification. Typically, students will not generate a list as complete as that provided to the facilitator on the right side of their page.

In subsequent visits with the patient the order of the structured format will be repeated. To avoid making the case dry and repetitive, appropriate dialogue should be inserted. The dialogue may involve all present individuals. In the case above, the dialogue could be between the patient and physician. It could also be between parent and patient, parent and physician, or could include the medical student who is "participating" in the case and the attending physician.

Case lab results are usually included in the text on the left side of the page. It is convenient to present these in tabular format, keeping the format consistent within and between cases. Appropriate units should always be included; normal or reference values may also be provided.

Imaging results and photographic exhibits are placed at the end of the case, with one image per page. These images (i.e., photographs, lab results) are linked to the text via generically labeled hyperlinks (e.g., Exhibit 1, Exhibit 2, etc.). In other words, the name of the hyperlink should not provide any information about the image. The hyperlink allows students to "jump" to the image at the end of the case. The page containing the image is labeled with the exhibit number; there is no other written information on the page. The bottom of the image page includes a hyperlink for students to return to their place in the case once they have finished reviewing and discussing the image.

The printed facilitator guide, which contains the entire case, is clearly divided into PBL Days 1 to 3. This printed version also contains the case learning objectives, delineating testable material covered in the case. This list is inserted between the end of the case proper and the exhibits for the case. A case normally contains slightly more learning objectives than there are students in the PBL group (generally no more than 10 to 12). Case learning objectives may vary in scope and subject matter. In the example case pertaining to both an eating disorder and osteosarcoma, the case objectives might include the biochemistry of the fed and fasted state, human papillomavirus (HPV) vaccination for both males and females (because the patient in the case began but did not complete her HPV immunization schedule), chondroblastic osteosarcoma (presentation, diagnosis, treatment options, and common outcomes), mechanism of action of each drug in the patient's chemotherapy regimen, and the difference between palliative and hospice care, specifically outlining legal and medical implications of palliative care for children vs. adults. Depending on what student-identified learning objectives were covered in Day 2 presentations, students may decide to combine two related case learning objectives into one presentation for Day 3. The facilitator version of the case is limited to one side of the page so that information is not visible to students in the room as the facilitator follows the progress of the case or turns pages to see the notes on the right side of each page. In this format, the single-sided printed version of a PBL case is generally 30 to 45 pages in length.

Student Version of the Case

Students do not receive a printed version of the case. Once the facilitator version of the case is completed, three student versions must be generated as three separate files. The Day 1 file contains Day 1 materials and images. The Day 2 file contains materials from Days 1 and 2, including images from both days. The case learning objectives list appears after the case text and before the images. The Day 3 file is organized using the complete case text, the case learning objectives, and then the images.

The material from the facilitator's right column must be removed from the student versions. This is easier to do if the typeface in the facilitator's right column appears in a different color. The two-column facilitator guide formatting must also be removed. It is necessary to edit the student versions of the case and adjust the spacing. In doing so, students will not immediately see answers to the prompts. For example, if the prompt asks students to consider and justify what labs they would order, the next item to appear may be a table containing the lab tests and results. In this situation, the spacing should be adjusted to provide white space after the prompt. Students would determine their labs prior to scrolling through the case and seeing the actual lab orders and the lab results.

Finally, hyperlinks must be added to the student version of the case. Hyperlinks are inserted into the Word document prior to its PDF conversion. Once converted, it is important to check formatting and spacing as indicated above, and to ensure functionality of all hyperlinks.

As mentioned, all hyperlinks in the text are labeled Exhibit (plus a number). At the bottom of any image, another hyperlink allows the student to "jump" back into their place in the case. This minimizes the possibility of a premature reveal of the next image. This is important because most cases include more than one image; students should not view the next image until they arrive at the appropriate hyperlink in the text. Hyperlinks may be included on the cover page for the Days 2 and 3 student versions so that students can "jump" to the start for that day.

Generally, the course director goes through the entire case to ensure that the case learning objectives align with course learning objectives. They also provide suggestions and comments. In some institutions, there may be a designated physician case reader and/or a reader representing academic affairs.

FRIDAY WRAP-UP SESSION

Some institutions routinely conclude the week by bringing all PBL groups and facilitators together for a one-hour wrap-up session. The patient portrayed in the case (or a different patient with the same medical condition) appears in this session. The patient's physician, who is usually the author for the case, also appears at this session. Although the physician may start with a brief introduction of the patient, these sessions are often unstructured. Students have an opportunity to address questions to the patient or physician. Patients may come to these sessions accompanied by a spouse, parent, child, or friend. Students may also direct questions to these guests.

As mentioned, all students and faculty facilitators are required to attend Day 3's case wrap-up session. Students generally cite this as a favorite and extremely valuable part of the PBL process. They formulate thoughtful and insightful questions for both the patient and physician. Students appreciate the interaction between healthcare provider and recipient. They also enjoy the opportunity to personally thank the patient and physician.

The logistics of arranging these encounters are somewhat formidable but well worth the effort. Friday wrap-up sessions greatly enhance a PBL program. In fact, in one report, PBL wrap-up sessions were shown to have a significant correlation with medical students' ability to describe the psychosocial and humanistic aspects of the patient case of the week (Welfare, Nolan, & Vari, 2016).

FRIDAY FACILITATOR DEBRIEFING SESSION

It is imperative to include a regular faculty facilitator debriefing session at the end of each week. These one-hour sessions are attended by facilitators, the director of PBL, and the current course director. During this time, each page of the case is reviewed. Any errors or problems are noted and/or discussed. Debriefing sessions also provide facilitators time to discuss other issues concerning PBL group function during the week.

PBL FACILITIES, FACULTY AND STUDENT GROUPS

PBL requires appropriate physical space where small groups can meet. Ideally these will be dedicated PBL rooms that will accommodate seven to nine students and one facilitator. PBL rooms will be equipped with Internet access, a computer, a projector, a large screen, and at least one large whiteboard. PBL rooms should be in a quiet area and free of other distractions. If dedicated PBL rooms are not feasible, small classrooms or meeting rooms can also be adapted for this purpose.

Role and Training of the Faculty Facilitator

When PBL is working well, the faculty facilitator will provide limited active intervention during sessions. Because the facilitator will need to provide formative and summative feedback to students in the PBL group, most faculty members will spend some session time taking notes on individual students, documenting presentation quality, participation, and overall behavior.

A common task for the facilitator, especially with groups new to PBL, is helping the group avoid the tendency to rush through the case. This problem often begins with the cover page because the Leader reads the patient's name and immediately scrolls to the case text. At this juncture, the facilitator needs to stop the group and say, "Look at the patient. What do you see?" Students often respond with the patient's gender and apparent racial background. They may not try to arrive at the patient's age. In this event, the facilitator must intervene again and ask, "How old is this patient?" or "What do you mean by young? How young, exactly?" The facilitator must also pay attention to prompts. They must stop the group directly or via the Leader if the group is not adequately discussing prompts.

In general, it is preferable to encourage the Leader to lead. The facilitator should attempt to address suggested modifications to the Leader rather than directly to the group. For example, if there are simultaneous side conversations in the room, the facilitator can say to the Leader, "Did you hear what 'so-in-so' just said? I couldn't hear it because there was a lot of other noise." At this point, the Leader should remind the group that there should be only one person talking at any given time. If the week's Leader is unable or unwilling to do this task, the facilitator may need to intervene directly. It is also the role of the Leader to encourage quiet students and ensure that extroverted students do not dominate the session. The facilitator may want to discuss this with the Leader in private and agree on a discreet way to remind the Leader during the session that everyone's voice should be heard.

Facilitator training can be accomplished through various means. However, it should be extensive, rigorous, and a requirement for all PBL facilitators, including substitutes. Training may consist of several parts. For example, a trainee may be required to observe an entire week of PBL in a group with a seasoned facilitator. Alternatively, a group of six or seven facilitator trainees could assume the role of "students" as they are led through an entire PBL case, including a few "student" presentations. In this scenario, it is often difficult for the "students" not to break character during the mock PBL sessions. Allowing ample time for faculty questions at the end of each training session is a helpful technique. As a final stage of training, facilitators may be required to work with a group of students while under observation of live closed-circuit television or while being video recorded. In doing so, the new facilitator can receive feedback on his/her performance in a practice situation.

Composition of Student PBL Groups

PBL works best with groups of seven to nine students (seven being ideal). Larger groups (10 or more) are unwieldy and detract from the learning environment. The process requires a critical mass of at least six students. Groups of less than six participants force individual students to handle too much content. Also, small groups lack the dynamic energy that can be an effective component of a slightly larger group.

The composition of individual groups requires attention. Forming groups using a random-number generator may constitute a reasonable starting point. However, it is essential to balance the groups for gender and other factors (e.g., race, ethnicity). In the experience of the authors, allowing students to form their own groups results in a poor-quality learning environment for an unacceptably large proportion of the cohort.

As described, each week's case assigns one student Leader, one Researcher, and one Scribe. The Leader controls the pace used to progress through the case. The Leader may also remind students of the rules in the PBL room. Importantly, the Leader is the only person empowered to call breaks in the proceedings. Both the Scribe and Researcher, in addition to their specific jobs, also contribute to group discussions and take turns reading aloud. This can be difficult for the Scribe who may stand at the whiteboard for the entire session. These student jobs should rotate weekly. Ideally, each student will perform each job during a given course. These jobs should be viewed as opportunities for practice and improvement rather than areas for assessment.

PBL groups remain together for an extended period of time (e.g., an entire course/block in an institution that uses weekly PBL cases throughout the preclinical medical curriculum). Changing group composition and facilitators after each block/course provides students with diverse group interaction.

PBL Decorum

Appropriate behavior during PBL sessions is crucial to the effectiveness of the program. Students must be fully present and engaged in the process. To this end, no phones should be used while the session is in progress. Therefore, phones should not be visible. Only the Researcher should have access to a computer during group work. Although this restriction can be very unpopular with students, it is critical to encouraging full attention and engagement in the session. Similarly, note-taking should be discouraged.

Complete engagement of the group also means that all participants be present in the room while the session is in progress. Unexcused absences are not acceptable. The Leader can call a break at any time; other group members can ask the Leader to call a break at any time. Breaks should not occur, however, while a student presentation is in progress.

The faculty facilitator is expected to remain engaged during the entire session, avoiding use of phones, computers, or other reading materials during PBL. In addition, the faculty facilitator must honor the PBL process and categorically refrain from any form of teaching or providing the group with additional study materials.

It is extremely important that facilitators respect the PBL process so that all groups are equal. If students perceive that one group is enjoying an advantage due to facilitator concessions or augmentations, this will quickly become a contentious and disruptive situation. A facilitator may gently remind a group of things that could be done better or praise the group. However, providing feedback to individual group members should be confined to scheduled one-on-one assessment sessions. In the event of outright conflict or unacceptable behavior, the facilitator should address the problem immediately with the group or with the individuals involved.

PBL is also a form of professionalism training in that it involves hours of group cooperation in close quarters. In any circumstance where behavior is notably unprofessional, it is the duty of the facilitator to intervene and turn the situation into a learning opportunity. This includes unprofessional behavior directed at student colleagues, the faculty facilitator, the patient in the case, or any other patient the student may have encountered. Students will sometimes provide the necessary intervention. They are, however, often uncomfortable giving this type of feedback to their peers.

Students must be informed that PBL case material is confidential. Students are expressly prohibited from helping students in the class below them with a PBL case. Additionally, faculty facilitators also have an obligation to keep case content secure.

PBL CURRICULA: RATIONAL DESIGN VS. RETROFIT

As of this writing at the end of the second decade of the 21ˢᵗ century, there are new medical schools implementing PBL curricula by rational design. Some medical schools are also incorporating PBL into existing curricula via a retrofit process.

Building a PBL Curriculum *de novo* by Rational Design

Although it is easier to build a PBL curriculum *de novo* by rational design, there are challenges and benefits to this approach. One benefit of implementing PBL from medical school inception is the unifying influence of an agreed-upon philosophical approach to best practices in andragogy as it serves preclinical medical education. Regardless if an incipient medical school is going to involve new building construction, the decision to start as a PBL institution allows the creation of the correct number of appropriately sized PBL rooms prior to matriculation of the inaugural class. Rational design also provides the opportunity to hire administrators and faculty members who are experienced with the PBL format and have realistic expectations about the process. This includes educators with previous experience as faculty facilitators at another PBL medical school and physicians who were educated in PBL curriculum. Additionally, these experienced educators should be able to assist in the training of inexperienced PBL-naive faculty members. Finally, allopathic medical schools envisioning a PBL curriculum can reasonably expect to remain in compliance with the Liaison Committee on Medical Education (LCME) accreditation standard 6.3 "Self-Directed and Life-Long Learning" (LCME, 2019). Similarly, an osteopathic medical school incorporating PBL into the curriculum will be in compliance with the Commission on Osteopathic College Accreditation (COCA) accreditation element 6.7 "Self-Directed Learning" (COCA, 2019).

There are corresponding disadvantages to some of the advantages listed above. For example, even when a new school opens with enough small rooms for PBL, a later decision to expand class size could be limited by available physical space or could require new construction/remodeling. Although hiring experienced PBL educators is usually advantageous, some faculty facilitators with previous PBL experience may not be open to the implementation of PBL as envisioned by the new institution. Lastly, the LCME interpretation of what constitutes satisfactory compliance with accreditation standard 6.3 on self-directed learning may change over time. This could also be the case for the COCA interpretation of accreditation element 6.7.

Implementing a PBL Curriculum by Retrofit

Medical schools that are considering adding PBL by retrofit into an established curriculum may be doing so to achieve or augment compliance with LCME standard 6.3 or COCA element 6.7. By bringing existing programs into accordance with an accreditation standard or element, the institution is presumably offering a better learning experience for students. Such changes may foster both self-directed learning and enhanced metacognition among adult learners. Curricular changes that include the addition of PBL may also be undertaken as a part of the continuous quality improvement that medical schools are obliged to undertake.

According to anecdotal experience with institutions implementing PBL by retrofit, the inclusion of PBL in the preclinical curriculum constitutes a welcome change for students who have experienced the curriculum with and without PBL. A student cohort in this situation is also likely to present PBL in a favorable light when interacting with colleagues in the class below them.

Introducing PBL into an existing curriculum by retrofit does, however, present considerable challenges. Notably, at a minimum, there must be enough rooms available to accommodate the total number of PBL groups. In some institutions, the PBL schedule is the same for both preclinical years. This requires rooms to simultaneously accommodate PBL groups from two cohorts. The use of existing study rooms or classroom space for a new PBL program is only feasible if the furniture in the room can be rearranged so all students in a group are able to face each other. Rooms with immovable furniture result in students sitting in rows with their backs to one another. This is not compatible with best practices for PBL. All PBL rooms must be equipped with Internet access, a computer, a projector, a large screen, and at least one large whiteboard.

Although informal evidence suggests that medical students usually respond positively to the introduction of PBL in the preclinical curriculum, the necessary constraints of the format may seem onerous to some students. Aspects of PBL that students may take exception to are mandatory attendance, limitation of computer use, and the amount of work involved in preparing individual presentations. Some students may also feel insecure about not being given the "right answer" to the case learning objectives.

Another challenge involves training enough faculty facilitators for PBL. Retrofitting PBL into an existing curriculum will require the presence of at least one faculty member with considerable PBL experience. Another option is to hire someone who fits this description. Even if the institution has one or more experienced PBL faculty facilitators, most facilitators will be new to PBL and newly trained at the outset of the program. Although this does not necessarily constitute a crippling obstruction, this situation should be considered when evaluating early iterations of the program. It will be necessary to train more faculty members than the envisioned number of PBL groups because it is imperative that trained facilitators are available to serve as back-up in the event of faculty absence. Both the upper-level administration and most faculty members must support the decision to implement PBL. They must recognize the extent to which this will consume faculty time. Lastly, faculty members who are not fully informed about or in agreement with the PBL process may constitute an impediment to the retrofit introduction of PBL into an existing curriculum.

ADVANTAGES AND CHALLENGES OF PBL

Advantages of a PBL Curriculum

The advantages of PBL in undergraduate medical education extend beyond case-based content delivery. As mentioned, this type of curriculum is generally well-received by students in the preclinical years. Students appreciate opportunities to develop teamwork skills, practice public speaking through the formal presentation of student-identified or case learning objectives, and enhance their abilities to research and critically evaluate scientific and medical literature. It quickly becomes apparent to students that the faculty facilitator is also learning from the student presentations. Therefore, PBL may foster a more collegial interaction with faculty members. Students often express an appreciation for the extensive amount of time faculty facilitators invest in PBL. This recognition presumably legitimizes and lends gravitas to the PBL process in the eyes of the student. When implemented correctly PBL provides a safe, nonjudgmental space for students to work on aspects of professionalism, become more comfortable providing constructive feedback, and experiment with self-improvement in a group setting.

A PBL curriculum also affords the opportunity to create a medical education elective for year four students. This could require students to write a PBL case *de novo* with a faculty coauthor, undergo PBL facilitator training, and facilitate one or more weeks of PBL.

For allopathic schools, a PBL curriculum has the added advantage of being recognized by the LCME as self-directed learning, thus contributing to compliance with accreditation standard 6.3. For osteopathic schools this method of content delivery will contribute to compliance with COCA accreditation element 6.7.

Challenges of a PBL Curriculum

A major criticism of PBL is that it is very labor intensive. The high faculty-to-student ratio sequesters faculty facilitators for extensive periods of time. This concern is a significant factor in the adoption of a Team-Based Learning (TBL) curriculum in lieu of PBL. Faculty facilitators, although hopefully finding PBL a rewarding and usually educational experience, spend 6 to 10 hours per week in the PBL sessions, wrap-ups, and faculty debrief sessions.

Faculty facilitators, however, need not be full-time faculty members. Recently retired physicians and other community members with an MD, DO or PhD degree make excellent PBL facilitators and are often pleased to maintain a connection to the medical school while enjoying a flexible schedule. These facilitators are trained, have faculty status, and are paid a stipend. In the experience of these authors, many such facilitators will do PBL for two or three courses/blocks each year. As indicated above, creating a year four medical education elective will also produce a small, temporary supply of trained student PBL facilitators. Another approach to stretching faculty resources while incorporating PBL into a curriculum is to schedule sessions on a less frequent basis (e.g., one PBL week per course/block). Although this is not ideal, it is likely to be preferable to completely omitting PBL from the curriculum.

Construction of PBL cases is also an extremely time-consuming process. Ideally, a case will have both a physician author and a basic scientist author. In a best-case scenario, these authors will need at least one month to create a case *de novo*, have it appropriately vetted, and allow time for proper formatting and distribution. Once a case has been used, it will continue to need editing and improvements as medical best practices change.

There is also a notable dearth of outcome data directly documenting the efficacy of PBL on physician competency. Although there have been meta-analyses examining PBL outcomes, the data, collected from different institutions, are subject to the criticism that institutional implementation of PBL varies significantly (Hartling, Spooner, Tjosvold, & Oswald, 2010; Koh, Khoo, Wong, & Koh, 2008; Pluta et al., 2013; Taylor & Miflin, 2008; Yew & Goh, 2016). This makes comparisons and overall outcome conclusions difficult. This obstacle could potentially be addressed by medical schools, like Lake Erie College of Osteopathic Medicine, that offer parallel programs in which students can elect a PBL track or a lecture/discussion track to acquire curricular content (American Association of Colleges of Osteopathic Medicine, 2019). A comparative outcome study within one curriculum may, however, be affected by student self-selection. This may result in cohorts with disparate aptitudes in each track.

Finally, it may take time for students to fully appreciate the benefits of a PBL curriculum. Both anecdotal evidence and a small study on this topic indicate that student perception of the benefits of PBL is positively correlated with stage of training (Ely, LaConte, Fogel, & Vari, 2015). In other words, students may not realize the skills gained in the PBL process until they are interacting with patients, physicians, and other providers during clinical clerkships and rotations in the third and fourth years of medical school.

COMPARISON OF PBL AND TBL

By the end of 2019 the University of Vermont's Larner College of Medicine will have completely phased out lectures as a means of curriculum delivery. California Health Sciences University College of Osteopathic Medicine will use an exclusively TBL curriculum beginning with the inaugural class entering in 2020. This movement away from lecture-based medical school curricula in favor of active learning modalities such as PBL and TBL is becoming increasingly common in the US and abroad. Among the methods of passive learning (attending lectures, reading texts, watching live or video demonstrations) attending lectures has been shown to be the least effective mode of information transmission. Among active learning techniques (learning by doing, teaching others, and discussion groups), teaching others is by far the most effective (Hawkins, 2014). Passive learning encourages memorization, often at the expense of understanding and the development of critical thinking. Active learning, especially in a context relevant to the student, promotes higher order thinking (synthesis of materials, application of content and analytical skills) and aids in knowledge retention (Hawkins, 2014).

As used in medical school curricula, both PBL and TBL promote active learning by emphasizing the engaged role of the learner in andragogy. Although a detailed consideration of TBL is beyond the scope of this chapter, the TBL process is outlined below. The major similarities and differences that characterize PBL and TBL are also delineated. TBL is used for curriculum delivery in both allopathic and osteopathic medical education, as well as in a variety of other health profession educational platforms (American Association of Colleges of Osteopathic Medicine, 2019; Burgess, McGregor, & Mellis, 2014).

Team-Based Learning Overview

TBL requires learners to progress through three phases per session. Students are expected to prepare individually (i.e., assigned readings, watching videos) prior to the session. This constitutes the first phase of the process. Student understanding of this preparatory work is assessed at the outset of the TBL session via a multiple-choice readiness assessment test (RAT) first taken individually (iRAT) and repeated as a team (tRAT). This constitutes the second phase of the process. In the final application phase of the process, the group works together to apply this new knowledge to a clinical case-based problem (Gullo, Ha, & Cook, 2015; Levine & Hudes, 2014). Ideally, the amount of time spent on the application phase would be significantly longer than that spent on the readiness assessment phase (Pluta et al., 2013). The second and third phases of TBL occur in a classroom that accommodates multiple TBL teams and one or more trained facilitators. Both the RAT phase and the application phase should include adequate time for intrateam and interteam discussion managed by the facilitator. Another feature that characterizes TBL is the inclusion of a scheduled and structured format for peer assessment/evaluation (Levine & Hudes, 2014).

Similarities Between PBL and TBL

The most apparent similarity between PBL and TBL is the use of small groups of students working together and assuming responsibility for aspects of their own active learning. Additionally, in both cases, students are meant to be instrumental in teaching their peers. A corollary of these two concepts is the requirement that facilitators are prohibited from delivering content. In both PBL and TBL, a skilled facilitator will create or contribute to a safe, nonjudgmental learning environment using neutral comments when necessary to stimulate or maintain a dynamic process. In broad concurrence with positive medical student perception of the PBL process as mentioned, attitudes regarding TBL were shown to be similarly positive (Parmelee, DeStephen, & Borges, 2009).

In the event of extensive modification to established format and/or delivery principles, both PBL and TBL are subject to significant erosion possibly resulting in ineffective curriculum delivery. Similarly, construction of small groups for either PBL or TBL should be done strategically. Neither case should invite students to form their own groups (Burgess et al., 2014; Levine & Hudes, 2014).

Differences Between PBL and TBL

The most notable difference between PBL and TBL is the vast disparity in facilitator-to-student ratio. PBL ideally provides one facilitator for every seven students. In contrast, one skilled TBL facilitator can simultaneously lead a roomful of 20 teams or more comprising a total in excess of 140 students (Dolmans, Michaelsen, Merriënboer, & Van Der Vleuten, 2015).

This difference also has implications for physical space requirements. TBL can be carried out in existing classrooms large enough to accommodate all teams at once. However, tiered lecture halls with immovable furniture are not ideal TBL spaces (Yoon, Burns, & Michaelsen, 2014). A large TBL room with multiple teams working simultaneously may, however, make it significantly more difficult for a sole facilitator to identify students who are not fully participating in the process.

There are several differences between PBL and TBL that impact individual students. Unlike PBL, individual preparation is required prior to a TBL session. This added requirement may explain the observation that, in one study, weaker students showed a larger difference in improved TBL topic-related test scores vs. topic-unrelated test scores as judged by performance on comprehensive course exams and as compared to stronger students in the cohort (Koles, Stolfi, Borges, & Nelson, 2010). Individual assessments in the form of iRATs at every session may be of greater benefit to weaker students. TBL also permits the facilitator to employ a direct, Socratic method of questioning individual students. Although this would not be permissible in PBL, it provides TBL students with practice answering direct questions, a skill that is likely to be appreciated in the clinical phase of medical education.

Additionally, TBL normally includes a structured requirement for peer evaluation. Practicing peer evaluation is likely to be beneficial to both the student evaluator and the evaluee. Although there is no formal peer-to-peer evaluation process in PBL, this can be added as described. It may also be easier to ensure that students leave TBL sessions with a clear understanding of what it is they need to know. While this can also be accomplished in a PBL curriculum by appropriate construction and wording of case learning objectives, achieving this understanding may be more difficult in a PBL format. Lastly, TBL affords all students in the session a uniform experience whereas 10 PBL groups working on the same case will have 10 slightly different encounters.

TBL is a more definitively structured process than PBL. Therefore, it may be somewhat less suscep-tible to variations in implementation by individual faculty facilitators and encroaching modifications that reduce efficacy over time.

Finally, as mentioned, the TBL facilitator sets session goals and provides resources. Therefore, TBL does not meet the specifications for self-directed learning as currently delineated by LCME accredita-tion standard 6.3 (LCME, 2019). TBL does, however, meet the specifications for self-directed learning as currently outlined by COCA accreditation element 6.7 (COCA, 2019).

CONCLUSION

Based on collective experience with the implementation of PBL curricula at three institutions by rational design and retrofit, the authors conclude that this approach to preclinical medical education is worth the effort at institutions with fairly small student cohorts and access to appropriate physical facilities. Par-ticularly, allopathic medical schools that wish to establish or enhance compliance with LCME standard 6.3 may find that PBL constitutes a good solution.

Schools with PBL as a curricular component will want to describe PBL on the school website, ideally including a brief video of their students engaging in the PBL process. During on-campus interviews, schools will also want to include a short and engaging PBL demonstration session conducted by a skilled facilitator with the entire applicant group. This should be highly interactive, with candidates taking turns reading aloud from a case and answering the prompts. Even ten-to-fifteen minutes of this exercise (i.e., just the beginning of a captivating well-written case) should help candidates understand the process. The interview day PBL demonstration needs to be extensive enough to allow candidates evaluate whether or not they are a good fit for a PBL curriculum.

What type of learner is a good fit for PBL? Students in a PBL curriculum may feel that they get the most benefit out of preparing and delivering their presentations that address group-identified gaps in knowledge. However, the majority of students in a PBL curriculum are also successfully learning cur-ricular content from the PBL cases, from other student presentations and from the dynamic group process itself. An extroverted natural leader who enjoys public speaking may find PBL a fun and effortless way to learn. Introverted students may find the PBL experience more challenging but will benefit from the chance to interact with peers in a safe, non-judgmental setting while mastering content. Students who are insecure about public speaking will profit from the numerous PBL presentations that they will deliver during two years of pre-clinical medical education. These students will find this experience helpful as they begin to interact with patients and preceptors in their third and fourth years of medical school. In summary, and in the experience of these authors, most adult learners thrive in a PBL environment.

ACKNOWLEDGMENT

The authors would like to acknowledge assistance from the following colleagues: Chris Burns at California Health Sciences University College of Osteopathic Medicine, Tracy Yarbrough at California Northstate University College of Medicine, and Nehad El-Sawi at Des Moines University.

REFERENCES

American Association of Colleges of Osteopathic Medicine. (2019). *2019-2020 student guide to osteopathic medical colleges*. Bethesda, MD: American Association of Colleges of Osteopathic Medicine.

Barrows, H. (1986). A taxonomy of problem-based learning methods. *Medical Education, 20*(6), 481–486. doi:10.1111/j.1365-2923.1986.tb01386.x PMID:3796328

Barrows, H. (1994). *Practice-based learning*. Springfield, IL: Southern Illinois University School of Medicine.

Burgess, A., McGregor, D., & Mellis, C. (2014). Applying established guidelines to team-based learning programs in medical schools: A systematic review. *Academic Medicine, 89*(4), 678–688. doi:10.1097/ACM.0000000000000162 PMID:24556770

Commission on Osteopathic College Accreditation. (2019). *Accreditation of Colleges of Osteopathic Medicine: COM Continuing Accreditation Standards*. Chicago, IL: American Osteopathic Association.

Dolmans, D., Michaelsen, L., Merriënboer, J., & Van Der Vleuten, C. (2015). Should we choose between problem-based learning and team-based? No, combine the best of both worlds! *Medical Teacher, 37*(4), 354–359. doi:10.3109/0142159X.2014.948828 PMID:25154342

Ely, S., LaConte, L., Fogel, S., & Vari, R. (2015). *Student perception of patient-centered problem-based learning in one medical school curriculum varies with stage of training; a mid-study report*. Poster presented at the 19th Annual Meeting of the International Association of Medical Science Educators, San Diego, CA.

Gallagher, S. A. (1997). Problem-based learning: Where did it come from, what does it do, and where is it going? *Journal for the Education of the Gifted, 20*(4), 332–362. doi:10.1177/016235329702000402

Gullo, C., Ha, T., & Cook, S. (2015). Twelve tips for facilitating team-based learning. *Medical Teacher, 37*(9), 819–824. doi:10.3109/0142159X.2014.1001729 PMID:25665624

Hartling, L., Spooner, C., Tjosvold, L., & Oswald, A. (2010). Problem-based learning in pre-clinical medical education: 22 years of outcome research. *Medical Teacher, 32*(1), 28–35. doi:10.3109/01421590903200789 PMID:20095771

Hawkins, D. (2014). Creating a team-based learning pedagogical culture. In D. Hawkins (Ed.), *A team-based learning guide for faculty in the health professions* (pp. 89–95). Bloomington, IN: AuthorHouse LLC.

Kinkade, S. (2005). A snapshot of the status of problem-based learning in U.S. medical schools, 2003-04. *Academic Medicine, 80*(3), 300–301. doi:10.1097/00001888-200503000-00021 PMID:15734817

Koh, G., Khoo, H., Wong, M., & Koh, D. (2008). The effects of problem-based learning during medical school on physician competency: A systematic review. *Canadian Medical Association Journal, 178*(1), 34–41. doi:10.1503/cmaj.070565 PMID:18166729

Koles, P., Stolfi, A., Borges, N., Nelson, S., & Parmelee, D. X. (2010). The impact of team-based learning on medical students' academic performance. *Academic Medicine, 85*(11), 1739–1745. doi:10.1097/ACM.0b013e3181f52bed PMID:20881827

Liaison Committee on Medical Education (LCME). (2019). *Function and structure of a medical school, standards for accreditation of medical education programs leading to the MD degree.* Washington, DC: Association of American Medical Colleges and American Medical Association.

Nendaz, M. R., & Tekian, A. (1999). Assessment in problem-based learning medical schools: A literature review. *Teaching and Learning in Medicine, 11*(4), 232–243. doi:10.1207/S15328015TLM110408

Norman, G. R., & Schmidt, H. G. (1992). The psychological basis of problem-based learning: A review of the evidence. *Academic Medicine, 67*(9), 557–565. doi:10.1097/00001888-199209000-00002 PMID:1520409

Parmelee, D., DeStephen, D., & Borges, N. (2009). Medical students' attitudes about team-based learning in a pre-clinical curriculum. *Medical Education Online, 14*(1), 4503. doi:10.3402/meo.v14i.4503 PMID:20165515

Pluta, W. J., Richards, B. F., & Mutnick, A. (2013). PBL and beyond: Trends in collaborative learning. *Teaching and Learning in Medicine, 25*(1), S9–S16. doi:10.1080/10401334.2013.842917 PMID:24246112

Taylor, D., & Miflin, B.Taylor & Miflin. (2008). Problem-based learning: Where are we now? *Medical Teacher, 30*(8), 742–763. doi:10.1080/01421590802217199 PMID:18946818

Welfare, L., Nolan, M., & Vari, R. (2016). Patient-centered learning curricula: Evaluating the impact of the Friday wrap-up on student conceptualization of patient psychosocial characteristics. *Medical Science Educator, 26*(4), 543–546. doi:10.100740670-016-0315-y

Yew, E., & Goh, K. (2016). Problem-based learning: An overview of its process and impact on learning. *Health Profession Education, 2*(2), 75–79. doi:10.1016/j.hpe.2016.01.004

Yoon, M., Burns, C., & Michaelsen, V. (2014). Team-based learning in different classroom settings. *Medical Science Educator, 24*(2), 157–160. doi:10.100740670-014-0024-3

ADDITIONAL READING

Burrows, H. (2000). *Problem-based learning applied to medical education.* Springfield, IL: Southern Illinois University School of Medicine.

Gilkison, A. (2003). Techniques used by 'expert' and 'non-expert' tutors to facilitate problem-based learning tutorials in an undergraduate medical curriculum. *Medical Education, 37*(1), 6–14. doi:10.1046/j.1365-2923.2003.01406.x PMID:12535110

Levine, R., & Hudes, P. (2014). *How-to guide for team-based learning. IAMSE Manual 1.* SBN: 978-1-4575-6665-0. Retrieved from www.iamse.org

Mezirow, J. (1991). *Transformative dimensions of adult learning* (1st ed.). San Francisco, CA: Jossey-Bass.

Michaelsen, L., Parmelee, D., McMahon, K., & Levine, R. (2008). *Team-based learning for health professions education*. Sterling, VA: Stylus Publishing.

Rogers, C. (1969). *Freedom to learn: A view of what education might become*. Columbus, OH: C. E. Merrill.

Seel, N. (2012). Assimilation theory of learning. In *Encyclopedia of the sciences of learning* (pp. 324–326). New York, NY: Springer.

Van Berkel, H., Scherpbier, H., Hillen, H., & van der Vleuten, C. (Eds.). (2010). *Lessons from problem-based learning*. Oxford, UK: Oxford University Press. doi:10.1093/acprof:oso/9780199583447.001.0001

KEY TERMS AND DEFINITIONS

Active Learning: Any method that seeks student engagement by requiring students to assume responsibility for aspects of their own learning.

Andragogy: Adult learning (as opposed to pedagogy, which formally pertains to learning by children).

Metacognition: Self-reflection regarding one's own educational advancement, in other words learning about learning.

PBL Clinical Case: A real but deidentified case, or amalgamation of cases, that portrays a clinical problem via narrative, dialogue, medical examination, and lab and/or imaging results.

Problem-Based Learning (PBL): A small-group active learning modality in which students work through a problem together (e.g., a clinical case), identifying gaps in their knowledge, constructing learning objectives to address their knowledge gaps, researching identified topics, and presenting their findings to peers in their group and their faculty facilitator.

Self-Directed Learning: Learning in which the student identifies gaps in her/his knowledge and seeks to correct those deficiencies by doing research, evaluating the quality of the new information sources, imparting the new information to peers, and receiving feedback from peers and faculty members.

Team-Based Learning (TBL): A structured, small group active learning framework that involves preclass assignments or preparation by individuals followed by in-class readiness assurance tests (RATs) taken first as an individual (iRAT) and then as a group/team (tRAT). Thereafter, an extensive application phase occurs in which newly learned concepts are put into practice and discussed by the team and by the entire class.

Chapter 7

Preparing the Next Generation of Physician Leaders:
Teaching Management Skills to Medical Students and Residents

I. Michael Leitman

https://orcid.org/0000-0001-7094-5657
Icahn School of Medicine at Mount Sinai, USA

Brian Nickerson
Icahn School of Medicine at Mount Sinai, USA

ABSTRACT

Formal training in leadership development has become increasingly popular among physicians. There is a growing interest to provide this educational content to medical students and residents so that they will have these skills upon the start of their clinical or academic medical practice. It is possible to provide the proper management skills to medical trainees so they will have the opportunity to utilize and master these competences during their education. This chapter provides an overview of the available content and the literature to support the integration of this curriculum into formal undergraduate and graduate medical education. This chapter provides a template for the development of a longitudinal experience and the necessary proficiencies to allow trainees to develop as effective clinical leaders.

INTRODUCTION

Medical students and residents must master a large amount of medical knowledge and a skill set in patient care for their desired specialty. In addition to becoming competent for independent practice, those physicians who enter medical education, academic medicine, or leadership positions in health care must acquire an additional skill set in order for them to succeed beyond the primary or specialty care of patients. The primary objective of this chapter is to review the emerging efforts at integration of management skills training into graduate medical education in order to better prepare and develop physician leaders.

DOI: 10.4018/978-1-7998-1468-9.ch007

BACKGROUND

Will we have enough candidates to fill leadership positions in academic medicine in the next few decades? Physician education in the 21st century faces a number of challenges, including an increasingly complex health care system, rapid changes in technology, increasing regulation of working and learning hours, and reductions of resources for student and resident education. While most physicians eventually complete the long process of multidimensional growth needed to become a competent practitioner, only some continue their careers as medical leaders or educators, and fewer seek to become educational leaders in undergraduate and graduate medical education. Medical school, residency, and fellowship have always prepared learners to organize, communicate, educate, and administer, but today's physicians who choose a career path outside of the traditional practice model, or perhaps even within it, need to acquire additional skills that were often not part of traditional medical education.

The seemingly growing refrain for more management and leadership education of physicians, even at the very early career stage, is not new. For instance, in 2004, the Institute of Medicine (IOM) recommended that academic medical centers "develop leaders at all levels who can manage the organizational and system changes necessary to improve health through innovation in health professions education, patient care, and research." Furthering this charge as it relates to graduate medical education, in 2014 the IOM issued consensus suggestions urging greater outcome measurement of education aimed at such areas as increasing value and health care delivery system effectiveness, as well as improving physician interpersonal skills around coordination of care, communication skills, and patient engagement. Similarly, Jardine et al (2015), as a member of the Council of Review Committee Residents, Leadership Subcommittee of the Accreditation Council for Graduate Medical Education (ACGME), advocated on behalf of residents and fellows for a national leadership curriculum. As a result, this educational content is consistent with the Common Program Requirements for residency and fellowship programs, beyond the development of skills in patient safety and quality improvement.

Moreover, according to Martins (2010), management education for internists should be "spiral," starting from medical school and expanding to incorporate new activities and responsibilities as the physician matures. A 2015 study by Frich and Brewster conducted a systematic review of the literature and found no fewer than 35 reports on leadership training programs designed exclusively for physicians. The vast majority of these programs focused on skills training and substantive knowledge, while only a small number used more high-impact educational practices involving interactive techniques to increase self-awareness or stressed system-level, as opposed to only individual-level, impact.

On a broader scale, the American Medical Association (AMA) jointly issued with the American Hospital Association (AHA) a "discussion document" identifying principles for developing successful physician, as well as interprofessional, leadership to achieve better integrated health systems. In addition to the mastery of a number of core operational functions (e.g., financial planning), the AMA and AHA emphasize development of strong interpersonal skill sets for physicians, including team-building, communication, and effective negotiation.

As academic medical centers continue to integrate management education into their curricula, current trainees and practicing physicians can access such education through a combination of workshops, residential courses, and online courses. This chapter describes essential managerial and leadership skills and associated learning activities during the graduate medical education phase of training for those who will manage the education of future physicians.

CREW RESOURCE MANAGEMENT SKILLS

As patient care becomes more complex, it becomes even more important to teach attitudes and behaviors that learners will need in order to work successfully with other members of the health care team. A physician in training must become competent in managing a team that may include members from a variety of educational and experiential backgrounds. These skills may be taught in a number of ways.

TeamSTEPPS™

Developed by the United States Department of Defense and the Agency for Healthcare Research and Quality (AHRQ), Team Strategies and Tools to Enhance Performance and Patient Safety (TeamSTEPPS™) is an evidence-based system for health care professionals that improves teamwork skills, communication, and patient safety within an organization. In addition to teaching conflict resolution through improved information sharing, TeamSTEPPS increases team awareness and clarifies team roles and responsibilities, eliminating key barriers to quality and patient safety. Meier et al. (2012) introduced TeamSTEPPS to senior medical students and found that the curriculum led to improved self-evaluation and medical knowledge acquisition. In addition, improved team skills during simulated immersive patient encounters were observed.

The AHRQ holds free TeamSTEPPS master training events and provides curriculum tools and materials at no charge. These resources provide teaching techniques for students and residents, who must ultimately learn to manage effective medical teams that optimize the use of information, people, and resources to achieve the best possible clinical outcomes.

Team Training Programs in Medical School

A simulation-based curriculum for team training among medical students was described by Meurling, Hedman, Felländer-Tsai, and Wallin (2013). Students participated in a half-day simulation-based team training exercise that included three video-recorded scenarios. Self-efficacy was assessed before and after training. For each scenario, the individual teamwork behaviors, concentration, and stress and the team's clinical performance were evaluated, and the researchers found that self-efficacy improved. Leaders experienced higher mental strain and concentration than did followers.

Team Training in Residency Programs

Dedy, Zevin, Bonrath, and Grantcharov (2013) conducted a survey of program directors in surgery in North America. Almost one-third of respondents conducted specific team training interventions for residents. Three main strategies were identified: combined approaches using simulation and didactic methods in 42%, predominantly simulation-based approaches in 37%, and didactic approaches only in 21%.

TEACHING LEADERSHIP SKILLS IN UNDERGRADUATE MEDICAL EDUCATION

A literature review of leadership training in medical school by Webb et al. (2014) suggested that a majority of curricula (71%) were longitudinal and delivered over periods ranging from one semester to four years. The most common setting was the classroom (50%). Curricula were frequently provided to both preclinical and clinical students (46%), and many (28%) employed clinical faculty as instructors. The majority (79%) addressed at least three Medical Leadership Competency Framework domains; the most common were "working with others" (88%) and "managing services" (75%). The authors also found that most studies did not demonstrate changes in student behavior or quantifiable results.

Stringfellow et al. (2015) studied medical leadership skills development during undergraduate medical education in the United Kingdom. Using questionnaires, they found that 65% of schools valued or highly valued the importance of teaching medical leadership topics, compared with 93.2% of students. Students favored simulation exercises (76%) and quality improvement (QI) projects (77.8%) over small-group discussions, reflective logbooks, or portfolio entries.

TEACHING LEADERSHIP IN GRADUATE MEDICAL EDUCATION

While faculty have great expectations for residents as leaders, leadership training is lacking in most residency programs. Overall, teaching hospitals provide very little formal education to help residents prepare for leadership opportunities. Ackerly et al. (2011) distinguished accidental from cultivated leadership development, and described a reduction in physicians graduating from a combined MD and MBA program. With approval from the American Board of Internal Medicine in 2009, they started a curriculum of Management and Leadership Pathway for Residents (MLPR) at Duke University School of Medicine, targeting residents who had already completed graduate management training or who had several years of prior management experience. The MLPR features a focused educational curriculum, practical management rotations, a longitudinal project, and committed mentorship by a physician executive. The 15-month program adds one additional year to an internal medicine residency program.

In a study of 43 senior residents who were taught management skills during surgical residency, Hanna, Mulder, Fried, Elhilali, and Khwaja (2012) reported that, after the course, 35% felt that management topics were "well addressed," and 44% felt that management topics had been "very well addressed." Residents noted a significant improvement in their ability to perform the following skills after the course: giving feedback, delegating duties, coping with stress, effective learning, and effective teaching. Sixty percent of residents rated their performance as "good" or "excellent" after the course, compared to only 49% before the course ($P=.02$). Residents also noted a statistically significant improvement in their ability to perform the managerial duties necessary for the establishment of a surgical practice.

According to Eubank, Geffken, Orzano, and Ricci (2012), adaptive leadership skills should be learned during family medicine residency. They developed a curriculum to enhance residents' skills in personal mastery, communication, collaboration, systems thinking, and change management through workshops and seminars, followed by an improvement project, over the course of two years. They concluded that these skills prepare residents to enter a primary care workforce with the ability to design, implement, and sustain true patient-centered medical homes based on patient-focused care and healing relationships.

At the U.S. Naval Academy, Edler, Adamshick, Fanning, and Piro (2010) provided a year-long curriculum for pediatric anesthesia residents in leadership and clinical decision-making skills. The latter part of the training required the fellow to be a team leader. At the end of the year, both quantitative assessment and qualitative reflection from residents and faculty members noted significantly improved clinical and administrative decision-making. The second-year residents' performance showed further improvement even one year after completing the training.

In a pediatric residency program, Kuo, Thyne, Chen, West, and Kamei (2010) developed the Pediatric Leadership for the Underserved (PLUS) program. The PLUS program incorporated leadership development into the framework of standard pediatric clinical training by providing specific sessions in personal leadership development and in related skills such as team-building, negotiation, and conflict management. In addition, the curriculum included sessions to develop and implement a three-year longitudinal child health project. Trainees were organized into advising groups to provide structured faculty and peer-to-peer advising. The authors reported that it was important to have a skill-based, rather than a topic-based curriculum, and that it was imported to present concrete examples of the many career paths of physician leaders. From 2004 to 2009, 38% entered with additional relevant degrees (e.g., MPH, MPA, JD). Fifteen of 16 residents who graduated from the program reported on their experience in the program. All responses were in the moderate-to-significant range: overall satisfaction with the program (3.73 on a scale of 1 to 4 (1 = none; 2 = limited; 3 = moderate; 4 = significant)); impact on long-term career goals (3.55); positive impact on plans to influence population health and health policy (3.53); positive impact on plans to serve minority or underserved populations (3.47); improvement of competence as a leader (3.40); and positive impact on clinical education/skills (3.18).

The following sub-sections address a sampling of specific types of leadership development efforts across the GME spectrum, including managerial skills, emotional intelligence, academic pathways, clinical educator tracks, and chief resident training.

Acquisition of Managerial Skills in Residency

Paller, Becker, Cantor, and Freeman (2000) described the Physician Management Pathway, in which they provided a curriculum for internal medicine residents consisting of a monthly seminar series, a preceptorship experience in the second year, and a supervised project in the third year. The program was designed not to assist residents in the attainment of competency in management but to allow them to explore careers that include management responsibilities. Lectures included information about health care delivery systems, health care economics, and population-based medicine. The four-week rotation in the second year was an opportunity to work with a health care executive in a quaternary-care university hospital, a community-based integrated delivery system, an HMO-owned teaching hospital, and an HMO or insurance company. The residents observed mid- and upper-level management meetings, learning many aspects of hospital management such as human resources, professional services, quality improvement, strategic planning, and financial budgeting. During the final year of residency, residents were given the opportunity to undertake an elective management project involving extensive study and exposure to an area of particular interest (Table 2).

The development of management skills in inpatient child and adolescent psychiatry units was described by Malloy and others (2010a). This setting can be an important site for mentoring and teaching early-career psychiatrists who choose to pursue leadership roles and must learn to meet challenges imposed by organizational structure, health care regulation, the accreditation process, and financial issues. Education in organization and quality improvement enables academic psychiatrists to provide better outcomes for their patients and their own academic careers by mastering proper planning skills and applying their educational and research endeavors to their clinical and administrative work.

The ambulatory care environment is rapidly increasing in importance as a site for primary care medicine training. Residents often learn and develop quality and patient safety initiatives in their continuity clinics. According to Colbert et al. (2012), such an activity allowed for the development of systems thinking and systems-based care skills, improved the quality of patient care, improved clinic efficiency, gave residents a feeling of ownership of patients, created the need for improved communication of practice changes, and became a springboard for further research.

Emotional Intelligence

A necessary skill for leaders, emotional intelligence (EI) includes a set of constructs, each with a set of competencies that can be taught and learned. EI competencies should be taught serially and iteratively to match the specific needs of physician learning at various stages of training. Lobas (2006) advocated measuring and using EI as a criterion for selecting physician leaders. The four component competency domains of EI are self-awareness, self-management, social awareness, and relationship management. Self-awareness includes emotional self-awareness, the ability to perform accurate self-assessment and the development of self-confidence. Self-management is emotional self-control, transparency, adaptability, achievement orientation, initiative, and optimism. Social awareness is learned during residency and includes empathy, organizational awareness, and service orientation. Finally, fellows and faculty learn relationship management, which includes professional development of others, inspirational leadership, influence, teamwork and collaboration, ability to bring about change, and conflict resolution (Goleman, Boyatzis, and Mckee 2004).

These skills are usually taught in specific phases of medical education. For example, medical students must learn self-awareness and self-management, while relationship management is typically emphasized during and after residency. Stoller, Taylor, and Farver (2013) suggest that EI should be an essential component of medical education, and that EI education should be tied to the phases of learning in undergraduate and graduate medical education.

To foster greater effectiveness of training in this area, there is a highly validated and normed assessment tool, the Emotional Quotient-Inventory 2.0 (Bar-On 2006, EQ-i 2.0), which helps measure a person's emotional intelligence toward social functioning, performance, and well-being. The tool enables trainers to work with physicians to improve self-awareness and expression, interpersonal skills, decision-making, and stress management. In 2018, Shahid reported on a pediatrics resident training curriculum at the Loyola University Health System that successfully employed the EQ-i2.0 to particular address stress management and well-being. While the longer-term effects of such training are unknown, the EQ-i 2.0 tool offers a systematic way to address training on this important topic.

Preparation for Academic Medical Careers

Coleman, Blatt, and Greenberg (2012) described a summer program for medical students who had an interest in an academic medical career at George Washington University in Washington, DC. Drawing medical students from across the United States, this week-long program placed an emphasis on developing teaching skills, the principles of leadership, medical education scholarship, and the building of a career in academic medicine career-building. The following teaching skills were taught: adult learning, teaching a skill, feedback, teaching in the presence of the patient, case-based teaching, lecturing/presentation skills, and observations of teaching in clinical settings.

The program utilized a variety of learning scenarios that included reflective practice, shared pairs, small- and large-group discussions, student-directed faculty panels, student presentations, observation of clinical teaching and learning in the ambulatory and inpatient settings, and interactions with standardized learners. Students received lectures on faculty career paths; scholarship in medical education; using technology effectively; how to build an academic medical career; the structure and regulation of academic medicine; and how to balance an academic medical career.

Coates et al. (2012) described a core curriculum for education scholarship in emergency medicine. They developed a consensus among education leaders in emergency medicine that a fellowship in medical education focusing on research methodology might lead to improved scholarship. Physicians graduating from these fellowships would be ready to start their academic careers with the tools needed to become education scholars in academic emergency medicine departments. Such faculty would possess skills in teaching and evaluating students and residents, would understand education research methods, and would produce scholarly work based on hypothesis-driven studies that could be applied to multiple institutions. These fellowship graduates would have the potential to positively affect patient care outcomes. The authors suggested a framework for a two-year fellowship in education emergency medicine scholarship.

Mentoring plays a major role in academic career development. Steele, Fisman, and Davidson (2013) reported that having role models increased faculty commitment to developing an academic career. Junior faculty reported that mentorship experience during residency training was an incentive to pursue academic medicine, and that they had identifiable mentorship experiences. Female faculty highlighted several difficulties and issues, including the lack of researcher role models, a range of perceptions regarding the benefits of formal versus less formal mentoring, and the idea that mentors should provide advice on academic promotion and grants. Males valued advice on financial issues, while females were more focused on a work–life balance.

The core competencies for medical educators are vastly different from the six core competencies in graduate medical education that have been promulgated by the ACGME. They are listed in Table 1.

Leadership Positions for Clinician-Educators

What is a clinician-educator? According to a study by Sherbino, et al (2014), medical school deans and department chairs described clinician-educators as being active in clinical practice, applying education theory to practice, and engaging in education scholarship. Holding a particular departmental administrative position was not an essential attribute of being a clinician-educator. Eighty-five percent endorsed the need for physicians to pursue advanced training in medical education in order to serve as clinician-educators. A majority of respondents felt that assessment, communication, curriculum development, education theory, leadership, scholarship, and teaching were essential domains of clinician-educator competence. With regard to training requirements, 55% endorsed a master's degree in education as effective preparation, whereas 39% considered faculty development programs effective.

The first opportunity for a physician to play the role of educator is as a resident, when they interface with medical students on clerkship. The quality of residents as teachers is associated with medical student educational outcomes. Better resident teachers have been associated with improved medical student academic performance during the clerkship (Griffith, Wilson, Haist, & Ramsbottom-Lucier 1998) and resident role modeling directly influences medical student career choices (Wright, Wong, & Newill 1997).

There are several roles for faculty who have an interest in developing a leadership career in academic medicine. Residency program directors play a pivotal role in developing curricula for residents. They must understand evaluation techniques and the unique challenges of adult learning. There is support for program directors from the ACGME, various program director associations, and institutional sponsors of residency programs.

Sanfey et al. (2012a) described the details of a career development resource to develop future vice chairs for surgical education. They suggest that creating a balance of clinical, teaching, research, and administrative responsibilities is necessary to provide leadership in surgical education. Resources to obtain the necessary leadership skills include master's degree courses in education, well-organized continuing medical education courses such as the American College of Surgeons' "Surgeons as Educators" and "Surgeons as Leaders" courses, and the Association for Surgical Education's surgical education research fellowships. In their survey, the authors concluded that vice chairs for education in surgery expressed needs for faculty development in conducting educational research and developing resident selection systems and mentorship programs. The skills deemed to be of greatest importance were effective communication, personnel conflict resolution, and change implementation.

The Chief Resident Year

The chief resident year presents a unique opportunity for trainees to refine their clinical and technical skills, and also to acquire administrative, leadership, and teaching skills. Specialty boards recognize the need for all physicians to master some aspects of leadership during the final year of training.

For internal medicine residents, Berg and Huot (2007) used organizational theory to examine the role of chief residents as "middle managers." The chief residents' work during this additional year consists of "up work" with those above them in the medical and academic hierarchies, "down work" with residents and interns below them in the program, "lateral work" with hospital and administrative staff outside of the residency program, and the "internal work" that chief residents must do with other chief residents. The chief resident role is marked by the tension of these constituencies' multiple and sometimes competing needs, demands, and concerns.

Biese, Leacock, Osmond, and Hobgood (2011) described multiple leadership roles for emergency medicine chief residents in addition to traditional administrative responsibilities, including medical student education, resident education, journal club, resident reading, ultrasonography, resident research, information technology, and high-fidelity simulation. The authors determined that there was a benefit to the program and each resident by having multiple leaders who would work to advance the goals of a residency while simultaneously enhancing resident learning through experience. This model also provided a larger group of residents with the opportunity to develop lifelong professional skills.

In family medicine, Deane and Ringdahl (2012) described the chief resident year as an "incubator for future leaders in family medicine." In their national survey of family medicine residency programs, 97% had a chief resident, and 84% of these are in their third year of training. However, the responsibilities, preparation, and selection for this role varied widely. At the University of Missouri, they developed a leadership curriculum to enhance training for this important role that included attendance at leadership conferences, acquisition of specific skills such as time management and communication, defined responsibilities, and administrative time to complete duties. A survey of the chief residents found that leadership training and increased exposure to faculty were most valued, while scheduled tasks were the least desirable. Chief residents who were trained were more likely to teach medical students or residents compared to those who were not.

A chief resident for education position in psychiatry residency was described by Ning and Lamdan (2009). By learning educational methods such as adult learning theory and concepts such as clinical self-efficacy during an additional year, clinically trained psychiatrists were able to develop as academic clinician-educators.

According to Weiss, Hassell, and Parks (2013), pathology chief residents need organized management training; management topics need greater visibility in mainstream pathology literature; and residents and program directors need pathology milestones–oriented tools for developing leadership and laboratory management skills. The authors described how residents learn to delegate authority, solve complex organizational problems, and develop survival skills. Finally, they describe how chief residents use the final months of their chief residency to transition into the next part of their career.

What attributes and competencies demonstrate leadership qualities? According to a survey of Canadian urology program directors and clinical chairs reported by Robinson and others (2013), only 8% of respondents in urology held an additional master's-level degree, compared to 45% in other specialties. Additional leadership training had been completed by 54%. A majority reported no clearly defined job description for their leadership role (54%). The top responsibility reported by leaders was mentoring residents (67%), followed by advising staff (62%). Excellence in patient care and teaching were seen as the most important professional characteristics, whereas integrity was the most important personal quality. Leaders reported that 17% of their income came from their leadership role, about equal to the time required for position duties (19%). "Time management" was listed as the greatest challenge (54%). Leadership style was reported as "democratic" by 92%.

To challenge educational perspectives that only consider fixed points of time within physician development or ignore that physicians often feel they have to gain additional training to manage and lead effectively in health care, we now scan programs beyond the scope of GME. The objective here is to identify potential topics and approaches that could be incorporated within, or bridged to, the GME experience.

ADVANCED DEGREE PROGRAMS FOR PHYSICIANS

According to Barzansky and Etzel (2011), 40% of U.S. medical schools have established medical doctorate (MD) and master of business administration (MBA) dual-degree programs. Patel et al. (2014) examined graduates with both degrees over a 30-year period. Among the 148 respondents, 118 respondents reported entering residency. Among respondents within their first decade after graduation from the MBA program, 46.2% reported clinical practice as their primary work sector, compared with 39.5% among respondents 11 to 20 years after graduation and 19.2% of respondents 21 to 30 years after graduation. Twenty-nine respondents of the 148 did not enter residency. Almost all of these entered biotechnology, pharmaceuticals, medical device manufacturing, consulting, marketing, investment banking, hedge fund or equity management, entrepreneurship, startups, or venture capital.

Baker and Daginawala (2011) surveyed all allopathic medical schools in the U.S. to identify the number of MD/MPH and MD/MBA degree programs available to medical students. Program directors were contacted to assess the number of MPH or MBA courses of study administratively related to their residencies. Also, a survey was sent to members of the Society of Chairs of Academic Radiology Departments inquiring whether each chairperson had earned an additional degree. Eighty-one allopathic medical schools in the United States offer MD/MPH degrees, and 52 offer MD/MBA degrees. Six residencies in radiology provide access to MPH programs, and three residencies in radiology provide the opportunity to pursue an MBA during residency. Twenty-six percent of the chairs surveyed had advanced degrees other than MDs.

Some have advocated new fellowship programs for medical education. Yarris and Coates (2012) described a two-year educational fellowship in emergency medicine. The goals and objectives for this program are for learners to apply basic concepts of adult learning theory, to employ multiple strategies for effective clinical teaching, to create, implement, and evaluate curricula and enduring educational materials, and to develop an educator's portfolio. They described the necessary steps needed to achieve academic appointment, advancement and promotion as a clinician-educator, function as an academic leader (such as a clerkship director, residency program director, assistant dean, or chair of a national education-related organization or committee). They also described the need for teaching design and implementation of methodologically sound medical education research projects.

Additionally, the popularity of master's of health administration (MHA) degrees has risen considerably in the last several years. The National Center for Education Statistics (2017) reports that 9,254 master's degrees were issued in academic year 2015–2016, which is a 47% increase on the 6,279 degree conferrals in academic year 2009–2010. Also, as of May 2019, gradschools.com lists no fewer than 473 master's programs in health care administration. While no reported summary data yet exists about either the number of physicians or MD students enrolled in health care administration master's programs, the AAMC reports (2019) that 3.5% of medical graduates pursue dual master's degrees or other qualifications and 80 medical schools assist students in pursuing a dual medical doctor/master's of public health degree.

NATIONAL HEALTHCARE LEADERSHIP TRAINING PROGRAM

Guidance can also be gained by examining how national professional associations train health care leaders to prepare for advanced roles. One such long-standing group is the American Association of Physician Leadership (AAPL; formerly the American College of Physician Executives). As part of a Certified Physician Executive credentialing program, the AAPL offers a Fundamentals of Physician Leadership program, approved by the Accreditation Council for Continuing Medical Education, for early-career physicians who are at least three years' post-residency or fellowship. The program, completed by over 3,000 physicians over the last 45 years, provides more than 20 hours of content around the core areas of communication, negotiation, influence, finance, and quality, with the primary goal of establishing a growth-based mindset in leadership roles. Within this training framework, the AAPL incorporates the use of a psychometric assessment, known as DiSC, essentially designed to make professionals more effective in team settings by increasing self-knowledge of conflict responses, motivation, stress triggers, preferred problem-solving styles, communication strategies, and what other team members need to be successful.

Table 3 provides a broad overview of effective practices and areas for consideration. The training process should not be limited to didactics as problem-solving exercises; longitudinal study and research provide a framework for lifelong learning. Deliberate and effective mentorship can play a vital role, both in attracting trainees and aiding career development for future leaders in academic medicine. These elements need to be carefully coordinated and will certainly incur costs, but a well-designed program can address commonly cited gaps in physician training.

CONCLUSION

The development of a leader in academic medicine is a long and complex process. Medical school introduces concepts of teamwork, interdisciplinary communication, and emotional intelligence. Residency provides greater exposure to educational theory and practice, and a variety of opportunities to develop

Table 1. Core competencies for family medicine educators

Leadership
Exhibits integrity, knows self, recognizes and accepts strengths and weaknesses in self and in others
Communicates clearly, openly, honestly, and concisely
Listens to individual's perspectives and encourages individual's initiative and growth
Resolves conflicts, negotiates well, fosters collaboration and cooperation
Establishes trust, values diverse perspectives and talent
Encourages individual initiative, mentors individuals to achieve success
Administration
Communicates effectively in oral, written, and electronic form
Uses technology relevant to one's job
Identifies personal style preferences and how to interact with others
Manages time, sustains one's well-being, balances work and personal needs
Conducts effective meetings with clear agenda and action plan
Plans a career strategy and accurately assesses one's strengths and weaknesses
Works within the confines of mission-based management
Understands ethical underpinnings of one's job and acts accordingly
Teaching
Demonstrates content knowledge
Organizes and conveys major teaching points at a level appropriate to audience
Engages learners, keeps on task, avoids domination
Solicits questions, summarizes main points to reinforce learning
Identifies learner needs
Negotiates learning objectives and selects appropriate teaching methods
Presents a lecture on a clinical or educational topic
Enhances presentation with effective audiovisual aids and handouts
Designs and uses evaluation to make improvements
Uses learner strengths and deficiencies to establish future learning activities
Demonstrates one-on-one teaching
Facilitates small-group sessions
Research
Teaches skills of accessing, analyzing, and applying medical literature to clinical practice
Role models the practice of evidence-based medicine for learner
Becomes an expert in a body of knowledge
Formulates researchable questions; designs, collects, and analyzes data
Evaluates findings and draws conclusions based upon findings
Participates actively as a member of a research team, including statistical consultants
Adheres to guidelines and regulations regarding the ethical conduct of research and use of human subjects
Balances competing faculty obligations to achieve research goals

continued on following page

Table 1. Continued

Leadership
Medical Informatics
Reads and accesses medical literature on the World Wide Web
Evaluates medical literature and translates into clinical and professional practice
Demonstrates basic computer knowledge and skills, utilization of hardware and software
Demonstrates communication skills using e-mail, networking, centralized and distributed integrated systems, multimedia work stations, medical language and classification, database management systems
Understands, teaches, and practices evidence-based medicine
Care Management
Discusses the history and financing of health care, principles of cost control, and resource allocation
Defines principles of shared financial risk among provider, patient, and payor
Discusses increased provider accountability for quality of care delivered, role of reimbursement in influencing care decisions
Teaches vocabulary and principles for effective functioning in managed care organizations (MCOs) and integrated health systems
Acquaints learners with models for assessing performance and delivery
Explains and implements utilization review concepts
Explains and applies concepts of cost-benefit analysis to determine best quality of care at minimum cost
Describes the barriers to health care access
Multiculturalism
Promotes individual self-awareness of multicultural differences and practices nonjudgmental interactions at all levels of medical training and practice
Describes changing demographics of various populations locally and nationally
Identifies the cultural epidemiology of health and illness problems of specific ethnic groups
Meets defined local health needs of selected minority, ethnic, and at-risk populations
Discusses the effects of cultural perspectives on medicine, health, illness-seeking behavior
Advocates for cultural competence in health care organizations and professional groups

From Harris, D. L., Krause, K. C., Parish, D. C., & Smith, M. U. (2007). Academic competencies for medical faculty. *Family Medicine, 39*(5), 343–350.

leadership skills. Residents can further their knowledge through specialized curricula or advanced degrees. Some residency programs offer specific educational tracks, but most do not. Master's-level advanced degree programs are helpful and may accelerate promotion, but are not absolutely essential; the majority of educational leaders do not have advanced degrees beyond their medical degrees. Workshops and other professional development programs are available to junior faculty to further develop their educational skills. Within such programs, the use of psychometric tools such as EI-Q 2.0 and DiSC should be considered important in increasing self-awareness.

Table 2. Resident rotations that provide opportunities for managerial skill development

1. Health system management and operations.
2. Financial management and planning.
3. Quality improvement and safety.
4. Information technology/informatics.
5. Technology transfer.
6. Global strategy and program development.
7. Research enterprise management.
8. Clinical service enterprise management.
9. Supply chain management.

Table 3. Overview of effective leadership development practices

Program and teaching elements	Content/topic areas
Lecture/didactic for baseline content Interactive workshops Supported by e-learning platform Self-assessment tools (EQ-I 2.0, DiSC) Multiple feedback mechanisms Competency-based assessment systems (especially ones that mitigate bias) Sequenced or progressive skills/topics Retreats (off-site, full day) Capstone projects	*Interpersonal skills:* Communication skills Team-building Emotional intelligence Conflict management Crisis management Coaching Stress management/wellness *Health care delivery systems knowledge:* Clinical and hospital operations Checklist debriefing processes Health care finance and insurance Health care policy

REFERENCES

Ackerly, D. C., Sangvai, D. G., Udayakumar, K., Shah, B. R., Kalman, N. S., Cho, A. H., ... Dzau, V. J. (2011). Training the next generation of physician–executives: An innovative residency pathway in management and leadership. *Academic Medicine, 86*(5), 575–579. doi:10.1097/ACM.0b013e318212e51b PMID:21436663

American Association of Physician Leadership. (n.d.). *Fundamentals of Physician Leadership.* Retrieved June 3, 2019, from https://www.physicianleaders.org

American Hospital Association and American Medical Association. (n.d.). *Integrated Leadership for Hospitals and Health Systems: Principles for Success.* Retrieved June 3, 2019, from https://www.ama-assn.org/sites/ama-assn.org/files/corp/media-browser/public/about-ama/ama-aha-integrated-leadership-principles_0.pdf

Association of American Medical Colleges. (2019). *Applying to Dual-Degree Programs.* Retrieved June 3, 2019, from https://students-residents.aamc.org/applying-medical-school/article/directory-md-mph-educational-opportunities

Baker, S., & Daginawala, N. (2011). Leadership training for radiologists: A survey of opportunities and participants in MBA and MPH programs by medical students, residents, and current chairpersons. *Journal of the American College of Radiology*, *8*(8), 563–567. doi:10.1016/j.jacr.2011.02.013 PMID:21807350

Bar-On, R. (2006). The Bar-On model of emotional-social intelligence (ESI). *Psicothema*, *18*(Suppl), 13–25. PMID:17295953

Barzansky, B., & Etzel, S. I. (2011). Medical schools in the United States. *Journal of the American Medical Association*, *306*, 1007–1014. PMID:21900145

Berg, D. N., & Huot, S. J. (2007). Middle manager role of the chief medical resident: An organizational psychologist's perspective. *Journal of General Internal Medicine*, *22*(12), 1771–1774. doi:10.100711606-007-0425-8 PMID:17940827

Biese, K., Leacock, B. W., Osmond, C. R., & Hobgood, C. D. (2011). Engaging senior residents as leaders: A novel structure for multiple chief role. *Journal of Graduate Medical Education*, *3*(2), 236–238. doi:10.4300/JGME-D-10-00045.1 PMID:22655148

Classic, D. I. S. C. 2.0 Profile. (2019). John Wiley & Sons. Retrieved June 3, 2019, from https://www.everythingdisc.com/Home.aspx

Coates, W. C., Lin, M., Clarke, S., Jordan, J., Guth, T., Santen, S. A., & Yarris, L. M. (2012). Defining a core curriculum for education scholarship fellowships in emergency medicine. *Academic Emergency Medicine*, *19*(12), 1411–1418. doi:10.1111/acem.12036 PMID:23279248

Colbert, C. Y., Myers, J. D., Cable, C. T., Ogden, P. E., Mirkes, C., McNeal, T., & Skeen, S. (2012). An alternative practice model: Residents transform continuity clinic and become systems thinkers. *Journal of Graduate Medical Education*, *3*(2), 232–236. doi:10.4300/JGME-D-11-00133.1 PMID:23730447

Coleman, M. C., Blatt, B., & Greenberg, L. (2012). Preparing students to be academicians: A national student-led summer program in teaching, leadership, scholarship, and academic medical career-building. *Academic Medicine*, *87*(12), 1734–1741. doi:10.1097/ACM.0b013e318271cfd6 PMID:23095923

Deane, K., & Ringdahl, E. (2012). The family medicine chief resident: A national survey of leadership development. *Family Medicine*, *44*(2), 117–120. PMID:22328478

Dedy, N. J., Zevin, B., Bonrath, E. M., & Grantcharov, T. P. (2013). Current concepts of team training in surgical residency: A survey of North American program directors. *Journal of Surgical Education*, *7*(5), 578–584. doi:10.1016/j.jsurg.2013.04.011 PMID:24016367

Edler, A., Adamshick, M., Fanning, R., & Piro, N. (2010). Leadership lessons from military education for postgraduate medical curricular improvement. *The Clinical Teacher*, *7*(1), 26–31. doi:10.1111/j.1743-498X.2009.00336.x PMID:21134139

Eubank, D., Geffken, D., Orzano, J., & Ricci, R. (2012). Teaching adaptive leadership to family medicine residents: What? Why? How? *Families Systems & Health*, *30*(3), 241–252. doi:10.1111/j.1743-498X.2009.00336.x 10.1037/a0029689

Frich, J. C., Brewster, A. L., Cherlin, E. J., & Bradley, E. H. (2015). Leadership development programs for physicians: A systematic review. *Journal of General Internal Medicine, 30*(5), 656–674. doi:10.100711606-014-3141-1 PMID:25527339

Goleman, D., Boyatzis, R. E., & Mckee, A. (2004). *Primal leadership: Learning to lead with emotional intelligence.* Boston, MA: Harvard Business School Press.

Griffith, C. H., Wilson, J. F., Haist, S. A., & Ramsbottom-Lucier, M. (1998). Do students who work with better housestaff in their medicine clerkships learn more? *Academic Medicine, 73,* S57–S59. doi:10.1097/00001888-199810000-00045 PMID:9795652

Hanna, W. C., Mulder, D. S., Fried, G. M., Elhilali, M., & Khwaja, K. A. (2012). Training future surgeons for management roles: The resident-surgeon-manager conference. *Archives of Surgery, 147*(10), 940–944. doi:10.1001/archsurg.2012.992 PMID:23117834

Harris, D. L., Krause, K. C., Parish, D. C., & Smith, M. U. (2007). Academic competencies for medical faculty. *Family Medicine, 39*(5), 343–350. PMID:17476608

Institute of Medicine. (2004). *Academic health centers: Leading change in the 21st century.* Washington, DC: National Academy Press.

Jardine, D., Correa, R., Schultz, H., Nobis, A., Lanser, B. J., Ahmad, I., ... Hinds, B. (2015). The need for a leadership curriculum for residents. *Journal of Graduate Medical Education, 7*(2), 307–309. doi:10.4300/JGME-07-02-31 PMID:26221472

Kuo, A. K., Thyne, S. M., Chen, H. C., West, D. C., & Kamei, R. K. (2010). An innovative residency program designed to develop leaders to improve the health of children. *Academic Medicine, 85*(10), 1603–1608. doi:10.1097/ACM.0b013e3181eb60f6 PMID:20703151

Lobas, J. G. (2006). Leadership in academic medicine: Capabilities and conditions for organizational success. *The American Journal of Medicine, 119*(7), 617–621. doi:10.1016/j.amjmed.2006.04.005 PMID:16828636

Malloy, E., Butt, S., & Sorter, M. (2010). Physician leadership and quality improvement in the acute child and adolescent psychiatric care setting. *Child and Adolescent Psychiatric Clinics of North America, 19*(1), 1–19. doi:10.1016/j.chc.2009.08.008 PMID:19951803

Malloy, E., Butt, S., & Sorter, M. (2010a). Physician leadership in residential treatment for children and adolescents. *Child and Adolescent Psychiatric Clinics of North America, 19*(1), 21–30. doi:10.1016/j.chc.2009.08.001 PMID:19951804

Martins, H. M. G. (2010). Why management and leadership education for internists? *European Journal of Internal Medicine, 21*(5), 374–376. doi:10.1016/j.ejim.2010.04.014 PMID:20816587

McCoy, K. L., & Carty, S. E. (2012). There is no "i" in "team": Comment on "a surgical simulation curriculum for senior medical students based on TeamSTEPPS.". *Archives of Surgery, 147*(8), 766–767. doi:10.1001/archsurg.2012.1573 PMID:22911076

Meier, A. H., Boehler, M. L., McDowell, C. M., Schwind, C., Markwell, S., Roberts, N. K., & Sanfey, H. (2012). A surgical simulation curriculum for senior medical students based on TeamSTEPPS. *Archives of Surgery, 147*(8), 761–766. doi:10.1001/archsurg.2012.1340 PMID:22911075

Meurling, L., Hedman, L., Felländer-Tsai, L., & Wallin, C. J. (2013). Leaders' and followers' individual experiences during the early phase of simulation-based team training: An exploratory study. *BMJ Quality & Safety, 22*(6), 459–467. doi:10.1136/bmjqs-2012-000949 PMID:23293119

National Academies of Sciences, Engineering, and Medicine. (2018). *Graduate medical education outcomes and metrics: Proceedings of a workshop.* Washington, DC: The National Academies Press. doi:10.17226/25003

National Center for Education Statistics. (2017). *Bachelor's, master's, and doctor's degrees conferred by postsecondary institutions, by sex of student and discipline division: 2015-16.* Retrieved June 3, 2019, from https://nces.ed.gov/programs/digest/d17/tables/dt17_318.30.asp

Ning, G. D., & Lamdan, R. M. (2009). The chief resident for education: Description of a novel academic teaching position. *Academic Psychiatry, 33*(2), 163–165. doi:10.1176/appi.ap.33.2.163 PMID:19398635

Paller, M. S., Becker, T., Cantor, B., & Freeman, S. L. (2000). Introducing residents to a career in management: The physician management pathway. *Academic Medicine, 75*(7), 761–764. doi:10.1097/00001888-200007000-00025 PMID:10926031

Patel, M. S., Arora, V., Patel, M. S., Kinney, J. M., Pauly, M. V., & Asch, D. A. (2014). The role of MD and MBA training in the professional development of a physician: A survey of 30 years of graduates from the Wharton Health Care Management Program. *Academic Medicine, 89*(9), 1282–1286. doi:10.1097/ACM.0000000000000366 PMID:24979286

Robinson, M., Macneily, A., Afshar, K., McInnes, C., Lennox, P., Carr, N., ... Arneja, J. (2013). Leadership in Canadian urology: What is the right stuff? *Journal of Surgical Education, 70*(5), 606–612. doi:10.1016/j.jsurg.2013.04.013 PMID:24016371

Sanfey, H., Boehler, M., DaRosa, D., & Dunnington, G. L. (2012a). Career Resources Career development resource: Educational leadership in a department of surgery: Vice chairs for education *American Journal of Surgery, 204*, 121–125. doi:10.1016/j.amjsurg.2012.04.003 PMID:22704712

Sanfey, H., Boehler, M., DaRosa, D., & Dunnington, G. L. (2012b). Career development needs of vice chairs for education in departments of surgery. *Journal of Surgical Education, 69*(2), 156–161. doi:10.1016/j.jsurg.2011.08.002 PMID:22365859

Shahid, R. J., Stirling, J., & Adams, W. (2018). Promoting wellness and stress management in residents through emotional intelligence training. *Advances in Medical Education and Practice, 9*, 681–686. doi:10.2147/AMEP.S175299 PMID:30310341

Sherbino, J., Frank, J. R., & Snell, L. (2014). Defining the key roles and competencies of the clinician-educator of the 21st century: A national mixed-methods study. *Academic Medicine, 89*(5), 783–789. doi:10.1097/ACM.0000000000000217 PMID:24667507

Steele, M. M., Fisman, S., & Davidson, B. (2013). Mentoring and role models in recruitment and retention: A study of junior medical faculty perceptions. *Medical Teacher*, *35*(5), e1130–e1138. doi:10.310 9/0142159X.2012.735382 PMID:23137243

Stoller, J. K., Taylor, C. A., & Farver, C. E. (2013). Emotional intelligence competencies provide a developmental curriculum for medical training. *Medical Teacher*, *35*(3), 243–247. doi:10.3109/014215 9X.2012.737964 PMID:23360483

Stringfellow, T. D., Rohrer, R. M., Lowenthal, L., Gorrard-Smith, C., Sheriff, I. H. N., Armit, K., ... Spurgeon, P. C. (2015). Defining the structure of undergraduate medical leadership and management teaching and assessment in the UK. *Medical Teacher*, *37*(8), 747–754. doi:10.3109/0142159X.2014.971723 PMID:25301039

Webb, A. M. B., Tsipis, N. E., McClellan, T. R., McNeil, M. J., Xu, M. M., Doty, J. P., & Taylor, D. C. (2014). A first step toward understanding best practices in leadership training in undergraduate medical education: A systematic review. *Academic Medicine*, *89*(11), 1563–1570. doi:10.1097/ ACM.0000000000000502 PMID:25250751

Weiss, R. L., Hassell, L. A., & Parks, E. R. (2014). Progress toward improved leadership and management training in pathology. *Archives of Pathology & Laboratory Medicine*, *138*(4), 492–497. doi:10.5858/ arpa.2013-0288-RA PMID:24678679

Wright, S., Wong, A., & Newill, C. (1997). The impact of role models on medical students. *Journal of General Internal Medicine*, *12*(1), 53–56. doi:10.100711606-006-0007-1 PMID:9034946

Yarris, L. M., & Coates, W. C. (2012). Creating educational leaders: Experiences with two education fellowships in emergency medicine. *Academic Emergency Medicine*, *19*(12), 1481–1485. doi:10.1111/ acem.12042 PMID:23240922

ADDITIONAL READING

Aluise, J. J., Schmitz, C. C., Bland, C. J., & McArtor, R. E. (1989-1990). Administrative skills for academy physicians. *Journal of Healthcare Education and Training*, *4*(3), 7–13. PMID:10304246

Baumgartner, W. A., & Greene, P. S. (2000). Developing the academic thoracic surgeon: Teaching surgery. *The Journal of Thoracic and Cardiovascular Surgery*, *119*(4, Pt 2), S22–S25. doi:10.1067/ mtc.2000.104721 PMID:10727957

Bellonci, C. (2010). Physician leadership and quality improvement in the acute child and adolescent psychiatric care setting. *Child and Adolescent Psychiatric Clinics of North America*, *19*(1), 1–19. doi:10.1016/j.chc.2009.08.008 PMID:19951803

Butani, L., Paterniti, D. A., Tancredi, D. J., & Li, S. T. (2013). Attributes of residents as teachers and role models – a mixed methods study of stakeholders. *Medical Teacher*, *35*(4), e1052–e1059. doi:10.3 109/0142159X.2012.733457 PMID:23137246

Cordero, L., Hart, B. J., Hardin, R., Mahan, J. D., & Nankervis, C. A. (2013). Deliberate practice improves pediatric residents' skills and team behaviors during simulated neonatal resuscitation. *Clinical Pediatrics*, *52*(8), 745–753. doi:10.1177/0009922813488646 PMID:23671270

Pidikiti, R. D., Marshall, H. E., & Bartolucci, A. A. (1991). Administrative physiatry. *Archives of Physical Medicine and Rehabilitation*, *72*(6), 413–416. PMID:2059110

Rader, M. (2008). Developing leadership skills: A resident's perspective. *Bulletin of the American College of Surgeons*, *93*(10), 21–23. PMID:19469364

Roberts, D. H., Schwartzstein, R. M., & Weinberger, S. E. (2014). Career development for the clinician-educator. Optimizing impact and maximizing success. *Annals of the American Thoracic Society*, *11*(2), 254–259. doi:10.1513/AnnalsATS.201309-322OT PMID:24575995

KEY TERMS AND DEFINITIONS

Constituencies: The group of people involved in or served by an organization.

Feedback: A process in which information about the past or the present influences the same phenomenon in the present or future.

Interprofessional: A group of health care professionals from diverse fields who work together in a coordinated fashion toward a common goal for the patient.

Management: Health information management (HIM) is the practice of acquiring, analyzing, and protecting digital and traditional medical information vital to providing quality patient care by combining business, science, and information technology.

Psychometric Assessment: The process of psychological and mental testing and of a person's psychological traits or attitudes or mental processes.

Self-Awareness: An awareness of one's own personality or individuality.

Simulation: The modern-day methodology for training health care professionals through the use of advanced educational technology. Medical simulation is the experiential learning every health care professional will need but does not necessarily have the opportunity to see in regular practice.

Chapter 8
The Role of Humanities
in Medical Education

Arthur L. Frank
Drexel University, USA

ABSTRACT

This chapter considers the role and value of the study of the humanities in medical education. Most authors on this subject believe the study of the humanities results in a better physician. However, few papers document this almost universally accepted idea. This chapter cites the available literature on the subject and also considers how the study of the humanities has become more common in countries beyond the United States. The study of the humanities is thought to improve physician communication and to influence ethical behaviors, ultimately improving patient care.

INTRODUCTION

A patient presented with a complex oncologic problem, and five teams of oncologists spent considerable time deciding on the best course of treatment for this patient. When the best course was finally agreed upon, the patient was transferred to the ICU for monitoring because of the complexity of the treatment plan and the potential side effects. The ICU attending physician, a professor and anesthesiologist, while doing admission planning for this patient, immediately wrote orders dismissing the care plan, writing a "usual" set of orders and neglected the complex needs of the patient. A young physician, still in his oncologic training, then fought with the attending physician over the discontinuation of the carefully crafted treatment plan. They exchanged words, sometimes at too loud a volume in public. Eventually, the care of the patient went forward as originally planned by the oncologists. The young doctor let it be known that he had challenged the professor because the teams of oncologists had come up with the best plan for his patient, and that plan should be carried out as ordered. But due to his efforts on behalf of his patient, he became concerned that he was in jeopardy. He had gotten into an argument with the professor. Fortunately, no serious negative repercussion resulted. But a more humane and professional approach to this matter, and less grandstanding by the professor, would have made for a better situation. A doctor needs to appreciate situations from the perspectives of the patient and of one's colleagues.

DOI: 10.4018/978-1-7998-1468-9.ch008

This episode highlights that patients now often receive complex and fragmented care and how better care might be given by including humanities training in medical education. Medical education too has become quite complex. Just as this is occurring, the use of electronic medical records often de-humanizes doctor-patient interactions and may more easily perpetuate incorrect medical information due to "cutting and pasting'. Updating medical records to reflect changes in a patient's status may become more difficult. In addition to learning to give traditional inpatient care, physicians now learn to care for patients in outpatient settings, are often taught about the business aspects of medicine, and also included is significant training for physician-scientists, the medical researchers and educators of future generations. As time goes on, the amount of science and technical information to be mastered becomes greater and more complex. But medical education, however demanding, should still include training in the humanities. The successful practice of medicine requires far more knowledge than what students learn in courses on technology and science alone.

The premise offered by this author, and as seen through much of the literature on the subject of teaching humanities in medical education, is that there are benefits from such training in helping to create better physicians. A large amount of literature takes this view, but there is a dearth of studies that actually measure this belief. Ousager & Johannessen (2010) found 245 articles on teaching medical humanities with over 200 praising such coursework. Only ten had a "reserved" attitude, and less than ten actually measured long-term impact.

The humanities fields that may be included as part of medical education include history, literature, sociology, anthropology, philosophy, art and music. Foreign language training can even be included, to increase intercultural understanding. To some degree, this is already occurring. The American Association of Medical Colleges notes that almost all allopathic medical schools in the United States have required courses in the humanities, and a lesser number allow electives rather than requirements. New joint MD/PhD programs have included studies in such fields as anthropology, bioethics, sociology, religion, and health behavior.

The great pathologist Virchow felt that medicine as a discipline is a subset of anthropology, the study of humans. He understood that the study of humans needs to take place in its broadest sense, including the appreciation of attitudes, language, and culture, as well as science and genetics. Until a few decades ago, however, the humanities were not thought to be essential in medical training. Fortunately, this is changing. An elective course offered to medical students at the University of Pennsylvania occurs at the Philadelphia Museum of Art, where students study art in order to sharpen their observational abilities. There is other evidence that humanities training such as this help to create better physicians.

As noted by Jones (2014), literature can assist in seeing the world from a number of perspectives. Poetry, as suggested by Shapiro & Rucker (2003), with other art forms, can have medical students focus on becoming a doctor, or a patient's experience of illness, or the interactions between doctors and patients. Music can focus attention on active listening.

Models of Medical Education

There are two primary contemporary models of medical education. The European model, used in much of Asia as well, takes individuals who have finished their secondary education and puts them through a six- or seven-year period of medical training, with almost all of the curricular activities devoted to various sciences and medical training. The American model of medical education, which has its roots in the Flexner Report, released at the beginning of the twentieth century, requires most physician trainees to attend a college or university for four years of undergraduate education before they attend medical school, from which they graduate with medical degrees. Traditionally, most American medical students have studied one of several sciences, such as biology or chemistry. At American universities, some training in the humanities and a broad range of subjects are usually required no matter what a student's ultimate degree area may be. Admission to medical school, and the testing that goes with that, now better reflect an understanding of humanistic principles and the social aspects of humanity. For reasons not well understood, several authors (Warren, 1984, Schwartz, Abramson, Wojnowich, Accordino, Ronan & Riffkin, 2009) report that students who enter medical school with a humanities rather than a science background perform better as measured by academic grades and national board examination scores.

What Constitutes Humanities in Medical Education?

Most who write about the inclusion of humanities in medical education do not specify what components should be included. Humanities range from literature and arts to music and history, often the history of medicine. They can create better understanding of societal issues and the differences among different ethnic, religious, and cultural groups, which would benefit many physicians. The author has served as an ethics officer in several medical settings and has thus far become aware of the need not to impose one's personal views and beliefs on others. Doctors must recognize that resolving difficult problems in unfamiliar cultural settings requires an understanding of varied cultural norms.

For example, what if two patients in need of a drug, but only one dose is available? If one of the patients is young and the other old, cultural differences might well dictate how this single dose is utilized. In many settings, the dose would be used for a young person, justified by the view that this person has much of their productive life ahead of them. Yet, in cultures in which the old are held in great reverence, the decision might well be to use the medication for the older person, who may be a well-established and revered community leader. Or perhaps, even though a full dose is thought to be needed to cure someone, it may be suggested, in fairness, that the dose be split in half, with the understanding that neither may be cured. For another example, Jehovah's Witnesses are forbidden to accept blood transfusions. Unless physicians have some understanding of varied values in diverse settings, they may well have difficulty providing effective and appropriate care.

The Rationale for the Humanities in Medical Education

Since the 1960s, there have been discussions of the importance of including the humanities in medical education in the United States. Several authors have recently reviewed this issue and changes over time (Bleakley, 2015, Horton, 2019). Potential desired outcomes include making doctors more holistic, ethical, and compassionate, all of which can assist with communication between doctor and patient and among physicians (MacNaughton, 2000). Some authors have written more specifically that students' future work as physicians will be enhanced by the study of literature (Hunter, Charon & Conlehan, 1995) and suggest that the inclusion of literature in medical education promotes a clarity of observation and expression, as well as helping to develop the clinical imagination and perhaps a set of ethical values. Anyone who has read George Bernard Shaw's, *The Doctor's Dilemma*, can appreciate those thoughts. In this work, both a long essay and a play, Shaw, who disliked doctors (and lawyers) writes of the moral decline of putting profits before patients, a phenomenon we see all too often in current American medical practice. When future physicians internalize the teaching of the humanities, they can become better equipped as physicians to combine scientific complexity with cultural sensitivity to their patients. For example, a case of lead poisoning might be caused not by paint, the usual culprit, but by the use of lead-containing cosmetics, even by children, in some Asian cultures. Authors have noted that, while medical education has become scientifically more complex, other skills are needed to perform well in medicine (Cooke, Irby, Sullivan & Ludmerer, 2006). It has been suggested by MacNaughton (2000) that the study of humanities in medical education allows physicians to improve their writing skills, which is highly valuable, as communication through medical records and verbally is an important part of patient care. It may become increasingly difficult to excel at chart notes, however, given the fact that, in many settings, electronic medical records are replacing handwritten records.

There is increasing competition for curriculum time among the various medical specialties. Without a stated commitment to the inclusion of the humanities in medical education, they may well be pushed out. Not only is there an ever-increasing amount of science that must be mastered, but other coursework is intruding into the medical curriculum. Even from a business standpoint, however, humanities education matters because a humane and caring physician is much less likely to be sued for malpractice or have complaints made than a physician who is a poor communicator, regardless of the quality of medical care given (Ha, Anat & Longnecker, 2010, Halperin, 2018). Good communication between patient and physician may well give rise to better medical outcomes, as well (Simpson, Buckman, Stewart, Maguire, Lipkin, Novack & Till, 1991). The Internet and television advertisements have made this aspect of care more difficult, because they sometimes offer misinformation, and humanities training may also help physicians deal diplomatically with issues of patient information and misinformation.

Where Should the Humanities Be Taught within Medical Education?

At one point in his career, this author was the head of a department of preventive medicine and environmental health. He was asked by the dean of the medical school to include training in ethics in the preventive medicine department's curriculum. His rejoinder was that it was entirely inappropriate to segregate such training to one department. It should be a mandate of medical education that all departments teach ethics, patient communication, and other areas affected by the study of the humanities. If only one department discusses this, then ethical issues in medicine will not be seen as a critically important area of medicine, even more so if the department asked to do this is not one of the classically important departments in the eyes of students, such as medicine, surgery, or pediatrics. This prejudicial view has been noted and written about in the scientific literature on medical education. If these aspects of medical education are quarantined, then more humane physicians may not be the outcome. Some have questioned the need for training in these areas over the past fifty years (Reynolds & Carson, 1976), and some writers have concerns that, even if these areas are taught, their segregation from the rest of the medical curriculum may undermine the desired outcomes (Stempsey, 1999).

Along the same lines, some writers have suggested that, when humanities are made voluntary in medical education, then the outcomes improve (MacNaughton, 2000). One author notes, for example, that when medical students take an elective humanities course, they adapt more readily to their work in the dissection laboratory, compared to students who did not (Bertman & Marks, 1985). Yet a clear potential disadvantage of making such courses voluntary is that self-selection will occur. Those who have a strong humanities background or with a more open-minded attitude toward the humanities may be more likely to take such electives, whereas students who maybe in greater need of such education may well opt out.

The Internationalization of Humanities Training in Medical Education

As noted above, the view that the humanities should be included in medical education goes back a considerable period of time in the United States (Reynolds & Carson, 1976). In other countries, it is a newer concept. But already there are places recognizing that students may actually do better in medical school and become better physicians if they incorporate principles gained from the study of humanities into their thinking and actions.

For example, Australian medical education has recently adopted such insights (Gordon, 2005). Similarly, the teaching of humanities in the medical education in Korea has begun (Meng, 2007). Greek educators have made a case for humanities training as well (Batistatou, Doulis, Tiniakos, Anogiannaki & Charalabopoulos, 2010). Canadians have followed their North American brethren with humanities training but find such teaching in conflict with the better regarded evidenced-based approach to medical education. The humanities in Canada are not as systematically taught (Kidd & Connor, 2008). Varied approaches to medical humanities teaching have been documented in both Canada and the United States (Lehman, Kassoff, Koch & Federman, 2004). The British have been concerned about the lack of medical humanities training for some years (McManus, 1995), but are still struggling to elucidate a proper teaching model (Evans & Greaves, 2010). Some in Britain still question the usefulness of humanities education (Blease, 2015).

India represents an interesting case study. As a multicultural society with a longstanding tradition of medical care, medical philosophy, and traditional medicine, as well as deep spiritual traditions, it has only recently begun considering the inclusion of the humanities in its system of medical education. The number of medical schools has grown tremendously there. At the time of partition and the beginning of the modern state of India, there were twenty or fewer medical schools through India, now there are about four hundred. Some have suggested that including the humanities is necessary in India's medical school curricula to counteract what is considered to be dysfunctional behavior among Indian physicians. One example of this is the common but illegal practice of the selective abortions of female fetuses (Mavani, 2007). Some have written about the role of the humanities in Indian medical education with the hope that such studies would create more holistic, compassionate, and ethical physicians (Chattopadhyay, 2007, Reddy, 2009, Gupta, Singh & Kotru, 2011).

Evaluation of the Teaching of Humanities in Medical Education

With the major new focus on the need for teaching humanities in medical education, one might well ask what the literature to date reveals about such teaching. Have outcomes been scientifically evaluated, and if so, what do they reveal? As noted earlier, a detailed literature review by Ousager & Johannessen (2010) found some 245 articles on the teaching of humanities in medical education. Surely there must have been many opportunities for assessment and outcome evaluation, but among these 245 articles, less than ten attempted to review long-term impacts. So, while there is a general consensus that including humanities in medical education is a good idea, there is not yet much scientific evidence available to show that such teaching is beneficial. A paper by Belling (2010) takes issue with Ousager and offers a competing view as to the value that has been proven for humanities training. Doukas, McCollough & Wear (2012) have noted that training in medical ethics and humanities is essential in America and required for accreditation. If scholars believe that it is relevant to teach humanities, which clearly makes some sense, then we need more scientific assessment of the outcomes. The narrower issue of medical-ethics training has had some assessment models developed (Favia, et al., 2013). The work of Hojat, et al. (2002) found that empathy was linked to better clinical performance as a medical student, and more frequently found among females. This raises the issue that outcomes may be somewhat pre-ordained, and dependent on the medical school admissions process.

Although one might wish for better assessments of the effects of the teaching of humanities to medical students, there does not appear to be any rational assessment at all of the effects of teaching many other areas within medicine. It is empirically recognized that students need to learn anatomy and physiology, but other aspects of medical education might not be as well supported. Assessments are needed for all aspects of medical education.

CONCLUSION

Physicians need to gain certain qualities to function more effectively in their generally exalted roles within society. Humanities training can improve their communication skills, ethical behavior, and imagination and could lead to a better understanding of the cultural contexts that their patients inhabit. Aronson (2014) claims that physician empathy leads to increased diagnostic accuracy, better patient outcomes, fewer errors, happier doctors, and more satisfied patients. It is unfortunate that there is not more scientific support to underlie the general recognition that teaching humanities to physicians-in-training is beneficial. Based upon the actions being taken worldwide to teach medical humanities in medical education, and the materials presented in this chapter, it is reasonable to expect that physicians who gain a better understanding of the humanities will do better as medical practitioners.

REFERENCES

Aronson, L. (2014). *The fundamentals of medical training: Every second counts.* Arnold P. Gold Foundation website, accessed July 19, 2019.

Batistatou, A., Doulis, E. A., Tiniakos, D., Anogiannaki, A., & Charalabopoulos, K. (2010). The introduction of medical humanities in the undergraduate curriculum of Greek medical schools: Challenge and necessity. *Hippokratia, 14*(4), 241–243. PMID:21311630

Belling, C. (2010). Commentary: Sharper instruments: On defending the humanities in undergraduate medical education. *Academic Medicine, 85*(6), 938-940. DOI:10.1097/ACM. Obo13e 318dc 1820

Bertman, S. H., & Marks, S. C. Jr. (1985). Humanities in medical education: Rationale and resources for the dissection laboratory. *Medical Education, 19*(5), 374–381. doi:10.1111/j.1365-2923.1985.tb01340.x PMID:4058336

Bleakley, A. (2015). *How the medical humanities can shape better doctors.* London, UK: Routledge. doi:10.4324/9781315771724

Blease, C. (2015). In defense of utility: The medical humanities and medical education. *Medical Humanities, 42*(2), 103–108. doi:10.1136/medhum-2015-010827 PMID:26842744

Chattopadhyay, S. (2007). Religion, spirituality, health and medicine: Why should Indian physicians care. *Journal of Postgraduate Medicine*, *53*(4), 262–266. doi:10.4103/0022-3859.33967 PMID:18097118

Cooke, M., Irby, D., Sullilvan, W. & Ludmerer, K.M. (2006). American medical education 100 years after the Flexner report. *New England Journal of Medicine, 355, 1339-1344. DOI: 055445*. doi:10.056/NEJMra

Doukas, D. J., McCullough, L. B. & Wear, S. (2012). Perspective: Medical education in medical ethics and humanities as the foundation for developing medical professionalism. *Academic Medicine, 87*(3), 334-341. DOI:. 0b013e318244728c. doi:10.1097/ACM

Evans, H. M., & Greaves, D. A. (2010). Ten years of medical humanities: A decade in the life of a journal and discipline. *Medical Humanities, 36*(2), 66-68. DOI:. 2010.005603 doi:10.1136/jmh

Favia, A., Frank, L., Gligorov, N., Birnbaum, S., Cummins, P., Fallar, R., Ferguson, K.... Rhodes, R. (2013). A model for the assessment of medical students' competency in medical ethics. *AJOB Primary Research, 4*(4), 68-83. DOI:. doi:10.1080/21507716.2013.768308

Gordon, J. (2005). Medical humanities: To cure sometimes, to relieve often, to comfort always. *The Medical Journal of Australia, 182*(1), 5–8. doi:10.5694/j.1326-5377.2005.tb06543.x PMID:15651937

Gupta, R., Singh, S., & Kotru, M. (2011). Reaching people through medical humanities: An initiative. *Journal of Educational Evaluation for Health Professions, 8*, 5. doi:10.3352/jeehp.2011.8.5 PMID:21716596

Ha, J. F., Anat, D. S., & Longnecker, N. (2010). Doctor-patient communication: A review. *The Ochsner Journal, 10*, 38–43. PMID:21603354

Halperin, E. C. (2010). Preserving the humanities in medical education. *Medical Teacher, 32*(1), 76–79. doi:10.3109/01421590903390585 PMID:20095779

Hojat, M., Gonnella, J. S., Mangione, S., Nasca, T. J., Veloski, J. J., Erdman, J. B. ... Magee, M. (2002). Empathy in medical students as related to academic performance, clinical competence, and gender. *Medical Education, 36*(6), 533-527. DOI: . 1365-2923.2002.01234.x. doi:10.1046/j

Horton, M. E. K. (2019). The orphan child: Humanities in modern medical education. *Philosophy, Ethics, and Humanities in Medicine. 14*(1), 1. DOI:130-018-0067-y. doi:10.1186

Hunter, K. M., Charon, R., & Conlehan, J. L. (1995). The study of literature in medical education. *Academic Medicine, 70*, 787–794. PMID:7669155

Jones, D. S. (2014). A complete medical education includes the arts and humanities. *AMA Journal of Ethics, 16*(8), 636–641. doi:10.1001/virtualmentor.2014.16.8.msoc1-1408 PMID:25140687

Kidd, M. G., & Connor, J. H. (2008). Striving to do good things: Teaching humanities in Canadian medical schools. *The Journal of Medical Humanities, 29*(1), 45–54. doi:10.100710912-007-9049-6 PMID:18058208

Lehman, L. S., Kasoff, W. S., Koch, P., & Federman, D. D. (2014). A survey of medical ethics education at US and Canadian medical schools. *Academic Medicine, 79*(7), 682–689. doi:10.1097/00001888-200407000-00015

MacNaughton, J. (2000). The humanities in medical education: Context, outcome, structure. *Medical Humanities, 26*(1), 23–30. doi:10.1136/mh.26.1.23 PMID:12484317

Mavani, P. S. (2007). Restructuring medical education. *Indian Journal of Medical Ethics, 4,* 62–63. PMID:18630222

McManus, I. C. (1995). Humanity and the medical humanities. *Lancet, 346*(8983), 1143–1145. doi:10.1016/S0140-6736(95)91806-X PMID:7475609

Meng, K. (2007). Teaching medical humanities in Korean medical schools: Tasks and prospects. *Korean Journal of Medical Education, 19*(1), 5-11. DOI:. 2007.19.1.5. doi:10.3946/KJME

Ousager, J., & Johannessen H. (2010). Humanities in undergraduate medical education: A literature review. *Academic Medicine, 85*(6), 988-998, D0l:. doi:10.1097/ACM.Ob013e3181dd226b

Reddy, M. S. (2009). Humanities in medical education. *Indian Journal of Psychologic Medicine, 31*(2), 57. DOl:. doi:10.4103/0253-7176.63573

Reynolds, R. C., & Carson, R. A. (1976). Editorial: The place of humanities in medical education. *Journal of Medical Education, 51,* 142–143. PMID:1249830

Schwartz, A. W., Abramson, J. S., Wojnowich, I., Accordino, R., Ronan, E. J., & Rifkin, M. R. (2009). Evaluating the impact of the humanities in medical education. *Mount Sinai Journal of Medicine, 76*(4), 372-380. DOl:. doi:10.1002/msj.20126

Shapiro, J., & Rucker, L. (2003). Can poetry make better doctors? Teaching the humanities and arts to medical students and residents at the University of California, Irvine, College of Medicine. *Academic Medicine, 78*(10), 953–957. doi:10.1097/00001888-200310000-00002 PMID:14534086

Simpson, M., Buckman, R., Stewart, M., Maguire, P., Lipkin, M., Novack, D., & Till, J. (1991). Doctor-patient communication: The Toronto Consensus Statement. *British Medical Journal, 303*(6814), 1385–1387. doi:10.1136/bmj.303.6814.1385 PMID:1760608

Stempsey, W. E. (1999). The quarantine of philosophy in medical education: Why teaching the humanities may not produce humane physicians. *Medicine, Health Care, and Philosophy, 2*(1), 3–9. doi:10.1023/A:1009936630946 PMID:11080973

Warren, K. S. (1984). The humanities in medical education. *Annals of Internal Medicine, 101*(5), 697-701. DOl:. 4819-101-5-697. doi:10.7326/0003

Chapter 9
Using the Intercultural Development Inventory (IDI) With First-Year, Pre-Med Students:
Impacting the Human Side of Healthcare

Robin Arnsperger Selzer
University of Cincinnati, USA

Rohan Srivastava
University of Cincinnati, USA

Alexis Huckleberry
Vanderbilt University, USA

ABSTRACT

Medical education emphasizes cross-cultural training programs to meet the needs of diverse patients and understand social determinants of health as root causes leading to healthcare disparities. The question remains about how to best accomplish this in the curriculum. Students in pursuit of medical education need intercultural training early to examine implicit biases, treat the patient not just the disease, and become patient advocates before they practice. This chapter addresses critical issues related to the human side of healthcare. The Intercultural Development Inventory® (IDI®) and accompanying reflection prompts were administered to 40 pre-med students. Findings revealed students overestimated their intercultural understanding and 97.5% had monocultural mindsets. Six themes demonstrated how the IDI® can be used to develop critically reflective future healthcare providers: Reframing Reactions, Lack of Exposure to Other Cultures, Lack of Cultural Self-Awareness, Bi-cultural Identity and Fitting In, Healthcare Connections, and Diversity and University Opportunities.

DOI: 10.4018/978-1-7998-1468-9.ch009

INTRODUCTION AND BACKGROUND

More than 40% of the United States population will be comprised of minorities by 2030; and 20% of the United States population does not currently speak English at home (Price, 2019). Literature in medical education has emphasized the need for cross-cultural training programs to meet the needs of increasingly diverse patient populations (Jernigan, Hearod, Tran, Norris, & Buchwald, 2016). Additionally, training programs that focus on health equity have been recommended to understand social determinants of health as root causes of structurally embedded healthcare disparities (Tervalon & Murray-Garcia, 1998). Social determinants of health are defined as the "conditions in the environments in which people are born, live, learn, work, play, worship, and age that affect a wide range of health, functioning, and quality-of-life outcomes and risks" (Office of Disease Prevention and Health Promotion, 2019). Studies show that 80% of healthcare outcomes involve the influences of social determinants (Heath, 2019). Relatedly, patients often report that these determinants aren't acknowledged, leading them to feel a lack of respect from healthcare providers. Yet the question remains about how to best address these problems. Social determinants of health and health equity are essential topics in the medical school curriculum so students can develop the necessary competencies to reduce health disparities. The long-standing argument is that the science-heavy curriculum is too full to incorporate this material. Wear, Zarconi, Aultman, Chyatte, and Kumagai (2017) purport that the existing medical education curriculum actually inadequately addresses healthcare disparities. Furthermore, she maintains that a "silent curriculum" exists in which individual bias is invisible--and individual bias can affect health outcomes. Attending one-off trainings or including a lecture into coursework will not effectively address this problem (Mgbako, 2019). Intercultural understanding is also not simply acquired with experience as many assume.

The extant medical education literature does not adequately address these topics with pre-med undergraduate students (Lin et al., 2013). This chapter seeks to address that gap as a critical issue related to the human side of healthcare. The authors introduce the use of the Intercultural Development Inventory®, commonly referred to as the IDI®, as an innovative training tool for developing intercultural competence. Findings of this study demonstrate merit for using the IDI® in medical education training programs to increase student's cultural self-understanding, identifying blind spots and implicit biases, and shifting student's mindsets to become more empathetic to cultural differences in others. Empirical evidence has demonstrated that "what happens to students prior to entering medical school affects their performance during medical school and beyond" (Lin et al., 2013). The addition of the IDI ® to curriculums is only one component to a more complete system of medical education; yet when done in the early years of pre-medical education, it can offer students an opportunity to reflect and then develop their cultural readiness before entering medical school. Waiting until students in pursuit of medical education have achieved their goal of becoming a practicing physician is too late. The curriculum must evolve to address the diversity that exists in 21st century healthcare.

Medicine is constantly changing and the 21st century physician will be different than that of the past. When the MCAT underwent its' 5th revision in 2015 to focus on psychological, social and behavioral foundations of behavior, it became clear that addressing the human side of healthcare is a priority. "If members of the professional school admissions committee truly desire humanists, the hard numbers [GPA and test scores] can be but one aspect of the selection process" (Solomon, 2016, p. 17). Becoming the best, most compassionate, and respectful doctor is more than the Flexner report's prescription for rote science memorization (Morris, 2016). The wide acceptance of holistic admissions policies has been one way that medical education has changed to create more diverse environments. "In fields such as healthcare, diversity literally saves lives. Prior research has shown that diversity ensures better access to care, improves the quality of care, and strengthens trust between patients and providers" (Ono, 2016, para 5).

Still, transformation of medical education involves more than changing a test or admission processes. "As more and more campuses incorporate diversity training programs into their undergraduate curriculum, the IDI® is one of the most valid and reliable instruments currently available to the education community to assess the efficacy of such programs" (Wabash College, 2019).

Medical educators should invite lasting change with students by pushing them out of their comfort zones early (Barnes & Souza, 2019). Students pursuing healthcare careers need training to listen to cultural differences while understanding our common humanity, particularly in today's polarized political climate where a lack of civil discourse has been heavily documented. One study documented that patients have approximately 11 seconds to explain the reasons for their visit before they are interrupted by their doctors (Singh Ospina, et al., 2019). Culturally responsive patient care requires active listening. Pre-med students are capable of developing these professional skillsets as early as their freshman year. "This empathy can be learned, and the structure of medical training programs should include more strategies to traverse these differences" (Mgbako, 2019).

Due to the increased emphasis on the human side of healthcare in medical education, more practicing physicians are speaking up and sharing personal reflections about the importance of building trust with patients and connecting across cultural differences. Critical reflection is defined by first identifying gaps in one's knowledge and then seeking ways to close this gap (Ash & Clayton, 2009). Doctors are leading the way by calling into question their own privileges, implicit bias, and behavior. For example, Cohan (2019) writes,

If I truly want to be part of the solution, I need to explore those parts of me that are most unwholesome, embarrassing, unflattering, and generally not discussed in the context of one's career. My goal is to dismantle the insidious thoughts that reinforce a hierarchy based on race, education, and other markers of privilege that separate me from others. These thoughts, fed by implicit bias, are more common than I find easy to admit. Although I know not to believe everything I think, I also know that thoughts guide attention, and attention guides actions. Until I bring to light and hold myself accountable for my own racist tendencies, I am contributing to racism in health care (p. 806).

Medical education training programs that prioritize critical reflection must be created. If physicians know themselves well, they can practice better self-care, in turn affecting the disturbing trend of physician burnout (Ariely & Lanier, 2015). The practice of critical reflection for healthcare providers may even make them more resilient (West et al., 2014). In short, critical reflection is a necessary part of cultivating tough-to-teach 21st century skills like cross-cultural communication that are highly valued in healthcare providers.

The renowned patient advocate and global health expert, Dr. Paul Farmer argued, ''Medical education does not exist to provide students with a way of making a living, but to ensure the health of the community. Physicians are the natural attorneys of the poor, and the social problems should largely be solved by them'' (as cited in Verghese, 2003, para. 6). Given this, it is the authors contention that students in pursuit of medical education should have formal training in intercultural preparation as early as possible. This way they can take the first steps towards examining their implicit biases and prepare to treat the patient and not just the disease. Hopefully this leads to becoming advocates for under-served patient populations (Levinsohn et al., 2017). The concept of implicit bias has gained recent attention in medical education (IHI Multimedia Team, 2017). Implicit bias is something everyone experiences and should therefore be addressed as a concept to be explored in without guilt and with responsibility in mind (Sukhera & Watling, 2018). Additionally, the concept of medical professionalism has evolved to include conduct that protects "patient welfare, patient autonomy, and social justice" (DeAngelis, 2015). With medical education paying increased attention to impacts on the human side of healthcare, the art and science of medicine must come together early. Students can then recognize the importance of being both a scientist *and* a humanist. Seeing patients as fully human requires listening, empathy, critical reflection, and perspective-taking across cultural differences. In summary, this topic is important because increasingly diverse patient populations require that physicians have an understanding of social determinants of health, implicit bias, health disparities and equity, and intercultural understanding to build trust and mutual respect. For physicians to lead in a culturally diverse and globally interconnected world, they need to commit to a lifelong process of critical reflection on the human side of healthcare; and that should begin as early as possible in their medical educational training.

POTENTIAL SOLUTION: IMPLEMENTING CROSS-CULTURAL ASSESSMENTS

Implementation of a cross-cultural assessment tool during the medical education journey can help establish a baseline for developmental growth and be an effective way to promote critical reflection related to diverse patient care. Yet many training programs omit these tools, even though employers consistently state they need employees with excellent soft skills like the ability to adapt, communicate, collaborate, and problem-solve across differences. In fact, intercultural awareness is ranked as #4 in the top 10 work skills needed for the future (Institute for the Future, 2011). However, most people do not receive any formal training or education to become interculturally effective. These skills are now more essential than soft (Blumenstyk, 2019). Students must obtain them during their undergraduate education to sustain the pipeline into medical school and then succeed in the workplace afterwards. With medical schools placing a growing emphasis on soft skills, some form of baseline assessment is necessary.

Cross-cultural assessments typically measure cultural competence. Cultural competence is defined as "having the knowledge, understanding, and skills about a diverse cultural group that allows the health care provider to provide acceptable cultural care" (Giger et al., 2007, p. 100). There are numerous cross-cultural assessments, including but not limited to, Cultural Intelligence (CQ), Inclusive Behaviors Inventory (IBI), Harvard's Implicit Association Test (IAT), and the Intercultural Development Inventory® (IDI®). Situational judgment tests, like the Computer-Based Assessment for Sampling Personal Characteristics (CASPer®), are also used in some medical school admissions and assess soft skills related to cultural understanding such as communication, empathy, equity, and ethics. This being said, the American Council of Education's working group on intercultural learning was charged with researching 20 assessment instruments and concluded that the IDI® was 1 of only 2 assessments that met their standards (Intercultural Development Inventory®, 2019). Moreover, The Society for Education, Training, and Research found that the IDI® was the most widely used assessment tool by professionals in the intercultural field (IDI®, 2019). According to the IDI®'s website, there are over 60 IDI®-related published articles and 80 PhD dissertations completed using the tool.

For the purposes of this research study, authors used the term "cultural humility" with student participants rather than cultural competence because the word "competence" conveys there is an end point. However, actively engaging with cross-cultural learning is a lifelong process of reflection and self-critique that requires humility (Tervalon & Murray-Garcia, 1998)). Cultural humility involves critically reflecting on our limitations as an opportunity to develop rather than trying to become fully competent or an expert in someone else's culture. This critique of cultural competence led to the discovery of the term, "intercultural competence." Bhawuk & Bruslin (1992) said, "To be effective in another culture, people must be interested in other cultures, be sensitive enough to notice cultural differences, and then be willing to modify their behavior" (p. 416). Intercultural competence is defined as appropriate shifting of one's mindset and behavior based on successful navigation and bridging of commonalities and differences to incorporate multiple perspectives into one's worldview. It relates to one's "capacity to generate perceptions and adapt behavior to cultural context" (IDI®, 2019). While the word competence is used, the emphasis is developmental in nature and places onus on the person for intentional growth. The IDI® measures intercultural competence and can help medical educators gain a better understanding of how to achieve diversity and inclusion goals. Corporations, non-profit, organizations, governmental organizations, primary/secondary schools, and colleges and universities use the IDI®. By examining intercultural competency from a developmental perspective, training can be targeted better based on where the individual or group is developmentally situated towards a deeper understanding of cultural differences.

UTILIZING THE IDI® AS A CROSS-CULTURAL ASSESSMENT TOOL

The IDI® is an online psychometric assessment that can be completed in 20 minutes. To be clear, the IDI® is not a personality test or opinion survey. It is a scientific test that calculates developmental mindsets, not typological traits or skills. It costs $12 each for the student version of the assessment. The IDI® centers understanding "culture" as the starting point for all intercultural efforts. Therefore, respondents are asked to think about which culture groups they feel they belong to first. The assessment asks respondents to think of a culture with which you have had personal, direct experience that has shaped how you experience the world. The IDI® includes 50 statements that track rigid to complex thinking patterns about cultural difference and are scored on a five-point Likert agreement scale. After the 50 statements, the IDI® also includes four open-ended contexting questions that allow respondents to describe their intercultural experiences:

Contexting question 1: What is your experience across cultures?
Contexting question 2: What is most challenging for you in working with people from other cultures?
Contexting question 3: What are key goals, responsibilities or tasks you and/or your team have, if any, in which cultural differences need to be successfully navigated?
Contexting question 4: Please give examples of situations you were personally involved with or observed where cultural differences needed to be addressed within your organization, and: • The situation ended negatively—that is, was not successfully resolved. • The situation ended positively—that is, was successfully resolved.

The IDI® must be purchased and administered by a Qualified Administrator (QA). Qualified Administrators also have the ability to add up to six unique multiple-choice questions. One can become a QA by undertaking the Qualifying Seminar which requires taking the IDI® assessment, participating in a debrief, and completing other training materials including authorizing a licensing agreement to use the tool ethically and appropriately. Upon completion of the assessment, a customized, graphic IDI® profile report and an actionable intercultural development plan (IDP) with suggestions for growth are generated by the QA and distributed by email to the respondents. The QA also provides feedback in an individual or group debrief session. An IDI® profile report may not be distributed without feedback. The IDI® profile is confidential unless the respondent shares it.

The IDI® statements are categorized into different constructs that are organized into 1 of 5 orientation scales on the Intercultural Development Continuum (IDC): 1) Denial, 2) Polarization, 3) Minimization, 4) Acceptance, and 5) Adaptation. These orientations explain how individuals and groups make meaning of and behave in their interaction with cultural differences. Orientations move from monocultural/ethnocentric to intercultural/ethno-relative. Monocultural mindsets are characterized by making sense of cultural differences/commonalities based on one's own cultural values/practices. Intercultural mindsets are characterized by making sense of differences/commonalities based on one's own and others culture values and practices. Individual profile results communicate the perceived orientation (PO) where they place themselves and the developmental orientation (DO) where the IDI® actually placed them on the IDC, in order to determine a meaningful difference. The key factor is that people engage difference from their developmental orientation (DO). The IDP gives participants a chance to clarify intercultural goals that are important and leads to positive action plans. Figure 1 illustrates the IDC, provides a brief explanation of each orientation, and distinguishes between monocultural mindsets at the bottom and intercultural mindsets at the top.

Denial is characterized by two parts: disinterest and avoidance. Those in Denial have limited experience with other cultural groups and tend to ignore or avoid cultural difference. Often, they use stereotypes about the cultural other. The goal for those with a Denial orientation is to recognize observable cultural differences like food or music and also behaviors they have in common with other cultures. The following sample IDI® statement illustrates Denial: "People should avoid individuals from other cultures who behave differently." The next IDI® orientation is Polarization. Those placed in Polarization judge differences as "us vs. them." Polarization can be experienced in two ways: Defense and Reversal. Polarization Defense occurs when individuals view their culture as superior and cultural difference as threatening to their own way. Someone in Polarization may agree with the following sample IDI® statement: "Our culture's

Figure 1. Intercultural Development Continuum

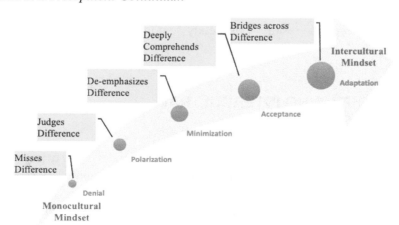

way of life should be a model for the rest of the world." Polarization Reversal is when an individual is overly critical of their own culture and uncritical towards other cultures. This sample IDI® statement, "People from our culture are less tolerant compared to people from other cultures" represents Polarization Reversal. A goal for people in Polarization is to encourage recognition of when they may not fully understand difference and may be overemphasizing it. Minimization is the most common orientation and focuses on cultural similarities and universal values while masking differences. This is a transitional orientation and can take on different meaning depending on one's positioning as part of a dominant or non-dominant group. Dominant groups can hyper-focus on similarities, while non-dominant groups may minimize difference to blend in as a survival strategy. Overall, those in Minimization "go along to get along." A participant in Minimization is likely to agree with the following sample IDI® statement: "Our common humanity deserves more attention than cultural difference." The goal for people in Minimization is to facilitate a deeper cultural self-understanding along with trying to draw out and identify differences.

Acceptance is the first orientation with an intercultural mindset, meaning the cultural values of others are taken into consideration along with their own. Those in Acceptance see commonality amongst cultures and appreciate cultural differences. Difference feels understood, but not fully engaged. They see other's perspective as valid but may still lack the ability to appropriately adapt to cultural difference. Here is a sample IDI® statement that reflects Acceptance: "I evaluate situations in my own culture based on my experiences and knowledge of other cultures." Adaptation is the final intercultural orientation on the IDC. Those in Adaptation value and fully engage cultural diversity while utilizing strategies to adapt their perspectives and behaviors in a culturally appropriate way. This is a sample IDI® statement representing Adaptation: "When I come in contact with people from a different culture, I find I change my behavior to adapt to theirs." In summary, Denial, Polarization, and Minimization orientations are monocultural mindsets. Acceptance and Adaptation orientations are as intercultural mindsets.

In addition to the assignment of orientations, the IDI® calculates a Cultural Disengagement score between 1.0-5.0. Cultural Engagement measures a person's sense of disconnection from their primary cultural group. Those who fall below a 4.0 are classified as unresolved, while participants with scores of 4.0 or higher are classified as resolved. Cultural Disengagement is not part of the IDC. An IDI® sample statement that gauges a participant's Cultural Disengagement is: "I do not identify with any culture, but with what I have inside." In May 2019, the IDI® is making changes and Cultural Disengagement will no longer be included so that the debrief can focus on their developmental orientation. In summary, implementing a cross-cultural assessment tool like the IDI© during the medical education journey is recommended as a first step to address the lack of training and intentional opportunities to critically reflect on diverse patient care. The results of this study demonstrate it is an effective way to bring about desired change.

FINDINGS FROM THE USING INTERCULTRAL DEVELOPMENT INVENTORY IDI®

The primary author of this chapter is a QA and administered the IDI® with 40 first-year, Medical Science majors who identify as pre-med at a large, public, urban research university. All students were enrolled in an Exploring Health Professions course as a required part of their major. The goal was to help them explore how they adapt across cultural differences as future healthcare providers. All research activities were approved by the university's Institutional Review Board. Thirty-nine students signed consent forms to participate. The population was high achieving as measured by admissions criteria to their major including minimum ACT score of 29/SAT score of 1360 and high school GPA of 3.5 or above. They were mindful that there might be a desire to achieve the top point of the IDC continuum. The process was confidential. Participants were not expected to share their results with one another. Ninety-seven percent of participants were ages 18-21. United States was the primary country of citizenship for 92% of participants. 10% of participants had lived in another country for 1-2 years.

After taking the assessment, students received their IDI® results and Individual Development Plan (IDP) by email. They were asked to complete a reflection assignment to 1) consider what their results mean 2) share insights about their goals and challenges, and 3) list 3 intercultural goals they would like to accomplish next. The reflections were made anonymous and used as data. The last step in the research design was to provide a group debrief which is mandated by the IDI®. The group debrief took place in the classroom where group's perceived and developmental orientation, cultural engagement, and con-texting question results were presented. Students were encouraged to discuss their thoughts and feelings about the results and what they plan on doing in response. Using the IDI® provided a shared language.

Figure 2 displays the student's perceived orientations. Figure 3 presents their developmental (actual) orientations. The orientation gap between their perceived and developmental orientation is indicated on a scale of 55-145 in Figure 4. A gap of 7 points on the scale is significant.

These results showed significant overestimation of their developmental orientation and that 97.5% of students have a monocultural mindset. This means they have a less complex perception and experi-ence of cultural difference. Overpredicting one's mindset is common because people generally think of themselves as accepting of others. They equate being exposed to differences as being interculturally competent, especially if they have life experience, have traveled, or moved a lot. Participant 34 illustrated this assumption: *"My family did take frequent vacations, visiting places like Canada, Mexico, France, Germany, Czech Republic etc. I considered myself cultured after being exposed to so many."*

This is why it is important to highlight the IDI® as a developmental tool from the beginning. It is also critical to emphasize the curiosity and humility required in this process upfront. Because the IDI® placed the majority (59.5%) of students in Minimization, the class debrief was helpful in processing that in the United States, many people are raised to believe that *"everyone is equal regardless of race, color, creed, or sexual orientation"* (Participant 29). This can lead to an overemphasis on searching for

Figure 2. IDI® group results: perceived orientation

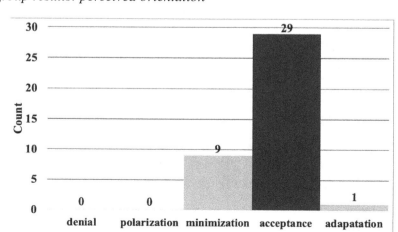

Figure 3. IDI® group results: developmental orientation

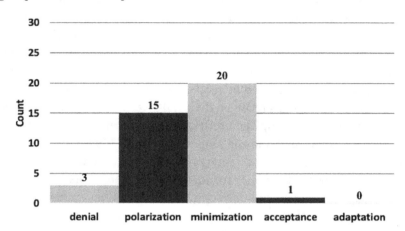

commonalities and downplaying differences. Participant 8 shared a thoughtful reflection on Minimization when stating, *"I still believe the common unity all people share through humanity is important, but I now understand that the recognition of the diversity and differences among cultural values are just as vital, if not more."* Participants need to have time and space to process to critically reflect after they have taken the assessment.

The Cultural Disengagement group score result was 3.76 of 5.0, indicating some lack of connection with a primary cultural community. The pie chart in Figure 5 represents the percentage of individual students who are resolved (no sense of disconnection) and unresolved (sense of disconnection).

Participant 8's cultural engagement score was 3.2 of 4.0 and wasn't surprised. This student stated, *"I've never truly felt a part of any one culture. This lack of belonging is a contributing factor to why I cast cultural distinctions aside at times."*

The QA added 3 additional questions regarding influences on intercultural development, why intercultural awareness is important to their future healthcare career, and whether they think they had a monocultural or intercultural mindset coming into college. The bar chart in Figure 6 shows 50% percent of students said intercultural awareness is important to their future healthcare career because it will allow them to achieve the best health outcomes for patients, indicating that students see the clear connection to their future healthcare careers. The bar chart in Figure 7 shows education was found to have the most significant influence on shaping their intercultural development, with family not far behind. Knowing the influence education has on intercultural growth is important because integration of the IDI® into curriculum could add impact.

Figure 4. Group orientation gap. adapted from group profile ©1998-2019, IDI®, LLC.

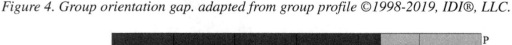

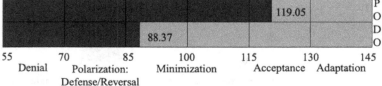

Figure 5. Cultural disengagement results

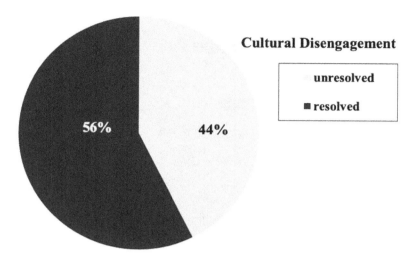

In the final stage of data analysis, authors reviewed reflection responses regarding the student's IDI® results. The three reflection prompts were: 1) consider what your results mean 2) share insights about your goals and challenges, and 3) list three intercultural goals you would like to accomplish next. The responses were analyzed for repetition of key words to identify similarities across experience. Codes were denoted in the transcripts to determine context and as a way to generate themes. Six themes were identified as salient in demonstrating how the IDI® can be used to develop critically reflective future healthcare providers: *Re-framing Reactions, Lack of Exposure to Other Cultures, Lack of Cultural Self-Awareness, Bi-cultural Identity and Fitting In, Healthcare Connections, and Diversity and University Opportunities.*

Figure 6. Reasons to value intercultural development. Adapted from the group profile provided by ©1998-2019, IDI®, LLC

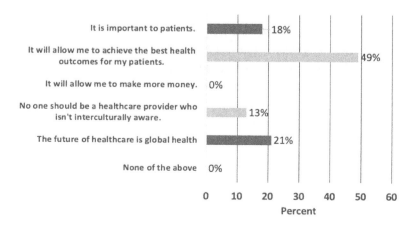

Figure 7. Influences on intercultural development. Adapted from the group profile provided by ©1998-2019, IDI®, LLC

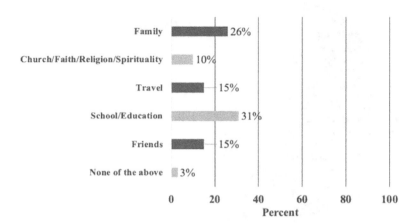

Reframing Reactions

Students experienced an initial uncomfortable reaction to their IDI® results because it was not what they expected. In fact, 28% of students used the word "*surprised*" as their specific reaction. Other reactions included response words like, "*shock, stunned, concerned, upset, appalling, embarrassed, discouraged, confused, insecure, and defensive.*" Participant 12 did not agree with the results. Other students called it "*a wakeup call,*" "*eye opener,*" and "*metaphorical smack in the face*" (Participants 8, 15, 29). For instance, participant 27 said, "*Before this, I believed as long as you acknowledge cultural difference, it was okay to ignore it. I need to learn how to adapt to other people's expectations.*" With the opportunity to reflect, students were able to re-frame the results in a more open-minded way and showed flexibility when changing how they viewed their results. Some even began to agree with their results. For instance, many students conveyed surprise because they thought they were "*a very open person when it came to culture*" or because they "*try to be an inclusive and accepting person*" (Participants 20, 16). Overall, the range of emotions involved some skepticism and nervousness before they took the IDI®, but moved towards a deep interest in the opportunity to grow interculturally. This reframing example is from Participant 7 in Polarization:

When initially reading my IDI® report, I denied the fact that my cultural competence could fall in such an exclusive mindset—one that critically evaluates my own culture or another culture. I do not actively discriminate or regularly compare my own culture and self to the cultures and beings of people around me (especially to people unlike me), but I realized I may subconsciously engage in such prejudices. Trying to find and explanation for this, I considered my upbringing; for my entire youth, I lived in suburbs with people just like me. My neighbors went to the same school as I did, spoke the same language as I did, and had similar backgrounds (in terms of family and experiences) as I did. With an unvaried environment, I understand how I could have slipped in a mindset that polarizes my cultural competence.

A second reframing example from Participant 17 in Minimization represents the common assumption that intercultural awareness just happens without intention:

I felt that I would be higher because I have lived abroad for two years in Turkey, and I have also taken 5 years of Spanish. However, I was only 8 when I lived in Turkey, and most of my life was spent on an Air Force Base surrounded mostly by other Americans. Overall, while I was upset when I originally read the report, I find myself excited for the future, as it means I am not starting off in a bad place, and I can only improve myself from here.

Overall, the fact that first-year pre-medical students were able to reframe their reactions to results as a learning opportunity to grow rather than resisting and shutting down was one of the most significant and promising outcomes of the study. Evidently, they may be a desirable population to work with on this topic because of their strong motivation to achieve as illustrated by Participant 21's reflection: "*I am going to try to hold on to my indignation from when I first got my results and strive to improve myself instead of remaining stagnant.*" Intercultural growth includes personal discomfort and medical educators must ask their students to rise to the occasion.

Lack of Exposure to Other Cultures

Many students cited an absence of surprise at their results due to lack of exposure to cultural difference prior to coming to college. *For instance, Participant 30 "grew up in a homogenous region"* and Participant 13 *shared, "because I grew up in a predominantly White, Christian atmosphere without much exposure to other cultures, I can partially understand these results."* Participant 16 even cited the media: "*I am not surprised by my results. I recognize I have a level of cultural ignorance due to where I lived, how I was raised, and ideas imprinted on me by the media growing up.*" Again though, students were able to reframe their results as a learning and growth experience.

This quote exemplifies how Participant 14 took accountability for the results despite a lack of exposure to cultural differences:

My first reaction was to make excuses for myself. I come from a small town, where everyone is primarily White, straight, middle-class, and Republican. I tried to tell myself that I haven't been exposed to cultures to possess an intercultural mindset. But then I realized I can't make excuses because there are all kinds of cultures out there. Men and women deal with situations differently. There are mannerisms that older people care about more than younger generations that I have witnessed in my part-time high school job. Just because where I grew up isn't considered racially diverse doesn't mean I have any reason not to develop an intercultural mindset.

Some students indicated they need additional support on how to navigate communicating across difference. For example, Participant 5 stated, "*A lot of the time a conversation with someone of a different culture is difficult because I don't know the right questions to ask or I don't want to offend the person.*" Still others realized culture is more than surface-level objective artifacts when saying, "*I want to learn more about other cultures on a deeper level than just how they eat and dress*" (Participant 14). Many students cited their lack of exposure to racial diversity in particular and named being from predominately White backgrounds. In the end, cultural "other" awareness was recognized as important and the desire to see new perspectives showed the development of empathy.

Lack of Cultural Self-Awareness

"Before now I never really thought about my own culture" (Participant 5). *"I never previously thought about what my culture was and how it affected me"* (Participant 26). *"I don't really know what my own culture is"* (Participant 28). Different than the lack of exposure to other cultures, these quotes were indicative of another salient theme, lack of cultural self-awareness. Students who fell into this category realized they *"need to be aware of what is important to me and how my culture has influenced my worldviews before I can begin to understand other cultures"* (Participant 17). Participant 18 wanted *"to look further into how my culture treats other cultures"* and provided examples of joining cultural affinity groups on campus like the Muslim Student Association. Participant 15 expressed a desire to *"travel around Ireland to truly understand where my family comes from, and how growing up Irish Catholic has affected me into the present day."* Participant 25 explored more dimensions of cultural self-awareness when stating,

The most important thing I need to do is feel connected to a culture before I can fully comprehend other cultures. Therefore, to connect to a culture I need to look deeper than my ethnicity. Currently one of the most significant aspects is my sexual orientation. Being bisexual I feel most connected to the LGBT community. Throughout my time at the university, I want to get more involved in this community, so I can have a group of people like me. Once I have a group that I relate to, I will be able to better comprehend other culture.

Participant 12 mentioned, *"College is the first time I have actually formed relationships with people of other cultures, because where I'm from, there aren't other cultures."* The premise of the IDI® is every individual has a culture(s). These reflection prompts are part of the debrief process and provide an opportunity to discuss how students define their own culture. It might also be an opportunity to discuss how students might conflate culture with race or ethnicity. According to American Association of Medical Colleges [AAMC] (2018), about half (49.6%) of United States medical school matriculants self-identify as White. It would be interesting to determine if they also self-identify with White culture or acknowledge the homogeneity of their experiences as many have done in this study.

Without taking the IDI®, students would not have been faced with having to ask themselves these tough questions about their own culture. Participant 25 shared, *"Taking the IDI® caused me to truly think about how I view other cultures and how I even look at my own culture."*

Bi-cultural Identity and Fitting In

23% of participants identified as having a bi-cultural identity. In some cases, having a bi-cultural identity led participants to overpredict their intercultural awareness. For example, Participant 20 stated, *"I am influenced by Indian and American cultures heavily, making it seem as if I would have a much higher developmental orientation score."* Participant 22 shared, *"Growing up in a household that grappled with balancing both Pakistani and American culture, I learned to be accepting of others as I understood the struggle of formulating an identity from two contrasting cultures."* Having a bi-cultural identity also played a role in processing why students may view one culture as superior over another. Participant 21 explains how bi-cultural identity can feel contradicting and makes sense of the Polarization mindset:

I am now more aware that I see my Korean culture and American culture separately which probably is where the us versus them judgment came from. I was immersed in the Korean culture at home and at church while I was immersed in the American culture at school. I spend almost every summer in Korea and have a chance to really feel the culture in its origin. The experiences were really separate from each other and did not mix really well. The fact that my experiences with each culture were completely separate probably contributed to my developmental orientation. I need to challenge myself to bridge the differences in between them.

Participant's ownership of this identity helped process the results, particularly how the Minimization mindset overemphasizes similarities and downplayed differences. For instance, several students cited the interplay of national identities as Americans and ethnic backgrounds as Indian or Pakistani as leading them to constantly adapt to "fit in." Participant 1 shared,

These results reflect my own complicated history with integrating the different American culture that I grew up with everywhere and the Indian culture that followed me home whenever I visited India. Minimization occurs as a way to navigate different values and practices created by the dominant culture and this is why I struggled when I was younger. I would accept certain beliefs or ideas in school to 'get along' while trying to connect them to what I was told at home and because of that I masked the unique qualities teach culture has.

Participant 2 said,

Being that I was born into a Muslim household, the expectations for me differed between home, school, and friends—and I was many different people being pulled along. Because I was always surrounded by differences, I tried to find similarities between the people in my life to feel like there wasn't such a gap between what was expected of me and who I was depending on where I was.

Minimization is the most common orientation and is meant to be a transitional developmental stage. This approach of minimizing differences to blend in can be a survival strategy.

Healthcare Connections

Several students made the explicit connection between healthcare and intercultural awareness in their reflections. They addressed intercultural awareness as *"vital for providing quality healthcare"* (Participant 16). For example, Participant 7 opened the reflection by stating,

The concept of cultural competence in a medical setting proves itself a fundamental foundation for providing and encouraging proper patient care. One's religion, skin tone, accent, culture, orientation, and identification should never affect the distribution of individualized, reliable, and effective healthcare. As a future medical professional, I aim to increase my cultural competence so that I may perform my duties with utmost inclusiveness and the least biases.

Participant 10 stated, *"The ability to give the same care despite cultural, social, age or gender differences seems to me to belong in the category of medical professionalism."* This focus on uniform and equal treatment of patients indicates further conversation about health equity, but still showed progress in their thinking. Participant 10 made the connection between intercultural awareness and building trust with future patients:

My goal as a healthcare professional is to provide care to all individuals in a way that they are comfortable and don't have to worry about trusting me. I want my patients' only concern to be about improving their health. I don't want them to have to worry about any sort of disparity concerning their health on account of any cultural, social, gender age, difference. As a doctor, I will be seeing many different people from different cultures. My number one goal is to make sure every patient is comfortable and well taken care of. Having an intercultural mindset will be imperative in this goal.

This type of mature concern as a freshman points to the promise the IDI® has for developing future healthcare providers who identify as patient advocates. It is also worth noting that a few students made healthcare connections to global health. For example, Participant 8 stated, "*The future of health is global health. Mastering a global health mindset is incredibly important to being a health professional in this day and age.*"

Diversity and University Opportunities

Students in this study were enrolled in a large, public urban, research university. Therefore, many of them discussed exposure to the university's *diversity as an opportunity to help them grow in their intercultural awareness. For example, students commented that the university "*is the perfect backdrop because of how ethnically diverse it is*" (Participant 1). Participant 29 stated, "*It wasn't until I arrived here at the university that I began to experience what diversity truly meant.*" The word "diversity" is denoted with an asterisk above because of the difference between the perception versus reality of diversity. In terms of race and ethnicity, the demographic data indicates the composition of Associate's and Baccalaureate degree-seeking students was 75% White; while 19.5% of faculty were considered minorities (University of Cincinnati's Office of Equity and Inclusion, 2018). Another student declared that "there are so many international students." The University of Cincinnati's Office of Institutional Research (2018) cites 7.7% of students are international students. Often dominant group cultures perceive that a large amount of diversity exists, but those in a minority culture do not experience the same perception. Sometimes perception can be the reality though. Therefore, what matters for the goal of this study is that the students thought that being at a university would allow them to take action on their intercultural growth. For instance, Participant 25 compared a lack of past exposure to difference to current opportunities:

I went to a predominantly White high school which caused me to experience practically no cultural diversity. Due to this, I was never able to fully develop intercultural competence while in high school. I can look back on this now and see what was wrong with that, but at the time I thought it was normal to go to school with people that are all the same. Now being at a university with significant amount of diversity, I will be able to improve my intercultural competence.

Overall, the size of campus is an advantage for allowing exposure to other cultures and as Participant 14 noted, "*Hopefully, attending a large school will give me many opportunities to meet many people from different cultures.*" In addition, opportunities to study abroad may be enhanced as a result of being at a large, public, research university as well.

Finally, students were asked what they would do next to grow in their intercultural awareness and to set 3 actionable goals to increase accountability. This aligned with the goals of the IDP which helps the participant understand that it's not only about what orientation the IDI® placed them in, but what they are committed to doing to develop their intercultural growth. Thus, the agency is on them. The IDP furthers the reflective process and specifies that 30-50 hours of concentrated effort can move people forward into a new orientation. Since many of the students made reference to a lack of exposure to other cultures and the IDI® placed the majority of them in Minimization, it made sense that most students' intercultural goal was to "*get out of their comfort zone*" and intentionally gain more interaction and engagement with cultures different than their own in a respectful way (Participant 20). Students wanted to attend programs and events and named LGBTQ, Hispanic, African American, and Indian cultural communities specifically, along with socioeconomically different youth. Traveling or study abroad ranked second highest with students noting place like Columbia, Africa, and Northern Asia as potential destinations. Participant 29 showed a depth of critical reflection related to this goal when saying,

I plan to research where I am travelling before stepping on the soil. My greatest fear is that I will be viewed as the stereotypical American tourist: someone who expects everyone to speak English, expects a McDonalds on every corner, and who views other cultures as taboo. I am going to do everything in my power to go in with an open mind and heart to every country.

Next many students wanted to deepen their own cultural self-awareness" (Participant 28). Some also cited reading more books, paying more attention to international news, or exploring arts, film, and music to understand cultural differences. Finally, a few students mentioned work on not making assumptions or using stereotypes. The goal setting reflection paired with the IDP supports the initiation of intercultural development efforts and is an important part of the assessment process.

FUTURE RESEARCH DIRECTIONS, LIMITATIONS AND RECOMMENDATIONS

There are limitations in this study. If the IDI® was administered to pre-med students at another type of university or from a population not considered 'high-achieving', their reflection on opportunities for intercultural growth might be different. While the participation rate was very high, another limitation is the small number of participants. As a mixed method study, the intent of this study was not to generalize findings from this pre-med sample, but rather to use this sample to describe how gaps in undergraduate and graduate medical school curriculums can be addressed using the IDI®. These results provide foundational knowledge from which further research can be developed. Finally, the IDI® must be ordered and administered by a QA. Institutions need to be willing to spend funding to hire a QA or to send a person to training. While this study explored use of the IDI®, it is only one example of the benefits of using a cross-cultural assessment tool to expand curricula. Other tools may be used as well.

Overall, participants were glad they took the assessment. They said things like:

- *I view my results as a baseline from which I can grow in my future career as well as in my life in general. I am excited to take my newfound awareness and implement my intercultural goals into my life* (Participant 8)
- *I am glad I got this information at this point in my education and in my life, so that by the time I get to the healthcare field, I can find myself being more aware and considerate of others from various backgrounds, as well as using my relative privilege to become an advocate for those in need of care* (Participant 30).

Therefore, it is recommended that future research studies like this be replicated, and a pre-and-post test of the IDI® be conducted so intercultural growth could measure progress over time. For example, it could be administered during undergrad, medical school, into residency, and even practice.

CONCLUSION

Below are key take-aways from this chapter:

1. The capacity for critical reflection is important in medical education. The results of this study reveal that students can develop this skill as early as their freshman year. They are capable of analyzing and re-framing their reaction in accordance with developmental feedback about their intercultural growth. This demonstrates flexibility and resilience. They also see the direct connection between intercultural understanding and their future healthcare careers treating a diverse patient population.
2. Practicing humility is a necessary part of intercultural development and growth. The results of this study signify that students can also exhibit this skill early. The philosophy behind the IDI® tool aligns with prioritizing humility because most respondents overestimate their intercultural developmental (actual) orientation. The concept of humility can be viewed as counter cultural in medical education because of the emphasis on training to become fully competent medical experts who shy away from acknowledging mistakes or failure.
3. The majority of students in this study overestimated their intercultural awareness, but also used it as an opportunity for growth. Most students were in Minimization and mentioned coming from homogenous backgrounds. Students in pursuit of medical education need early exposure to cultural diversity because the results of this study indicate many have been raised with a focus on treating people equally, which can lead to over-focusing on similarities. Exposure to perspective-taking of the cultural other can increase empathy and support future patient advocacy. These findings reinforce the importance of the holistic admissions process to increase diverse environments in medical education. Prior to coming to college, education was found to be the most significant influence shaping intercultural development. This carries forward as the university has been identified as an opportune place to intentionally take accountability for exposure to cultural difference.
4. Students with a bi-cultural identity may experience a struggle and overemphasize similarities as a way to fit in with the dominant culture.
5. Students in pursuit of medical education need time and space to develop their own cultural self-understanding. How can they achieve a deeper understanding of other cultures if they feel confused about which culture(s) they belong to?

6. The incorporation of an assessment tool in intercultural understanding is needed in medical education curriculums to determine baselines and benchmarking of growth over time. Because 31% of students remarked that education shaped their intercultural development before college, using the curriculum to continue that type of development makes sense. This study has shown that high-achieving students are motivated to intentionally develop their intercultural proficiency because of their drive for self-improvement.

All of these points relate to changes needed in medical education training programs and systems and impact the human side of healthcare. If medical education aims to improve the quality of diverse patient care and outcomes through creating self-aware physician leaders able to work across difference in today's polarized climate, it needs to evolve. What better time to explore these issues with students than as early as possible in their medical education journey? The expectation for future physicians can be set forward from the onset of the college experience. Conducting a cross-cultural assessment, like the IDI®, with students in pursuit of medical education can be a first step. This study has shown the efficacy of using the IDI® to provide an opportunity to pre-med students for critical reflection of their own intercultural experiences. This finding elucidates the influence the IDI® can have on the personal and professional development of future physicians. This significantly impacts their learning about human side of healthcare.

ACKNOWLEDGMENT

This research was supported by Central Association of Advisors in the Health Professions with a $500 research grant. The IDI® costs were covered by a University of Cincinnati Equity and Inclusion grant.

REFERENCES

American Association of Medical Colleges. (2018). Matriculants to U.S. medical schools by race, selected combinations of race/ethnicity and sex, 2015-2016 through 2018-2019. Retrieved from https://www.aamc.org/download/321474/data/factstablea9.pdf

Ariely, D., & Lanier, W. L. *Disturbing trends in physician burnout and satisfaction with work-life balance: Dealing with malady among the nation's healers.* doi:// doi:10.1016/j.mayocp.2015.10.004

Ash, S. L., & Clayton, P. H. (2009). Generating, deepening, and documenting learning: The power of critical reflection in applied learning. *Journal of Applied Learning in Higher Education, 1*(1), 25–48.

Barnes, E., & Souza, T. (2019). Intercultural dialogue partners: Creating space for difference and dialogue. Retrieved from https://www.facultyfocus.com/articles/teaching-and-learning/intercultural-dialogue-partners-creating-space-for-difference-and-dialogue/

Bhawuk, D., & Bruslin, R. (1992). The measurement of intercultural sensitivity using the concepts of individualism and collectivism. *International Journal of Intercultural Relations, 16*(4), 413–436. doi:10.1016/0147-1767(92)90031-O

Blumenstyk, G. (2019). Do your academic programs actually develop 'Employability'? There's an assessment for that. Retrieved from https://www.chronicle.com/article/Do-Your-Academic-Programs/246120

Cohan, D. (2019). Racist like me - A call to self-reflection and action for white physicians. [doi]. *The New England Journal of Medicine, 380*(9), 805–807. doi:10.1056/NEJMp1814269 PMID:30811907

DeAngelis, C. D. (2015). Medical professionalism. *Journal of the American Medical Association, 313*(18), 1837–1838. doi:10.1001/jama.2015.3597

Giger, J., Davidhizar, R. E., Purnell, L., Harden, J. T., Phillips, J., & Strickland, O. (●●●). American academy of nursing expert panel report: Developing cultural competence to eliminate health disparities in ethnic minorities and other vulnerable populations. *Journal of Transcultural Nursing, 18*(2), 95–102. doi:10.1177/1043659606298618

Hammer, M. R. (2011). Additional cross-cultural validity testing of the Intercultural Development Inventory. *International Journal of Intercultural Relations, 35*(4), 474–487. doi:10.1016/j.ijintrel.2011.02.014

Heath, S. (2019). Hospitals need targeted plan for social determinants of health. Retrieved from https://patientengagementhit.com/news/hospitals-need-targeted-plan-for-social-determinants-of-health

Institute for Healthcare Improvement Multimedia Team. (2017). How to reduce implicit bias. Retrieved from http://www.ihi.org/communities/blogs/how-to-reduce-implicit-bias

Institute for the Future. (2011). Future working skills 2020. Retrieved from http://www.iftf.org/future-workskills/

Intercultural Development Inventory®. (2019). IDI general information: external, prestigious reviews of the IDI. Retrieved from https://idiinventory.com/generalinformation/external-prestigious-reviews-of-the-idi/

Jernigan, V. B., Hearod, J. B., Tran, K., Norris, K. C., & Buchwald, D. (2016). An examination of cultural competence training in US medical education guided by the tool for assessing cultural competence training. *Journal of Health Disparities Research and Practice, 9*(3), 150–167. PMID:27818848

Levinsohn, E., Weisenthal, K., Wang, P., Shahu, A., Meizlish, M., Robledo-Gil, T., ... Berk-Krauss, J. (2017). No time for silence: An urgent need for political activism among the medical community. *Academic Medicine: Journal of the Association of American Medical Colleges, 92*(9), 1231–1233. doi:10.1097/ACM.0000000000001724 PMID:28422815

Lin, K. Y., Parnami, S., Fuhrel-Forbis, A., Anspach, R. R., Crawford, B., & De Vries, R. G. (2013). The undergraduate premedical experience in the united states: A critical review. *International Journal of Medical Education, 4*, 26–37. doi:10.5116/ijme.5103.a8d3 PMID:23951400

Mgbako, O. (2019). The unicorn. *Journal of the American Medical Association, 321*(2), 149–150. doi:10.1001/jama.2018.21048 PMID:30644986

Morris, N. P. (2016, May 12). It's time to retire premed. Retrieved from https://blogs.scientificamerican.com/guest-blog/it-s-time-to-retire-premed/?redirect=1

Office of Disease Prevention and Health Promotion. (2019). Social determinants of health. Retrieved from https://www.healthypeople.gov/2020/topics-objectives/topic/social-determinants-of-health

Oliveira, A. C. P., Machado, A. P. G., & Aranha, R. N. (2017). Identification of factors associated with resilience in medical students through a cross-sectional census. *BMJ Open, 7*(11). doi:10.1136/bmjopen-2017-017189 PMID:29133319

Ono, S. J. (2016, April 1). Holistic admissions: What you need to know. *The Association of Governing Boards - Trusteeship, 24.* Retrieved from https://agb.org/trusteeship-article/holistic-admissions-what-you-need-to-know/

Price, M. (2019, Feb. 7). How do you say 'Culturally competent care' in Korean? Retrieved from https://medium.com/@mirissaprice/how-do-you-say-culturally-competent-care-in-korean-3cadf7a5eac6

Singh Ospina, N., Phillips, K. A., Rodriguez-Gutierrez, R., Castaneda-Guarderas, A., Gionfriddo, M. R., Branda, M. E., & Montori, V. M. (2019). Eliciting the patient's agenda- secondary analysis of recorded clinical encounters. *Journal of General Internal Medicine, 34*(1), 36–40. doi:10.100711606-018-4540-5 PMID:29968051

Solomon, H. F. (2016, June). Pre-professional health advising in the eighties. *The Advisor, 36*(2), 15–17.

Sukhera, J., & Watling, C. (2018). A framework for integrating implicit bias recognition into health professions education. *Academic Medicine: Journal of the Association of American Medical Colleges, 93*(1), 35–40. doi:10.1097/ACM.0000000000001819 PMID:28658015

Tervalon, M., & Murray-Garcia, J. (1998). Cultural humility versus cultural competence: A critical distinction in defining physician training outcomes in multicultural education. *Journal of Health Care for the Poor and Underserved, 9*(2), 117–125. doi:10.1353/hpu.2010.0233 PMID:10073197

University of Cincinnati's Office of Equity and Inclusion. (2018). Diversity datapoints. Retrieved from https://www.uc.edu/inclusion/latest/diversitydata.html

University of Cincinnati's Office of Institutional Research. (2018). Student diversity & internationalization. Retrieved from https://www.uc.edu/provost/about-us/peopleandoffices/institutional_research/institutional-dashboards/student-data/student-diversity.html

Verghese, A. (2003, Sept. 14). A season in hell. *The New York Times*, pp. 7007011. Retrieved from https://www.nytimes.com/2003/09/14/books/a-season-in-hell.html

Wabash College. (2019). Using the intercultural development inventory to assess liberal arts outcomes. Retrieved from https://www.wabash.edu/news/displaystory.cfm?news_ID=2646

Wear, D., Zarconi, J., Aultman, J. M., Chyatte, M. R., & Kumagai, A. K. (2017). Remembering freddie gray: Medical education for social justice. *Academic Medicine: Journal of the Association of American Medical Colleges, 92*(3), 312–317. doi:10.1097/ACM.0000000000001355 PMID:27580436

West, C. P., Dyrbye, L. N., Rabatin, J. T., Call, T. G., Davidson, J. H., Multari, A., & Shanafelt, T. D. (2014). Intervention to promote physician well-being, job satisfaction, and professionalism: A randomized clinical trial. *JAMA Internal Medicine, 174*(4), 527–533. doi:10.1001/jamainternmed.2013.14387 PMID:24515493

ADDITIONAL READING

Hammer, M. R. (2008). The Intercultural Development Inventory® (IDI®): An Approach for assessing and building intercultural competence. In M. A. Moodian (Ed.), *Contemporary leadership and intercultural competence: Understanding and utilizing cultural diversity to build successful organizations.* Thousand Oaks, CA: Sage.

Hammer, M. R., Bennett, M. J., & Wiseman, R. (2003), The Intercultural Development Inventory®: A measure of intercultural sensitivity, in R.M. Paige (Guest Editor), Special Issue on the Intercultural Development Inventory®, International Journal of Intercultural Relations, 27, 421-443.

Kruse, J. A., Didion, J., & Perzynski, K. (2014). Utilizing the Intercultural Development Inventory® to develop intercultural competence. *SpringerPlus*, *3*(1), 334. doi:10.1186/2193-1801-3-334 PMID:25077059

Paige, R. M. (2004). Instrumentation in Intercultural Training. In D. Landis, J. M. Benett, & M. J. Bennett (Eds.), *Handbook of intercultural training* (3rd ed., pp. 85–128). Thousand Oaks, CA: Sage. doi:10.4135/9781452231129.n4

Sklar, D. P. (2018). Cultural Competence. *Academic Medicine*, *93*(9), 1259–1262. doi:10.1097/ACM.0000000000002322 PMID:30153157

Sptizberg, B. H., & Changnon, G. (2009). Conceptualizing intercultural competence, in D. Deardorf (Ed), The Sage Handbook of Intercultural Competence (1-52), Thousand Oaks, CA: Sage.

Stuart, D. (2009). Assessment instruments for the global workforce. In M. A. Moodian (Editor). Contemporary leadership and intercultural competence (175-190). Thousand Oaks, CA: Sage. doi:10.4135/9781452274942.n14

Williams, D. R., & Mohammed, S. A. (2013). Racism and Health I: Pathways and Scientific Evidence. *The American Behavioral Scientist*, 57(8), . doi:10.1177/0002764213487340

KEY TERMS AND DEFINITIONS

Cultural Competence: Having knowledge, understanding, and skills to work effectively with diverse cultural groups.

Diversity: The presence of difference or representation in an organization.

Empathy: Connecting with a feeling inside of yourself to feel with other people.

Health Disparities: Preventable differences in health across many dimensions including race, age, gender, sexual orientation, class etc.

Implicit Bias: Unconscious prejudice and stereotyping of people.

Inclusion: Making sure diverse people count, feel valued and engaged.

Self-reflection: Introspective exploration of thoughts and feelings.

Social Determinants of Health: Conditions where people work, live, play, and pray that affect their health.

Social Justice: Equitable distribution of wealth, opportunities, and privileges.

Chapter 10
Transition Courses in Medical School

Vinita C. Kiluk
University of South Florida Morsani College of Medicine, USA

Alina R. Zhu
University of South Florida Morsani College of Medicine, USA

Antoinette C. Spoto-Cannons
University of South Florida Morsani College of Medicine, USA

Dawn M. Schocken
University of South Florida Morsani College of Medicine, USA

Deborah J. DeWaay
 https://orcid.org/0000-0002-4755-6714
University of South Florida Morsani College of Medicine, USA

ABSTRACT

Across the nation, many medical schools have begun to include short courses during key transition points in the curriculum to help prepare students to succeed in the new area where they will be learning. This chapter introduces the reader to these "transition courses" that were not a part of medical education 20 years ago. These courses utilize combinations of high- and low-fidelity simulation, standardized patients, small group sessions, team-based learning and didactics. The authors explore four key transition areas that have seen an influx of these short courses: Orientation to Medical School, Return to Clerkship, Orientation to Clerkship, and Capstone or Boot camp. Each of these four courses is examined in content and relevance in preparing the medical student for the transition in their academic career.

DOI: 10.4018/978-1-7998-1468-9.ch010

INTRODUCTION

It has been recommended that a transition course "should help in developing the coping skills (the student) need(s) to effectively deal with the challenges presented by new environments" (Teunissen 2011); otherwise, the course may not advance the students learning in an effective way. This chapter endeavors to familiarize the reader with this discourse. Throughout this chapter a review of the literature specific to each type of course will be described. Despite a paucity of scholarship of these courses in general, their emersion is not surprising. Dreyfus described the Five-Stage Model of Adult Skill Acquisition to include the novice, the advanced beginner, the competent learner, the proficient and the expert. This model has been applied to medical education across the spectrum from medical student to attending physician. However, if it were to be applied to being a medical student, one could argue that the first-year medical student is the novice and the graduating senior, although still a novice clinician, should either be a proficient or expert medical student. These courses fall in the natural transitions where student would be transitioning from one developmental phase of being a medical student to another.

In designing new transition courses, medical schools should consider the course's goals, objectives, and what would be of value to the student. As with any other course, a needs assessment must be done. Extraneous or redundant material should not be included, but many will find that transition courses are ideal for covering LCME (Liaison Committee on Medical Education) requirements that do not fit elsewhere in the curriculum. The course should fill gaps within the curriculum, and an assessment should be done to see if the redundancies created are necessary, or do changes in other courses need to be made accordingly. Additionally, as core educators become more involved with the administrative aspects of the clerkships and courses they run, transition courses provide an opportunity to work one-on-one with students. This practice helps decrease psychological size of administrators, increase accessibility to administration and keep administrators in the trenches with students so that they understand student needs. Some institutions run longitudinal, interwoven transition courses by having the same faculty involved in all the transitions in their curriculum, thereby building strong relationships. Transition courses provide core administrators and educators the opportunity to instill the core values of the institution, thereby battling the hidden curriculum, while students are outside of other required coursework. Having no other coursework is more conducive bonding between peers as they go through these stressful transitions together.

In general, there are seven steps to implement a medical curriculum that are applicable to transition courses: identify resources (personnel, time, facilities, and funding), obtain support from the administrative authority, develop administrative mechanisms to support the curriculum, anticipate barriers, pilot the curriculum, fully implement the courses, and plan for enhancement and maintenance (Thomas, 2016). This implementation is no small feat from an administrative perspective.

The most important question that has to be asked before embarking is, "how does this curriculum improve the ability of students to meet the objectives of the program?" Standard 8.1 of the LCME standards states, "A medical school has in place an institutional body that oversees the medical education program as a whole and has responsibility for the overall design, management, integration, evaluation, and enhancement of a coherent and coordinated medical curriculum." This body is traditionally called the "Curriculum Committee". With the establishment or enhancement of any transition course from the perspective of central administration, the first step must be to decide how the curriculum advances the students' abilities to meet the objectives of the program. There are many great curricular ideas that exist, but not all of them fit into the big picture of a particular program. The second step is to describe the objectives of the curriculum and how those objectives fill a gap or eliminate a redundancy in the curriculum. The third step is to outline the activities of the curriculum. Once this is done, approval to pilot or for full implementation must be obtained from the curriculum committee (LCME, 2019).

It is best to get the support from the educational dean's office early so that they can be a participant and guide through the process. The curriculum dean is an important consultant to the Curriculum Committee, and the committee will ask her/his opinion before proceeding. In addition, if significant funding is needed for implementation, the educational dean's office will be the office that procures that funding.

At the end of this chapter, the reader will be able to outline and discuss transition courses available for their programs. The italicized sections throughout this chapter represent the voice of the medical student who is undergoing the transition from one part of the medical school education to another.

TRANSITION COURSES COVERED IN THIS CHAPTER

- **Beginning medical school orientation courses:** These courses have sprouted up across the United States, replacing the one-day orientation of the past. Many medical schools have an orientation that includes a White Coat Ceremony (WCC) and many other aspects intended to prepare the student for medical school coursework. For these institutions, orientation is a very important part of the academic year. Three domains that are generally covered during an orientation week have been described as "cultural, social and practical" (Ellaway, 2014).
- **Return to clerkship courses:** These courses have been created in undergraduate medical education for students who have taken time off from their medical school career due to illness, pursuit of research, or other personal reasons. How long the medical student has been away from the medical curriculum determines how much intervention is needed. There is no data regarding this type of transition course in the literature, but it is something that the reader should consider at their institution to accommodate the various needs of these returning learners.
- **Beginning clerkship transition courses:** These courses have been created to help decrease the anxiety and stress that comes with leaving the classroom and beginning to see patients on a regular basis. During the first two years of medical school, students begin to learn about basic clinical skills, but they do not get the opportunity to practice these skills on a daily basis due to time constraints. Many students come to their third year of medical school with the need for a refresher. A review of the literature states "the evidence supports clinical skills refreshers, clarification of roles and expectations, demystification of healthcare hierarchy and assessment processes and student-student handovers (Surmon, 2016)" during such courses.
- **Boot camp/Capstone courses:** These courses have been created to help with the transition from an undergraduate medical student to a residency program intern. Participation in specialty type boot camps during the fourth year of medical school have been shown to increase intern confidence upon beginning the specialty (Lewis, 2017). These courses also present the possibility for final assessment of student achievement in the core entrustable professional activities, as defined in 2014 by the Association of American Medical Colleges (AAMC) (Ryan, 2016). Some schools use this time not just to brush up on specialty specific clinical skills but to also discuss contemporary ethical issues that the student may encounter as an intern and to learn the communication skills to navigate these difficult conversations. Some capstone courses include other topics that might not have been covered elsewhere in the medical curriculum but are important skills for join-

Table 1. Overview description of the transition courses

Institution Core Values	• **Interprofessionalism:** We understand the roles and responsibilities of others while communicating effectively across teams, merging professional expertise, and collaborating to improve health outcomes for our communities. • **Compassion and Passion:** We have a deep awareness and kindness for all, and a strong enthusiasm for Making Life Better. • **Accountability:** We accept responsibility for our actions, attitudes, and performance and do the right thing when no one is looking. • **Respect and Inclusion:** We embrace all diversity and treat one another with dignity and empathy. • **Excellence:** We perform at the highest level. We are resilient lifelong learners with grit and strive to continuously improve.
Types of Transition Courses	Content to deliver

Medical School Orientation Courses	• Values of the institution
	• Intro to professional identity formation
	• Resilience and wellness
	• School resources
	• Financial aid resources and planning
	• Expectations of the institution and the course directors
	    o Evaluation and feedback
	    o Interprofessional education
	• Opportunity to lay a foundation for content important to the art of medicine
	    o Social determinants of Health
	    o Special patient populations
	    o Implicit bias
	• Opportunities to have discussions with near-peers
	• Tasks for on-boarding
	    o Review of Blood Bourne Pathogens
	    o BLS
	    o TB testing
	• White Coat Ceremony

Return After a Gap Year Courses	• History taking practice
	• Physical exam practice
	• Clinical Reasoning Practice
	    o Creating differential diagnoses
	    o Using appropriate support from the history and physical exam for the differential diagnosis
	• Beginning practice with reasonable management plans
	• Presentation practice
	If further help is needed:
	• Medical improvisation workshop to help with confidence and interpersonal skills
	• 1:1 Student to preceptor practice at clinical sites
	• Physical exam review with standardized patients

Welcome to Clerkship Courses	• Electronic medical record review
	• Tasks for on-boarding
	    o Review of Blood Bourne Pathogens
	    o HIPPA training
	    o BLS
	    o TB testing
	• Introduction/Review of Skills
	    o Radiology session
	    o Procedure session (IV placement, foley placement)
	    o Scrubbing, gowning & gloving
	    o Note writing (H&P versus progress note)
	    o Presentation
	    o Rounding
	    o Time management with chart review
	    o ABG, EKG reviews
	    o Fluid status of patients
	• Resilience and wellness
	• Expectations of the institution and the clerkship directors
	    o Evaluation and feedback
	    o Student abuse and mistreatment: reporting and resources for support
	    o Proper etiquette
	        ■ What to wear
	        ■ Absence requests: illness vs. personal
	• Discussion of the values of the institution
	• Chronic disease, end of life, suffering and emotions
	• Balancing clinical work with studying for exams
	• Revisit professional identity formation
	• Creation of an individual learning plan by the student for the year
	• Opportunity to reinforce important curriculum
	    o Opioid use disorder
	    o Social determinants of health
	    o Medical Improvisation
	• Opportunities to have discussions with near-peers
	• Clerkship Site visit/ opportunity to locate parking and other essential locations for first day of clerkship
	• Ending ceremony to signify entering the clinical world and the Oath of Commitment Ceremony

continued on following page

Table 1. Continued

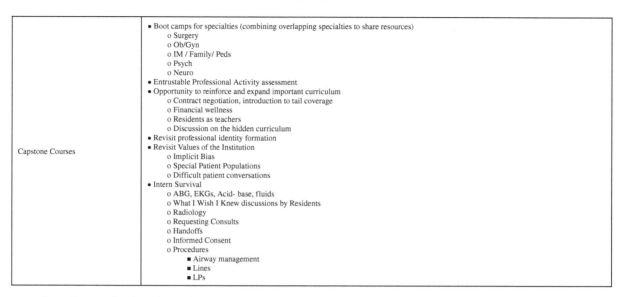

Capstone Courses	• Boot camps for specialties (combining overlapping specialties to share resources)
	    o Surgery
	    o Ob/Gyn
	    o IM / Family/ Peds
	    o Psych
	    o Neuro
	• Entrustable Professional Activity assessment
	• Opportunity to reinforce and expand important curriculum
	    o Contract negotiation, introduction to tail coverage
	    o Financial wellness
	    o Residents as teachers
	    o Discussion on the hidden curriculum
	• Revisit professional identity formation
	• Revisit Values of the Institution
	    o Implicit Bias
	    o Special Patient Populations
	    o Difficult patient conversations
	• Intern Survival
	    o ABG, EKGs, Acid- base, fluids
	    o What I Wish I Knew discussions by Residents
	    o Radiology
	    o Requesting Consults
	    o Handoffs
	    o Informed Consent
	    o Procedures
	        ■ Airway management
	        ■ Lines
	        ■ LPs

ing the professional world, such as introductions to contract negotiations, forming professional identities, and teaching residents to be teachers.

MEDICAL SCHOOL ORIENTATION COURSES

As an inbound medical student, I anticipated orientation to be a time of great change. It was for me both a finish line and a start line; a bookend on my years of preparing, and the onset of many more years of becoming. In this first step, my classmates and I could celebrate the many different paths we took to get here, and the shared mission we looked forward to. It was, of course, exciting and commemorative.

Looking back, I also see orientation as a time of focus: a big, deep breath. More than my self-exploratory years of undergraduate, more than my years of working in fields that orbited around my hopes of becoming a physician, the transition into medical school represented a commitment to this path. I looked at the long road ahead with no small amount of trepidation.

I certainly can't recall every detail of my orientation experience, but two particular aspects have stayed with me even past my first year of proverbially sticking my head in front of the academic firehose. First, the scale of attention dedicated to facilitating a better understanding of ourselves and each other illustrated to me how determined our school was that we should not only learn but also grow together from our time here. And second, fervent efforts by the faculty to arm us with resources characterized the institutional culture with a fierce sense of caring. Even as Prologue and POH become more and more distant, I remember them as a period when excitement and stress together were channeled into a sense of purpose. From that experience grew a rapid, profound kinship among my classmates and a deep sense of mutual support. These have only grown so far in our professional journey, and I expect that growth to continue.

Medical School Orientation Course Background

Relative to other medical school transitions that have received more thorough attention in the literature, orientation has been the subject of limited research and recommendations. Whether it falls within or outside the realm of legitimate medical education, as well as which offices should administrate it, are debatable (Ellaway, 2014). Nonetheless, the advantages are clear: orientation programs introduce curricula and learning resources, as well as classmates and faculty in a manner conducive to helpful future practices (like small group study) (Shankar, 2014). Orientations have grown over the years, in length of time as well as purpose. Existing literature has divided orientation into three distinct domains: cultural, social, and practical (Ellaway, 2014). They are crucial to managing expectations for students who are acclimated undergraduate education.

Orientation serves the important purpose of introducing students to the medical culture and values of the institution that will guide them in the formation of a professional identity. While the traditions and ceremonies that play key roles in this objective vary between schools, the WCC has become a landmark event in medical school orientation. Since its first appearance in 1993 at the Columbia College of Physicians and Surgeons (Scheinman, 2018), the WCC has become a widespread tradition signifying the first step into the mysterious world of healthcare professionals.

The ceremony has drawn criticism and defense alike for the symbolism tied to the white coat. However, a textual analysis into the WCCs of eighteen schools performed by Karnieli-Miller and colleagues (2013) found an overwhelming emphasis on compassion, service, and humility, with statements about obligation occurring three times more frequently than statements about privilege. The adoption of a physician identity—seen as a difficult but valuable journey—has been a dominating focus of the ceremony (Ellaway, 2014), and the WCC is an invitation to affirm this pursuit. Students solemnly answer the physician's call by donning the white coat as a symbol of humanism before the witness of family, friends, and a new professional community (Karnieli-Miller, 2013).

The WCC also commonly includes an oath recitation, expressing the student's acknowledgement of an ethical and professional code. While more ubiquitously a feature of commencement rather than orientation, a 2018 survey by Scheinman and colleagues (Scheinman, 2018) found that more than half of schools utilized a modified oath at the WCC or comparable introductory ceremony. The majority of oaths are modern variants of the Hippocratic Oath, the Declaration of Geneva, Lasagna's oath, or other standard oaths. Compared to commencement oaths, WCC oaths were more likely to include calls to have empathy, humility, and "injunctions to care for oneself; become a lifelong learner; and not lie, cheat, or steal". These variations reflect the early stage of professional identity formation, as well as students' shared commitment to their obligation to patients and the demanding curriculum ahead of them.

While ceremonies unite the incoming class of students through shared purpose, other, less-ritualistic aspects of orientation bring students together into a cohesive class. These commonly take the form of fun group activities—not only the universal icebreakers, but also "Med Olympics" and other dedicated team-building activities. While academic medical literature is not explicit about whether class solidarity primarily benefits the student, the institution, or both, the cohesiveness of the class is widely seen as a desirable outcome, building support among peers for the trials ahead. Through socializing events and discussions, students also build relationships with faculty and senior students. An unofficial yet important facet of social orientation occurs outside of the medical school when students gather in private homes or at local events and attractions (Ellaway, 2014). Thus, orientation is a period of not only developing relationships with faculty and peers but also grounding oneself in the community.

Though the practical aspects of orientation are perceived as less significant than the cultural or social domains, they occupy a significant portion of the orientation schedule and provide the incoming students with important resources. Students not only receive information on their upcoming curriculum and the expectations of the institution but also practical advice on how to succeed. Orientation has been designated as an ideal time to ensure all students are up to speed in specific skills—for example, computer-based research methods that medical school curriculums of the past were otherwise slow to incorporate (Gibson, 2000). More recently, Nyland and colleagues (2017) developed an interactive workshop intended to teach evidence-based study techniques to medical students early in their first year. Orientation serves as an ideal time to introduce these and other foundational areas of medical school.

Finally, orientation is an excellent time to not only introduce students to academic resources, but also to initiate discussions on mental health and resiliency. Medical students, while widely known to face significant personal distress at some point during their professional journey, have been found to begin medical school with better-than-average mental health (Brazeau, 2014). Thus, orientation—a period when students are likely to be engaged and receptive—serves as an important time to introduce students to wellness resources and services, affirming the institution's dedication to student health and wellbeing.

Orientation Courses At Morsani College Of Medicine

The Morsani College of Medicine (MCOM) offers several distinct introductory transition courses. First is the Medical Science Skills Development Program (MSSD), an optional three-week pre-matriculation program that facilitates the adjustment to the rigorous academic demands of medical school. The small group learning curriculum has three essential components: an introduction to the medical sciences curriculum, consisting of introductory lectures followed by engaged learning sessions; weekly patient-oriented case presentations; and assessment and development of specific academic skills, such as learning, reading, and test-taking (MSSD Program, 2018). The program is geared towards those who would benefit from an in-depth review and a more facilitated transition into the pace of learning expected during medical school.

Second, the Scholarly Excellence, Leadership Experiences, Collaborative Training (SELECT) program at MCOM—which comprises approximately 30% of each matriculating class—has its own three-day orientation known as Prologue that takes place prior to class-wide orientation. The SELECT program seeks to recruit and develop students with high emotional intelligence from diverse backgrounds into physician leaders. This process occurs through two years of educational experiences at MCOM followed by two clinical years at the Lehigh Valley Health Network. SELECT has several distinct curricular features, including a professional development curriculum, both physician faculty and peer coaching, research mentoring, and the completion of capstone projects integrating leadership, patient values, and health systems analysis (SELECT, 2018). Prologue prepares SELECT students for the unique demands of the program, including the relocation for third and fourth year clinicals, separate from the rest of the class comprising the alternate core program. This program has a strong focus on the cultural and social domains of orientation. Large-group sessions introduce students to the SELECT domains and program expectations; small group-based activities focus on personal values exploration and longitudinal peer bonding. Prologue is highly effective at socializing the SELECT students prior to integration with the larger class. The group dynamics and support systems formed in these early stages are integral to the physician development curriculums which take place over the next four years.

Finally, Professions of Health (POH) is the two-week, class-wide orientation program that transitions all medical students into the medical school curriculum. POH covers many practical necessities of concern during this transition period, including introduction to academic, research, financial, and safety resources, Basic Life Support certification, and white coat fittings. The curriculum also features smaller group-based workshops, providing overviews and facilitated discussions in topics such as effective communication, professionalism, conflict resolution, building resiliency, and the Myers-Briggs Type Indicator. In following with MCOM's emphasis on early and frequent clinical exposure, students are also introduced during orientation to standardized patient encounters and history-taking skills. POH also provides the opportunity for integration of medical school curricular components not covered in other courses. This includes seminars on the social determinants of health, humanistic goals of compassionate care, special patient populations, and identifying and addressing implicit biases. Overall, POH serves the role of both a traditional orientation and a gradual acceleration into the normal class schedule.

The POH curriculum has undergone continuous development, expansion, and improvement based on program needs and student feedback. From 2013 to 2019, longitudinally-collected responses to POH evaluations from 391 first-year students show that the majority of students (85%) thought that POH was a good course, and most (77%) reported that they understood what was expected of them in order to successfully progress through medical school and graduate after POH. A smaller majority (54%) thought that POH was organized and administered well, indicating both the need for the curricular changes already implemented, as well as an ongoing need for continued development.

RETURN TO CLERKSHIP COURSES

I took time off following my second year of medical school, as I had the opportunity to work in a research lab that would help me gain critical insights into the pathways of clinical medicine that I was not able to put together during my third year. I worked in the lab thirty hours a week, and shadowed physicians in the hospital and in the clinics for the remainder of my time; this helped me with essential learning opportunities that I did not take advantage of while I was studying so hard for all my exams.

This past year, I have grown tremendously. I feel confident in my research skills, but I also feel a sense of knowing how the first two years of medical school relate to the care and management of my patients. I have a deeper understanding of the relevance of the intersection between my basic sciences classes and the clinical care of my patients. I am going to apply my experiences to the clerkships and beyond, and now I will be practicing medicine with greater clarity.

Return To Clerkship Background

No academic literature exists regarding this type of transition course. Google Scholar and PubMed searches did not yield any results for the following terms: "Return to Clerkship Courses"; "Return to Medical School Courses"; "Leave of Absence" and "Medical School"; "medical school after leaving"; "time off" and "medical school"; "medical school leave of absence"; "research year" and "medical school" and "gap year" and "medical education". A Google search of "return to medical school after time off" brought up blog posts and other checklists, including one from the AAMC for students considering taking time off from medical school.

Table 2. Planning document/example planner for transition course: Medical school orientation course.

Session Title	Session Action

Welcome Session	• Invite deans and associate deans at least 4 months in advance to clear their clinical schedule
	  o Give timings
	    ■ 10-15 minutes per person
	  o What do the Deans need to portray
	    ■ Congratulations on matriculating into medical school
	    ■ What you need to know starting your first year
	    ■ Pearls on How to be Successful

Plenary Sessions
  • Who are we?
  • Security and Safety
  • Canvas 101
  • Intro to Anatomy
  • Intro to Radiology
  • Blood Bourne Pathogens
  • ExamSoft 101
  • Financial Aid
  • Careers in Medicine
  • Social Determinants of Health
  • Intro to History Taking
	• Invite lecturers at least 4 months on advance to clear their clinical schedule
	• Discuss slides/handouts/follow up sessions for the plenary talks
	• Reserve auditorium one year in advance

Workshops
  • Anatomy workshop
  • Communications Skills
  • Professionalism
  • Social Media Savvy
  • MBTI
  • Safe Zone
  • Intro to IPE
  • Grit
  • Financial Aid Entrance
  • Social Determinants and Humanism
	• Start discussions with faculty at least 6 months in advance to make sure they are available and can send slides for the manual.
	• Reserve classroom space for workshops

Breakout Sessions
  • BLS Training
  • Bootcamp Training
  • FIT Testing
	• Start discussions at least 6 months in advance to begin to recruit residents / fellows to teach the Breakout Session courses.
	• Need to have a preceptor for each session (16 preceptor residents)
	• Send review to MS IVs to determine if they have any other interests to be offered for their course.
	• Reserve small group rooms, clinical space and simulation training rooms for various sessions

Return To Clerkship At Morsani College Of Medicine

Reasons listed for making the decision to take time off from medical school include but are not limited to illness, family issues, need for time to reboot after a difficult year, pursuit of research, and opportunity for international clinical exposure. Due to the time away, these students require more preparation than the standard "Introduction to Clerkships" (I2C) transition course provides. While away, some of the students, were able to volunteer in clinical settings, but many others did not. In order to help these students to become as successful as possible, MCOM uses this transition course to help to assess where they stand relative to others who will be entering third year with them, to help students develop their skills up to par with their peers, and to help students gain confidence before re-joining clerkships.

Once the student has notified Student Affairs that they intend to return to school, they are instructed to contact the team in charge of running the Return to Clerkship course. The enrichment team is comprised of the Director of the Simulation center and the course director for the enrichment elective. Depending on the need of the students that are returning to the clerkship, other members included on the team are primary care and surgical preceptors who provide clinical experience for the students. To augment the skills that are deemed necessary for the returning students, fourth year MD students help with tailored focused history taking and physical exam skill practice. These fourth-year students have undergone special training in education prior to being considered ready to help with these returning students. At any time, the team may consist of two to seven members. The team has the student perform baseline standardized patient cases to evaluate problem-focused history and physical exam skills, presentation skills, clinical reasoning skills, and note writing skills. These cases are similar to those that the students complete at the end of second year as part of the end-of-the-year exam for the longitudinal Doctoring Two course at MCOM. Based on the student's performance with these baseline cases, a plan is made to rejoin medical school successfully. Some students show that their performance is on par with their peers from this first baseline activity, so they are offered non-mandated practice opportunity. Other students need a little more work prior to the start of clerkships to be deemed on par, so a plan is mandated for them. Depending on needed areas of improvement, the following have been included in students' individual plans:

- SP work to practice:
  - History taking.
  - Physical exam.
    - Some SPs are trained in advanced physical exam skills, so they can work one on one with returning student.
    - Near-peer teaching from upper level students help with PE skills.
- Medical Improvisation workshops to help with empathy, connectedness and confidence.
- Joining a ward team or clinic team that does not have other students on service to help with time management skills, organization, history taking, and physical exam skills

Some students will work with the team for two weeks, but others may need a month. In addition, students can request more practice.

After the students have completed the required learning plan for the return to clerkships, the feedback from the SPs, preceptors, and the students is reviewed. These evaluations are used to determine if the student is ready to join the clerkship with the rising third year class at I2C. If other work is deemed necessary, the student may practice more after I2C and join clerkships late, or it is recommended that the student complete a two-week elective during their current clerkship to help solidify the skills that were re-visited during this course (this is a very rare scenario).

During the time that the clinical skills team runs this course, many students have commented on the increase in confidence with their skills due to this course. Having time away from clinical practice gave them a feeling of inadequacy, and this course gave them an opportunity to feel like they belonged with their class. While the team has not formally reviewed the success of this course, anecdotally, the students are thankful and happy that they were able to practice before re-joining medical school. Other medical schools should consider the inclusion of such a transition course as more students opt for leave of absences during their medical school training. Things to consider when taking on such a course would be the time and other resources that are needed to help the students to become successful. Some students do require a more labor-intensive schedule to help them reach the level of their new class cohort. We have used near peer preceptors in these instances to help the returning students on the daily basis that they require. The returning students that participate in this course are not formally matriculated and there is no charge for the course. Due to these reasons, they are not eligible for financial aid at our institution, but this could be something to consider at other institutions when considering starting such a course.

INTRODUCTION TO CLERKSHIP COURSES

I took my Step 1 and completed all the required on-boarding prior to the start of I2C. I initially felt a bit lost and confused—not sure what I want to be when medical school ends, but hopeful that I would find my people during my clerkship year—and the first two days back at school after my long time off seemed tedious, involving lectures about how I should behave this year. The following week was a lot more interactive and certainly gave me a broad look into what clerkships could be like.

Table 3. Planning document/example planner for transition course: Return after a gap year course.

Session Title	Session Action
Prior to Start of Course	Stay in contact with Student Affairs: • To have an idea of how many off cycle students will join the clerkship this academic year • When the students will be taking their Step 1 (if they have not taken it yet). • When would student affairs recommend contacting these students (if the students have not yet contacted the team). Begin to reserve rooms at the Simulation center (the sim center will give us priority for rooms for this course and our remediation course so that we do not have to reserve rooms one year in advance): • What will be the room availability for the expected dates that the students will begin • SP availability • Preceptor availability Contact students to find out when they will return to town. If they will not return (we have a third year Campus in Pennsylvania) or would like to start practicing before they return to town begin the process of setting up videoconferencing options to do the baseline activity, as well as other SP activities. Contact preceptors to work with students on a 1:1 basis in the clinical setting to find out when they have no other student learners present to maximize the time the returning medical student has with the preceptor.
Baseline session	Aim for four to six baseline cases that the student will be able perform problem focused history and physical exams on. The students will write-up half of the cases and present in real time the other cases to a preceptor.
After baseline assessment • If student performed on par with other rising 3rd year medical students • If the student if determined to be close to par • If the student is far from par	• Resources for review prior to the start of clerkship are provided and opportunities for more practice are offered. • A schedule is created for the returning medical student that consists of similar standardized patient cases that were used during the baseline assessment. Depending on the amount of time prior to the start of clerkships, this student may complete 4 cases a day for 2-4 weeks • Resources for review prior to the start of clerkship are provided • A schedule is created for the returning medical student that consists of similar standardized patient cases that were used during the baseline assessment. Depending on the amount of time prior to the start of clerkships, this student may complete 4 cases a day for 2-4 weeks • The student will spend 1-3 weeks in the clinical setting working 1:1 with preceptor • The student will participate in a 1-week medical improvisation workshop • The student will work with SPs trained in physical exam skills or with graduating MS4s to work on physical exam skills • Resources for review prior to the start of clerkship are provided

I arrived for the Introduction to Clinical Care and met up with my 4ᵗʰ year to learn how to scrub, then got gowned and gloved and went to the "OR." It was fascinating to see all the instruments, and I was able to interview a patient heading to the OR. I followed this patient through the continuity of his care, from the OR to the inpatient setting and then as a follow up in the outpatient clinic. I realized the power of the patient story, the depth of compassion you need to care for critically ill patients, and the exhilaration you feel when they are no longer in the hospital. Practicing presenting my patient gave me insights and clarity into caring for my future patients.

I realized with a profound sense of purpose that this was going to be a year filled with great emotions. I was going to be asked to take care of others, their lives in my hands, as I made decisions on their behalf. My goal was to be open to feedback from my residents, my attendings, and the team who were helping me in the care and management of my patients.

Introduction To Clerkships Background

Medical schools recognize that it is imperative for students to be prepared for entering the clinical years. While the pre-clinical years of medical school are challenging, the method of instruction and learning is similar to their elementary schooling through undergraduate education. Once students begin their clinical years, they enter a high-stakes clinical environment where they are expected to become an integral part of the clinical team in the ambulatory or inpatient setting and operating room. Additionally, they are expected to care for patients while continuing to acquire and synthesize knowledge. Thus, medical schools have found it is very important to help with this transition and have implemented multiple strategies.

As simulated and real-world experiences are the best ways to learn, many medical schools have implemented longitudinal courses that teach history, physical examination, documentation, oral presentation skills and clinical experiences in their preclinical years. While these courses and experiences have been found to be beneficial, students continue to find the transition to clerkships stressful and challenging (Jacobs, 2005; Shacklady, 2009; van Hell, 2008; Haglund, 2009). Medical students continue to have difficulty adjusting to the different clinical settings and understanding their roles, responsibilities, and expectations (O'Brien, 2007; Prince, 2005).

In 2003, Poncelet and O'Brien conducted a Web-based survey of curriculum deans at 125 U.S. medical schools in order to identify whether or not students participated in a transition to clerkship course and determine the purpose of the course (Poncelet, 2008). Of the 56 of the 125 (45%) deans contacted who responded, 30 reported having a transition to clerkship course lasting one day to seven weeks and taking place immediately preceding clerkships. The majority (83%) of courses were from one day to one week. While seven school identified their course objectives and purpose, all of the schools presented "new information and skills", and 53% also used this course to increase "student well-being and stress reduction" and for "review and application of preclerkship knowledge, skills, and attitudes in a clinical setting" (Poncelet, 2008).

O'Brien and Poncelet repeated a Web-based survey in 2008, reaching out to curricular deans and transition course directors at 142 U.S. and Canadian medical schools with an improved response of 78 out of 126 (62%) of US and 5 out of 16 (31%) Canadian medical schools. All five of the Canadian schools and 68 out 78 of the U.S. schools reported having a transition to clerkship course lasting anywhere between one to 18 days with the majority lasting one week or less. Two of the 10 schools with no transition course offered a half-day transition session and another one had a half-day transition session prior to each clerkship orientation. Interestingly, all of the schools with a transition to clerkship course identified that the purpose of the course was "to increase student well-being and reduce stress" and the majority of schools also used this course "to present new information and skills not covered in the preclerkship curriculum" and "to review and apply knowledge, skills, and/or attitudes previously learned in a clinical setting". Thus, the content of transition courses was stratified into "preparation to participate in authentic tasks/activities", such as oral presentations, notes, orders, and basic procedure; "relationships in the workplace"; and "introduction to routines, rules, norms, and culture of the workplace" with feedback and mentoring utilizing both faculty and peers. An increasing number of schools are recognizing the need for a transition to clerkship course, and it is most important to provide real-world experiences and focus on tasks the students will experience in their first clerkship (O'Brien, 2010).

Introduction To Clerkship (I2C) At Morsani College Of Medicine

The I2C transition course at MCOM has existed in its current form for five years. The authors have reviewed the data from the years 2013 through 2018 as these years resemble the most recent iterations of the course. The course was rated as "useful to somewhat useful" by 77% 527 third-year medical students after having completed the course. Ninety-two percent of the same 527 students felt that I2C oriented them for their third year of medical school "adequately or better".

The I2C course is a six-day course prior to the start of clerkship for the new third year students. During this time, the students revisit clinical skills that they learned during their first two years of medical school in a short refresher course. Students are also introduced to concepts that apply specifically to being on a clerkship such as required didactics, professional attire and absence requests. A list of the course objectives as well as the planning document are located below this section.

A well-received aspect of the I2C course is the standardized patient sessions called "Introduction to Clinical Care" and "Introduction to Pediatrics". During the clinical care session, the students follow the same "SP" from the OR to the inpatient wards and then to the outpatient setting. While in the OR, the students practice scrubbing, gowning, gloving and learn OR etiquette in the simulation center OR. They learn how not to contaminate themselves and what to do in case of a needle stick. Throughout this simulation, the students have the opportunity to touch drains, Foleys, chest tubes and other equipment that they would see in the hospital setting. They learn the differences between surgery notes and IM notes. Students practice presenting and writing notes about the patient in the inpatient and outpatient settings. The "Introduction to Pediatrics" session is similar in the other session in that the students see SPs in the inpatient and outpatient setting. We use SPs as the parents and low fidelity baby dolls play the patients. These sessions allow the students to practice their presentation skills while allowing them to learn the difference between SOAP notes and admit notes.

CAPSTONE / BOOTCAMP COURSES

I'd recently matched into my first choice of the Family Medicine Residency programs to which I'd applied. It was close to graduation and I had one more requirement to complete, the Capstone TIPS course. I pulled out my Individual Learning Plan and surveyed the course offering to determine what sessions would help me meet my personal goals. The Family Medicine Bootcamp, run by the Chief Resident in

Table 4. Planning document/example planner for transition course: Transition to clerkship - Introduction to Clerkships Course (I2C).

Session Title	Session Action

Welcome Session	• Invite UME deans and associate deans at least 4 months in advance to clear their clinical schedule
	   o Give timings
	     ■ 10-15 minutes per person
	   o What the Deans would talk about
	     ■ Your first day of clerkship
	     ■ Pearls on How to be Successful
	• Invite clerkship directors and coordinators at least 4 months in advance to clear their clinical schedule
	   o Give timings
	     ■ 10-15 minutes per person
	   o What you would like them to talk about
	     ■ Your first day of clerkship
	     ■ Pearls on how to be Successful

Didactic Sessions • Student Abuse • Evaluation (PRIME) • Resilience, Etiquette, Thriving	Invite lecturers at least 4 months in advance to clear their clinical schedule Reserve auditorium one year in advance
EMR training	Start discussions at least 6 months in advance to make sure students will be able to write notes on day one of clerkship
On-boarding	Start discussions with hospitals at least 6 months in advance to make sure students will be able to report to clinical site on day one of clerkship
Bloodborne pathogens TB testing	Review requirements and invite for TB placement at least 4 months in advance
Introduction to clinical care OR session IM session	• Review scripts, faculty and student guides at least two months in advance • Split students so there are no more than 12 students in a small group for these sessions • Reserve two OR rooms, six inpatient rooms, six outpatient clinical rooms and three classroom/ debrief spaces in Sim center one year in advance • Needs for OR session (reserve at least four months in advance): • 2-6 preceptors (attendings, rising MS4s and graduated MS4s) • 2 SPs • At least one for each student- Scrub soap, gown, gloves, booties, hair bouffant, mask • Needs for IM session (reserve at least four months in advance): • 12 SPs (6 for inpatient case/6 for outpatient case) • 6 preceptors (attendings, rising MS4s and graduated MS4s)
Intro to Pediatrics	Review scripts, faculty and student guides at least two months in advance Split students so there are no more than 12 students in a small group for these sessions Reserve six clinical rooms and one debrief space in Sim center one year in advance Needs: 6 SPs (3 for inpatient case/ 3 for outpatient case) 6 preceptors (attendings, rising MS4s and graduated MS4s)
Simulation (codes)	Reserve two team training rooms and a debrief space in Sim center one year in advance. Inform sim center of high-fidelity mannequins that will be used at least four months in advance Needs: 1-2 preceptors
Procedures	Reserve one room in Sim center one year in advance. Inform sim center of the task trainers that will be required at least four months in advance Needs: 2 preceptors IV supplies -enough for each student to try one stick Foley supplies- enough for each student to try once

continued on following page

Table 4. Continued

Session Title	Session Action
BLS	Reserve one room in Sim center one year in advance. Inform sim center of that 14 BLS mannequins will be required at least four months in advance Needs: 2-4 preceptors
Narcan session	Reserve one room in Sim center one year in advance. Inform sim center four mannequins will be required at least four months in advance Needs: 1 preceptor 12 Narcan nasal inhaler practice devices Bottled water to refill inhalers
Individual Learning Plan	Reserve one room in Sim center one year in advance. Needs: 1 preceptor
ALS session	Reserve auditorium and small group rooms one year in advance Ensure accessible parking will be available for panel members one year in advance Needs: Depending on how many panel members available: • 6-8 small group preceptors • 1 preceptor to introduce the panel • Ask for 6-8 patient panel members but realize there may be far fewer depending on their health the day of the session
Near Peer Lunch sessions • How to Thrive • Resilience	• Reserve auditorium one year in advance • Contact rising MS4 speakers 4-6 months in advance
Intro to Medical Improvisation	Reserve auditorium and small group rooms one year in advance Needs: 8-16 SPs who will be the lead facilitators for this session because they have undergone special training. 8-16 medical preceptors to help with encouraging participation and explaining take home points of the session
Oath of Commitment Ceremony	Reserve auditorium one year in advance Needs: 1 patient speaker to speak about what the Oath means to them as a patient

Family Medicine, was clearly my first choice, covering the essentials of Family Medicine: "what I need to know," "cases for cross coverage," "resiliency in residency," and "how to call a consult."

I also completed some of my EPA requirements with the airway management 'hand-offs' session, the lumbar puncture 'Informed Consent' session, and the vascular access session. It was great to sign off on these before graduation.

Arriving at the course, I was excited; there was so much energy in the auditorium. I had not seen some of my friends for a while and realized how nice it was to just talk with others who were as nervous as I was. My classmates asked thoughtful questions and as we headed for lunch, we realized that our lives are going to change so much in the next few years. After lunch, we did a workshop on "Pearls of Internship," filled with terrific hands-on advice on how to manage the first few weeks as an Intern.

The two days helped me feel more confident in my skills, and I picked up valuable tips on what to expect during my residency in a few weeks. While this phase of my life is ending, I know now that the field of medicine is filled with brilliant minds taking care of sick people who need our help, and I have committed myself to do just that.

Capstone / Bootcamp Courses Background

Bootcamp / Capstone courses have been created in many medical schools as a method to transition from undergraduate medical student to intern in a residency program. Each school may offer specialty specific type bootcamps during the fourth year of medical school, which have been shown to increase intern confidence upon beginning the specialty (Lewis, 2017).

There is an abundance of support in the medical education literature that advocates for a course that transitions an individual from an undergraduate medical student to the graduate medical resident/intern (Lewis, 2017; Ryan, 2016). These courses are titled a variety of names, including "bootcamps", "capstone courses", "intern preparatory course", and "transition course" (Lewis, 2017). While these courses are recent additions to many medical schools' curricula, the course is an actual requirement in 59% of the 136 medical schools in the United States (Ryan, 2016). Ranging in length of a few days to several weeks, the content is specifically designed to provide the students with an opportunity to prepare for their roles as interns following graduation.

Topics covered by these courses include specific patient care management, relevant basic science topics, learning to work in teams, professionalism, communication skills, and technical skills. The students are given a menu of options and are required to fulfill a number of specified tasks linked to their EPAs.

Capstone Tips At Morsani College Of Medicine

The two-day transition course at MCOM is called Capstone Tools for Internship Preparedness and Success (TIPS) Course. This course is offered as an interprofessional educational opportunity for graduating medical, advanced practice nursing, and pharmacy students for them to learn about their transition from the school environment to the work environment as they begin their professional careers. The course covers a large menu of topics that are not traditionally offered in the academic setting. Sessions such as contract negotiation, coding, billing, and financial planning help the graduating learner to be prepared for the next phase of their career. Sessions on 'what I wish I knew…' from the senior residents' perspectives give the students an opportunity to ask about their discipline specific preparedness for entry into the internship year.

The TIPS course also offers the opportunity to complete required competencies that may have been overlooked over that past year. The Entrustable Professional Acts (EPAs) that medical schools state are entrustable acts are reviewed and checked off during this transition course. It is a method to review the students' competencies are met just prior to graduation. Simulations of real-life scenarios, like utilizing Narcan with a patient on the street, are reviewed and offered to assure all of the graduates feel as competent as they can before their first day of residency.

FUTURE RESEARCH DIRECTIONS

Many medical schools are working to implement and/or already have transition courses in their curriculum. It will be important to determine the future trends of these transition courses as they become more

Table 5. Planning document/example planner for transition course: Bootcamps capstone course.

Session Title	Session Activity

Welcome Session	• Invite deans and associate deans at least 4 months in advance to clear their clinical schedule
	    o Give timings:
	        ■ 10-15 minutes per person
	    o Discuss what the Deans will talk about:
	        ■ Congratulations on graduation
	        ■ What you need to know starting your intern year
	        ■ Pearls on how to be Successful

Plenary Sessions: • Opioid Addiction • Pain Management	• Invite lecturers at least 4 months on advance to clear their clinical schedule • Discuss slides/handouts/follow up sessions for the plenary talks • Reserve auditorium one year in advance
Workshops: • Intern Survival Guide • Resilience • Financial Planning • Investments 101 • Developing your professional identity	• Start discussions with faculty at least 6 months in advance to make sure they are available and can send slides for the manual. • Reserve classroom space for workshops
Breakout Sessions: • EKGs • ABGs • Radiology • Recognition of Skin Cancers • What I wish I knew (done by residents) • Residents as Teachers • Airway Management Handoffs check off • Advanced Communications check off • Informed Consent / lumbar puncture case check off • Vascular Access • Ultrasound training • Billing and Coding • Social Determinants of Health • Understanding the Hidden Curriculum • Calling Consults • Pharmacology Escape Room	• Start discussions at least 6 months in advance to begin to recruit residents / fellows to teach the Breakout Session courses. • Need to have a preceptor for each session (16 preceptor residents) • Send review to MS IVs to determine if they have any other interests to be offered for their course. • Reserve small group rooms, clinical space, and simulation training rooms for various sessions
Bootcamps: • Family Medicine • Ob/Gyn • Pediatrics • Emergency Medicine • Internal Medicine • Surgery • Neurology • Psychiatry	• Review requirements for each Bootcamp and invite Senior Residents to run the program specific Bootcamp for the MS IVs at least 4 months in advance • Reserve teaching and simulation space to provide small group sessions and task training in each three-hour bootcamp • Order supplies and reserve equipment needed

ubiquitous. Further research is needed to assure that these transition courses are effectively allowing the medical student to move smoothly from one phase of their medical career to the next. Identifying key terms such as professional identity formation and measurement of EPAs would be the most logical future platform to measure key successes in these courses.

CONCLUSION

Transition courses provide a framework for the many important topics that may not fit well elsewhere in the medical school curriculum. The courses discussed in this chapter have used these transitions to introduce and revisit the core values of the institution. As they take place at crucial times for medical students, transition courses are key for addressing professional identity formation. The process of creating an identity as a medical student—versus undergraduate or other professional student—can be discussed in detail during orientation. Transition to clerkship courses can prompt students to think further on how their professional identity will change with moving into a clinical environment. Moreover, during Capstone courses, students can reflect on entering the profession of doctors: what society expects from doctors, what they expect from themselves as doctors, and what that means to their professional identity formation.

These periods of change can be tumultuous times for students. Transition courses are the ideal setting to discuss resilience, self-care and resources that exist for the student's benefit. In addition, the usage of simulation in these courses nurtures confidence in the student going forward into the pre-clinical, clinical, and then residency worlds. The process of transitioning well into new roles will continue to be important during students' professional journeys, as they one day contemplate what it means to be a resident versus a full attending, and what growth in their professional identity comes with attending status. These are important questions to explore explicitly with the students during these transition courses to foster lifelong reflection on what it is to be a doctor and a professional in the United States.

REFERENCES

Brazeau, C. M., Shanafelt, T., Durning, S. J., Massie, F. S., Eacker, A., Moutier, C., ... Dyrbye, L. N. (2014). Distress among matriculating medical students relative to the general population. *Academic Medicine, 89*(11), 1520–1525. doi:10.1097/ACM.0000000000000482 PMID:25250752

Dreyfus, S. (2004). The Five-Stage Model of Adult Skill Acquisition. *Bulletin of Science, Technology & Society, 24*(3), 177–181. doi:10.1177/0270467604264992

Ellaway, R. H., Cooper, G., Al-Idrissi, T., Dube, T., & Graves, L. (2014). Discourses of student orientation to medical education programs. *Medical Education Online, 19*(23714). PMID:24646440

Gibson, K. E., & Silverberg, M. (2000). A two-year experience teaching computer literacy to first-year medical students using skill-based cohorts. *Bulletin of the Medical Library Association, 88*(2), 157–164. PMID:10783971

Haglund, M. E., aan het Rot, M., Cooper, N. S., Nestadt, P. S., Muller, D., Southwick, S. M., & Charney, D. S. (2009). Resilience in the third year of medical school: A prospective study of the associations between stressful events occurring during clinical rotations and student well-being. *Academic Medicine, 84*(2), 258–268. doi:10.1097/ACM.0b013e31819381b1 PMID:19174682

Health, U. S. F. (2018). *Medical Science Skills Development Program.* Retrieved from https://health.usf.edu/medicine/mdprogram/diversity/prematriculationprogram

Health, U. S. F. (2018). *The SELECT Experience*. Retrieved from https://health.usf.edu/medicine/md-program/select/experience

Health, U. S. F. (2019). *Institutional Core Values*. Retrieved from https://health.usf.edu/care/hr/Culture

Jacobs, J. C., Bolhuis, S., Bulte, J. A., Laan, R., & Holdrinet, R. S. (2005). Starting learning in medical practice: An evaluation of a new introductory clerkship. *Medical Teacher, 27*(5), 408–414. doi:10.1080/01421590500087001 PMID:16147793

Karnieli-Miller, O., Frankel, R. M., & Inui, T. S. (2013). Cloak of compassion, or evidence of elitism? An empirical analysis of white coat ceremonies. *Medical Education, 47*(1), 97–108. doi:10.1111/j.1365-2923.2012.04324.x PMID:23278829

LCME Functions and Structures of a Medical School. (2019). Retrieved from http://lcme.org/publications/

Lewis, J. S. D., Dubosh, N., & Ullman, E. (2017). Participation in an emergency medicine bootcamp increases self-confidence at the start of residency. *Western Journal of Emergency Medicine: Integrating Emergency Care with Population Health, 18*(5), s22.

Nyland, R. L., Sawarynski, K. E. (2017). Setting students up for success: A short interactive workshop designed to increase effective study habits. *MedEdPORTAL, 13*(10610).

O'Brien, B., Cooke, M., & Irby, D. M. (2007). Perceptions and attributions of third-year student struggles in clerkships: Do students and clerkship directors agree? *Academic Medicine, 82*(10), 970–978. doi:10.1097/ACM.0b013e31814a4fd5 PMID:17895662

O'Brien, B. C., & Poncelet, A. N. (2010). Transition to clerkship courses: Preparing students to enter the workplace. *Academic Medicine, 85*(12), 1862–1869. doi:10.1097/ACM.0b013e3181fa2353 PMID:20978432

Peña, A. (2010). The Dreyfus model of clinical problem-solving skills acquisition: A critical perspective. *Medical Education Online, 15*(6). doi:10.3402/meo.v15i0.4846 PMID:20563279

Poncelet, A., & O'Brien, B. (2008). Preparing medical students for clerkships: A descriptive analysis of transition courses. *Academic Medicine, 83*(5), 444–451. doi:10.1097/ACM.0b013e31816be675 PMID:18448897

Prince, K. J., Boshuizen, H. P., van der Vleuten, C. P., & Scherpbier, A. J. (2005). Students' opinions about their preparation for clinical practice. *Medical Education, 39*(7), 704–712. doi:10.1111/j.1365-2929.2005.02207.x PMID:15960791

Quinn, J., & White, B. (2019). Cultivating Leadership in Medicine. Dendall Hunt Publishers. 155-164.

Ryan, M. S., Lockeman, K. S., Feldman, M., & Dow, A. (2016). The gap between current and ideal approaches to the core EPAs: A mixed methods study of recent medical school graduates. *Medical Science Educator, 26*(3), 463–473. doi:10.100740670-016-0235-x

Scheinman, S. J., Fleming, P., & Niotis, K. (2018). Oath taking at U.S. and Canadian medical school ceremonies: Historical perspectives, current practices, and future considerations. *Academic Medicine, 93*(9), 1301–1306. doi:10.1097/ACM.0000000000002097 PMID:29239902

Shacklady, J., Holmes, E., Mason, G., Davies, I., & Dornan, T. (2009). Maturity and medical students' ease of transition into the clinical environment. *Medical Teacher, 31*(7), 621–626. doi:10.1080/01421590802203496 PMID:19811146

Shankar, P. R. (2014). Designing and conducting a two day orientation program for first semester undergraduate medical students. *Journal of Educational Evaluation for Health Professions, 11*(31). PMID:25417865

Surmon, L., Bialocerkowski, A., & Hu, W. (2016). Perceptions of preparedness for the first medical clerkship: A systematic review and synthesis. *BMC Medical Education, 16*(89). PMID:26968816

Teunissen, P. W., & Westerman, M. (2011). Opportunity or threat: The ambiguity of the consequences of transitions in medical education. *Medical Education, 45*(1), 51–59. doi:10.1111/j.1365-2923.2010.03755.x PMID:21155868

Thomas, P. A., Kern, D. E., Hughes, M. T., & Chen, B. Y. (2016). *Curriculum Development: A Six-Step Approach for Medical Education* (3rd ed.). Baltimore, MD: Johns Hopkins University Press.

Van Hell, E. A., Kuks, J. B., Schonrock-Adema, J., van Lohuizen, M. T., & Cohen-Schotanus, J. (2008). Transition to clinical training: Influence of pre-clinical knowledge and skills, and consequences for clinical performance. *Medical Education, 42*(8), 830–837. doi:10.1111/j.1365-2923.2008.03106.x PMID:18564098

Chapter 11
Passing the Baton:
The Role of Targeted Transition Programs in Medical Education at an Urban Medical School

Andrea A. Anderson

The George Washington School of Medicine and Health Sciences, USA

Yolanda C. Haywood

The George Washington School of Medicine and Health Sciences, USA

Juliet Lee

The George Washington School of Medicine and Health Sciences, USA

Claudia U. Ranniger

The George Washington School of Medicine and Health Sciences, USA

Grace E. Henry

The George Washington School of Medicine and Health Sciences, USA

ABSTRACT

Transitions in medical school are a recognized point of stress for learners. Overall, stress is a known aspect of any period of transition, where the unknown looms large and new skills need to be acquired to achieve mastery of the next step. As the medical needs of the population grow, medical schools are admitting larger and more diverse classes. These students will undergo several major points of transition in their undergraduate medical education careers including the period of matriculation to the first year and the transition from the preclinical years into the clinical years. The George Washington School of Medicine has developed a longitudinal approach including two specific programs to support students during these recognized points of academic transition. The Prematriculation Program (PMP) and the Foundations of Clinical Practice course address the specific needs of these stages. The authors contend that an intentional approach to support students at periods of known academic risk is a beneficial aid to student success.

DOI: 10.4018/978-1-7998-1468-9.ch011

INTRODUCTION

This chapter aims to describe two successful programs at an urban medical school which address common points of transition in medical education. The authors will emphasize the process of the development of these programs with attention to future steps to increase the impact these programs can have on medical students at known points of critical transition.

BACKGROUND

A Brief History of the George Washington School of Medicine and Health Sciences (GW SMHS)

Founded in 1824 as a medical department within Columbian College (now known as The George Washington University), the George Washington (GW) Medical School was the eleventh medical school founded in the US and the first in the nation's capital. GW has long offered curricular innovations designed with the goal of graduating "Physician Citizens" committed to local, national, and global public service through excellent patient care, scholarly inquiry, leadership, and advocacy for change and innovation.

GW has developed a comprehensive curriculum with aspects of the curriculum intentionally designed with the aim to support select student cohorts through known periods of academic and professional identity transition in medical education. The authors will discuss two GW programs which highlight the importance of curricular innovations to support UME students through transitions. As evidenced from student feedback, these programs have been associated with success in mitigating these transitions.

The Pre-Matriculation Program (PMP) is an academic four-week summer pre-enrollment program which provides pre-clinical content exposure to prepare select incoming medical students for the academically rigorous learning environment of the GW medical school. After the second year, the baton is passed to the Foundations of Clinical Practice course—a course which prepares students to make the move from the preclinical to the clinical years. Finally, the baton is passed to the Transition to Residency course, which prepares fourth-year students for internship and residency. The authors will discuss the first two courses, highlighting their more innovative aspects. All in all, these courses are specially designed to bring learners to the next step of their learning and professional identity development.

Pre-Matriculation Programs

Background

Most educators are united in their commitment to preparing students for academic success in medical school. Over the last several years, many schools have implemented Pre-Matriculation Programs to help prepare students transition into the first year (Crump and Fricker 2015, Schneid et al, 2018). As mentioned earlier, the phenomenon of the stressors associated with transition is not unique to medical schools. However, it is arguable that what is unique to medical education is the requirement that students be able to navigate a large volume of scientific information in a short amount of time (Schneid et al, 2018). Medical school is rigorous for all, but it is known that there are certain factors that predispose students from certain groups to be at increased risk for academic difficulty. These factors include, but are not limited to (Andriole and Jeffe 2010; Huff and Fang 1999; Kleshinski et al 2009), the following:

1. Longer intervals between college graduation and the start of medical school
2. Lower scores on standardized tests such as the MCAT or USMLE
3. Lower undergraduate GPAs

Students entering with one or more of these variables are more likely to fail to complete their medical school training, or to graduate without having passed the United States Medical Licensing Examination Step 1 or Step on the first attempt. Most schools have a successful passing of Step 1 and Step 2 Clinical Knowledge and Clinical Skills as requirements for graduation. Thus, these factors have a significant impact on the predicted successful graduation of the student body. Furthermore, experiencing academic difficulty can have a significant impact on student confidence and can result in increased rates of depression (Stewart et al, 1995).

Medical schools have employed various strategies to mitigate the potential academic risk associated with transition. For example, some schools offer a more flexible schedule that provides additional study time. Other schools offer a decelerated curriculum that extends the length of the medical school curriculum. In recent years, many schools have instituted the use of Pre-Matriculation Programs. Some schools offer the program to all admitted students, while others target students identified during the admissions process to have a potential for academic risk (Shields 2010). Overall, the goal of these programs is to increase study skills, develop familiarity with pre-clinical content, acculturate students with the campus, and create peer social support groups. Limited data from these programs show that students feel more familiar with school supports, engage more in social activities, and feel more confident when beginning the school year. In all, while limited, the data suggest that these programs can help students succeed in the first year of medical school (Schneid et al, 2018).

The Pre-Matriculation Program at the GW School of Medicine and Health Sciences (PMP)

Prior to 2013, the GW School of Medicine and Health Sciences (SMHS) offered a decelerated program as a suggested option to assist students with a factor that could place them at risk of academic difficulty. This program enrolled a select number of students into a decelerated 5-year medical program in which the first year of medical school was separated into two years (Year 1A and Year 1B). Students were selected by the admissions committee to participate in this program, and admission was contingent on participation. The program was successful in giving students who are at potential risk for academic difficulty increased confidence by participating in the curriculum at a slower pace as compared to students admitted to the traditional MD program. Later, the School of Medicine underwent a massive review and revision of its curricular offerings. The result was an innovative new curriculum incorporating more longitudinal learning and multiple ways to employ the use of the new state-of-the-art clinical simulation center. With the implementation of this revised curriculum, the administrators of the George Washington University SMHS found that enrolling students into a decelerated program was substantially more complex, and the decision was made to eliminate the five-year decelerated program. However, the need to support admitted students identified to be at potential risk for academic difficulty when adjusting to the rigors of medical school remained.

In 2013, a Pre-Matriculation Program was designed by relevant stakeholders throughout the medical school community after studying similar programs in the area and after reviewing the medical literature. The initial program was based largely on the long-standing program in place at the Howard University School of Medicine which employed MD candidates who completed the first year of medical school as tutors. The GW pilot Pre-Matriculation Program enrolled students that would have otherwise been admitted to the decelerated five-year program. The current iteration is structured as a four-week pre-matriculation program to selected accepted students. The program is offered to students identified to have one or more risk factors that might place them at risk of academic difficulty at the time of acceptance. In addition to the risk factors mentioned earlier in the chapter, the school looks at additional factors including the quantity or quality of an applicant's undergraduate science preparation. This program provides an enriching academic, social, and environmental adjustment to medical school and the local community. This program is offered by invitation only to students who self-identify as underrepresented-in-medicine, socioeconomically disadvantaged, first-generation college graduate, or as a student whom the Committee on Admissions believes would benefit from the program. If selected, an invitation for this required experience is made at the time of the offer of admission. This offer of admission is contingent upon full participation in the Pre-Matriculation Program. The program is housed in the Office of Diversity and Inclusion.

On average, about 10–12 students attend the program each year. All participants are offered on-campus housing and are provided a stipend. The program mentors are rising second year students who have the summer to experience areas of professional enrichment. The program provides early content and eases the transition into the first-year M.D. program curriculum. Workshops are provided on study and test-taking skills, stress reduction, and other strategies for success. The curriculum is designed as a four-week intense introduction to the material covered during the first block of medical school. In addition, the curriculum is supplemented with peer counseling, focus groups, clinical reasoning skills, study skills, clinical skills, and informational workshops designed to help students maintain a healthy and balanced lifestyle while in medical school.

Mission

The Pre-Matriculation Program aims to:

1. Prepare incoming medical students for the speed and depth of medical studies,
2. Provide mentorship to offer social support through peer-mentoring relationships,
3. Support students in their transition to the medical school environment, and
4. Introduce learning topics that will be covered during the first semester of medical school.

Program Curricular Overview

Currently, the course material covered during the program is taken from portions of the first and second blocks of the first semester of medical school. These blocks cover Foundations of Medicine as well as Inflammation, Hematology, Immunology, and Infection. The Immunology portion of the academic year curriculum has been found by previous students to be particularly challenging; and thus, it is well represented in the PMP curriculum.

Students are also introduced to clinical skills and professional development. Students learn how to conduct a patient interview and physical exam with a rudimentary introduction to developing a differential diagnosis and plan for therapeutic intervention. In addition, students are provided with non-technical, supplemental skills of which mastery is crucial to a successful medical school experience.

Use of Peer Mentors

Studies have shown us that the peer-group has one of the strongest influence[s] on behaviors and outcomes. The GW [P]re-[M]atriculation [P]rogram leverages this reality to help prepare students for the challenge of medical school. High achieving [,] rising [,] second-year medical students are selected as mentors who develop the month-long curriculum. Their proximity to the experience of the first-year allows the mentors to identify concepts that they, themselves, found challenging [—] and [,] in turn [, to] share strategies and lessons learned. Most importantly, the peer mentors serve as role models of and testaments to the reality that successfully making it through the first year of medical school is possible. (Grace Henry, Ed.D., Dir. of Diversity and Inclusion; Adjunct Asst. Prof. of Medicine)

Table 1. A sample schedule of week 1 of the PMP

	Monday	Tuesday	Wednesday	Thursday	Friday
8:30				Energy Mobilization and Metabolism	Quiz 2
9:00	Icebreaker	DNA Damage, Replication, and Repair	Quiz 1		PDX Core Maneuvers
9:30	Introductions		CSR History Taking		
10:00					
10:30	IDs	Transcription and Replication of Gene Expression		Nutrition and Body Weight Homeostasis	
11:00			Intro to Chest Anatomy and Physiology		
11:30	IT Logistics				
12:00	Lunch				
1:00	Organelle Structure	Early Embryonic Development and Tissue Differentiation	Intro to Pharmacology	Molecular Regulation of Cell Death	Biochemistry Review
2:00	Intro to Anatomic Terminology		Intro to Pharmacodynamics	Regulation of Cell Cycle/ Mitosis	Independent Study
3:00		Medical School Study Skills and Survival Guide	How to be Successful in Medical School	Independent Study	
4:00	Intro to Diagnostic Terminology				

An innovative aspect of the GW Pre-Matriculation Program is that the curriculum is redesigned each year by rising second-year students who can both serve as mentors regarding, and subject matter experts, on the rigors of transitioning to the first year. In this way, program participants can see themselves reflected in the confidence and successes of students who are one year removed from their experience. Selection preference is offered to students who are members of the Medical Education and Leadership Scholarly Concentration. This is one of nine extra-curricular "tracks" offered to all students in the MD program. The Medical Education & Leadership Scholarly Concentration is intended to attract students with a special interest in academic medicine and who foresee a future as members of a medical school faculty. Students from this concentration who serve as mentors in PMP are able to satisfy the track requirement to participate in a scholarly activity during the summer after the first year of medical school. Mentors are required to have satisfactorily completed all coursework during the first year of medical school. Mentors participate in a series of training sessions facilitated by staff of the Office of Diversity. These sessions are intended to help the mentors understand their own learning styles, areas of talent, and areas of challenge as it relates to serving in the position of educator and coach. Additionally, fundamentals of adult learning and the value of active learning are emphasized. Each year, the mentors are tasked with preparing a four-week curriculum that models what the participants will experience during the MD program. The goal is to identify key lectures and sessions on topics considered as being either particularly difficult to conceptualize or as representing key foundational information. A consistent theme in terms of preparing the curriculum is to expose the participants to the kind of volume of information presented during medical school. Even the most successful students often lament that they were least prepared for was the quantity of information and the time required to adequately prepare for demonstrations of understanding and competence.

An unexplored potential benefit of using peer mentors is the possibility that participating in the Pre-Matriculation Program as a mentor actually improves the mentors' academic performance. Teaching information is well known to be an active method of acquiring knowledge and retaining it. The program mentors face the first step of the medical licensing exam within a year of participating in the program; and the knowledge content that has been reinforced by their teaching role in the program is represented in Step 1 of the United States Medical Licensing Examination.

The authors contend that the use of peer mentors as teachers and leaders is one of the more innovative aspects of this program. Both the participants and the student mentors benefit from the camaraderie and bonding experience that comes from a shared common experience. The mentors can share wisdom and insights from a student perspective and can obtain a level of mastery over the material that can only come from feeling confident to teach the material. The confidence that the peer mentors achieve is passed on to the student participants; and many are inspired to follow this model.

I enjoyed having two student mentors who seemed very interested in helping us through our first year of medical school. I felt inspired by their leadership and abilities to create workshops and lectures that promoted our success in the Foundations courses. I was surprised by how many second-year students took the time to volunteer to teach the incoming students. I liked that the program was not only about mentoring incoming students, but [that] it [also] gave the second-year students the opportunity to hone their skills in providing lectures, workshops and answering questions. (Dr. Dalila Gittens, GW SMHS Class of 2019)

Finally, the authors assert that the advising for this program is another curricular innovation that contributes strongly to its success. The Office of Diversity and Inclusion employs a self-described intrusive advising model in which PMP students are proactively monitored. Cohort members receive encouraging emails before all medical school examinations throughout their undergraduate medical career; and they always have a place to reach out to in the event of early signs of academic difficulty. By reaching out immediately and often, the administrators give the student alumnae the sense that they are being supported. It is this type of proactive and continued mentorship—both from peer mentors and the administration—that can serve, in part, as a kind of buoy, keeping many of these students afloat as they pass through the sometimes choppy waters of medical education.

Evaluations

Students are formally evaluated using cumulative examinations for both the written and practical aspects of the courses. This assessment method was chosen because it best emulates the methods in which the students will be assessed during the academic year. Exam questions are approved by the respective professors whose content material is covered. For example, during one year, the students subjected themselves to a PowerPoint-projected team-based learning exercise with 15 questions (five from each tested subject) of testing material from the first week of the program. At the end of the third week, students had an individual PowerPoint-projected 18-question quiz (six questions from each tested subject) of testing materials from the third week of the program.

Since 2013, GW SMHS has enrolled a cohort of pre-matriculation students each summer. The cohort is generally comprised of anywhere from 8–12 students. The Office of Diversity and Inclusion anticipates twelve students will matriculate into the program for the 2019–2020 year. Approximately 50 students have completed the program since its inception. To date, none of these students has experienced significant academic difficulty during the first year of medical school. One student received below passing grades in more than one course during the second year of medical school and was required to repeat the year. The student then completed the additional year without difficulty. Another student withdrew from the MD program for personal reasons after successfully completing all the pre-clinical requirements.

Faculty members who participate in presenting material to participants in the Pre-Matriculation Program have a favorable view of the content selected for review by the mentors and the potential that the program represents in terms of student retention. One faculty member wrote,

For several years now, I have given a few lectures in the Pre-[M]atriculation Program at GWU SMHS. This program is designed to give promising students from challenging backgrounds a kind of head start on our full MD program ... I think that this program is useful for getting recent college graduates an orienting perspective on the content and level of coverage of typical lectures. I also provide some representative examination questions. It is the aim of this program to provide incoming students the tools needed to help them make the sometimes difficult transition from undergraduate studies to the more difficult and demanding work required in our medical school. In my opinion, the program is highly relevant, helping new students adjust to the rigors of our Core Curriculum. (Kurt Johnson, PhD. Professor of Anatomy and Cell Biology)

In all, the program is well received by the participants. Dr. Dalila Gittens, a recent SMHS graduate and program alumna, said of the program:

I believe that having lectures and exams on material that would be taught was very helpful ... I felt less overwhelmed with the material as a result and felt more prepared for the exams. I remember doing physical exam maneuvers for the first time and putting on our white coats and stethoscopes. I enjoyed learning the physical exam maneuvers with my classmates. I felt that I was in a safe and non-judgmental space to practice the maneuvers. During the first few PDX sessions, I was eager to demonstrate the maneuvers to other classmates who were not in the [P]re-[M]atriculation [P]rogram. I also got to meet people who were also new students and one of them wound up being my closest friend in medical school. (Dr. Dalila Gittens, GW SMHS Class of 2019)

Another student alumna characterized her experience as follows:

In the very first week of Foundations 1[,] I knew that I had a leg up after being a part of the PMP program. All of the nerves associated with the first day of medical school were pretty much dissipated. I [had] already formulated a study plan ... after [having made] necessary mistakes during the summer. For instance, I learned very quickly that I am not someone who benefitted from just reading lecture slides over and over. I realized that I retain things better if I actively reorganized my notes and made outlines of the lectures. It was nice to have realized this when in PMP [,] because [there] I could fumble around without jeopardizing my grade in the actual course.

More importantly ... PMP provided me with a group of friends that I still keep today! We got really close during the summer as we studied in groups and explored the District ... I had a reliable group of people from [D]ay 1[,] and that allowed me to hit the ground running.

Overall, PMP was a great eye-opener into the intensity of med school[,] without the associated stakes. The mentors were very open about their experiences[,] and I felt like I knew the system well before I even got there. I would say that this program greatly impacted my academic performance (especially in the first year) and helped me feel more comfortable in such a demanding environment. Plus[,] we had a lot fun! (Gifty Dominah, GW SMHS Class of 2021, MD anticipated)

LIMITATIONS

The authors recognize that formal assessment data of this program is limited. Furthermore, it is difficult to attribute student participant academic success or the lack thereof to a single factor. To date, much of the feedback comes from anecdotal evidence from graduates of the program. However; a formal mixed methods assessment is planned in the near future. The authors acknowledge that this more formal assessment of the program's graduates would be instrumental in determining future programmatic direction. It is difficult to ascertain which, if any, aspect of the PMP is instrumental in the future success of these students—or if other factors such as admissions committee selection or other pre-existing factors present at the time of the student's admission to the MD program are at play. A longitudinal study that follows students' post-medical school completion and examines future success may also be warranted.

The process of transition continues, as students make the transition from the preclinical years into the clinical years. At GW, this process is supported by the Foundations of Clinical Practice course, which aims to prepare students for the transition by beginning to weave together the preclinical factual and discrete knowledge domains into a tapestry of application to clinical practice.

PRECLINICAL TO CLINICAL TRANSITION COURSES

The transition from the pre-clinical curriculum to the clinical clerkship rotations in medical school can be an exciting and highly anticipated time, but may also be associated with stress and challenge (Firth, 1986; Radcliffe, 2003). This stress is underpinned by the finding that many students feel unprepared to begin their clerkship (Seabrook, 2004; O'Brien, 2007; Surmon, 2016). Students express concerns about the volume of knowledge to be acquired (Atherley, 2016; Godefrooij, 2010, Small, 2008; Greenberg, 2010; Surmon, 2016), clinical workload, extended work hours (Godefrooij, 2010), time management and self-care (Small, 2008). Both students and clerkship directors highlight concerns regarding roles and responsibilities, adjusting to the culture of patient care, and being able to adapt basic science knowledge and skills to the clinical situation. Clerkship directors echo concerns about preparedness (Windish, 2004; O'Brien, 2007) and also feel that students do not engage in adequate self-assessment as learning changes from an education-centric paradigm to one of experiential learning in a patient-centric environment. This transition requires students to adjust their learning styles while also having to navigate the complex social order of the clinical settings. In addition, students must transition to an environment where performance is measured through subjective evaluations of clinical skills, reasoning, and patient care – on the job performance- instead of objective standardized examinations.

Multiple studies have demonstrated that the challenges medical students face while transitioning to clinical clerkships can affect learning and performance (Pekrun, 2002; McConnell, 2012). Organizational socialization theory describes a process in which novice learners acquire knowledge, skills, and attitudes that help them to be successful in a workplace environment (Bauer, 2011). Successful 'onboarding' is enhanced when both newcomer and institution engage in deliberate activities to manage the uncertainties inherent in a new job. The theory, which describes success as a function of newcomer characteristics and attitudes, information-seeking and network-building behaviours, and organizational integration efforts and culture, can be applied to clerkship transitions.

Organizational socialization theory has been used to explore the determinants that affect success in the transition to the medicine clerkship (Atherley, 2016). Students who have a positive attitude or belief system are more successful in transitioning to clinical medicine. Peer to peer knowledge transfer has the potential for both positive and negative effects on student attitudes, whereas prior first-hand clinical experience reduces stress. This finding is supported by other studies that indicate that early patient contacts can minimize the shock of clinical practice (Diemers, 2007; Diemers, 2008; Godefrooij, 2010; Soo, 2016).

Students find that team integration (network building) is both important and difficult, and that their relative lack of clinical and institutional knowledge - usefulness to the team - are barriers to effective integration (Atherley, 2016). Students, when handing off generational knowledge to successors, prioritize information about workplace culture and normative behaviors, effective learning techniques and logistics – all essential for team function (Masters, 2013). Students who actively seek performance feedback from other members of the team feel more successful in integrating, whereas students who have little guidance feel isolated (Atherley, 2016).

Students who are integrated into the medical team with defined roles or responsibilities are more invested in patient care and learning (Atherley, 2016). Having real responsibilities in patient care, compared to experiences that only included shadowing and observation, enhances student desire to learn (Soo 2016). Acquisition of patient care skills and clinical reasoning is improved when students can associate a particular disease entity with an actual patient as a frame of reference.

Thus, adequate attention to student attitudes, organizational integration, and team building opportunities can improve student satisfaction and learning potential during the transition to clerkships. Organizations can facilitate this transition by providing a comprehensive orientation that outlines schedules, expectations, and assessments and by providing structure (Atherley, 2016). Clinical faculty may underestimate the support and guidance that newcomers to clinical practice need (Dornan, 2007). In addition, providing a nurturing environment in which faculty and housestaff are engaged may foster team building and optimize learning (O'Brien, 2007; Benbassat, 2013).

Overview of Transition Courses

Many medical schools have overhauled their curricula in order to provide exposure to clinically oriented courses that teach skills such as interviewing, physical examination, communication skills, and professional comportment and responsibility. A 2004 survey of US medical school deans (a survey with a response rate of 45%) found that 30 schools held some type of transition course (Poncelet, 2008). Most preclinical to clinical transition courses have been designed for one or more of three specific purposes:

- To present new skills needed for the clerkship phase,
- To review previously taught knowledge with an emphasis on clinical application, and/or
- To increase student wellbeing through better preparedness for the wards (O'Brien, 2010).

Some schools integrate essential clinical materials into the pre-clinical years in the form of clinical skills courses, while others administer specific transition courses during the pivotal transition time just before starting clerkships (Chumley, 2005; Jacobs, 2005; Van Gessel, 2003). Just-in-time transition courses are supported by research suggesting that critical intensive learning can occur just prior to a transition (Kilminster, 2011; Corbett, 2007; George, 2013; Taylor, 2014; Spura, 2016). In addition, workplace learning theory suggests that learners should practice authentic skills and tasks that accurately simulate skills for the workplace prior to the transition (Chittenden, 2009; Poncelet, 2008).

Most transition courses last between one day and one week; are mandatory; and occur just before the start of clerkships. Course duration affects course design, objectives, and instructional approaches. Course objectives are documented for 40% of transition courses that are 2–7 weeks in duration—but are documented only for 13% of transition courses that are a mere 1–4 days in duration (Poncelet, 2008). Poncelet et al. recommended three essential features of transition courses:

1) Address aspects that students, faculty, and clerkship directors recognize as being problematic;
2) Articulate specific, measurable objectives; and
3) Ensure the use of instructional approaches and learning objectives that meet the needs of the students.

They also suggest that these courses should be at least one week in length in order to meet learning objectives, provide assessments of students, and provide opportunities for students to experience day-to-day activities.

The George Washington University School of Medicine and Health Sciences (GW SMHS) underwent a curricular revision (starting with the class which matriculated in 2014), with the development of a pre-clinical curriculum based on organ system blocks. The blocks cover content in core organ systems in a sequential manner. Themes, including ethics, humanities, teamwork, human development throughout the life cycle, diversity and cultural competence, clinical skills and reasoning, public health, and evidence-based medicine are overlaid longitudinally on these blocks throughout the pre-clinical curriculum.

In order to help students transition to clinical clerkships, a new four-week course—Foundations of Clinical Practice (FCP)—was developed in 2016. Although the new block-based curriculum integrates basic sciences with clinical presentations, it does not provide the opportunity to explore the interactions between organ systems. Thus, the Transitions course is uniquely situated to highlight the multiorgan physiology of disease processes, while simultaneously using organizational socialization theory to prepare students for clerkships. Moreover, the Transitions course is designed to promote systems thinking and help students to understand the concept that medical issues arise within the context of the patient's overall physiologic status and within a healthcare system.

Needs Assessments

Needs assessments are an essential part of Kern's approach to curriculum design. The needs for transition courses vary, and are dependent on the stakeholders—medical schools, faculty, and the students themselves. National standards for medical student skills (Mileder, 2014) or expert consensus (Blohm, 2014) may be used to identify needed general skills and expectations for performance.

Pre-clinical students have identified history taking and physical examination; proficiency in oral presentations; and the generation of a differential diagnosis as being essential skills (Small, 2008). In comparison—and in retrospect—third-year students prioritize interpersonal skills, history taking and physical examination, and time management skills. When transitioning to a new clerkship, students hand off information about learning strategies effective for the clerkship—thus suggesting that this skill is also important for success (Masters, 2013).

In contrast, faculty members expect moderate competence in communications and interviewing and examination skills (Wenrich, 2004). Faculty emphasize the development of clinical reasoning skills and knowledge integration (Jacobson, 2010), and expect students to be good at receiving feedback (Windish, 2004). Faculty want students to understand the multidimensional aspects of patient care, including interdisciplinary clinical care mechanisms and overall hospital systems (Spura, 2016).

The authors in their role as co-directors of the FCP course conducted a needs assessment—soliciting input from students, residents, pre-clinical and clinical faculty, and clerkship directors in order to identify these groups' perceived needs for clerkship matriculation. In addition, the course directors queried the curriculum task force's list of essential content areas and skills for clinical practice in order to identify gaps in the preclinical curriculum which could be reasonably addressed in a Transitions course. Finally, longitudinal theme directors were engaged to ensure continuity between preclinical to clinical theme content. Integration of data from these sources yielded a combination of cognitive, teamwork and procedural skills that should be represented in clerkship preparation. These areas included clinical reasoning skills; diagnostic testing; distinguishing sick versus well patients; interprofessional teamwork; diversity;

patient advocacy and patient safety; procedural skills such as BLS and establishing a peripheral IV; writing notes; and using an electronic medical record.

Course Objectives and Structure

Poncelet (2008) found that of the 30 transition courses discussed in their review, only seven had learning objectives—and few had assessments or evaluations of the students. Most objectives were related to improving student comfort in clinical settings or with procedures; or were related to easing the transition into clerkships. O'Brien (2007) categorized transition course objectives from a survey of medical schools as being related to specific tasks, workplace culture and rules, or interpersonal skills in the workplace. Subsequent literature on transition courses (George, 2013; Taylor, 2014) provide more specific learning objectives which also fall into these broad categories.

The FCP course focuses specifically on the transition to inpatient medicine, as the medical school provides out-patient clinical experiences during the pre-clinical phase of the curriculum through a clinical apprenticeship program. FCP course objectives—outlined in Table 1—emphasize clinical knowledge acquisition; teamwork and communications skills; familiarity with the organizational structures of hospital-based care; and lifelong learning. The course objectives address educational needs identified by the clerkship needs assessment, organizational socialization theory, and workplace learning theory; and they are linked to GWU SMHS program objectives.

Learning Environment

Workplace learning theory suggests realistic work experiences are essential to learning. Transition programs may use one or more learning environments. Students may be paired with clinicians longitudinally outside a formal Transitions course (Turner, 2012; Miller, 2018) in order to facilitate understanding of the workplace and help contextualize learning. Several transition courses incorporate clinical experience on the wards (Chittenden, 2009; Jacobs, 2005) or immersive clinical experiences (Miller, 2018).

Table 2. Foundations of Clinical Practice Course Objectives

• Apply the principles of basic science in a clinical context.
• Define the process in which a patient enters and in which, with the help of health care professionals, the patient navigates the in-patient hospital system from admission to discharge.
• Practice introductory patient care skills (including writing admission and in-patient progress notes; oral presentations; writing admission and daily orders; ordering and interpreting labs; and radiologic imaging).
• Demonstrate the ability to perform common procedures (including CPR and basic life support; placement of peripheral IVs; and skills specific to the first rotation of the cohort).
• Demonstrate the initial evaluation and management of emergent clinical situations.
• Discuss the role of the student in an inter-disciplinary and inter-professional care team.
• Demonstrate the ability to use an electronic medical record.
• Explain the importance of quality improvement and patient safety in a clinical context.
• Apply principles of ethics, teamwork, cultural competence, public health, and professionalism in a clinical context.
• Identify goals for continuous learning moving forward to the clinical rotations.

These may include either closely supervised clinical care, or the development of a shadow team in which transitioning students perform activities related to patient admission and care in parallel with the patient's primary team (Chittenden, 2009). In this format, students perform all of the relevant patient care activities in a safe environment, in which they are not graded and their clinical decisions do not impact patient care. This approach, however, is both time consuming and difficult to implement with large numbers of students.

As an alternative to immersive clinical care, clinical vignettes—in which videotaped, written, or standardized patient actors must be admitted to the hospital and receive care—are often used to simulate the clinical realm (Taylor, 2014). These vignettes may be augmented by electronic medical records which include relevant physiologic, laboratory, and diagnostic imaging data in order to emulate real world data sources. Students practice knowledge integration and plan treatment, write notes, and give oral presentations. However, the essential steps of data acquisition are limited due to the artificial construct of the cases.

The FCP course utilizes a variety of environments to provide students with virtual workplace learning experiences. Throughout the month, students manage the inpatient care of three virtual patients in internal medicine, pediatrics, and surgery who are admitted to the hospital, are evaluated for pathology, clinically deteriorate, and are eventually are discharged. All didactic content—which is built on course objectives and which emphasizes clinical reasoning, diagnostic testing, communications skills, patient safety, and teamwork—is linked to the care of these patients, either directly or through weekly note writing or simulation exercises. Table 2 illustrates the linkages between global course content and longitudinal patient presentations. Patients are presented via a prerecorded (video) history and physical examination. Students use this material in order to generate initial written admission documents. Subsequent encounters take place via updates in the electronic medical record and in the simulation lab where high-fidelity mannequins are used to demonstrate the clinical deterioration of each of the virtual patients. In this setting, students are able to practice real-time data acquisition from the EMR and from the patient, and must rapidly develop a problem representation. These virtual patient experiences are supplemented with a ward-shadowing experience, during which transitioning students are paired with third-year clerks on a team corresponding to their first in-patient clinical assignment. In this environment, students gain temporally-appropriate experience and benefit from peer-to-peer knowledge transfer, yet without requiring additional clinical faculty resources. The hybrid model uses didactics, low-fidelity (video), and higher-fidelity (simulation and observed ward) experiences. This model balances the competing pressures of realistic training venues with the inherent limitations in ward availability.

In keeping with educational best practices, classroom-based sessions are limited to half-days throughout the course; the remaining time is spent in small-group or simulation exercises (as shown in Figure 1).

Didactic Content

Didactic content can be divided into several broad content areas. Core medical content reviews medical knowledge basics for the wards, framed as patient treatment options. Procedural skills sessions provide hands-on training for new skills such as IV placement, and also provide opportunities to operationalize the clinical knowledge during simulated patient events. Ward preparation sessions encompass an overview of the clerk's daily tasks in each of the clerkships—as well as an introduction to the hospital system, interdisciplinary teams, quality improvement, and patient safety. Teamwork and communica-

Figure 1. Over 50 faculty members participate in teaching this course (one week of the FCP schedule is shown; large group sessions are listed horizontally, while small group sessions are shown vertically)

	Monday	Tuesday	Wednesday	Thursday	Friday
6:00 / 7:00		Ward Shadowing	Ward Shadowing	Ward Shadowing	Ward Shadowing
8:00		Treating Pediatric Patients Across Clerkships: Presentation and Small Group Study	Basic Life Support / IV skills / Interview Practice / Differential Diagnosis		
9:00	Orientation and EPA		IV skills / Interview Practice	Introduction to Clinical Laboratory Medicine	Writing a Problem List and Plan
10:00	Public Health: Foundations of Obesity		IV Skills / Interview Practice	EBM 1: Clinical Prediction Rules	Overview of Medical Imaging
11:00					
1:00	Basic Life Support / IV skills / Interview Practice	Basic Life Support / IV skills / Interview Practice / Differential Diagnosis	Oral Presentations	Basic Life Support / IV skills / Interview Practice	Basic Life Support / IV skills / Interview Practice
2:00	IV skills / Interview Practice	IV skills / Interview Practice		IV skills / Interview Practice	IV skills / Interview Practice
3:00	IV skills / Interview Practice	IV skills / Interview Practice	Caring for the Geriatric Patient	IV skills / Interview Practice	
4:00	IV skills / Interview Practice	IV skills / Interview Practice		IV skills / Interview Practice	
5:00					

Table 3. Longitudinal cases in medicine, surgery, and pediatrics in the Foundations course

Concept	Medicine ("Linda Stewart")	Surgery ("Gloria Adams")	Pediatrics ("Caden Alvarez")
Chief Complaint	Dyspnea	Palpitations	Dyspnea
Diagnosis	COPD exacerbation in an elderly patient with multiple comorbidities and dementia	Pulmonary embolus in a postoperative bariatric surgery patient	Bronchiolitis in the setting of undiagnosed ventricular septal defect
Enter Healthcare	Transfer from nursing home	Direct admission	Emergency department
Barriers to Care	Dementia Power of attorney	Stigma of obesity	Language Access/insurance
Complication	Aspiration pneumonia and delirium	Retroperitoneal hematoma	Pulmonary edema
Handoff Tool	SBAR	SIGNOUT	I-PASS
Discharge Plan	NH/Rehab	Home	Home with services

tions sessions emphasize the student's role in the medical team, and describe best practices in oral and written communication with medical providers and patients.

Core Medical

Although some transition courses include clinical content (Jacobson 2010; George 2013), the rationale for content selection has not been well described in the literature. The clinical content for GW's FCP course was selected by course and clerkship directors in order to replicate common diagnostic and treatment questions encountered on the wards. Diagnostic sessions include identifying sick patients, or ordering and interpreting diagnostic imaging and laboratory testing. Additional clinical sessions review common treatment modalities—ones such as fluid and blood product administration, antibiotic use and infection control measures, pain control, and nutrition. Information about daily care orders is provided in an online format. Clinical content is explicitly linked to the care of the three longitudinal patients (as demonstrated in Table 3), so that students have an opportunity to directly apply the relevant knowledge in note writing, order sets, or the simulated environment.

Procedural Skills

Procedural skills training serves to improve student self-confidence (Miller, 2018) and comfort in the clinical environment (data on whether students use the skills that they were taught). Transition courses typically include procedural skills such as IV placement, wound care and suturing, and team skills such

Table 4. Clinical content for the longitudinal cases in medicine, surgery, and pediatrics

Clinical Content	Medicine ("Linda Stewart")	Surgery ("Gloria Adams")	Pediatrics ("Caden Alvarez")
Chief Complaint	Dyspnea	Palpitations	Dyspnea
Diagnosis	COPD exacerbation in an elderly patient with multiple comorbidities and dementia; develops aspiration pneumonia	Pulmonary embolus in a postoperative bariatric surgery patient; develops retroperitoneal bleed	Bronchiolitis in the setting of an undiagnosed ventricular septal defect; develops congestive heart failure
Laboratory Testing	Acid/base analysis	Serial hemoglobin Frequency of testing	Overutilization of laboratory testing
Diagnostic Imaging	Chest X-ray	Computed tomography	Echocardiogram
Antibiotic Stewardship and Infection Control	Antibiotic selection in pneumonia	Evaluation of the post-operative fever	Isolation precautions
Medication Orders	Insulin dosing Polypharmacy	Heparin dosing and anticoagulant use	Weight-based medications
Fluids	Bolus and maintenance fluids	Blood transfusion	Diuresis
Nutrition	Diabetic diet Aspiration risk	Bariatric diet	Growth curves Enteral feeding
Nursing Orders	Nursing care for delirium prevention		Measurement of fluid intake and output
Sick/Not Sick	Vital signs Septic shock	Vital sign trends Hypovolemic shock	Pediatric vital signs Cardiogenic shock

as BLS (Blohm, 2014; Chittenden, 2009; Chumley, 2005; Mileder, 2014). Little data is provided on the level of training or mastery learning in transition courses.

The authors have used two approaches to skills training in the FCP Transitions course. IV placement, a skill generally agreed by clerkship faculty to be universally useful, is taught to mastery level in the simulation environment. Students are trained in essential steps of the skill, and are required to demonstrate skill mastery by placing an IV in a mannequin arm while interacting with a standardized patient who is averse to needles. Students are expected to both perform all essential steps of the procedure correctly, and engage in compassionate communication with the patient. The goals of this training are not only to teach an essential skill, but also to engage students in the processes of deliberate practice, mastery learning, and the need to attend to patients' emotional needs in complex situations. Students are asked to reflect on the learning process so that lessons learned can be applied to future skills acquisition.

Other skills—including suturing, intubation, foley placement, and the manipulation of a laparoscopic camera—are provided as electives, as faculty recognize that students who are not participating in a surgical clerkship early in the clinical year may have no need for these skills yet, and no mechanism for skills retention. However, students request these sessions because the desire to have 'useful' skills reduces anxiety about clerkship preparedness and increases learner enthusiasm—both of which are positive learner attitudes that can contribute to success.

Ward Preparation and Orientation

Many transition courses include preparatory knowledge and skills that are relevant to all clerkships such as writing notes (Small, 2008; Soo, 2016; Sakai, 2012; Taylor, 2014; Chittenden, 2009), providing resources to search the literature (Small, 2008), and providing guidance on teamwork and inter-disciplinary hospital care (Soo, 2016; Sakai, 2012; Taylor, 2014). In addition, student responsibilities within the health care system, identification of medical errors and reporting, and patient safety were also stressed (Small, 2008; Soo, 2016; Sakai, 2012). Sakai et al. also provided an opportunity for students to meet with each clerkship director and clerkship administrative staff and coordinators.

The FCP Transitions course includes educational sessions that expose the students to each of the core clerkships and specialties. In addition to the six core clerkships of Internal Medicine, Obstetrics and Gynecology, Internal Medicine, Pediatrics, Psychiatry, and Surgery, the course includes additional specialties that are integral to patient care—specialties such as Geriatrics, Emergency Medicine, and Neurology. These sessions are not intended to be an orientation to the clerkships, but rather an opportunity to demonstrate how each specialty approaches clinical problems; to review and introduce knowledge and skills within the specialty; and to highlight specific areas of documentation that differ from the usual admission and progress notes.

In an effort to place a student's role in the context of the larger health care system, sessions on inter-disciplinary teams and social work, patient safety and quality improvement, and patient experience are delivered by hospital administrators. These sessions serve to demonstrate how students can influence patient safety and how students can use resources to optimize patient care.

The course provides opportunities for students to learn about the electronic medical record (EMR) by conducting searches for medical data and documenting patient care plans for the longitudinal patients. In addition, students practice access to the curriculum and evaluation management system; and they record duty hours.

Teamwork and Communications Skills

Transition courses provide an opportunity to develop and review essential communications skills. Roughly half of existing transition courses include written or oral communications activities (O'Brien, 2007), and 20% include specialty-specific oral presentation content.

Prior to the Transitions course, GW students all participate in a longitudinal Clinical Skills and Reasoning (CSR) course. It introduces history taking and physical examination, development of differential diagnoses, writing office-based notes, and providing oral presentations. The FCP course exposes students to the broad variety of notes that they will encounter clinically. Problem lists—which identify not only the primary presenting problem, but also identify ongoing medical and social issues—are introduced in the context of the admission history and physical examination documentation. Interactions between problems (such as the effects of steroids—given for COPD exacerbation—on blood glucose in the diabetic patient) are highlighted in order to illustrate the interconnected nature of various physiologic processes and to encourage systems thinking—in line with the course's goal of integrating preclinical block knowledge. SOAP notes, transfer notes, and discharge summaries are also reviewed and practiced for the virtual patients described above.

Students learn oral presentations during their CSR course. In order to better prepare students for clerkship-specific rounds, content and format of oral presentations are reviewed for each of the major clerkships. Communications protocols for patient handoff are discussed and practiced. Elements of a successful consult are reviewed. Finally, communications strategies for emergent situations are reviewed and then practiced in the simulation environment. Discharge discussions, including anticipatory advice, are practiced with standardized patients as the virtual patients are discharged from the hospital.

Students have the opportunity to practice teamwork in clinical settings through a series of simulation activities. After obtaining Basic Life Support (BLS) licensure, student teams care for simulated patients who require rapid assessment, early intervention, and handoff to residents. These rapid response/code blue simulation sessions expand on team roles learned in BLS with an emphasis on team communication in order to gather information and plan actions.

A final simulation event lets students care for the three longitudinal patients who become critically ill. Teams must evaluate the patients, perform critical early interventions, gather information from the patient and medical record, order and interpret diagnostic testing, determine a treatment plan, communicate with the patient or family, consult specialists, and hand the patient off to the ICU. In this setting, students are able to operationalize the didactic content as well as the clinical, communications, and teamwork skills that have been reviewed over the past month.

Student Evaluation

Few transition courses include evaluations of student performance. Taylor developed end-of-course assessments using a multi-station OSCE that tested a range of skills including writing admission histories; physical exam, CXR and EKG interpretation; searching the medical literature; and suturing and knot tying. On evaluation during the medicine clerkship, the first student cohort scored significantly better on the CXR and EKG reading than their historical peers, suggesting that knowledge acquired from this transition course was retained (Taylor, 2014). Students also expressed improved confidence in their clinical abilities.

During the FCP Transitions course, students receive formative assessment of weekly progress notes and order sets, oral presentations, teamwork and clinical skills during simulation events, and discharge conversations with simulated patients. A weekly 'roundup' session enables faculty to clarify common note and order writing errors, and provides an open forum for student questions. Summative evaluations are provided only for the intravenous catheter (IV) skills placement, and a final exam. The IV skills examination—which includes consent, interpersonal communications with an anxious patient, the safe placement of an IV, and a procedure note—is graded using a 13-point technical skills checklist and a nontechnical skills evaluation. Students who are not successful must retrain, and must repeat the examination, until passing performance is demonstrated. A final open book, short answer, and multiple-choice examination is administered to teams of students. It guides students through the admissions process and orders for both a medical and a surgical patient.

Student Self Evaluation and Preparation for Wards Learning

The AAMC has proposed a framework for clerkship evaluations via the core Entrustable Professional Activities (EPA). Many schools, including GWU SMHS, are working to implement EPA evaluation metrics as a part of the clinical evaluation process. The EPAs are presented to students during the FCP Transitions course in order to provide a framework for aspirational and expected behaviors for the clerkships. Students are encouraged to consider learning and professional development in the context of both course objectives and EPAs. Students are asked to undergo regular self-assessment within each clerkship using the EPAs as one group of metrics to assess their progress. The EPAs are linked to core content in the FCP Transitions course, as shown in Table 4. Students self-assess with EPAs at the beginning and end of the Transitions course using a published scale (Klapheke). Combined scores from three years of courses demonstrate self-reported skills improvements in all EPAs as a result of the FCP course (Figure 2). Unfortunately, large-scale curricular revisions that occurred simultaneously preclude comparison of wards' performance with prior cohorts.

FUTURE RESEARCH DIRECTIONS

Both the Pre-Matriculation Program and the Foundations of Clinical Practice Course could benefit from more expensive long-term evaluation of their effects on student performance at regular intervals. The authors plan a longitudinal research study in order to assess student performance and the perception of the effects of these transitions programs at regular intervals following students' completion of these respective programs.

CONCLUSION

Providing targeted support to students during known phases of stressful transition during their medical education is beneficial to students' overall academic performance, confidence, and well-being. The authors have described two successful programs at an urban United States medical school. Transitions programs should be tailored to the needs and contexts of the student participants in order to be maximally effective.

Table 5. Entrustable Professional Activities and Corresponding FCP Transitions course Sessions

EPA	FCP Transitions course Session
1. Gather a history and perform a physical examination	History and physical examination Critical care simulation
2. Prioritize a differential diagnosis following a clinical encounter	Patient care documentation (H and P, progress, transfer, and discharge notes) Oral case presentations Critical care simulation
3. Recommend and interpret common diagnostic and screening tests	Introduction to clinical lab medicine Imaging Patient care documentation Oral case presentations Critical care simulation
4. Enter and discuss orders and prescriptions	Asynchronous 'orders' module Patient care documentation and orders Critical care simulation EMR
5. Document a clinical encounter in the patient record	Patient care documentation
6. Provide an oral presentation of a clinical encounter	Oral case presentations
7. Form clinical questions and retrieve evidence in order to advance patient care	Evidence-based medicine Diagnostic bias Critical care simulation
8. Give and receive a patient handover in order to transition care responsibility	Handoff session, with in-class simulation Transfer note Critical care simulation
9. Collaborate as a member of an inter-professional team	Elective ward shadowing Nutrition Ancillary services Interdisciplinary rounds Handoff and consult sessions
10. Recognize a patient requiring urgent or emergent care and initiate evaluation and management	BLS certification Sick or not sick? Critical care simulations
11. Obtain informed consent for tests and/or procedures	Peripheral intravenous catheter (IV) placement: practice and test
12. Perform general procedures of a physician	IV placement Elective skills stations
13. Identify system failures and contribute to a culture of safety and improvement	Patient safety and quality improvement Patient experience

Figure 2. Self-reported EPA confidence before and after FCP Transitions course. The data represents 3 years of student self-evaluations (n=528). All pre-post differences are statistically significant via student's t test with p<0.01

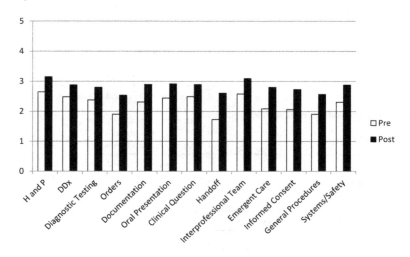

REFERENCES

Andriole, D., & Jeffe, D. (2010). Pre-matriculation variables associated with suboptimal outcomes for the 1994–1999 cohort of US medical school matriculants. *Journal of the American Medical Association*, *304*(11), 1212–1219. doi:10.1001/jama.2010.1321 PMID:20841535

Atherley, A. E., Hambleton, I. R., Unwin, N., George, C., Lashley, P. M., & Taylor, C. G. (2016). Exploring the transition of undergraduate medical students into a clinical clerkship using organizational socialization theory. *Perspectives on Medical Education*, *5*(2), 78–87. doi:10.100740037-015-0241-5 PMID:26951164

Bauer, T., & Erdogran, B. (2011). Organizational socialization: The effective on boarding of new employees. In S. Zedeck (Ed.), *Maintaining, expanding, and contracting the organization* (pp. 51–64). Washington, DC: American Psychological Association. doi:10.1037/12171-002

Benbassat, J. (2012). Undesirable features of the medical learning environment: A narrative review of the literature. *Advances in Health Sciences Education: Theory and Practice*, *18*(3), 527–536. doi:10.100710459-012-9389-5 PMID:22760724

Blohm, M., Krautter, M., Lauter, J., Huber, J., Weyrich, P., Herzog, W., ... Nikendei, C. (2014). Voluntary undergraduate technical skills training course to prepare students for clerkship assignment: Tutees' and tutors' perspectives. *BMC Medical Education*, *14*(1), 71. doi:10.1186/1472-6920-14-71 PMID:24708782

Bullock, A., Fox, F., Barnes, R., Doran, N., Hardyman, W., Moss, D., & Stacey, M. (2013). Transitions in medicine: Trainee doctor stress and support mechanisms. *Journal of Workplace Learning*, *25*(6), 368–382. doi:10.1108/JWL-Jul-2012-0052

Chittenden, E. H., Henry, D., Saxena, V., Loeser, H., & O'Sullivan, P. S. (2009). Transitional clerkship: An experiential course based on workplace learning theory. *Academic Medicine, 84*(7), 872–876. doi:10.1097/ACM.0b013e3181a815e9 PMID:19550179

Chumley, H., Olney, C., Usatine, R., & Dobbie, A. (2005). A short transitional course can help medical students prepare for clinical learning. *Family Medicine, 37*(7), 496–501. https://www.ncbi.nlm.nih.gov/pubmed/15988643 PMID:15988643

Crump, W., & Fricker, R. (2015). A medical school prematriculation program for rural students: Staying connected with place, cultivating a special connection with people. *Teaching and Learning in Medicine, 27*(4), 422–430. doi:10.1080/10401334.2015.1077709 PMID:26508001

Diemers, A. D., Dolmans, D. H., Santen, M. V., Luijk, S. J., Janssen-Noordman, A. M., & Scherpbier, A. J. (2007). Students' perceptions of early patient encounters in a PBL curriculum: A first evaluation of the Maastricht experience. *Medical Teacher, 29*(2–3), 135–142. doi:10.1080/01421590601177990 PMID:17701623

Diemers, A. D., Dolmans, D. H., Verwijnen, M. G., Heineman, E., & Scherpbier, A. J. (2007). Students' opinions about the effects of preclinical patient contacts on their learning. *Advances in Health Sciences Education: Theory and Practice, 13*(5), 633–647. doi:10.100710459-007-9070-6 PMID:17629786

Dornan, T., Boshuizen, H., King, N., & Scherpbier, A. (2007). Experience-based learning: A model linking the processes and outcomes of medical students' workplace learning. *Medical Education, 41*(1), 84–91. doi:10.1111/j.1365-2929.2006.02652.x PMID:17209896

Firth, J. (1986). Levels and sources of stress in medical students. *British Medical Journal, 292*(6529), 1177–1180. doi:10.1136/bmj.292.6529.1177 PMID:3085772

George, P., Macnamara, M. M., Gainor, J., & Taylor, J. S. (2013). An integrated virtual family curriculum to introduce specialty-specific clinical skills to rising third-year medical students. *Teaching and Learning in Medicine, 25*(4), 342–347. doi:10.1080/10401334.2013.827977 PMID:24112204

Godefrooij, M. B., Diemers, A. D., & Scherpbier, A. J. (2010). Students' perceptions about the transition to the clinical phase of a medical curriculum with preclinical patient contacts; a focus group study. *BMC Medical Education, 10*(1), 28. doi:10.1186/1472-6920-10-28 PMID:20367885

Gohara, S., Shapiro, J., Jacob, A., Khuder, S., Gandy, R., Metting, P., & Kleshinski, J. (2011). Joining the conversation: Predictors of success on the United States Medical Licensing Examinations (USMLE). *Learning Assistance Review, 16*(1), 11–20.

Greenberg, L., & Blatt, B. (2010). Perspective: Successfully negotiating the clerkship years of medical school: a guide for medical students, implications for residents and faculty. *Academic Medicine, 85*(4), 706–709. doi:10.1097/ACM.0b013e3181d2aaf2 PMID:20354392

Hesser, A., & Lewis, L. (1992). Evaluation of a summer prematriculation program for black and other nontraditional students. *Academic Medicine, 67*(4), 270–272. doi:10.1097/00001888-199204000-00016 PMID:1558602

Hesser, A., & Lewis, L. (1992). Prematriculation program grades as predictors of black and other nontraditional students' first-year academic performances. *Academic Medicine*, *67*(9), 605–607. doi:10.1097/00001888-199209000-00015 PMID:1520422

Huff, L., & Fang, L. (1999). When are students most at risk of encountering academic difficulty? A study of the 1992 matriculants to U.S. medical schools. *Academic Medicine*, *74*(4), 454–460. doi:10.1097/00001888-199904000-00047 PMID:10219232

Jacobs, J., Bolhuis, S., Bulte, J., Laan, R., & Holdrinet, R. (2005). Starting learning in medical practice: An evaluation of a new introductory clerkship. *Medical Teacher*, *27*(5), 408–414. doi:10.1080/01421590500087001 PMID:16147793

Jacobson, K., Fisher, D. L., Hoffman, K., & Tsoulas, K. D. (2010). Integrated cases section: A course designed to promote clinical reasoning in Year 2 medical students. *Teaching and Learning in Medicine*, *22*(4), 312–316. doi:10.1080/10401334.2010.512835 PMID:20936581

Kilminster, S., Zukas, M., Quinton, N., & Roberts, T. (2011). Preparedness is not enough: Understanding transitions as critically intensive learning periods. *Medical Education*, *45*(10), 1006–1015. doi:10.1111/j.1365-2923.2011.04048.x PMID:21916940

Klapheke, M., Cubero, M., & Johnson, T. (2017). Assessing entrustable professional activities during the psychiatry clerkship. *Academic Psychology*, *41*(3), 345–349. doi:10.100740596-017-0665-9

Masters, D. E., O'Brien, B. C., & Chou, C. L. (2013). The third-year medical student "grapevine.". *Academic Medicine*, *88*(10), 1534–1538. doi:10.1097/acm.0b013e3182a36c26

McConnell, M. M., & Eva, K. W. (2012). The role of emotion in the learning and transfer of clinical skills and knowledge. *Academic Medicine*, *87*(10), 1316–1322. doi:10.1097/ACM.0b013e3182675af2 PMID:22914515

Mileder, L., Wegscheider, T. & Dimai, H. P. (2014). Teaching first-year medical students in basic clinical and procedural skills – A novel course concept at a medical school in Austria. *GMS Zeitschrift fuer Medizinische Ausbildung, 31*(1): Doc6.Doi:10.3205/zma000898

Miller, S., Shipper, E., Hasty, B., Merrell, S. B., Lee, E. L., Lin, D., & Lau, J. N. (2018). Introductory surgical skills course: Technical training and preparation for the surgical environment. *MedEdPORTAL*, *14*(10775). doi:10.15766/mep_2374-8265.10775 PMID:30800975

O'Brien, B., Cooke, M., & Irby, D. M.O'Brien. (2007). Perceptions and attributions of third-year student struggles in clerkships: Do students and clerkship directors agree? *Academic Medicine*, *82*(10), 970–978. doi:10.1097/ACM.0b013e31814a4fd5 PMID:17895662

Pekrun, R., Goetz, T., Titz, W., & Perry, R. P. (2002). Academic Emotions in Students Self-Regulated Learning and Achievement: A Program of Qualitative and Quantitative Research. *Educational Psychologist*, *37*(2), 91–105. doi:10.1207/S15326985EP3702_4

Poncelet, A., & O'Brien, B. (2008). Preparing medical students for clerkships: A descriptive analysis of transition courses. *Academic Medicine*, *83*(5), 444–451. doi:10.1097/ACM.0b013e31816be675 PMID:18448897

Radcliffe, C., & Lester, H. (2003). Perceived stress during undergraduate medical training: A qualitative study. *Medical Education, 37*(1), 32–38. doi:10.1046/j.1365-2923.2003.01405.x PMID:12535113

Sakai, D. H., Fong, S. F., Shimamoto, R. T., Omori, J. S., & Tam, L. M. (2012). Medical school hotline: Transition to clerkship week at the John A. Burns School of Medicine. *Hawai'i Journal of Medicine & Public Health: A Journal of Asia Pacific Medicine & Public Health, 71*(3), 81–83. PMID:22454819

Schneid, S., Apperson, A., Laiken, N., Mandel, J., Kelly, C., & Brandl, K. (2018). A summer prematriculation program to help students succeed in medical school. *Advances in Health Sciences Education: Theory and Practice, 23*(3), 499–511. doi:10.100710459-017-9808-8 PMID:29340892

Seabrook, M. A. (2004). Clinical students initial reports of the educational climate in a single medical school. *Medical Education, 38*(6), 659–669. doi:10.1111/j.1365-2929.2004.01823.x PMID:15189263

Shields, P. (1994). A survey and analysis of student academic support programs in medical schools focus: Underrepresented minority students. *Journal of the National Medical Association, 86*(5), 373–377. PMID:8046766

Small, R. M., Soriano, R. P., Chietero, M., Quintana, J., Parkas, V., & Koestler, J. (2008). Easing the transition: Medical students' perceptions of critical skills required for the clerkships. *Education for Health, 20*, 1–9. PMID:19967639

Soo, J., Brett-Maclean, P., Cave, M., & Oswald, A. (2015). At the precipice: A prospective exploration of medical students' expectations of the pre-clerkship to clerkship transition. *Advances in Health Sciences Education: Theory and Practice, 21*(1), 141–162. doi:10.100710459-015-9620-2 PMID:26164285

Spura, A., Werwick, K., Feissel, A., Gottschalk, M., Winkler-Stuck, K., Bernt-Peter, R., ... Stieger, P. (2016). Preparation courses for medical clerkships and the final clinical internship in medical education – The Magdeburg Curriculum for Healthcare Competence. *GMS Journal for Medical Education, 33*(3), 2366–5017. PMID:27275505

Stewart, S., Betson, C., Marshall, I., Wong, C., Lee, P., & Lam, T. (1995). Stress and vulnerability in medical students. *Medical Education, 29*(2), 119–127. doi:10.1111/j.1365-2923.1995.tb02814.x PMID:7623698

Surmon, L., Bialocerkowski, A., & Hu, W. (2016). Perceptions of preparedness for the first medical clerkship: A systematic review and synthesis. *BMC Medical Education, 16*(1), 89. doi:10.118612909-016-0615-3 PMID:26968816

Taylor, J. S., George, P. F., MacNamara, M. M., Zink, D., Patel, N. K., Gainor, J., & Dollase, R. H. (2014). A new clinical skills clerkship for medical students. *Family Medicine, 46*(6), 433–439. https://fammedarchives.blob.core.windows.net/imagesandpdfs/pdfs/FamilyMedicineVol46Issue6Taylor433.pdf PMID:24911298

Turner, S. R., White, J., Poth, C., & Rogers, W. (2012). Preparing students for clerkship. *Academic Medicine, 87*(9), 1288–1291. doi:10.1097/ACM.0b013e3182623143 PMID:22836844

Van Gessel, E., Nendaz, M. R., Vermeulen, B., Junod, A., & Vu, N. V. (2003). Development of clinical reasoning from the basic sciences to the clerkships: A longitudinal assessment of medical students' needs and self-perception after a transitional learning unit. *Medical Education, 37*(11), 966–974. doi:10.1046/j.1365-2923.2003.01672.x PMID:14629409

Wenrich, M., Jackson, M. B., Scherpbier, A. J., Wolfhagen, I. H., Ramsey, P. G., & Goldstein, E. A. (2010). Ready or not? Expectations of faculty and medical students for clinical skills preparation for clerkships. *Medical Education Online, 15*(5295). doi:10.3402/meo.v15i0.5295 PMID:20711483

Wilson, W., Henry, M., Ewing, G., Rehmann, J., Canby, C., Gray, J., & Finnerty, E. (2011). A prematriculation intervention to improve the adjustment of students to medical school. *Teaching and Learning in Medicine, 23*(3), 256–262. doi:10.1080/10401334.2011.586923 PMID:21745061

Windish, D. M., Paulman, P. M., Goroll, A. H., & Bass, E. B. (2004). Do clerkship directors think medical students are prepared for the clerkship years? *Academic Medicine, 79*(1), 56–61. doi:10.1097/00001888-200401000-00013 PMID:14690998

KEY TERMS AND DEFINITIONS

Clerkship: A course of clinical medical training in medical school that usually lasts a minimum of several weeks and occurs during the third and fourth years of undergraduate medical education.

Clinical: referring to the third and fourth years of undergraduate medical education.

Curriculum Design: The purposeful, deliberate, and systemic organization of a curriculum within a class or a course in undergraduate medical education.

Foundations of Clinical Practice: A transition course offered at the GW SMHS to support students during their transition from the preclinical to the clinical phase of their undergraduate medical education.

GW SMHS: The George Washington School of Medicine and Health Sciences.

Peer Mentor: a person, in this case a student, who has lived through a specific experience who can guide a student new to that experience.

Preclinical: Referring to the first, largely foundational and theoretical, stage of undergraduate medical education.

Pre-Matriculation Programs: Programs designed to support students in the period of time between enrollment and beginning an educational course of study.

Chapter 12
Psychometric Post–Examination Analysis in Medical Education Training Programs

Emanuele Fino
Aston Medical School, UK

Bishoy Hanna-Khalil
Aston Medical School, UK

ABSTRACT

Assessment in medical education has changed dramatically over the last two decades. The current, global call for medical practitioners has encouraged medical schools to open their doors and expand their curricula, generating an increasing demand for guidance with regards to the assurance and improvement of the quality of training programs and systems. This chapter provides the reader with an overview of psychometric post-examination analysis. The authors' view is that these are strategic educational assets that can help medical educators to understand and evidence the extent to which assessment data and their interpretation reflect the achievement of learning objectives, and the validity of assessment methods implemented in medical education programs.

INTRODUCTION

Assessment in medical education has changed radically over the last two decades (Norcini & McKinley, 2007; Swanwick, Forrest, & O'Brien, 2019). Traditional methods of examinations such as the written papers, based on open-ended questions, and oral examinations are being replaced with standardized written tests of applied knowledge and objective structured clinical exams. These are guided with the intention of making assessment more reliable, valid and acceptable. Recent developments in psychometric theory and access to advanced computational technology have favored such changes, allowing educators to improve methods and tools used to assess students through their academic progression and transition into the medical profession.

DOI: 10.4018/978-1-7998-1468-9.ch012

The use of psychological measurement in medical education has a long-standing history, originating from the need of educators to make high-stake decisions and provide multiple stakeholders (students, regulatory bodies, health systems, communities) with results in which measurement error is minimized. The vast majority of assessment methods and techniques will ultimately produce indirect observations of latent constructs (Finch & French, 2018), which are assumed to represent part of the fundamental toolkit of knowledge, competences, and skills that a doctor is required to develop (e.g. functional knowledge of basic sciences, diagnostic reasoning, and communication skills). Unfortunately, educational measures differ from the measurement of attributes of physical objects in that they entail a higher degree of variation or error, which in turn need to be inspected and properly addressed to consider the assessment results as reliable and valid, and to allow educators to make confident decisions. This makes the pursuit of precision and the calibration of assessment methods cost or effort dependent, however necessary to satisfy decision-making requirements (Bond & Fox, 2015; Jackson, Jamieson, & Khan, 2007).

Psychometrics represent a set of evidence-based theoretical test models that can help to validate the fundamental assumption that a test score, usually expressed in numeric terms, will represent a certain degree of a medical student's capacity within a defined domain of scientific knowledge or clinical skills and competencies (Kline, 2014; Norman, 2016). Such models are necessary to clarify and evidence the relation between the measured or observed score, the underlying latent construct that the test is aiming to measure (De Champlain, 2010), and to provide clear and evidence-based recommendations to educators with regards to a process that will determine academic progression and ultimately medical licensing.

It is important to remind the reader that assessment in medical education occurs within a situated system of learning practices and in relation to a curriculum, and the pursuit of a constructive alignment of curriculum and assessment is key in this process (Orsmond & Merry, 2017). The process is meant to be cyclic and guided by the definition and implementation of clear, specific learning outcomes informing all further steps, from the choice of core content to learning, teaching, and assessment methods (Harden, 2007). Assessment will generally serve the purpose of verifying whether medical students have attained – and, to what extent – the desired learning outcomes. Tavakol and Dennick (2011, p. 448) distinguish between two major phases of the assessment process, namely measurement and evaluation. They define measurement as the "process of assigning a numerical value in order to assess the magnitude of the phenomenon being measured", while drawing upon Tyler's (1949) classic definition, they conceptualize evaluation as "the process of determining to what extent the educational objectives are being realized". It is at this point that psychometric post-examination analysis comes into place, based on the fundamental aim of evaluating and interpreting the characteristics of a test (e.g. central location and dispersion of scores, internal consistency, construct validity) in relation to the results observed in a group of examinees and the pre-specified learning outcomes of a medical program.

Therefore, in this conceptualization, the importance of psychometric post-examination analysis does not reside just in the attempt to summarize student performance, but rather it represents a step that shall precede and inform decision making in medical education, providing educators with insight into the constructive alignment of curriculum and assessment, and robust interpretation of test scores supporting progression decisions.

It is a fact that the content and learning outcomes of medical education globally are continuously evolving (Sundberg, Josephson, Reeves, & Nordquist, 2017). There is a basic core corpus of knowledge, competence, and skills which survives across generations, however current medical programs are also called to account for public health, educational, and political scenarios that are rapidly changing, characterized by the significant impact of digital technologies and evidence-based medicine on learning and professional practice, and the impact these have on the public understanding of health.

The recent affirmation in U.S. Medical Schools of integrated curricula has determined a number of curricular reforms to ensure that graduating physicians are immediately prepared to apply their knowledge and skills into real-world clinical scenarios. These include, for example, a short pre-clerkship that has led several schools to adapt the timing of the exam to after students have completed their clerkships. Recent literature has shown that although such curricular reforms are determining a number of pedagogical benefits, several challenges arise and shall be addressed. Pock, Daniel, Santen, Swan-Sein, Fleming, & Harnik (2019, p. 775), identified the following:

- lack of student preparation due to poor development and / or consolidation of basic science knowledge;
- risk of weaker students progressing due to lack of insight and appropriate methods to identify and help them;
- inadequateness of students to clerkship;
- extension of study times;
- uncertainty and anxiety about future specialty choices;
- reduced time to pass board exams.

The strategies that Pock et al. (2019, p. 775) identified to overcome these potential challenges are: effective "communication with all stakeholders; curricular design and assessments that facilitate integration of basic and clinical sciences; and proactive student coaching and advising."

In this regard, it is the authors' opinion that U.S. Medical Schools could certainly benefit from the integration of psychometrics in their quality assurance, supporting their design and implementation of curricular design to tackle such challenges. In fact, lack of preparation, poor knowledge and skills could be identified in a timely manner and addressed by thorough psychometric post-examination analysis, helping educators to spot false positives and false negatives and require additional testing before progressing. By identifying weaker students based on robust scientific evidence, medical schools could then tailor communication, remediation and coaching of students, and inform stakeholders about the progress of those students who are approaching clerkship, with a higher degree of confidence, facilitating judgement over the quality of their knowledge and their integration of basic science and clinical skills.

In this chapter, the authors will aim to provide the reader with a comprehensive view of psychometric post-examination analysis, considering it a strategic asset in the implementation of a robust, valid and transparent approach in medical programs that satisfies the requirements of multiple and diverse stakeholders.

With a worldwide need for medical practitioners, medical schools are accepting more students and expanding their curricula, eliciting an increasing demand for guidance with regards to the assurance and improvement of the quality of training programs and systems. This chapter will serve as an important resource for educators and learning practitioners working within medical education, particularly those involved in the measurement and evaluation of student learning.

BACKGROUND

Historically, three main theoretical models have attempted to provide a comprehensive framework to the psychometric approach of the analysis of assessment results. These are: Classical Test Theory (CTT), Generalizability Theory (GT), and Item Response Theory (IRT).

CTT relies on the fundamental assumption that the score a test-taker obtains can be decomposed into two components: the 'true' score, i.e. the variance corresponding to the expected value, fully representing the ability of interest in a hypothetical, infinite number of test administrations, and 'error', i.e. the variance that represents any factor other than the ability being tested (Allen & Yen, 2001; De Champlain, 2010; Lord & Novick, 2008; Sijtsma, 2009; Walsh, 2013).

Considered an extension of CTT, GT provides a comprehensive theoretical framework and a set of statistical procedures to decompose and differentiate test variance in multiple components, called facets (Brennan, 2010; Cronbach, Gleser, Nanda, & Rajaratnam, 1972; Shavelson & Webb, 1991). GT has the great advantage of requiring few distributional assumptions, and produces unbiased estimators (Bloch & Norman, 2012; Shavelson & Webb, 1991). An important advancement of GT compared to CTT is that it allows researchers to separate the proportion of variance in test scores that is attributable to test-takers' abilities, and the proportion of variance accounted for by other variables affecting scoring, such as examiners, setting and time. This allows the researcher to decide if the variability of each facet is due to measurement error. Reliability is therefore expressed in terms of generalizability of test scores to a set of facets (e.g., items, examiners), and depends on the sources of variance that the researcher will consider as part of the 'error' variance, and whether the test scores will be interpreted using norm-referencing or criterion-referencing (G-Study). Ultimately, the researcher will have of a powerful set of statistical procedures to make decisions over the improvement of the reliability of future measurements occasions, for example by estimating the change in reliability obtained by increasing the number of items, examiners, or even a combination of both (D-Study).

Finally, IRT (Baker, 2001; Embretson & Reise, 2000; Lord, 1980) represents a family of models based on the fundamental assumption that a test-taker's response to an item is a function of both their ability and the level of difficulty of the item (Bond & Fox, 2015). In contrast to CTT and GT, IRT primarily concentrates on the analysis of the information that one can extract from the individual item-level, rather than a test as a whole. Three IRT models, known as three-, two-, and one-parameter models are mainly utilized in educational measurement (with the one-parameter model often referred to as the 'Rasch' model, named after Georg Rasch who introduced it in 1961). These models offer a number of advantages compared to CTT, particularly with regards to person and item scaling. In general, because the probability of answering an item correctly is a function of both the ability of the person and the difficulty of the item, these two can be measured on the same scale and compared through a conversion of scores into success-to-failure odds that indicate the location of the person and of the item along a continuous scale. Reliability is hence defined in terms of 'information', i.e. as a function of the model parameters. Furthermore, IRT parameter estimations do not depend on the specific characteristics of a sample of examinees taking a test. However, IRT models tend to make stronger assumptions than CTT, including sample size requirements and verification of some fundamental characteristics of the test, such as unidimensionality and local independence (Bond & Fox, 2015), and their application require complex computational procedures. Figure 1 shows a comparison chart between different theoretical models.

The chapter will focus on examples of applications of CTT, guiding the reader to develop a thorough understanding of their meaning and implications for the quality improvement of medical education

Figure 1. Comparison of different theoretical models in psychometric post-exam analysis

	Classical Test Theory	Generalizability Theory	Item Response Theory
Main focus and scope	Item difficulty, discrimination, correlation with the total, internal consistency of an exam paper.	Variance components impacting a set observed scores (e.g. students, examiners, location, circuit, etc), reliability and the Standard Error of Measurement measured at the overall exam level	Student ability as a function of item difficulty and discrimination, reliability measured at the item level.
Assumptions	Low	Low	High (sample size, unidimensionality, local independence)
Expertise required to be applied	Low	Medium/High, depending on the complexity of the model under investigation	High
Level of detail deriving from the analysis	Low	Medium/High, depending on the complexity of the model under investigation	High

programs by using a practical, applicative perspective (rather than theoretical-speculation), embracing the analysis of measures of central location, dispersion, test validity, reliability, standard setting, and item performance. In particular, it will concentrate on the post-examination evaluation of the three basic domains from Miller's (1990) pyramidal model of clinical competence, namely knowledge and application of knowledge (both assessed through Applied Knowledge Tests [AKTs]), and demonstration of knowledge (usually assessed through Objective Structured Clinical Examinations [OSCEs]). Cases of how these principles apply to the medical education community will be provided throughout the chapter, focusing on how applying psychometric principles could assist in the development of exam questions and papers on a practical level.

The Construct Validity of Medical Assessments

The analysis of validity in medical education is based on the modern theorisation provided by Messick (1994; see also Colliver, Conlee, & Verhulst, 2012; Downing, 2003). In this theoretical framework, validity is conceptualized in hypothetical terms, representing the extent to which the information collected and observed through a test corresponds to what the test was originally aimed to observe (Messick, 1994). Therefore, in order to consider an assessment as valid, assessors need to collect, analyze, and present sufficient evidence to support such a hypothesis. This approach represents a development of the original view of validity as divided in content, criterion, and construct validity (Crossley, Humphris, & Jolly, 2002), shifting the focus onto construct validity as the only type of validity that can be investigated.

In the context of assessment in medical education, construct validity represents the extent to which an assessment is ultimately capable of measuring what it aims to measure (Cronbach & Meehl, 1955). In turn, constructs are defined as "intangible collections of abstract concepts and principles which are inferred from behavior and explained by educational or psychological theory" (Downing, 2003, p. 831). In the specific case of medical education, assessors are interested in measuring educational attainment by looking at learners' use of knowledge and their mastery of clinical and practical skills (e.g. history-taking, examination, communication) through targeted tests. For these reasons, the validity of an assessment requires medical educators to focus onto a specific set of sources that can help them assess the extent to which the measurement of educational attainment in examinees has been achieved. In particular, five sources of evidence have been identified and discussed in the literature, and these should always be considered in a robust investigation of validity in medical assessments (Downing, 2003; Messick, 1994). These are: (1) core content coverage, (2) appropriateness of the response process, (3) the internal consistency of the assessment, (4) the statistical convergence with other valid tests measuring the same variables, and (5) the implications of validity to the examinees' learning and their progression in the program. Following, these sources are presented and discussed.

1.   Core content coverage.

Blueprinting is considered best practice in modern medical education programs (Patil, Gosavi, Bannur, & Ratnakar, 2015). Blueprinting represents the process of pre-determining the core content that a program should implement into its curriculum, mapped against learning outcomes and stages of learning. In the interest of assessment validity, the link between curriculum and assessment then assumes a crucial role. Assessors should make sure that every assessment thoroughly represents the curriculum blueprint, and that assessment items adequately cover the learning outcomes and core content for that particular stage of learning. Best practice requires medical assessors to then liaise with item writers and teaching staff in order to collaborate on the production and quality improvement of items and assessment tests that are representative of the blueprint and the range of learning activities included in the program.

2.   Appropriateness of the response process.

The format of items and stations should be familiar to examinees, and dedicated assessment training sessions for staff are warranted throughout the curriculum. The quality of the scoring process and the combination of different scores forming a common marking scale are also key in preventing random and systematic error, and ultimately in determining robust and defensible pass-fail decisions. Nevertheless, scores also require an accurate and evidence-informed interpretation, especially when open-ended formats are used (e.g., short answer questions), and in clinical exams (OSCEs). Medical assessors will then need to carefully provide staff and test writers with adequate training, monitor their performance and progress, and moderate when the quality of item writing and interpretation is not mirroring pre-defined standards.

3.   *The internal consistency of an assessment*

This represents the degree to which all assessment items are measuring the same construct. This concept refers to the wider field of reliability, and there are a number of ways to help evaluate the internal structure of a test, from the analysis of the reliability of the test as a whole, including the analysis of the dimensionality, consistency and generalizability of the test (GT), to a detailed item analysis including the investigation of individual item difficulty and discrimination, correlation of the item with the total (CTT), item characteristic curves, and differential item functioning (Rasch and IRT).

4.   Statistical convergence with other valid tests measuring the same variables.

The analysis of the test validity in convergence with other valid measures of the same construct can help medical educators to interpret the validity of the test itself. It is therefore important to investigate correlations between a test and both valid measures of the same construct and valid measures of non-related constructs. For this reason, assessors should always perform correlation analyses aiming to investigate the relation between a current assessment and results observed in previous tests. Convergence shall has been attained only when correlations are sufficiently high (≥ 0.7). In all other cases, results should prompt a timely and thorough review of the assessment.

5.   The implications of test validity to the examinees' learning and their progression in the program.

Finally, best practice requires medical educators to ensure that a pass-score is set for an assessment, and that this is solid and defensible, based on the recognition that the assessment will have significant consequences on the progression of examinees in their academic and professional pathway (including licensing and practicing). The post-examination analysis of standards is therefore key, aiming at reviewing any random or systematic errors in standard setting, and to put timely interventions in place, whenever required.

Case study 1: Reviewing the content validity of an Undergraduate Summative Knowledge Test

A cohort of 100 students in their first year of undergraduate medical program is required to sit and pass an applied knowledge test composed of 80 Single Best Answer Questions in order to progress to the second year. By incorporating Messick's (1994) definition of construct validity, the following steps could be implemented in order to optimize and quality assure the process of designing and delivering a valid test:

1.   Blueprint (core content). By blueprinting teaching and assessment you should aim to account for the content and learning outcomes delivered through the curriculum, for example by commissioning Block Leads to write items that tackle a specific set of domains (e.g. cell biology, genetics, introduction to clinical practice, etc.), specialties, and skills (e.g. diagnosis, data gathering, communication etc). Continuing work will include tagging each item to a condition, and ensuring that learning outcomes and core content are adequately represented in the assessment as well as in your item bank

2.   Familiarize students with the response process. Preparing students to the exam format is key, and it could be accomplished by introducing a number of preparatory sessions in the curriculum, formative exams, and dissemination of material aimed at increasing their assessment literacy. Before and after exams ask students for continuous feedback about their level of confidence and perceived self-efficacy with the item format.

3.   Analyze the internal consistency of the exam. Make sure you analyze the internal consistency of the exam by running a Cronbach's alpha analysis over students' observed scores, identify any questions that would increase internal consistency if removed, signal them to internal staff as candidates for review, and keep a record of any changes or modifications in your item bank.

4.   Check convergence with other exams. Make sure you check whether results from the exam correlate with results of the same cohort at formative as well as previous summative exams, for example by running a Pearson's correlation analysis. If you find a low correlation (< 0.5), reflect on the possible, underlying motivations, for example poor blueprinting, inadequate learning and teaching,

difficulty of the exam compared to other tests, etc and keep a record of any hypothesized flaws. This will reveal particularly useful in approaching and preparing your next exam diets.

5.   Think of the possible consequences for students. If this is a summative assessment, you really want to make sure that your exam is allowing educators to make informed decisions. Therefore, you may want to review any items that would increase the reliability if deleted, including items where low-performing students did better than top, single best answer items where more than one correct option was available, and introduce post-exam moderation (e.g. if more than one correct option was available, it may be reasonable to award a mark to students who selected either option).

In the following paragraphs, several techniques for the investigation of such sources of validity are discussed, particularly the analysis of descriptive statistics and the analysis of items to inform the evaluation of the content coverage, performance, quality of assessment items, post-examination review of standards, and analysis of the reliability of assessments.

The Preliminary Screening And Description Of Assessment Results

This paragraph will focus on the basic descriptive statistics that any post-examination analysis should extract from a set of raw assessment data. Beyond their basic nature, descriptive statistics can be extremely important in providing a preliminary overview of the distribution of scores, quantitative descriptions of the information collected, and identification of any errors derived from data coding and entering.

There are two main types of statistics that can help assessors describe the data: measures of central tendency and measures of spread of a given distribution of data.

Measures of central tendency identify the central location within a pattern of scores observed in a cohort of students sitting an exam. Several measures exist, and the most common are the mean, median, and mode. The mean represents the average score from a distribution. The median is the middle score, obtained by reordering the data from the lowest to the highest, and identifying the value that splits the distribution into two equal parts. The mode is the most frequent number in a distribution.

Measures of dispersion describe the degree of variability or spread of a distribution of scores. Several measures exist, and the most common are variance, standard deviation, and range. Variance represents the squared deviation from the mean observed for a given item, and it is obtained by calculating the squared distance between each individual score and the mean, and then averaging the results. Standard deviation is the square root of the variance, and provides a view over the dispersion of data from the mean in a format that allows comparison of the spread of data against the mean. Range is the difference between the maximum and minimum value from a distribution of scores.

In the example presented below, results from the descriptive analysis of a simulated dataset of dichotomous data are presented. In particular, these statistics were computed both for each of the 10 items and for the total score, the latter obtained by summing up scores from all items (Table 1).

The inspection of the descriptive statistics can provide useful information on the assessment. Firstly, the mean computed at the item level can reveal the level of difficulty of an item, also known as the difficulty index. For example, in Table 1, Item 1 represents the easiest item in the set, having 73% correct answers by the hypothetical cohort of examinees, whilst Item 10 represents the most difficult item, with only 18% correct answers. Assessments require a range of item difficulties to target students with different abilities (Bond & Fox, 2015) and to ensure learning outcomes and core content are adequately covered throughout. The median can inform evaluation of the total score. Compared to the mean, the

Table 1. Example of descriptive statistics from a simulated dichotomous (0-1) assessment data set

Item	Mean	Median	Mode	Variance	Standard Deviation	Range
1	0.73	1	1	0.20	0.45	1
2	0.71	1	1	0.21	0.45	1
3	0.69	1	1	0.22	0.46	1
4	0.65	1	1	0.23	0.48	1
5	0.51	1	1	0.25	0.50	1
6	0.42	0	0	0.24	0.49	1
7	0.40	0	0	0.24	0.49	1
8	0.30	0	0	0.21	0.46	1
9	0.28	0	0	0.20	0.45	1
10	0.18	0	0	0.15	0.39	1
Total	**4.88**	**5**	**4**	**5.70**	**2.39**	**10**

median is more informative in skewed distributions to describe central tendency, because the mean tends to be influenced more by outliers. The skew of a distribution can be understood by looking at the mode calculated for the total score. In Table 1, the mode is equal to 4, indicating a slightly positive skew to the left side of the distribution, signaling that the test was more difficult than expected, and that less difficult items are required for future assessments.

Regarding the spread of the distribution, variance computed at the total test level is equal to 5.70 and the standard deviation is equal to 2.39. They are both relevant to the variation of scores within the dataset, but the standard deviation provides a direct indication of how far results are from the mean value. The larger the standard deviation is, the greater the dispersion of scores and the error of measurement. Finally, the range is a measure that provides a useful indication of the extreme values in a distribution of scores. In particular, the range can help to clarify any discrepancies between expected scores and possible encoding error. For example, any value higher than 1 in a dichotomous data set is clearly signalling error in data encoding or entering, and that should prompt a review of the raw data before proceeding with any further analyses.

The Review of Standards

The review of standards represents another important step in a post-examination analysis, assuming a crucial role in medical assessments. In fact, to meet the standards of good medical practice, medical graduates must demonstrate that they possess and master sufficient knowledge and skills. The process of identifying minimally competent students and making fair decisions regarding progression and credentialing is known as standard setting (Cusimano, 1996). The importance of standard setting is evident in medical education, as it is necessary to determine a standard of minimal competence against a the learning outcomes and core content of a program, and the extent to which it is possible to link assessments to the curriculum (George, Haque, & Oyebode, 2006).

Various methods and approaches to standard setting exists. One basic distinction is between norm-referenced methods and criterion-referenced methods (Cizek, 2012). Norm-referenced methods are based on the assumption that a pre-established proportion of examinees will pass the assessment, and for this reason they are often described as relative methods. On the other hand, the need for an absolute criterion to rely on in decision-making characterizes criterion-based standard-setting methods, in which the standard is set against specific learning outcomes, competences, and skills that medical students are required to demonstrate in order to progress in their academic and professional pathway. Criterion-referenced methods are the most utilized in medical education, so the present chapter will focus on the review of standards obtained from two common methods, namely the Angoff method and borderline regression, usually applied to AKTs and OSCEs, respectively.

The Angoff method is considered the gold standard in medical education (Cizek, 2012). It is named after William H. Angoff, an American educationalist who first introduced the method in 1971. The Angoff method is based on the definition of the 'minimally competent' or 'borderline' student, i.e. a student with some knowledge who has a 50% probability of either passing or failing the exam, depending on the specific content of questions, the characteristics of the exam, or other circumstances. Five to ten medical experts gather to read the exam papers and provide an estimate for each question. This estimate, from 0 to 1, represents the probability that the minimally competent student would answer the question correctly. After providing estimates for all questions, experts are asked to defend and discuss their estimates for those questions where the range of estimates was equal to or higher than 0.2, and to see if, as informed by the discussion, a consensus can be achieved. Although it is allowed and desirable, experts are not required to modify their estimates if they think those represent a genuine point of view for the individual item and the estimated performance for a minimally competent student (C. Clauser, E. Clauser, & Hambleton, 2014).

Although the general procedure does not vary across contexts, several modifications to the application of the methods exist. For example, the minimum range required to trigger a discussion over individual items, the number of experts, the definition of a 'minimally competent' or 'borderline' student and the anchor statement. In some cases, the first round may even be delivered online, by means of dedicated educational software.

In all cases, however, the process ends with individual estimates being averaged across items and summed up across experts, determining a standard of minimal competence. This standard represents the cutoff score that students will need to achieve in order to get a pass score and progress. In some contexts, particularly high-stakes examinations and postgraduate assessments, this standard is considered inadequate for evaluation of the examinee's competence, as the students ranking in the 'borderline' area may be required to provide additional evidence to demonstrate that they are competent enough to progress. For this reason, one standard error of measurement (SEM) is usually added to the cutoff score. The reader will find a detailed definition and formulae to calculate the SEM in the following paragraph on the analysis of reliability, however in the interest of clarity, the SEM is a measure that decrease as the reliability increases, determining the upper boundary of a confidence interval above the cut to screen for false positives and false negatives.

The SEM is also utilized in the context of OSCEs. However, as anticipated above, the elective standard setting method in OSCEs is borderline regression. Similarly to the Angoff, borderline regression relies on the definition of the 'borderline' student, but it accounts for two different types of information that are derived directly from the evaluation of examinees' performance by OSCE examiners. Specifically, these are (1) a checklist, or domain-based score, i.e. a score that is usually expressed in the form of a Likert scale, which summarizes the examinee's performance at a particular station and in a specific domain, and (2) a global rating, i.e. a judgement provided by the examiner regarding the student's overall performance at the station. For each station the OSCE is composed of, checklist scores are eventually regressed against global ratings across the whole cohort of examinees, and regression parameters are the standard for minimal competence that examinees will have to achieve in order to progress.

The review of standards represents a crucial step in a thorough psychometric post-examination analysis, aimed at informing medical educators of the validity of the standard setting process, the robustness and fairness of the derived standards, and the confidence in the decisions made on this basis. This process helps to close the loop that standard setting actually represents, going back to the original definition of learning outcomes and core content for the exam, and attempting to inform educators about the correlation between outcomes, content, standards and performance of the examinee.

In practical terms, when setting standards of minimal competence, experts and examiners will not only be required to set a generic standard for a medical student, but to specifically link that standard to the learning outcomes and the stage of learning that the particular assessment originated from. This aspect is of extreme importance, and failures in linking learning outcomes to standards is likely to determine assessment cutoff scores that may result into either standards that are too low or too high, compared to what is required at that particular stage of learning.

Case study 2: Applying the SEM in high-stakes exams

A cohort of 100 students sit a final assessment at your Medical School. The exam consists of two tests, namely an applied knowledge test made of 80 items and an Objective Structured Clinical Exam including 12 practical and clinical stations. Each test accounts for the 50% of the total score, and there is no cross-compensation between the two (students must pass both independently in order to progress). The pass-score for the applied knowledge test is 55.40%, obtained through the Modified Angoff Method, and the pass-score for the OSCE is 51.43%, obtained through borderline regression. The pass-score for the assessment, overall, is 53.42%.

One student out of 100 obtained a total score lower than 53.42%. Hypothetically, she/he should be the only not allowed to progress. However, post-examination analysis of reliability of the exam shows a combined Cronbach's alpha of 0.723 and a standard deviation of 7.56%. Try to import this information in an electronic spreadsheet, and enter the formula: $= 7.56 * SQRT(1-.723)$. The result is 3.98%: This is the SEM. By adding 3.98% to the pass-score, four more students would not pass the exam.

As this is a final exam and you want to make robust progression decisions, and you may want to consider keeping the SEM and ask those total five students to re-sit the exam.

The process of reviewing the standard set post-hoc may contribute to understanding in this regard. For example, estimating Pearson's correlation coefficient between the actual performance of minimally competent students and the average Angoff estimate, can help identify any major discrepancies between the standard estimates and the actual performance of examinees. However, the reader should note that this carries a number of risks. Firstly, it relies on the assumption that, although a high correlation is expected and desired, a low or negative correlation should not necessarily prompt intervention to modify the previously established standards, for the reason discussed above (i.e. standards must be set as informed by robust criteria, namely the achievement of specific learning outcomes and the development of adequate skills, rather than norm-referencing to the actual performance of a cohort of examinees). Secondly, students in the cohort may not have achieved the standard due to a mismatch between curriculum and assessment, so although the standard is fair and robust, they may be struggling to achieve it due to problems related to their learning. Thirdly, it is best practice to make sure this process does not necessarily lead to alterations of standards, which might cause serious repercussions in terms of licensing and patients' safety, especially in high-stake exams. For these reasons, caution in interpreting this analysis is warranted, given that its main function should consist of providing assessors and educators with the opportunity to review the standard setting process, informing the future standard setting and assessment diets, and intervening by modifying the current standard as the extrema ratio for those cases in which the standard setting may result in a flawed process.

The Analysis of The Reliability And Internal Structure of Tests

The analysis of reliability is generally considered a core phase of every valid psychometric post-examination analysis. In this section, it will be outlined by discussing two major psychometric approaches, namely CTT and GT.

The quest for a 'true' score and the differentiation between this and both measurement and systematic error is what ultimately characterizes the analysis of reliability (Cronbach et al., 1972). Now some examples will be considered. In an OSCE station, is the variance across examiners measurable and should it be considered part of the error, rather than contribute to the students' score? If the OSCE is delivered over two different sites, is it reasonable to assume that there was no effect of the site on the performance of the examinees? What if one of the two sites was not adequate in terms of organization, physical environment or temperature? These questions are not only legitimate, but they should be asked and covered in any valid psychometric evaluation of medical assessments.

From a CTT point of view, there are a number of indices that can clarify the internal consistency and the reliability of a test. In this chapter, three of the most utilized psychometric indices of reliability will be considered: Cronbach's alpha, Guttman's lambda, and McDonald's Omega.

Cronbach's alpha is an extension of the Kuder–Richardson Formula 20 (KR-20), and is one of the most widely used measures of reliability across a number of fields (Sijtsma, 2009). It is named after the American psychologist Lee Cronbach, who introduced it in 1951, and is based on the assumption of tau-equivalent measurement, i.e. a model in which all factor loadings (i.e. the contribution of individual items to the latent 'true' factor) are assumed to be equivalent.

Alpha tends to increase as the between-score correlation increases, so it is usually referred to as a measure of internal consistency, rather than, more specifically, reliability. The difference is that reliability should inform the extent to which the test items contribute to identify a single, latent construct (true ability score). However, research has shown that often Cronbach's alpha fails to do so, and that its use is recommended in those cases when multiple, substantive factors underlie a higher-order, global construct (Sijtsma, 2009; (Tavakol & Dennick, 2011a). Values equal to or higher than 0.7 are considered acceptable, however, only values equal to or higher than 0.8 are recommended in undergraduate medical education (0.9 in high-stakes examinations).

An interesting contribution of GT to the analysis of reliability is to allow educators to measure and separate the effects of a number of components on the total variance observed in an exam. For example, by running a generalizability study over multiple cohorts, a 'cohort' may be introduced in the model as a so-called 'facet of stratification' (Brennan, 2010), i.e. a variable that stratifies the sample of students into multiple groups and whose effect onto students' performance can be estimated and therefore evaluated separately. This could reveal information of vital importance for the assessment of the quality of exams over a number of cohorts, sites, circuits, allowing educators to identify any pitfalls in the organization and delivery of assessments, and intervene in a timely manner by introducing, for example, curricular changes, changes to the blueprint, assessment format, and assessors' training.

The SEM, as previously mentioned, is a measure of variation of test scores around a hypothetical 'true' score, expressed as the standard deviation of error measurement observed in the assessment. It is often utilized to determine the proportion of measurement error arising from the observation of assessment scores, and to address any concerns regarding the performance of students whose scores are located close to the cut-off.

The SEM is usually utilized in association with a reliability coefficient, having the specific aim of helping assessors to evaluate the internal consistency and generalizability of the assessment, and the amount of error measurement. However, the type of information that a reliability coefficient can provide is not sufficient *per se* to describe the measurement error observed in a test, and for this reason the SEM is estimated as a function of both the degree of variability of test scores (standard deviation) and the reliability of a test (a hypothetical, perfectly reliable test is assumed to have an SEM equal to zero).

Assessors may benefit from using the SEM in their assessment policy for a number of reasons. Firstly, assessors would be able to set up effective remediation models, both for borderline pass and borderline fail students. In the former case, based on the fact that those students might pass but require further support in future assessment diets, and in the latter case based on the fact those students might not pass but they could be helped to fill a relatively smaller gap in knowledge and skills to be successful in future diets. Secondly, students in both groups may end up with either false positive or false negatives results, providing assessors with a strong justification for requiring further evidence in order to let them progress. Thirdly, based on the previous point, assessors may decide to utilize the SEM differently, especially in high-stake assessments. For example, adding one or more SEM to the cut-score, so that the minimal score for examinees to achieve a pass would be 53.68% from the previous example, attempting to reduce the probability of letting a student who would have failed as the result of further testing progress (Pell, Fuller, Homer, & Roberts, 2013).

The Analysis of Items

This final section presents the reader with an overview of item analysis from the point of view of CTT. CTT includes a number of statistical techniques and measures supporting the evaluation of assessment items. In particular, the objectives of item analysis are: (1) to extract information about the difficulty of an item; (2) to investigate the extent to which an item can help differentiate between high-performing and low-performing examinees and address any anomalies; (3) to consider the relation between an individual item and the total assessment score; (4) to analyze the variation in the internal consistency of an assessment that would occur if the item was deleted; ultimately, to inform the post-examination moderation of items when required, and the retention of items that are candidates for future assessment diets.

There are four main measures that medical assessors should take into account when performing item analysis, which can help to complete those objectives. These are the Facility Index, the Discrimination Index, the Correct Item-Total Correlation Coefficient, and the value of Cronbach's alpha if item is deleted. They are presented and discussed as follows.

The Facility Index, sometimes referred to as the difficulty of an item, is defined as the "proportion of a specified population passing or failing the item" (Guilford, 1936). It is computed by calculating the proportion of examinees who answered an item correctly over the whole cohort attending the exam. Values range from 0 to 1, with values close to 1 indicating a very easy item, and values close to 0 indicating a very difficult item. Ideal values of facility are considered to range between 0.7 for five-option MCQs to 0.85 for true-false items (Lord, 1952), with acceptable values usually between 0.3 and 0.7.

Such values are desired in the interest of maximizing the discrimination of an item, since items that are either too difficult or too easy are likely to result in negative discrimination between the high-performing examinees and the low-performing examinees.

The concept of item discrimination is defined as the "extent to which success on an item corresponds to success on the whole test" (Kelley, Ebel, & Linacre, 2002). A commonly utilized way to compute discrimination is to identify two groups within the cohort of examinees, based on their observed performance: the top 27% performers and the bottom 27% performers (Kelley, 1939). The Discrimination Index is then obtained by subtracting the proportion of correct responses in the bottom performers from the proportion of correct responses in the top performers. Values range from −1 to 1, with values above 0.4 considered ideal, values between 0.2 and 0.4 considered fair, and values below 0.2 considered poor. Items with no discrimination or negative discrimination challenges the validity of a test item, highlighting that either the content or the structure of an item has determined a higher proportion of correct responses amongst those who performed less well at the overall assessment. Items with negative discrimination should prompt timely review and possible moderation, aiming at understanding whether, for example, the content of the item had not been adequately covered in the curriculum, partially covered, or only covered to the benefit of a smaller group (e.g. if covered only in one Problem-Based Learning session attended by few students), or if the scenario, the lead-in question, and the distractors are not clear or appropriate and it is therefore not possible to determine the correct answer, or there are two or more distractors that could be considered as correct. Moderation is needed especially in high-stake assessments, when one item is likely to determine significant shifts in exam results and affect the ranking or progression of examinees.

The Corrected Item-Total Correlation is the Pearson Product Moment Correlation Index computed between the scores observed at one item and the remaining set of items composing the assessment, corrected by ruling out the former item from the total. This index represents the extent to which an item effectively measures the same construct measured by the overall assessment, assuming that all items should tackle one factor of educational attainment (Bond & Fox, 2015; Tavakol & Dennick, 2011b). Values range from −1 and 1, with ideal values being above 0.5, acceptable values between 0.4 and 0.49, fair values between 0.3 and 0.39, and poor values below 0.3. Negative values should prompt a review of the item in relation to the overall assessment, aiming at understanding whether the item is actually measuring knowledge or skills that are different compared to the rest of the paper, or whether there are any problems in content or structure that make the item flawed.

It is important to highlight that these measures are not useful to capture students' differential attainment and item differential functioning. Although a number of measures and techniques exist, usually a descriptive item analysis of differential attainment by gender, age, ethnicity, learning group, etc. can help educators shed a light on any possible differences derived from any differential attainment in learning, and the analysis of mean differences through *t*-test and one-way ANOVA, where appropriate, may help them accept or reject the hypothesis of equality in students' attainment, and put in place effective interventions (e.g. randomise students across groups in case of Problem-Based Learning, identify possible systematic gaps in learning and implement remediation strategies, etc).

These measures can be applied to both AKTs and OSCEs, and can help medical assessors understand the fundamental properties of assessments and their items, and make informed decisions about the progression of students. However, there are other measures that can more specifically help understand the quality of OSCE stations by looking at their performance, as introduced by Pell, Fuller, Homer, and

Roberts (2010). The next section will focus on the two of these measures: the coefficient of determination and the inter-grade discrimination.

The coefficient of determination (R^2) quantifies the linear relation assumed between checklist or domain-based scores and global ratings of an OSCE, and is obtained by squaring Pearson's correlation coefficient determined through linear regression. To describe the relationship between the two different types of rating from an OSCE a correlation of at least 0.5 is expected, meaning that 50% of variation in the global ratings of the cohort at that station is explained by the variation in checklist or domain-based scores. This assumes even more importance as assessors should be trained to avoid direct arithmetical translation of checklist or domain-based scores into global ratings, as this may cause an inflating R^2.

Inter-grade discrimination represents the slope of the linear regression between checklist or domain-based scores and global ratings. In particular, Pell et al. (2010) recommend that such discrimination, measured at station level, should be in the order of a tenth of the maximum available checklist or domain-based score. This is because a low value in this index may be a symptom of unsatisfactory performance of the station, especially if associated with a low R^2, indicating an overall inconsistency in scoring between checklist or domain-based scores and global ratings, or excessive variability of marks across assessors. On the other hand, an inter-grade discrimination that is too high may represent a violation of the assumption of linearity between types of scores, usually determined by a low cut-off or outlying students that may have performed at a very low level.

Case study 3: An OSCE station with low R2 (and possible consequences)

A Year 2 cohort sits an OSCE made of 10 stations. Post-examination analysis shows that all stations have a satisfactory R2 (> 0.7), but one station (0.39) does not. By removing that station, two students would not pass the exam, and in theory would need to repeat the year.

Because R2 quantifies the linear relation assumed between checklist or domain-based scores and global ratings of an OSCE, a low value is indicative of flaws arising from either standard setting, marking or both. In this specific case, assume that your investigation discloses that four out of nine examiners at the flawed station did not attend examiner training. In fact, those four had not fully understood how to award marks based on your checklist and global rating, and as a result their marks are scattered compared to the global rating scale.

The problem now is that you are not allowed to make decisions about the performance of the two students, and you may need to remove the station and ask those who did not pass to sit an additional test in order to make informed decisions.

As reported previously, a number of additional methods and measures exist, informed by modern psychometric theory and approaches. However, these go beyond the scope of the present chapter, and the reader is referred to specialized literature (Bond & Fox, 2015; de Ayala, 2013; Embretson & Reise, 2000; McDonald, 1999).

Psychometrics for Educator And Curriculum Assessment

The role of psychometrics extends beyond the analysis and evaluation of exams, items, or stations and plays a role in the assessment of educators and curricula.

Educators take on a number of complex and challenging tasks in medical education programs, from designing and delivering programs, blueprinting, standard setting, writing assessment items, marking, moderating, to name but a few. The importance of quality assuring all these processes is vital to ensure concordance of educators' behaviour and performance across a number of learning outcomes and educational activities.

Reviewing the performance of educators should then become routine in medical schools, with the primary objective to help them calibrate and develop their role rather than merely being judged and disempowered. In this regard, a descriptive analysis of the performance of standard setters at a Modified Angoff Session, a comparative analysis of markers' spread of scores in an OSCE can be extremely informative about potential 'hawk' and 'dove' effects, requiring medical schools to elaborate and implement timely intervention. These may include providing additional training, and where expertise is not available, outsourcing training and professional development of internal assessors. Moreover, keeping a record of standard setters' and assessors' performance is key to monitoring their performance over time, and providing them with appropriate guidance when required.

With regards to the assessment of curricula, Khalil and Kibble (2015, p. 199) recently argued that "successful curriculum integration and evaluation are key elements for a solid faculty development." In fact, medical schools are increasingly asked to be accountable in developing and integrating their curricula according to standards of quality, learning outcomes, and core scientific as well as clinical content. In their interpretative analysis, the authors discuss the challenges of negotiating an understanding of learning outcomes and pedagogical methods for teaching and assessment with multiple stakeholders and provided recommendations applicable to curricular reforms in established medical schools as well as for developing competency-based curricula. These include:

- a clear vision and goals for curriculum design and governance as well as efforts to translate vision into practice;
- defining and negotiating integration among faculty members at different stages;
- constructing multiple, diverse faculty teams;
- providing a solid infrastructure to facilitate horizontal and vertical integration;
- sharing and negotiating with stakeholders the understanding of intent of pedagogy;
- adequate resourcing for faculty development and ongoing support.

They suggest that faculty members should be surveyed about how their experience, and management should be open to integrate faculty experience into curricular updates and continuous improvement. This include assessment curriculum integration, learning objectives, course framework design, development instructional materials, writing assessment items, and faculty collaboration, concluding that "open-ended items addressed the effective strategies and challenges when developing an integrated curriculum" (p. 201).

It is the opinion of the authors that a qualitative assessment and review of human judgment over curricular integration is warranted in medical education. If on one hand it is true that "no universal solution, based on an approved pedagogical approach, exists to parametrically describe, effectively manage, and clearly visualize a higher education institution's curriculum, including tools for unveiling relationships inside curricular datasets." (Komenda et al., 2015; p. 1), then on the other hand, medical educators can benefit from a number of assessment initiatives involving the use of feedback from faculty and staff about their experience and approach to the curriculum.

CONCLUSION

The medical profession is a dramatically changing field, with unique landmarks that the generation of today's and tomorrow's doctors are called to achieve. Such changes are also affecting education and learning. Medical schools are increasingly required to engage and evidence quality assurance procedures that reflect the needs of multiple stakeholders, and ensure that those who graduate are fit to practise and prepared to undertake further specialist education, adhering to high standards of professionalism. New methodologies for developing knowledge, and transferring and consolidating skills are available, multiplying the opportunities for learning and opening unexplored scenarios for the future development of medical education.

This chapter presented a number of fundamental techniques that are currently used in medical education to inform the post-exam psychometric analysis of assessment data, with focus on its implications on learning and its impact on training programs and systems in medical education. The main aim of the chapter was to provide the reader with a fundamental toolkit of knowledge and methods that can help understanding of how the quality of medical programs can be measured, evaluated, and improved, in the attempt to link assessment and the curriculum.

As highlighted by Tavakol and Dennik (2011), assessment holds a key role in facilitating learning, and medical assessors are called to provide a robust, transparent, and defensible approach to three main questions: firstly, they should identify, develop, and implement clear and detailed learning objectives that guide the journey of medical trainees in the program, with specific instructions about what they are required to know and know how to do in order to progress. Secondly, they should implement adequate management and leadership to make sure assessment matches the curriculum and the learning objectives, translating into targeted learning and teaching activities. Thirdly, they shall ensure that the attainment of learning objectives is measured and evaluated carefully by means of evidence-based methods that would inform all interested stakeholders.

It is in this perspective that the psychometric post-examination analysis of assessment data constitutes part of a more comprehensive, systematic approach that medical schools should take globally to assure the quality of training programs. In fact, notwithstanding the large plethora of approaches, options and further modifications that characterizes the choice of assessment methods in medical programs, often observed even at the local level, the need for a thorough, transparent approach represents a common denominator to ensure that medical graduates are fit to practise, adhere to standard patient safety measures, and master a sufficiently wide corpus of knowledge and skills to practise medicine in a variety of settings.

Overall, psychometrics can have a significant impact onto medical education, evident in at least five consequences:

- They help educators increase the solidity of their decisions over student learning, providing them with evidence-based information to determine student progression and professional licensing.
- They help educators in making assessment processes and procedures smoother and more efficient, relying on powerful analytics, information processing, and feedback.
- They can shed a light on assessment methods, instrument, and practices, indicating what works and what does not work in the assessment of knowledge and skills, contributing to improved assessment, timely implementation of changes if required, overall increased fairness, and transparency in medical education.

- They signal possible strengths and limitations of the curriculum, as emerging through the analysis of assessment data, allowing educators to implement effective changes and restructuring when required.
- They can provide stakeholders with evidence on the quality of learning and assessment of medical students, and inform whether the latter has achieved a sufficient standard to operate in real-world clinical contexts, in the interest of patients and the community.

The need for this has dramatically expanded in the last two decades. Doctors are no longer just asked to master knowledge and fundamental clinical skills, but rather are they called to operate in complex contexts and settings where communication patterns, languages, and competencies are diverse. Similarly, patients and their approach to health and illness have profoundly changed, in light of the recent diffusion of digital technologies and their use to address public understanding of science and medicine. In this altered scenario, the set and quality of skills that medical trainees are required to develop is much richer and more diverse, posing a number of challenges to medical educators, particularly with regards to the assessment of learning in medical programs, its measurement and evaluation.

Using a systematic approach in the implementation, measurement, and evaluation of assessment in medical programs is therefore necessary to support high-stake decision making (Pell, Homer, & Roberts, 2008), compared to traditional unsystematic approaches. The advantages of such approaches are "in that it is absolutist, carefully standardized for all candidates, and assessments are clearly designed and closely linked with performance objectives. These objectives can be clearly mapped against curricular outcomes, and where appropriate, standards laid down by regulatory and licensing bodies, that are available to students and teachers alike" (Pell, Fuller, & Homer, 2010, p. 802).

In summary, psychometric post-examination analysis of assessment data represents a useful set of methodologies and techniques that can help medical educators to understand and evidence the extent to which assessment data and their interpretation reflect the achievement of learning objectives for a changing profession, and that the assessment methods utilized are valid and are accepted by stakeholders, ultimately contributing to enhance the quality of training programs and systems in medical education.

REFERENCES

Allen, M. J., & Yen, W. M. (2001). *Introduction to Measurement Theory*. Waveland Press.

Baker, F. B. (2001). *The Basics of Item Response Theory* (2nd ed.)., Retrieved from https://eric.ed.gov/?id=ED458219

Bloch, R., & Norman, G. (2012). Generalizability theory for the perplexed: A practical introduction and guide: AMEE Guide No. 68. *Medical Teacher*, *34*(11), 960–992. doi:10.3109/0142159X.2012.703791 PMID:23140303

Bond, T., & Fox, C. M. (2015). *Applying the Rasch Model: Fundamental Measurement in the Human Sciences* (3rd ed.). Routledge. doi:10.4324/9781315814698

Brennan, R. L. (2010). Generalizability Theory and Classical Test Theory. *Applied Measurement in Education*, *24*(1), 1–21. doi:10.1080/08957347.2011.532417

Cizek, G. J. (2012). *Setting Performance Standards: Foundations, Methods, and Innovations*. Routledge. doi:10.4324/9780203848203

Clauser, J., Clauser, B., & Hambleton, R. (2014). Increasing the Validity of Angoff Standards Through Analysis of Judge-Level Internal Consistency. *Applied Measurement in Education, 27*(1), 19–30. doi:10.1080/08957347.2013.853071

Colliver, J. A., Conlee, M. J., & Verhulst, S. J. (2012). From test validity to construct validity … and back? *Medical Education, 46*(4), 366–371. doi:10.1111/j.1365-2923.2011.04194.x PMID:22429172

Cronbach, L. J., Gleser, G. C., Nanda, H., & Rajaratnam, N. (1972). *The Dependability of Behavioral Measurements: Theory of Generalizability for Scores and Profiles*. New York: John Wiley & Sons.

Cronbach, L. J., & Meehl, P. E. (1955). Construct validity in psychological tests. *Psychological Bulletin, 52*(4), 281–302. doi:10.1037/h0040957 PMID:13245896

Crossley, J., Humphris, G., & Jolly, B. (2002). Assessing health professionals. *Medical Education, 36*(9), 800–804. doi:10.1046/j.1365-2923.2002.01294.x PMID:12354241

de Ayala, R. J. (2013). *The Theory and Practice of Item Response Theory*. Guilford Publications.

De Champlain, A. F. (2010). A primer on classical test theory and item response theory for assessments in medical education. *Medical Education, 44*(1), 109–117. doi:10.1111/j.1365-2923.2009.03425.x PMID:20078762

Downing, S. M. (2003). Validity: On meaningful interpretation of assessment data. *Medical Education, 37*(9), 830–837. doi:10.1046/j.1365-2923.2003.01594.x PMID:14506816

Dunn, T. J., Baguley, T., & Brunsden, V. (2014). From alpha to omega: a practical solution to the pervasive problem of internal consistency estimation. *British Journal of Psychology (London, England: 1953), 105*(3), 399–412. doi:10.1111/bjop.12046

Embretson, S. E., & Reise, S. P. (2000). *Item Response Theory for Psychologists*. L. Erlbaum Associates.

Finch, W. H., & French, B. F. (2018). *Educational and Psychological Measurement*. Routledge. doi:10.4324/9781315650951

Guilford, J. P. (1936). The determination of item difficulty when chance success is a factor. *Psychometrika, 1*(4), 259–264. doi:10.1007/BF02287877

Harden, R. M. (2007). Learning outcomes as a tool to assess progression. *Medical Teacher, 29*(7), 678–682. doi:10.1080/01421590701729955 PMID:18236255

Jackson, N., Jamieson, A., & Khan, A. (2007). *Assessment in Medical Education and Training: A Practical Guide*. Radcliffe Publishing.

Kelley, T., Ebel, R., & Linacre, M. (2002). Item discrimination indices. *Rasch Measurement Transactions, 16*(3), 883–884.

Kelley, T. L. (1939). The selection of upper and lower groups for the validation of test items. *Journal of Educational Psychology, 30*(1), 17–24. doi:10.1037/h0057123

Khalil, M. K., & Kibble, J. D. (2014). Faculty reflections on the process of building an integrated pre-clerkship curriculum: A new school perspective. *Advances in Physiology Education, 38*(3), 199–209. doi:10.1152/advan.00055.2014 PMID:25179608

Kline, P. (2014). *The New Psychometrics: Science, Psychology and Measurement.* Routledge. doi:10.4324/9781315787817

Komenda, M., Víta, M., Vaitsis, C., Schwarz, D., Pokorná, A., Zary, N., & Dušek, L. (2015). Curriculum Mapping with Academic Analytics in Medical and Healthcare Education. *PLoS One, 10*(12). doi:10.1371/journal.pone.0143748 PMID:26624281

Lord, F. M. (1952). The relation of the reliability of multiple-choice tests to the distribution of item difficulties. *Psychometrika, 17*(2), 181–194. doi:10.1007/BF02288781

Lord, F. M. (1980). *Applications of Item Response Theory to Practical Testing Problems.* Routledge.

Lord, F. M., & Novick, M. R. (2008). *Statistical Theories of Mental Test Scores.* Information Age Pub.

McDonald, R. P. (1999). *Test Theory: A Unified Treatment.* Taylor & Francis.

Messick, S. (1994). Validity of Psychological Assessment: Validation of Inferences from Persons' Responses and Performances as Scientific Inquiry into Score Meaning. *ETS Research Report Series, 1994*(2), i–28. doi:10.1002/j.2333-8504.1994.tb01618.x

Miller, G. E. (1990). The assessment of clinical skills/competence/performance. *Academic Medicine, 65*(9), S63–S67. doi:10.1097/00001888-199009000-00045 PMID:2400509

Norcini, J. J., & McKinley, D. W. (2007). Assessment methods in medical education. *Teaching and Teacher Education, 23*(3), 239–250. doi:10.1016/j.tate.2006.12.021

Norman, G. (2016). Is psychometrics science? *Advances in Health Sciences Education: Theory and Practice, 21*(4), 731–734. doi:10.100710459-016-9705-6 PMID:27501689

Orsmond, P., & Merry, S. (2017). Tutors' assessment practices and students' situated learning in higher education: Chalk and cheese. *Assessment & Evaluation in Higher Education, 42*(2), 289–303. doi:10.1080/02602938.2015.1103366

Patil, S. Y., Gosavi, M., Bannur, H. B., & Ratnakar, A. (2015). Blueprinting in assessment: A tool to increase the validity of undergraduate written examinations in pathology. *International Journal of Applied & Basic Medical Research, 5*(4Suppl 1), S76–S79. doi:10.4103/2229-516X.162286 PMID:26380218

Pell, G., Fuller, R., Homer, M., & Roberts, T. (2010). How to measure the quality of the OSCE: A review of metrics - AMEE guide no. 49. *Medical Teacher, 32*(10), 802–811. doi:10.3109/0142159X.2010.507716 PMID:20854155

Pell, G., Fuller, R., Homer, M. S., & Roberts, T. (2013). Advancing the OSCE: Sequential testing in theory and practice. *Medical Education, 47*, 569–577. doi:10.1111/medu.12136 PMID:23662874

4. Identify the differences between advising, mentoring and coaching, and when each might be useful for supporting the medical student.

BACKGROUND

The Liaison Committee on Medical Education (LCME) accredits medical schools in the United States, and has standards around student support services. The most pertinent to academic support is:

11.1 Academic Advising

A medical school has an effective system of academic advising in place for medical students that integrates the efforts of faculty members, course and clerkship directors, and student affairs staff with its counseling and tutorial services and ensures that medical students can obtain academic counseling from individuals who have no role in making assessment or promotion decisions about them. (LCME, 2019)

While this leaves substantial room for interpretation, the intent is clear. Students must have academic support from the school that is multi-pronged in approach, easily accessible, and safe to use. The complexity of creating an environment of academic support has led many schools to hire learning specialists to help guide these efforts. The learning specialist can help design and administer programs designed to build academic support including peer tutoring, remediation of academic deficiencies, and test-taking skills. Academic advising for the individual student can be achieved by designing programs using different models of advising, mentoring or coaching, depending on the intent and resources.

ACADEMIC SUPPORT

Learning Specialists

Student learning support specialists typically have master degrees or higher, and work with students on learning strategies, time management, test taking strategies, and academic resilience. There is a dearth of evidence-based information about learning specialists in the medical education literature. A search of PubMed in October 2019 for the phrase "learning specialist" garnered a single, non-relevant match. Therefore, this chapter will focus on the programs that a learning specialist would support. The programs are generally focused in one of three ways: 1) reactive-deficit, in which students who are identified as struggling in some way are helped to develop their skills, 2) proactive-deficit, in which students who are identified at risk of struggling are helped to develop their skills, and 3) proactive-developmental, in which all students are given skills to help improve performance. (Kebaetse MB, 2018) Ideally, the learning specialist will involve him or herself in the use of all three of these approaches.

When working with specific struggling students (i.e. taking the reactive-deficit approach), the learning specialist is providing a "learning consult." An example of an intake form may be found in Appendix 1. Particular attention should be made to the possibility of learning disabilities, which may require a referral to the Office of Student Access for confidential evaluation or accommodations as protected under the Americans with Disability Act (ADAAA). Learning support specialists will also need to advocate for students who are found to have other challenges affecting their ability to succeed in school, such as challenges in their personal life. This may be best addressed by referral to the student affairs official (e.g. Assistant Dean for Student Affairs) if the student agrees, but may also include referral to a wellness/ mental health provider or financial consultant depending on the challenge. The learning specialist will need to have full familiarity with support offerings within the school and institution.

The proactive-deficit approach plays a key role for targeting specific, at-risk groups with resources to prevent failure. If risk factors for struggling in the curriculum are known (e.g. humanities majors with little science background), then specific interventions (e.g. pre-matriculation study tools) can be targeted at those persons. This becomes particularly important if the intervention is highly resource-intensive (e.g. one-on-one faculty mentoring for students who are first-generation college graduates or under-represented minority students.)

As highly trained educators, learning support specialists also may take the proactive-developmental approach and provide student and/or faculty development workshops to improve the skills of all students. Student workshops may include test-taking skills, study strategies, or resilience skills. Faculty workshops may include best practices in teaching, such as how to teach to different learning styles, how to create effective study materials or how to approach the struggling student. This may be in conjunction with other teaching and learning educators in the institution to create maximal impact. In theory, any approach that involves all students is likely to require more effort and resources to implement compared to a more targeted deficit focused plan. However, creating a culture of proactive development of students and a positive learning environment is generally well received. In addition, if this effort prevents student failure, this will recoup a significant portion of the invested time and energy.

An institution or the medical school may administer learning support. Benefits of central administration at the level of the institution include:

- Greater efficiencies in offering support over multiple programs
- Possibility of increased specialization in support staff (e.g. one person dedicated to working with students on test-taking skills, one person dedicated to working with tutors, etc.)
- Easily identifiable student support for university level accreditation requirements.

However, the level of support required by medical students is high, and cannot be compromised by resource utilization by other schools in the university or institution when examined for LCME accreditation. In fact, the needs are frequently enough to support a full time learning specialist dedicated specifically to the medical school alone, and this is quickly becoming the norm in UME.

In order to provide sufficient academic support, it is imperative that learners see those who are providing academic support and guidance as helpful, approachable, and available. There are various ways to be visible to learners, but certainly some places will make a more significant impact. Times that may provide extra stress and require extra support when they are introduced to their new learning environment, during programmatic shifts, and at milestones. The highest impact visibility for UME learners are at the transition to medical school (particularly during orientation as it sets the stage for later interactions), and the transition to clinical experiences/rotations. It is critical that the learning specialist has a role in these times beyond introducing him or herself. Beyond being visible at specific points in time in the UME program, it can also be helpful to have student learning support specialists present during the learners' courses. This allows the learner to see the learning specialist as someone who understands what is happening in the classroom. Additionally, it allows the learners to walk up and chat, get to know the learning specialist and schedule appointments.

For those individuals that provide advising, there are many spaces in which they want to be visible to their learners. The relationship that exists between student affairs deans and students is different than that of the learning specialist and might need to be cultivated in different spaces. Those could include student affairs coffee hours, meet the deans town halls, or various wellness activities. One unexpected space that provides access to students is student committees. By inserting learning support, services, and student affairs at student committees, the learners will be reminded again and again of the services (for both learning support and advising) and will likely reach out prior to academic crisis.

Tutoring

Many medical schools are turning to formalized tutoring programs to provide academic support to their students who need additional content and academic assistance to supplement what they learn in classrooms and in labs. Faculty are stretched thin with teaching and clinical responsibilities. Formal peer tutoring programs can provide student academic content support, as well as providing leadership opportunities for those students who are tutors. Peer-assisted learning is defined in the literature as "people from similar social groups who are not professional teachers helping each other to learn (Burgess, 2004)." Similarly, a near-peer teacher is "someone at least one year senior to their near-peer learner (de Menezes, S. & Premnath, D. 2016)". For example, in UME, a near-peer teacher could be a second-year medical student working with a first-year medical student. For the remainder of this section of the chapter, a tutor is someone who is a student, but is also a near-peer.

At most medical schools, learning support offices coordinate and manage tutoring programs by recruiting and training the tutors, as well as mentorship around best teaching practices. The benefits of formal peer tutoring programs are numerous, clear and have been reported in the literature. For example, a tutoring program can provide affective support to all participating students as the tutors appreciate the opportunity to solidify their own knowledge and gain confidence in teaching, while the tutees feel supported by more senior students (Burgess, A. 2016). The goal of this section of the chapter is to discuss the framework for creating and supporting a formal peer-tutoring program within UME.

Recruiting

Prior to a new class of students starting, applications for new tutors should be made available. This application should include the job description, time commitment, and hourly rate of pay (if applicable). In addition, the application should include the following questions:

- Why are you interested in serving as a formal peer tutor?
- What relevant experiences have you had that relate to working as a tutor?
- What relevant skills do you possess?
- What skills and assets would you like to develop?
- How does this position fit into your academic and career goals?
- Is there anything else we should know as we consider your application?

These questions can help you identify which students you would like to hire after you filter for grades, as the ability and interest of the tutor will help set the learning climate for the tutees. In addition, this information can inform the tutor training for maximal impact.

Training

All hired tutors should be required to complete a tutor training. This training should be based on educational theories to help support your tutors as they embark on working with their peers. One of the most beneficial outcomes for the tutors, aside the intrinsic value they place on helping their peers, is that they receive training and practice in teaching. The tutors value this training and many wish they received more training in teaching (Clarke, 2015). Tutor training should include modules around effective classroom management, facilitation, learning strategies, motivation, and student development theories. Below are two education theories to incorporate into tutor training:

- **Cognitive Learning Strategies:** Active learning processes help students create new knowledge and relate this knowledge to prior knowledge, thus allowing the student to recall the information (Weinstein & Mayer, 1986). Examples include rehearsal strategies, active vs. passive learning, organizational strategies, and elaboration strategies. Each of these examples should be explained for the tutors to be able to demonstrate and teach to their students.
- **Vygotsky's Zone of Proximal Development:** Vygotsky's (1978) theory explains that there is a difference between what a student can do with help and without assistance. Although a student may not be able to do a task on their own, when a student is in the zone of proximal development for a particular task, the student can receive the appropriate guidance and then achieve the task. This is facilitated by social interactions with a more knowledgeable person (the tutor) who can help the student observe and practice skills. Helping tutors understand how they can serve to help students recognize their own content deficits and overcome them is one way to incorporate this theory into the tutor training.

Beyond formal tutor training, all formal peer tutoring programs should include a tutor handbook that includes the procedures around eligibility for tutoring, professionalism standards, scheduling sessions, best practices in tutoring, and assessment practices. Lastly, robust tutoring programs must include goals and objectives to ensure adequate program assessment.

Tutoring Sessions

Group tutoring can be a valuable tool for de-stigmatizing tutoring services. To this end, tutoring sessions should be made available to all students regardless of performance on assessments. Depending upon the curriculum and scheduled assessments within the institution, the amount of group tutoring sessions offered each week will vary. Table 1 gives an example of the types of group tutoring sessions that could be made available throughout an academic block. The goal is to have a variety of sessions offered during the week so each student can find a tutor and a style that fits their needs.

Individual tutoring should be made available to students who meet specific criteria. The eligibility requirements can be tied to whether or not they have remediated past blocks, failed weekly quizzes,

Table 1. Group tutoring sessions offered during one pre-clerkship course at Oregon Health & Science University

Title	Format	Optimal Number of Students	Goals of the Tutoring Session
Sunday Preview Session	Large group tutoring, 1-2 tutors; 2 hours/week	15-30 students	• Preview the week's content • Familiarize the student with what to expect
Weekly Tutoring Session	Large group tutoring, 1-2 tutors; 2 hours/week	15-30 students	• Review weekly concepts • Question and answer format if applicable
NBME Preparation	Small group tutoring, 1 tutor; 1-3 hours	10 students	• Work through NBME style questions as a group
Final Preparation	Small group tutoring, 1 tutor; 1-3 hours Large group tutoring, 1-2 tutors; 2 hours	10 students	• Review high-yield topics from the block • Answer questions from students
Anatomy Tutoring	Small group tutoring in anatomy lab; 1 tutor; 1-2 hours/week	6 students	• Review anatomical dissections with students • Answer questions

or some other form of academic measurement. These sessions are individualized and should focus on meeting the needs of the struggling student for a short period of time.

Effective Program Evaluation

Regular evaluation is important in order to ensure that the tutors are effective, the goals of the program are being met, and that the students are satisfied with the program. Evaluations can take place in multiple formats such as tutor observations with feedback sessions and student evaluations.

It is important that the tutors are observed at a minimum of two times during the academic year. These observations should be fully formative and intended as a learning opportunity for the tutor. The observer should follow a rubric with sections that link back to the goals of the program (Table 2). For example, the rubric can include sections on engagement in tutoring, promoting self-empowerment, and effective communication. These observable qualities can be rated on a continuum from 'needs growth' to 'exemplary.' A follow-up meeting with the tutor to go over the observation will aid in the growth and development of the tutor's teaching and facilitation skills and help the tutor identify areas they want to work on for the next period of time.

Maps to Learning Objective:

Apply their knowledge and skills in a collaborative learning environment

Student satisfaction surveys provide a second source of feedback for peer educators. These can be distributed to students during the previously described observed session and/or at other times throughout the academic year. The questions asked on the survey should also mapped back to the goals and learning objectives of the tutoring program. Dissemination of the results of the surveys should include a debrief of the overall results, as well as action items that the tutor wants to work on in the near future. Results

Table 2. Example of how tutor observation rubric maps back to tutor program learning objectives

	Needs Growth	Emerging	Solid	Exemplary	Notes
Student feels welcome, Tutor greets students					
Tutor is knowledgeable					
Tutor provides a student perspective on learning and student access					

may also be given to the administration to demonstrate effectiveness independently and in advance of the AAMC Graduation Questionnaire.

Formal peer tutoring programs are an opportunity for UME programs to connect near-peers to each other and have them engage in meaningful ways. There must be structure, continued trainings for the tutors, and meaningful assessment to ensure that all of the students are benefiting from this mutually advantageous relationship.

Remediation Approaches

Assessment during the UME curriculum can be both formative and summative. Designing assessments that meet the needs of today's UME learners should include opportunities for students to remediate when they stumble. In fact, approximately 10% of all medical students will experience academic failure at some point during their training (Holland, 2015). Remediation is defined as "the act of facilitating a correction for trainees who started out on the journey towards becoming a physician but have moved off course" (Kalet & Chou, 2014, p. 17). Depending on the size of your program and the resources available at your institution, remediation practices can be applied to both formative and summative assessments. This section of the chapter will outline two different remediation approaches.

Before discussing the two suggested approaches for remediation, it is important to note that this is not an exhaustive manual on how to develop remediation policies within your school. There are entire books (Kalet & Chou, 2017) and articles with step-by-step guides that focus solely on this topic. This section is devoted to the argument that has been made in the literature that remediation policies should be grounded in sound educational theories (Cleland, 2013). Additionally, all remediation practices must take a holistic approach, both in terms of the professionals working with your students and from the standpoint of the learner.

Educational Theories

While many remediation practices are intended to confirm mastery attainment after failure, not all are adequately grounded in theory. Below are the brief definitions of a few pertinent educational theories to consider when devising remediation practices:

- **Cognitive Constructivism:** Knowledge systems of cognitive structures are actively constructed by learners based on pre-existing cognitive structures.
- **Meta-cognition:** Awareness and understanding of one's own thought processes.
- **Self-efficacy:** Bandura (1977) defined self-efficacy as one's belief in his or her own ability to succeed in specific situations or accomplish a task.
- **Self-regulated learning theory**: A cyclical process that includes goal setting, process selection, and reflection to achieve adaptive change over time.

When working with a student who is academically struggling, it is often hard to pinpoint the exact cause for why they might be in academic jeopardy. Given the complexity of why a student might struggle, holistic approaches can address the multitude of reasons for the academic concern, rather than fix the problem temporarily (Table 3).

In order to address the multiple factors that can contribute to a student's inability to pass an exam or course, a truly multidisciplinary team of professionals can help get a student back on track, as well as address the actual problems affecting them. This multidisciplinary team consists of course faculty, assessment staff, learning specialists, and staff from the student health and counseling center. Instead of the burden falling solely on the faculty teaching the course, which is often the case, the student can feel supported and receive the appropriate needed resources for what they might be experiencing.

Rapid Remediation

The first approach is Rapid Remediation. This involves the learner remediating the material as quickly as possible so not too much time passes between the old content and the new content. Rapid Remediation is built on Perry's Cognitive Constructivism theory (Perry, 1999) and Bandura's Self-Efficacy theory (Bandura, 1977). This type of remediation works best for formative assessments or low-stakes summative assessments. Aside from content mastery, reflective practice is an essential component for Rapid Remediation. For the formal reflective practice component, the student should ask themselves the following questions:

- How did I prepare for this assessment?
- What were my goals?
- What can I do differently next time?

Table 3. Factors affecting the learning process

External	Emotional & Social	Individual Learning
Family/relationship stressors	Depression	Attention span
Time burden from extracurricular activities	Anxiety	Prior knowledge
Part-time employment	Burnout	Intellectual ability
Financial stress	Motivation	Learning preferences
		Learning disabilities
		Secondary resource overload (knowing which to use)

Should a student not meet the passing threshold on a particular assessment, specific ways of implementing this type of remediation include:

- Requiring the student to submit written explanations of the incorrect answers within a certain amount of time to the course director/remediation leader for review.
- Requiring the student to review their incorrect answers with a peer tutor and submit explanations of incorrect answers within a certain amount of time to the course director/remediation leader for review.
- Requiring the student to retake the assessment before the next formative assessment.
- Requiring the student to meet with other students who did not meet the passing threshold and create test questions together on the content to submit to the course director/remediation leader for review.

The goal of implementing these processes would be to allow for rapid reflection on the content, while actively working to engage with the content, evaluate gaps in knowledge, and construct new meanings and connections with the knowledge to ensure learning.

Individualized Remediation

The second approach of remediation discussed in this chapter is called Individualized Remediation. This approach is based on the work of Durning and colleagues (2011) who use a learner-center and theory-based remediation strategy called Self-Regulated Learning – Microanalytic Assessment and Training. Individualized Remediation allows the student to truly be a self-directed learner. In order to allow for individualized remediation, it is important that all M1s be taught the fundamentals of self-regulated learning strategies. This includes the "before, during, and after phases of learning," as these are the basic tenants of the Individualized Remediation approach.

Should a student not meet the passing threshold on a particular assessment, one specific way of implementing this type of remediation includes:

- Requiring the student to submit to the course director/remediation leader a written plan for how he or she will plan to remediate the content.
- Areas of specific individualization for the student:
  ○ The necessary resources, which may include tutors, faculty time, counseling or time-off.
  ○ How gaps in knowledge will be covered.
  ○ When the exam will be retaken, and how the material will be tested.

This approach will maximize reflection on the material, as well as the agency the student has over his or her own learning.

STANDARDIZED TEST PREPARATION

USMLE Step 1

After the initial shock of medical school has worn off, students begin thinking and preparing for the USMLE Step 1. The USMLE Step 1 consists of seven one-hour blocks of approximately 40 questions and tests the students' knowledge of basic biomedical science content. The timing of Step 1 is variable. Most students take Step 1 prior to the start of clerkships; however, a growing number of schools are now positioning it after the clerkships. Passing Step 1 has implications for both medical schools and the students. For the schools, first-time pass rates are reported out which may affect both accreditation as well as recruitment of students. For the students, many residency programs look to Step 1 scores as a first filter for sorting through applications.

Due to the high-stakes nature of Step 1, some medical schools have sought to look within their data, including both admissions and assessment, to create predictive models for Step 1 performance. While there is supporting research that indicates that those who struggled with the Medical College Admissions Test (MCAT) might struggle with Step 1 (Coumarbatch, Robinson, Thomas, Bridge, 2010), the literature points out that schools working towards predictive models are also including their own assessment data. Assessment data points can include end of course or block cumulative assessments, bottom quartile class rank, and remediation data. While predictive models can aid in early identification of students who need resources, there are plenty of examples of students who struggled with coursework and still passed Step 1, or performed extraordinarily throughout the curriculum but did not pass Step 1. Therefore, caution should be used when focusing on predictive models.

The literature on which study techniques can lead to a successful outcome of USMLE Step 1 is sparse and is complicated by the lack of ability to determine which exact technique or resource led to success. However, what is known is that spaced-repetition of concepts, having an individualized study plan, active retrieval of concepts (e.g., utilization of a question bank), self-monitoring of progress (understanding test practice scores), and appropriate resource utilization all play important roles for the student during the study period for Step 1. Students may be assisted in their preparation for the exam by the school by having specific time allotted for studying, providing resources such as question banks, and workshops for specific study skills (Table 4).

Beyond workshops aimed at meeting the needs of many students at one time, having individual consultations is vital both before and during the dedicated study period. These consultations aid students in fine-tuning their study plan and schedule, identifying which resources are most appropriate for their learning, and most importantly, help student's track and monitor progress towards readiness to take Step 1. If your school has the resources to check-in with students during the dedicated study period, this is encouraged. Students need to feel supported, rather than isolated, during this incredibly demanding and daunting time in their medical training.

Shelf Exam/USMLE Step 2 CS and CK

For many students, the transition from the didactic portion of their medical training to the clinical portion of their training is considered one of the most challenging (Knobloch, Ledford, Wilkes, Saperstein, & 2018). Once medical students begin their clinical rotations, they are still required to take exams, such as the NBME Shelf Exams. This is a point during UME that can easily get overlooked in terms of aca-

Table 4. Examples of workshops to support students preparing for USMLE Step 1

Workshops	Timing	Theory to Support Practice	Content	Presented by
Introduction to Step 1	4-6 months prior to dedicated study time		• General information on registering for Step 1 • What resources/workshops are coming up • General timeline	Multidisciplinary team: • Assistant Dean for Student Affairs • Learning Specialist • Support Staff
How to Utilize a Question Bank	Immediately before dedicated study time	• Active Recall • Testing Effect • Moving from (content) input to application	Advising students about how to use a question bank • Timed vs. Tutor function • Active vs. passive techniques • How many questions to get through • Subject based vs. random	Learning Specialist
Creating a Dedicated Study Plan	1-4 months before dedicated with optional follow-up appointment during dedicated	• Motivational theories • Content Chunking Strategies • Time management • Stress management	Discussing with students about how to create an individualized study plan. Important to focus on: • This is your plan! • 8-10 hours/day • Must include time for wellness/self-care • Optimal amount of time is ≈ 40 days • When to take practice tests • Resources to use	Learning Specialist
Managing Stress and Anxiety During Dedicated	1 month prior to dedicated	• Stress management • Anxiety reduction • Stress physiology	Working with students about ways to manage stress and anxiety during dedicated study periods including: • Resources • Signs of when to seek help • Strategies	Student Health and Counseling

demic support because learners are rotating throughout the hospital and clinical settings. Nonetheless, these learners still need to be provided with academic support around shelf exams and USMLE Step 2 CS/CK in order to succeed.

The academic support that individual students find helpful for shelf exams is variable. Yet, the common pitfalls that students face on the shelf exams, such as failing to work through resource books or practice tests, and failing to practice questions on "timed mode" to account for differences between clinical subject exams and Step 1, can be counteracted through starting all students off with equitable resources. Timely access to appropriate resources and study strategies can lead to improved learning on the wards and eventual passing scores on shelf exams. One way to do this is for the learning specialist to offer a session during a transition to clinical experiences curriculum. Because every student will be taking each of the shelf exams, they need to have a solid understanding of what resources are available, how the shelf exams are different that USMLE Step 1, and best practices for ensuring a passing score of the shelf exams.

Suggested content for the session is as follows:

Content Resources: A thorough list of resources by rotation should be made available to students. This resource list would include books, videos, websites that are appropriate for the shelf exam. Not all of these resources are required or necessary, however having a resource list organized by shelf exam is helpful for the student.

Question Banks: A list of appropriate question banks to utilize to study organized by shelf exam. This can also include books that are question based, or cased-based questions.

NBME Science Subject Practice Tests: How and when to utilize these should be discussed.

Integrated learning on the ward and studying for the shelf: Overall, the process of studying for the shelf exams can be feeling like an independent learning activity aside from studying for the clerkship. Helping students understand what it takes to be successful on the clerkship and how to integrate studying for the shelf exams at the same time can only benefit the student, the patients, and the experience overall.

After they have successfully studied and passed their shelf exams, most learners feel more confident about USMLE Step 2 CK feels and studying for it becomes less burdensome. Regardless, information and resources need to be made available to students at each school around Step 2 CS/CK so that they feel supported and can continue to be successful in the examination process (Table 5).

In addition to the above-mentioned workshops, webinars, and in-class presentations, having a student learning support specialist who can work individually with students will always be important. This trained professional can work individually with students to provide guidance to students who are struggling to make a study plan, selecting which resources to utilize, or to help identify readiness to take the exam.

ACADEMIC ADVISING

Advising

The traditional way for UME programs to formally facilitate the growth of students is via advising. Advising is a pedagogical construct in which information is generated from the teacher or expert (advisor) and transmitted to the learner (advisee), who plays a relatively passive role in the relationship. It is an efficient way of conveying information from an expert to a non-expert. Advisors may be assigned for short term, specific problems. This may be particularly useful for scenarios in which there is less need for personalization of the information. One example of this is in preparation of residency applications;

Table 5. Examples of USMLE Step 2 preparation offerings

Exam	Format	Content Covered	Delivered by
Step 2 CK	Workshops	• Study plan • Resource utilization • Timing	Learning Specialist
Step 2 CS	Webinar	• Timing • Overview of exam	Assistant Dean of Student Affairs
Step 2 CS	Simulation	• Clinical encounters	• Clinician course director • Simulation team

advice for a student will vary little from one applicant to the next for a given specialty. An extreme example of this is "Speed Advising" for students interested in Emergency Medicine, in which students met with seven faculty for eight minutes each, saving each faculty an estimated 7.3 hours (McGrath, 2016). Alternatively, advisors may be assigned for longer periods of time up to the duration of the program. In this context, meetings may be expected to occur at some regular interval, such as semi-annually or quarterly. Advisors may be sought from a volunteer pool of faculty or recruited, and are frequently assigned with minimal input from the student. Although advising as a process can make use of speed and efficiency, it does have drawbacks. Advisees may be less active and engaged in the process leading to less buy-in and commitment to change if the approach is being used for development.

Mentoring

Mentoring may be a less-formal construct than advising, in which the teacher or expert (mentor) has a mutually beneficial relationship with the learner (mentee). A proto-typical mentor-mentee relationship may be found in research, in which a mentor may help a mentee with their project design, support for resources to carry out a project, or knowledge of how to navigate funding, while the mentee is assisting the mentor by furthering growth of knowledge in the mentor's lab, or providing the mentor with a sense of giving back. Other mentorships may develop between mentors who are prominent in a field and mentees who wish to gain entrance into the field or specialty. Mentoring is relational, and mentor-mentee pairings usually form more organically from mutual interests of both parties, as opposed to being strictly assigned. Frequently the learner primarily initiates the relationship, as the mentor is presumably more engaged in his or her work activities. When the relationship arises ad hoc, there is less likely to be explicit expectations around how the relationship works, such as how often will they meet or who is responsible for reaching out. Without explicit discussion of expectations, there may be a higher likelihood of disappointment on the part of either the mentor or the mentee. Formalizing the mentor-mentee relationship, and training both mentors and mentees on their shared responsibilities can help ameliorate the chance of miscommunication and disappointment in the relationship.

Coaching

Coaching has been a concept used for traditionally used for sports and transitioned to executive leadership in business. This concept is now being adapted and incorporated in medical education. DeIorio (2016) evaluated multiple sources to try to define academic coaching and found the closest parallels with executive coaching. She proposed the following definition:

An academic coach is a person assigned to facilitate learners achieving their fullest potential. Coaches work with learners by evaluating performance via review of objective assessments, assisting the learner to identify needs and create a plan to achieve these, and helping the learner to be accountable.

Coaching differs from advising and mentoring in that the learner (coachee) is the driver of the relationship. The coach does not necessarily need content expertise, but instead facilitates the growth of the coachee by helping the learner focus on his or her goals and how he or she may best achieve them. This model conceptually increases self-directed reflection and improvement consistent with the development of life-long learning. Indeed, coaching has been shown to facilitate improved outcomes in performance/

skills, well-being, coping, work attitudes, and goal-directed self-regulation in organizational settings (Theeboom, 2014). Key differences between the models are described in Table 6.

Most science faculty use mentoring and advising synonymously (Titus, 2013), and few have any experience with academic coaching. Therefore, any model chosen will benefit from development of the faculty to best fill their role. As most faculty have not had experience in coaching, this model is likely to require the most faculty development to be successful. Although the learner is driving the content of the discussions, the coach plays a very active role in guiding the learner. It is very common for a coach to slip back into an advisory role to more efficiently "solve the problem" the learner has, instead of allowing the learner to work through the problem himself or herself. This is more than a new skill for most coaches; it is a new way of thinking about learning and change, and will take substantial practice.

Multiple modalities may be used to enhance the ability of faculty to effectively coach. At the most basic level, workshops with readings and presentations can be used. However, more extensive training may be helpful with this new skill. Kopachek (2017) described how faculty coaches at The Ohio State University met for a full day of development. This included training in how to evaluate student reflections, as well as Observed Structured Teaching Evaluations (OSTE) with actors playing standardized learners. Orr (2019) described pairing coaches together to observe coaching episodes with learners either in person or recorded, and then coaching each other alternately for reflection and improvement in the COACH2COACH model.

Coaching Tools

Coaches, especially early in their development, may benefit from specific checklists and tools to use during their coaching meetings. Checklists that prompt the coach as to which examinations the student will have recently completed, and what evaluations will be expected to be available will be useful to the early coach. Additionally, items that need specific planning and attention at certain times in the curriculum would be helpful to note (e.g. study planning for USMLE Step1, planning and progress for a capstone project, etc.).

R2C2: There are multiple other coaching tools that can be specifically used by a coach to help prompt reflection and growth. One model is the R2C2 model (Sargeant, 2018). This is a four-step model designed to specifically facilitate the reflection of a coachee for change by the coach. Use of the R2C2 model is well accepted and promotes learner reflection and improvement plan creation in residents. The steps and possible questions to use for each step include:

Table 6. Comparison of advisor, mentor and coach relationship

	Advisor	**Mentor**	**Coach**
Domain/Goal	Offer advice & give direction to learner	Role-model to learner Mutually beneficial	Coach to facilitate learning & results
Relationship	Assigned	Organic	Assigned
Expertise	High content expertise Granular advice	High content expertise General wisdom	Content expertise variable
Meetings	Formal/Regular	Informal or formal/Time Variable	Formal/Time Variable

Step 1:   **R**elationship Building. How are you doing? What things are going well for you?

Step 2:   Exploring **R**eactions to the Feedback. What do you think about these evaluations? How does this make you feel?

Step 3:   Exploring Understanding of Feedback **C**ontent. What is the most important part of this feedback to you? What do you think about this evaluation?

Step 4:   **C**oaching for Change. What are you going to do to improve?

WOOP: Another useful tool for coaching is the WOOP (Oettingen, 2000). WOOP is also known as Mental Contrasting with Implementation Intentions. It is designed to give the coachee the tools to overcome obstacles to desired change by recognizing and pre-planning responses to those obstacles. It is very easy to understand and use, and may be used either in conjunction with the R2C2 or as a stand-alone. The specific steps include having the coachee reflect on:

Step 1:   What is the **W**ish?

Step 2:   What is the desired **O**utcome?

Step 3:   What is your main inner **O**bstacle?

Step 4:   Make a **P**lan. (Oettingen, 2000)

Use of the WOOP tool has been shown to be more effective for helping people make change in behaviors compared to just wishful planning in many environments. Specifically in medical education, residents spent significantly more time studying towards a goal when using the WOOP once at the beginning of a rotation compared to residents who just made a plan (Saddawi-Konefka, 2017).

Models of Delivery

Unfortunately, at this time there is no evidence to suggest that advising, mentoring or coaching has better outcomes in medical education. Therefore, consider the goals of the program and resources available when attempting to design an academic advising program. Many schools are now beginning to center their academic advising, mentoring or coaching in Learning Communities. Learning Communities are common now, with 46 medical schools as members of the Learning Community Institute ("LCI Members", n.d., list 1). One common model is having a faculty who is the advisor/mentor/coach for 5-8 students per class. This is known as the "molecule" in the Genes to Society Curriculum at the Johns Hopkins School of Medicine (Frosch, 2019). With subsequent classes stacking on to each other, it becomes the "macro-molecule," so that each faculty member has five students x four years for a total of twenty students in a cohort. Multiple macro-molecules join to create a "college". Coaching models such as this will frequently financially support the coaches at the 0.1-0.3 FTE level. This protects the time for the coach to meet with their coachees and participate in faculty development.

Variations on this model include designating near-peer mentors from senior classes to specifically mentor junior students in a cohort. This is the model at the University of Texas Health Science Center at San Antonio School of Medicine, where the near-peer mentors are called "Mentors in Medicine" or MiMs (Andre, 2017). Reported benefits included facilitating discussion that may have been sensitive for faculty to discuss, and extending the reach of mentoring such that faculty mentors had eleven students x four years for a total of forty-four students. As expected in a mentoring relationship, the near-peers appreciated the opportunity to "give back" to the junior students.

One caution to be aware of is that the advisor/mentor/coach may be conflicted if they happen to work with the learner and are asked to assess the performance of a mentee/coachee. With a limited number of faculty in an institution, this happens on occasion. One way of dealing with this is to ban a coach from clinically assessing a coachee under any circumstance. This eliminates any possible discussion or worries of conflict of interest, and allows the coach to always be the advocate for the learner. This approach works more successfully in a large academic center where there are adequate additional faculty members to evaluate learners. A specific plan may be needed for highly engaged faculty who frequent both curriculum and advising roles.

CONCLUSION

Academic support and advising are necessary components to medical education. Learning specialists that have expertise in education may play important roles in supporting students. Students may need particular help with remediation, but all students may wish more support with standardized national exams. Advising, mentoring and coaching are all distinct processes, and each may have a role in medical education. Faculty development is critical to ensuring success for the students.

REFERENCES

Andre, C., Deerin, J., & Leykum, L. (2017). Students helping students: Vertical peer mentoring to enhance the medical school experience. *BMC Research Notes*, *10*(1), 176. doi:10.118613104-017-2498-8 PMID:28464902

Bandura, A. (1977). Self-efficacy: Toward a unifying theory of behavioral change. *Psychological Review*, *84*(2), 191–215. doi:10.1037/0033-295X.84.2.191 PMID:847061

Burgess, A., Dornan, T., Clarke, A. J., Menezes, A., & Mellis, C. (2016). Peer tutoring in a medical school: Perceptions of tutors and tutees. *BMC Medical Education*, *16*(1), 85. doi:10.118612909-016-0589-1 PMID:26956642

Burgess, A., & Nestel, D. (2014). Facilitating the development of professional identity through peer assisted learning in medical education. *Advances in Medical Education and Practice*, *5*, 403–406. doi:10.2147/AMEP.S72653 PMID:25378965

Clarke, A. J., Burgess, A., Menezes, A., & Mellis, C. (2015). Senior students' experience as tutors of their junior peers in the hospital setting. *BMC Research Notes*, *8*(1), 743. doi:10.118613104-015-1729-0 PMID:26631241

Cleland, J., Leggett, H., Sandars, J., Costa, M., Patel, R., & Moffat, M. (2013). The remediation challenge: Theoretical and methodological insights from a systematic review. *Medical Education*, *47*(3), 242–251. doi:10.1111/medu.12052 PMID:23398010

Coumarbatch, J., Robinson, L., Thomas, R., & Bridge, P. (2010). Strategies for identifying students at risk for USMLE Step 1 failure. *Family Medicine*, *42*(2), 105–110. PMID:20135567

De Menezes, S., & Premnath, D. (2016). Near-peer education: A novel teaching program. *International Journal of Medical Education*, *7*, 160–167. doi:10.5116/ijme.5738.3c28 PMID:27239951

DeIorio, N., Carney, P., Kahl, L., Bonura, E., & Miller Juve, A. (2016). Coaching: A new model for academic and career achievement. *Medical Education Online, 21*(1). doi:10.3402/meo.v21.33480 PMID:27914193

Durning, S., Cleary, T., Sandars, J., Hemmer, P. A., Kokotailo, P., & Artino, A. R. (2011). Perspective: Viewing "strugglers" through a different lens: How a self-regulated learning perspective can help medical educators with assessment and remediation. *Academic Medicine, 86*(4), 488–495. doi:10.1097/ACM.0b013e31820dc384 PMID:21346503

Frosch, E., & Goldstein, M. (2019). Relationship-Centered Advising in a Medical School Learning Community. *Journal of medical education and curricular development*, 6. doi:10.1177/2382120519827895

Grover, S., Sood, N., & Chaudhary, A. (2019). Reforming pathology teaching in medical college by peer-assisted learning and student-oriented interest building activities: A pilot study. *Education for Health, 30*(2), 126–132. doi:10.4103/efh.EfH_267_16 PMID:28928342

Kalet, A., & Chou, C. (2014). Preface. In A. Kalet, & C. Chou (Eds.), *Remediation in Medical Education. (xvii-xxi)*. New York, NY: Springer. doi:10.1007/978-1-4614-9025-8

Kalet, A., Guerrasio, J., & Chou, C. (2016). Twelve tips for developing and maintaining a remediation program in medical education. *Medical Teacher, 38*(8), 787–792. doi:10.3109/0142159X.2016.1150983 PMID:27049798

Kebaetse, M. B., Kebaetse, M., Mokone, G., Nkomazana, O., Mogodi, M., Wright, J., ... Park, P. (2018). Learning support interventions for Year 1 medical students: A review of the literature. *Medical Education, 52*(3), 263–273. doi:10.1111/medu.13465 PMID:29058332

Knobloch, A., Ledford, C., Wilkes, S., & Saperstein, A. (2018). The Impact of near-peer teaching on medical students' transition to clerkships. *Family Medicine, 50*(1), 58–62. doi:10.22454/FamMed.2018.745428 PMID:29346691

Kopachek, J., Bardales, C., Lash, A., Walker, C. Jr, Pfeil, S., & Ledford, C. (2017). Coaching the Coach: A Program for Development of Faculty Portfolio Coaches. *Teaching and Learning in Medicine, 29*(3), 326–336. doi:10.1080/10401334.2016.1273781 PMID:28632014

Learning Communities Institute Members. (n.d.). In Learning Communities Institute Website. Retrieved from http://www.learningcommunitiesinstitute.org/content/schools

McGrath, J., Bischof, J., Greenberger, S., Bachmann, D., Way, D., Gorgas, D., & Kman, N. (2016). 'Speed advising' for medical students applying to residency programs: An efficient supplement to traditional advising. *Medical Education Online, 21*(1), 31336. doi:10.3402/meo.v21.31336 PMID:27056564

Morgan, K. M., Northey, E. E., & Khalil, M. K. (2017). The effect of near-peer tutoring on medical students' performance in anatomical and physiological sciences. *Clinical Anatomy (New York, N.Y.), 30*(7), 922–928. doi:10.1002/ca.22954 PMID:28726243

Oettingen, G. (2000). Expectancy effects on behavior depend on self-regulatory thought. *Social Cognition, 18*(2), 101–129. doi:10.1521oco.2000.18.2.101

Orr, C., & Sonnandara, R. (2019). Coaching by design: Exploring a new approach to faculty development in a competency-based medical education curriculum. *Advances in Medical Education and Practice*, *10*, 229–244. doi:10.2147/AMEP.S191470 PMID:31118862

Perry, W. G. (1999). *Forms of Ethical and Intellectual Development in the College Years*. San Francisco, CA: Jossey-Bass Publishers.

Saddawi-Konefka, D., Baker, K., Guarino, A., Burns, S. A., Oettingen, G., Gollwitzer, P. M., & Charnin, J. E. (2017). Changing resident physician studying behaviors: A randomized, comparative effectiveness trial of goal-setting versus use of WOOP. *Journal of Graduate Medical Education*, *9*(4), 451–457. doi:10.4300/JGME-D-16-00703.1 PMID:28824757

Theeboom, T., Beersma, B., & van Vianen, A. (2014). Does coaching work? A meta-analysis on the effects of coaching on individual level outcomes in an organizational context. *The Journal of Positive Psychology*, *9*(1), 1–18. doi:10.1080/17439760.2013.837499 PMID:26640507

Titus, S., & Ballou, J. (2013). Faculty members' perceptions of advising versus mentoring: Does the name matter? *Science and Engineering Ethics*, *19*(3), 1267–1281. doi:10.100711948-012-9366-7 PMID:22660987

Vygotsky, L. S. (1987). Thinking and speech. In R. W. Rieber, & A. S. Carton (Eds.), The collected works of L. S. Vygotsky, Volume 1: Problems of general psychology (pp. 39–285). New York: Plenum Press. (Original work published 1934.)

Weinstein, C., & Mayer, R. (1986). The teaching of learning strategies. In M. C. Wittrock (Ed.), *Handbook of research on teaching* ((3rd ed., pp. 315–327). New York, NY: Macmillan.

KEY TERMS AND DEFINITIONS

Advising: The process of giving information or knowledge by an expert to a person wishing to have input on an issue.

Coaching: A developmental process by which a learner meets regularly with a coach to create goals, manage existing and potential challenges, and improve performance toward the goal of reaching the learner's highest potential.

Cognitive Constructivism: Knowledge systems of cognitive structures are actively constructed by learners based on pre-existing cognitive structures.

Learning Communities: Intentionally designed groups that are actively engaged in learning with and from each other.

Mentoring: A mutually beneficial relationship in which an expert mentor is able to guide a less experienced mentee towards success in a specific project or career.

Meta-Cognition: Awareness and understanding of one's own thought processes.

Self-Efficacy: Bandura (1977) defined self-efficacy as one's belief in his or her own ability to succeed in specific situations or accomplish a task.

Self-regulated Learning Theory: A cyclical process that includes goal setting, process selection, and reflection to achieve adaptive change over time.

APPENDIX

Appointment Intake Form

Please take a few minutes to answer the following questions. Answering these questions as completely and honestly as possible will enable us to provide you with more effective assistance. All information on this form is confidential unless required to be disclosed by law.

Name: _____Date: _

College/Program: _____Projected Year of Graduation:_____

Date of Birth:_____ Age: _____

Primary Phone Number: _____

Alternate Phone Number: _____

Email: _____

Emergency Contact:_____Phone:_____

Relationship to Emergency Contact: _____

Referred by: _____

Is English your first/primary language? □ YES □ NO If no, specify:_____

Do you have a disability/disabilities (physical, learning, emotional, etc.)? □ YES □ NO
If yes, please specify: _____

Are you employed? □ YES □ NO If yes, how many hours a week?_____

What are your family responsibilities?_____

Do they impact your school performance? □ YES □ NO

What brings you to Student Academic Support Services?

_____

What would you like to accomplish from your SASS appointment(s)?

_____

Describe your current study and test preparation strategies:

_____
_____
_____

Do you use a study schedule? □ YES □ NO If so, explain: _____
_____

Courses which present or have presented more challenges:_____

_____

Academic History

Courses/Block Currently Enrolled In Grades to date

_____ _____
_____ _____
_____ _____
_____ _____
_____ _____

GPA prior to this term (if applicable): _____

Is there any additional information you would like for us to know?_____

_____

_____

Section 4
Professional Identity and Career Development Across the Continuum

Chapter 14
The Premedical Years

Stephanie Chervin
University of Michigan, USA

Mariella Mecozzi
University of Michigan, USA

David Brawn
University of Michigan, USA

ABSTRACT

The premedical baccalaureate period is critical to shaping a high-achieving, diverse, and service-oriented medical school applicant pool. The focus on achieving superior academic performance in premedical coursework captures the attention of most premedical students, but equal attention must be paid to developing the personal qualities and experiences that will form the foundation of their future capacity to understand and communicate with patients. Premedical students are best served to major in a field for authentic intellectual reasons regardless of the field's immediate connection to the health care field. There is a growing trend for applicants to have a gap year or more between the undergraduate period and medical school. The authors discuss the role of letters of evaluation and the premedical committee in the application process. The authors have more than 40 years of combined experience in premedical academic and career advising at a large, research-focused public institution.

INTRODUCTION

The demands, competition, and anxiety of the premedical college experience shape the formative years in the lives of thousands of students. Some remember these years as stressful, consuming, and disappointing. Others remember an awakening of fascination with science, ambition to help individuals in need, and determination to make a societal impact. The difference in the premedical experience may prove critical, not only for individual happiness and fulfillment, but for the future wellbeing of countless patients who benefit the most when their physicians feel professionally satisfied, helpful, and capable rather than burned out.

DOI: 10.4018/978-1-7998-1468-9.ch014

This chapter will consider the landscape of the premedical period encompassing the entirety of the college experience in the setting of a large research-focused public institution. The authors will address premedical students' choice of major, prerequisite coursework, MCAT preparation, how students engage in meaningful exploratory healthcare experiences, letters of evaluation, and the application stage. It is the authors' intent that medical school educators will find this perspective valuable for the enhancement of their ability to interpret applications to their programs. Insight they will gain from this review could improve their understanding of the particular challenges and unique opportunities that exist in the contemporary undergraduate premedical experience.

BACKGROUND

The roots of the modern American medical education model can be traced to the late nineteenth century when medical educators first called for a premedical education period leading to a baccalaureate degree or its equivalent in preparation for medical training. These recommendations were established to ensure that medical trainees were properly prepared in the sciences and classics such that they would possess the academic fitness to complete a medical doctor degree that was becoming increasingly based on scientific practice (Fishbein, 2001). Decades later in 1910, in his comprehensive review of the American and Canadian medical education system, Abraham Flexner of the Carnegie Foundation concluded that "a two-year college training, in which the sciences are featured is the minimum basis upon which modern medicine can be successfully taught" and advocated further for medical departments to adopt a stricter standard of a prerequisite baccalaureate degree (Flexner, 1910). The 1920s saw the development of the the Moss Test, a forbearer of the Medical College Admission Test (MCAT), a tool designed to objectively assess an applicant's intellectual qualities with the aim of reducing the medical school attrition rate which had climbed to as high as 50% in that period (McGaghie, 2002). In the postwar period, under the direction of the Association of American Medical Colleges (AAMC), the exam evolved into a multiple-choice test of verbal, quantitative, and science ability and knowledge of "modern society." The MCAT has undergone numerous revisions and updates with the latest in 2015. The MCAT and the undergraduate record continue to be the key indicators of academic readiness in the medical school application process (Schwartzstein, Rosenfeld, Hilborn, Oyewole, & Mitchell, 2013).

This uniquely American rite of passage has played out for generations in elite liberal arts colleges and universities, the most prized recruiting grounds for medical schools. The decades that followed have witnessed considerable debate about the objectives of this premedical education period, and while such debates are still ongoing, a baccalaureate degree for the modern American premedical student is *de rigueur*. In an undergraduate experience characterized by competition, sacrifice and persistence (Richardson, Mulvihill, & Latz, 2014), the premedical student not only must demonstrate excellence in coursework, research, and service and achieve a high MCAT score, but also demonstrate mature personal development and obtain formal letters of support from several faculty. The numbers are not in the premedical student's favor with fewer than 50% of applicants each year gaining admission to U.S. MD-granting schools (*Applying to Medical School: 2018 AMCAS Medical School Applications by the Numbers,* 2019).

Like any large system, the U.S. medical school preparation and application process is susceptible to inequities. Institutionalized discrimination, endemic poverty, and poor educational opportunities focused in urban and rural environments are key drivers each year behind the underrepresentation of the poor in general and specific populations among competitive applicants to medical schools in the United States; African Americans perhaps chief among these underrepresented-in-medicine (URiM) populations. This has resulted in a population of physicians that skews toward affluence which in turn has resulted in a scarcity of doctors and ongoing barriers to acceptable medical care in disadvantaged parts of the country (Smith, Rose, Schroeder, & Long, 2015). For premedical students from minority and disadvantaged backgrounds particularly, the competitive and complex undergraduate period can contribute to the "leaky pipeline" effect, or the decline in interest in a medical career (Barr, Gonzalez, & Wanat, 2008; Freeman, Trevino, Grande, Shea, & Shea, 2016). With the following, the authors offer their view of the fundamental features of the undergraduate premedical period and point attention to aspects that present particular vulnerabilities to the URiM population.

ROLE OF THE BACCALAUREATE MAJOR

The selection of a major field of study is perhaps the most significant act of self-definition that a premedical student confronts. In this act, a student formally joins a community of like-minded scholars and adopts a new layer of identity distinct from the "premed" label. The authors underscore that from the standpoint of the goals of a liberal arts and sciences education, the premedical student is best served to pursue a major that is most personally meaningful, regardless of any immediate connection of the major to the health care or biomedical field. The reasons for this recommendation are twofold: 1) a diversity of academic specialization brings richness to the practice of medicine, and 2) for the many freshmen who embark on the premedical path and choose a life-science major reflexively, some may abandon a premedical path entirely or ultimately may not gain admittance to a medical program and are then burdened with an academic preparation they chose for arbitrary reasons rather than intrinsic interest.

Concerning the latter case, consider a student who listlessly pursues a cellular biology major without an authentic interest in the field and under the misguided impression that such a choice will "look good" to a medical school admissions committee. This student finds herself in a precarious position should she arrive at graduation with no medical school acceptances (a fate shared by over 50% of the MD applicant pool) and with a degree that she did not enjoy nor thrive in. Had this student declared a major that truly reflected her intellectual interest, a viable plan B would be in place. More significantly, her college journey would have been an authentic one, not an instrumental one.

An examination of the premedical student population at the authors' institution[1] shows that the majority of premedical students applying majored in a life-science related field in recent years (Table 1). The American Association of Colleges of Osteopathic Medicine reports a similar trend wherein 70% of the DO applicant pool majored in a life science (*Data Reports in Osteopathic Medical Education* 2017). Among the MD applicant pool, a small majority (56%) specialized in the biological sciences with a broader distribution among the physical sciences, social sciences, humanities and other fields (*MCAT and GPAs for Applicants and Matriculants to U.S. Medical Schools by Primary Undergraduate Major, 2018-2019*, 2019). The dominance of life-science majors among the premedical population is not surprising given that a commitment to a future career in health care might incline a student toward a major that draws a linear connection to human medicine. Undoubtedly for some in this group, the choice of a life science major was informed not by an intrinsic interest for the field but by the notion that medical schools admissions committees prefer life science majors or that these majors are efficient routes toward completing medical school-specific prerequisites. A closer examination of this institution's applicant cohort reveals that dozens of non-science majors are represented – from English to history to business – and students who major in these subjects experience similar medical school acceptance outcomes to traditional life-science majors.[2]

In the modern era, countless medical journal commentaries have called for increased intellectual diversity among the medical school applicant pool with considerable interest in supporting premedical students with an academic focus in the humanities (e.g. English, cultural studies, religion, philosophy). Thirty years ago, the Mount Sinai School of Medicine Humanities and Medicine Program opened a new pathway to obtaining a medical degree that encouraged premedical students to engage in a truly broad liberal arts education by way of guaranteeing medical school admittance to select humanities students in the sophomore year (Rifkin, Smith, Stimmel, Stagnaro-Green, & Kase, 2000). The Mount Sinai program is joined by a growing number of formal undergraduate programs in medical humanities built upon the idea that the study of empathy, communication, and ethical reasoning prepares premedical students to serve as expertly-skilled, patient-centered physicians (Lamb, Berry, & Jones, 2019). Investigations of undergraduate humanities and social science majors have substantiated that as physicians, they have a greater tendency to choose primary care specialties (Hall, Woods, & Hanson, 2014), have superior interpersonal competencies, and are more informed of the factors that lead to health disparities than their science-major prepared colleagues (Metzel, Petty, & Olowojoba, 2018).

PREREQUISITE COURSEWORK AND ACADEMIC COMPETENCIES

As the American medical education model evolved over the last century, a broad consensus emerged that applicants to medical school should be required to show a mastery in biology, chemistry, physics, and

Table 1. Undergraduate majors of University of Michigan students who entered the MD application pool in the period of 2014-2018. Students with double majors are included in both major cohorts, respectively. Majors with fewer than 25 students are not shown. S. Chervin (author) collected these data.

Undergraduate Major	Number
Neuroscience	1233
Biology-related	1102
Psychology/Biopsychology	946
Biochemistry	491
Engineering-related	285
Kinesiology	201
Foreign language	179
Anthropology	105
History/Political Science	98
Economics/Business	97
Sociology-related	41
English	30
Mathematics	26

mathematics coursework at the undergraduate level as evidence of readiness to engage in the medical school curriculum (Alpern, Belitsky, & Long, 2011). At its most general, the modern prerequisite list continues to emphasize coursework in the sciences: one year each of general chemistry, organic chemistry, and physics; two years of biology; and a semester of biochemistry. Beyond these sciences, particular medical schools may require additional coursework in math or statistics (a requirement for calculus has become rare), an English composition, or social science (*Medical School Admission Requirements*[TM], 2019; *Student Guide to Osteopathic Medical Colleges*, 2019). Over the course of a baccalaureate degree, the medical school-specific courses amount to roughly half of all the academic courses a student will take. For some students, the prerequisite coursework will align efficiently with their chosen major, and for others, these courses will be completed alongside a major in a non-science field.

Where a premedical student completes these prerequisite courses appears to influence admissions outcomes. Students who begin their undergraduate experience at a two-year community college experience lower admission rates than students who matriculate at four-year undergraduate institutions even when controlling for MCAT scores and GPA (Talamantes et al., 2014). This finding is particularly concerning because a higher proportion of underrepresented minority and first-generation college students attend community colleges and thus complete much of the introductory premedical science coursework in these less-competitive settings (Saguil & Kellermann, 2014). In a recent commentary (2018), Amanda Kost speaks about the broken promise of a community college pipeline to medical school and challenges medical schools to "take a hard look at how we think about medical school admissions and the value we assign community college education versus a traditional 4-year degree. Community college should not be a barrier for medical school admission. On the contrary, it should be valued for not only the education it provides, the spaces it builds and offers disadvantaged students, but also for the pipeline it creates for those who otherwise could not apply to medical school."

Theoretically, once community college students arrive as transfer students to a four-year college or university, they have the opportunity to demonstrate academic prowess equivalent to that of the students who have been at such institutions from the beginning by performing well in upper-level science courses. However, it is the authors' (admittedly anecdotal) observation that the factors that initially led those students to begin at community colleges follow them to the four-year school and exacerbate what was likely to have been a challenging transition to begin with. Low SES status still requires them to work and sets them apart from an otherwise affluent student population. Lack of familiarity with the intensity and academic cultures associated with the new school's science courses may be an impediment to immediate success. The fact that they arrive with only two years to finish can force the transfer student to make an expedient curricular choice rather than a scholarly one. All of these factors can militate against the transfer student's academic success, even as they imbue in precisely the breadth of perspective, resilience, and empathy for the struggle of others that medical schools are looking for.

In 1988, the University of Pennsylvania School of Medicine moved away from the traditional model requiring a particular amount of credit hours in target coursework and toward a competency model. This model has slowly been adopted[3] by a small number of other programs (Burg, Croll, Ruff, & Stemmler, 1988). At its core, the competency model defines a benchmark set of knowledge and skills deemed essential for the study of human medicine (e.g., demonstrated skills in laboratory-based problem solving, knowledge of eukaryotic cell function, knowledge of the molecular underpinnings of life). Under this model, the premedical student is given freedom to master these competencies through a range of curricula and experiential options; they may demonstrate mastery by coursework, certainly, but also by extensive research in the content area, completing low-cost online courses or by other kinds of focused experiences. The underlying goals of the competency model were to provide medical schools with a greater degree of flexibility when it comes to identifying acceptable applicants and to encourage broad intellectual exploration at the undergraduate level. The developers of this model hoped that in freeing premedical students from the credit-hour economy, the competency model would have a liberating effect on the undergraduate premedical experience and support the development of innovative interdisciplinary leaders in the field. The Association of American Medical Colleges, in partnership with numerous consulting committees, developed a list of core personal and academic competencies to guide students both in their preparation for medical school and undergraduate institutions in their efforts toward curriculum reform (*Core Competencies for Entering Medical Students*, 2019). These core competencies encompass four areas of personal development and knowledge:

- Interpersonal:
  - Service orientation.
  - Social skills.
  - Cultural competence.
  - Teamwork.
  - Oral communication.
- Intrapersonal:
  - Ethical responsibility to self and others.
  - Reliability and dependability.
  - Resilience and adaptability.
  - Capacity for improvement.
- Thinking and Reasoning:
  - Critical thinking.
  - Quantitative reasoning.
  - Scientific inquiry.
  - Written communication.
- Science:
  - Living systems.
  - Human behavior.

The existence of the competency model poses the dilemma that unless a vast majority of medical schools adopt similarly liberal admission standards, the premedical student will forever be confined to complete the traditional prerequisite course list. Consider that on average applicant applies to sixteen medical programs in hopes of landing an interview at a handful of these schools (*FACTS: Applicants, Matriculants, Enrollment, Graduates, MD-PhD, and Residency Applicants Data*, 2018). In casting such a sizeable net, the applicant is beholden to complete the most particular coursework requirements among the set regardless of the existence of a more flexible plan among them. Thus, the traditional coursework model continues to hold sway over the lives of the modern premedical student.

PREPARING FOR THE MCAT

A superior performance on the Medical College Admission Test (MCAT) is essential to an applicant's competitiveness and accordingly the test is a dominant feature of the undergraduate premedical experience. With a substantial reform in 2015 (Schwartzstein et al., 2013), the MCAT shed its previous final exam-like quality and shifted to a format that emphasizes the foundational nature of the natural and behavioral sciences to the practice of human medicine. The seven-hour multiple-choice exam measures knowledge of the natural and behavioral sciences and assesses problem solving and critical reasoning skills. With the 2015 update, the AAMC introduced a variety of free and low-cost test preparation materials, including a comprehensive set of online tutorial videos produced in partnership with the Khan Academy, low-cost question packs, flashcards, and practice tests. While these AAMC resources are key to providing access to quality test prep for all applicants, many students nevertheless are compelled to invest in expensive commercial test preparation services, leaving low-income students vulnerable. From the authors' vantage, it appears that formal undergraduate institutional MCAT support is uneven and largely dependent upon the institution's philosophy. Does the institution consider pre-professional education core to its mission or does it prioritize intellectual development over "teaching to the test"?

With the mean MCAT score of an MD program matriculant at the eighty-third percentile (511.2) (*FACTS: Applicants, Matriculants, Enrollment, Graduates, MD-PhD, and Residency Applicants Data*, 2018) and sixtieth percentile (503.8) for a DO program matriculant (*AACOMAS Applicant and Matriculant Profile Summary Report*, 2018), students are aware of the high-stakes nature of the exam. The worry about outscoring the majority of other test takers contributes to the tendency for students to adopt a competitive mindset when it comes to learning and preparing for the exam (Lin et al., 2014). In the authors' view, the MCAT is an exam best taken once and after the student has completed the entirety of the premedical coursework. Students who take the exam before they are ready with the idea that they will sit for multiple times, find themselves on a continual loop of exam preparation which takes away from the effort that they could be devoting to other worthwhile experiential and educational opportunities. Within the framework of this high-stakes competition, those who advise and teach undergraduates must work to ensure that premedical students have a learning experience that is not solely focused on completing an academic checklist based on prerequisites and the MCAT, but one that sparks fascination and fosters life-long learning.

EXPERIENCES IN HEALTHCARE AND SERVICE

While the focus on achieving superior academic metrics captures the attention of most premedical students, equal attention must be paid to developing the personal qualities and experiences that will form the fabric of their future bedside manner. Strong GPAs and MCAT scores will often grant an applicant a review, but without meaningful exposure to the health care setting and related service-oriented experience, students have little chance of landing an in-person interview. These non-academic factors grow in importance as admissions committees move toward a final decision post interview (Dunleavy, Sondheimer, Castillo-Page, & Beer Bletzinger, 2011). It is now commonplace for premedical students to have spent hundreds of hours volunteering in clinical environments, nursing homes, hospice centers, or similar contexts during their undergraduate years (*Applying to Medical School: 2018 AMCAS Medical School Applications by the Numbers*, 2019). In addition to providing evidence to medical schools of an applicant's capacity to become a humane (and not just technically competent) physician, the interaction with patients helps premedical students found their decision to pursue a career in medicine on a realistic understanding of what this career can entail. Beyond patient interaction, medical schools also place enormous emphasis on the value of volunteer work of all kinds. This emphasis comes from the philosophical position that medicine is a service profession, and thus substantive involvement in some volunteer service in local, national, or international contexts is indicative of an applicant's ability to thrive in medical service.

Often, access to shadowing opportunities and high-profile internships favors students with the social capital to arrange for these opportunities. A student who is the first in their family to attend college, for example, cannot rely on a well-connected family member to offer her easy entry into a clinic or hospital. Premedical students who are underrepresented-in-medicine cite that difficulties connecting to a physician mentor was a contributing factor to their decision to leave the premedical track (Freeman et al., 2016). To address this disparity in access with an aim to promote diversity in the future physician workforce, several innovative partnerships between medical schools and undergraduate institutions have been developed. In 2001 at the University of Michigan, the Health Science Scholars Program (HSSP) was launched to connect low-income and first-generation college students to structured clinical observation and mentorship by health professionals in the setting of a first-year living-learning community (Morgan, Haggins, Lypson, & Ross, 2016). Dr. Helen K. Morgan, a clinical associate professor of obstetrics and gynecology at the University of Michigan and former faculty director of HSSP puts forth that medical schools have a responsibility to support premedical education in such direct ways. Morgan states (2016), "leaders in academic medicine should be involved in 'matching' underprepared, underrepresented students with concrete college experiences that promote their success. The HSSP is one example of how developing innovative collaborations can help to nurture and sustain interest in these promising students."

There is little doubt that learning communities providing formalized access to opportunities such as shadowing and courses designed to develop a deep understanding of healthcare help the students in profoundly valuable ways. The question remains, however, as to whether such programs can contain enough students to provide sufficient opportunity to address the current inequities of access to resources at a scale that matches the need. The resources, typically in the form of low faculty/staff to student ratios and specialized courses that such programs provide typically come at a high cost and therefore the programs serve only a small subset of the students who would benefit. For example, HSSP enrolls 120 students each year, while the entering class at the University of Michigan regularly includes approximately 6000 students. Among these students, about 2000 declare some interest in a healthcare career. Advisors who work with students who are part of the general population (rather than those in small learning communities) engage in a different strategy, one that requires the collaboration of medical school admissions personnel. Specifically, those students who do not have access to formal exploratory opportunities are forced to find such experiences on their own and in the process develop the reflective practice that allows them to learn well from the work they are doing. For example, advisors commonly spend a great deal of time helping students see the connection between the experiences they develop in activities ranging from research, to tutoring, to tending bar at home to help pay for school to the competencies expected by medical school admissions committees. By the same token, advisors are frequently a medium for conveying explanatory context about the idiosyncrasies of the institution's sprawling curricula and programs to the medical schools frequently targeted for application by their students.

A specific instance of this kind of work has to do with the opportunities offered by third party commercial organizations who look to profit from zeal found in the large populations of premedical students at public schools. It is not uncommon to encounter a premedical student who is eager to demonstrate his or her capacity to engage in hands-on medical care under the mistaken notion that admissions committees will be impressed by their capacity to diagnose, assist with surgery, or otherwise practice medicine with no official training. Such opportunities are thankfully rare in the United States, but for a hefty fee, some less-than-reputable medical "voluntourism" junkets will provide students the ability to act as a health care provider under local supervision in a short-term "medical mission" trip abroad. On the surface, these trips appear laudable for providing students a mechanism to learn about the challenges of healthcare delivery in a developing country, but they create a situation that has the potential to put patients at real risk for harm. Reports of undergraduates engaging in activities that would never be allowed stateside (e.g., extracting teeth and performing physical examinations) led the AAMC to develop guidelines for students participating in medical experiences abroad (*Guidelines for Premedical and Medical Students Providing Patient Care During Clinical Experiences Abroad*, 2011). This statement emphasizes the importance of ethical decision-making concerning the welfare of the patient and provide cautionary statement about the risks to the applicant when ethics aren't foremost. Premedical advisors commonly take responsibility for conveying this information to student organizations that focus on work abroad, usually in the form of direct outreach.

EXPERIENCES IN RESEARCH

Premedical students generally articulate their motivation to pursue a career in medicine as stemming from a desire for a career that combines helping others and doing science (Pacifici & Thomson, 2011). However, much of their premedical science coursework centers on learning and applying long-established scientific principles that do not afford them the opportunity to actually engage in the scientific methods of research. Only through authentic research experiences can students truly practice the art of scientific inquiry and work to create a new understanding of natural phenomena. Scientific inquiry is among the fifteen core competencies for entering medical students, as outlined by the AAMC, and it is identified as a key experience leading to the development of the thinking and reasoning skills of the applicant. Medical school admissions committees, and particularly those affiliated with research universities, value substantial hypothesis-driven research experience as an indicator that the applicant is adept at the type of analytical thinking that will promote innovation in medical science and practice. A perusal of the Medical School Admission Requirements publication of the AAMC finds that all medical schools report that a vast majority of their matriculating students had research experience in the premedical period with an average of over 1,200 hours reported (*Applying to Medical School: 2018 AMCAS Medical School Applications by the Numbers*, 2019). In this context, nearly all premedical students will seek to engage in a faculty-mentored research experience either at their home institution or through short-term summer research fellowships in external academic or industrial settings.

For students aiming for a career as a physician-scholar via the highly competitive MD-PhD dual degree pathway, research experiences dominate the undergraduate years. Although the majority of MD-PhD programs are intended to support those pursuing careers in translational biomedical research, MD-PhD training has grown to encompass academic inquiry from across the natural sciences, social sciences, and humanities. Regardless of their intended academic focus, undergraduates pursing an academic path need a strong, intrinsic motivation for research and demonstrated independence, creativity, and productivity in the research setting.

APPLICATION TIMING AND GAP YEARS

Depending on the institution's ability to provide dedicated premedical advisors on staff or faculty, applicants can benefit from expert guidance through the medical school application process. Such advisors provide a wealth of knowledge about navigating the primary and secondary applications, assist students in crafting a target medical school list appropriate for their philosophy and goals, and provide critical feedback about essays and written material. For underrepresented students and those with little social capital in the professional community in particular, such guidance is critical to their success.

Considering the present landscape, there are about 180 medical degree programs in the United States with thirty-five of these leading to the osteopathic degree (DO) and the remainder leading to the allopathic degree (MD). The authors have observed strong interest in both degree paths among their institution's premedical population.[4] Applications to both MD and DO programs are robust, with nearly 7,000 applications to DO programs annually with the top feeder institutions being the University of Florida, Michigan State University, and the University of California-Los Angeles (*Data Reports in Osteopathic Medical Education*, 2017). MD programs receive approximately 50,000 applications annually with the top feeder schools being the University of California-Los Angeles, University of Florida, and the University of Michigan (*FACTS: Applicants, Matriculants, Enrollment, Graduates, MD-PhD, and Residency Applicants Data*, 2018).

When is a premedical student ready to apply to medical school? The answer to this question is unique to the individual, and is a measure of an applicant's academic preparedness, maturity, and experience. A generation ago, the premedical student could assume that he or she would apply to medical school early senior year and proceed from college graduation ceremony directly to white coat ceremony. In the present day, the straight-through path is not a given with the median age of a white-coat inductee at twenty-four and thus a few years post-college or after lengthy part-time undergraduate status (*FACTS: Applicants, Matriculants, Enrollment, Graduates, MD-PhD, and Residency Applicants Data*, 2017).

Recent trends at the authors' institution find that about one-third of premedical students who achieve a spot in a medical school do so directly out of undergraduate education, leaving two-thirds who have completed at least one gap year or are planning for a glide year.[5] A postbaccalaureate gap period is a valuable detour for students with the motivation to expand their knowledge and experience into an area that is complementary to their professional and personal goals. The experiences students pursue in this period range from formal master's degree programs (e.g., MBA, MFA, MPH) to service opportunities (e.g., Peace Corps, City Year) to research experiences and beyond. A gap year experience, chosen thoughtfully and with an understanding of how the opportunity marries the premedical student's overall narrative, can bring unique perspectives and innovations to the practice of medicine.

POSTBACCALAUREATE PROGRAMS

The over two-hundred formal postbaccalaureate programs in the United States deserve consideration given their prominent position in the preparation of substantial numbers of medical school aspirants. These programs were developed over the last four decades to address the needs of two groups of premedical students: the career-changers who developed a late awareness of their desire to pursue a career in medicine; and the academic enhancers who in the face of lackluster performance in medical school prerequisites at the undergraduate level seek a mechanism to improve their academic record. The career-changer focused programs are typically administered by undergraduate colleges and provide the late-decider with an efficient route to fulfill all of the medical school prerequisites in twelve to eighteen months of study. In contrast, the academic enhancing-focused programs build upon the prerequisite coursework and challenge the student with up to two years of graduate level coursework in the applied life sciences and often lead to a master's degree. Both categories of programs frequently include personalized advising, professional development opportunities, and application support. Particularly advantageous are programs with linkage agreements to a medical school, which offers assurance that upon successful completion of the program, a student will earn an interview to at least one medical school.

A long-term study of medical practice outcomes of students who completed postbaccalaureate programs of any type prior to medical school matriculation (about 12% of the medical student pool) found that such participants had an increased likelihood of practicing medicine in an underserved area and that participants in career-changing-focused programs had a slight edge in gaining admissions to medical school over those who had completed an academic enhancing program (Andriole & Jeffe, 2011). Both types of programs, and particularly those with formal ties to a medical school, have been implicated as impactful methods to support minority and disadvantaged premedical students of promise (Blakely & Broussard, 2003). Typically these programs are small and selective, with cohorts of twenty to thirty students. Program candidates are evaluated on the basis of the candidate's potential to gain admittance to medical school or other health professional graduate programs and consider the student's overall undergraduate record, commitment to health care, and educationally disadvantaged status. The fees for these programs remain relatively high (into the range of 40K) and arranging financial aid can be a challenge especially for the career-changer programs, which do not lead to a terminal degree.

PREMEDICAL COMMITTEES AND LETTERS OF EVALUATION

In the high-volume and competitive world of medical school admissions, letters of evaluation can play a critical role in helping admissions committee differentiate their applicants. The unique insights that well-crafted letters can provide also support medical schools' efforts to engage in more holistic admission practices. However, the interests of a medical school committee, whose main charge is to admit the best-qualified and diverse applicants, do not align perfectly with the interests of premedical advisors, whose main charge is to support their students.

For the letters to help medical school admission committees discern the personal qualities and attributes among their applicants, they need to be relevant and more evaluative than descriptive. They should focus on information that either would not be otherwise available to the reader or that should help make sense of the information provided. The fact that medical schools insist on requiring multiple letters of evaluation also reinforces the importance of gathering *multiple* perspectives about an applicant.

However, the world of letters of evaluation is rife with unevenness. The guidelines for writing letters of evaluation developed by the AAMC have been a useful tool in clarifying expectations for such documents, while providing critical structure and, ideally consistency in addressing applicants' relevant personal attributes as well as skills and abilities (*Guidelines for Writing a Letter of Evaluation for a Medical School Applicant*, 2019). The fact, however, that these guidelines are optional and that writers may operate within different contexts and mechanisms (e.g., premedical committees, advising offices, commercial services) create great variances both in the process and the end-product.

Admissions committees are challenged to understand this very complex landscape in which letters are generated and place letters in the appropriate context. For example, when it comes to format, they review committee letters, letter packets, and individual letters. Although some medical schools prefer committee letters, not all do. Regardless, applicants must support their application with letters generated via whatever mechanism their primary undergraduate institution or post-baccalaureate program provides. In fact, some undergraduate schools have the resources *and* applicant pools small enough to make committee letters possible, but that is not the reality of larger undergraduate institutions or under-resourced premedical advising offices.

The presence or absence of rankings adopted by certain undergraduate institutions; cryptic code words to express overall support of an applicant; different philosophies around rating scales and even the professional responsibility to ensure that the "right" individuals enter the medical profession (vs. succumbing to the pressure of ensuring a better medical school "placement" rate for their school). Each of these factors can negatively impact how a letter is written and perceived. More examples of unevenness include the internal institutional criteria that an applicant has to meet to be able to avail themselves to the services of their premedical committee; the "gate keeping" role that some premedical committees take on; and different undergraduate schools' policies around disclosure of disciplinary action in letters of evaluation.

Premedical advisors at institutions with a premedical committee often painfully feel the pull between the time devoted to writing letters versus advising their students. Advisors at large institutions without a premedical committee struggle to educate all their students' letter writers – especially those external to the school. While they may lament the generic endorsements that may come out of faculty teaching large science introductory courses, they cannot help being sympathetic to their plight of being bombarded with requests (often in a short period of time) or even more basically the fact that they are not receiving any institutional recognition or support for the enormous investment in time and resources to write these letters.

In addition, a changing landscape in the world of employment and graduate school admissions (with increasing reliance on phone references for the former and the required use of centralized application services for the latter) has gradually but inexorably inhibited the ability of university-based reference letter services to continue to handle the files of their students and alumni, forcing them to outsource their operation to external commercial services. This new reality has put even more distance and potential disconnect between the letter writers, the advisors, and the applicants in the absence of a committee or university-based letter service. For example, "unmonitored" delays in submitting letters can have dire effects on the timely review of an applicant's file. Similarly, with the protection of the waived right to access a letter and the lack of an internal review for the fitness of individual letters, sometimes unsubstantiated or ill-spirited comments can greatly hinder an applicant's viability. Moreover, the disclosure of information around protected categories and unwanted impact of such disclosures presents another tricky area.

In light of the issues stemming from different letters of evaluation mechanisms at various undergraduate institutions and the unique challenges that non-traditional and under-represented applicants may encounter, it is clear that flexibility and context are essential to review letters of evaluation in the appropriate light.

CONCLUSION

Much of this discussion has been grounded by the experience and observations of the authors, who acknowledge and lament the sparse formal research about the premedical years in general. This observation has been made by others calling for the need for "up-to-date, high quality empirical research on the premedical period." (Lin et al., 2013) The authors can only speculate as to why the premedical period has been largely neglected, but proffer the observation that the mission of liberal arts and sciences institutions are sometimes at odds with the goals of a pre-professional focused education. There is much focus for example, on understanding Science, Technology, Engineering, and Math (STEM) curriculum pathways as routes to STEM careers and professorships, but medicine has decidedly been excluded from the STEM focus (Granovskiy, 2018). Furthermore, the liberal arts and sciences philosophy calls for faculty to teach to their area of expertise— be it molecular biology or organic chemistry— as content relevant for further disciplinary focus, not as stepping stones to the applied medical school curriculum. In this environment, the premedical student is at risk for marginalization as a student whose career-focused directive is counter to the liberal arts philosophy.

The challenge at hand is to craft a college experience that preserves and cultivates humanism along with both intellectual and experiential diversity among the premedical ranks. In doing so, colleges will prepare applicants who can withstand the rigors of medical training and form the foundations for an effective, empathic, and well-balanced professional career. Likewise, colleges with the help of medical schools need to ensure that students from all backgrounds are invited to consider a career in medicine and are mentored and supported throughout their preparatory years. The success of those premedical years should not be judged solely by a college's ability to place students into competitive medical programs, but ultimately by the well-being of the medical profession itself and the premedical students' future patients.

The authors leave the reader with the following considerations:

Will The Goals of the Competency Prerequisite Model Be Met?

The competency model was introduced with the notion that it would free the premedical student from a lock-step credit hour economy and thereby encourage individualized and diverse curricular paths. The model has been slow to be adopted by the majority of medical schools. Given that the average student applies to over a dozen medical schools, unless the majority of medical schools adopt the competency model, the student still is bound to complete the standard credit hours of premedical science and math coursework. Undergraduate institutions are unsure how, or even if, to respond to the competency model in their curricular planning. What is the future for the competency model? Furthermore, should the majority of schools eventually adopt it, will the MCAT ascend as the primary academic metric by which knowledge of the premedical content is judged?

Is There a Downside to The Rise in the Average Age of a Medical School Matriculant?

With the average age of an incoming medical student approaching twenty-five in the United States, many future physicians are facing a training period that will extend well into their thirties. The anticipated effects of a lengthy premedical period can be heard in the anxieties expressed by undergraduates imagining their future. Potentially delaying a medical school application by even a year or two brings forth questions fundamental to the structuring of an adult life (e.g., *When can I have a child? When will I earn a real salary?*) and points to the personal sacrifice inherent to the arduous medical training process. While applicants with gap year experiences bring perspective and maturity to a medical school class, what is the personal cost to our future physician workforce when taking a gap year (or two) becomes the rule?

What is The Role of Physician Shadowing in Preparation for Medical School?

It has become increasingly difficult for undergraduates to obtain physician shadowing opportunities, a key experience especially for those students not socialized to a career in medicine. Those who do get substantive shadowing hours as undergraduates are typically either related to physicians or otherwise involved in a privileged relationship with someone in a clinical profession. Less well-connected applicants are faced with increasingly dense barriers to shadowing formed by references to HIPAA regulations and ignored requests. In the authors' experience, medical school representatives also seem to be less emphatic about the value of shadowing, citing its passive nature. Is shadowing experience valued by admissions committees and if so, how are barriers to finding it best addressed and by whom?

What is the Future for the Letter of Evaluation in the Application Process?

This report has described the inequities inherent to the current state of play embodied by letters of evaluation. Committee letters are common among private schools, where premedical programs provide a reliable process and an equally reliable product, but perhaps reproduce the privilege that feeds such institutions. Applicants from schools without premedical committees have a much harder time finding faculty evaluators who can and will write substantive letters. A tremendous amount of faculty time and effort is devoted to writing letters of evaluation, a task for which few are properly recognized. Consider the science professor tapped to produce letters by dozens of medical school applicants year after year; how can he or she not tire of a ritual that arguably provides little distinguishing insight into the non-academic characteristics of the applicant? The authors ask for clarity from medical school admissions committees about what information they most value from these recommendations and ask furthermore if letters are ultimately the most efficient vehicle to deliver that information. Are there alternatives? Perhaps the situational judgement tests (e.g., CASPer®) now part of several medical school evaluation processes, will fulfill their promise to provide a robust and objective characterization of an applicant's personal strengths. Eventually, will letters of evaluation and committee evaluations decrease in prominence for these more objective tools?

Are Relationships Between Premedical Advisors and Medical School Admissions Personnel as Effective as they Should Be?

The faculty and staff who teach and advise premedical students are uniquely positioned to encourage undergraduates of promise to seek a career in medicine and as such should be considered partners in the medical education process. In the authors' view, strong professional relationships with medical school admissions personnel are vital to their ability to effectively support students throughout the premedical education period. An open, regular exchange between admissions directors and premedical advisors about all matters that shape the applicant pool would help to identify areas for collaboration to promote a shared interest in supporting a more diverse applicant pool. Key areas of focus for such exchanges might include:

- Many medical schools are extraordinarily generous with information about and access to their program's mission, curriculum, and admissions procedures. This is immensely helpful to advisors. More formalized opportunities for advisors from the undergraduate institutions (e.g., those that provide high numbers of applicants for a given school) to return the favor by providing information about the educational and socioeconomic dynamics in the undergraduate school to medical school admissions personnel might provide similar benefits.

- More specifically, case studies, demographic data, and discussions of curricular particularities from the undergraduate institution might provide a foundation for more nuanced decisions involving students from disadvantaged backgrounds, with possible benefits for the effort to diversify the population entering medical school.

- Much of an advisor's ability to help a student negotiate the most challenging decisions about medical school preparation is based on accumulated anecdotal information: When is additional, costly record enhancing post-baccalaureate work a reasonable option? What constitutes a viable MCAT score in the context of holistic review? What criteria do medical schools think applicants should use when compiling a list of target schools?

ACKNOWLEDGEMENT

The authors would like to thank Jean Song, Assistant Director at the Taubman Health Sciences Library at the University of Michigan, for her expertise in conducting a literature review. Her work was immensely helpful to the authors.

REFERENCES

AACOMAS Applicant and Matriculant Profile Summary Report. (2018). Retrieved from https://www.aacom.org/docs/default-source/data-and-trends/2018-aacomas-applicant-matriculant-profile-summary-report.pdf?sfvrsn=28753a97_12

Alpern, R. J., Belitsky, R., & Long, S. (2011). Competencies in premedical and medical education: The AAMC-HHMI report. *Perspectives in Biology and Medicine, 54*(1), 30–35. doi:10.1353/pbm.2011.0001 PMID:21399381

Andriole, D. A., & Jeffe, D. B. (2011). Characteristics of medical school matriculants who participated in postbaccalaureate premedical programs. *Academic Medicine, 86*(2), 201–210. doi:10.1097/ACM.0b013e3182045076 PMID:21169786

Applying to Medical School: 2018 AMCAS Medical School Applications by the Numbers. (2019). Retrieved from https://aamc-orange.global.ssl.fastly.net/production/media/filer_public/43/1b/431bc986-9e69-424f-8066-5fc95eba4a44/aamc-2018-amcas-medical-school-applications-by-the-numbers-infographic.pdf

Barr, D. A., Gonzalez, M. E., & Wanat, S. F. (2008). The leaky pipeline: Factors associated with early decline in interest in premedical studies among underrepresented minority undergraduate students. *Academic Medicine*, *83*(5), 503–511. doi:10.1097/ACM.0b013e31816bda16 PMID:18448909

Blakely, A. W., & Broussard, L. G. (2003). Blueprint for establishing an effective postbaccalaureate medical school pre-entry program for educationally disadvantaged students. *Academic Medicine: Journal of the Association of American Medical Colleges*, *78*(5), 437–447. doi:10.1097/00001888-200305000-00004 PMID:12742777

Burg, F. D., Croll, S. R., Ruff, G. E., & Stemmler, E. J. (1988). Competency requirements. A new approach to medical school admissions. *Journal of the American Medical Association*, *259*(3), 389–391. doi:10.1001/jama.1988.03720030049032 PMID:3336163

Core Competencies for Entering Medical Students. (2019). Retrieved from https://www.aamc.org/admissions/dataandresearch/477182/corecompetencies.html

Data Reports in Osteopathic Medical Education. (2017). Retrieved from https://www.aacom.org/docs/default-source/data-and-trends/gme-special-report-2017.pdf?sfvrsn=dfb22c97_6

Dunleavy, D., Sondheimer, H., Castillo-Page, L., & Beer Bletzinger, R. (2011). *Medical school admissions: More than grades and test scores*. Retrieved from https://www.aamc.org/download/261106/data/

FACTS: Applicants, Matriculants, Enrollment, Graduates, MD-PhD, and Residency Applicants Data. (2018). Retrieved from https://www.aamc.org/data/facts/

FACTS: Applicants, Matriculants, Enrollment, Graduates, MD-PhD, and Residency Applicants Data Table A-6. (2017). Retrieved from https://www.aamc.org/download/321468/data/factstablea6.pdf

Flexner, A. (1910). *Medical Education in the United States and Canada. A Report to the Carnegie Foundation for the Advancement of Teaching*. Retrieved from http://archive.carnegiefoundation.org/pdfs/elibrary/Carnegie_Flexner_Report.pdf

Freeman, B. K., Trevino, R., Grande, D., Shea, J. A., & Shea, J. A. (2016). Understanding the leaky pipeline: Perceived barriers to pursuing a career in medicine or dentistry among underrepresented-in-medicine undergraduate students. *Academic Medicine*, *91*(7), 987–993. doi:10.1097/ACM.0000000000001020 PMID:26650673

Granovskiy, B. (2018). *Science, Technology, Engineering, and Mathematics (STEM) Education: An Overview*. Retrieved from https://fas.org/sgp/crs/misc/R45223.pdf

Guidelines for Premedical and Medical Students Providing Patient Care During Clinical Experiences Abroad. (2011). Retrieved from https://www.aamc.org/download/181690/data/guidelinesforstudentsprovidingpatientcare.pdf

Guidelines for Writing a Letter of Evaluation for a Medical School Applicant. (2019) Retrieved from https://www.aamc.org/download/349990/data/lettersguidelinesbrochure.pdf

Hall, J. N., Woods, N., & Hanson, M. D. (2014). Is Social Sciences and Humanities (SSH) Premedical Education Marginalized in the Medical School Admission Process? A Review and Contextualization of the Literature. *Academic Medicine, 89*(7), 1075–1086. doi:10.1097/ACM.0000000000000284 PMID:24826852

Lamb, E. G., Berry, S. L., & Jones, T. (2019). *Health Humanities Baccalaureate Programs in the United States*. Retrieved from https://www.hiram.edu/wp-content/uploads/2019/03/Health-Humanities-Program_2019_final.pdf

Lin, K. Y., Parnami, S., Fuhrel-Forbis, A., Anspach, R. R., Crawford, B., & De Vries, R. G. (2013). The undergraduate premedical experience in the United States: A critical review. *International Journal of Medical Education, 4*, 26–37. doi:10.5116/ijme.5103.a8d3 PMID:23951400

MCAT and GPAs for Applicants and Matriculants to U.S. Medical Schools by Primary Undergraduate Major, 2018-2019. (2018). Retrieved from https://www.aamc.org/download/321496/data/factstablea17.pdf

McGaghie, W. C. (2002). Assessing readiness for medical education: Evolution of the Medical College Admission Test. *Journal of the American Medical Association, 288*(9), 1085–1090. doi:10.1001/jama.288.9.1085 PMID:12204076

Medical School Admission Requirements™. (2019). Retrieved from https://students-residents.aamc.org/applying-medical-school/applying-medical-school-process/medical-school-admission-requirements/

Metzel, J. M., Petty, J., & Olowojoba, O. V. (2018). Using a structural competency framework to teach structural racism in pre-health education. *Social Science & Medicine, 199*, 189–201. doi:10.1016/j.socscimed.2017.06.029 PMID:28689630

Morgan, H. K., Haggins, A., Lypson, M. L., & Ross, P. (2016). The Importance of the Premedical Experience in Diversifying the Health Care Workforce. *Academic Medicine, 91*(11), 1488–1491. doi:10.1097/ACM.0000000000001404 PMID:27603037

Pacifici, L. B., & Thomson, N. (2011). Undergraduate science research: A comparison of influences and experiences between premed and non-premed students. *CBE Life Sciences Education, 10*(2), 199–208. doi:10.1187/cbe.11-01-0005 PMID:21633068

Richardson, T., Mulvihill, T., & Latz, A. O. (2014). Bound and Determined: Perceptions of Pre-Med Seniors Regarding Their Persistence in Preparing for Medical School. *Journal of Ethnographic and Qualitative Research, 8*(4), 222–238.

Rifkin, M. R., Smith, K. D., Stimmel, B. D., Stagnaro-Green, A., & Kase, N. G. (2000). The Mount Sinai humanities and medicine program: An alternative pathway to medical school. *Academic Medicine, 75*(10Supplement), S124–S126. doi:10.1097/00001888-200010001-00040 PMID:11031196

Saguil, A., & Kellermann, A. L. (2014). The community college pathway to medical school: A road less traveled. *Academic Medicine, 89*(12), 1589–1592. doi:10.1097/ACM.0000000000000439 PMID:25076201

Schwartzstein, R. M., Rosenfeld, G. C., Hilborn, R., Oyewole, S. H., & Mitchell, K. (2013). Redesigning the MCAT Exam: Balancing Multiple Perspectives. *Academic Medicine, 88*(5), 560–567. doi:10.1097/ACM.0b013e31828c4ae0 PMID:23524933

Smith, M. M., Rose, S. H., Schroeder, D. R., & Long, T. R. (2015). Diversity of United States medical students by region compared to US census data. *Advances in Medical Education and Practice*, *6*, 367–372. PMID:26028982

Student Guide to Osteopathic Medical Colleges. (2019). Retrieved from https://www.aacom.org/student-guide

Talamantes, E., Manigone, C. M., Gonzalez, K., Jimenez, A., Gonzalez, F., & Moreno, G. (2014). Community college pathways: Improving the U.S. physician workforce pipeline. *Academic Medicine*, *89*(12), 1649–1656. doi:10.1097/ACM.0000000000000438 PMID:25076199

ENDNOTES

[1]   The University of Michigan is a large, research-focused public institution with a total undergraduate population of about 30,000.

[2]   Data not shown. S. Chervin.

[3]   Competency-based models have been adopted by University of California, Los Angeles David Geffen School of Medicine in 2018; University of Michigan Medical School in 2017, and Albert Einstein College of Medicine in 2014, among others.

[4]   In a given application cycle about 1,200 students from the University of Michigan will apply to MD and DO programs combined, with about 800 applying to MD programs and 300 applying to DO programs and a portion of these students applying to both.

[5]   Glide year vs. gap year: The timing of the application dictates that the application is submitted a full year prior to medical school matriculation. For an applicant who submits the summer immediately following college graduation, the *glide year* describes the year spent between college graduation and medical school matriculation. For the applicant who engages in a year-long experience prior to making an application, the term *gap year* applies. The gap year experience often features prominently in the application and for these applicants, actually a period of two years passes between college graduation and medical school matriculation.

Chapter 15
Early Medical Education Readiness Interventions:
Enhancing Undergraduate Preparedness

Amber J. Heck

https://orcid.org/0000-0002-0758-2950

TCU and UNTHSC School of Medicine, USA

Courtney E. Cross

TCU and UNTHSC School of Medicine, USA

Veronica Y. Tatum

TCU and UNTHSC School of Medicine, USA

ABSTRACT

Medical educators have long debated how to address one pivotal question: Which students will succeed in medical school? Traditionally, the approach to guaranteeing success in undergraduate medical education focused heavily on a rigorous admissions process. While student selection processes have evolved over time, so have the multiple categories of interventions to prepare students for success in medical school. These interventions are most often aimed at enhancing either academic or emotional preparedness in future or current students and are perhaps best described as early medical education readiness interventions. This chapter organizes these programs into the three overarching categories of preadmissions, prematriculation, and postmatriculation interventions, and will discuss the history and current landscape of each of these categories in detail. Further, the authors make recommendations for medical school administrators and directors of such programs to consider when designing their institutional approach to early medical education readiness interventions.

DOI: 10.4018/978-1-7998-1468-9.ch015

INTRODUCTION

In U.S. medical schools, the attrition rate hovers around 4% (Association of American Medical Colleges, 2018a). Students who leave medicine during training report a plethora of contributing factors, including individual motivation, academic underperformance, and personal problems. The most common reason for leaving medical school is "academic" and the majority of academic problems occur during the pre-clinical years (Huff & Fang, 1999; O'Neill, Wallstedt, Eika, & Hartvigsen, 2011). On the other hand, roughly half of all medical students lost to attrition reported nonacademic reasons, including personal reasons related to health, family, change in career interest, and, most concerning, psychological distress, including depression, burnout, and low quality of life (Dyrbye et al., 2010).

The transition into medical school is challenging, and results in a significant increase in stress for student doctors. Upon matriculation, medical students express lower rates of burnout and depression symptoms than age-matched college graduate peers (Brazeau et al., 2014). However, in a 2008 study of more than 4,000 medical students across seven universities, 49.6% of students reported burnout, and an alarming 11.2% reported suicidal ideation (Dyrbye et al., 2008). In a 2006 systematic review, Dyrbye, Thomas, & Shanafelt found that most published longitudinal studies on medical student psychologic distress in U.S. and Canadian schools focused on first-year students. The majority of those studies found that symptoms associated with depression and anxiety increased over the course of the first year. Together, this evidence supports concerns that medical education makes students vulnerable to the deterioration of mental health during training.

Academic concerns, leading to learning difficulty and underachievement, are also a major contributing factor in medical school attrition (O'Neill et al., 2011). The predictive factors associated with academic success can be divided into four categories: Demographic factors, aptitude or performance measures such as the Medical College Admissions Test (MCAT) and undergraduate GPA, noncognitive factors related to personal and interpersonal dispositions, and other background factors such as undergraduate major and institution (Krupat, Pelletier, & Dienstag, 2017). Among these, sociodemographic factors, such as ethnicity, low income, and minority group membership, have been associated with disadvantages related to achievement (Kumwenda, Cleland, Walker, Lee, & Greatrix, 2017). A variety of preadmission and prematriculation programs targets these students to address the shortage of diverse backgrounds in medicine. Together with postmatriculation interventions, these programs strive to reduce the number of medical school students facing academic challenges.

Whatever the contributing factors may be, around 10% of medical school matriculants will encounter academic failure at some time during their undergraduate medical education (UME). For the majority of these students, academic failure in the past was rare, and therefore has a significant impact on motivation and feelings of lack of personal accomplishment (Holland, 2016).

BACKGROUND

In order to address these issues, medical schools offer a variety of interventions, which are aimed at enhancing either academic or emotional preparedness in future or current students. The authors organize these programs into three categories: Preadmissions, prematriculation, and postmatriculation interventions. Preadmissions programs serve to bolster a student's preparedness prior to the medical school application process. Prematriculation interventions include orientation programs and prematriculation courses (PMCs), which are delivered to accepted students prior to matriculation into the academic program. Postmatriculation interventions are delivered during the UME curriculum and preemptively target content and characteristics known to, or believed to, affect medical school readiness.

Some of the earliest programs which are documented in the literature appear in the 1970s and describe preadmissions programs, or programs targeting undergraduate or K-12 students prior to entering medical school admissions. The aim of these early preadmissions programs was enhancing the academic preparedness of minority and socioeconomically disadvantaged students for medical school (Heck, Gibbons, Ketter, Furlano, & Prest, 2017). The authors, among others, believe this is to reflect the increase in social activism taking place at this time. In 1964, black students were vastly underrepresented within medical schools, comprising only 0.5% of the U.S. medical student population. In response, at the 1968 Annual Meeting of the Association of American Medical Colleges, a task force was charged to make recommendations to improve this statistic. Thus, by 1974, the situation had improved to the point that 10% of U.S. medical students were underrepresented minorities (Nickens, Ready, & Petersdorf, 1994; Reede, 2003). At that time, the major obstacle to increasing the admittance and retention of minority students in medical school was thought to be inadequate preparation in the sciences during primary and secondary education (Jackson, 1972; Nickens et al., 1994). Consequently, schools created preadmission programs to address this perceived deficiency in the prerequisite sciences.

Today, the majority of preadmissions programs delivered by U.S. medical schools still focus on K-12 and undergraduate outreach to underrepresented or underserved individuals. The proportion of minorities, women, rural, first-generation or immigrant, LGBTQ, and low-income individuals in medicine has not kept pace with their representative populations (Castillo-Page, 2016). A survey of potential medical and dental underrepresented minority students identified four themes as barriers to matriculation: Inadequate institutional support, limited personal resources, lack of mentoring, and societal barriers (Freeman, Landry, Trevino, Grande, & Shea, 2016). Thus, the authors believe that effective preadmissions interventions must address multiple barriers to significantly impact minority readiness and acceptance to medical school.

Prematriculation programs are designed to acclimate medical students to the rigors of the academic program and offer resources for transitioning (Heck, 2014). While they are generally viewed as value added student experiences, a lack of information exists in the literature to indicate whether any best practices for these programs exist, based on program efficacy (Heck et al., 2017). Differences in program structure and content abound in these programs, with many of them existing based solely upon well-intentioned historic precedent, which indicates either a lack of evidence-based practice or a disinterest in pursuing evidence to support program effectiveness.

Postmatriculation programs are traditionally predicated on short-term remedial study programs, which are aimed at enhancing study practices and therefore preventing academic failure (Holland, 2016). Recently, a small number of medical schools have begun to offer short-term mind-body skills programs to provide medical students with a variety of tools to reduce the high levels of stress, sleeplessness, and burnout that have become so prevalent among them (Gordon, 2014).This chapter will explore the current landscape of postmatriculation interventions and build an argument for their inclusion in the undergraduate medical curriculum.

A lack of evidence to support the efficacy of most of these interventions, coupled with a lack of evidence to support historic student selection criteria for these programs, led the authors to evaluate multiple aspects of these early medical education readiness interventions. There is a serious need to explore what practices positively impact student academic and personal readiness and whether current views of early medical education readiness programs are capable of delivering this effect.

ENHANCING READINESS FOR UNDERGRADUATE MEDICAL EDUCATION

What Defines Readiness?

At the core, intervention programs are tools deployed with the intent to enhance readiness of medical school matriculants. What defines readiness? Readiness is a multifactorial state of preparation. One component, historically well studied and heavily scrutinized in the medical school admissions process, is academic preparedness. However, personal and professional attributes contribute a great deal to student readiness for medical school (McGaghie, 2002).

Readiness Assessment

In medical school admissions, educators and administrators strive to identify students who are likely to succeed in the curriculum and beyond by examining evidence of previous academic performance and factors known to be associated with future academic performance. The MCAT is perhaps the most influential tool medical schools utilize when selecting students for their academic program. The MCAT has served as the foremost standard for evaluating readiness in medical school applicants since 1928, and is generally regarded as an objective and standardized measure of readiness (McGaghie, 2002). It primarily assesses foundations of biomedical sciences and behavior, critical analysis, and reasoning skills, and is consistently revised to address changes in medical education (Kirch, Mitchell, & Ast, 2013). It was shown to be a reliable predictor of academic performance in the preclinical years and performance on the U.S. Medical Licensure Exam (USMLE) (Gauer, Wolff, & Jackson, 2016; Veloski, Callahan, Xu, Hojat, & Nash, 2000). However, the MCAT is often criticized for its scope and inability to broadly assess the skills that holistically contribute to academic performance. Undergraduate grade point average (GPA) is likely the second most relied upon variable which is used in medical school admissions. Though slightly less reliable than the MCAT, undergraduate GPA, in both science and nonscience coursework, has been found to predict academic performance in the preclinical and clinical years, and performance on the USMLE (Veloski et al., 2000). As a result of this evidence, admissions programs have traditionally relied heavily on these measures of cognitive performance to ascertain readiness, placing arguably less emphasis on noncognitive measures.

Evidence for Readiness

There is much to learn from the general education literature regarding adult readiness for learning. Multiple large-scale international surveys of adult educational competencies and skills have explored the causes and consequences of these skills in relation to success in generalizable settings. They identify an individual ability or readiness to learn as being key to attaining job or education-specific skills and body of knowledge, and define readiness as a composite derived from themes that occur in educational psychology and adult education literature. Among these are learning strategies, study behaviors, cognitive processing, metacognition, critical thinking, and self-regulation. Along with educational attainment and age, readiness to learn does significantly predict adult learner skill (Murray et al., 2015; Smith, Rose, Smith, and Ross-Gordon, 2015). Thus, a substantial body of existing literature supports a holistic approach to defining and affecting student readiness for medical school.

Academic Readiness

Self-directed learning (SDL), a component of self-regulation, is the process by which individuals implement learning practices based on self-identified learning needs (Knowles, 1985). Self-directed learners can determine what strategies they need to attain a goal. They regularly set specific goals, manage time, and monitor performance (Zimmerman, 2002). In 2004, the Liaison Committee on Medical Education endorsed medical college accreditation standards that promote medical students' skill acquisition in SDL, increasing the interest in and emphasis on exploring this process in medical education literature (Simon & Aschenbrener, 2005). Increasing complexities in health care systems and the rapid turnover of medical information make continuous learning a vital requirement for practicing physicians (Soliman & Al-Shaikh, 2015). The same is true of medical education. The content within the undergraduate medical curriculum is ever expanding, while the length of time remains the same. As such, it is increasingly important for medical students to have skill in SDL. Further, parallel SDL board-study during preclinical years is positively correlated with higher USMLE Step 1 scores (Burk-Rafel, Santen, & Purkiss, 2017). Evidence of the connection between prematriculant SDL readiness and success in medical education is currently inconclusive. However, it has been established that age and previous academic experience contribute to SDL readiness in medical students (Slater & Cusick, 2017).

Metacognition, or cognition about cognition, can impact student academic performance (Cao & Nietfeld, 2007). Metacognition relies on three component processes: Planning, monitoring, and evaluating personal cognitive performance. During the learning process, metacognition drives how students apply their knowledge of information and strategies, monitor their use of this information and strategies, and control when and where to employ them. In addition, skill in metacognitive control can greatly influence the time and effort medical students dedicate to learning (Medina, Castleberry, & Persky, 2017). High-achieving medical students demonstrate greater knowledge of the strategies they apply to learn and lower-achieving counterparts are less likely to adopt strategic approaches to learning (Holland, 2016). Ample research has shown that metacognitive practice is not a reflex process for many learners but is a teachable skill (Zimmerman, 2002). There is much overlap between SDL and metacognition, namely identifying resources, implementing and monitoring processes, and evaluating the processes. As in SDL, deliberately including training in metacognitive strategies early on for medical students can support board preparation and life-long learning.

Intrapersonal Readiness

Similarly, self-regulation of action and affect can be learned. Emotional intelligence (EI) is the result of collecting information about one's own and others' emotions, and using this information in the process of self-regulation. Furthermore, EI is related to empathy and is understood to impact communication skills (Mayer & Salovey, 1993). Several studies have found a statistically significant positive relationship between EI and academic performance upon matriculation into a UME program (Cook, Cook, & Hilton, 2016). Finally, self-regulation has been associated with well-being in many contexts. This relationship is based on the personal and professional success that comes with skill in identifying one's own needs, deploying strategies to meet these needs, and the ability to evaluate and adapt these plans as necessary (Gagnon, Durand-Bush, & Young, 2016).

A preponderance of evidence now shows that an academic "mindset", or the set of beliefs one holds about his/her academic abilities, can substantially influence learning, motivation, and success. More specifically, a "growth mindset," one that sees intelligence as malleable, is associated with improved performance and greater resilience in case of challenging tasks (Dweck, 2006, 2013). An academic mindset provides the foundation for one's motivation to learn, which is also recognized to affect academic performance (Cook, Castillo, Gas, & Artino, 2017). Medical students are generally highly vocationally motivated, which may drive them to learn deeply for the good of their future profession or rely on surface learning to overcome the pressures of the medical education learning environment and achieve their ultimate goal of becoming a doctor. Moreover, when they are faced with obstacles or failure, medical student motivation may be affected (Holland, 2016). Dweck (2013) demonstrated that students in general, when faced with failure, will adopt strategies based on either a fixed mindset, attributing failure to a lack of ability which they see as a final determination, or a growth mindset, characterizing ability as malleable and adapting strategies to further develop it incrementally. When medical students faced with failure have a fixed mindset or performance-driven motivation, they may begin to have negative feelings about learning and personal achievement, and self-efficacy may suffer, leading to questions about whether to continue in the academic program (Holland, 2016).

Finally, resiliency has been offered as the ultimate character virtue which is required for overcoming the challenges of medical education. Resiliency, which is defined as the ability to manage or withstand adversity while maintaining capabilities, is positively associated with favorable personality traits and coping skills, and negatively associated with psychiatric symptoms in college students (Campbell-Sills, Cohan, & Stein, 2006). Thus, resilient medical students better cope with, and therefore endure, the stressors and challenges inherent to medical education. Yet again, research suggests that resiliency is a dynamic trait and can be nurtured through intervention (Dyrbye & Shanafelt, 2012). Taken together, this evidence suggests that readiness for medical education is complex, and there are many opportunities for early intervention.

Preadmissions Interventions

Pipeline Programs

The 2018 Association of American Medical Colleges (AAMC) Matriculating Students Questionnaire identified that up to13.5% of first-year medical school students participated in some type of preadmission intervention program (Association of American Medical Colleges, 2018b). These programs serve to recruit and retain a diverse group of students by providing multifactorial support to enhance readiness. A 2011 survey identified five areas addressed in K-12 or undergraduate preadmissions interventions, which those authors referred to as pipeline programs: Outreach, mentoring, academic enrichment, test preparation, and scholarship. Outreach was the most common method, with almost 70% of schools performing outreach to undergraduate students, and 52% performing outreach to K-12 students. In contrast, and despite identified needs, only 31% of schools provide mentorship and 25% of schools provide academic enrichment to K-12 students (Danek & Borrayo, 2012). Focus groups of underrepresented minorities at undergraduate institutions identified a variety of barriers to entering a medical career, including academic readiness, shadowing opportunities, finances, nonacademic skills, and mentoring

(Freeman et al., 2016). This highlights a significant need to provide multifactorial support to enhance readiness of potential medical school students.

Several existing programs, including some of the oldest, seek to provide multifactorial longitudinal support starting during K-12 education and demonstrate positive outcomes. One of the earliest preadmissions programs was developed in 1971 by the Rutgers New Jersey Medical School. This pipeline program begins in K-12 and continues into the first year of medical school. Early on, the focus is academic readiness and health career awareness for both the student and their family, then transitions to include nonacademic skills. 36% of the program participants have entered health profession schools (Soto-Greene, Wright, Gona, & Feldman, 1999). The nationally recognized Stanford Medical Youth Science Program began in 1988 for very low-income students, and has expanded to include personalized admissions counseling, long-term mentorship, and preparation for academic transitions (Winkleby, 2007). Ninety percent of participants earned a 4-year degree. Forty-seven percent of them completed or are in graduate or medical school, and 44% entered health and science professions (Crump, Ned, & Winkleby, 2015). The Joint Admission Medical Program (JAMP) was established in Texas in 2003 to address enrollment disparities across all Texas medical schools. Socioeconomically disadvantaged undergraduate students who completed JAMP activities and maintained an acceptable GPA were automatically accepted to medical school. The program also offers a limited amount of scholarships. As of 2006, 57% of participants successfully matriculated to medical school (Dalley et. al., 2009). A limited number of similarly structured preadmissions programs exist which focus on enhancing enrollment and retention of American Indians and Alaskan Natives in medical education under the Indians into Medicine federal grant funding program. Only one such program, at the University of Washington, has published data thus far, demonstrating that 102 of the 477 total participants have matriculated into medical school (Acosta & Olsen, 2006).

Newer programs also recognize the need for nonacademic readiness interventions delivered alongside academic programs. The Morehouse School of Medicine and Emory School of Medicine run a joint 11-week mentoring and medical exposure program for inner-city high school students. It addresses issues of financial literacy and introduces strategies to both matriculate into undergraduate schools and fulfill premedical requirements while in college. So far,100% of their graduates enrolled in undergraduate schools, with 66% in a premedical program (Danner et al., 2017). In Baltimore, the Medical Education Resources Initiative for Teens program assists low-income, predominantly African-American, students in achieving entrance to medical school by providing longitudinal coaching and training in health disparities, financial literacy, and personal identity formation. In total, the program provides seven years of social and academic support. 100% of program graduates have enrolled in bachelor's degree programs, compared to 20% of students overall from their public-school district (Mains, Wilcox, & Wright, 2016). These newer programs cannot yet be evaluated for success in matriculation to medical school; however, the focus on nonacademic support, long-term mentorship, and personal growth is likely to serve them well.

A limited number of medical schools offer shorter exposure-based or academic-only programs, and some note significant barriers based on the punctuated approach. The University of Kentucky offers a two-day program to college students with a tour, lectures, workshops, and financial aid information. The program identified a lack of financial support for the students to attend, potentially limiting the number of low-income participants (Achenjang & Elam, 2016). The Mentoring in Medicine Program which is offered through the Albert Einstein College of Medicine is an after-school education program primarily serving high school students. The students gained significant knowledge in the health sciences and increased their self-efficacy. Students who did not complete the course noted conflicts with other demands and a lack of active learning activities (Holden, Berger, Zingarelli, & Siegel, 2015). Some preadmissions programs focus efforts on enhancing readiness for the admissions process itself. The Northeast Kentucky Area Health Education Center developed a program that pairs MCAT preparation with guidance on writing, interviewing, and communication skills. So far, this program has successfully matriculated 87% of participants to medical school (Gross, Mattox, & Winkleman, 2016). Though one should question whether this approach prepares students for the UME curriculum.

Postbaccalaureate Programs

A significant amount of preadmissions academic enrichment occurs after obtaining a bachelor's degree in the form of postbaccalaureate (postbac) programs. A portion of these programs target underrepresented and underserved students and report success in matriculation, graduation, and residency. However, students still face high barriers to admission to postbac programs, usually due to poor undergraduate GPA, and increased premedical debt, due to the extended length of their education. The AAMC Postbaccalaureate Premedical Programs database lists 238 postbac programs (Association of American Medical Colleges, 2019). The 2018 AAMC Matriculating Students Questionnaire reports that 6.9% of first-year medical school students participated in a postbac program to strengthen academic skills, while 8% participated to complete premedical requirements (Association of American Medical Colleges, 2018b). A survey of physicians in 2015 shows that postbac graduates are more likely to come from a low socioeconomic household, more likely to be the first college graduate in their family, have lower parental education levels, and less likely to have parents in the health care field (McDougle et al., 2015). High-quality postbac programs address these barriers, recognizing the need for multifactorial support to successfully matriculate to medical school.

The first postbac program was established at Columbia University in 1955. It provides an academic and clinical experience program for non-science majors, and is not targeted to underserved students. The program reports up to 90% of students in a given year matriculate to medical school, but lacks published data on graduation rates. The remainder matriculate to dental or veterinary school or choose another path (Columbia University, 2019). One of the oldest postbac programs to recruit disadvantaged students was established in 1972 by the Southern Illinois University School of Medicine. The school offers tuition waivers to at least 66% of its students yearly, and partial scholarships to the remainder of the students. This multifactorial program addresses academic readiness in the form of MCAT preparation, basic science courses, and learning evidence-based study techniques to enhance readiness. Students also receive professional development training, application development, peer mentors, and frequent counseling sessions. Overall, alumni with an MCAT score at the 45th percentile or higher had a 93% medical school graduation rate (Metz, 2017).

Some postbac programs target disadvantaged medical school applicants who were not accepted. Meharry Medical College began offering academic intervention programs in the early 1990's to underserved applicants who were rejected due to GPA or MCAT scores. Acceptance rates of their postbac alumni averaged 73%, and no significant differences occurred between alumni and traditional students in overall USMLE Step 1 or Step 2 pass rates, though alumni were more likely to fail during the first take. Additionally, there was no significant difference in years to graduation between alumni and traditional students (Epps, 2015). Michigan State University's postbac program has successfully matriculated over 96% of their students to a medical school, with a 7% attrition rate (Lipscomb, Mavis, Fowler, Green, & Brooks, 2009). Ohio State University's postbac program was established in 1990 and recruits underrepresented minorities and those from disadvantaged backgrounds who did not successfully matriculate to medical school. Program alumni have an 89% graduate rate from medical school (McDougle, Way, & Rucker, 2010; McDougle, Way, & Yash, 2008). The University of North Texas Health Science Center (UNTHSC) offers a 1-year academic and practice interview program to students who were not accepted to the Texas College of Osteopathic Medicine (TCOM). This program does not target underserved students, therefore the percentage of minority students is much lower than other programs, at 25%. Sixty-nine percent of alumni successfully matriculated to medical school, while 10% decided to not reapply to medical school, instead opting to complete other programs at UNTHSC. Alumni did as well or better than traditional students at TCOM (Reeves, Vishwanatha, Yorio, Budd, & Sheedlo, 2008).

There is a paucity of published literature on the success of postbaccalaureate programs regarding medical school matriculation and graduation. With such a lack, it is difficult for schools to establish a new program or modify an existing program using evidence-based best practices. Careful consideration should be made regarding what constitutes readiness, including training in metacognitive practices and SDL.

Prematriculation Interventions

Orientation Programs

Prematriculation interventions are delivered to accepted students prior to matriculation into the UME program, and include orientation programs and PMCs. Although orientation programs are a consistent part of academic calendars and are generally considered to be a valuable, there is a paucity of literature describing the design, practice or efficacy of these programs. Orientation programs characteristically provide an inclusive and welcoming culture to foster teamwork and professional relationships, and introduce students to campus support and resources (Canavan et al., 1993). Despite this, much of the literature has focused on similar roles of white coat ceremonies.

A recent discourse analysis of medical orientation in the literature, based on data from a survey of Canadian institutions' approaches, aimed to develop a framework for medical school orientation thinking and practice, and to examine the role of scholarship in shaping orientation practices. Orientation was typically defined as a series of organized events that took place shortly before, at or shortly after an entering class of medical studies began their studies. Three domains of orientation programs were identified, namely cultural, social, and practical. Cultural orientation included the symbolic and ceremonial aspects related to professionalism and physician identity development, such as white coat ceremonies, stethoscope ceremonies, Hippocratic oath ceremonies, and anatomy memorial services. Social orientation included the group activities intended to coalesce students together as a coherent class unit, such as team-building activities and student organization-led events. Practical orientation included providing students with the information needed to function in the program, such as curricular structure, campus tours and exposure to student support resources. Based on the survey data and despite cultural orientation being the smallest component of most schools' orientation calendar, the significance of cultural orientation was perceived to be greater than that of social or practical orientation (Ellaway et al., 2014). In the absence of reported measured outcomes and best practices, the limited existing literature suggests that faculty responsible for orientation program design have mainly relied on rituals as opposed to evidence-guided practice.

Prematriculation Courses

The other major category of prematriculation intervention, which has increased in prevalence, is the PMC. The term PMC describes a course that enrolls accepted students prior to their matriculation in a collegiate program. One of the earliest medical PMCs the literature describes was Boston University School of Medicine's Preentrance Enrichment Program. The program began in 1973 and was a six-week program offered to minority and other financially or educationally disadvantaged students. Participation was voluntary, and the goal of the program was to enhance these students' curriculum preparation graduation rates. The program offered students instruction in anatomy, histology, biochemistry, study skills, and test-taking skills the summer prior to matriculation. The data collected demonstrated significantly higher percentages of participants passing or receiving honors in two courses, and slightly higher, though not significant, percentages of participants passing or receiving honors in six other courses of the nine first-year medical school courses, compared to their nonparticipant minority peers (Ugbolue, Whitley, & Stevens, 1987). This seminal work may have established a precedent for PMC course design that is still heavily relied upon today.

Much of the current literature regarding PMCs consists of descriptions of individual schools' programs whose experimental design cannot support interprogram comparison. Review of the literature yields several common themes among existing PMCs (Heck, 2014). One recurring theme is that PMCs selectively target minority or "at-risk" students, who are historically defined as being less likely to reach established measures of competency in academics, when they are compared to their peers (Kaufman & Bradbury, 1992). A second commonality among PMCs is the primary focus on delivery of curricular content knowledge (Lindner et al., 2013; Wilson et al., 2011). The areas of greatest concentration are often basic sciences that students encounter early in their preclinical training, such as anatomy, histology, cell biology, biochemistry, and physiology, with some introduction of clinical skills. Some programs have taken a broader approach by also addressing learning, study, and interpersonal skills (Kornitzer et al., 2005). A third trend among PMCs are their timing and length, with the majority taking place in the summer prior to matriculation and lasting four to six weeks. As the results of a recent multi-institutional survey suggest, the current design of PMCs at United States medical schools is likely based primarily upon tradition, rather than evidence-based best practices (Heck et al., 2017). However, there are some notable outlying models for medical educators to consider as they embark on planning a PMC.

Recently, the primary author described a one-week and faculty-led PMC that focused on the acquisition of metacognitive awareness and skill development. The course utilized a combination of educational psychology, basic science, and clinical medicine content, which was delivered in standard formats, including lectures, flipped-classroom application sessions, and standardized patient experiences. Learning outcomes were assessed using pre- and postcourse surveys, board-style multiple test questions and standardized patient evaluations. Results demonstrated a statistically significant increase in student knowledge and confidence, and student feedback in the end-of-course survey was overwhelmingly positive (Heck & Underwood, 2016).

A newer trend in line with a new generation of technologically driven learners, online PMCs allow for self-selection and self-pace. Authors from Des Moines University described an online PMC that was offered to all incoming students and consisted of faculty-developed biochemistry and physiology modules. Results showed statistically significant, but modest, increased performance on the biochemistry exams of students who accessed vs. students who did not, and no statistically significant differences in physiology exam scores between the two groups (Wilson et al., 2011). Although the authors note that this example is overwhelmingly similar to traditional, content-focused PMCs which were delivered in the past, the online format and opportunity for self-selection are desirable features.

Most PMCs share a common goal of improving students' academic performance. Reported outcome measures range from PMC grades, to attrition rates, to individual course grades, and to cumulative year 1 grades (Heck et al., 2017), which complicates one's ability to compare measure of success across publications. Further confounding are reports demonstrating the ineffectiveness of PMCs in improving academic performance (Heck et al., 2017; Seifert & Harper, 2007). Though there are publications both supporting and opposing the efficacy of PMCs, the lack of comparability makes higher order evaluation difficult.

There are a multitude of factors for medical educators to consider when embarking on planning efforts for prematriculation interventions. The authors have presented several examples using various methodologies and learning theories to help provide medical educators a framework as they begin designing and implementing their own prematriculation interventions. Although there remains an overall lack of empirical evidence to support the efficacy of these programs in improving academic performance, they are still generally considered a valuable part of the medical school experience by both students and faculty.

Postmatriculation Interventions

Postmatriculation intervention refers to programs which are delivered once a student has matriculated into the UME curriculum. Research has identified that objective measures of medical knowledge during the curriculum can predict subsequent performance on licensing examinations and clinical competence after medical school (Gonnella, Erdmann, & Hojat, 2004). Thus, there is general agreement among all medical school stakeholders that struggling students are identified and supported early in their medical training. These interventions have traditionally been reactionary measures predicated on short-term and remedial study programs for medical students who have failed to achieve program standards (Holland, 2016). However, due to the inability to determine the long-term effectiveness of these interventions, there is growing interest to look beyond traditional deficit-driven and reactive support, and incorporate more proactive and developmental approaches that can benefit all students. This section will focus on the two major categories of postmatriculation intervention: Academic and noncognitive programs.

Academic Remediation

Academic interventions can be further defined by the concepts of academic remediation and academic preparation. Academic remediation is defined as having three components: Identification of deficiency in knowledge or skills through assessment, attempt to provide remedial education targeting the deficiency, and reassessment of the areas of deficiency (Hauer et al., 2009). A recent review of the literature revealed that remediation in medical education appears to be an increasingly important area of research (Cleland et al., 2013). The majority of studies focus solely on performance on a specific examination, such as retaking a course exam, retaking a standardized national exam, or the next standard examination in a program. Those of most interest are the few studies that explicitly attempted to tease out what methodologies and practices have impact, and what populations of students may respond best to remediation.

One such study from authors at the University of Michigan utilized two levels of remediation for students who failed an OSCE station(s). They demonstrated that remediation combining review, reflection, and self-assessment had a statistically significant effect, showing improvement on both students' performance and self-assessment between first and second attempts on failed OSCE stations. Additionally, no significant changes were found between self-assessed and faculty-guided remediation (White et al., 2009). Winston, Van der Vleuten, and Scherpbier (2010) published a series of particularly informative linked studies, one of which explicitly stated the evidence used to design their intervention. They first noted a key issue with voluntary remediation programs in that weak students who are in most need of assistance often fail to seek it. Second, interventions seemed to be more effective once the need had become manifest, such as after a failed examination. Third, there was growing consensus that interventions should focus on content boosting and skills development. Fourth, exemplary programs used in nonmedical colleges and universities relied on skilled faculty-led tutoring and focused on group, rather than individual interventions. In keeping with these principles, the authors designed a 14-week mandatory remediation course for medical students repeating their first semester. This course incorporated a combination of basic science course work, cognitive and metacognitive skills sessions, and individual mentorship. Compared to nonparticipant peer controls, participants had a significant improvement in semester pass rates, which persisted as they progressed through the three subsequent school semesters (Winston et al., 2010).

A review of the literature points to some practical implications for medical educators as they design these interventions. First, the more recent and successful interventions tend to use self-regulation, metacognition, reflection, and feedback as conceptualizing theories (Holland, 2016). Second, programs that supported study skills development were most effective when they were need-related and learner-driven, occurred over the course of several weeks, and included some form of learning needs assessment focusing on learning skills study techniques, examination skills, metacognitive self-regulation, and self-efficacy approaches (Winston, van der Vleuten, & Scherpbier, 2014).

Academic Preparation

In contrast to academic remediation, academic preparation is defined as a proactive and developmental approach that focuses on personal and professional growth for all students, regardless of academic risk or performance, by developing life-long learning skills (Sandars, Patel, Steele, & McAreavey, 2014). One such program at the Leeds Institute of Medical Education, described the development and evaluation of a "learning to learn" course that was fully integrated within the first-year medical curriculum. The course consisted of three one-hour facilitated small groups sessions, prior to which students completed two online questionnaires that were designed to provide an individual score for dimensions of SDL. In each session, discussions focused on a different set of SDL dimensions and incorporated student reflection on the implications for the new approaches they were learning. Student perceptions on usefulness of the course were positive, with the majority of students agreeing the course helped to improve their understanding of their own learning, study skills, and academic performance (Sandars & Homer, 2012). Another study which evaluated student perceptions of using an appreciative inquiry approach to discover good learning and study strategies showed similar favorable student responses (Kumar & Chacko, 2010).

Currently, the literature reveals a predominant focus on academic remediation, suggesting a lack of programs which are targeted at academic preparation. As the evidence supporting academic preparation has thus far been anecdotal, further research to provide empirical evidence of the efficacy of this proactive and developmental approach is necessary.

Noncognitive Programs

The second category of postmatriculation interventions, which are termed noncognitive programs, provide medical students the opportunity to learn and employ a variety of tools to help prevent the deleterious consequences resulting from the inherently high levels of stress and burnout associated with medical education (Dyrbye et al., 2008). As described by Gordon (2014), the evolution of these programs began in the 1970s, when several medical schools and hospitals were implementing strategies they modeled on sensitivity training groups that had been previously used with patients, health professionals, and in the corporate world to teach medical professionals to better handle stress and its consequences. Over the next two decades, the emphasis shifted from sensitivity training toward stress management, prompted by the accumulating scientific evidence that physiologic systems are positively affected by mind-body techniques (Gordon, 2014). Studies in medical students who practiced mind-body techniques demonstrated similar results, and reported outcomes included decreased levels of depression (Rosenzweig, Reibel, Greeson, Brainard, & Hojat, 2003) and greater general well-being (Rakel & Hedgecock, 2008).

A small number of medical schools in the U.S. have begun to offer short-term mind-body skills programs, based on the Mind-Body Skills Group model that was developed at the Washington DC-based Center for Mind-Body Medicine in the 1990s. In the original model, each small-group meeting has a similar structure which includes meditation, sharing experiences, and discussing the scientific rationale for a new mind-body technique to be learned, such as meditation, relaxation techniques, deep breathing, biofeedback, and autogenic training, or a form of self-expression, such as guided imagery or a written dialogue. The group then practices the new technique together. Following the experiential practice, participants reflect on the exercise. Georgetown University and the University of Washington have the most comprehensive programs, but at least 13 other medical schools have or do offer Mind-Body Skills Groups to their students (Gordon, 2014).

Research from the Georgetown Mind-Body Skill Groups demonstrated efficacy using both qualitative and quantitative measures. In one qualitative analysis of student experiences and attitudes regarding the program, the authors found that students reported improved experiences in five areas: Connections, self-discovery, stress relief, learning, and medical education. Students reported that the program was a unique and valuable experience that helped them to dispel feelings of isolation, become more aware of their own priorities and limitations, become more attentive to their state of mind, perform better in school, and reduce their overall stress levels (Saunders et al., 2007). In another study that sought to assess the stress-reducing effects of the program by measuring physiological changes, the authors found that participants did not have the expected increase in salivary cortisol at exam time compared to nonparticipating peers, indicating a lower physiologic stress response (Maclaughlin et al., 2011). Programs such as the Mind-Body Skills Groups offer students a variety of tools with which they can improve self-care and potentially reconnect to the idealism and passion that first led them to choose a career in medicine. Given the well-documented and serious consequences that result from the inherently high levels of stress, burnout, and sleeplessness which are associated with the medical education, a strong argument can be made for the inclusion of such noncognitive postmatriculation interventions.

CONCLUSION

The purpose of this chapter is to contribute to the body of knowledge in medical education literature by exploring what contributes to readiness for the UME program, and describe the current landscape of interventions meant to address this. There is a substantial need to address the underlying reasons for medical school attrition, including psychological distress and academic failure in healthy individuals who were high academic achievers upon matriculation. Furthermore, institutional and academic barriers to matriculation continue to prevent promising students from entering the academic program, suggesting further needs to identify better indicators of readiness for medical education.

In this chapter, for the first time, the authors have described the continuum of interventions which are aimed at enhancing early medical education readiness, and categorized them according to the student's academic progression, which includes preadmission, prematriculation, and postmatriculation. Though mention of these programs does occur in the literature, the limited number of studies, range of intended outcomes, and variability in experimental design among them, to date, have prevented any higher order evaluation to determine which practices demonstrate efficacy in affecting readiness. Some evidence suggests that these programs are often based on traditional beliefs or historic precedent that academic readiness is wholly dependent on prior content knowledge or evidence of good academic performance. This contributes heavily to the current practices, which are often directed at enhancing foundational content knowledge and targeting student populations who are seen as "at-risk" or in need of remediation. Despite some evidence supporting this approach, a greater body of knowledge in the educational literature points towards a combination of cognitive and noncognitive traits which significantly contribute to academic readiness and can be developed in adult learners.

Even with this knowledge, readiness intervention programs exhibit high variability regarding program goals and the populations they serve. In this research, the authors have found that preadmissions readiness interventions generally vary greatly in structure and intended outcomes. However, most share common goals of delivering multifaceted and longitudinal support to sociodemographically disadvantaged populations to enhance readiness. The current literature on such programs supports their continued use. In order to reinforce this approach, the authors offer the conclusion that multiple barriers to recruitment and acceptance exist in this learner population. Thus, the authors urge medical educators to consider and articulate how these barriers impede academic readiness. Shorter duration and exposure-based programs, which are less prevalent in the literature, note significant barriers to reaching intended populations, and admissions-focused programs may fall short of addressing readiness for the academic curriculum at all. As such, the authors recommend program directors seek to offer long-term multifaceted programs, which provide holistic support. Postbac programs are common and growing in popularity in the U.S., but scantly appear in the literature. The authors implore medical educators who are involved in such programs to explore the effects of these interventions, particularly on medical education readiness, and disseminate this knowledge of program design and outcomes through peer-reviewed publications.

Despite prematriculation interventions being the most recognized intervention category aimed at enhancing either academic or emotional preparedness in accepted students, there remains a lack of consistent efficacy data and evidence-based best practices for both orientation programs and PMCs. In designing these programs, the authors encourage medical educators to think outside the box. They should consider incorporation of cognitive and metacognitive skills, such as learning skills, study skills, self-regulation, and self-assessment, that can benefit all incoming students. Lastly, the authors encourage medical educators to take these lessons learned in preadmission and prematriculation interventions, and offer similar preparation-focused interventions to currently enrolled medical students. In general, there is much that these three categories of interventions can learn from one another.

In conclusion, the authors have identified several themes in early medical education readiness interventions and made several recommendations for the future. These programs are generally aimed at enhancing learner readiness, or their state of preparation for UME. However, the complex and multifactorial nature of readiness for education has resulted in such extensive variability between studies that it may be difficult for program directors to determine direction or consult evidence to support their own programs. The authors recommend that medical educators consider and articulate goals and intended learning outcomes for these programs, which explicitly give attention to how readiness is addressed. Further, the authors recommend that medical educators formulate hypotheses and design experiments to demonstrate their program's effectiveness in achieving these outcomes and disseminate this knowledge, with the purpose of influencing best practices. In general, the authors encountered themes related to cognitive and noncognitive interventions throughout the literature on these intervention programs. They recommend medical educators look toward the evidence base that exists in the education literature to explore what types of knowledge, skills, and traits contribute to readiness for education, and pursue student outcomes in cognitive areas such as self-regulation and metacognition, and noncognitive areas, such as mindset, motivation, and resilience.

REFERENCES

Achenjang, J. N., & Elam, C. L. (2016). Recruitment of underrepresented minorities in medical school through a student-led initiative. *Journal of the National Medical Association, 108*(3), 147–151. doi:10.1016/j.jnma.2016.05.003 PMID:27692354

Acosta, D., & Olsen, P. (2006). Meeting the needs of regional minority groups: The University of Washington's programs to increase the American Indian and Alaskan Native physician workforce. *Academic Medicine, 81*(10), 863–870. doi:10.1097/01.ACM.0000238047.48977.05 PMID:16985341

Association of American Medical Colleges. (2018a). *AAMC data snapshot.* Washington, DC: Association of American Medical Colleges.

Association of American Medical Colleges. (2018b). *Matriculating student questionnaire 2018. All schools summary report.* Washington, DC: Association of American Medical Colleges.

Association of American Medical Colleges. (2019). *Postbaccalaureate premedical programs.* Washington, DC: Association of American Medical Colleges.

Brazeau, C. M., Shanafelt, T., Durning, S. J., Massie, F. S., Eacker, A., Moutier, C., ... Dyrbye, L. N. (2014). Distress among matriculating medical students relative to the general population. *Academic Medicine, 89*(11), 1520–1525. doi:10.1097/ACM.0000000000000482 PMID:25250752

Burk-Rafel, J., Santen, S. A., & Purkiss, J. (2017). Study behaviors and USMLE Step 1 performance: Implications of a student self-directed parallel curriculum. *Academic Medicine, 92*(11S), S67–S74. doi:10.1097/ACM.0000000000001916 PMID:29065026

Campbell-Sills, L., Cohan, S. L., & Stein, M. B. (2006). Relationship of resilience to personality, coping, and psychiatric symptoms in young adults. *Behaviour Research and Therapy*, *44*(4), 585–599. doi:10.1016/j.brat.2005.05.001 PMID:15998508

Canavan, M. M., Saavedra, R., & Russell, A. Y. (1993). A health science center's pre-matriculation retreat. *Academic Medicine*, *68*(5), 358–359. doi:10.1097/00001888-199305000-00017 PMID:8484847

Cao, L., & Nietfeld, J. L. (2007). College students' metacognitive awareness of difficulties in learning the class content does not automatically lead to adjustment of study strategies. *Australian Journal of Educational Developmental Psychology*, *7*, 31–46.

Castillo-Page, L. (2016). *Diversity in medical education: Facts & figures 2016*. Washington, DC: Association of American Medical Colleges.

Cleland, J., Leggett, H., Sandars, J., Costa, M. J., Patel, R., & Moffat, M. (2013). The remediation challenge: Theoretical and methodological insights from a systematic review. *Medical Education*, *47*(3), 242–251. doi:10.1111/medu.12052 PMID:23398010

Columbia University. (2019, n.d.). At a glance. Retrieved from https://gs.columbia.edu/postbac/postbac-at-a-glance

Cook, C. J., Cook, C. E., & Hilton, T. N. (2016). Does emotional intelligence influence success during medical school admissions and program matriculation? A systematic review. *Journal of Educational Evaluation for Health Professions*, *13*, 40. doi:10.3352/jeehp.2016.13.40 PMID:27838916

Cook, D. A., Castillo, R. M., Gas, B., & Artino, A. R. Jr. (2017). Measuring achievement goal motivation, mindsets, and cognitive load: Validation of three instruments' scores. *Medical Education*, *51*(10), 1061–1074. doi:10.1111/medu.13405 PMID:28901645

Crump, C., Ned, J., & Winkleby, M. A. (2015). The Stanford Medical Youth Science Program: Educational and science-related outcomes. *Advances in Health Sciences Education: Theory and Practice*, *20*(2), 457–466. doi:10.100710459-014-9540-6 PMID:25096792

Dalley, B., Podawiltz, A., Castro, R., Fallon, K., Kott, M., Rabek, J., ... Smith, Q. (2009). The Joint Admission Medical Program: A Statewide Approach to Expanding Medical Education and Career Opportunities for Disadvantaged Students. *Academic Medicine*, *84*(10), 1373–1382. doi:10.1097/ACM.0b013e3181b6c76b PMID:19881424

Danek, J., & Borrayo, E. (2012). *Urban universities: Developing a health workforce that meets community needs*. Washington DC: Urban Universities for Health. Retrieved from http://urbanuniversitiesforhealth.org/media/documents/Urban_Health_Workforce_Final_Report.pdf

Danner, O. K., Lokko, C., Mobley, F., Dansby, M., Maze, M., Bradley, B., ... Childs, E. (2017). Hospital-based, multidisciplinary, youth mentoring, and medical exposure program positively influences and reinforces health care career choice: "The Reach One Each One Program early Experience. *American Journal of Surgery*, *213*(4), 611–616. doi:10.1016/j.amjsurg.2016.12.002 PMID:28040097

Dweck, C. S. (2006). *Mindset: The new psychology of success*. New York: Random House.

Dweck, C. S. (2013). *Self-theories: Their role in motivation, personality, and development*. New York: Psychology Press. doi:10.4324/9781315783048

Dyrbye, L., & Shanafelt, T. (2012). Nurturing resiliency in medical trainees. *Medical Education*, *46*(4), 343. doi:10.1111/j.1365-2923.2011.04206.x PMID:22429167

Dyrbye, L. N., Thomas, M. R., Massie, F. S., Power, D. V., Eacker, A., Harper, W., ... Shanafelt, T. D. (2008). Burnout and suicidal ideation among U.S. medical students. *Annals of Internal Medicine*, *149*(5), 334–341. doi:10.7326/0003-4819-149-5-200809020-00008 PMID:18765703

Dyrbye, L. N., Thomas, M. R., Power, D. V., Durning, S., Moutier, C., Massie, F. S. Jr, ... Sloan, J. A. (2010). Burnout and serious thoughts of dropping out of medical school: A multi-institutional study. *Academic Medicine*, *85*(1), 94–102. doi:10.1097/ACM.0b013e3181c46aad PMID:20042833

Dyrbye, L. N., Thomas, M. R., & Shanafelt, T. D. (2006). Systematic review of depression, anxiety, and other indicators of psychological distress among U.S. and Canadian medical students. *Academic Medicine*, *81*(4), 354–373. doi:10.1097/00001888-200604000-00009 PMID:16565188

Ellaway, R. H., Cooper, G., Al-Idrissi, T., Dube, T., & Graves, L. (2014). Discourses of student orientation to medical education programs. *Medical Education Online*, *19*(1). doi:10.3402/meo.v19.23714 PMID:24646440

Epps, A. C. (2015). The strategic impact of a post baccalaureate pre-medicine intervention program on medical school academic performance. *Journal of Health Care for the Poor and Underserved*, *26*(1), 8–20. doi:10.1353/hpu.2015.0008 PMID:25702723

Fralick, M., & Flegel, K. (2014). Physician burnout: Who will protect us from ourselves? *Canadian Medical Association Journal*, *186*(10), 731. doi:10.1503/cmaj.140588 PMID:24890102

Freeman, B. K., Landry, A., Trevino, R., Grande, D., & Shea, J. A. (2016). Understanding the leaky pipeline: Perceived barriers to pursuing a career in medicine or dentistry among underrepresented-in-medicine undergraduate students. *Academic Medicine*, *91*(7), 987–993. doi:10.1097/ACM.0000000000001020 PMID:26650673

Gagnon, M.-C. J., Durand-Bush, N., & Young, B. W. (2016). Self-regulation capacity is linked to wellbeing and burnout in physicians and medical students: Implications for nurturing self-help skills. *International Journal of Wellbeing*, *6*(1), 101–116. doi:10.5502/ijw.v6i1.425

Gauer, J. L., Wolff, J. M., & Jackson, J. B. (2016). Do MCAT scores predict USMLE scores? An analysis on 5 years of medical student data. *Medical Education Online*, *21*(1). doi:10.3402/meo.v21.31795 PMID:27702431

Girdano, D., Everly, G. S., & Dusek, D. E. (1996). *Controlling stress and tension: A holistic approach*. Needham Heights, MA: Allyn & Bacon.

Gonnella, J. S., Erdmann, J. B., & Hojat, M. (2004). An empirical study of the predictive validity of number grades in medical school using 3 decades of longitudinal data: Implications for a grading system. *Medical Education*, *38*(4), 425–434. doi:10.1111/j.1365-2923.2004.01774.x PMID:15025644

Gordon, J. S. (2014). Mind-body skills groups for medical students: Reducing stress, enhancing commitment, and promoting patient-centered care. *BMC Medical Education*, *14*(1), 198. doi:10.1186/1472-6920-14-198 PMID:25245341

Gross, D. A., Mattox, L. C., & Winkleman, N. (2016). Priming the physician pipeline: A regional AHEC's use of in-state medical school data to guide its health careers programming. *Journal of Health Care for the Poor and Underserved*, *27*(4A), 8–18. doi:10.1353/hpu.2016.0194 PMID:27818409

Hauer, K. E., Ciccone, A., Henzel, T. R., Katsufrakis, P., Miller, S. H., Norcross, W. A., ... Irby, D. M. (2009). Remediation of the deficiencies of physicians across the continuum from medical school to practice: A thematic review of the literature. *Academic Medicine*, *84*(12), 1822–1832. doi:10.1097/ACM.0b013e3181bf3170 PMID:19940595

Heck, A. (2014). Students' activities in a pre-matriculation course as a predictor of initial academic performance in medical school. *Medical Science Educator*, *24*(3), 239–243. doi:10.100740670-014-0050-1

Heck, A. J., Gibbons, L., Ketter, S. J., Furlano, A., & Prest, L. (2017). A survey of the design of pre-matriculation courses at us medical schools. *Medical Science Educator*, *27*(2), 229–236. doi:10.100740670-017-0379-3

Heck, A. J., & Underwood, T. (2016). A pre-matriculation course that focuses on a metacognitive approach to learning. *Medical Science Educator*, *26*(4), 515–516. doi:10.100740670-016-0320-1

Holden, L., Berger, W., Zingarelli, R., & Siegel, E. (2015). After-school program for urban youth: Evaluation of a health careers course in New York City high schools. *Information Services & Use*, *35*(1-2), 141–160. doi:10.3233/ISU-150773 PMID:26316659

Holland, C. (2016). Critical review: Medical students' motivation after failure. *Advances in Health Sciences Education: Theory and Practice*, *21*(3), 695–710. doi:10.100710459-015-9643-8 PMID:26443085

Huber, S. (2003). The white coat ceremony: A contemporary medical ritual. *Journal of Medical Ethics*, *29*(6), 364–366. doi:10.1136/jme.29.6.364 PMID:14662817

Huff, K. L., & Fang, D. (1999). When are students most at risk of encountering academic difficulty? A study of the 1992 matriculants to U.S. medical schools. *Academic Medicine*, *74*(4), 454–460. doi:10.1097/00001888-199904000-00047 PMID:10219232

Jackson, R. E. (1972). The effectiveness of a special program for minority group students. *Journal of Medical Education*, *47*(8), 620–624. PMID:5057182

Kaufman, P., & Bradbury, D. (1992). *Characteristics of at-risk students in NELS: 88. National education longitudinal study of 1988. Statistical analysis report. Contractor report. NCES 92-042. (0160380111).* Jessup [ED Pubs]. *MD Medical Newsmagazine*, 20794–21398.

Kirch, D. G., Mitchell, K., & Ast, C. (2013). The new 2015 MCAT: Testing competencies. *Journal of the American Medical Association*, *310*(21), 2243–2244. doi:10.1001/jama.2013.282093 PMID:24302080

Klamen, D. L., & Williams, R. G. (2011). The efficacy of a targeted remediation process for students who fail standardized patient examinations. *Teaching and Learning in Medicine*, *23*(1), 3–11. doi:10.1080/10401334.2010.536749 PMID:21240775

Knowles, M. S. (1975). *Self-directed learning: A guide for learners and teachers*. New York: New York Association Press.

Knowles, M. S. (1985). Application in continuing education for the health professions: Chapter five of "Andragogy in action". *Mobius, 5*(2), 80–100. doi:10.1002/chp.4760050212 PMID:10271191

Kornitzer, B., Ronan, E., & Rifkin, M. R. (2005). Improving the adjustment of educationally disadvantaged students to medical school: The summer enrichment program. *The Mount Sinai Journal of Medicine, New York, 72*(5), 317–321. PMID:16184295

Krupat, E., Pelletier, S. R., & Dienstag, J. L. (2017). Academic performance on first-year medical school exams: How well does it predict later performance on knowledge-based and clinical assessments? *Teaching and Learning in Medicine, 29*(2), 181–187. doi:10.1080/10401334.2016.1259109 PMID:28098483

Kumar, L. R., & Chacko, T. V. (2010). Using appreciative inquiry on learning styles to facilitate student learning. *Medical Education, 44*(11), 1121–1122. doi:10.1111/j.1365-2923.2010.03842.x PMID:20946485

Kumwenda, B., Cleland, J. A., Walker, K., Lee, A. J., & Greatrix, R. (2017). The relationship between school type and academic performance at medical school: A national, multi-cohort study. *BMJ Open, 7*(8). doi:10.1136/bmjopen-2017-016291 PMID:28860227

Lindner, I., Sacks, D., Sheakley, M., Seidel, C., Wahlig, B. C., Rojas, J. D., & Coleman, M. T. (2013). A pre-matriculation learning program that enables medical students with low prerequisite scores to succeed. *Medical Teacher, 35*(10), 872–873. doi:10.3109/0142159X.2013.786812 PMID:24050196

Lipscomb, W. D., Mavis, B., Fowler, L. V., Green, W. D., & Brooks, G. L. (2009). The effectiveness of a postbaccalaureate program for students from disadvantaged backgrounds. *Academic Medicine, 84*(10Suppl), S42–S45. doi:10.1097/ACM.0b013e3181b37bd0 PMID:19907383

Maclaughlin, B. W., Wang, D., Noone, A. M., Liu, N., Harazduk, N., Lumpkin, M., ... Amri, H. (2011). Stress biomarkers in medical students participating in a mind body medicine skills program. *Evidence-Based Complementary and Alternative Medicine, 2011*, 950461. doi:10.1093/ecam/neq039 PMID:21799696

Mains, T. E., Wilcox, M. V., & Wright, S. M. (2016). Medical education resources initiative for teens program in Baltimore: A model pipeline program built on four pillars. *Education for Health, 29*(1), 47–50. doi:10.4103/1357-6283.178935 PMID:26996799

Mayer, J. D., & Salovey, P. (1993). The intelligence of emotional intelligence. *Intelligence, 17*(4), 443–442. doi:10.1016/0160-2896(93)90010-3

McDougle, L., Way, D. P., Lee, W. K., Morfin, J. A., Mavis, B. E., Matthews, D. A., ... Clinchot, D. M. (2015). A national long-term outcomes evaluation of U.S. premedical postbaccalaureate programs designed to promote health care access and workforce diversity. *Journal of Health Care for the Poor and Underserved, 26*(3), 631–647. doi:10.1353/hpu.2015.0088 PMID:26320900

McDougle, L., Way, D. P., & Rucker, Y. L. (2010). Survey of care for the underserved: A control group study of practicing physicians who were graduates of The Ohio State University College of Medicine premedical postbaccalaureate training program. *Academic Medicine, 85*(1), 36–40. doi:10.1097/ACM.0b013e3181c46f35 PMID:20042818

McDougle, L., Way, D. P., & Yash, C. (2008). Effectiveness of a premedical postbaccalaureate program in improving medical college admission test scores of underrepresented minority and disadvantaged students. *Journal of the National Medical Association, 100*(9), 1021–1024. doi:10.1016/S0027-9684(15)31438-3 PMID:18807429

McGaghie, W. C. (2002). Assessing readiness for medical education: Evolution of the medical college admission test. *Journal of the American Medical Association, 288*(9), 1085–1090. doi:10.1001/jama.288.9.1085 PMID:12204076

Medina, M. S., Castleberry, A. N., & Persky, A. M. (2017). Strategies for improving learner metacognition in health professional education. *American Journal of Pharmaceutical Education, 81*(4), 78. PMID:28630519

Metz, A. M. (2017). Medical school outcomes, primary care specialty choice, and practice in medically underserved areas by physician alumni of MEDPREP, a postbaccalaureate premedical program for underrepresented and disadvantaged students. *Teaching and Learning in Medicine, 29*(3), 351–359. doi:10.1080/10401334.2016.1275970 PMID:28632012

Murray, T. S., Clermont, Y., & Binkley, M. (2005). *Measuring adult literacy and life skills: New frameworks for assessment*. Ottawa, Canada: Statistics Canada.

Nickens, H. W., Ready, T. P., & Petersdorf, R. G. (1994). Project 3000 by 2000. Racial and ethnic diversity in U.S. medical schools. *The New England Journal of Medicine, 331*(7), 472–476. doi:10.1056/NEJM199408183310712 PMID:8035847

O'Neill, L. D., Wallstedt, B., Eika, B., & Hartvigsen, J. (2011). Factors associated with dropout in medical education: A literature review. *Medical Education, 45*(5), 440–454. doi:10.1111/j.1365-2923.2010.03898.x PMID:21426375

Rakel, D. P., & Hedgecock, J. (2008). Healing the healer: A tool to encourage student reflection towards health. *Medical Teacher, 30*(6), 633–635. doi:10.1080/01421590802206754 PMID:18677663

Reede, J. Y. (2003). A recurring theme: The need for minority physicians. *Health Affairs, 22*(4), 91–93. doi:10.1377/hlthaff.22.4.91 PMID:12889755

Reeves, R. E., Vishwanatha, J. K., Yorio, T., Budd, M., & Sheedlo, H. J. (2008). The post-baccalaureate premedical certification program at the University of North Texas Health Science Center strengthens admission qualifications for entrance into medical school. *Academic Medicine, 83*(1), 45–51. doi:10.1097/ACM.0b013e31815c641c PMID:18162749

Rosenzweig, S., Reibel, D. K., Greeson, J. M., Brainard, G. C., & Hojat, M. (2003). Mindfulness-based stress reduction lowers psychological distress in medical students. *Teaching and Learning in Medicine, 15*(2), 88–92. doi:10.1207/S15328015TLM1502_03 PMID:12708065

Russell, P. C. (2002). The White Coat Ceremony: Turning Trust Into Entitlement. *Teaching and Learning in Medicine, 14*(1), 56–59. doi:10.1207/S15328015TLM1401_13 PMID:11865752

Sandars, J., & Homer, M. (2012). Pause 2 Learn: A "learning to learn" course to help undergraduate medical students to become more effective self-regulated learners. *Education for Primary Care*, *23*(6), 437–439. PMID:23232136

Sandars, J., Patel, R., Steele, H., & McAreavey, M. (2014). Developmental student support in undergraduate medical education: AMEE Guide No. 92. *Medical Teacher*, *36*(12), 1015–1026. doi:10.3109/0142159X.2014.917166 PMID:25072412

Saunders, P. A., Tractenberg, R. E., Chaterji, R., Amri, H., Harazduk, N., Gordon, J. S., ... Haramati, A. (2007). Promoting self-awareness and reflection through an experiential mind-body skills course for first year medical students. *Medical Teacher*, *29*(8), 778–784. doi:10.1080/01421590701509647 PMID:17852720

Simon, F. A., & Aschenbrener, C. A. (2005). Undergraduate medical education accreditation as a driver of lifelong learning. *The Journal of Continuing Education in the Health Professions*, *25*(3), 157–161. doi:10.1002/chp.23 PMID:16173065

Slater, C. E., & Cusick, A. (2017). Factors related to self-directed learning readiness of students in health professional programs: A scoping review. *Nurse Education Today*, *52*, 28–33. doi:10.1016/j.nedt.2017.02.011 PMID:28229917

Smith, M. C., Rose, A. D., Smith, T. J., & Ross-Gordon, J. M. (2015). Adults' readiness to learn and skill acquisition and use: An analysis of PIAAC. *Adult Education Research Conference*. Retrieved from http://newprairiepress.org/aerc/2015/papers/50

Soliman, M., & Al-Shaikh, G. (2015). Readiness for self-directed learning among first year Saudi medical students: A descriptive study. *Pakistan Journal of Medical Sciences*, *31*(4), 799–802. PMID:26430406

Soto-Greene, M., Wright, L., Gona, O. D., & Feldman, L. A. (1999). Minority enrichment programs at the New Jersey Medical School: 26 years in review. *Academic Medicine*, *74*(4), 386–389. doi:10.1097/00001888-199904000-00032 PMID:10219218

Ugbolue, A., Whitley, P. N., & Stevens, P. J. (1987). Evaluation of a preentrance enrichment program for minority students admitted to medical school. *Journal of Medical Education*, *62*(1), 8–16. PMID:3795249

Veloski, J. J., Callahan, C. A., Xu, G., Hojat, M., & Nash, D. B. (2000). Prediction of students' performances on licensing examinations using age, race, sex, undergraduate GPAs, and MCAT scores. *Academic Medicine*, *75*(10Suppl), S28–S30. doi:10.1097/00001888-200010001-00009 PMID:11031165

White, C. B., Ross, P. T., & Gruppen, L. D. (2009). Remediating students' failed OSCE performances at one school: The effects of self-assessment, reflection, and feedback. *Academic Medicine*, *84*(5), 651–654. doi:10.1097/ACM.0b013e31819fb9de PMID:19704203

Wilson, W. A., Henry, M. K., Ewing, G., Rehmann, J., Canby, C. A., Gray, J. T., & Finnerty, E. P. (2011). A prematriculation intervention to improve the adjustment of students to medical school. *Teaching and Learning in Medicine*, *23*(3), 256–262. doi:10.1080/10401334.2011.586923 PMID:21745061

Winkleby, M. A. (2007). The Stanford Medical Youth Science Program: 18 years of a biomedical program for low-income high school students. *Academic Medicine, 82*(2), 139–145. doi:10.1097/ACM.0b013e31802d8de6 PMID:17264691

Winston, K. A., van der Vleuten, C. P. M., & Scherpbier, A. J. (2010). An investigation into the design and effectiveness of a mandatory cognitive skills programme for at-risk medical students. *Medical Teacher, 32*(3), 236–243. doi:10.3109/01421590903197035 PMID:20218839

Winston, K. A., van der Vleuten, C. P. M., & Scherpbier, A. J. (2014). Prediction and prevention of failure: An early intervention to assist at-risk medical students. *Medical Teacher, 36*(1), 25–31. doi:10.3109/0142159X.2013.836270 PMID:24083365

Zimmerman, B. J. (2002). Becoming a self-regulated learner: An overview. *Theory into Practice, 41*(2), 64–70. doi:10.120715430421tip4102_2

KEY TERMS AND DEFINITIONS

Academic Preparation: A proactive and developmental approach that focuses on personal and professional growth for all students, regardless of academic risk or performance, by developing life-long learning skills.

At-Risk: The condition of a student who is less likely to reach established measures of competency in academics as compared to their peers.

Attrition: The loss of students through non-completion of a medical program.

Cognitive Skills: Skills related to thinking, learning, reasoning, and memory.

Metacognition: An awareness or analysis of one's own learning or thinking processes.

Mindset: A student's belief about their own academic abilities.

Noncognitive Skills: Skills related to motivation, integrity, and interpersonal interaction.

Pipeline Program: A program that serves to recruit and retain a diverse group of students by providing multifactorial support to enhance readiness.

Postmatriculation: Existing or occurring after matriculation.

Preadmission: Existing or occurring prior to admission.

Prematriculation: Existing or occurring prior to matriculation.

Self-Directed Learning: The process by which individuals implement learning practices based on self-identified learning needs.

Chapter 16
Professional and Career Development of Medical Students

Sophia Chen
Rutgers New Jersey Medical School, USA

Christin Traba
iD https://orcid.org/0000-0001-6367-297X
Rutgers New Jersey Medical School, USA

Sangeeta Lamba
Rutgers New Jersey Medical School, USA

Maria Soto-Greene
Rutgers New Jersey Medical School, USA

ABSTRACT

This chapter reviews the steps for professional and career development of medical students. While the two overlap, there are distinct differences in preparation of students for lifelong professional vs. career development. Professional development involves professional/social identity as well as professional competence. Authors describe curricular implementation to help students achieve professional competence, including specific tools to form professional/social identities and recognize unconscious biases, essential for personal growth, psychological health, and successful careers of future physicians. In parallel to professional development, career specific advising must start in Year 1 of medical school as well. This chapter delineates the differences in academic vs. career advising, advising versus counseling, and a stepwise approach by medical school year to help guide students to their ultimate career path exploring career specialties to choosing one and ultimately preparing for residency.

DOI: 10.4018/978-1-7998-1468-9.ch016

INTRODUCTION

Physicians have a unique professional identity as a "doctor". These qualities include a mission-driven spirit committed to helping others, the ability to inspire trust and the deep sense of responsibility that comes with the intense and personal relationships with patients. Training in medical school therefore does not only include mastery of medical knowledge but also developing this social and professional identity as well as finding a career fit in a discipline of practice. In addition, physicians have a professional responsibility to be lifelong learners in order to keep up with new discoveries so they may provide the best care to their patients. This chapter will address the evolution of the benchmarking and best practices for medical student professional and career development. Organizational structures and models that are recommended to support these activities and related accreditation standards will be discussed.

PROFESSIONAL DEVELOPMENT OF MEDICAL STUDENTS

Background

Professional development as a doctor involves the formation of the professional/social identity and professional competence. Professional identity may be described as how individuals think of themselves in the profession. Social identity is how individuals think of themselves based on membership within social groups. This professional identity with its associated skills is essential for personal growth, psychological health, and a successful career as a future physician. Professional competence is the habitual and judicious use of communication, knowledge, technical skills, clinical reasoning, emotions, values, and reflection in daily practice for the benefit of the individual and community being served (Epstein & Hundert, 2002). General considerations for medical student professional development under domains of professional competence, professional identity, and curricular implementations are described below.

Students often matriculate to medical school from college. They are familiar with their role as a student but may have never held a job, or held the responsibility for an organization's outcomes or received difficult or negative feedback. Therefore, it is critical that medical schools empower students to act and think as professionals and this involves providing students the tools to form their professional and social identity. The 5 key skills for a student's professional and social identity formation include 1) self- awareness and understanding unconscious biases, 2) accountability and professional standards, 3) teamwork and communication, 4) leadership skills, and 5) resilience.

Professional and Social Identity Formation

1. **Self- awareness and understanding unconscious bias**: It is important to provide students the tools to help them understand their social identity and become aware of their own biases. This will have an impact on the type of care they provide to patients as well as help them determine the type of physician they aspire to become.

    Biases are part of the pattern recognition processes and brain short cuts that are meant to increase efficiency and handle external information. These biases may be conscious (or explicit) and unconscious (or implicit). Conscious bias refers to a set of attitudes, beliefs and deliberate thoughts that an individual has against others as a result of a perceived threat and this type of bias is easier to recognize. Unconscious or implicit bias refers to "the attitudes or stereotypes that affect our understanding, actions, and decisions in an unconscious manner." These associations (both positive and/or negative) are without an individual being aware of them. Unconscious biases develop over the course of a lifetime through exposure to direct and indirect messages and social media is often cited as a contributing cause (Staats et al., 2015). These unconscious biases may not only affect a student's attitudes towards other people based on characteristics such as race and ethnicity but also have the potential to impact their future career decisions. For example, a woman medical student may not initially consider orthopedics due to an unconscious bias that favors men as surgeons.

Teaching medical students about unconscious bias and giving them the tools to mitigate these biases is therefore important. This includes moving them from recognition and self-awareness to action so they can mitigate bias. One such tool to use is the Implicit Association Test (IAT) that can be freely accessed at https://implicit.harvard.edu/implicit/takeatest.html. The IAT measures attitudes and beliefs that individuals may be unwilling or unable to report. Debriefing with faculty facilitators in a safe space for discussion and self-reflection allow a student to process this information further. For example, a student may believe that they harbor no gender bias but the IAT may show that they (like many others) associate men with science more. The curriculum would ideally then build on this self-awareness to offer facilitated workshops that allow for practice of tools and frameworks to mitigate the uncovered biases (DallaPiazza et al., 2018).

2. **Accountability and Professional Standards:** "Society permits medicine to set standards of ethical and professional conduct for physicians. In return, medicine is expected to hold physicians accountable for meeting those standards and to address lapses in professional conduct when they occur (AMA, 2019)."

Students begin medical school with often high ideal values and a commitment to serve the profession and others. In school, they may witness unprofessional behavior from colleagues or faculty that goes unchecked and results in the interpretation that such behavior is the norm or acceptable. In this way the hidden curriculum may erode their ideal values. The rigor of medical school may compel students to take shortcuts to meet competing demands that could result in questionable professional behavior such as signing in an attendance sheet for another. Faculty witnesses do not always provide timely or any feedback, reinforcing -this behavior. As a result, medical schools need to not only have clearly defined professional expectations/standards but have a process for addressing breaches in professional conduct. Policies that describe acceptable (or not) behavior, steps for student remediation and language when a student is remediated, as well as student grievance procedures are important aspects.

These expectations and processes should be clearly communicated to students so they have access to and knowledge of all the professional standards set forth by the medical school, including those for student promotion and graduation. Many institutions also ask students to read and attest to the document at the beginning of medical school and at critical points such as transition to clerkship. A system for evaluation and remediation would involve the following steps (Arnold et al., 2007):

◦ Create policies and guidelines and describe the process of remediation
◦ Develop an evaluation form where professionalism is evaluated by the faculty, peers, and patients. Although there is no gold standard for measuring competency in professionalism, schools can assess the students based on the standards set forth by the institution
◦ Determine if the evaluation forms will be anonymous. Anonymity may allow the individual to be forthcoming in their feedback

- Provide faculty and resident development on how to give effective feedback (both negative and positive)
- Assess and provide feedback on student professionalism constantly and consistently, e.g., through each course and clerkship
- Provide formative and summative feedback to the student and remediate when necessary
- Remediation may involve meeting with the Dean of Student Affairs, Dean of Education, or Vice Dean. Document the discussion of unprofessional behavior and a corrective plan of action. Assigning a mentor may be helpful and would help ensure that the steps to remediating the unprofessional behavior are being met

3. **Teamwork and Communication:** Integral to shaping a professional identity is understanding oneself and managing relationships with the patient and family, community, and with other healthcare professionals. "An effective team is one in which the team members communicate with one another as well as combining their observations, expertise and decision-making responsibilities to optimize patient care (Human Resources for Health Global Resource Center, 2019)." Darrell Kirsch MD during his presidential address at the Association of American Colleges called for focus upon ''collaboration, shared accountability, and team performance (Kirch, 2007)."

Teaching medical students to work together, share knowledge, and work on clinical diagnosis and management as a team is an essential early part of medical education. A framework of the characteristics of successful teams to set expectations is recommended. For example, The Council on Medical Student Education in Pediatrics (COMSEP) framework identifies three key elements of highly effective teams (Bannister et al., 2014):
- Identifying a common purpose that all members of the team can articulate
- Being open and engaged in order to effectively communicate with other team members,
- Understanding the roles and skills of the other team members and what they contribute

Teaching modalities such as case studies, simulation, problem based learning, team based learning, and flipped classrooms encourage team work, collaboration, and communication. For example, Team-Based Learning implementation is based on four underlying principles (Michaelsen & Richards, 2005):
- Diverse groups of students should be created to work together for the entire course.
- Students groups are responsible for the pre learning and for work in their assigned teams.
- Team assignments must promote both learning and team development.
- Students must receive frequent and immediate feedback.

Interdisciplinary and interprofessional collaborative practice experiences, in both simulated and real practice settings, similarly build teamwork skills. Examples include participating in multidisciplinary rounds, volunteering for a global mission trip or a clinic with other health profession students.

4. **Leadership skills:** Physicians are expected to lead teams and manage or resolve conflicts. Individuals acquire these skills through life and real-world experiences. In medical school, there may be a much heavier emphasis on the medical and technical aspects of the curriculum than on teaching leadership skills.

Understanding individual strengths, and management styles in order to effectively lead is part of this journey. For example, the Medical Leadership Competency Framework (MLCF) developed by the National Health Service, describes the following five domains: (NHS Institute for Innovation and Improvement, 2010).

- ○ Demonstrating personal qualities: Developing self-awareness, the capability of managing oneself, continuing personal development, and acting with integrity.
- ○ Working with others: Learning how to develop networks, building/maintain relationships, and working with a team.
- ○ Managing services: Planning and achieving service goals, understanding resources to address diverse needs, directing and motivating others, and holding themselves and others accountable.
- ○ Improving services: Teaching how to critically evaluate the services and systems, patient safety, and innovating to provide the best care for patients.
- ○ Setting direction: Identifying context for change, applying evidence-based knowledge, making and evaluating decisions.

5. **Resilience:** Providing students the tools to manage and cope with degrees of distress, mental health, and wellness early medical education is valuable. This helps nurture coping skills and growth of good habits that maintain emotional and social well-being through their careers. The first step to addressing resilience may be to have the student self-reflect on personal experiences of stress and how they coped with it. Students can then engage in reflective exercises to understand the difference between their own adaptive and maladaptive responses to stress (Epstein & Krasner, 2013). Session topics may include: an orientation to lay the framework and expectations, how to manage time and workload, depression, burnout, substance abuse, performing acts of kindness, how to journal and be thankful, and many others. Interactive sessions with follow-up and faculty feedback are critical. Some programs therefore use assigned faculty mentors for ongoing guidance. Students may need encouragement and guidance to constantly apply these learned techniques in order to foster resilient future physicians.

Professional Competence

"Professional competence is developmental, impermanent, and context-dependent (Epstein & Hundert, 2002)." Critically and reflectively assessing own weaknesses and strengths and developing a learning plan to address and remedy the gaps are critical to maintaining professional competence. Emerging and important aspects of professional competence that are included in the undergraduate medical education (UME) include 1) clinical reasoning, 2) self and peer assessments, 3) feedback, and 4) lifelong learning.

1. **Clinical Reasoning:** The ability to make a diagnosis and decisions for management require application of clinical reasoning. Traditional medical education consisted of teaching content in the first two years of medical school such that students learned normal vs. abnormal processes first and the integration and application occurred during the clerkship phases when students interacted with patients. Students were challenged to seek clinical relevance and to learn the most critical higher thinking and reasoning processes on their own. The shift from a discipline based to an integrated organ system or symptom-based curriculum has allowed for better integration of explicit clinical reasoning teaching in the early years. Though teaching clinical reasoning can be complex, making the process more visible to the students and providing a step wise framework may be helpful. A framework that students can apply to each patient presentation based on the chief complaint is useful as is asking students to document the information so that they can also see their thought process and make adjustments. A simple clinical reasoning framework is:

- ◦ Begin with a chief complaint.
- ◦ Generate a broad differential diagnosis list.
- ◦ Gather information through history and physical examination tailored to differentials.
- ◦ Create a problem list for the patient.
- ◦ Develop a summary statement based on the data that frames the main issues and context.
- ◦ Revisit, revise, and reorder the differentials based on the problem list.

Assigned faculty mentor or coach may help monitor the learner's thought process and provide feedback by helping them identify learning gaps and piecing clinical information together (Kassirer 2010).

2. **Feedback:** Giving and receiving feedback is an essential element for professional growth. Traditionally feedback is often informal during small group sessions and bedside rounds. However, students may not realize that they are receiving feedback or the critique gets buried in positive words such that students do not take the necessary steps to improve on their skills. There are many models and methods for giving feedback. Some core concepts for feedback include:

- ◦ Setting expectations early: This allows learners to recognize the importance of feedback in medical education and sets the expectation that they will be giving and receiving feedback on an ongoing basis.
- ◦ Providing guidelines to supervising peers and faculty on how to give feedback will help the process be more meaningful, for example, providing bad vs. good examples of feedback, being specific rather than vague etc.
- ◦ Providing dedicated time for timely feedback also allows the students to process the information given to them and develop steps to improve the skills with the guidance of a faculty member. Small group session of the doctoring course and mid clerkship feedback sessions are two such examples.

Medical students need to be able to review, monitor and regulate their own learning processes and to engage in lifelong learning to reflect the real-life complexity of integrating knowledge into clinical competence (Soemantri et al., 2018). Asking them to self-reflect followed by faculty feedback on behaviors or events that the student may not identify may be useful. Often a summary of the discussion with an action plan is necessary to help the student make the necessary changes to the behavior.

3. **Self and Peer assessments:** Students self-assessment process covers the domains of knowledge, skills attitudes, beliefs, and behaviors in the clinical performance and is formative in nature (Epstein, 2007). The peer assessment process also addresses the domains of professional demeanor, work habits, interpersonal behavior, and teamwork and is also formative. Teaching students the importance of ongoing self-assessment will help them evaluate and seek ways to address their own performance gaps. Peer assessment is a powerful tool to identify gaps in skills that may not have been self-identified. Samples in curriculum include:

- ◦ Preparing students, setting expectations, and explicit time for students to self-assess and work on action plans (through the medical school years—often in the doctoring course)
- ◦ Providing opportunities to practice delivery of peer feedback (both narrative verbal and written).
- ◦ Evaluating their peers' work and having their own work evaluated is a learning tool that helps students with enhancing their own learning goals and improvements.

4. **Lifelong learning:** Motivating students to pursue the acquisition of knowledge on an ongoing basis is critical to provide the best evidence based care for patients. To be an effective lifelong learner,

the student must direct their own development by identifying the learning needs and meeting those needs. The American Medical Association (AMA) is calling for medical schools to teach students how to learn so they can learn for a lifetime (AMA, 2017)

"4 phases of adaptive learning (Brendan, 2017)"

- Planning: Student identifies a knowledge gap
- Learning: The learner must first appraise the resources—are they the right solutions to the problem then go about digesting the information so it sticks.
- Assessing: A combination of self-assessment and external feedback in which the learner determines if the findings would require a change in practice.
- Adjusting: The learner applies any necessary changes to practice while determining the scope and scale at which they should be implemented.

Some medical schools use the Learning Style Survey, VARK or ASSIST questionnaire to help students understand their own learning styles (Samarakoon, 2013) and where they may have strengths. Partnering with library resources on campus also assists students in practicing and identifying valid resources to seek information.

Curricular Implementations to Support Student Professional Development

Reflective professional practice and learning plans that guide student professional development are powerful tools in the curriculum. Faculty mentors who guide and provide longitudinal feedback to the student for ongoing growth and development are critical for constant re-enforcement.

1. **Reflective professional practice**: Reflecting on an ongoing basis for continuous professional and personal growth is an important skill set to foster in medical students. Sessions that discuss the importance of this activity, different types of reflections (journaling, verbal reflection, assignment specific reflection feeding into a portfolio), how to effectively link it to teaching and clinical experiences, and how to develop action plans set the stage for reflective practice. Timely and deliberate reflections built in the curriculum allow for practice: For example, if first year students are learning to elicit a medical history, an effective way for a student to improve these skills can be though a longitudinal patient experience where students submit a written reflection on their history taking before the experience, midway, and at the end of the experience. As with other skills, faculty feedback and debriefing is critical in helping students close behavioral, content based, and clinical performance gaps and address emotions so they can move forward.

    If students are asked to submit written reflections, a reflective portfolio in a learning management system may allow them to not only stay organized but see the improvements, and personal, emotional, and professional growth they have made. Ideally, the reflective portfolio would include all the components of professional/social identity and professional competence.

2. **Individualized Learning Plans**: One of the most underutilized modalities is building student skills in formulating their own plans for personal and professional goals. Since students have varying backgrounds, life experiences, and learning styles, the learning plans are best tailored to each individual need. The reflective portfolio often provides data for the students to generate these plans. The learning plans often have the following sections:

    - Standards and expectations
    - Self-assessment and reflection on targets for improvement

- ○ Faculty feedback
- ○ Establishing short term goals
- ○ Plan of action with timelines

Finally, organizational aspects such as a structure of Office of Student Affairs for academic and professional support and models such as Learning Communities are ways to support a medical student's professional development. Learning communities (faculty lead and peer role models) can provide crucial role modeling by allowing the students to observe and imitate behavior that is fundamental to the acquisition of a professional identity and the longitudinal guidance to foster the process.

CAREER DEVELOPMENT OF MEDICAL STUDENTS

Background

Professional and social identity formation as well as career development of medical students occur across a continuum and many elements and skills such as self-assessment, reflection, and resources such as faculty mentoring overlap across these growth domains. In the section below we further discuss elements related to a student's career development.

Career development in medical school follows a step-wise approach, with shift in focus from understanding oneself as a first year student to choosing a specialty in third year and then preparing for future career as a fourth year student. This requires active participation on behalf of the student under the guidance of faculty, including clerkship directors, residency program directors, student affairs faculty, as well as fellow students. There must be a structured approach to career advising, which includes required career advising sessions, self-assessment, confidential and individualized student assistance, and a continual needs assessment of both students and faculty.

The LCME standard 11 (Medical Student Academic Support, Career Advising, and Educational Records) requires that each medical school "provides effective academic support and career advising to all medical students to assist them in achieving their career goals and the school's medical education program objectives. All medical students have the same rights and receive comparable services (LCME, 2019)."

11.1 Academic Advising

A medical school has an effective system of academic advising in place for medical students that integrates the efforts of faculty members, course and clerkship directors, and student affairs staff with its counseling and tutorial services and ensures that medical students can obtain academic counseling from individuals who have no role in making assessment or promotion decisions about them.

11.2 Career Advising

A medical school has an effective career advising system in place that integrates the efforts of faculty members, clerkship directors, and student affairs staff to assist medical students in choosing elective courses, evaluating career options, and applying to residency programs.

The LCME (2019) clearly denotes that each student must have access to academic counseling from individuals that have no role in assessment or promotion decisions about them. This is an important distinction to make. In order to accomplish this, students must be provided with confidential advisors. Further, schools may also choose to provide "confidential" advisors within specialties who do not have a role in the residency selection process. Students are often concerned to discuss their performance and career options with the faculty whom are directly involved in their specialty of choice's residency recruitment.

The term advising is often used in conjunction with or even in lieu of counseling. While there is over-lap between the two, there are distinct differences. Kuhn et al. (2006) developed an advising-counseling continuum to delineate responsibilities as listed below:

Informational Advising is the first on the continuum and involves basic questions and providing in-formation only (no interpretation). For example, a student asks for the name of a USMLE Step 1 review course.

Explanatory Advising provides clarification of information which the student then will use to make a decision/act. For example, the student requests to do an international elective and asks regarding the application process for credit.

Developmental Advising provides insight into the students learning plans, which involves discussion options and values within the context of the students' own personal situation and goals. For example, a student originally thought they wanted to apply for a general surgery residency but now after completing their obstetrics/gynecology clerkship, they are unsure of which specialty is the better choice for them.

Mentoring is the most personal of these relationships, providing an ongoing relationship as a role model, providing them with support and encouragement to achieve their goals.

Personal Counseling is utilized when the students' individual concerns/problems extend beyond the expertise of the advisor. Adjustment and mental health concerns should be referred to trained counselors and therapists.

While advising and counseling often overlap, academic advisors focus on developing skills for the student to meet the requirements for academic success and ultimately graduation/employment. Coun-selors focus on skills to help students learn better coping and behavioral skills to make better personal decisions (Kuhn et al., 2006).

While the core foundational elements may be similar, individual schools have varied approaches to the structure of career and academic advising. Academic advising is generally housed within the Office of Student Affairs in order to provide students with confidential advising (specifically by individuals who do not have a role in the grading/evaluation of the student). For career specific advising, options (not mutually exclusive) include:

1. Careers in Medicine Division
   a. Placed within the Office of Student Affairs or the Office of Education.
   b. Usually includes a specific director (outside of the Offices of Student Affairs /Education deans)
2. Designated Learning Community Faculty
   a. Faculty time may be bought out (10-20% FTE) depending on their individual responsibilities; larger % is bought out if they participate in core faculty teaching as well (e.g. facilitation of small group activities in the pre-clerkship years).

       b.   Faculty are often matched with students in Year 1 of medical school and thus are often not related to their specialty choices.

3.   Specialty Specific Advisors
       a.   Each specialty has a core faculty contact(s) which the students readily have access to so that they can reach out in real time to discuss career options (faculty contact information often available on a central website).
       b.   Each specialty can also consider having a "confidential" advisor, one whom does not have any role in selection of students for residency positions.

In 2017, Canadian National Guidelines were published for integrating career advising into medical school curricula (Howse et al., 2017). These were in accordance to the current LCME standards. The five essential elements are as follows:

1.   A structured approach to career advising

Each school must integrate career advising into the curriculum with mandatory career advising sessions with a longitudinal approach covering career options, elective guidance, and applying to residency at a minimum. All students should be engaged in self-assessment and self-reflection with faculty available for assistance/guidance in debriefing. Confidential career guidance should be available to each student.

2.   Information about available career options

Early and diverse exposure to various clinical and community experiences should be available to all students, including interest groups, electives, community service, research, shadowing opportunities.

3.   Elective guidance

A core group of faculty should provide elective guidance with additional specialty specific career advisors available for additional assistance.

4.   Preparation for residency application

Students need to be prepared for all aspects of residency applications, including overall timelines, medical school performance evaluation (MSPE) letters, curriculum vitae, personal statements, letters of recommendation, and interviews.

5.   Social accountability

This is unique to Canada as their medical schools have a social accountability mandate. However, this information can be useful to US medical students – providing them with data on societal needs and health care resource projections which can be extremely helpful in deciding their future careers.

The above elements are discussed in greater detail by medical school year to provide a timeline of career advising.

Year 1-2 of Medical School: Self-Assessment and Self-Reflection

Student: During the first few months of medical school, the initial focus is on appropriate study habits and skills as they transition from undergraduate studies to the demands of medical school. As they develop a structured individualized study plan, there needs to be a shift towards self-assessment and self-reflection. Through the Association of American Medical Colleges (AAMC) Careers in Medicine (CiM), students can utilize various self-assessment tools to address specific characteristics and attributes, such as interests, values, skills, and personality type and learning style. Examples include:

1. **Medical Specialty Preference Inventory (MSPI)** is a 150 item self-assessment, measuring preference for specific activities, tasks, and experiences within medicine comparing them to 18 selected areas of medicine and 16 major specialties. This provides students with options to explore over the course of their medical school education (CiM AAMC, 2019).

2. **Physician Values in Practice Scale (PVIPS)** is a 60 item self-assessment to "identify how you prioritize six core values found in physician careers: autonomy, management, prestige, service, lifestyle, and scholarly pursuits." A student's scores are then categorized as low, moderate, and high for each of the six core values. This can help guide a student in qualities they are looking for in their future career, including location of practice: i.e., community-based hospital versus academic medical center versus private practice (CiM AAMC, 2019).

3. **Physician Skills Inventory (PSI)** is a 47 item self-assessment identifying an individual student's strengths in psychomotor, problem-solving, and counseling skills. The individual student's scores are then compared to skills identified by currently practicing physicians in primary care, medical, surgical, and technical specialties (CiM AAMC, 2019).

4. Personality Assessments are available via the Myers-Briggs Type Indicator (MBTI). The MBTI provides preferences in each of the following four pairs (Stilwell et al., 2000):
    ◦   Extraversion or Introversion (E or I). An extravert focuses on action, objects, and persons, whereas the introvert focuses on concepts and ideas.
    ◦   Sensing or Intuition (S or N). A sensing person uses the immediate and practical facts of life to obtain information while the intuitive person looks beyond the immediate to see the possibilities and underlying meaning of an experience.
    ◦   Thinking or Feeling (T or F). A thinker judges objectively, evaluating the causes of the events as well as the effects of decisions. The feeler judges subjectively and on a personal level, evaluating how choices may affect others.
    ◦   Judging or Perceiving (J or P). The judger prefers to plan, regulate and control events while the perceiver is flexible and adapts to life's events.

After completing the assessment, an individual receives a four-letter "type" (e.g., ISTP). As there are 4 pairs, there are 16 possible types. Stilwell et al. (2000) performed a retrospective study looking at changes in the MBTI profiles of US and Canadian medical students over a 40-year period of time. The "type" distribution of medical students remained relatively stable over time. When comparing E-I and T-F types, feeling (F) types and introverts (I) were significantly more likely to select primary care and less likely to select surgical residencies.

Faculty: Self-assessments can be useful in career choices for a student, however, they can also be overwhelming and/or confusing when results do not match a student's perceptions and/or existing career goals. No assessment is meant to decide a specialty for a student. Thus, it is essential that a faculty career advisor help guide the student through their individual results. In order to accomplish this, the advisor should complete these self-assessments themselves to get a better understanding of these tools, how they are completed, and how their own results match with their specialty/career.

Experiential Learning

Student: While a significant portion of Years 1 and 2 are spent in the classrooms and small group settings, there are a variety of ways to provide early clinical exposure as these are critical to shaping their future career plans:

- Primary care clinical preceptorships: These are often in primary care specialties either within the academic setting or in the local community.
- Subspecialty experiences may involve more shadowing due to limited clinical skills early in the student's career. However, they can be useful in allowing a student to develop a mentorship, including a glimpse into the day-to-day work of a specific specialty as well as work-life balance.
- Interest groups provide peer as well as faculty support and allow students to explore multiple specialties.
- Non-credit electives exploring specialty-specific topics can provide students with not only medical knowledge, but also opportunities to meet faculty from their specialty of interest, building relationships for future scholarly and clinical collaborations.
- Career nights sponsored through student affairs can bring together specialties across the medical school. Often a "speed-dating" approach is used to allow students to spend brief periods of time with multiple different specialties. These can involve both faculty and residents, either in one unified event or separate.
- Summer research is highly sought after by students, especially those who may be interested in competitive specialties. Provide students with structured research opportunities such as a research night.

Faculty: As an advisor, the faculty often guide the students through not only their clinical experiences for first and second year but also in selecting the best sequence of Year 3 clerkships and choosing electives. As elective time is often limited in core clerkship Year 3 phase and exposure to some specialties being limited within the required clerkships, students must be strategic with their choices.

Years 3-4: Exploring and Choosing a Specialty

Student: As students gain further clinical experience in Year 3, their perceived interests may change significantly. Thus, students are encouraged to retake the above self-assessments done in Years 1 and 2 as the results may change with the gained "real-life" experiences. Elective experiences remain essential for students to explore specialties further. This is especially crucial in the first half of Year 3 as students are often ranking sub-internship choices and applying for away electives by the mid-point of the academic year.

The AAMC does offer a clinical rotation evaluation tool to highlight your likes and dislikes for each clerkship (CiM AAMC, 2013). Whether a student uses this formal tool or simply documents in a journal, self-reflection is essential throughout Year 3 as a student's career choices are being finalized. Often a student is so engrossed within the clerkship and trying to balance clinical "work" week with studying that they lose sight of the bigger picture. Students should ask themselves these questions:

- Can I see myself practicing in this specialty and/or setting in the next 5 years? 10 years?
- Do I feel "at home" or "fit" in this specialty?
- Are my likes/dislikes related to the patient care/pathology seen or the specific individuals I was working with?

By spring of Year 3 (at the latest), students should be meeting with a faculty advisor/mentor within their field of interest (s) to discuss their individual competitiveness as well as the overall competitiveness of the specialty. This is the time to develop a strategic plan for obtaining strong letters of recommendation. As it is never too early to ask for a letter of recommendation – this can be done within the core clerkships of third year. Students must be strategic in scheduling of subinternships, away rotations, and electives in order to ensure they will obtain a minimum of three letters.

Students should research each specialty to obtain the following information:

- Understanding of the day to day work within a specialty,
- Requirements for residency,
- Specialty statistics to assess competitiveness.

This can be obtained through the AAMC, Fellowship and Residency Electronic Interactive Database Access (FREIDA), faculty mentors, as well as formal residency information sessions. The program director or other designated faculty hold an information session for students in the spring of Year 3 to address many of these concerns as well as set aside time to meet with students individually to assess their application strengths and weaknesses.

Faculty

Byerley and Tilley (2018) created a pyramid model for career guidance in graduate medical education (i.e. residencies), which can be applied at the student level as well.

Assets: Utilizing the students' self-assessments, the faculty advisor should first have the student self-reflect on their individual strengths as well as explore the students' USMLE scores, scholarly activity, etc., in order to provide the student with an assessment of their competitiveness.

Joy: Ask the student to list what the student enjoys most about medicine: i.e. challenge of the unknown, direct communication with patients, teaching.

Pride: In thirty years, what does the student hope to be known for? Is it a specific research or clinical area? Is it related to service or the community as a whole? This may help a student prioritize specialty choices.

Purpose/Social accountability: What societal or clinical needs does the student feel compelled to address?

In the 1993 AAMC Medical School Graduation Questionnaire (GQ), over 8,000 Year 4 medical students rated the influence of 36 factors on their specialty choice using a 0-4 Likert-type scale (4=major influence). The following factors received a rating of 3-4 (strong to major influence): types of patient problems encountered, consistent with personality, opportunity to make differences in people's lives, interest in helping people, intellectual content of the specialty, challenging diagnostic problems, and diversity in diagnosis and therapy (Kassebaum & Szenas, 1994). Now, over 25 years later, these factors often still hold true. Most importantly, the faculty must listen to the student, process the student's strengths and vision for the future, and assess their "match" within that field, and provide individualized feedback.

Peer

Year 4 students can provide invaluable advice regarding their journey in choosing a specialty. This can be done in several ways. A formal mentorship program can be structured to have select Year 4 students available in each of the specialties as points of contact for Year 3 students. Schools that use the Learning Community model often have senior students hold sessions. Match panels by specialty are also helpful to provide a variety of perspectives in one setting. It is important for faculty to be engaged in the process so they can suitably guide the students to avoid over-generalizing and be sure to include their unique attributes as much as possible to contextualize the peer advice.

Preparing for Residency

While choosing a specialty is an enormous first step, it is only the beginning of the application process. Students are overwhelmed with not only the application process itself but also the large number of residency programs with confusion on how to narrow down their program lists.

Step 1:   Selecting Desired Program Qualities

AAMC Careers in Medicine has Residency Preference Profile (2019) tool which students can use to self-assess in the following categories: educational factors, clinical duties/patient care, workplace environment, compensation/benefits, staff characteristics, quality of life, work/life balance.

Step 2:   Create a Potential Program List

Create an initial list of residency programs using AMA's FREIDA online database, which will allow a student to search for programs by specialty, state, institution, program size, and specialty training tracks (looking for qualities noted in Step 1 as well as linking it now to geographic location).

Step 3:   Narrow the Program List

Narrow the program list based on the following:

- Utilize Residency Preference Exercise to prioritize program qualities.
- Research individual residency programs through the CiM residency program profiles (CiM AAMC, 2019).
- Review list of programs with specialty-specific advisor and/or dean of student affairs. They can offer insight into quality of programs outside the traditional on-line statistics (i.e. their own personal experiences as well as those of recent graduates).
- In conjunction with the specialty-specific advisor and/or dean of student affairs:
  - Review students' competitiveness
    - USMLE Step Scores
    - Class rank (if utilized)
    - AOA status

- Clinical clerkship grades
- Research/scholarly activity
- Service/ Leadership experiences
  - Review the specialty's competitiveness
    - American Medical Association (AMA) Fellowship and Residency Electronic Interactive Database (FREIDA) Online can provide minimum Step 1 and Step 2 scores to be considered for interview.
    - National Resident Matching Program (NRMP) Data Reports provides outcomes from previous matches, including number of positions offered and filled for each program by year.
  - Match the two together to create a reasonable list
    - Encourage application to highly competitive programs while ensuring the student applies to moderately competitive "target" and "safety" programs as well.
    - Connect students with recent graduates in the specialty of their choice to get additional feedback on individual residency programs.

How does a student decide on the number of programs to apply to? Based on AAMC ERAS data on applicants in select specialties from 2011-2016, researchers used the number of programs an applicant applied to, most recent USMLE Step 1 score, and the applicant's type (U.S. MD, etc.) to predict whether an applicant entered a residency program in the application year. The research demonstrated that "there is a point at which submitting one additional application results in a lower rate of return on the applicant's likelihood of entering a residency program," which varies based on USMLE Step 1 scores as well as specialty and applicant type. As expected, applicants with higher USMLE Step 1 Scores required fewer applications and competitive specialties required more applications. AAMC has published data for multiple specialties, including anesthesiology, dermatology, diagnostic radiology, emergency medicine, internal medicine, internal medicine-pediatrics, pediatrics, plastic surgery, etc. For example, as a US MD applicant applying to pediatrics with a Step 1 Score >/= 230, the point of diminishing return is 12 applications. Whereas for a US MD applicant applying to internal medicine-pediatrics with a Step 1 Score >/= 238, the point of diminishing return is 17 applications (CiM AAMC, 2019).

Preparation of Curriculum Vitae (CV)

While students will complete the CV portion of the residency application in the ERAS template, they still need to formulate a traditional CV to be distributed to their letter of recommendation writers. Often students ask whether they should include work experiences from high school or even college on their CV. In general, any experience that can either showcase the student's dedicated ongoing interest in a specific field or demonstrate skills essential to being a physician should be included. For example, a prior career in teaching or even teaching demonstrates skills as an educator which are essential for becoming an effective physician (teaching students, residents, peers, and patients). Experience as a camp counselor demonstrates their abilities to lead, multi-task, and communicate or their passion to care for children for a pediatrics career. Service (school as well as community-based activities) should be highlighted. Shadowing experiences in high school on the other hand are often used as exposure to clinical medicine and entry to medical school and unless they demonstrate significant passion for a specific patient cohort or specialty, may be excluded.

If a student participated in specific interest groups/clubs, they should note their specific role (i.e. highlight leadership roles) as well as a brief description of the group/club if appropriate unless it has a national presence (such as American Medical Student Association, etc.). Hobbies/interests can also be highlighted and are often used as a talking point at the residency interview. Thus, be sure that the student is ready to discuss all components of their CV, whether it be research or hobbies. If they note they are avid runners, they should be able to have a conversation about such in an interview.

Preparation of Personal Statement

Personal statements are the next step in the application journey. This is the first glimpse into the unique qualities and/or story of the applicant. This is not meant to rehash the CV. The personal statement should be just that – "personal." The best way to accomplish this is for the student to tell the story of their journey in choosing the specialty. General outline of the personal statement should be as follows:

1. Opening paragraph can summarize why the student entered medicine overall.
2. Student's journey to choosing this specific specialty.
3. How the student's personality/characteristics/interests fit with their chosen specialty and why the specialty fits the student.
4. A patient example (or life example) that demonstrates the above.
5. Student should consider explaining any circumstances surrounding "red flags" on your application, such as course repeats, Step failures, etc. However, this should be discussed with the dean of student affairs.
6. Student should then describe what they are looking for in a program. Be cautious in avoiding too specific of details so that the student does not exclude programs on their list.

It should never be longer than one page and readability is important. Everything written in the personal statement is fair game on the interview. The student should always have multiple persons review their personal statement in advance of submission: someone who knows the student well but is outside of medicine (family, significant other, friend), someone who knows the student well and is in medicine (can be peer), someone in the specialty they are applying for (faculty).

Mock Interviews

Mock interviews are essential in a student's preparation for residency applications. These are generally coordinated by the Office of Student Affairs and/or the careers in medicine director. Ideally, the mock interviewers are performed by faculty who are directly involved in medical student and/or residency education. Mock interviewers should be provided with sample interview questions (Wong, 2019).

Students should be instructed to treat the mock interview as "real" in every way, including wearing appropriate attire. Faculty should provide feedback on every aspect of the interview including attire, overall demeanor, communication skills, and the content of their answers.

Special Situations

MD/PhD students are unique in their advising/mentoring needs. First, while completing their PhD, they are generally removed from any clinical work for at least 2-3 years if not longer. As a result, their transition back into their clinical clerkships can be challenging, both in patient care skills as well as standardized test taking skills. If possible, starting the students on a longer clinical clerkship (such as medicine) can be helpful to provide them with a longer adjustment time. In addition, schools may provide a clinical "immersion" before starting their 3rd year clerkship such as an early responder course to hone their clinical skills.

Career advising may require dual advising in areas of clinical medicine as well as research depending on their career goals. However, it is just as important for the dual career advisors to connect and perhaps even meet all together with the student to avoid providing conflicting information.

Decelerated students will require additional support through the Office of Student Affairs as well as their individual career counseling. This is a complicated topic as the guidance needs to be individualized to each student to their own circumstances as advising will defer greatly from a student whom decelerated for a personal/family emergency versus academic difficulties.

In highly competitive specialties, more students are now completing a *Scholars Year* in order to increase their publications/scholarly activity to improve their chance at matching into their specialty and/or program of choice. While this can be an excellent opportunity for research, this can also set the student up for challenges in successful completion of the USMLE Step 2 Clinical Skills and Clinical Knowledge exams. As many students will have little clinical exposure during this year, advisors should discuss strategies and timelines for completion of the students USMLE exams so that it will not affect their performance and/or residency applications.

Non-clinical career options may be a first choice for a medical student or may be the best choice based on their medical school performance. While there are organizations now specializing in non-clinical career options, each medical school should have a list of resources as well as contact information for potential advisors currently in non-clinical careers for students.

Parallel tracks may be needed when a student's level of competitiveness does not match with their top specialty choice. This often requires a multi-prong approach with the individual student's advisors (academic and career) to come together with the student to develop a parallel track or "back-up" plan. The student needs to reflect on the qualities that attracted them to their top specialty and explore specialties that may have overlapping or similar qualities.

Challenges for Students and Faculty

In a national survey of pediatric clerkship directors in 2013, 68% of clerkship directors had a formal role in advising with over half of these (58%) also playing a role in the intern selection process at their own institution and 39% serving on the intern selection committee (Ryan, 2015). This illustrates the importance of identifying "confidential" advisors within each specialty whom do not have a role in resident recruitment.

Over the last decade, the number of applications per student has grown exponentially across all fields. Mean applications per US/Canada applicant has grown in nearly every specialty, from primary care to emergency medicine to surgical subspecialties (Chang & Erhardt, 2015). In a survey of fourth year medical students in 2014, students applied to a mean of 21.7 residency programs in psychiatry to a high of 58.2 in surgery. Of these, the average number of residency interviews ranged from 10.7 in psychiatry to a high of 16.9 in radiology (Benson, 2015). While a change in competitiveness of applicants has not been demonstrated, students are often counseled to increase their number of applications to "overinsure" their match. This is creating an undue financial burden on students (application costs and travel expenses) as well as a time burden on residency program directors to sort through and select appropriate applicants (Callaway, 2017).

When reviewing unmatched U.S. allopathic seniors in the 2015 main residency match (N=299), the mean step score was 225.2 compared to a mean of 233.6 for the matched U.S seniors (P<.001). Based on USMLE Step 1 scores, applicants were rated as "strong" if 1 standard deviation higher than mean in their specialty; "solid" if between mean and 1 SD higher than the mean; "marginal" if between mean and 1 SD below mean; and "weak" if more than 1 SD lower than the group mean. Not surprisingly, the majority of unmatched applicants had USMLE scores more than 1 SD below the mean for their specialty. Marginal and weak U.S. seniors also applied to more than twice the number of programs than they received interviews for. However, the strong unmatched U.S. seniors applied to twice as many programs on average with roughly the same number of interviews as their matched colleagues (Liang, 2017). This suggests that program directors are now using other modalities to screen for interviews. The NRMP Program Director Survey demonstrates an increased focus on letters of recommendation in the specialty as well as the medical school performance evaluation (MSPE) due to negative evaluations correlating with problem behavior (NRMP, 2018).

Noting such a rapid increase in the number of applications per student, some schools such as the University of Maryland School of Medicine instituted an electronic interview tracking tool to help improve advising and match outcomes. They created a homegrown student and curriculum management system called MedScope. Students' residency applications are downloaded from ERAS and uploaded into MedScope after the September 15th opening date, which provides a list of residency programs each student applied to. This also maintains a master file of all programs the UMSOM students have applied to and/or matched in the preceding 10 years so that long-terms trends can be utilized. Students are then reminded to update data such as callback status, interview status, and optional comments. The office of student affairs deans then review on an ongoing basis and provide additional counseling to students, such as when to reach out to residency programs they have not heard from and safety vs reach programs. Utilizing this system, they noted an increase in their match rate from 86% in 2015 to 94% in 2017 (Frayha, 2019).

In addition, the University of Texas Southwestern Medical Center has developed a nationally available tool, Texas STAR (Seeking Transparency in Application to Residency) which "acts as an information clearinghouse for participating medical schools that complete the annual survey." Matched 4th year medical students provide their own data on board exam scores, rank, publications, programs applied to vs interviewed at, and where they matched (UT Southwestern Medical Center, 2019).

FUTURE RESEARCH DIRECTIONS

As medical school curriculum evolves in becoming a truly individualized curriculum with increasing portions of on-line learning, small group exercises, and earlier clinical immersion, further studies need to be done to assess the effectiveness and utility of various learning community models. Learning community models vary widely across schools. While some have a cross-over model between professional development, academic advising, educators, as well as career advising, others have separated each of these areas out to have parallel advisors. As we transition to individualized learning plans for students, should we also be creating individualized professional and career development plans with advising integrated as well? Future research directions will focus on predictors of successful residency match while balancing number of interviews/financial burden on the students as well as ways to streamline medical student data such as creation of uniform data collection such as standard letters of recommendation in Emergency Medicine.

SUMMARY/CONCLUSION

Professional and career development are woven together in a lifelong longitudinal experience. At the core of professional development, students must become self-aware, reflect on their own unconscious biases, and learn to work together as part of an effective inter-professional team. Through this process, leadership skills emerge as the learner recognizes their individual strengths and identifies management styles to effectively lead as they evolve in their journey while building resilience to cope with the stresses of physician life. Clinical reasoning and feedback are core underlying principles for the individual to both learn as well as eventually teach others. At every point in this process, career advising is essential to assist the student to explore their future goals and link them back to the reason why they entered medicine.

Professional and career development of medical students are just as important as learning the foundations of basic sciences and how to apply it to clinical sciences as well as the basic clinical skills every physician needs to know. Thus, each medical school must create the core structure and provide students as well as faculty with the essential tools for self-assessment and self-reflection, including recognition of unconscious biases, and ability for individualized academic and career counseling. The core skills for lifelong learning, development of professional behaviors, and choosing the right specialty for an individual student are essential in developing successful medical students and ultimately successful physicians who continue to find the joy in medicine as well as serve their communities.

REFERENCES

American Medical Association. (2017). *Creating a community of innovation.* Retrieved June 9, 2019, from https://www.ama-assn.org/sites/ama-assn.org/files/corp/media-browser/public/about-ama/ace-monograph-interactive_0.pdf

American Medical Association. (2019). *Code of medical ethics: professional self-regulation.* Retrieved June 9, 2019, from https://www.ama-assn.org/delivering-care/ethics/code-medical-ethics-professional-self-regulation

Arnold, L., Shue, C. K., Kalishman, S., Prislin, M., Pohl, C., Pohl, H., & Stern, D. T. (2007). Can There Be a Single System for Peer Assessment of Professionalism among Medical Students? A Multi-Institutional Study. *Academic Medicine, 82*(6), 578–586. doi:10.1097/ACM.0b013e3180555d4e PMID:17525545

Bannister, S. L., Wickenheiser, H. M., Kin, B., & Keegan, D. A. (2014). Key elements of highly effective teams. *Pediatrics, 133*(2), 184–186. doi:10.1542/peds.2013-3734 PMID:24446450

Benson, N. M., Stickle, T. R., & Raszka, W. V. Jr. (2015). Going "Fourth" From Medical School: Fourth-Year Medical Students' Perspectives on the Fourth Year of Medical School. *Academic Medicine, 94*(3), 348–342. PMID:27002891

Brendan, M. (2017). *4 phases to making goal of lifelong physician learner a reality.* Retrieved June 9, 2019, from https://www.ama-assn.org/education/accelerating-change-medical-education/4-phases-making-goal-lifelong-physician-learner

Byerley, J., & Tilly, A. (2018). A Simple Pyramid Model for Career Guidance. *Journal of Graduate Medical Education, 10*(5), 497–499. doi:10.4300/JGME-D-18-00028.1 PMID:30386473

Callaway, P., Melhado, T., Walling, A., & Groskurth, J. (2017). Financial and Time Burdens for Medical Students Interviewing for Residency. *Family Medicine, 49*(2), 137–140. PMID:28218940

Careers in Medicine (CiM), Association of American Medical Colleges (AAMC). (2013). *Clinical rotation evaluation.* Retrieved June 9, 2019 from https://www.aamc.org/cim/download/382812/data/clinicalrotationevaluation.pdf

Careers in Medicine (CiM), Association of American Medical Colleges (AAMC). (2019). *About self-assessment.* Retrieved June 9, 2019 from https://www.aamc.org/cim/specialty/understandyourself/472322/aboutself-assessment.html

Careers in Medicine (CiM), Association of American Medical Colleges (AAMC). (2019). *Residency preference exercise.* Retrieved June 9, 2019 from https://www.aamc.org/cim/residency/programs/residencypreferenceexercise/

Careers in Medicine (CiM), Association of American Medical Colleges (AAMC). (2019). *Apply smart: new data to consider.* Retrieved June 9, 2019 from https://www.aamc.org/cim/480276/applysmartnewdatatoconsider.html

Chang, C. W. D., & Erhardt, B. F. (2015). Rising Residency Applications. *Otolaryngology - Head and Neck Surgery, 153*(5), 702–705. doi:10.1177/0194599815597216 PMID:26243024

DallaPiazza, M., Padilla-Register, M., Dwarakanath, M., Obamedo, E., Hill, J., Soto-Greene, M. L. (2018). Exploring racism and health: an intensive interactive session for medical students. *MedEdPORTAL, 14*, 10783.

Epstein, R. M. (2007). Assessment in medical education. *The New England Journal of Medicine, 356*(4), 387–396. doi:10.1056/NEJMra054784 PMID:17251535

Epstein, R. M., & Hundert, E. M. (2002). Defining and assessing professional competence. *Journal of the American Medical Association, 287*(2), 226–235. doi:10.1001/jama.287.2.226 PMID:11779266

Epstein, R. M., & Krasner, M. S. (2013). Physician resilience: What it means, why it matters, and how to promote it. *Academic Medicine, 88*(3), 301–303. doi:10.1097/ACM.0b013e318280cff0 PMID:23442430

Frayha, N., Raczek, J., Lo, J., Martinez, J., & Parker, D. (2019). An Electronic Interview Tracking Tool to Guide Medical Students Through the Match; Improvements in Advising and Match Outcomes. *Academic Medicine, 94*(3), 348–352. doi:10.1097/ACM.0000000000002522 PMID:30431454

Howse, K., Harris, J., & Dalgarno, N. (2017). Canadian National Guidelines and Recommendations for Integrating Career Advising into Medical School Curricula. *Academic Medicine, 92*(11), 1543–1548. doi:10.1097/ACM.0000000000001720 PMID:28445219

Human Resources for Health Global Resource Center. (2019). *Why is teamwork in health care important?* Retrieved June 9, 2019, from https://www.hrhresourcecenter.org/HRH_Info_Teamwork.html

Kassebaum, D. G., & Szenas, P. L. (1994). Factors influencing the specialty choices of 1993 medical school graduates. *Academic Medicine, 69*(2), 163–170. doi:10.1097/00001888-199402000-00027 PMID:8311892

Kassirer, J. P. (2010). Teaching Clinical Reasoning: Case-Based and Coached. *Academic Medicine, 85*(7), 1118–1124. doi:10.1097/ACM.0b013e3181d5dd0d PMID:20603909

Kirch, D. G. (2007). *Culture and the Courage to Change.* AAMC President's Address 2007 Annual Meeting. Retrieved June 9, 2019, from https://www.aamc.org/download/169722/data/kirchspeech2007.pdf

Kuhn, T., Gordon, V. N., & Webber, J. (2006). The Advising and Counseling Continuum: Triggers for Referral. *NACADA Journal, 26*(1), 24–31. doi:10.12930/0271-9517-26.1.24

Liaison Committee on Medical Education. (2019). *Functions and structure of a medical school: standards for accreditation of medical education programs leading to the MD degree.* Retrieved June 9, 2019, from http://lcme.org/publications/

Liang, M., Curtin, L. S., Signer, M. M., & Savoia, M. C. (2017). Unmatched U.S. Allopathic Seniors in the 2015 Main Residency Match: A Study of Applicant Behavior, Interview Selection, and Match Outcome. *Academic Medicine, 92*(7), 991–997. doi:10.1097/ACM.0000000000001501 PMID:28657556

Michaelson, L., & Richards, B. (2005). Drawing conclusions from the team-learning literature in health-sciences education. *Teaching and Learning in Medicine, 17*(1), 85–88. doi:10.120715328015tlm1701_15 PMID:15691820

National Resident Matching Program. (2018). *Results of the 2018 NRMP Program Director Survey.* Retrieved July 26, 2019, from https://mk0nrmp3oyqui6wqfm.kinstacdn.com/wp-content/uploads/2018/07/NRMP-2018-Program-Director-Survey-for-WWW.pdf

NHS Institute for Innovation and Improvement and Academy of Medical Royal Colleges. (2010). Medical leadership competency framework: enhancing engagement in medical leadership. 3rd ed. Retrieved June 9, 2019, from https://www.leadershipacademy.nhs.uk/wp-content/uploads/2012/11/NHSLeadership-Leadership-Framework-Medical-Leadership-Competency-Framework-3rd-ed.pdf

Ryan, M. S., Levine, L. J., Colbertz-Getz, J. M., Spector, N. D., & Fromme, H. B. (2015). Advising Medical Students for the Match: A National Survey of Pediatric Clerkship Directors. *Academic Pediatrics, 15*(4), 374–379. doi:10.1016/j.acap.2015.03.009 PMID:25922334

Samarakoon, L., Fernando, T., Rodrigo, C., & Rajapakse, S. (2013). Learning styles and approaches to learning among medical undergraduates and postgraduates. *BMC Medical Education, 13*(1), 42. doi:10.1186/1472-6920-13-42 PMID:23521845

Soemantri, D., Mccoll, G., & Dodds, A. (2018). Measuring medical students' reflection on their learning: Modification and validation of the motivated strategies for learning questionnaire (MSLQ). *BMC Medical Education*, *18*(1), 274. doi:10.118612909-018-1384-y PMID:30466427

Staats, C., Capatosto, K., Wright, R. A., & Contractor, D. (2015). *State of the Science Implicit bias review 2015*. Retrieved June 9, 2019, from http://kirwaninstitute.osu.edu/wp-content/uploads/2015/05/2015-kirwan-implicit-bias.pdf

Stillwell, N. A., Wallick, M. M., Thal, S. E., & Burleson, J. A. (2000). Myers-Briggs Type and Medical Specialty Choice: A New Look at an Old Question. *Teaching and Learning in Medicine*, *12*(1), 14–20. doi:10.1207/S15328015TLM1201_3 PMID:11228862

The University of Texas Southwestern Medical Center. (2019). *Texas STAR*. Retrieved July 26, 2019, from https://www.utsouthwestern.edu/education/medical-school/about-the-school/student-affairs/texas-star.html

Wong, J. G. (2019). *The real questions behind three challenging interview questions and how to answer them*. Careers in Medicine (CiM), Association of Medical Colleges. Retrieved June 9, 2019, from https://www.aamc.org/cim/residency/application/interviewing/338086/interviewquestions.html

KEY TERMS AND DEFINITIONS

Advisor: For purposes of this chapter, refers to individuals providing academic and career instruction. An advisor may provide clarification to procedures within the institution, insight into a student's academic performance and how that relates to future career goals, including career options.

Clinical Reasoning: Also known as clinical judgment; the process of obtaining history and physical exam findings (signs/symptoms), then processing this information to understand the problem(s), develop a differential diagnosis, and implement a management plan.

Conscious Bias: A set of attitudes and beliefs that we have toward an individual or group at a conscious level; deliberate thoughts in response to a perceived threat.

Counselor: For purposes of this chapter, this refers to individuals with graduate-level training to provide personal counseling services.

Feedback: Discussing observations and recommendations with a learner with the goal to either improve specific behaviors or reinforce specific good behaviors.

Mentor: While a mentor can be considered an advisor, this implies an ongoing relationship, often being a role model for the student and providing the student with longitudinal time and support.

Unconscious Bias: Also known as implicit social cognition or implicit bias; attitudes or stereotypes that affect our understanding, actions, and decisions in an unconscious manner.

Chapter 17
Clinical Educator Track Resident Programs:
Lessons Learned From Innovative Programs

Michael W. Stumpf
Louisiana State University Health Sciences Center, USA

Sonya D. Hayes
(iD) https://orcid.org/0000-0002-6826-2117
The University of Tennessee, USA

ABSTRACT

Medical residents have a growing responsibility to educate their fellow residents and serve as the primary teachers for medical students; however, many residents have reported lacking the skills needed to be effective teachers. Clinical educator tracks (CET) were designed to provide a more intense and diverse opportunity for residents to receive training in areas of learning theory, teaching, evaluation and assessment, curriculum design, research, and leadership. This chapter highlights promising practices in established CET programs in the United States and spotlights one CET program in Louisiana as an example. Based on a review of the literature, CET programs have the following promising practices in common: a commitment to teaching and learning, continuous improvement through program design and evaluation, and a focus on leadership and mentoring. The authors elaborate on the CET program at LSU Health Center and discuss future trends in CET programming.

INTRODUCTION

In the past decade, medical education has seen an increased demand for faculty with expertise in teaching (Knight et al., 2017). Medical residents have a growing responsibility to educate their fellow residents and serve as the primary teachers for medical students within teaching hospitals, providing between one-

DOI: 10.4018/978-1-7998-1468-9.ch017

third and two thirds of medical students' education (Smith, McCormick, & Huang, 2014). Recognizing the significant role that residents have in medical education, accreditation organizations require that residents are adequately prepared for teaching roles. Resident-as-teacher programs were developed to address teaching skills but were limited in their scope. Based on faculty development programs, clinical educator tracks were designed to provide a more intense and diverse opportunity for residents to receive training in areas of learning theory, teaching, evaluation and assessment, curriculum design, research, and leadership. Despite a growing demand for skilled teachers in graduate medical education, clinician-educator tracks for residents are few and far between (Heflin et al., 2009).

Career development as a medical educator requires careful planning to ensure that residents acquire various knowledge and skills (Roberts et al., 2014), including the ability to design and develop optimal and innovative curriculum, instruction, and assessment. Clinician-Education Tracks (CET) can prepare residents for a career in education and assist residents in developing their skills in curriculum, instruction, and assessment. CET programs offer improvement in medical education by preparing residents to be effective teachers. By highlighting innovative and quality CET programs in medical education, we can examine how learning is developed through real-time experiences in the residency.

Our purpose in this chapter is twofold. First, we review the literature on clinical educator track (CET) programs for residents and elaborate on the methods and procedures for creating an optimal clinical education program. To achieve this purpose, we reviewed descriptive studies on clinical education track programs in the United States and synthesized the data from these programs to highlight current practices and trends in CET programming and training. Second, we describe a clinical educator track program at Louisiana State University's (LSU Health Baton Rouge) Internal Medicine Residency in Baton Rouge. LSU Health Baton Rouge's CET program offers residents a unique experience to explore and engage in teaching and leading in medicine, including an opportunity to collaborate with LSU's School of Education.

BACKGROUND

Medical education is currently comprised of three areas: undergraduate, postgraduate and the continuing professional development of established clinicians; however, this was not always the case (Swanwick, 2014). In the 19th century, medical education in the U.S.A. took place in small "proprietary schools with limited facilities, few formal requirements, and little academic content" (Barchi & Lowery, 2000, p. 899); however, by the turn of the 20th century, medical schools had established four-year formalized training programs with clinical requirements. The required clinical component of medical schools primarily fell on practicing physicians who taught residents in an apprentice-type model. Many practicing physicians reported increase workloads and longer hours as they maintained their patient loads and taught residents, and they were not compensated for their additional role and responsibilities (McCullough, Marton, Ramnanan, 2015). Consequently, many of these physicians chose not to engage or continue as clinical educators. As medical schools found it increasingly difficult to recruit and retain physicians willing to teach students and residents, clinical educator track programs emerged (Kubiak, Guidot, Trimm, Kamen, & Roman, 2012). Clinical educator track programs typically place more emphasis on preparing residents for teaching and clinical skills. Over the past three decades, clinician-educators have become critical to the success of medical education (Barchi & Lowery, 2000; Levinson & Rubenstein, 2000; Lin et al., 2016), and as such, clinical-educator tracks have become equally important.

The role of clinician-educators in post-graduate medical education has steadily changed due to the growth of medical education research that supports effective practices in teaching (Helfin, Pinheiro, Kaminetzky, & McNeill, 2009). CET programs are designed to develop teaching skills (Ahn, Martin, Farnan, & Fromme, 2018), and an increasing number of residents have expressed an interest in becoming clinician-educators (Chen, Miloslavsky, Winn, & McSparron, 2018). Benefits of residents participating in CET programs include: improved content knowledge, mentoring skills, clinical instruction, enthusiasm for teaching, learner-centered teaching, and a better understanding of educational theory and practices (Ramani, Mann, Taylor, & Thampy, 2016). The Liaison Committee on Medical Education (LCME) and the Accreditation Council of Graduate Medical Education (ACGME) require that residents engage in teacher training to develop skills as educators (Borges, Navarro, Grover, & Hoban, 2010), but they do not offer guidelines for how to prepare residents as teachers (Ahn et al., 2018). Once residents become clinician educators, they are expected to: a) develop the knowledge and skills for effective clinical teaching; b) design new research-based curricula; c) evaluate student learning and provide meaningful feedback; d) evaluate program effectiveness and make recommendations for improvement; and e) develop the skills (e.g. visioning, strategic planning, supervision, etc.) needed to become a capable administrator, leader, and change agent. Developing clinical educators to effectively address all of these requirements is the primary goal of clinical educator track (CET) programs.

RESEARCH STRATEGIES FOR BOOK CHAPTER

We conducted an extensive search of the literature published between 2000 and 2019, using ERIC, Medline, PubMed, and Google Scholar databases, with key terms: *medical education, clinical educator track programs,* and *residents.* Our initial query found over 868 articles and books on clinical educators and medical education. We narrowed the scope to only peer-reviewed articles and found 693 articles. We narrowed the search again by focusing only on educator programs within medical education and found 65 articles.

After reviewing and categorizing these 65 articles, we identified ten CET programs in the United States mentioned in the literature. Various scholars (Adamson, Goodman, Kritek, Luks, Tonelli, & Benditt, 2015; Ahn, Martin, Farnan, & Fromme, 2018; Chen, Wamsley, Azzam, Julian, Irby, & O'Sullivan, 2017; Heflin, Pinheiro, Kaminetzky, & McNeill, 2009; Jibson, Hilty, Arlinghaus, Ball, McCarthy, Seritan, & Servis, 2010; Lin, Sattler, Yu, Basaviah, & Schillinger, 2016; Schnapp, Fant, & Gisondi, 2017; Smith, McCormick, & Huang, 2014) discuss these different programs and offer descriptions of practices and program features for each one. We synthesized the information about each program to determine current practices and trends in clinical educator track programming. The ten CET programs are:

1. The Graduate Medical Education Scholars Track, The Pritzker School of Medicine, University of Chicago
2. Clinical Scholars Track at the University of Michigan
3. The Clinician-Educator Track at Baylor College of Medicine
4. The Resident Educator Track at the University of California Davis School of Medicine
5. The O'Connor Stanford Leaders in Education Residency (OSLER) track at O'Connor Hospital, Stanford University
6. Clinical Educator Track at Beth Israel Deaconess Medical Center, Harvard Medical School

7. Health Professions Education Pathway at the University of California San Francisco
8. Emergency Medicine Scholarly Track in Education at Northwestern University
9. The Clinician-Educator Track of the University of Washington Pulmonary and Critical Care Medicine Fellowship Program
10. Clinician-Educator Track at Duke University Medical Center

PROMISING PRACTICES

Through an analysis of various published articles on these clinical educator track (CET) programs, we determined that CET programs have the following promising practices in common: a commitment to teaching and learning, continuous improvement through program design and evaluation, and a focus on leadership and mentoring.

A Commitment to Teaching and Learning

A primary practice that all CET programs have in common is a commitment to developing clinical educators as effective teachers. Given the many skills required to be both a physician and a teacher, residents who can teach effectively are more likely to be competent physicians (Smith, Newman, & Huang, 2018). Srinivasan et al. (2011) developed a conceptual framework to identify six core competencies required of an effective teacher in medical education. These competencies include:

1. Medical (or content) knowledge in which competent educators are experts in their field;
2. Learner centeredness in which medical educators are committed to their students' growth and success;
3. Interpersonal and communication skills in which medical educators have flexible teaching styles to meet the needs of their students;
4. Professionalism and role modeling in which medical educators demonstrate best teaching and clinical practices and model these practices for their students;
5. Practice-based reflection and improvement in which medical educators exhibit life-long learning and a commitment to improving their instruction for their students;
6. Systems-based learning in which medical educators utilize available resources within medical education to advocate for students and optimize learning. (pp. 1214-1215)

These six competencies reflect what is expected of competent clinical educators in the area of teaching in order to support student learning. Additionally, as teachers, clinical educators facilitate active learning, leverage principles of adult learning, utilize needs assessments to design curricula, lead interactive small and large group discussions, provide effective feedback, experiment with innovative pedagogy, identify opportunities to use education technology, and develop appropriately challenging assessments (Roberts, Schwartzstein, & Weinberger, 2014).

Residents in CET programs need formal training in classroom teaching, meaningful feedback, curriculum development, assessment, and educational theory (Jibson et al., 2010), and they should have the ability to demonstrate their ability to teach, provide feedback, and develop curriculum (Srinivasan et al., 2011). Residents can further their teaching skills through direct teaching activities such as leading small groups of medical students on clinical rounds, presenting lectures, or professional development workshops (Adamson, Goodman, Kritek, Luks, Tonelli, & Benditt, 2015). Miloslavsky, Boyer, Winn, Stafford, and McSparron (2016) highlight several strategies that can support residents in developing their teaching skills:

- Include medical education topics in core curricula
- Integrate teaching into daily responsibilities
- Design specific teaching roles for residents on clinical rotations
- Encourage residents to engage in teaching junior trainees as part of their clinical responsibilities (e.g., teaching the primary team during consultation)
- Have expert faculty observe residents teaching on a regular basis and provide feedback
- Obtain feedback from trainees regarding resident teaching skills
- Emphasize teaching as a focus of the division
- Include medical education topics in division conferences
- Provide faculty development to enhance teaching and feedback skills
- Support educators within the division to model effective teaching and provide feedback. (p. 467)

By finding ways for residents to practice their teaching, they become more confident in their content knowledge and their instructional knowledge.

A major component of developing teaching skills is an obligation of providing specific and timely feedback. Residents in CET programs should be observed teaching and given high-quality feedback from faculty members (Miloslavsky et al., 2016); moreover, teaching residents how to give constructive feedback in clinical settings is equally important. Residents need to learn that when giving feedback, it is best to a) be honest and offer feedback as soon as possible; b) be direct with ways to improve; c) give an opportunity for the person receiving the feedback to reflect on their performance; d) offer support; and e) acknowledge the good things. Residents can practice giving meaningful and constructive feedback through peer observations and role-playing in class as faculty mentors supervise and offer support and advice.

Learning in CET programs is fundamentally based on adult learning theory. Not only should faculty in CET programs develop their instruction and class lessons using adult learning theory, but residents need to possess a strong understanding of adult learning theory for their future roles as clinician educators. Adult learning theories are relatively recent in education and focus on how adults learn. A pioneer in adult learning theory, Malcolm Knowles (1950), felt there were key differences between how adults and children learn. Knowles noted that instructional methods associated with the art and science of educating children were not as effective in educating adults, and he argued that adults need to know *why* they need to learn something before undertaking to learn it. He asserted that the characteristics of adult learners are different from children in self-concept, experience, readiness to learn, the orientation of learner, and in the motivation to learn. The key characteristics of Knowles' adult learning theory include: a) adults are motivated to learn; b) adult's orientation to learning is life-centered; c) experience is the richest resource of adult learning; d) adults have a deep need to be self-directed; e) individual differences among individuals increase with age. Knowles' theories should provide a foundation for CET curriculum development and be incorporated in the CET courses for the participants to apply to their learning, teaching, and curriculum design.

Clinician-educators also need more than an understanding of teaching and learning—they need "specific knowledge and skills in curriculum design and evaluation in order to effect growth and change in individual learners, entire educational systems and communities" (Helfin et al., 2009, p. e237). In addition to using adult learning theory to guide curriculum design and instruction in CET programs, residents need to be able to identify learning goals and develop learning activities designed to meet those goals (Chen et al., 2018). Some of the CET programs (e.g. Helfin et al., 2009; Schnapp, Fant, & Gisondi, 2017) teach residents Kern's (1998) six steps of curriculum development in medical education in which curriculum developers: a) identify a problem by conducting a needs assessment; b) identify targeted learners and their learning needs; c) set learning goals and objectives; d) create strategies to meet the learning goals; e) implement the strategies through classroom instruction; and f) evaluate the learning and provide feedback.

Clinical educator track residents are also taught the process of curriculum evaluation. Curriculum evaluation requires residents to identify knowledge deficiencies, to locate available resources, to assess preferred learning styles, and to gauge administrative support. Active learning strategies are emphasized in the clinical educator track, and residents are introduced to active teaching strategies that can be utilized in large group (e.g. think-pair-share), small group (e.g. problem based learning, flipped classroom), and independent learning (e.g. concept mapping, mind mapping).

Continuous Improvement through Program Design and Evaluation

Another promising practice in CET programs is fostering a culture of continuous improvement in program design and evaluation. To implement and sustain an effective program, it is necessary to build a fellow-faculty coalition who support cycles of inquiry and improvement by conducting needs assessments and using data to drive the program (Konerman, Alpert, & Sinha, 2016). In order for a CET program to be effective and sustainable, program directors need to foster a culture of continuous program by creating organizational systems, trouble-shooting problems, and regularly collecting data from faculty, students, and alumni (Konerman et al., 2016; Lin et al., 2016). Learning about improvement cycles, such as Plan-Do-Study-Act, can benefit program directors and faculty as they engage in program design and evaluation.

Program evaluation needs to be a significant responsibility of a CET program director. Olson (2014) explains the basics of program evaluation:

The goal of program evaluation is to establish the value or worth of a program based on a systematic assessment of the program results, where the term "program" refers to resources and activities directed towards accomplishing some goal or goals. Where feasible, program evaluation also attempts to establish the extent to which the measured results can be attributed to the program activities. Program evaluation is similar to research in that it requires selecting an appropriate evaluation design, devising the right methods for data collection, and analyzing those data properly. (p.27)

Program directors can employ both quantitative (surveys) and qualitative (interviews, open-ended responses) to gain valuable feedback from both current and past students. By using data to drive improvement, CET program directors and faculty members can identify both strengths and weaknesses of the program and make adjustments as needed. When conducting a program evaluation, program directors need to collect data on specific aspects of the program (e.g. curriculum, mentoring, guest speakers, etc.) in order to make targeted improvements.

Focus on Leadership and Mentoring

Collaboration among the residents and with the CET faculty is also a valued practice in CET programs. A building block in the CET program is a collaborative relationship with a faculty mentor (Coates, Hobgood, Birnbaum, & Farrell, 2008; Jibson et al., 2010). Clinical educator track (CET) programs need a cadre of physicians with advanced expertise in education, who can serve as leaders and mentors in medical education (Sherbino, Frank, & Snell, 2014). In identifying the qualities of role models in CET programs, Sherbino, Frank, & Snell (2014) asserted that mentors need to be active in clinical practice, have the ability to connect theory to practice, and engage in education scholarship. Effective clinical educators should be leaders and role models in the field, who have a dual perspective as both a practitioner and an educator, and who can serve as a mentors to other health professionals on education questions and issues (p. 785).

Mentors in clinical education should not only be respected within the field, they need to believe in and be committed to the professional development process of the CET residents (Castiglioni et al., 2012). Mentors should be able to work with residents to center their learning on their personal and professional needs and the needs of their patients. The mentor needs the ability to help CET residents set goals, identify opportunities for learning, provide constructive feedback, and encourage reflection of experiences. Mentors should be able to build and maintain their relationships with their mentees based on mutual trust, respect, and professionalism; moreover, they should be able to create a relationship that encourages their mentee to honestly share and reflect upon their experiences (Ragins & Kram, 2007).

In order to develop the leadership skills that CET residents need, faculty mentors should primarily focus on activities and strategies that emphasize learning and improved patient outcomes. Furthermore, mentors need to understand the importance of developing the resident's leadership confidence by being engaged in ways that enable them to become leaders, such as supervising medical students, building leadership capacity in others, creating a vision, and goal-setting. CET residents need support, encouragement, affirmation, information and resources in order to build their leadership capacity (Schnapp et al., 2017). In essence, they need a mentor to listen to them and to show concern for their success by giving them encouragement and affirmation to their work. Through this mentoring relationship, CET residents learn the needed skills to help them become leaders in clinical education and mentors for a future generation of medical students.

Example of A Clinical Educator Track Program

One of the purposes of this book chapter is to describe LSU Health Baton Rouge's internal medicine residency program and the CET program associated with LSU Health Baton Rouge. We address this purpose by providing an overview of the program, explaining how the CET program correlates with the promising practices discussed in the literature review, and highlighting the perceptions of the resident associated with the CET program. We also discuss a collaboration with LSU's School of Education in supporting both the faculty and the residents in the CET program.

Overview of LSU Health Baton Rouge's Medical Residency Program

LSU Health Baton Rouge internal medicine residency program has a philosophy that:

1. nurtures the development of critical thought in a manner that moves beyond the redundant acquisition and retention of information;
2. encourages the application of evidence based medicine to enhance critical thinking, to provide a forum for evaluation of current medical philosophy and practice, and to stimulate interest in the foundation of the art of medicine;
3. provides a relaxed educational atmosphere, understanding that to promote the learning process there must be opportunity for humor, casual interactions, self-reflection, and constructive criticism;
4. centers around education in a hospital equipped with the full array of medical and surgical specialties;
5. provides a comprehensive foundation in internal medicine and subspecialty care under the guidance of experienced and purpose driven faculty.

The residency program is a three-year program with a select few residents chosen by program leadership to be Chief Residents for a fourth year. Residents participate in a mix of inpatient general medicine rotations, consult services, and outpatient clinics. During their second and third years, residents develop and present resident conferences (standard presentation), morbidity and mortality conferences (discuss a medical error they were involved in), and journal club (critical look at research). At the end of their third year, residents are required to research and analyze a controversial, disputed or unresolved topic in medicine and then resent their findings for critical review. Residents are expected to attend and participate in morning reports every day at 7:30am where a student or resident presents a patient, and the program director facilitates a discussion based on the pathophysiology of the patient. Finally, all residents are expected to participate in simulation sessions where they work through clinical scenarios as a team followed by a debriefing during which educational points are discussed with faculty.

LSU's CET Resident Program

The CET is an extracurricular program available to LSU Health Baton Rouge internal medicine residents. Participation is voluntary and limited to three to five residents in order to maintain a small group dynamic. First year internal medicine residents are eligible to apply provided they are in good standing with the program. The application includes a copy of their curriculum vitae and a description of the following:

1. Specific teaching and education interests;
2. Past and current teaching and education responsibilities (formal and informal);
3. A specific educational strength you've noted in your program **and** a specific educational weakness you've noted in your program (could be from any of the domains: teaching and learning; evaluation and assessment; curriculum; leadership);
4. A brief description of your career plans (e.g., vision or goals to be achieved in the next 3-5 years), especially in terms of teaching and education;
5. What you hope to gain from participation in the Clinical Educator Program.

Each application undergoes a blinded review process and participants are selected prior to beginning the second year of residency.

The CET program runs during the second and third year of residency. Sessions are held monthly and are loosely structured in order to promote discussion. Prior to each session participants are expected to complete pre-assigned reading or engage in reflection about the pertinent topic. After each session participants are tasked with utilizing any skills learned in the session in the clinical environment and reporting their observations at the next session. In the first year of CET program (2nd year of residency), residents are instructed in the following topics:

1. Strategic Planning and Development: students identify personal core values, develop mission and vision statement development and perform SWOT (strength, weakness, opportunities, threat) analysis;
2. Adult Learning Theory: students explore Knowles' theory through real clinical scenarios and discuss how the theory connects to practice;
3. Teaching Strategies I: students learn about public speaking, vocal tone, verbal arrangement, and the awareness of facial expression;
4. Teaching Strategies II: students learn effective teaching strategies, develop their teaching philosophy, and understand how to make effective teaching presentations, students learn PowerPoint presentation tips;
5. Evaluation and Feedback: students understand the meaning of feedback, how feedback is effectively delivered, and how it is effectively measured;
6. Library Sciences: students learn how to develop effective research questions and how to perform efficient and effective literature searches;
7. Understanding Educational Research: students learn how educational research is different from medical research, how to read a research article, the differences between quantitative and qualitative data, research terminology, and survey development;
8. Curriculum Development: students learn what curriculum is, how to use standards to drive curriculum, and how to develop curriculum using backwards by design;
9. Leadership: students learn the qualities of a good leader, how to lead effectively, differentiating a leader from a manager, and supervision.

In the second year of program (3rd year of residency), residents utilize the information and skills learned during the first year of the program to develop and complete a research project, a problem-based learning case, and teaching sessions which are observed by faculty who provide detailed feedback. The residents also have the opportunity to further explore and area of education by attending a conference or observing an expert at another academic institution in a field of their interest. The CET residents have been able to learn about Problem Based Learning (PBL) at the University of Missouri school of Medicine, Inter-professional Learning at Vanderbilt School of Medicine and attend a leadership conference in Philadelphia.

Clinical educator track participants utilize the skills learned in the program during small and large group teaching sessions. These skills include providing feedback to medical students; educating patients; improving research skills and utilizing library databases. Additionally, the majority of the clinical educator track participants are asked by program administration to remain in the department as a chief resident where they function as internal medicine faculty for one additional year. LSU's CET program exhibits many of the promising practices of effective programs discussed in the literature review.

A Commitment to Teaching and Learning

Faculty in the LSU Health clinical educator tract foster a learning environment that supports residents in understanding the principles of effective teaching and learning. Faulty in the program both directly teach adult learning theory and model the principles of andragogy while instructing students. Residents are exposed to a variety of teaching methods that are designed to engage adult learners; consequently, residents have a strong understanding of the adult learner and how to utilize the principles of andragogy to improve their own teaching strategies. Residents are required to design lessons that demonstrate an understanding of how to engage and instruct adult learners.

Faculty in the CET program also practice and model a *backwards by design* (Wiggins & McTighe, 2005) curriculum model in which they begin designing lessons with the end-goals in mind. By utilizing backwards by design, faculty develop course curriculum by identifying desired student outcomes (what students need to know and be able to do), determining acceptable evidence of learning (how students will demonstrate their learning), and then planning their instruction and activities to ensure that students meet the desired outcomes. The residents are also taught how to use backwards by design and are required to model a lesson using this strategy.

Finally, one or two faculty members in the CET program are academic scholars, and they teach the CET residents how to be academic researchers and scholars. Residents are exposed to lessons in advanced research design and research strategies. Residents are taught how to utilize library resources and how to conduct literature reviews through databases such as *PUBMED*. A website with landmark studies was also developed as a reference for residents and includes a tutorial on how to critically read journal articles.

A Focus on Leadership and Mentoring

One of the primary objectives of LSU Health's CET program is to develop competent and caring leaders in the medical profession. Residents are exposed to a variety of opportunities to develop their leadership skills.

1. Communication. Residents are taught about effective communication skills in working with both interns and patients. Residents learn how to give both informal and formal feedback and offer constructive feedback and reflection. They are also taught how to improve their presentation skills via PowerPoint design in order to effectively communicate their message.
2. Professional Development. Residents have an opportunity to take an elective in which participants can explore a specific area of education and observe an expert in the field by either visiting an institution (e.g. Vanderbilt) or attending a conference (e.g. PBL conference in Missouri or leadership conference in Philadelphia).
3. Mentoring. Residents are taught about mentoring and how it differs from coaching, supervising, advising and managing. They are encouraged to seek out a mentor and complete a mentoring agreement. Faculty are also asked to volunteer as mentors and receive similar education about the role of mentors and are asked to complete a mentoring profile so the Program Director can attempt to match mentors and mentees.

Continuous Improvement through Program Design and Evaluation

As LSU Health CET program is committed to continuous improvement, the program director and faculty engage in both program and course evaluations to improve the CET experience for residents. All residents are expected to complete course evaluations at the end of each year, and these evaluations are analyzed by faculty to improve course curriculum and instruction. Residents are also asked to participate in both qualitative (interviews) and quantitative (surveys) feedback sessions with the program director in order to gauge resident satisfaction with the overall quality of the program. These data are used to determine program quality and effectiveness, and from these data, the program director has tracked how CET graduates are performing and has used feedback to make adjustments to the program structure.

Student Successes:

- One graduate is currently working with the city policy makers to provide healthy food options to patients in lower socioeconomic areas. This program started with a project the resident designed and implemented through the CET program.
- A PBL curriculum for medical interns was developed by a CET resident and is in its second year of implementation at LSU Health.
- Out of 8 CET participants 6 have been asked to be chief residents.
- Former CET students are now being added as faculty and instructors.

Program Successes and Changes:

- Largest class is starting in 2019 with four participants.
- Changing the second year to more project focused on concepts introduced in the first year based on participant feedback.
- One resident working at Vanderbilt asserted that the strategies he learned in the CET gave him the ability and confidence to teach internal medicine residents and EM residents. He stated, "Some of the lessons you imparted on me both as a mentor and through the clinical educator track have been the most insightful of my residency."

Resident Students' Perceptions

Part of the LSU Health Baton Rouge CET Resident Program is the collection of annual evaluations. The program director uses a qualitative open-ended evaluation protocol so residents have the opportunity to reflect on both the program and their learning to offer constructive feedback. Based on the open-ended surveys, we analyzed the LSU program's strengths and areas of improvement.

Strengths

One of the primary strengths of the CET program is the focus on teaching and learning. All of the residents commented that they enjoyed the various strategies faculty used to engage them in their learning. Students mentioned small group settings, dynamic lectures, diversity of faculty, clinical projects and guest speakers as varying ways faculty connected with them. One of the students wrote,

The small groups, different teachers, and focused sessions were very beneficial. I felt like each learning session had a specific focus with solid points that we learners could take away from the session. I learned so much about teaching, leading, learners, and myself this year. It was a great experience to be so well-rounded as a future educator.

The students appreciated focused sessions on specific topics with varying faculty and guest speakers and how the program supported learning and new ways of thinking:

The program goes away from more traditional conventions that I was familiar with and offered new ways to think about education. It also offers ways have this practically applied and incorporate this into a project. This can help cement some of the techniques and further expand on their application not previously talked about.

Many of the students discussed how much they enjoyed their learning, one student wrote, "What I enjoyed the most was learning about adult learning theory, and I've enjoyed thinking of ways to apply many of the lessons to my every day work." Not only did students appreciate learning about various education theories, such as adult learning theory, some also commented on how learning about these theories impacted their own ideas on teaching. One student stated,

I have learned that there are many effective ways to reach your target audience, and that specifically with adults conveying motivation and a reason to learn is as important as the information itself. Once you have the motivation a lot of learning can take place outside of traditional teaching methods like lectures, and these can often be superior.

Since CET programs are primarily focused on developing residents as teachers, it is imperative that teaching and learning be at the forefront of the program. One of the residents commented, "I have learned that teaching requires a very thoughtful approach including preparation about your audience, topic, goals of the lesson, and ways to assess teaching. Too often I think teaching is approached as an afterthought." As students completed the program, they became more confident in their ability to teach others, and many asserted that they "feel far more confident in teaching my colleagues, patients, and even superiors" and they are "encouraged to pass the knowledge" they have gained to others. One student summarized the importance of the CET program in improving residents as teachers by stating, "Many people say that they like to teach, but few actually understand the theory behind teaching, or how to engage the learner. CET provides these essential foundations, and it is one of the things I have enjoyed most."

Another strength of the program is the flexibility afforded to students in the program design. The CET Resident Program at LSU Health Baton Rouge allows students to participate in an elective course of their choosing, and all of the residents commented how much they appreciate this option. One student commented, "I enjoyed the opportunity to participate in an elective course of my choosing, which ended up being a 2 week trip to Vanderbilt University to discuss the principles behind inter-professional education, and how they have incorporated IPE into the core curriculum of their medical education." This student had the opportunity to visit another medical program to learn about a specific topic of interest. By allowing students the opportunity to choose an elective in an area of interest, the CET program enhances their students' passion for lifelong learning.

Areas of Improvement

The students also indicated areas in which the CET program could be improved. Some of the suggestions included curriculum design, specifically when topics are introduced and taught. One student stated, "I think one area that could be more fully explored is curriculum design. The talks on constructing lectures was somewhat late in the year." Another student agreed by stating," Consideration could be given to moving up talks on constructing lectures in order to allow for more practice while preparing our lectures throughout the year." One of the residents also mentioned starting the senior projects earlier.

Another area of improvement is the level of mentoring and support the residents receive. Students mentioned "having more advice and assistance with projects" or having the opportunity to work with faculty not in the CET program to learn new teaching styles. The students would like more immediate feedback and the "opportunity to practice the skillset [they] just learned in session." One of the residents also mentioned the lack of support at the institutional level. This student commented, "Interest level within the program can be low as the program does not allow residents to have any official credit for participation."

The Partnership with LSU's School of Education

The CET Program Director took the initiative to contact faculty in the School of Education at Louisiana State University to form a collaborative partnership focused on improving teaching and learning within the CET program. One of the professors from Education Leadership collaborated with the Program Director to teach sessions on leadership, review course material, and help with curricular and instructional design. From this collaboration came the idea to have doctoral students in education, who are master teachers in K-12 schools, work with the residents in developing their teaching skills. The vision for the partnership was to have a combined class of medical residents and education doctoral students where the students, under the supervision of School of Education and CET faculty, could work together to develop curriculum, practice instructional strategies, and role play on assessing learning and giving feedback. The partnership would be mutually beneficial for both School of Education students and medical residents as residents would have the opportunity to learn from master teachers and scholars, and education students could learn from medical residents how to be better teacher leaders, instructional coaches, and supervisors.

Although the partnership between LSU's HSC CET program and LSU's School of Education is an emerging idea with excellent potential, it has had its challenges. The largest challenge involves a change in personnel. Both faculty members in the LSU School of Education who worked with the CET program accepted a new position at other institutions in two different states. When these faculty members left LSU, the partnership between the medical school and the School of Education temporarily stalled. The Director of the CET program found a way to continue partnering with the School of Education by working directly with the education doctoral students. Doctoral students in the School of Education, under the direction of the CET Director, have been teaching CET residents various modules, including teaching strategies, curriculum, supervision, and leadership. While the vision of having a joint class between CET resident students and education doctoral students has been temporarily suspended until a new faculty member in the School of Education is hired to continue the program, both the doctoral students and the CET residents have reported positive feelings about working together. The residents have enjoyed working with the education doctoral students and learning from them, and the education doctoral students have enjoyed developing their adult teaching skills. Because the residents found it beneficial to work with the education doctoral students and vice versa, the collaboration between the CET program and LSU School of Education will continue as a promising practice.

PROGRAM CONCERNS

Time

One of the concerns of the CET program is how faculty manages the time constraints of residents. The LSU Health CET faculty recognizes that their students' primary responsibility is the residency, and the faculty responds by being well-prepared with scheduling and being flexible. The program director conducts a planning meeting at the beginning of the year in which faculty coordinates schedules, considering clinical rounds, impatient care, vacations, major holidays, and major community events. Classes are scheduled to work with the residents' schedules, and most classes are schedules on Friday afternoons, in the evenings, or on weekends. Consideration is also given to avoid classes being scheduled in December and June. The faculty also look for ways to minimize wasted time: a) pre-class readings reduces class time; b) post-class assignments are designed to be incorporated in resident's clinical duties (e.g. observe teaching in real time and reflections on topics in their current rotations).

The residents are also told in advance the expectations of the program and the time commitment. The first year is course intensive, but the second year is designed for residents to work at their own pace. During the second year, residents engage in PBL and work on projects that allow the resident to implement lessons learned during the first year. Finally, if the program director has any concerns about a resident's ability to fulfill his/her duties, then the program director can prevent the resident from applying to the CET program.

Residents and Faculty

Another challenge of the program is how faculty engages residents in the teaching and learning focus of the CET program while handling the changing focus of medicine. Both residents and faculty are responsible for documentation, billing, electronic medical records, and avoiding lawsuits which decreases the personal aspects of medicine. Faculty and residents have to remain focused on the primary objective of the CET program which is to develop residents as teachers. The flexibility of the CET program supports residents in their desire to become teachers and engages them in courses that are scheduled around the residents' work schedules. Class sessions are protected from clinical responsibilities, and the faculty ensure a trusting and environment by making the course sessions open learning environments where residents are safe to speak freely about their learning and teaching experiences. Moreover, faculty and student relationships are valued, and course sessions are traditional face-to-face meetings so faculty can build interpersonal relationships with residents and mentor and support them.

FUTURE DIRECTIONS OF CET PROGRAMS

Clinical educator track (CET) programs have become a valuable approach to enhancing the knowledge, skills, and dispositions of medical residents in developing their skills to be effective teachers both in hospitals and academic institutions. Although we found literature on how emerging CET programs are developed and on promising practices in effective programming, there are some emerging trends that warrant further consideration.

1. Program Directors may want to explore formal collaborations with schools from the main university. The School of Education seems like a natural fit, but other schools may also benefit from a collaboration with a CET program. The School of Mass Communication could provide medical residents an opportunity to learn about public perception/persona and improving public speaking skills, while the mass communications students would be exposed to future professionals and provide them with opportunities to develop projects around the health profession.
2. Program Directors may want to consider offering a stream-lined program for residents who are chosen to be chief residents but are not students in the CET. In most residency programs, chief residents are considered junior faculty and are responsible for attending on inpatient services, preempting outpatient clinic, and lecturing to resident and medical students. For chief residents who did not participate in a clinical educator track, a stream-lined course could be offered as a preparatory opportunity for a resident transitioning into the chief resident role.
3. Program Directors may want to expand the research skills of resident students by exploring how intervention skills learned through CET are utilized in the community and measuring the effects of the intervention. Students could discover whether or not approaching patient education differently translates into medical outcomes (e.g. better diabetes control, blood pressure control, compliance with medication, less emergency room visits). One of the LSU graduates focused her teaching around healthy eating and is now working on community programs to teach patient's about healthy diet and working with local government on providing resources to food-insecure areas. As many CET students will secure positions in the academic field, program directors should explore ways to support students with projects that bridge their research with their practice.
4. Finally, Program Directors may want to consider expanding the program to other health professionals. A number of other health professionals (e.g. nursing educators, pharmacy educators, etc.) are responsible for teaching their colleagues and may not have had formal training in education. A clinical educator track program could improve the effectivity of health profession education by supporting the learning of the teachers in health education.

CONCLUSION

The word *doctor* originates from the Latin verb docēre, meaning to teach. Although medical doctors are primarily charged with patient care, many are called on to teach and to develop the next generation of physicians. Teaching is a craft that not is not necessarily innate, and the best teachers are lifelong learners who continuously hone their craft to meet the needs of their students. Medical students are taught fundamentals and advances in medicine, but they are rarely taught the art and craft of teaching. There are nuances in education that must be mastered before a teacher can impact student learning. Nuances, such as curriculum design, learning theory, instructional design, and mentoring, are all skills that are not innate within the human psyche, and they must be deliberately taught and learned by educators in order to support learning. Clinical educator track (CET) programs are designed to teach medical students how to master these skills in order to be educators.

As more residency programs begin to offer CET programs, it is necessary to learn from established programs in order to implement an effective model. Through this chapter, we highlighted some of the promising practices at established CET programs in the United States, including a commitment to teaching and learning, continuous improvement through program design and evaluation, and a focus on leadership and mentoring. Residents studying how to be clinical educators need to learn effective practices in teaching learning, and faculty in CET programs should be committed to designing a program that focuses on developing quality educators through effective curriculum and instructional design and mentoring. As faculty mentor residents and model best instructional strategies, they empower them to become better educators for future generations. The role of the clinical educator in developing competent and caring physicians is too important to leave to chance. Preparation for this role should be thoughtfully and purposefully developed through clinical educator track programs.

REFERENCES

Adamson, R., Goodman, R. B., Kritek, P., Luks, A. M., Tonelli, M. R., & Benditt, J. Clinician-Educator Track of the University of Washington Pulmonary and Critical Care Medicine Fellowship Program. (2015). Training the teachers: The clinician-educator track of the University of Washington pulmonary and critical care medicine fellowship program. *Annals of the American Thoracic Society*, *12*(1), 480–485. doi:10.1513/AnnalsATS.201501-032OT PMID:25763811

Ahn, J., Martin, S. K., Farnan, J. M., & Fromme, B. (2018). The graduate medical education scholars track: Developing residents as clinician-educators during clinical training via a longitudinal, multimodal, and multidisciplinary track. *Academic Medicine*, *93*(2), 214–219. doi:10.1097/ACM.0000000000001815 PMID:28678096

Barchi, R., & Lowery, B. (2000). Scholarship in the medical faculty from the university perspective: Retaining academic values. *Academic Medicine*, *75*(9), 899–905. doi:10.1097/00001888-200009000-00011 PMID:10995611

Borges, N. J., Navarro, A. M., Grover, A., & Hoban, J. D. (2010). How, when, and why do physicians choose careers in academic medicine? A literature review. *Academic Medicine*, *85*(4), 680–686. doi:10.1097/ACM.0b013e3181d29cb9 PMID:20354389

Castiglioni, A., Aagaard, E., Spencer, A., Nicholson, L., Karani, R., Bates, C. K., ... Chheda, S. G. (2012). Succeeding as a clinician educator: Useful tips and resources. *Journal of General Internal Medicine*, *28*(1), 136–140. doi:10.100711606-012-2156-8 PMID:22836953

Chen, D. C., Miloslavsky, E. M., Winn, A. S., & McSparron, J. I. (2018). Fellow as Clinical Teacher (FACT) curriculum: Improving fellows' teaching skills during inpatient consultation. *MedEdPORTAL*, *14*(10), 1–6. PMID:30800928

Chen, H. C., Wamsley, M. A., Azzam, A., Julian, K., Irby, D. M., & O'Sullivan, P. S. (2017). The health professions education pathway: Preparing students, residents, and fellows to become future educators. *Teaching and Learning in Medicine*, *29*(2), 216–227. doi:10.1080/10401334.2016.1230500 PMID:27813688

Coates, W. C., Hobgood, C. D., Birnbaum, A., & Birnbaum, A. (2008). Faculty development: Academic opportunities for emergency medicine faculty on education career tracks. *Academic Emergency Medicine*, *10*(10), 1113–1117. doi:10.1197/S1069-6563(03)00369-5 PMID:14525747

Helfin, M. T., Pinheiro, S., Kaminetzky, C. P., & McNeill, D. (2009). So you want to be a clinician-educator: Designing a clinician-educator curriculum for internal medicine residents. *Medical Teacher*, *31*(6), e233–e240. doi:10.1080/01421590802516772 PMID:19296370

Jibson, M., Hilty, D., Arlinghaus, K., Ball, V., McCarthy, T., Seritan, A., & Servis, M. (2010). Clinician-educator tracks for residents: Three pilot programs. *Academic Psychiatry*, *34*(4), 269–276. doi:10.1176/appi.ap.34.4.269 PMID:20576984

Kern, D. E. (1998). *Curriculum Development for Medical Education: A Six Step Approach*. Baltimore, MD: Johns Hopkins University Press.

Knight, C. L., Windish, D. M., Haist, S. A., Karani, R., Chheda, S., Rosenblum, M., ... Aagaard, E. M. (2017). The SGIM TEACH program: A curriculum for teachers of clinical medicine. *Journal of General Internal Medicine*, *32*(8), 948–952. doi:10.100711606-017-4053-7 PMID:28409434

Knowles, M. S. (1950). *Informal adult education*. New York, NY: Association Press.

Konerman, M. C., Alpert, C. M., & Sinha, S. S. (2016). Learning to be a clinician-educator: A fellow-driven curricular reform. *Journal of the American College of Cardiology*, *67*(3), 338–342. doi:10.1016/j.jacc.2015.11.032 PMID:26796400

Kubiak, N. T., Guidot, D. M., Trimm, R. F., Kamen, D. L., & Roman, J. (2012). Recruitment and retention in academic medicine: What junior faculty and trainees want department chairs to know. *The American Journal of the Medical Sciences*, *344*(1), 24–27. doi:10.1016/S0002-9629(15)30914-9 PMID:22744375

Levinson, W., & Rubenstein, A. (2000). Integrating clinician-educators into academic medical centers: Challenges and potential solutions. *Academic Medicine*, *75*(9), 906–912. doi:10.1097/00001888-200009000-00012 PMID:10995612

Lin, S., Sattler, A., Yu, G. C., Basaviah, P., & Schillinger, E. (2016). Training future clinician-educators: A track for family medicine residents. *Family Medicine*, *48*(3), 212–216. PMID:26950910

McCullough, B., Marton, G. E., & Ramnanan, C. J. (2015). How can clinician-educator training programs be optimized to match clinician motivations and concerns? *Advances in Medical Education and Practice*, *6*(1), 45–54. doi:10.2147/AMEP.S70139 PMID:25653570

Miloslavsky, E. M., Boyer, D., Winn, A. S., Stafford, D. E. J., & McSparron, J. I. (2016). Fellows as teachers: Raising the educational bar. *Annals of the American Thoracic Society*, *13*(4), 465–468. PMID:26835749

Olson, L. E. (2014). Articulating a Role for Program Evaluation in Responsible Conduct of Research Programs. *Accountability in Research*, *21*(1), 26–33. doi:10.1080/08989621.2013.822265 PMID:24073605

Ragins, B. R., & Kram, K. E. (2007). *The handbook of mentoring at work: Theory, research, and practice*. Thousand Oaks, CA: Sage.

Ramani, S., Mann, S., Taylor, D., & Thampy, H. (2016). Residents as teachers: Near peer learning in clinical work settings. *Medical Teacher, 38*(7), 642–655. doi:10.3109/0142159X.2016.1147540 PMID:27071739

Roberts, D. H., Schwartzstein, R. M., & Weinberger, S. E. (2014). Career development for the clinician-educator: Optimizing impact and maximizing success. *Annals of the American Thoracic Society, 11*(2), 254–259. doi:10.1513/AnnalsATS.201309-322OT PMID:24575995

Schnapp, B. H., Fant, A. L., & Gisondi, M. A. (2017). A ten-year program evaluation of an emergency medicine scholarly track in education using a qualitative approach. *Society for Academic Emergency Medicine, 1*, 215–220. PMID:30051037

Sherbino, J., Frank, J. R., & Snell, L. (2014). Defining the key roles and competencies of the clinician-educator of the 21st century: A national mixed-methods study. *Academic Medicine, 89*(5), 783–789. doi:10.1097/ACM.0000000000000217 PMID:24667507

Smith, C. C., McCormick, I., & Huang, G. C. (2014). The clinician-educator track: Training internal residents as clinician-educators. *Academic Medicine, 89*(6), 888–891. doi:10.1097/ACM.0000000000000242 PMID:24871239

Smith, C. C., Newman, L. R., & Huang, G. C. (2018). Those who teach, can do: Characterizing the relationship between teaching and clinical skills in a residency program. *Journal of Graduate Medical Education, 10*(4), 459–463. doi:10.4300/JGME-D-18-00039.1 PMID:30154980

Srinivasan, M., Li, S. T., Meyers, F. J., Pratt, D. D., Collins, J. B., Braddock, C., ... Hilty, D. M. (2011). Teaching as a competency: Competencies for medical educators. *Academic Medicine, 86*(10), 1211–1220. doi:10.1097/ACM.0b013e31822c5b9a PMID:21869655

Swanwick, T. (2014). Understanding medical education. In T. Swanwick (Ed.), *Understanding Medical education: Evidence, theory and practice* (2nd ed.). Medford, MA: John Wiley & Sons.

Wiggins, G., & McTighe, J. (2005). *Understanding by design*. Alexandria, VA: ASCD.

Chapter 18
The Clinician as Educator:
Redefining the Medical Educator's Role and Toolbox

Barbara A. Schindler
Drexel University College of Medicine, USA

ABSTRACT

The changing landscape of medical practice, the explosion of medical knowledge, and the introduction of new technologies and teaching methods have impelled a re-examination of the various roles of the medical educator. This chapter examines each of those roles -- content expert, competency expert, role model, teacher of critical thinking, promoter of life-long learning, patient educator -- from both a historical and modern perspective. The overall requirements for faculty development are described and, for each of the educator's roles, specific faculty development suggestions are put forth to meet the evolving needs of modern medical educators.

INTRODUCTION

I swear by Apollo the physician, and Aesculapius the surgeon, likewise Hygeia and Panacea, and call all the gods and goddesses to witness, that I will observe and keep this underwritten oath, to the utmost of my power and judgment.

I will reverence my master who taught me the art. Equally with my parents, will I allow him things necessary for his support, and will consider his sons as brothers. I will teach them my art without reward or agreement; and I will impart all my acquirement, instructions, and whatever I know, to my master's children, as to my own; and likewise, to all my pupils, who shall bind and tie themselves by a professional oath, but to none else. (Adams, 1939)

The essential role of physicians and healthcare providers as educators dates back to the ancient Greeks. The original and subsequent versions of the Hippocratic Oath focus on the primacy of the physician as

DOI: 10.4018/978-1-7998-1468-9.ch018

teacher. In the current era, with shifting paradigms of clinical practice, medical economic pressures, the explosion of medical knowledge, the integration of technology into healthcare and medical education, and generational differences in current learners, the vital role of physicians and scientists as educators has become an important topic of discussion and debate (Cooke, Irby, & O'Brien, 2010; ten Cate, 2014). These forces combine to affect the delivery of medical scientific content in the classroom or at the bedside, the traditional modalities most familiar to medical faculty. The role of the academic clinician as "bedside" teacher of students and patients is further challenged by significantly shorter hospital stays, briefer clinic visits, and wide access to information on the internet (Sherbino, Frank, & Snell, 2014). While these many changes test the skills and established roles of medical educators, they have created exciting opportunities to more clearly define or redefine the clinician's role as medical trainee and patient educator. These changes have also focused attention on the need for clearer and more specific faculty development to engage the commitment and enthusiasm of medical educators in training the next generation of healthcare providers (Feinberg & Koltz, 2015). This chapter addresses that need and proposes ways to meet it.

BACKGROUND

A significant driver of educational changes has been technological advances in conjunction with the dramatic increase in basic biomedical knowledge and medical treatment options. The age of the internet has allowed almost universal access and transmission of basic and clinical scientific content to patients, trainees and practitioners alike through a variety of web-based clinical resources. This information, often scientifically unfiltered and even speculative, can be overwhelming to trainees and patients alike. Practitioners themselves increasingly rely on technology to make diagnoses and decide on treatment, thereby raising concerns about how students can learn data collection and physical examination skills and develop critical diagnostic thinking and assessment skills.

While current students of medicine are typically far more adept than their faculty in accessing ever-expanding digital modalities, they often lack the knowledge and experience to use that information effectively. At the same time, many educators continue to see the traditional classroom lecture as the best way to impart their extensive knowledge and skills. In response, students are clearly speaking with their feet, routinely avoiding the lecture hall, opting instead to view the material online at their preferred time, location and speed. Students feel quite comfortable accessing needed or supplemental information and content from a variety of mostly digital resources: digital textbooks, medical school created online lectures, review books, Wikipedia, YouTube, Kahn Academy, practice examinations, etc. (Prober 2013). However, students cannot develop the clinical skills and professional identity formation, attitudes and behaviors needed to become the next generation of health care providers, proficient in the art and science of medicine, without educational goals, objectives and assessments created by experience medical educators. Local, national and international faculty collaboration facilitates greatly the generation of general and discipline-specific objectives and assessment tools.

The current dynamic changes in medical education have become intellectual as well as personal struggles for many medical school faculty who were themselves trained in the centuries-old didactic traditions (Norman, 2012). Most basic scientists and clinicians had, as trainees themselves, limited opportunities to learn how to become medical educators, which is a similar problem for faculty in other academic disciplines (Anderson, 1996). A major concern cited by many faculty is whether students have the ability to acquire necessary information without being told directly what they need to know while, at another level, faculty appreciate that trainees need to develop life-long learning skills. Faculty also note that they miss the interpersonal, though sometimes only non-verbal, interactions with students in the classroom setting. In fact, some highly motivated educators take personal offence because students do not physically attend their lectures which, in their view, were developed with the goal of transferring important discipline-specific, often hard-earned, knowledge and skills. After all, most teachers are teachers because of their passion for personally transmitting their knowledge, skills and clinical stories to the next generation of practitioners. It may be difficult for some educators to appreciate that students readily utilize the objectives, notes and lectures that have created and have been posted online. Similarly, Topol's predictions about mostly digital interactions with patients as an integral part of the future of healthcare raise both concerns and excitement on the part of medical educators, especially how technology will impact on medical education and how that will affect the clinician-patient relationship and its critical role in prevention, diagnoses and treatment (Topol, 2013; Topol, Steinhubl, & Torkamani, 2015). Finally, clinical faculty may be concerned about financial support for their educational endeavors, with academic administrators comparing their teaching hours to billable clinical hours.

THE MODERN MEDICAL EDUCATOR; ISSUES AND SOLUTIONS

Given the challenges of adopting new and potentially exciting teaching modalities, how do we continue to engage committed educators in their essential role in training the next generation of healthcare providers? How do we maximize the mutually gratifying learning relationship between faculty and students, with both seeking to improve their knowledge and skills to enhance patient care? We will need a clear definition/redefinition of the evolving role of faculty. Redefining the essential established role of faculty will require faculty development to educate faculty about their changing but critical educational role and to facilitate their appreciation and development of newer methods to deliver medical education. Engagement of faculty in this work should start by acknowledging and focusing on the enormous knowledge and clinical and problem-solving skills that the experienced clinician brings to the education of trainees, and to their role as healthcare professionals and teachers of patients.

The development of competent healthcare providers is a multifactorial educational process that requires knowledge of various educational modalities, including testing of knowledge and venues to assess clinical competence and professional behavior (Sherbino, Frank, & Snell, 2014). Defining educational and behavioral objectives and evaluating trainees' achievement of those objectives requires careful curriculum planning with significant faculty input. Understanding of the principles of adult learning theory and appreciation of millennial generation trainees' different learning styles, including the time needed to become competent in defined discipline-specific areas, are key to successful educational outcomes (Abela, 2009; Eckleberry-Hunt &Tucciarone, 2011; Kaufman, 2003, Merriam & Bierema, 2013). Educational strategies such as the use of the flipped classroom, team-based learning and problem-based learning with skilled small group facilitators, and medical simulation experiences need to be designed to promote life-long learning in trainees (Kamei, Cook, Puthucheary, & Starmer, 2012; McMahon, 2005; Norman, 2012; Prober & Kahn, 2013).

Gone are the days of the giants in medicine, such as Oliver Wendell Holmes, Sr. and Sir William Osler, when bedside teaching with a skilled clinician could maximize a trainee's learning experience. In its place are short hospital stays, with much healthcare provided in the ambulatory setting and a shift from lecture halls and hospital rooms to brief ambulatory patient visits, small group settings, emergency departments and simulated patient care scenarios.

Medical educators need to maintain awareness of the impact of the ever-changing healthcare and thus learning environments. High demands for clinical educational sites for trainees can put students into settings where teaching practitioners may be less well prepared to meet trainees' educational needs despite a willingness to teach. Some of these educational settings may be less than ideal for teaching, especially with their own financial, clinical and non-clinical stressors that may actually create toxic learning environments which impede learning and need to be monitored and addressed (Cook, Arora, & Rasinski, Curlin, & Yoon, 2014; Shochet, Colbert-Getz, Levine, &Wright, 2013).

While our knowledge of normal and abnormal clinical entities and treatment modalities and the role of technology in healthcare and medical education are changing rapidly, there are unchanging basic educational principles and needs observed and documented long ago by giants of medicine including Hippocrates and Sir William Osler (Adams, 1939; Silverman, Murray, & Bryan, 2007). The current shifts in the healthcare and medical education environments provide an excellent opportunity to reaffirm and redefine the essential roles of medical educators which go far beyond the delivery of lecture content and bedside teaching (Branch, Kroenke, & Levinson, 1997), to demonstrating critical thinking skills in patient care and patient education, to serving as role models and mentors, and to being promoters of life-long learning. Faculty development programs, critical to supporting medical educators in their evolving roles, should focus on appreciating faculty motivation to teach (Dahlstrom et al., 2005) and then providing the necessary content, educational skills, and assessment expertise to support that motivation.

The Medical Educator as Content Expert

Basic science and clinical medical school faculty, with their many years of training, patient care and research experiences, are the obvious content experts in their own disciplines. These faculty have the expertise to define both curriculum content and the requisite competencies for medical trainees at each educational level. The educational challenge for these specialized discipline-specific educators is to integrate their basic and clinical science with defined educational and behavioral outcome measures appropriate for trainees' developmental stages. This complex process has been facilitated to some degree by various organizations such as the National Board of Medical Examiners, the Accreditation Council for Graduate Medical Education (ACGME), the Association of American Medical Colleges, specialty organizations and specialty boards that have defined discipline-specific educational objectives, competencies, Entrustable Professional Activities (EPAs), and milestones, and that have created assessment tools to evaluate outcomes. While there are significant commonalities in medical education programs, each institution has its own unique characteristics, based on its history, mission and culture. Faculty play a distinctive role in ensuring that these unique institutional characteristics are fully integrated into curriculum content and delivery.

Faculty development should focus on exploring the expanding spectrum of educational modalities: problem-based learning, team-based learning, and electronic or web-based options for delivering content, e.g. the flipped classroom and on promoting promote life-long learning skills. Specific goals should include identifying students' learning needs particularly as healthcare shifts toward prevention, population-based medicine and socioeconomic issues; skill building strategies for students; creating appropriate simulation experiences; assessment tools; how to provide timely formative and summative feedback; using students' feedback to improve curriculum and curricular content.

The Medical Educator as Competency Expert

In recent years medical educators at the graduate medical education level have focused on the development and implementation of core competencies and specialty specific milestones which provide a framework for evaluating residents' readiness to practice medicine. Competencies required by the ACGME include patient care, medical knowledge, practice-based learning and improvement, systems-based practice, professionalism, and interpersonal skills and communication. At the undergraduate level, educational competencies, milestones and EPAs, have been developed and will facilitate educators' assessment of student performance and enhance both the faculty's and each student's ability to develop individual educational improvement plans (Jones, Rosenberg, Gilhooly, & Carraccio, 2011; ten Cate, 2013).

In addition to teaching and assessing student performance, faculty play a central role in helping trainees evaluate and integrate available medical information into the clinical care of patients. While Generation X and Y millennial students readily access digital data, they need experienced clinician educators to guide them on the practical use of evidence-based data and practice guidelines in both routine patient care and the care of patients who are outliers.

Faculty development should focus on educating clinical teachers on general educational competencies and discipline-specific milestones, on assessment tools, and on providing feedback to students on their achievement of those competencies and milestones.

The Medical Educator as Teacher of Critical Thinking

As students progress through their education they move from mastering facts required to pass examinations to the complex role of clinicians. For a student to master that role requires an ability to recognize, understand, and address clinical patient presentations. This ability is based on knowledge of basic and clinical science; clinical skills in history-taking and physical examination; interpretation of laboratory data; familiarity with current peer reviewed-literature and practice guidelines; and reflection on all data collected. However, beyond that, experienced clinical faculty need to help students develop the "critical thinking" skills required to integrate this information and apply it to the diagnosis and treatment of patients. Those faculty need support and guidance as they demonstrate and teach these skills and provide trainees with feedback appropriate to their level of training. An equally key role for faculty is in helping trainees think through and deal with those inevitable clinical situations where there is inadequate data and there is an urgency to make a diagnosis and begin treatment. That is, faculty can help students to recognize and accept, as well described by Osler, *"Medicine is a science of uncertainty and an art of probability"* (Silverman et al., 2007).

Patients have been described as the best teachers. "Textbook" cases, those patients who present with classic symptoms of a disease, make diagnosis and treatment easy. But there are times when the outcomes of apparent "textbook" cases may be a different story. Faculty play an essential role in helping trainees understand and appreciate the many variables that can affect patient presentations and outcomes. Demonstrating how to utilize known and potentially evolving patient data and utilizing evidence-based practices with an openness to changing diagnoses and treatment approaches is important in fostering critical thinking in trainees. In addition, faculty are invaluable in helping trainees recognize "outliers" and how to approach their diagnosis and treatment, especially when practice guidelines may not apply to the clinical situation (Mercuri, et al., 2015).

Faculty development should focus on assisting clinical educators to appreciate their own role as critical thinkers as they deal with ambiguity and uncertainty in medical practice, and on helping them to guide students as they develop the critical thinking skills needed to recognize and deal with that ambiguity and uncertainty. Faculty development programs should focus on helping experienced clinicians understand and identify the cognitive skills they routinely utilize as they approach a complex clinical situation, thus making the components of the critical thinking process more explicit to themselves and their learners (Sharpless et al 2017).

The Medical Educator as Patient Educator

As noted already, patients have long been recognized as the best medical teachers and attentive clinicians are always learning from their patients. Indeed, as Osler stated, *"To study the phenomena of disease without books is to sail an uncharted sea, while to study books without patients is not to go to sea at all"* (Silverman et al., 2007). This implies that patient engagement is critical for successful clinical outcomes and emphasizes the clinician's role in engaging and educating their patients. Indeed, the same educational principles that create a successful healthcare provider are also essential to the development of the competent clinician's role as a patient educator.

The role of healthcare providers as patient and patient family educators has been receiving more attention in an age of personalized medicine. Issues such as escalating healthcare costs and patient non-adherence have brought this topic into clearer focus (McCann & Blossom, 1990). In this context, the clinician-patient relationship, so vital to the successful diagnose and treatment of any medical problem, plays a central role in establishing patient trust and engagement and contributes significantly to successful diagnosis and treatment outcomes. Thus, successful outcomes in patient care depend on the clinician's ability to create appropriate rapport with patients, to assess their knowledge and understanding of their illnesses, to identify their learning styles, and to establish settings that facilitate their learning about their illnesses and treatment needs.

The skill set that makes a clinician an excellent student educator also is directly applicable to the role of patient educator. Helping patients navigate and understand medical information acquired through the media, including the internet, is similar to helping students navigate the massive amount of medical material available to them. The ability to understand cultural and generational differences, to ask patients the sometimes-challenging questions about their understanding of their illness and its treatment, and to explore potential reasons for non-adherence and treatment failures, is similar to guiding trainees in critical thinking and promoting life-long learning. Helping patients understand the integrated nature and various roles of their healthcare team mirrors the clinical educator's role in describing and modeling integrated healthcare for trainees. The very communication skills needed to be a competent patient educator are the same skills necessary to be a good student educator: possessing strong interpersonal skills, creating a non-threatening environment, listening carefully, eliciting what is known or not known by the patient or trainee, and being non-judgmental.

Faculty development should focus on the similarity of the roles of student educator and patient educator by demonstrating the common skill set required for success in both areas. The communication skills vital in this process should reviewed and be emphasized.

The Medical Educator as Role Model

Faculty serve as educators who both teach and demonstrate the art and science of medicine and serve as powerful role models of professional behavior. The oft-quoted adage -- *videre unum, noli unum, docent:* see one, do one, teach one – is central to medical education as a time-tested mechanism for transferring information from one generation of learners to the next. Clinicians are generally comfortable in demonstrating their interviewing/history taking and physical examination skills and in systematically demonstrating the integration of the biopsychosocial aspects of health and illness as well as the social determinants of health including health disparities as they create differential diagnoses and appropriately prioritized treatment plans for patients. Through this process, faculty can assist and assess trainees as they learn how to deal not only with straightforward clinical situations, but also with the complex determinants of health and illness. Faculty can articulate the ambiguity and uncertainty in some clinical situations and help trainees understand why practice guidelines may have exceptions in the context of complex situations (Mercuri, et al., 2015).

Faculty are responsible for creating and sustaining a positive student-centered learning environment. This includes identifying potential sources of student mistreatment and providing appropriate interventions when it occurs. Faculty also model professional behavior and promote the development of professional behavior and identity in trainees.

Faculty attitudes and professional behavior are regularly noted and copied by their students and play an important recruitment role for their discipline (Stahn & Harendza, 2014). Students routinely look for mentors in their area of interest who are willing to serve as career advisors and counselors, both in training and later in practice. Trainees observe and learn from how faculty deal with the daily stressors of medical practice, how they manage their work-life balance, and how they cope with potential burnout, a major challenge in the current healthcare environment.

While clinical practice stressors are continually changing, the basic tenets of professional medical practice remain the same. Understanding of current stressors by trainees and faculty can be mutually beneficial. For example, appreciation of the use of social media and its impact on the physician-patient relationship can create an excellent opportunity for constructive dialogue between the several generations working together in the educational, each with its own expectations.

Content area topics taught and discussed in the classroom, online, or in small group settings still rely heavily on clinical role models to ensure integration into students' developing clinical skills. Open discussions of the hidden curriculum of topics such as patient safety, staff-staff interactions, interdisciplinary team collaboration, conflict resolution in the clinical setting, management of heath care resources, personal time management, clinician-patient boundaries, management of disruptive patients or medical staff, dealing with adverse outcomes, etc., all can provide the trainee with critical role modeling.

Sharing clinical stories with trainees allows students to learn from unusual and/or stressful patient situations. More importantly, it helps clinicians deal in an open, reflective and transparent manner with their stresses in clinical practice which can include missed diagnoses, difficult treatment decisions, adverse patient outcomes, and patient losses. Trainees look to faculty role models to learn how to deal with stressful clinical situations. Helping others learn from challenging clinical experiences can be both gratifying and helpful to clinicians as they deal with the day-to-day pressures of clinical practice. The satisfaction of seeing trainees grow in their clinical roles and knowing that they will have a positive effect on the lives of their own patients can help prevent burnout in their faculty mentors.

Finally, as an added bonus, many clinicians report that, despite multiple other demands, teaching promotes their own satisfaction, health and well-being and their legacy, consistent with Osler's words: *"I desire no other epitaph... than the statement that I taught medical students in the wards, as I regard this as by far the most useful and important work I have been called upon to do"* (Silverman et al., 2007). Indeed, faculty play such a crucial role in creating the next generation of medical teachers that students regularly cite their best teachers as their own inspiration to become medical educators.

Faculty development should focus on the importance of faculty as mentors and role models in medical education and should provide mentoring and advising skills for faculty, including a well-defined curriculum for professional identity formation in trainees (Cruess, Cruess, Boudreau, Snell, & Steinert, 2015).

The Medical Educator as Promoter of Life-Long Learning

The overwhelming amount of new information available on almost every aspect of medical practice requires that faculty become both teachers and promoters of life-long learning. The clinical setting provides experiential learning and is an ideal site in which to make the educational shift from pedagogy to the use of adult learning processes (Abela, 2009; Kaufman, 2003; Merriam & Bierema, 2013). By creating a collaborative learning environment within the healthcare team, clinicians can also share the responsibility for teaching and learning within the context of trainees' clinical experience as the team explores what they know, what they need to know, and the latest treatment and practice guidelines. Trainees' access to the most recent online information can be very helpful to the team while faculty can provide essential input into evaluation of the validity of that information. At the same time trainees will learn that even a master clinician does not and cannot "know it all" and cannot be expected to be an expert on every disease process and its treatment. In fact, clinicians who share their self-assessment about what they know and what they do not know and what needs to be learned serve as powerful role models as they emphasize the importance of life-long learning and problem-solving skills. Beyond that, the ability of faculty to accept feedback from trainees without becoming defensive, and to make changes based on that feedback, emphasizes the mutual educational opportunities within the clinical team, ultimately increasing everyone's knowledge and skills and enhancing patient care.

Faculty development should focus on helping teachers understand adult learning theories and established educational modalities such as problem-based learning and team-based learning that facilitate and promote self-directed learning for trainees and themselves (Abela, 2009, Kaufman 2003, Merriam & Bierema, 2013).

CONCLUSION

Overall Faculty Development Needs

Medical education administrators and faculty development professionals must recognize the major changes taking place in the healthcare system and the effect of new technologies on medical education and especially on medical educators. In response to changing learner needs and recognition of the many roles that faculty play in the creation of the next generation of medical practitioners, traditional methods of teaching are being modified or even abandoned (Ramani, 2006), sometimes without input or engagement of front-line clinical educators. These roles include content expert, competency expert, teacher of critical thinking, patient educator, role model, and promoter of life-long learning. Each of these roles requires targeted faculty development programming that should capitalize on clinician educators' commitment to and enthusiasm for preparing the next generation for the practice of medicine. Faculty are quite receptive to faculty development programs so long as those programs recognize their commitment and desire to participate, are structured appropriately for their needs, and are respectful of their feedback and time and potential financial resources they dedicate to participate.

REFERENCES

Abela, J. C. (2009). Adult learning theories and medical education: A review. *Malta Medical Journal*, *21*(1), 11–18.

Adams, F. (1939). *The Genuine Works of Hippocrates*. Baltimore, MD: The Williams & Wilkins Company.

Anderson, M. (1996). *Imposters in the Temple: A Blueprint for Improving Higher Education in America*. Palo Alto, CA: Hoover Institution Press.

Branch, W. T., Kroenke, K., & Levinson, W. (1997). The clinician- educator --- present and future roles. *Journal of General Internal Medicine*, *12*(S2supplement 2), S1–S3. doi:10.1046/j.1525-1497.12.s2.16.x PMID:9127237

Cook, A. F., Arora, V. M., Rasinski, K. A., Curlin, F. A., & Yoon, J. D. (2014). The prevalence of medical student mistreatment and its association with burnout. *Academic Medicine*, *89*(5), 740–754. doi:10.1097/ ACM.0000000000000204 PMID:24667503

Cooke, M., Irby, D. M., & O'Brien, C. S. (2010). *Educating Physicians: A Call for Reform of Medical School and Residency*. San Francisco, CA: Jossey-Bass.

Cruess, R. L., Cruess, S. R., Boudreau, J. D., Snell, L., & Steinert, Y. (2015). A schematic representation of the professional identity formation and socialization of medical students and residents: A guide for medical educators. *Academic Medicine*, *90*(6), 718–725. doi:10.1097/ACM.0000000000000700 PMID:25785682

Dahlstrom, J., Dorei-Rag, A., McGill, D., Owen, C., Tymms, K., & Watson, D. A. (2005). What motivates senior clinicians to teach medical students? *BMC Medical Education*, *5*(1), 27–37. doi:10.1186/1472-6920-5-27 PMID:16022738

Eckleberry-Hunt, J., & Tucciarone, J. (2011). The challenges and opportunities of teaching "Generation Y". *Journal of Graduate Medical Education*, *3*(4), 458–461. doi:10.4300/JGME-03-04-15 PMID:23205190

Feinberg, R. N., & Koltz, E. F. (2015). Getting started as a medical teacher in times of change. *Medical Science Educator*, *25*(1), 69–74. doi:10.100740670-014-0098-y

Jones, M. D. Jr, Rosenberg, A. A., Gilhooly, J. T., & Carraccio, C. L. (2011). Perspective: Competencies, outcomes, and controversy --- Linking professional activities to competencies to improve resident education and practice. *Academic Medicine*, *86*(2), 161–165. doi:10.1097/ACM.0b013e31820442e9 PMID:21169788

Kamei, R. K., Cook, S., Puthucheary, J., & Starmer, C. F. (2012). 21st Century learning in medicine: Traditional teaching versus team-based learning. *Medical Science Educator, 22*(2), 57–64. doi:10.1007/BF03341758

Kaufmann, D. M. (2003). ABC of learning and teaching in medicine: Applying educational theory to practice. *British Medical Journal, 326*(7382), 213–216. doi:10.1136/bmj.326.7382.213 PMID:12543841

McCann, D. P., & Blossom, H. J. (1990). The physician as a patient educator. From theory to practice. *The Western Journal of Medicine, 153*(1), 44–49. PMID:2202158

McMahon, T. (2005). Teaching medicine and allied disciplines in the 21st century; lessons from Ireland on the continuing need for reform. *Radiography, 11*(1), 61–65. doi:10.1016/j.radi.2004.05.005

Mercuri, M., Sherbino, J., Sedran, R. J., Frank, J. R., Gafni, A., & Norman, G. (2015). When guidelines don't guide: The effect of patient context on management decisions based on clinical practice guidelines. *Academic Medicine, 90*(2), 191–196. doi:10.1097/ACM.0000000000000542 PMID:25354075

Merriam, S. B., & Bierema, L. L. (2013). *Adult Learning: Linking Theory and Practice.* San Francisco, CA: Jossey-Bass.

Norman, G. (2012). Medical education: Past, present and future. *Perspectives on Medical Education, 1*(1), 6–14. doi:10.100740037-012-0002-7 PMID:23316454

Prober, C. G., & Khan, S. (2013). Medical education reimagined: A call to action. *Academic Medicine, 88*(10), 1407–1410. doi:10.1097/ACM.0b013e3182a368bd PMID:23969367

Ramani, S. (2006). Twelve tips to promote excellence in medical teaching. *Medical Teacher, 28*(1), 19–23. doi:10.1080/01421590500441786 PMID:16627316

Sharpless, J. M., Oxman, A. D., Mahtani, K. R., Chalmers, I., Oliver, S., Collins, K., … Hoffman, T. (2017). Critical thinking in healthcare and education. BM J2017, 357, j2234 doi:10.1136bmj.j2234.

Sherbino, J., Frank, J. R., & Snell, L. (2014). Defining the key roles and competencies of the clinician-educator of the 21st Century: A national mixed-methods study. *Academic Medicine, 89*(5), 783–789. doi:10.1097/ACM.0000000000000217 PMID:24667507

Shochet, R. B., Colbert-Getz, J. M., Levine, R. B., & Wright, S. M. (2013). Gauging events that influence students' perceptions of the medical school learning environment: Findings from one institution. *Academic Medicine, 88*(2), 246–252. doi:10.1097/ACM.0b013e31827bfa14 PMID:23269291

Silverman, M., Murray, T. J., & Bryan, C. S. (Eds.). (2007). *The Quotable Osler.* Philadelphia, PA: American College of Physicians.

Stahn, B., & Harendza, S. (2014). Role models - major determinant of specialty choice and training program. *GMS Zeitschrift für Medizinische Ausbildung, 31*(4), 1–15. PMID:25489345

ten Cate, O. (2013). Nuts and bolts of entrustable professional activities. *Journal of Graduate Medical Education, 5*(1), 157–158. doi:10.4300/JGME-D-12-00380.1 PMID:24404246 ten Cate, O. (2014). What is a 21st-century doctor? Rethinking the significance of the medical degree. *Academic Medicine, 89*(7), 966–969. doi:10.1097/ACM.0000000000000280 PMID:24979164

Topol, E. J. (2013). *The Creative Destruction of Medicine: How the Digital Revolution Will Create Better Health Care*. New York, NY: Basic Books.

Topol, E. J., Steinhubl, S. R., & Torkamani, A. (2015). Digital medical tools and sensors. *Journal of the American Medical Association, 313*(4), 353–354. doi:10.1001/jama.2014.17125 PMID:25626031

Chapter 19
Continuing Professional Development:
Supporting the Complex Role of Today's Physician

Shari A. Whicker
Virginia Tech Carilion School of Medicine, USA & Carilion Clinic, USA

Alisa Nagler
American College of Surgeons, Duke University School of Medicine, USA

ABSTRACT

Continuing professional development is a critical responsibility within the complex role of today's physician. This chapter provides an overview of continuing professional development for physicians. The authors propose self-determination theory (SDT) as a foundational framework for discussing physician continuing professional development. They also address a variety of motivating factors for physicians being involved in continuing professional development. These factors include regulatory requirements, continued competence, career planning, and their own commitment to learn. Lastly, the authors include a discussion of various continuing professional development formats and the benefits of each, as well as challenges and barriers to effective continuing education.

INTRODUCTION

By this point in the book, readers will have already read descriptions of the joys and challenges of many years spent learning and training to finally begin their careers as practicing physicians. The formal medical education and training that physicians have participated in prior to the initiation of the practice phase of their career will generally have run anywhere between 7 and 15 years. Usually when one reaches such a monumental goal for which they have spent as many years preparing, he or she might see it as an end point, a finish line, or a destination. In the professional field of medicine, however, these accomplished individuals have achieved this feat, only to *begin* practicing. Merriam-Webster defines the term *practice*

DOI: 10.4018/978-1-7998-1468-9.ch019

as "To perform or work at repeatedly so as to become proficient" or "To train by repeated exercises" (Practice, 2019). Given the high stakes and constantly evolving nature of medicine, extensive continuing professional development is a necessary correlate to maintaining success throughout the duration of a physician's medical practice.

BACKGROUND

The concept of continuing professional development (CPD) has been described by many throughout the literature and includes a variety of permutations (Academy of Royal Medical Colleges, 1999; Filipe, Silva, Stulting, 2014); World Health Organization, 2010). For the purpose of this chapter, we will use the definition provided by the World Federation for Medical Education (WFME). The WFME describes continuing professional development as the following,

all activities that doctors undertake, formally and informally, in order to maintain, update, develop and enhance their knowledge, skills, and attitudes in response to the needs of their patients. Engaging in CPD is a professional obligation but also a prerequisite for enhancing the quality of health care. The strongest motivating factor for continuous professional life-long learning is the will and desire to maintain professional quality.

Worldwide, continuing professional development has evolved from continuing medical education (CME) and differs in a number of ways (Table 1). Continuing professional development is an expectation of practice in many professional fields. However, in medicine, physicians are not expected to practice using only what they have learned throughout their previous formal education and training. Each is, instead, expected to continue to grow and develop in areas not only directly related to clinical care, but also as a researcher, a leader, a teacher, someone who looks out for their own well-being as closely as they do for that of their patients, as well as other areas that contribute to them being well-rounded physicians in the current age. In a field as complex and high stakes as medicine, this can be a challenging and daunting feat. While the more recent generations of physicians seem to be acquiescing to the diverse demands of practicing today, gone are the days of the physician with expertise only in patient care.

Terms related to CPD are often used interchangeably and institutions may have varying definitions for each (e.g. faculty development, professional development, lifelong learning, continuing education, career development, continuing medical education, etc.). More recently, these terms have been more carefully defined, compared, and contrasted, advocating for each to retain their own identity while emphasizing the shared components and opportunities for complementing one another (Silver & Leslie, 2017; Davis et al., 2017). Understanding these distinctions and the role of each is certainly important, however, it is clear that all emphasize the need for continued learning beyond formal medical education training programs. More specifically, the critical point behind the lifelong learning that all of these terms represent, is that one must develop and enhance competence and a personal career path relevant to the complex nature of practicing medicine, while promoting and contributing to quality healthcare. For the purposes of this chapter, the term *continuing professional development (CPD)* will be used to encompass this overriding concept.

LIFELONG LEARNING IN MEDICAL EDUCATION

Lifelong learning is expected to occur across the medical education continuum, from UME (undergraduate medical education) to GME (graduate medical education) to CME (continuing medical education). This book has provided an in-depth overview of UME and even GME, as it relates to the role of the educator. In those cases, the Liaison Committee on Medical Education (LCME), and the Accreditation Council for Graduate Medical Education (ACGME) provide guidance and regulations related to the training of individuals pursuing a career in medicine. Upon graduation from a GME Program, one enters the field of independent practice. At that time, there are numerous external bodies dictating a physician's professional development, with requirements to obtain and maintain licensure, certification, and credentialing in order to practice medicine.

Ideally, and most often the case, those who choose to practice medicine have an inherent desire to not only maintain competence but also continue to learn and grow throughout their careers. The ever-evolving nature of medicine, changes in healthcare delivery, moving between practices, meeting the varying needs of changing patient populations, and/or personal responsibilities that may take one out of training or work for a period of time, all require on-going learning to maintain competence. Additionally, moving from novice to competence, to mastery or expert in their complex professional world is ideally the goal for most physicians in practice (Ericsson, 2004; Dreyfus, 2004). CPD is a critical element in the process for physicians to maintain competence and eventually achieve mastery.

MOTIVATION

There are numerous theories on what motivates one to continue learning throughout his or her profession, especially in the field of medical education, some of which are described by Cook and Artino (2016). Adult learning theory posits that a distinct difference between pedagogy and andragogy centers on motivational direction. Knowles (1980), known for his development of Adult Learning Theory, suggests that while children are primarily extrinsically motivated, adults are primarily driven by intrinsic motivators. Knowles theory suggests that, while there will always be tension between the balance of intrinsic and extrinsic motivational factors, adults are more satisfied with the learning process, more focused, more persistent, and more eager to apply their knowledge when they learn through experiences by which they are intrinsically motivated.

As is the case with adults in general, physicians are motivated both factors. Extrinsic motivation refers to performance in order to attain a separate outcome while intrinsic motivation refers to performance for the inherent satisfaction of the activity itself (Ryan & Deci, 2000). It is likely that, in order for physicians to reach and maintain their competence to ensure quality patient care, development as a well-rounded, thriving physician, both extrinsic and intrinsic motivations are at play. A complex web of professional requirements forces a sense of extrinsic motivation. Ambition and the desire to stay current, together with personal career planning, encourage activation of our intrinsic motivation. The drive for continued development is likely the result of both extrinsic and intrinsic motivation.

SELF-DETERMINATION THEORY AS A FOUNDATION FOR CPD

Deci and Ryan's theory of Self-Determination (2000) proposes that, while intrinsic motivation is the biggest driver for the positive potential for human nature, extrinsic factors are clearly meaningful contributors to individuals' behaviours. Many studies have shown that extrinsic factors such as "tangible rewards, threats, deadlines, directives, pressured evaluations, and imposed goals" (p. 70) undermine intrinsic motivation. As proposed by Knowles (1980), intrinsic motivation is ideal for adults to find the most value and meaning in an educational activity.

Thus, not only is it preferred for people to be motivated internally, but also there are findings that external motivations can be counterproductive. The field of medicine is full of external regulations and requirements for compliance. Therefore, in this professional world in which extrinsic motivators are prevalent, it is important to understand them and facilitate their integration into practice and lifelong learning.

Self-Determination Theory (SDT) (Ryan & Deci, 2000), emphasizes the importance of three main psychological needs that are the basis for positive self-motivation: competence, autonomy, and relatedness..SDT proposes that if these needs are met, the negative effects of extrinsic motivators can be minimized. This then informs that it is critical to foster competence, autonomy, and relatedness in a physician's CPD opportunities for learning.

Feelings of perceived competence on a given topic can enhance intrinsic motivation for a related action and minimize the negative impacts of extrinsic motivators. Effective feedback, for example, has been considered to be the "cornerstone of clinical teaching" (Cantillon & Sargeant, 2008). However, feedback is an extrinsic motivator that can hinder development if it is given ineffectively, is demeaning in any way, or is seen as an indicator of incompetence. To the contrary, if feedback is given effectively, constructively, and promotes positivity, it can promote a feeling of perceived competence and, thus, minimize the negative impact of feedback as an extrinsic motivator.

A sense of autonomy is the second psychological need that is essential to positive self-motivation under SDT. SDT suggests that feelings of competence must be accompanied by an internal perceived locus of control or sense of autonomy to facilitate the internalization. If an individual feels as if they have some sort of control, choice, and volition over his or her competence and participation in developmental efforts, that feeling of autonomy enhances their intrinsic motivation to engage in the activity (Deci & Ryan, 1985). For example, forcing individuals to participate in specific CPD activities that may or may not correspond with their own preferences (related to format, content, timing, teacher, etc.) may compromise the desired need for autonomy. To the contrary, if they have the option to choose from a variety of opportunities, autonomy may be enhanced.

Relatedness is the third essential psychological need that SDT relates to optimized motivation. As defined by Merriam-Webster related is defined as, "Connected by reason of an established or discoverable relation" (Related. 2019). Within the context of CPD, when activities or behaviours are encouraged, modelled, or participated in by significant others to whom individuals are positively connected or related, this need is fulfilled. For example, an individual might feel a greater sense of connectedness to an activity if it were recommended by his or her respected mentor rather than assigned en masse across the organization. Similarly, if the content being discussed or presented is "related" to the work they are doing and can, thus, be applied, it is likely to be much more meaningful. This again is likely to enhance one's internal motivation to use the opportunity for CPD.

Each physician will undoubtedly vary in their constellation of motivating factors. However, adult learning and SDT theories make it clear that attending to both extrinsic and intrinsic factors is critical to the success of CPD programs to maximize their professional growth potential.

CPD REGULATORY REQUIREMENTS

There is no escaping the numerous regulatory bodies and organizations that determine and monitor the requirements necessary for one to practice (and continue practicing) medicine. These serve as extrinsic motivation for CPD prescribing the necessary requirements needed to care for patients. SDT would emphasize the importance of careful attention to the three essential psychological needs in the face of this bevy of requirements to ensure the developmental process does not get waylaid.

Even with the simplest scenario, the ceaseless, fluctuating, and numerous requirements can be complicated and considerable for any busy physician. CPD is often a component of requirements put in place by State Medical Boards, Specialty Boards, and hospital or clinic employers. Individuals can utilize the external requirements as a form of guidance and organization. They establish the baseline or minimum required, fostering motivation to grow personally and professionally. Below is a brief description of the varied requirements in place for continued practice as a physician.

Specialty Board Requirements

Specialty Boards set the standards for *Certification*. Components of Maintenance of Certification (MOC) include 4 parts: 1.) Professionalism and Professional Standing; 2.) Lifelong Learning and Self-Assessment; 3.) Assessment of Knowledge, Judgement and Skills; 4.) Improvement in Medical Practice (American Board of Medical Specialties) (n.d.). Many Boards have included a high-stakes exam for those who have successfully completed their UME and GME training, in order to become *certified* initially. In the last 10 years, there have been many changes (and more on the horizon) to MOC, including many moving to a *continuous certification* model. There are similarities but also great variance in what each Board requires for one to obtain and maintain this certification throughout their career, many now moving away from a high stakes exam every 10 years, to this more *continuous certification* (and documentation of learning).

Despite highlights on websites, alerts sent via social media platforms, formal mailed letters, and discussions at national meetings, it is still difficult to remain abreast of the many, varied, and changing regulatory requirements. Thus, the onus is on the practicing physician to be proactive and seek out new information to stay updated. Individuals are encouraged to visit relevant Board websites, read the likes of relevant newsletters, seek out Board updates at national meetings, and/or help ensure such critical information is incorporated as part of one's day-to-day work. Physicians should seek out any regular communications within an organization or community they are connected to, such as one's Academic Medical Center Department, Specialty Society, private practice group, etc.

State Board Requirements

In order to practice in one's State, one must meet State Medical Board *Licensure* Requirements, which are likely different than (although often complementary with) Specialty Board Requirements. There has been a growth in the number, and perhaps breadth, of State requirements, with newer emphasis on requiring continuing education in certain content areas (U.S. Medical Regulatory Trends and Actions, 2018). More than half of the states now identify specific content (e.g. ethics, professionalism, risk management, opioid prescribing) as a component of one's required CME. The Federation of State Medical Boards tracks these requirements, as do a number of other entities working to support their members, employees, and/or diplomats (FSMB, 2019). In some cases, States require individuals to utilize the content they have developed or approved. For example, the Pennsylvania Medical Board requires all physicians complete two hours of *Recognition and Reporting of Child Abuse*, a biannual renewal requirement that can only be met by successfully completing the online modules offered by the Pennsylvania Medical Society.

In other cases, individuals are left on their own to identify educational content that will meet the requirement. Reporting structures also vary, with many states requiring only an attestation with periodic and random audits of one's documented education. As noted above, State requirements may be even more difficult to keep up with than specialty Board requirements. Thus, individuals are encouraged to identify a way or ways to stay current and not be surprised by a requirement, avoiding the need to scramble to find content to check off a box before receiving a formal reprimand, or even interrupting one's licensure to practice. Again, consider the opportunities to incorporate competence, autonomy and relatedness, converting these external requirements into meaningful CPD.

Employer and Other Requirements

Employers, such as hospitals and clinics, may also require specific education and training, often beyond what a State or Specialty Board requires, as part of *credentialing* and *privileging*. Depending on one's role in patient care, research, teaching, physician well-being, quality, leadership, etc., there are likely specific local CPD requirements. As examples, for those involved in patient care—there is the Health Insurance Portability and Accountability Act (HIPAA) training. Depending on one's area of expertise or specialty, there may be additional internal trainings or documentation of "counts" of procedures to be deemed competent to practice in that area. For those involved in research (bench, clinical, and or education)—there is the Institutional Review Board (IRB) training requirements. For those involved in interprofessional healthcare—there is the *Team Strategies and Tools to Enhance Performance and Patient Safety* or Teamstepps training (Agency for Healthcare Research and Quality, n.d.). For most involved in patient care—there is training related to "quality" and how to measure the impact of patient care for purposes of individual and institutional improvements.

Even more relevant to this Chapter, for those faculty working with medical students or GME residents/fellows in a teaching capacity, the external regulatory bodies, such as the Liaison Committee on Medical Education (LCME) and the Accreditation Council for Graduate Medical Education (ACGME) require core faculty to obtain/complete CPD related to "how to teach." These can be either local or institutional requirements

The growing complexity of regulations to practice medicine has led to considerable dialogue about whether these are the appropriate entities to be setting and mandating the continued CPD requirements. Recent discussions have included conversation regarding who is determining what is necessary for physicians to practice, how was the responsible party/parties determined, and on what are the requirements based. However, maybe more importantly is the question whether the requirements put into place are the appropriate ones to ensure safe and competent practice. There has been much recent discussion related to this very question (Boulet & Durning, 2019; Vandergrift, Gray, & Weng, 2018) which undoubtedly led to the major changes in Board Certification requirements (e.g. moving from a 10-year, high-stakes exam to continuous certification and assessment with formative feedback). However, one cannot always be sure of the origin or outcomes of many of these regulations. As examples—Does requiring two CME Credits of "ethics" content every two years make one a better doctor? Does the process that individuals use to complete Level Four of MOC (Improvement in Medical Practice) make them a safer doctor? Given these questions, the push to evaluate the effectiveness of CME is critical (Smith, Stark, Rayburn, Davis, & Turco, 2017; O'Sullivan & Irby, 2017; Davis, Rayburn, & Smith, 2017).

Whether the regulations lead to the best patient care or not, physicians must comply in order to practice medicine. Identifying convenient and meaningful ways to address the requirements and demonstrate compliance is critical. Just as requirements continue to evolve, so are the means of documenting compliance and demonstrating understanding. Gone are the days of manila folders overflowing with CME certificates and multiple-choice exams every 10 years, covering content one does not need for practice. It is important to identify a method for staying current on requirements at the state, specialty, and local levels, especially given the continuous revisions and additions.

It is also important to establish a means of organizing individual activities and progress toward meeting requirements. There are numerous hospitals, specialty societies, and/or paid services that allow for electronic storage of CME credit or documentation of CPD activities. Physicians do not want to find themselves surprised by a certification or licensure requirement with no time left to meet it. More importantly, physicians do not want to adhere to these requirements simply for the purpose of checking off a box. Instead, these regulations can serve as a road map and a set of minimal requirements to continuing one's professional development across a lifetime.

According to SDT, complex webs of requirements put the CPD process at risk for ineffective behaviour modification. They may or may not instill a greater sense of competence, but they contradict the concept of autonomy. Key to meeting these requirements in productive ways is to connect physicians with meaningful activities within which others may participate and to recommend to them activities that convey a sense of relatedness.

CONTINUED COMPETENCE

Maintaining continued competence and confidence is a strong motivator for physicians to engage in CPD and involves elements of both extrinsic and intrinsic motivation. Continued competence, by nature, is one of the psychological needs espoused by SDT. However, within the context of medical education, physicians are charged with balancing complex roles involving multiple facets for which they are held accountable making it challenging to achieve and maintain competence in all facets. As noted above, these facets may include clinical care, research, leadership, well-being, teaching, as well as areas such as professionalism, quality improvement, the business of medicine, and ethical excellence. These areas may appear to be disparate in nature, but all converge within the role of the physician across his or her career. Change is ubiquitous in medicine, and given the evolving nature of these areas, the profession makes it essential for physicians to regularly retool to keep up with advances and developments within each.

Clinical Care

Clinical care is fundamental to the role of a practicing physician. However, clinical practices change rapidly based on a variety of evolving factors, including advances in technology and techniques, research, patient demographics, innovations, and reimbursement. Imagine a point in time when smallpox was a major cause for concern in healthcare, but opioids were not. Consider when no one knew what the acronym LGBTQI stood for or what it might mean for his or her patients. A diagnosis of Human Immunodeficiency Virus (HIV) was once considered a death sentence. Advances in laparoscopy have so dramatically changed the surgical sciences, yet laparoscopic techniques were not always an option. While society has moved beyond these specific examples, new ones arise each day, and every subtle evolutionary point creates an additional learning opportunity for physicians. CPD is essential when it comes to physicians remaining current with the evolution of advancements in clinical care. Furthermore, each evolutionary point hinges on physicians and others to study, investigate, and improve upon what currently exists.

Research and Quality Improvement

The science of medicine would not exist without medical research. Medical research is critical to new discoveries, innovations, and evidence-based advancements in medicine. While formally trained researchers bear the brunt of the investigative work, it is essential for physicians who are involved in hands-on patient care to be familiar with the processes necessary to conduct basic research. CPD can support physicians in learning more about the process of formulating and investigating hypotheses in order to develop basic research skills that will benefit both themselves and their patients. Many of the basic research skills can also contribute to a better understanding of the quality improvement process that is so critical to a physician's role (Sargeant, Wong, & Campbell, 2018). Quality Improvements (QI) may include simple interventions to minimize patient wait time, improving cancer-screening rates, modifying the residency curriculum to be more meaningful, or reducing unnecessary blood draws in young children. These changes can significantly impact the patient, physician, clinical care team, and/or learner experience. However, it is difficult to implement, measure, and maximize such changes without following an appropriate Quality Improvement process. CPD can help physicians to be better equipped to take on these challenges.

Leadership

Whether it is related to clinical care, research, a part of their more formal career path, or any other of the myriad of responsibilities encompassed within a physician's role, physicians are often looked upon to be leaders (Storey, 2019; Angood & Birk, 2014; Grady & Hinings, 2018; Gunderman & Kanter, 2009). Often, immediately upon graduation from their GME training, physicians are expected to lead interprofessional healthcare teams. They may also be expected to lead the clinical discussions related to clinical research projects. There will be times when they are asked to lead the "business of medicine" charge within their practice. Furthermore, physicians often move into a variety of leadership roles without adequate guidance on how to be successful within them. These leadership skills are not generally learned during any part of the formal medical education continuum but can be incorporated into CPD.

Teaching

By virtue of their chosen profession, physicians are granted both the privilege and the responsibility to not only continue to learn throughout their careers, but also to share what they have learned. While many may not have consciously chosen a career as a teacher, an inherent element of practicing medicine is to teach. The word "doctor" is actually a derivative of the Latin word "docere," which means, "to teach." Teaching is well integrated into the daily role of a physician.

Physicians teach patients and patients' families about their general health, conditions, prevention, and treatments. The literature clearly shows a connection between effective physician teaching and patient compliance (Leung et al., 2015; Peter, 2014). Critical to the heart of the medical education continuum, physicians teach medical students,residents, and fellows. Sometimes, this is done in the classroom, but more frequently, this is done through hands-on patient care experiences and small group or one-on-one conversations. They also teach their peers, at times both directly and indirectly.

Teaching skills are not generally parts of the formal learning physicians receive through medical education or GME training. Therefore, regardless of how proficient they may be within their clinical specialty, they may not be effectively equipped to teach what they know. Effective teaching involves a variety of key elements, many of which can be provided through CPD. CPD related to teaching might include topics to enhance physicians skills at effectively providing feedback, assessing and evaluating learners, teaching at the bedside, using simulation to teach, working with challenging learners, and incorporating active learning techniques or technology into their teaching.

Interprofessionalism

In addition to engaging in CPD in the areas of teaching, patient care, and research, physicians must maintain competence and often serve as leaders of interprofessional teams (Dow & Thibault, 2017). Interprofessional education (IPE) emphasizes collaborative training and practice that aims at promoting the working relationships between different healthcare professions. There is growing literature on the impact of such training on patient care (Cox et al., 2016). Programs like TeamSTEPPS (Agency for Healthcare Research and Quality, n.d.) have been developed and utilized at numerous institutions, that focuses on improved teamwork and communication in health care. Given that IPE is essential (and somewhat new), there are growing efforts and newly developed programs available to offer faculty development for those providing such education (Watkins, 2016).

The topics addressed within this section represent a sampling of the main areas of faculty CPD needs for continued competence. Faculty do not need to be experts in all of these areas, but do need to be adequately familiar with them all and more. The field of medicine also offers them the opportunity to choose amongst these areas to develop an advanced level of expertise. Formal expectations for the number of areas within which each physician should develop a higher-level expertise will be variable by specialty, employment, and personal preference for career advancement.

CAREER PLANNING

Physicians engaged in career planning and seeking of CPD may be either and/or both extrinsically and intrinsically motivated. Ideally, physicians move from passive compliance to active personal commitment, as described by Deci and Ryan (2000), and perhaps this can be fostered by the way in which physicians are supported in their lifelong learning. As noted earlier, focusing on competence, autonomy, and relatedness is likely to foster intrinsic motivation. Regardless of the motivational direction, there are ample opportunities and tools to guide a physician in their career development as one's individual interests and needs evolve, and healthcare continues to change.

Annual Performance Evaluations

At a minimum, most employed physicians participate in a formal Annual Evaluation of Performance. A supervisor's evaluation of an individual may be supplemented with a 360 (a safe environment for an individual to receive candid feedback from peers, supervisors, subordinates, and other individuals with relationships key to their success), and an opportunity for individual employee self-reflection. An Annual Evaluation of Performance may even include patient satisfaction surveys or the review of relevant patient care outcomes, such as from an Electronic Medical Record (EMR) system or procedural registries. There is often short and long-term goal setting for the individual and, in some cases, an Individualized Education Plan (IEP) developed based on feedback, outcomes, and personal career goals. This is a wonderful opportunity for one to identify any gaps in practice and, thus, opportunities for CPD. It is often difficult for individuals to identify where deficiencies may be (Eva & Regehr, 2008; Ward, Gruppen, & Regehr, 2002). Thus, incorporating more objective data is important to inform one on potentially problematic deficits and/or opportunities for growth. If an annual evaluation with some of the elements described above is not a component of one's workplace and formally conducted by a supervisor, physicians should consider initiating something similar independently, either including a supervisor, or not.

Mentorship and Coaching

Both mentorship and coaching are important components of a physician's CPD (Geraci & Thigpen, 2017; Lovell, 2018). There are distinctions between the two that may be important as one is determining what is best for their CPD. Gawande (2011) introduced the idea of coaching for physicians, first as an opportunity for someone to offer individualized observation and feedback (Geraci & Thigpen, 2017; Lovell, 2018). It has been transformed as a strategy for implementing individualized education, allowing faculty to guide performance, competency, and career progression of an individual learner (Deiorio, Carney, Kahl, & Juve, 2016). Coaching and mentoring both use questioning and guiding. Mentorship includes more advising, counselling, and supporting in a way that coaching does not. Mentorships are generally long-term relationships, while coaching tend to be shorter-term relationships (6 to 12 months) and target a potential change in performance (Abiddin, 2007).

It is likely one will find themselves on either side of these of mentoring or coaching (mentor/mentee, coach/coached) relationships at some point in their career. While distinctions have been made in the literature, in both cases, mentors and coaches have been found to foster CPD. Numerous programs have reported improved career advancement as a result of mentoring programs. Programs also report enhanced peer networking and improved career satisfaction as a result of mentoring programs (Fleming, 2017; Pololi, 2015). There are examples of mentoring and coaching programs that have improved patient outcomes for the mentee and or the individual being coached (Sheri et al., 2019; Lyasere et al., 2016). CPD that reaches the top of Kirkpatrick's pyramid (impact on patient care) for program evaluation is a lofty goal and one which educators reach for in developing and offering educational programs (Kirkpatrick, 1994). This suggests mentorship and coaching can be quite impactful as a form or supplement to one's CPD. An effective coaching and/or mentoring relationship can truly enhance feelings of relatedness.

Promotion and Tenure

If employed within an academic medical center, one is almost always faced with the variability of the appointments, promotions and tenure (APT) process, stimulating individuals to select meaningful CPD activities and incorporate them as part of a career plan. Over the last decade, some individuals and institutions have moved to the use of an "education portfolio" as a way to document scholarly educational activities and, in some cases, promote oneself (Lewis & Baker, 2007; Heeneman & Driessen, 2017). This is yet another opportunity to utilize objective data to inform one's CPD and career planning. If used effectively, it is not just a laundry list of everything that an individual has done, but instead, hopefully, an illustration of thoughtfully designed, meaningful professional growth over time.

Being able to independently, and periodically, evaluate one's own performance for purposes of growth and improvement is critical to professional success. This process directly connects with an individual's need for perceived competence. However, this exercise can be less than ideally productive as it can also be detrimental to the development process as an extrinsic factor that compromises an individual's intrinsic motivation. Thus, if none of the above career planning mechanisms arein place, or better yet, to complement the above, it is critical for physicians to take charge of their own lifelong learning and CPD. Self-Directed Learning Theory (SDL) promotes an individual: 1.) Diagnosing their learning needs; 2.) Formulating learning goals; 3.) Identifying resources for learning; 4.) Selecting and implementing learning strategies; and 5.) Evaluating learning outcomes (Jeong et al., 2018). According to Jeong et al, "Self-directed learning (SDL) is a learning process considered to be one of the most appropriate strategies within Continuous Professional Development (professional development) for physicians to remain current with new evidence and maintain their competency" (Jeong et al., 2018).

Ideally, this all happens as part of a structured process, complementing an existing CPD plan put in place by one's employer or through another structured program (e.g. formal mentor/mentee program, employer orientation and annual reviews, offered by one's specialty society). However, once leaving the structured confines of a training program, it may be left to the individual to plan, steer, and implement their growth and development. This promotes autonomy but may also be challenging without further guidance. SDL may be the most effective when it comes to career development within CPD. SDL suggests that the more internally motivated one is, the better the results. Given this, the Accreditation Council for Graduate Medical Education (ACGME) now requires residents to develop SDL skills as part of their training, recognizing the potential for SDL to enhance learning in residency and beyond (Nothnagle, Anandarajah, & Goldman, 2011). This reinforces the idea that physicians must be at the center of identifying and planning their CPD. Davis et al (2011) found that physicians feel confident in identifying their own learning needs. There are few processes within professional development that contribute more authentically to a professional's incorporation of effective SDL practices during which he or she accurately identifies his or her areas of deficits, and then takes steps to mitigate them.

COMMITMENT TO LEARN

At the very top of Maslow's Hierarchy of Needs (Maslow, 1943), one finds self-actualization. Self-actualization involves an innate desire to grow and develop in the direction of one's values and reaching one's full potential. Similar to the way in which Maslow posited that self-actualization might be realized once other more basic needs are satisfied, a physician is able to focus on his/her own innate commitment to learn once he or she has addressed other requirements or guidelines for participating in CPD that may be more fundamental to success within his or her role.

The literature shows that once a physician's basic compliance and other external motivators are met, intrinsic factors are the most significant motivators for their behaviour change (Phipps & Shortell, 2016). Intrinsic motivation often accompanies a certain level of expertise. Expertise, as described by Dreyfus (2004), allows one to intuitively perform and make decisions at a high level while also adapting to variable situations with subtle modifications. Given the high level of constant change in medical practice, clinicians need to develop the competence and expertise to function efficiently on everyday tasks, but also to create solutions for novel workplace challenges (Mylopoulos & Regehr, 2009).

Cutrer et al. (2010) proposed the Master Adaptive Learner as a model for providing physicians with strategies for learning and improving in the ever-evolving healthcare environment, all while effectively managing the constant influx of new information and on-going change to efficiently and effectively maintain competence.

As a part of their daily, minute-by-minute work, physicians are constantly problem solving. Oftentimes, the solutions they reach are based on the knowledge and experience they have attained throughout their formal education, training, and practice. However, there are times during which they will be challenged by circumstances that require additional learning or innovations with which they are not yet familiar to provide the best care. Master Adaptive Learning fosters the development and use of adaptive expertise in practice. The Master Adaptive Learner describes a metacognitive approach to learning based on self-regulation that can foster the development and use of adaptive expertise in practice.

Dreyfus's (2004) model, presented in Figure 1, also describes a developmental approach that parallels metacognitive ability. The model suggests that once one attains a certain level of expertise, they are not only less focused on rules, more intuitively-driven, and more relevantly focused, but they are also more likely to be able to engage in the metacognitive process of self-regulated learning (Zimmerman & Schunk, 2001) that allows them to recognize their areas of strength and deficits, and then to thoughtfully address these areas with appropriate CPD. Self-regulated learning involves two main metacognitive elements: metacognitive monitoring and metacognitive control. Simply put, the metacognitive monitoring process guides an individual to recognize their strengths and deficits in knowledge, skills, and behaviours to adequately prepare him or her for the metacognitive control process. During the metacognitive control process, her or she would take appropriate developmental steps to maximize their strength potential and fill in his or her deficit gaps.

For example, a more novice practitioner who is well skilled in bedside teaching might attend a session on bedside teaching at a national conference because it is a topic of interest to him or her, despite the fact that he or she may receive very little developmental value from the activity. However, an expert practitioner would be more apt than a novice, advanced beginner, competent, or proficient practitioner to recognize his or her deficits in an area in which his or her skills are weaker and seek appropriate development opportunities to strengthen them. Therefore, an expert practitioner who is well-skilled in bedside teaching but recognizes his or her deficiencies (metacognitive monitoring) might forgo the bedside teaching session and instead choose to participate in a session that more directly addresses a topic area in which they may be deficient in an effort to maximize the developmental opportunity (metacognitive control).

The theory of Deliberate Practice illustrates the value of metacognitive monitoring and control in the development of expertise. The challenge at this point in the continuum is for experts to not become complacent and for them to continue to consciously seek further development (Ericsson, 2004).

Figure 1.

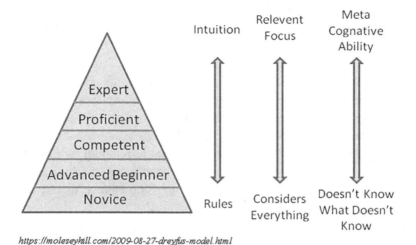

https://moleseyhall.com/2009-08-27-dreyfus-model.html

"Deliberate Practice" is a model that describes SRL through the development of expertise. It suggests the notion that individuals themselves assume responsibility for areas in which a teacher, coach, or mentor may have once been very valuable from an external perspective. Deliberate practice allows the individual to monitor and control their own development through the SRL process and engaging themselves in increasingly challenging variations to continue to enhance their knowledge, skills, and behaviours to the highest levels.

PROFESSIONAL DEVELOPMENT: FORMATS, BENEFITS & CHALLENGES

For many, CME evokes the concept of credits physicians are required to earn and claim to meet regulatory requirements. As others have described, CME has also been conceptualized as the CPD required to keep one up to date in their specific field (Davis, Rayburn, & Smith, 2017). As some have attempted to clarify and refine, CPD can be seen as the combination of "... CME, with its focus on content knowledge, and faculty development, with its focus on evidence-based learning methodologies, across the institution to produce a more robust, system-and outcomes-oriented program to facilitate both individual and organizational learning" (Davis et al., 2017). To meet the on-going needs of physicians, it is necessary for the CME system to evolve, including more innovative education and more opportunities for participation, which healthcare systems can recognize as providing strategic value in driving change (McMahon, 2016). This transition from CME to CPD reinforces a move away from simply counting CME credits, and a focus on staying current in one's field of practice (Filipe, Golnik, & Mack, 2018).

Similarly, to meet the learning needs of individuals, there is a move away from education as just a didactic and clinically-oriented activity, and more toward learning "which encompasses diverse activities, addresses diverse aspects of physicians' competency, and includes diverse professionals, highlighting the importance of team-based interprofessional education" (Kitto, Price, Jeong, Campbell, & Reeves, 2018). Additionally, there is much focus on the benefits of learning on the job and physicians have noted a desire for more credit for learning during patient care (Davis et al, 2011). While physicians must still count

CME credits and document completion of educational activities to meet many regulatory requirements, the goal is to help foster a love for learning, while making it convenient, accessible, and meaningful to ensure continued competence in the evolving healthcare field.

There are a multitude of options for physicians to participate in formal professional development. So many options offer the opportunity for physicians to engage in activities using methods with which he or she is most comfortable, often at times befitting to his or her busy schedule and/or offering additional benefits that may be personally meaningful. Allowing physicians to play an active role in their CPD plan and lifelong learning process, is more likely to lead toward successful outcomes by allowing them a greater sense of autonomy (Deci & Ryan, 1991). Deci and Ryan (1991) found that those whose motivation is more authentic (and less externally controlled) have more interest, excitement, and confidence that, in turn, leads to enhanced performance, persistence, and creativity. "Concomitantly, it is necessary for stakeholders and developers of accredited professional development programs to incorporate more SDL initiatives into their educational activities (Jeong et al., 2018)."

Oftentimes, physicians are challenged by identifying appropriate activities to meet their developmental needs. Thus, it is critical to have varied options allowing for preferences related to a variety of factors, including format (delivery), time available, cost, and, of course, content. As noted above, this still requires an individual to self-reflect and evaluate to identify *how* they learn best and *what* they need to learn to maintain competence, contribute to quality healthcare, reach for Maslow's self-actualization and meet individuals' need for autonomy. It is imperative that those engaged in the development of CME activities, faculty development, and or mentoring or coaching individuals recognize the importance of letting the learner lead the way. Table 1 for a list of potential CPD forums and the associated benefits each offers.

Table 1.

Venue (Activity Type)	On Demand	Collaborative	Certificate	CME Credit	Networking	Timely Feedback	Q&A
External Conferences	✗	✓	P	P	✓	✗	✓
Internal Conferences	✗	✓	P	P	✓	P	✓
Webinars	✗	✗	P	P	✗	✗	P
Journal Review	✓	✗	✗	P	✗	✗	✗
Journal Clubs	✗	✓	✗	P	✓	P	✗
Graduate Programs	P	✓	✓	P	✓	P	✓
Enduring Materials (online modules)	✓	✗	P	P	✗	P	✗
Point of Care Learning	✓	✓	✗	✓	P	✓	✓
Practice Test Questions	✓	P	✓	✓	✗	✓	✗
Fellowship	P	✓	✓	✗	✓	P	✓
Academies	P	✓	✓	✓	✓	P	✓

Legend: ✓ = Yes, ✗ = No, P = Potentially

Practical Implementation

One option for CPD stands out as particularly robust in its potential benefits to physicians. The concept of "academies" has become commonplace within the CPD world, and so directly resonates with the concept of relatedness. Academies are communities of practice through which "groups of people who share a concern or a passion about a topic, and who deepen their knowledge and expertise in this area by interacting on an on-going basis (Wenger, 1998)." People who belong to communities of practice do not necessarily work together every day, but commune related to their specific shared interest. For example, a group of physicians may vary in their clinical specialty, but have a shared interest in research, leadership, teaching, or something else altogether. These individuals might come together for various activities, collaborations, and/or to engage in meaningful discussions and innovations facilitated through a research, leadership, teaching, or other type of academy. More and more national organizations and academic medical centers (AMCs) are developing academies focused on one or more of these areas, promoting a community of individuals to support one another and fostering individual CPD.

In addition to academies, there are a multitude of options for identifying and accessing relevant, convenient and meaningful CPD opportunities, ranging from one hour twitter conversations to week long conferences or Master Degree programs. Most, if not all, AMCs offer various opportunities for CPD, either through a clinical department, academy (as noted above), Graduate Medical Education Office, or Office of Faculty Affairs or Professional Development. Additionally, Continuing Medical Education is a primary role of most Medical Specialty Societies, who sometimes even partner with relevant Specialty Boards to ensure regulatory requirements are being met through CPD opportunities. Medical Specialty Societies often offer an annual meeting, which is likely to include clinical, research, and teaching related sessions. There are also endless on-line resources available through commercial medical and education companies. Finally, there are lists of available CPD opportunities in academic journals, association websites, and repositories of opportunities such as ACCME's CME Finder (www.cmefinder.org). Conducting an on-line search for CPD related to specific topics elicits a myriad of opportunities.

Obstacles and Barriers

There can be many barriers or challenges to offering and participating in continuing education for physicians. See Table 2. For learners, in addition to motivation as discussed above, these barriers can stem from individual preferences, styles, priorities, and or personal reasons. Barriers for learners can also be a result of poor support from an employer, or a lack of relevant quality educational programs available and made known. Thus, it is critical for educators to conduct ongoing and robust needs assessments or gap analysis to hear from learners about what they want and need. It is also important to effectively market educational activities and opportunities to the appropriate audiences. Another barrier to individuals participating in continuing education may be their belief (or their employer's belief) that it won't be impactful and or a good use of time and resources. This speaks to the need for robust program evaluation and presentation of outcomes. As Moore et al (2009) and Kirkpatrick (1994) describe, positive educational outcomes can range from participant satisfaction, to changes in participant behaviour or practice, to improvements in system process, and ideally, to improvements in patient care.

For those involved in developing and delivering educational activities, the challenges and barriers may be very similar to that of learners. See Table 2. There may not be adequate time or resources to develop and deliver the kind of educational activity that is believed would be most beneficial. It may be

Table 2.

Barriers to CPD for Learners	Barriers to CPD for Educators
• Not enough time • Too expensive • Content not relevant • Not preferred format of delivery • Not accessible • Previous negative experiences • Lack of information on what's available • Resentment for required learning • Employer not supportive	• Did not conduct a needs assessment (lacking feedback from learners) • Not enough time to develop/implement • Too expensive to develop/implement • Unsure of timely topics to be addressed • Difficult to meet diverse learner needs • Lack of content area expertise • Identifying best day and time • Identifying best venue/delivery method • Learners not committed or participating

a challenge to keep up with what are the current topics or content areas that need to be addressed. Again, this speaks to the need for conducting research ahead of time to recognize what learners want and need. Identifying the most convenient time and delivery method (for the greatest number of learners) may be difficult, just as meeting the needs of diverse learners. There may also be occasions when despite the development and implementation of a quality educational program, learners are not engaged. This mitigates their learning potential and perhaps that of others around them (if a live activity). Recognizing and understanding the barriers listed below (for learners and educators) is critical so they may be addressed to help ensure meaningful continuing education for physicians.

CONCLUSION

CPD is fundamental to most professions. The importance of CPD in medicine is exacerbated by the complex, evolving, and multi-dimensional role of the physician. Individuals move from the safe and more closely regulated confines of UME and GME training programs with supervision, formative feedback, and clear learning objectives, to independent practice with responsibility for the health and well-being of patients on their own. This responsibility alone is immense, but add in the inherent evolving changes in medicine, a new teaching role, pressure to conduct research, healthcare team leadership responsibilities, an emphasis on measuring quality of care, and keeping oneself "well," among so many other things, and physicians are at risk for not doing any of these things very well. CPD is essential for physicians, as they must continue to grow and learn, especially given the changing nature of healthcare and their complex role.

There are extensive regulations and requirements in place for physicians, ranging from specialty boards, to State requirements, to employer requirements for lifelong learning. While one may not always be convinced of the effectiveness of these regulations and their role in motivating a physician to grow and learn, they exist to enhance and ensure physician competence and must be complied with if one wants to continue to practice medicine. While this may be an overabundance of educational requirements, working to motivate individuals extrinsically, as is made clear by the Self-Determination Theory, that fostering competence, autonomy, and relatedness as part of learning are foundational to motivation. Also known from a number of theories discussed is that individuals are motivated to learn, grow, and strive for self-actualization once their basic knowledge and skills are in place. Thus, if physicians meet those basic licensure and certification requirements, maybe they are then motivated to "self-determine" how best to maximize their developmental opportunities.

It is not completely clear what motivates an individual and, in this case, a physician, to engage in CPD. While one may want to believe that individuals should be intrinsically motivated, it may be safest to assume that individuals are motivated both extrinsically and intrinsically and that it differs substantially by individual. This confirms the need for a variety of educational opportunities to help ensure individuals get the content and learning format they need and desire to remain competent and fulfilled throughout their career. Table 1 lists a large (although not all inclusive) number of forums that can be utilized for CPD and the potential benefits of each. Again, individuals must be responsible for identifying the opportunities for learning that are most personally impactful. And, for those responsible for promoting CPD and or creating educational content, recognizing the diversity needed to appeal to each different individual, is critical.

CPD is not optional in the field of medicine, and learning cannot stop upon successful completion of a GME training program. Given the high stakes, constantly evolving nature of medicine, and variety of roles physicians end up playing, extensive physician CPD is necessary. There is not one formula that works for all, and education researchers will always be seeking new understandings related to what motivates individuals to learn and what is most effective. The key is accepting that learning continues across one's career and life and, for physicians, this translates to innovative medicine and quality patient care.

REFERENCES

Abiddin, N. Z. (2007). Mentoring and coaching the roles and practices. *J Human Res Adult Learn.*, 107–116.

Academy of Royal Medical Colleges. Ten Principles for CPD. 1999. Available from http://www.rcgp. org.uk/revalidation-and-cpd/~/media/Files/Revalidation-and-CPD/ACADEMY-GUIDANCE-CPD-HEADINGS.ashx

Agency for Healthcare Research and Quality. (n.d.). *Teamstepps.* Retrieved May 1, 2019 from https://www.ahrq.gov/teamstepps/index.html

American Board of Medical Specialties. (n.d.). *Board Certification.* Retrieved May 15, 2019 from https://www.abms.org/board-certification/steps-toward-initial-certification-and-moc/

American Board of Surgery. *Training and Recertification.* Retrieved May 10, 2019 from http://www.absurgery.org/default.jsp?exam-moc)

Angood, P., & Birk, S. K. (2014). The value of physician leadership. *Physician Executive*, *40*(3), 6–20. PMID:24964545

Boulet, J. R., & Durning, S. J. (2019). What we measure… and what we should measure in medical education. *Medical Education*, 53(1), 86–94. doi:10.1111/medu.13652 PMID:30216508

Cantillon, P., & Sargeant, J. (2008). Giving feedback in clinical settings. *BMJ (Clinical Research Ed.)*, 337(nov10 2), a1961. doi:10.1136/bmj.a1961 PMID:19001006

Cook, D. A., & Artino, A. R. Jr. (2016). Motivation to learn: An overview of contemporary theories. *Medical Education*, 50(10), 997–1014.

Cox, M., Cuff, P., Brandt, B., Reeves, S., & Zierler, B. (2016). Measuring the impact of interprofessional education on collaborative practice and patient outcomes.

Cutrer, W. B., Miller, B., Pusic, M. V., Mejicano, G., Mangrulkar, R. S., Gruppen, L. D., ... Moore, D. E. Jr. (2017). Fostering the development of master adaptive learners: A conceptual model to guide skill acquisition in medical education. Academic Medicine [PubMed]. *Journal. Association of American Medical Colleges*, 92(1), 70–75.

Davis, D. A., Prescott, J., Fordis, C. M. Jr, Greenberg, S. B., Dewey, C. M., Brigham, T., ... Tenner, T. E. Jr. (2011). Rethinking CME: An imperative for academic medicine and faculty development (2011). *Academic Medicine: Journal of the Association of American Medical Colleges*, 86(4), 468–473. doi:10.1097/ACM.0b013e31820dfacf PMID:21346497

Davis, D. A., Rayburn, W. F., & Smith, G. A. (2017). Continuing professional development for faculty: An elephant in the house of academic medicine or the key to future success? *Academic Medicine: Journal of the Association of American Medical Colleges*, 92(8), 1078–1081. doi:10.1097/ACM.0000000000001777 PMID:28562453

Deci, E. L., & Ryan, R. M. (1991). A motivational approach to self: Integration in personality. In R. Dienstbier (Ed.), *Nebraska Symposium on Motivation:* Vol. 38. *Perspectives on Motivation* (pp. 237–288). Lincoln, NE: University of Nebraska Press.

Deiorio, N. M., Carney, P. A., Kahl, L. E., & Juve, A. M. (2016). Coaching: A new model for academic and career achievement. *Medical Education Online*, 21(1), 1087–2981. doi:10.3402/meo.v21.33480 PMID:27914193

Doty, J., & Taylor, D. (2019). Developing physician leaders. *Current Sports Medicine Reports*, 18(2), 45. doi:10.1249/JSR.0000000000000561 PMID:30730339

Dow, A., & Thibault, G. (2017). Interprofessional Education-A Foundation for a New Approach to Health Care. *The New England Journal of Medicine*, 377(9), 803–805. doi:10.1056/NEJMp1705665 PMID:28854090

Dreyfus, S. E. (2004). The five-stage model of adult skill acquisition. *Bulletin of Science, Technology & Society*, 24(3), 177–181. Retrieved from https://moleseyhill.com/2009-08-27-dreyfus-model.html

Ericsson, K. A. (2004). Deliberate practice and the acquisition and maintenance of expert performance in medicine and related domains. *Academic Medicine: Journal of the Association of American Medical Colleges*, 79(10Suppl), 70–81. doi:10.1097/00001888-200410001-00022 PMID:15383395

Eva, K. W., & Regehr, G. (2008). I'll never play professional football and other fallacies of self assessment. *The Journal of Continuing Education in the Health Professions, 28*(1), 14–19. doi:10.1002/chp.150 PMID:18366120

Federation of State Medical Boards. (2018). *U.S. Medical Regulatory Trends and Actions 2018*. Retrieved May 10 from https://www.fsmb.org/siteassets/advocacy/publications/us-medical-regulatory-trends-actions.pdf

Filipe, H. P., Golnik, K. C., & Mack, H. G. (2018). Professional development? What happened to CME? CME and beyond. *Medical Teacher, 40*(9), 914–916. doi:10.1080/0142159X.2018.1471200 PMID:29793386

Filipe, H. P., Silva, E. D., Stulting, A. A., & Golnik, K. C. (2014). Continuing professional development: Best practices. *Middle East African Journal of Ophthalmology, 21*(2), 134–141. doi:10.4103/0974-9233.129760 PMID:24791104

Gawande, A. (2011). Personal best. *The New Yorker*. Oct. 3. Retrieved May 15, 2019 from http://www.newyorker. com/magazine/2011/10/03/personal-best

Geraci, S. A., & Thigpen, S. C. (2017). A review of mentoring in academic medicine. *The American Journal of the Medical Sciences, 353*(2), 151–157. doi:10.1016/j.amjms.2016.12.002 PMID:28183416

Grady, C. M., & Hinings, C. R. (2018). *Turning the Titanic: Physicians as both leaders and managers in healthcare reform. Leadership in Health Services*. Retrieved from 1108/LHS-09-2017-0058

Gunderman, R., & Kanter, S. L. (2009). Perspective: Educating physicians to lead hospitals. *Academic Medicine: Journal of the Association of American Medical Colleges, 84*(1348–1351).

Heeneman, S., & Driessen, E. W. (2017). The use of a portfolio in postgraduate medical education–reflect, assess and account, one for each or all in one? *GMS Journal for Medical Education, 34*(5). PMID:29226225

Jeong, D., Presseau, J., ElChamaa, R., Naumann, D. N., Mascaro, C., Luconi, F., ... Kitto, S. C. (2018). Barriers and facilitators to self-directed learning in continuing professional development for physicians in Canada: A scoping review. *Academic Medicine: Journal of the Association of American Medical Colleges, 93*(8), 1245–1254. doi:10.1097/ACM.0000000000002237 PMID:29642101

Kirkpatrick, D. L. (1994). *Evaluating Training Programs*. San Francisco, CA: Berrett-Koehler Publishers.

Kitto, S., Price, D., Jeong, D., Campbell, C., & Reeves, S. (2018). Continuing professional development. *Understanding Medical Education: Evidence. Theory into Practice*, 263–274.

Knowles, M. S. (1980). *The modern practice of adult education: From pedagogy to andragogy*. Wilton, CN: Association Press.

Leung, J. M., Mohit Bhutani, M., Leigh, R., Pelletier, D., Good, C., & Sin, D. D. (2015). Empowering family physicians to impart proper inhaler teaching to patients with chronic obstructive pulmonary disease and asthma. *Canadian Respiratory Journal, 22*(5), pp. 266-270. doi:10.1155/2015/731357

Lewis, K. O., & Baker, R. C. (2007). The development of an electronic educational portfolio: An outline for medical education professionals. *Teaching and Learning in Medicine, 19*(2), 139–147. doi:10.1080/10401330701332219 PMID:17564541

Lovell, B. (2018). What do we know about coaching in medical education? A literature review. *Medical Education, 52*(4), 376–390. doi:10.1111/medu.13482 PMID:29226349

Lyasere, C. A., Baggett, M., Romano, J., Jena, A., Mills, G., & Hunt, D. P. (2016). Beyond continuing medical education: Clinical coaching as a tool for on-going professional development. *Academic Medicine: Journal of the Association of American Medical Colleges, 91*(12), 1647–1650. doi:10.1097/ACM.0000000000001131 PMID:26910898

Maslow, A. H. (1943). A theory of human motivation. *Psychological Review, 50*(4), 370–396. doi:10.1037/h0054346

McMahon, G. T. (2016). What do I need to learn today?: The evolution of CME. *The New England Journal of Medicine, 374*(15), 1403–1406. doi:10.1056/NEJMp1515202 PMID:27074064

Moore, D. E. Jr, Green, J. S., & Gallis, H. A. (2009). Achieving desired results and improved outcomes: Integrating planning and assessment throughout learning activities. *The Journal of Continuing Education in the Health Professions, 29*(1), 1–14. doi:10.1002/chp.20001 PMID:19288562

Mylopoulos, M., & Regehr, G. (2009). How student models of expertise and innovation impact the development of adaptive expertise in medicine. *Medical Education, 43*(2), 127–132. doi:10.1111/j.1365-2923.2008.03254.x PMID:19161482

Nothnagle, M., Anandarajah, G., Goldman, R. E., & Reis, S. (2011). Struggling to be self-directed: Residents' paradoxical beliefs about learning. *Academic Medicine: Journal of the Association of American Medical Colleges, 86*(12), 1539–1544. doi:10.1097/ACM.0b013e3182359476 PMID:22030764

O'Sullivan, P. S., & Irby, D. M. (2011). Reframing research on faculty development. *Academic Medicine: Journal of the Association of American Medical Colleges, 86*(4), 421–428. doi:10.1097/ACM.0b013e31820dc058 PMID:21346505

Peter, D., Robinson, P., Jordan, M., Lawrence, S., Casey, K., & Salas-Lopez, D. (2015). Reducing readmissions using teach-back: Enhancing patient and family education. *J Nurs Adm., 45*(1), 35–42. Epub 2014/12/06. pmid:25479173.

Phipps-Taylor, T. M., & Shortell, S. M. (2016). More than money: Motivating physician behavior change in accountable care organizations. *The Milbank Quarterly, 94*(4), 832–861. doi:10.1111/1468-0009.12230 PMID:27995705

Pololi, L. H., Evans, A. T., Civian, J. T., Vasiliou, V., Coplit, L. D., Gillum, L. H., ... Brennan, R. T. (2015). Mentoring faculty: A US national survey of its adequacy and linkage to culture in academic health centers. *The Journal of Continuing Education in the Health Professions, 35*(3), 176–184. doi:10.1002/chp.21294 PMID:26378423

Practice. (2009). In *Merriam-Webster.com*. Retrieved January 22, 2019, from https://www.merriam-webster.com/dictionary/practice

Related. 2019. In *Merriam-Webster.com.* Retrieved May 11, 2019, from https://www.merriam-webster.com/dictionary/practice

Ryan, R. M., & Deci, E. L. (2000). Self-determination theory and the facilitation of intrinsic motivation, social development, and well-being. *The American Psychologist, 55*(1), 68–78. doi:10.1037/0003-066X.55.1.68 PMID:11392867

Sargeant, J., Wong, B. M., & Campbell, C. M. (2018). Professional development of the future: A partnership between quality improvement and competency-based education. *Medical Education, 52*(1), 125–135. doi:10.1111/medu.13407 PMID:28984354

Sheri, K., Too, J. Y. J., Chuah, S. E. L., Toh, Y. P., Mason, S., & Radha Krishna, L. K. (2019). A scoping review of mentor training programs in medicine between 1990 and 2017. *Medical Education Online, 24*(1), 1555435. doi:10.1080/10872981.2018.1555435 PMID:31671284

Silver, I., & Leslie, K. (2017). Comparing and contrasting faculty development and continuing professional development 2003-2019. In D. A. Davis, & K. Wolters, *W. F. Rayburn, & M. G. Turco,* Continuing Professional Development in Medicine and Health Care (1st ed.).

Smith, G. A., Stark, A. M., Rayburn, W., Davis, D., & Turco, M. (2017). Enhancing continuing professional development with insights from implementation science. In *Continuing Professional Development in Medicine and Healthcare: Better Education, Improved Outcomes, Best Care.* Philadelphia, PA: Wolters Kluwer.

Storey, V. A. (2019). Advancing healthcare leadership: Physicians as agents of change. In *Preparing Physicians to Lead in the 21st Century* (pp. 1–25). Hershey, PA: IGI Global.

U.S. Department of Health and Human Services. (n.d.). Agency for Healthcare Research and Quality Team Strategies and Tools to Enhance Performance and Patient Safety (TeamStepps). Retrieved July 15, 2019, from https://www.ahrq.gov/teamstepps/index.html

U.S. Medical Regulatory Trends and Actions. (2018). *Federation of State Medical Boards.* Accessed May 1, 2019 from https://www.fsmb.org/siteassets/advocacy/publications/us-medical-regulatory-trends-actions.professional development

Vandergrift, J. L., Gray, B. M., & Weng, W. (2018). Do state continuing medical education requirements for physicians improve clinical knowledge? *Health Services Research, 53*(3), 1682–1701. doi:10.1111/1475-6773.12697 PMID:28419451

Ward, M., Gruppen, L., & Regehr, G. (2002). Measuring self-assessment: Current state of the art. *Advances in Health Sciences Education: Theory and Practice, 7*(1), 63–80. doi:10.1023/A:1014585522084 PMID:11912336

Watkins, K. D. (2016). Faculty development to support interprofessional education in healthcare professions: A realist synthesis. *Journal of Interprofessional Care, 30*(6), 695–701. doi:10.1080/13561820.2016.1209466 PMID:27459591

Wenger, E. (1998). Communities of practice: Learning as a social system. *The Systems Thinker, 9*(5), 2–3.

World Federation for Medical Education (WFME). (2003). Continuing professional development of medical doctors: WFME global standards for quality improvement. Available at https://wfme.org/standards/cpd/

World Health Organization. (2010). Regional Guidelines for Continuing Medical Education (CME)/Continuing Professional Development (CPD) Activities. Available at https://www.wbginvestmentclimate.org/toolkits/health-in-africa-policy-toolkit/upload/WHO-CME-Requirements.pdf

Zimmerman, B. J., & Schunk, D. H. (Eds.). (2001). *Self-regulated learning and academic achievement: Theoretical perspectives* (2nd ed.). Mahwah, NJ: Lawrence Erlbaum Associates Publishers.

Section 5
Technology in Medical Education

Chapter 20
Using Technology to Teach and Teaching About Technology:
Synergies for the Digital Age

Shohreh V. Anand
LearnLong Institute, USA

Tejwansh S. Anand
University of Texas at Austin, USA & Columbia University, USA

ABSTRACT

This chapter analyzes the role played by technology in undergraduate medical education (UME) using two perspectives: how technology is used as a tool to facilitate teaching and how medical students are taught to use technology in the clinical setting. For each perspective, a survey of literature, published from 2009 to 2019, was conducted to understand the current state. Authors critically examine the current state and describe and analyze issues with it. Recommendations are made for improving the blending of medical education, technology, pedagogy, and clinical practice. The narrative in this chapter is at the intersection of digital technology, educational theories, and medical settings (educational and practice).

INTRODUCTION

Over the past 20 years, we have seen a convergence and an acceleration of the digital and information revolutions. Higher education, including medical schools, has not been immune to these revolutions. It is slowly, some would say in the face of strong resistance (Howard, 2013; Johnson, Wisniewski, Kuhlemeyer, Issacs, & Krzykowski, 2012), adapting to how curricula are shaped, pedagogies are evolved, and instruction and training are delivered (Orr, Weller, & Farrow, 2018). At the same time, encouraged by regulations and the need to manage costs and demonstrate quality outcomes, the clinical workplace is spending on technology at a feverish pace (Rossini, 2018; Sullivan, 2018). The clinical workplace now demands skills in utilizing digital tools and instruments, as well as competence in evaluating, understanding, and analyzing information. The AMA (2019a) considers "preparing future physicians to provide

DOI: 10.4018/978-1-7998-1468-9.ch020

care in the modern, technology-driven health care environment" as one of its mandates. Consequently, the inclusion of applications of technology in medicine and health information in medical curricula has been seen as a foregone conclusion for some time (Stead, Searle, Fessler, Smith, & Shortliffe, 2011; Triola et al., 2010).

Having come of age as digital natives, the millennial generation (born 1981-1996) of medical students are active users and adopters of digital devices and social media (Rideout, Foehr, & Roberts, 2010; Smith & Anderson, 2018). Additionally, most have seen the incorporation of technology in their secondary and tertiary educations, such as course presentation (white boards, online courses), content accessibility (eBooks, podcasts, digital open-source materials), and communicative applications (online gradebooks, e-Portfolios, course and learning management systems) (U.S. Department of Education, 2019). Incorporation into teaching activities of cutting-edge innovations, such as virtual reality (VR) devices and 3D printers, is steadily getting a foothold in high schools and colleges across the country (Griffith, de Cataldo, & Fogarty, 2016; Horton, 2017; Misak, 2018; Smiar & Mendez, 2016; Wood, 2018). These prior exposures to the use of technology in academic settings, the daily immersion in digital media, and facility in using digital devices, as well as the generational characteristics (Berk, 2009), are implicated in the millennial medical students' expectation, attitude, and usage of learning technologies (Chen & Scanlon, 2018; Roberts, Newman, & Schwartzstein, 2012).

Developing learning curricula that incorporate technology for learning and teach technological competencies for future work is seen as crucial. Accordingly, in this chapter we explore technology adoption in undergraduate medical education (UME) from two perspectives of using technology to teach medical students and teaching students about the technology used in the practice of medicine. One views technology as a teaching tool, the other as the tool of trade. After providing a brief background, we review the current state of each perspective through key factors influencing the adoption of technology, and through real examples and cases. Subsequently, we present our understanding of controversies and issues leading to the discussions and arguments of the central theses of the chapter. Finally, we bring these two perspectives together under recommendations and conclusions. The overall organizing framework of this chapter is depicted in Figure 1.

BACKGROUND

In writing this chapter, we surveyed the literature in the use of technology deployed in the North American UME published in the past decade (2009-2019). The intention was not to do a systematic review, but to gain an understanding of research related to the following:

- Influences that drive technology adoption in UME.
- Context-specific challenges, needs, and issues the use of technology was intended to solve.
- Descriptions of technology implementation and utilization.
- Pedagogical justifications that were presented, and how technology was integrated in the course design and learning/teaching context.
- Descriptions of how technology solutions addressed the issues and how their impact was evaluated within a learning/teaching context.

Figure 1. Chapter's organizational framework

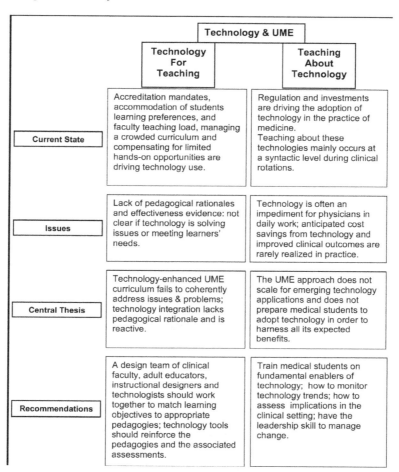

We looked in medical education, technology, and higher education journals, as well as performed a general search. Several studies were eliminated because they were conducted in a medical education context other than UME, or were conducted in settings outside North America. However, ultimately we did reference a handful of overseas studies for their evaluative insights.

Based on this literature survey, we examine the current state of technology adoption in UME with an eye toward influencing factors and challenges that seem to prompt such adoptions. We weave in our presentation brief descriptions of technologies and examples of real case implementations in UME. Our narrative is located at the intersection of digital technology, educational theories, and medical settings (educational and practice). We start off with technologies in service of teaching medicine followed by an examination of how technology is taught to students.

TECHNOLOGIES FOR TEACHING

Terms such as e-learning, blended or hybrid learning, online learning, and technology-enhanced learning, among others, have been used, interchangeably, to reference learning/teaching technologies. Whether operating synchronously or asynchronously, these terms are meant to convey the digital nature of full or partial delivery of what traditionally was done through face-to-face lectures, instruction, demonstration, prosection, and such. Digital delivery, digital content, and specialized programs and hardware (for simulation, for example) come together to create a technological backbone for teaching and learning. At stake is this blending of technology and pedagogy.

Current State

The current blending of technology and pedagogy in UME can be viewed through the lens of challenges and influencing factors propelling it. Some of these factors seen in the literature include:

- Accreditation standards
- A student-centered teaching/learning focus
- Expanding experiential and practical learning
- Accommodating students' learning preferences, faculty teaching loads, and managing a crowded curriculum

Accreditation Standards

The Liaison Committee on Medical Education (LCME) of North America, a jointly sponsored organization formed in 1942 by the Association of American Medical Colleges (AAMC) and the American Medical Association (AMA), is the accreditation body for North American medical schools that grant a Doctor of Medicine degree. At the time of this writing, 154 U.S. and 17 Canadian medical schools have been accredited (https://www.aamc.org/about). LCME standards on information technology resources delineate that a medical school needs to provide "access to well-maintained information technology resources sufficient in scope to support its educational and other missions" (LCME, 2020, 5.9). Furthermore, a medical library needs to have resources "sufficient in breadth of holdings and technology to support its educational and other missions" (5.8). Use of technology in support of "educational and other missions," therefore, is an institutional imperative. Technology can facilitate compliance with a number of LCME standards relating to the "educational mission" of a school, such as providing means for self-directed and lifelong learning experiences (6.3), exposure to elective opportunities (6.5), and providing comparable educational experience and assessment across multiple campuses (8.7). Technology is also indispensable in "other missions" of a school, such as collection and analysis of data for evaluation of educational program outcomes (8.4), collection of students' feedback (8.5), processes for monitoring students' time on required activities (8.8), and a centralized assessment mechanism (9.4).

According to AAMC, in 2017-2018, 53 medical schools have reported one or more regional campuses, and 14 schools were reporting expansion plans for new branch campuses. Providing comparable educational experiences and assessment across multiple sites, therefore, is a major policy driver for the adoption of technology. Such adoption can take different forms, from pre-recorded lectures used in conjunction with blended learning that can be shared among sites (asynchronous model) to real-time video conferencing and simultaneous environments for live lectures (synchronous model).

Lovell and Vignare (2009) state making "the learning experiences equivalent for all students at all campuses" (p. 55) as the main goal of an asynchronous technology solution for Year-1 basic science courses, across multi-campus Michigan State University (MSU) medical schools. The authors make note of other influencing factors. One is the reduced faculty time due to research pressures being at odd with students' desire for standardized instruction from the same faculty. This results in large classes. A blended learning strategy to address large class sizes, while maintaining hands-on lab experiences, was seen as a solution. Recorded audio and video for Year-1 basic science courses and some Year-2 courses had been available at MSU for a number of years. Creating a blended learning environment, however, consisted of a deliberate strategy to combine pre-recorded lectures, online modules, online histology lab exercises, and microbiology/immunology virtual interactive labs into course structures in a systematic manner.

Unlike the asynchronous model of MSU, Tummons, Fournier, Kits, and MacLeod (2018) reported on a technology-rich synchronous implementation in a Canadian medical school connecting two campuses, in two provinces, some 250 miles apart. Lecture halls, small seminar rooms, laboratories, and student lounges all were equipped with audio, video capturing and transmission devices, and large display screens. Additionally, cameras had mechanisms for the automated tracking of lecturers around the lecture halls, and projecting students' images on large screens when commenting/asking questions. Students' seats were fitted with push-to-talk microphones. Lectures were transmitted in real-time from the live-site (main campus) to the remote-site, and rarely the other way around. In this setup, technical assistants were present at both sites during lectures to manage capturing and transmission issues, and prior to classes to assure strict formatting of slides, images, and files for proper display.

A third example is Indiana University School of Medicine connecting two regional campuses, 111 miles apart, in a synchronous physiology class (Waite, Orndorff, Hughes, Saxon, & White, 2014). This example describes a single class implementation with a less-elaborate technology setup. In this variation, the course instructor, alternatively, attended the two sites, so both groups of students had a live lecture experience. In the absence of an instructor at one site, a facilitator was present to assist with the problem-based part of the class and to manage the class dynamic at the remote site. These interventions were intended to ameliorate limitations such as lack of spontaneity due to transmission delays, inability of an instructor to read cues and gauge the remote class, and the absence of "common out-of-class interactions, which typically humanize a course" (p. 141).

Given the crowded medical curriculum and pressures on students' time, technology is seen as a solution for meeting LCME's provisions for elective opportunities. Online courses offer attractive features such as flexible start and completion schedules, shorter durations, fewer demands on faculty time, and, increasingly, options for externally produced content. One such option, MOOCs (massive open online courses) on platforms such as Coursera, Udemy, Udacity, EdX, and FutureLearn, is based on the idea of open-access content delivery. Some medical schools have experimented with offering undergraduate courses and electives on these platforms. Examples include: the University of Pittsburgh's "Clinical Terminology for International and US Students" on Coursera; Southern Illinois University's "Medicine as a Business" on Udemy; the University of California, San Francisco's "Clinical Problem Solving" on Coursera, Duke University's "Medical Neuroscience" on Coursera, and an anatomy course in University Leeds, UK on FutureLearn.

"Medicine as a Business" is a fourth-year elective course offered by Southern Illinois University School of Medicine (SIU-SM) as a MOOC since 2014. Comparing the MOOC delivery of the course to the traditional 5-week in-person format showed no statistical difference in terms of students' reported rating of faculty effectiveness or overall evaluation of the course. The retrospective analysis of SIU-SM MOOC indicated that the primary advantage of MOOC format for the fourth-year elective course was the affordance of flexibility to students in terms of time and place for taking the course (Robinson, 2018).

What distinguishes MOOCs from other institutions' online offerings is the scale due to their public availability. MOOCs extend the institution's educational reach and allow the institution to be a participant in a disruptive innovation (White, 2018). Hollands and Tirthali (2014) suggest that perception of MOOCs as a disruptive innovation to the higher education business model motivates experimentation with MOOCs as a prudent approach for creating brand and hedging against the perceived uncertainty.

Notwithstanding the scale, with availability of a plethora of learning platforms and authoring tools, creating an online course is technically accessible to non-programmers. Innovative and thoughtful designs, pedagogical principles, authoritative content, engaging presentations, expertise of the presenters, and support for interactions with presenters and other learners are among the elements that set one technology-enabled learning implementation apart from another. Increasingly, such innovative offerings are produced outside the confines of institutions as FOAMEd (Free, Open Access Meducation). One example, modeled after Khan Academy's format, is MEDSKL. A number of medical schools are experimenting with this high-quality, externally produced content. The strategy allows for the incorporation of such offerings into curricula either as supplementary materials or as a way to ease faculty into flipping classes.

A Student-Centered Teaching/Learning Focus

The movement away from didactic lectures and toward more active and interactive engagement of students in the process of learning is at the heart of student-centered models of teaching and learning. These models aim to develop self-directed learners who take on more responsibility for curating content, conducting independent inquiry, and controlling the learning process.

The flipped classroom, sometimes referred to as blended learning in reference to how technology is integrated, is one of these models. Students are expected to engage with course content pre-class and participate in activities in class to augment, clarify, and consolidate their learning. Problem-based learning (PBL) and case-based learning (CBL), similarly, require prior engagement with materials followed by tutorials or discussion-based groupwork. In small groups, students work on a "problem" with the facilitation of a faculty member. The differences among these models stem from the pedagogical role the "problem" is intended to play, and the level of structure (open inquiry vs. guided inquiry) imposed on the group inquiry process by the guidance or facilitation of an expert (McLean, 2016; Miles, Lee, Foggett, & Nair, 2019; Srinivasan, Wilkes, Stevenson, Nguyen, & Slavin, 2007). Added to this mix is the model of self-directed learning (SDL) (Knowles,1975). This model is premised on the capability of adults to deliberately plan their learning activities, including controlling resource identification and access, as well as the learning tempo, duration, and place.

Technology can greatly facilitate access to learning resources, coalescing the elements of an active-learning curriculum design. In addition to static digital materials, interactive content through intelligent tutoring systems and computer-supported collaborative learning environments are readily available. The goal of these systems is to walk the students through materials, provide feedback, and individualize the learning. Built-in activity trackers and access-logs make students' usage statistics readily available for faculty monitoring.

In general, these technologies have been in the service of facilitating access, acquisition, and retention of a vast amount of theoretical knowledge needed to master and remember. Decreased clinical opportunities, a new focus on improving competencies, and issues and expenses associated with maintaining anatomy laboratories have created a demand for technologies that address experiential and practical learning.

Expanding Experiential and Practical Learning

Technology for experiential learning attempts to address the type of learning that occurs in labs or clinical settings through observation and haptic modes of knowing. Simulation, using a representation of an object or situation to mimic reality, has always been part of teachers' instructional props. Using technology to increase fidelity, the degree of realism, of such representations is the basis for high fidelity technology-enhanced simulation. Enabled by fast processing speed, high resolution displays, specialized hardware and algorithms optimized for massive calculations, 3D visualization, simulation of clinical settings, and virtual patients have entered the educator's toolbox.

The purpose of 3D visualization technology is to create a realistic 3D virtual space with the perception that one can manipulate objects within it. Virtual dissection tables (Anatomage table by Anatomage, Inc., and Sectra table by Touch of Life Technologies, Inc.), the 3D anatomy atlas, and virtual reality technologies provide realistic visualization through high resolution images, real cadaveric dissection image libraries, and features that convey physical characteristics like flow, motion, depth, scale, and topography. In addition to impressive realism, they offer interactivity (sizing, dissection, annotation, drawing) to facilitate not only an understanding of individual anatomical structures, but also the spatial relationships that exist among them. Although positively received by students (Gross & Masters, 2017) and embraced by some schools as replacement for cadaveric education, such tools are mostly hailed as adjuncts to more standard approaches in teaching anatomy (cadaveric dissection, plastinated prosection, plastic models).

Another area of rapid technology development with applications in medicine and education is simulated reality. The variants of this technology—virtual reality (VR), augmented reality (AR), and mixed reality (MR) —differ in the degree of graphical rendering and the mixing (if any) with real or live images. In an MR application, virtual objects appear as inserted or overlaid into live images captured in the viewer's physical space. The viewer, therefore, has an awareness of both. Using headsets or goggles such as HoloLens (Microsoft, Inc.), life-size, 3D holographic objects perceived to be in the viewer's environment can be manipulated through the use of gaze, gesture, voice commands, or hand controllers. The headset has the ability to map the room, adjust for the viewer's movement, and display a hologram in the observer's line of sight. Unlike the impression of rotating an object on a display screen, one has the illusion of moving around the object. Similarly, "zooming in" is invoked in response to the viewer taking steps toward the hologram, and "zooming out" is akin to stepping away. These illusions make the experience of interacting with holographically created anatomical objects feel immersive and situate the learner in the learning experience.

In 2016, Case Western Reserve University (CWRU), partnering with the Cleveland Clinic, created an anatomy app, HoloAnatomy, using HoloLens for pre-clinical anatomy materials covered in a standard dissection laboratory course. Wish-Baratz, Gubatina, Enterline, and Griswold (2019) reported on the uses of HoloAnatomy on HoloLens, with 170 first-year medical student volunteers, in supplemental faculty-facilitated review sessions at CWRU. Students found the device/app helpful and were enthused about using it for their reviews. In response to open-ended questions, 43 students (25%) listed physical complaints (headache, nausea, eye and neck strain) when using the device. These findings indicated a need for proper device calibration (brightness, pupillary distance) before use and the determination of an optimal usage time for students' comfort. Industry reviewers of HoloLens have noted the weight of the headset, the center of gravity of the device, and the limited field of view (34-degree) resulting in disappearance of holograms with the slightest head movement as major design flaws (Antunes, 2019). These flaws and the calibration issues were addressed in a 2019 release of the second generation HoloLens (HoloLens 2).

One limitation of visualization technologies is their reliance on visual processing and depth perception. They cannot provide for haptic learning of the kind (texture, pliability, elasticity, rigidity) obtained from a cadaver dissection experience. Using 3D printers to create anatomical models where different components can have distinct levels of rigidity (giving tissue fidelity) is one approach to ameliorate haptic shortcomings (Mogali & Yeong, 2017). Notwithstanding a number of challenges (cost, printing time, inability to create certain hollow structures), progress is rapidly being made. Among the challenges are creation of high-quality and accurate anatomical printing files; availability of 3D repositories and exchanges (NIH, 2017) for file sharing; development of new photopolymers and filaments with real tissue fidelity (Smith & Jones, 2018); and novel combination of 3D printing with other methods, such as injection molding techniques (Ghazi, Stone, Candela, Richards, & Joseph, 2017). These work will accelerate the use of 3D printers in medical education and the practice of medicine, such as surgery planning and prosthetics (Breining, 2016).

Lastly, Virtual Patients (VPs) are valued for providing situated learning in simulated clinical settings without the risk of harming patients. This is achieved through presentation of real clinical scenarios focusing on history taking, clinical reasoning and diagnostic, and therapeutic decision-making. The human interface component of VPs could be a text-based screen with or without multimedia features, a computer-controlled mannequin with haptic features (e.g., SimMan), or a system with Natural Language Processing capabilities (e.g., SimX). The underlying engine to advance the clinical scenario along could be based on a simple state-based model or a dynamic physiological model (e.g., HumMod, CAE Healthcare). Through the U.S. Department of Defense's TATRC (Telemedicine & Advanced Technology Research Center), open-source physiological modeling engines (e.g., BioGears, Pulse) with permissible licensing for commercial and research use have become available in recent years. Coupled with pharmacokinetic models of drug behavior (distribution, uptake, clearance), pharmacological interventions can be incorporated in the simulation (Bray et al., 2019). The University of North Carolina Center for Innovation in Pharmacy Simulation (CIPS)'s nXhuman virtual patient learning project is one such initiative, using a Pulse engine with psychological and sociocultural modeling, and a Unity video game engine for a mixed reality user interface.

To assess the usability and appropriateness of virtual patient technologies, most studies use constructs such as learners' satisfaction and perceived course effectiveness. Satisfaction is taken to indicate students' acceptance, enjoyment, ease in using the technology, or willingness to recommend the course to others. Effectiveness relies on the perceived knowledge and competency in using the technology, or the perception of the learning intervention's difficulty. Overwhelmingly, students have expressed high satisfaction and increased competency and knowledge in studies exploring the use of VPs. These perceptions are attributed to the interactive nature of technology, the freedom to make decisions and take risks without harming patients, the formative assessment and feedback provided by supervising faculty, and the elements of group collaboration and teamwork that are usually involved (Kwan, Bui, Jain, Shah, & Juang, 2017).

Controversies and Issues

For a number of decades, the proponents of the use of technology in education have enthusiastically lauded its promises of pedagogical "enhancement, transformation, and even 'liberation' from the shackles of time and place'" (Goodchild & Speed, 2018, p. 2). With the same vigor, the skeptics point to the lack of compelling evidence of its effectiveness, a cycle of shifting rhetoric from failing technologies to new hyperboles, and the vested interests of technology enterprise in perpetuating these myths (pp. 2-3). Similar patterns of high hopes and enthusiasm and deep disappointment and frustration exist among medical educators and practitioners. From "the game-changing digital transformation of medicine" (AMA, 2015) to "death by 1,000-clicks" (Fry & Schulte, 2019), the paradox is best captured by Goodman (2010) as the longstanding medical profession's "deeply ambivalent" relationship with "technological imperatives and technology run amok." Against this contested backdrop of debates, we suggest that the following issues are at the core of challenges facing UME in teaching with and learning about technology.

Underdevelopment of Medical Education Technology Scholarship

In our review of literature, the breadth of technologies covered was expansive. Every digital technology and application, including simulations, games, mobile-learning, social media, telemedicine, student generated wikis, artificial intelligence, EMRs, audience-response (clicker) technology, and more, was represented. The focus of most studies was on describing a given technology implementation and utilization. When assessment was included, it took the form of either a student-reported perception of effectiveness and satisfaction with the technology/course, or a comparison of course grades or the USMLE Step scores. Most studies reported high levels of student satisfaction and examination scores on a par with those without technology interventions. Rarely were there attempts to account for the role of confounding factors. The parity was framed as positive, or at most was viewed as needing further studies. Follow-up and longitudinal studies were rare. Given the focus on the technology itself, technological obsolescence limits long-term follow-ups.

As to research methodology, we found a stark absence of qualitative studies. Large technology undertakings, such as blended and distance learning, reshape and restructure not only how curriculum is delivered, but how faculty, students, and support staff have to work in new ways. Tummons et al.'s (2018) ethnographic study, cited earlier in this chapter, provided more insights into such longitudinal impact than any other study we located within the field. Using a sociological framework (Actor-Network Theory), the authors explored the relationships between human and non-human entities (including technology) and how they came together to accomplish the intended work. The study's main conclusion was that attributing educational comparability to technology alone is misguided. Behind the technology, a network of actors as "pedagogical partners" (p. 1920), made up of administrative, technical, and academic staff, had to work cooperatively for a "seamless enactment" of the curriculum at two campuses. Similarly, assessments of students' life-long learning development (enhanced critical thinking, reasoning, meta-cognition, etc.) and how technology is actually used by students and faculty alike are examples of topics that are best studied by qualitative methods.

In short, the main challenge we encountered in our survey of literature was studies' focus on technology itself and the lack of attention to how learning and teaching were mediated through technology. This, in our opinion, is a fundamental issue in understanding the role of technology in UME.

Mismatching of Learning Theories and Conflating Technology with Pedagogy

As reflected in the surveyed literature, learning theories were often cited without a clear explanation of how authors saw them being applicable to the way technology was adopted. An often-stated theory was self-directed learning (SDL). In many studies, technology was lauded as promoting SDL. How this occurred was rarely explained.

The SDL and lifelong learning theories are premised on the capability of adults' deliberately planning their learning activities and to continue to do so in their lifework. A large body of literature in education (Brockett & Hiemstra,1991; Candy, 1991; Chene, 1983; Guglielmino, 1978; Knowles, 1970; Phares & Guglielmino, 2010; Tough, 1971) offers a number of models for SDL. These models generally consist of three elements. The first is the personal characteristics or traits (e.g., autonomy, independence in judgment and decision-making, discipline and mastery of self, emotional detachment, personal responsibility orientation). The second is the external conditions in teaching/learning transactions (e.g., transfer of responsibility and authority from instructor to learner, learner's control of planning, implementation, and evaluation). The last element is the learning that occurs (e.g., development of knowledge, skill, attitude, and personal development, such as transformation and emancipation, etc.). The SDL models offer a complex and nuanced concept that actualizes on a continuum when these elements come together for adult learners. The narrow use of one aspect of one element of this theory (e.g., learner's control of planning and implementation) and coupling it with technology (e.g., online resources) is quite selective and unfortunate. When there is a high congruence between the levels of the self-directedness that learners are able to manage and the available and carefully planned opportunities, including those through technology and educational interventions, then self-direction in learning may be said to be supported.

Inadequate Consideration of Students' Readiness and Learning Needs in Adoption of Technology

The inadequacy of research into students' engagement with technology, stemming perhaps from the perception of them being digital natives, is another area of concern. There are two aspects to understanding this engagement. One is consideration of the suitability of a given technology for learners' level of readiness or ability (e.g,. novice vs. experienced learner). The second is the impact on the realities of students' lives by the imposition of technology.

Judd and Kennedy (2011) argue that the assumption of students entering medical school with information-seeking skills and discernment in the use of authoritative sources is naïve. According to Miflin (2004), the assumption that a majority of the students entering medical school have had mature experiences of adulthood may be unfounded as well. The millennium's own coinage of "adulting," as engaging in new, previously unencountered adult responsibilities, may support Miflin's argument. The SDL theory used as a justification for online learning is specifically premised on learners' traits and characteristics that are not generally seen in early adulthood.

Additionally, learners need a certain reservoir of knowledge before they can be self-directed. A number of reviewed studies noted differences among Year-1's and other cohorts' utilization of online resources, but did not pursue these differences further. Within high fidelity simulation environments, Talbot, Sagae, John, and Rizzo (2012) comment that, in practice, these might be counterproductive for novice learners who are in need of acquiring core knowledge (Cook & Triola, 2009). Simplification, abstracting the messiness of reality, and gradual ramping up complexity are tried and true teaching strategies for novices that cannot be overlooked in a rush for immersion in life-like simulations.

Overwhelmed with the amount of information to retain, skills to develop, and little time to do so, many students opt for the least time-consuming option. A randomized crossover study at the University of Minnesota Medical School (Prunuske, Henn, Bearley, & Prunuske, 2016) compared passively designed modules (30-40-minute PowerPoint video lecture presentation) with actively designed modules (questions with recommended sources, reflection on short video clips, picture drawing, online eye simulator interaction) for a neurological medicine course. When given a choice, students overwhelmingly chose the passive option. The sentiment expressed by one student was: "Looking things up takes a lot of time. I don't believe it is worthwhile" (p. 138). A three-year study at Loyola University Chicago's Stritch School of Medicine tracked audio and video lecture file access across five basic science courses in Year-1 and Year-2 (McNulty et al., 2011). The findings indicated, across all courses whether factual or conceptual, students accessed less than 10% of videos/audio files. Judd and Kennedy (2011) looked at usage logs during SDL sessions of first, second, and third year medical students, along with a survey of their perceptions of the reliability of sources. Google and Wikipedia were the most frequently consulted sites (69.8% and 51.0% of sessions), even when students had rated them as least reliable. eMedicine and NIH access rates were at 21.5% and 16.5%, respectively. Similar results by Choi-Lundberg, Low, Patman, Turner, and Sinha's (2016) showed the SDL gross anatomy resource with the highest preference to be Wikipedia.

Students preferring the "expediency" of Google or Wikipedia (Judd & Kennedy, 2011), bypassing modules designed for deep learning, and foregoing online resources because of lack of time upend the assumptions about millennials' insatiable use of technology. Students' readiness for and their decision-making regarding the use of technology need to be given consideration.

In the next section, we pivot our attention to teaching about technology in UME.

TEACHING ABOUT TECHNOLOGY IN UME

Apart from the perspective of technology as a teaching and learning tool, technology is incorporated and embedded in many aspects of clinical practice. It can be seen in the everyday work of attending to patients and in the running of the clinical business, as the tool of trade. The inability to employ these technologies effectively is becoming a barrier in enhancing the effectiveness of a practice in meeting both the needs of patients and the institutional needs for regulatory compliance, efficiency, and cost management. Should the medical curriculum include education on the adoption of clinical technology, and should medical schools play a proactive role in shaping clinical technology?

In the sections that follow, we describe the current state of teaching about technology in the UME curriculum. This is followed by an analysis of the issues raised by the current state.

Current State

Since the mid to late 1980s, characterized by Moore's Law (Moore, 1998), computers have become increasingly faster and cheaper. Network effects (Hendler & Goldbeck, 2008) have increased the usefulness of computers as more people connect to each other via computers. This has led to the availability of searchable digital content, automation, and the collection and analysis of data, which are changing how business is conducted.

Higher education has responded by mandating a course on technology literacy in the undergraduate curriculum, irrespective of the student's selected field of study. We have taught a technology literacy course at three higher educational institutions in the Northeast and Southwest United States. The curriculum across the institutions for this course is similar and includes a broad overview of the components of information technology and their increasing utility.

Our review of the UME curriculum in the U.S. does not provide evidence of any additional technology literacy courses specifically catered to the needs of future physicians. Mesko, who has pioneered digital literacy in medical schools (Mesko et al., 2015), provided a master class at the Stanford Medicine X conference in 2013 (Steakley, 2013), but we were unable to find evidence of this type of course being included in the UME curriculum.

While the medical curriculum does not include broad digital literacy education, there is evidence that some medical schools have made extensive efforts to establish curricula to train medical students narrowly on specific aspects of information technology, such as Electronic Health Records (EHRs), medical informatics, and the use of searchable, curated, digital content as electronic diagnostic reasoning tools. The majority of these efforts are focused on training medical students to use EHRs. These efforts are consistent with the Core Entrusted Professional Activities (EPAs) for entering residency developed by the AAMC (2014, 2017). Three of the 13 EPAs explicitly call out the need for information technology skills. These EPAs are EPA 4 (Enter and Discuss Orders and Prescriptions), EPA 5 (Document a Clinical Encounter in the Patient Record), and EPA 7 (Form Clinical Questions and Retrieve Evidence to Advance Patient Care). In 2013, the AMA launched its Accelerating Change in Medical Education initiative. The AMA (2019a) has so far awarded $14.1 million in grants to 37 leading medical schools to develop innovative curricula. Some of the medical schools have used a portion of their grant money to explore the teaching of information technology skills (Skochelak & Stack, 2017; Wald, George, Reis, & Taylor; 2014).

Next, we provide examples of information technology skills training from the literature, starting with EHR training.

EHR Training

In most cases, the EHR skills training commences with clinical clerkship in Year-3. In some cases, training is limited to the beginning of clerkship, while in other cases training continues throughout the two years of clerkship.

The Uniformed Services University of the Health Sciences (USU) in Bethesda, Maryland started providing EHR training prior to 2011. The students are given a half-day orientation to the Electronic Medical Record (EMR) used in the Military Health System at the beginning of the third-year clerkship period (Stephens, Corcoran, & Motsinger, 2011). For the purpose of this chapter, EMRs and EHRs are equivalent. At the Alpert Medical School of Brown University (AMS), the third-year clinical skills clerkship includes an initial training session in EHR use followed by a second "advanced" EHR training module (Wald et al., 2014). The Regenstrief Institute and the Indiana University School of Medicine have developed a fully functional teaching EHR populated with more than 10,000 deidentified patients to simulate EHR use and learning for medical students (Skochelak & Stack, 2017). In addition to these efforts, organizations such as the AMA Council on Medical Education, Association of Professors of Gynecology and Obstetrics Undergraduate Medical Education Committee, the Society of Teachers of Family Medicine (STFM), and the Alliance for Clinical Education have all developed recommendations, best practices, guides, and templates for teaching EHRs within the UME curriculum (Welcher, Hersh, Takesue, Elliott, & Hawkins, 2018).

Recent surveys have led to the conclusion that almost all U.S. medical schools accredited by the LCME now allow students limited access to EHRs at clinical training sites (Welcher et al., 2017). In addition, several medical schools have implemented simulated EHR training for medical students when they do not have consistent access to EHRs in clinical settings (Welcher et al., 2018). EHR training for medical students, as described in the literature, includes syntactic training. Medical students need to have the ability to review patient medical histories, add clinical notes, and place orders for tests and medications when they begin their residency.

The remainder of the section provides examples of teaching about other technology areas in medical schools.

Other Technology Training

Yazdani, Relan, Wilkerson, and Chung (2017) report that medical students at the University of California, Los Angeles (UCLA) were trained through a mandatory 1-hour interactive session, in a lecture hall setting, on using digital content. This content included popular pharmacopeia and other institutionally subscribed electronic resources. Separate training sessions were conducted at UCLA on using digitally available clinical guidelines and various medical databases. Through a survey, Yazdani et al. concluded that all medical students who participated in the survey reported using electronic diagnostic reasoning tools (EDRTs) for either generating differential diagnosis, confirming final diagnosis, or both across all patients, illnesses, and clinical settings. Skochelak and Stack (2017) describe a course at New York University School of Medicine called "Health Care by the Numbers." In this course students learn to analyze big-data sets from the New York Statewide Planning and Research Cooperative System and the National Health and Nutrition Examination Survey to answer questions about health care outcomes. Finally, based on an Internet search of UME curriculum at the various U.S. medical schools, the authors have identified a trend for elective courses related to biomedical informatics and evidence-based medicine. The content of such a course can be illustrated by the two-week "Introduction to Biostatistics and Evidence-Based Medicine" course on the principles of biomedical research, foundational statistics, medical informatics, and application of evidence to patient care (University of Louisville, n.d.).

In summary, a literature review of scholarly articles shows that the current state of teaching about technology in medical schools includes a focused effort on training students in the use of EHRs before they begin residency. It also includes isolated efforts to make students aware about medical informatics and the use of searchable, curated, digital content as electronic diagnostic reasoning tools. The current state also reflects the lack of training for broad digital literacy. It is our opinion that digital literacy should include a nuanced discussion of the societal implications of information technology, many of them unintended and unforeseen, as well as the challenges associated with the successful adoption of information technology and the requisite change management and governance.

The next section discusses issues with the current state of teaching about technology in medical schools.

Controversies and Issues

At a high level, there are three major types of issues with the current state of teaching about technology. First, there are tactical issues with the manner in which EHR training is currently conducted and perhaps consequently the lack of expected benefits from EHR implementation. Second, the current narrow focus of medical school training on EHRs, medical informatics, and digital content is problematic in achieving the goals of information technology implementation in health care of improved clinical outcomes and cost reduction. Finally, the current approach creates the challenge of being overwhelmed by new and emerging technology that is likely to impact more EPAs than the three that are currently being impacted.

In the current state, there are several impediments in the way of medical students' access to EHRs in a clinical setting (Welcher et al., 2018). This has led to students sometimes having read-only access to patient records. These limitations are usually the result of an overly broad interpretation of HIPPA regulations and concerns about violations of billing regulations if student's notes were to drive billing (Welcher et al., 2018; White, Anthony, WinklerPrins, & Roskos, 2017). Medical schools have attempted to address these limitations by creating simulated EHRs for teaching purposes. This is problematic because of the variation in EHR implementations across different clinical settings (Pereira, 2018). The authors, during their consulting, used to remind their clients that if they had seen one EHR implementation, then they had seen one EHR implementation.

To help physicians enter data into the EHR, most EHR systems provide guided data entry via clinical templates. While this can speed data, entry it can also have the unintended consequence of hindering student learning. A similar issue exists with access to patients' clinical data in the EHR, which has the advantage of strengthening real-time clinical reasoning skills. However, this capability can also preclude investigative pathways prematurely for a medical student. In some sense, teaching based on the capabilities in an EHR is a double-edged sword; while it is necessary, it also has the potential of negatively affecting student learning (Goodman, 2010; Skochelak & Stack, 2017; Wald et al., 2014; Welcher et al., 2018).

The final issue with the current state of teaching EHRs is that to date expected benefits from EHR implementation have not been realized. These expected benefits included better patient care coordination, patient engagement, fewer medical errors, reduced healthcare costs, increased productivity, and analytics fueled by data in the EHR to drive preventive care, personalized care, targeted healthcare policy, and treatment effectiveness research. By the end of 2017, 96% of all hospitals had a certified EHR (Office of the National Coordinator for Health Information Technology, 2017a), and 80% of office-based physicians had a certified EHR (Office of the National Coordinator for Health Information Technology, 2017b). The government has paid out subsidies of over $30 billion to accelerate the adoption of EHRs (Fry & Schulte, 2019; Hayes, 2015). CMS-funded studies (Buntin, Burke, Hoaglin, & Blumenthal, 2011; Chaudhry et al., 2006; Goldzweig, Towfigh, Maglione, & Shekelle, 2009; Jones, Rudin, Perry, & Shekelle, 2014) analyzed peer-reviewed published literature from 1994 to 2013 regarding the impacts of EHRs. These studies found that a vast majority of the literature has reported positive outcomes from EHR implementation, with a few negative impacts. Even accounting for publication bias, this is a stellar result.

However, this stellar result does not tell the whole story. Buntin et al. (2011) cite "human element" as a critical issue for information technology implementations in healthcare leading to negative provider satisfaction. This highlights the importance of strong leadership and staff "buy-in" that the syntactic training for EHRs does not address. This finding was further supported by a lengthy investigation conducted by Kaiser Health News and Fortune (Fry & Schulte, 2019) that reviewed documents associated with past and current litigations and other publicly available material as well as interviewed patients, physicians, administrators, and executives of technology companies. This investigation revealed several instances of patient harm related to either human error in using the EHR and/or severe defects in the underlying EHR software. One contention of this investigation was that EHR adoption was accelerated by a well-intentioned public policy before the EHR software and the healthcare organizations and stakeholders were ready for the change. This leads us to the next issue with the current state of teaching about technology.

The current narrow focus of information technology training in medical schools has contributed to the situation of the "tail wagging the dog," with the technology getting out front without a deliberate and critical understanding of the second-order and third-order implications. The physicians end up reacting to technology, sometimes incentivized by federal subsidy payments. The unintended consequences are silos of data, difficult-to-use, complicated software systems, bespoke implementations across health systems, critical software defects, false positive alerts that numb the physician, and highly impactful security breaches. Stress, overwork, and physician burnout are now being blamed on the EHR with a potential permanent alteration of how the physician-patient interaction is conducted. This is similar to the assessment from the World Health Organization (WHO, 2010) at the beginning of the decade that physicians are often insufficiently aware and trained to manage technology implementations, leading to inefficient health care at best, or adverse events at worst. The situation in healthcare mirrors the reasons that information technology projects in many business settings have not produced the expected benefits (Dwivedi, Wastell, Laumer, Henriksen, & Myers 2014).

The final issue with the current state of teaching about technology deals with the speed with which new technologies are emerging and their increasing rates of adoption. In 2016, the AMA encouraged training about telemedicine for medical students and residents. Recently, the AMA (2019b) adopted a policy advocating for the integration of augmented intelligence in physician training. In addition to the EHR, technologies related to artificial intelligence, wearable sensors, and digital collaboration (social media, text messaging, group messaging) are becoming important. We expect technology to start impacting six more EPAs beyond the three EPAs that the current state section described as being impacted by technology. These six EPAs are EPA 1 (Gather a History and Perform a Physical Examination), EPA 2 (Prioritize a Differential Diagnosis Following a Clinical Encounter), EPA 3 (Recommend and Interpret Common Diagnostic and Screening Tests), EPA 6 (Provide an Oral Presentation of a Clinical Encounter), EPA 8 (Give or Receive a Patient Handover to Transition Care Responsibility), EPA 9 (Collaborate as a Member of an Interprofessional Team), and EPA 10 (Recognize a Patient Requiring Urgent or Emergent Care and Initiate Evaluation and Management). All the EPAs are summarized in Table 1 with the name of the technologies that impact the EPA and the current state of adoption of that technology. If the current approach of teaching students about EHRs is adopted by the medical schools, they will find it difficult to keep pace with or scale their approach to the number of technologies and applications that are emerging. From a pedagogical perspective, the authors believe that Wald et al. (2014), who describe incorporation of adult learning approaches such as reflection, are headed in the right direction, even though their end objective is narrow, namely, EHR training. There are nascent efforts that are attempting a broader approach to teaching about technology by teaching medical students computer programming (Law, Veinot, Campbell, Craig, & Mylopoulos, 2019), creating an interdisciplinary telehealth course (Jonas, Duming, Zebrowski, & Cimino, 2019), and integrating engineering principles in teaching medicine by infusing basic sciences, clinical sciences, engineering and innovation, and medical humanities into all four years of the UME curriculum (UIUC, n.d.). These nascent efforts confirm the issue the authors are describing, but the authors believe more fundamental change is needed.

RECOMMENDATIONS

Literature review about the current state of how technology is used for teaching and how medical students are taught about technology within the UME curriculum has brought to light several issues that were elaborated in the previous section. An analysis of the issues leads to two central theses that then drive four recommendations.

The central thesis about *technology for teaching* is that the technology-enhanced UME curriculum fails to coherently address issues and problems prompting them, because technology integration lacks pedagogical rationale and direction, and is reactive and driven by outside forces. We believe the integration of technology tools to support the UME curriculum should be driven by a design team of clinical faculty, adult educators, instructional designers, and technologists. This design team should ensure that the support technology provides is congruent with the learning objectives of a course. At the same time, when a course is in progress, the design team should play the role of a support team that adapts the technology tools based on real-time student feedback and assessment of how the students are using the technology tools.

The central thesis for *teaching about technology* is that the UME's approach does not prepare medical students to adopt technology in order to harness all its expected benefits. This is partially due to the design of technologies that do not meet the needs of the clinical practice and partially due to the role expected of clinicians when technology is implemented in the clinical setting. Medical schools need to prepare students to proactively shape the technology that is designed for the clinical settings, as well

Table 1. Adoption status for EPA impacting technologies

Entrusted Professional Activity	Technologies	Adoption Status
EPA 1: Gather a History and Perform a Physical Examination	Telehealth	Early stage, likely to increase
EPA 2: Prioritize a Differential Diagnosis Following a Clinical Encounter	Digital content	Widely adopted
	Augmented intelligence	Early stage
EPA 3: Recommend and Interpret Common Diagnostic and Screening Tests	Augmented intelligence	*Ad hoc* adoption, likely to increase
EPA 4: Enter and Discuss Orders and Prescriptions	HER	Widely adopted
EPA 5: Document a Clinical Encounter in the Patient Record	HER	Widely adopted
EPA 6: Provide an Oral Presentation of a Clinical Encounter	Telehealth	Early stage, likely to increase
EPA 7: Form Clinical Questions and Retrieve Evidence to Advance Patient Care	HER	Widely adopted
	Digital content	Widely adopted
EPA 8: Give or Receive a Patient Handover to Transition Care Responsibility	EHR interoperability	*Ad hoc* adoption
	Augmented Intelligence	Early Stage
	Digital collaboration	*Ad hoc* adoption
EPA 9: Collaborate as a Member of an Interprofessional Team	Digital collaboration	*Ad hoc* adoption
EPA 10: Recognize a Patient Requiring Urgent or Emergent Care and Initiate Evaluation and Management	EHR interoperability	*Ad hoc* adoption
	Wearable sensors	Early stage
	Telehealth	Early stage
	Augmented Intelligence	Early stage

as to play a leadership role in managing the change that the introduction of technology will necessitate in the clinical practice. Such a training will pay greater dividends than training on narrow aspects of specific technology applications.

Deliberate Design of Technology for Teaching

To get the maximum benefit from the technology tools that are used in the UME curriculum, we recommend that a design team of adult educators, instructional designers, and clinical faculty work together to ensure that the learning objectives for each course match the pedagogies used in that course. The technology tools should reinforce the pedagogies, and the associated assessments should then be selected to teach the course. Such a deliberate design approach will help the design team analyze the balance among the different types of learning objectives. For example, if we categorize the types of learning objectives into those that promote conceptual understanding, awareness, and memorization of important knowledge facts, hands-on experience, inquiry, and analysis, then the design team can ensure that courses have the desired balance between these types of learning objectives. Once the desired balance has been achieved, the design team can start focusing on the pedagogies that support the learning objective.

For example, if the type of learning objective for a course is to promote conceptual understanding, then the pedagogies most conducive to attaining this learning objective are likely to be a combination of in-person didactic lectures, followed by case-based group work and asynchronous discussions on curated topics. The discussion groups can be monitored to assess understanding of the concepts. The technology that supports this learning objective would be classroom technology, threaded discussion groups available in most Learning Management Systems, and short videos that review each concept.

Similarly, if the type of learning objective is to promote awareness and memorization of knowledge facts, then the most appropriate pedagogies would include classroom lectures to help students locate and assess the credibility of digital content. Students would need access to digital content with varying degrees of veracity that cumulatively is a comprehensive source of the knowledge facts they need to acquire. The assessment for this learning objective could be frequent quizzes. The technology support for such a course would be digital content, tools for searching digital content, online outlines of topic areas and tools available in a Learning Management System for building quizzes, and digital flash cards.

The deliberate and team-based course-design should be mirrored in conducting studies in technology impact. The focus should be on how technology enhances or mediates learning. In this endeavor, consideration should be given to all research methodologies, including qualitative and mixed-methods.

Real-Time Feedback, Assessment, and Adaptation

To ensure that technology is configured appropriately to support varying learning styles and capabilities of students as well as teaching styles of faculty, we believe a course in progress should be supported by a team of adult educators, instructional designers, and technologists. This team will be charged with assessing if the technology tools are serving their intended purpose, gathering real-time feedback from students, and then adapting the supporting technology. Most of the technology tools being used by medical schools are facile and amenable to quick configuration changes.

For example, if videos to promote the learning and understanding of concepts are not being accessed by students, then through real-time feedback from students, the videos should be replaced by classroom lectures or other types of digital content. The support team should be agile in recognizing the situation and responding to it.

Proactive Shaping of Technology for Clinical Practice

Medical education is not informed by trends of emerging technology maturity and trains medical students on the syntactic use of technology applications after they have begun to be adopted. Health Information Technology (IT) companies that leverage emerging technology are developing products with very little understanding of the UME curriculum. Medical educators and IT companies working in isolation has resulted in the current situation where technology applications do not deliver on the expectations of reduced healthcare costs and improved clinical outcomes.

Our recommendation is for UME curriculum to train medical students on the fundamental enablers of information technology and the implications these enablers can have in the clinical setting. Students should also learn to monitor technology trends and assess their implications. With this training, medical students will be in a position to work with IT companies and give them requirements for the technology applications. This proactive shaping of technology for clinical practice is more likely to deliver the expected benefits, and since it is shaped by the clinicians, its need of syntactic training will be negligible.

Physician Leadership of Technology Adoption

An experience at any doctor's office, emergency room, urgent care facility, or recovery from an in-patient procedure vividly demonstrates that healthcare delivery is a team activity, sometimes a masterful choreography of clinicians from multiple disciplines working in concert to heal a patient (Edmondson, 2012). Our fourth recommendation is based on the recognition that a physician needs to become the leader of the team that drives successful technology adoption and exhibit behaviors of successful leaders who can drive change (Anand, 2014).

For a physician to function in this capacity, the UME curriculum should include training on change management and leadership based on adult development theories, such as those proposed by Kegan (Kegan & Lahey, 2009) and Torbert (Torbert & Associates, 2004). Such training is likely to be useful beyond the realm of technology adoption and should also build capacity for interprofessional collaboration.

CONCLUSION

This chapter looked at the role played by technology in UME using the perspectives of how technology is used as a tool to facilitate teaching as well as how medical students are taught to use technology in the clinical setting. For each perspective, a survey of literature, published from 2009 to 2019, was conducted to understand the current state. Technology helps medical schools meet accreditation standards, create a student-centered teaching/learning focus, and expand experiential and practical learning. The current state of technology used for teaching needs to deal with issues such as the underdevelopment of medical education technology scholarship, mismatch of learning theories and the conflation of technology with pedagogy, and the inadequate consideration of students' readiness and learning needs. The UME curriculum does not include broad digital literacy education, but instead trains medical students narrowly on specific aspects of information technology, such as EHRs, medical informatics, and the use of digital content. A majority of the effort is expended on EHR training. The main issue with the current state of teaching about technology is the narrow focus on syntactic training on specific technology applications (such as the EHR). This approach will not scale for the large number of technology applications that are emerging and will also not prepare physicians to shape technology implementations to ensure success. Considerations should be given to UME courses to be designed by a team consisting of clinical faculty, adult educators, instructional designers and technologists. The purpose is to utilize technology in course design such that it can support the carefully selected pedagogy to match the learning outcomes. We also recommend that clinical faculty be supported by adult educators, instructional designers and technologists who can adjust the technology tools based on real-time student feedback and assessment. Additionally, attempts should be made to replace the narrow syntactic training on technology applications with training on the fundamentals of technology, as well as the development of skills to monitor technology trends, and analyze the implications of technology for clinically practice. Lastly, the incorporation of leadership training so that medical students are prepared to lead the change in management aspects associated with technology application implementation should be considered.

As we previously stated, the blending of pedagogy and technology is at stake. This key principle should orient UMEs' efforts and vision to harness technology for better learning and practice outcomes.

REFERENCES

American Medical Association (AMA). (2015). *AMA president outlines physician leadership plan for digital health* [Press release]. Retrieved from https://www.ama-assn.org/press-center/press-releases/ama-president-outlines-physician-leadership-plan-digital-health/

American Medical Association (AMA). (2016). *AMA encourages telemedicine training for medical students, residents.* [Press release]. Retrieved from https://www.ama-assn.org/press-center/press-releases/ama-encourages-telemedicine-training-medical-students-residents

American Medical Association (AMA). (2019a). *AMA expansion of national effort creating medical school of the future* [Press release]. Retrieved from https://www.ama-assn.org/press-center/press-releases/ama-expansion-national-effort-creating-medical-school-future/

American Medical Association (AMA). (2019b). *AMA adopt policy, integrate augmented intelligence in physician training* [Press release]. Retrieved from https://www.ama-assn.org/press-center/press-releases/ama-adopt-policy-integrate-augmented-intelligence-physician-training

Anand, T. (2014). *Team learning to narrow the gap between healthcare knowledge and practice* [Doctoral dissertation]. Retrieved from ProQuest.

Antunes, J. (2019). Microsoft's HoloLens 2 mixed-reality headset: better specs, comfort, enterprise features. *Spar3D*. Retrieved from https://www.spar3d.com/news/hardware/microsofts-hololens-2-mixed-reality-headset-better-specs-comfort-enterprise-features/

Association of American Medical Colleges (AAMC). (2014). *Core entrustable professional activities for entering residency: Curriculum developer's guide*. Washington, DC: Author. Retrieved from https://store.aamc.org/downloadable/download/sample/sample_id/63/

Association of American Medical Colleges (AAMC). (2017). *Core entrustable professional activities for entering residency*. Washington, DC: Author. Retrieved from https://www.aamc.org/download/484778/data/epa13toolkit.pdf

Association of American Medical Colleges (AAMC). (n.d.). *Medical schools reporting regional campus information*. Retrieved from https://www.aamc.org/initiatives/ cir/406434/13a.html

Berk, R. (2009). Teaching strategies for the Net Generation. *Teaching and Learning Journal, 3*(2), 1–24.

Bray, A., Webb, J., Enquobahrie, A., Vicory, J., Heneghan, J., Hubal, R., ... Clipp, R. (2019). Pulse physiology engine: An open-source software platform for computational modeling of human medical simulation. *SN Comprehensive Clinical Medicine, 1*(5), 362–377. doi:10.100742399-019-00053-w

Breining, G. (2016, Sept. 29). 3D printers are revolutionizing medicine. *AAMCNews*.

Brockett, R., & Hiemstra, R. (1991). *Self-direction in adult learning: Perspectives on theory, research and practice*. London, UK: Routledge.

Buntin, M., Burke, M., Hoaglin, M., & Blumenthal, D. (2011). The benefits of health information technology: A review of the recent literature shows predominantly positive results. *Health Affairs, 30*(3), 464–471. doi:10.1377/hlthaff.2011.0178 PMID:21383365

Candy, P. (1991). *Self-direction for lifelong learning: A comprehensive guide to theory and practice*. San Francisco, CA: Jossey-Bass.

Carle Illinois College of Medicine (UIUC). (n.d.). *The Illinois model for medical education*. Retrieved from https://medicine.illinois.edu/education/paradigm-shifting-curriculum

Centers for Medicare and Medicaid Services (CMS). (n.d.). *National health expenditures by type of service and source of funds, CY 1960-2017*. Retrieved from https://www.cms.gov/research-statistics-data-and-systems/statistics-trends-and-reports/nationalhealthexpenddata/nationalhealthaccountshistorical.html

Chaudhry, B., Wang, J., Wu, S., Maglione, M., Mojica, W., Roth, E., ... Shekelle, P. G. (2006). Systematic review: Impact of health information technology on quality, efficiency, and costs of medical care. *Annals of Internal Medicine, 144*(10), 742–752. doi:10.7326/0003-4819-144-10-200605160-00125 PMID:16702590

Chen, P., & Scanlon, M. (2018). Teaching radiology trainees from the perspective of a Millennial. *Academic Radiology, 25*(6), 794–800. doi:10.1016/j.acra.2018.02.008 PMID:29573938

Chene, A. (1983). The concept of autonomy in adult education: A philosophical discussion. *Adult Education Quarterly, 1*(1), 38–47. doi:10.1177/0001848183034001004

Choi-Lundberg, D., Low, T., Patman, P., Turner, P., & Sinha, S. (2016). Medical student preferences for self-directed study resources in gross anatomy. *Anatomical Sciences Education, 9*(2), 150–160. doi:10.1002/ase.1549 PMID:26033851

Cook, D., & Triola, M. (2009). Virtual patients: A critical literature review and proposed next steps. *Medical Education, 43*(4), 303–311. doi:10.1111/j.1365-2923.2008.03286.x PMID:19335571

Dwivedi, Y., Wastell, D., Laumer, S., Henriksen, H., Myers, M., Bunker, D., ... Srivastava, S. C. (2014). Research on information systems failures and successes: Status update and future directions. *Information Systems Frontiers*, *17*(1), 143–157. doi:10.100710796-014-9500-y

Edmondson, A. (2012). *Teaming: How organizations learn, innovate and compete in the knowledge economy*. San Francisco, CA: Jossey-Bass.

Fry, E., & Schulte, F. (2019, March 18). Death by a thousand clicks: Where electronic health records went wrong. *Fortune*.

Ghazi, A., Stone, J., Candela, B., Richards, M., & Joseph, J. (2015). Simulated inanimate model for physical learning experience (SIMPLE) for robotic partial nephrectomy using a 3-D printed kidney model. *The Journal of Urology*, *193*(4SSupplement), e778. doi:10.1016/j.juro.2015.02.2285

Goldzweig, C., Towfigh, A., Maglione, M., & Shekelle, P. (2009). Costs and benefits of health information technology: New trends from the literature. *Health Affairs*, *28*(Supplement 2), w282–w293. doi:10.1377/hlthaff.28.2.w282 PMID:19174390

Goodchild, T., & Speed, E. (2018). Technology enhanced learning as transformative innovation: A note on the enduring myth of TEL. *Teaching in Higher Education*. doi:10.1080/13562517.2018.1518900

Goodman, R. (2010). Healthcare technology and medical education: Putting physical diagnosis in its proper place. *Academic Medicine*, *85*(6), 945–946. doi:10.1097/ACM.0b013e3181dbb55b PMID:20505391

Griffith, K., de Cataldo, R., & Fogarty, K. (2016). Do-it-yourself: 3D models of hydrogenic orbitals through 3D printing. *Journal of Chemical Education*, *93*(9), 1586–1590. doi:10.1021/acs.jchemed.6b00293

Gross, M., & Masters, C. (2017). Virtual dissection: Using active learning with the Anatomage Table to enhance student learning. The *FASEB (Federation of American Societies for Experimental Biology) Journal, 31*(1)-Supplement.

Guglielmino, L. (1978). Development of the Self-Directed Learning Readiness Scale. *Dissertation Abstracts International*, *38*, 6476A.

Hayes, T. (2015). Are electronic medical records worth the costs of implementation? *American Action Forum*. Retrieved from https://www.americanactionforum.org/ research/are-electronic-medical-records-worth-the-costs-of-implementation/

Hendler, J., & Golbeck, J. (2008). Metcalfe's Law, Web 2.0, and the Semantic Web. *Journal of Web Semantics*, *6*(1), 14–20. doi:10.1016/j.websem.2007.11.008

Hollands, F., & Tirthali, D. (2014). Why do institutions offer MOOCs? *Online Learning, 18*(3).

Horton, J. (2017). A content analysis of 3D printing policies at academic libraries. *Journal of Library Administration*, *57*(3), 267–281. doi:10.1080/01930826.2016.1258876

Howard, S. (2013). Risk-aversion: Understanding teachers' resistance to technology integration. *Technology, Pedagogy, and Education*. Retrieved from https://www.academia.edu/2042088/Risk-aversion_Understanding_teachers_ resistance_to_technology_integration/

Johnson, T., Wisniewski, M., Kuhlemeyer, G., Issacs, G., & Krzykowski, J. (2012). Technology adaptation in higher education: Overcoming anxiety through faculty bootcamp. *Journal of Asynchronous Learning Networks, 16*(2), 63–72.

Jonas, C. E., Durning, S. J., Zebrowski, C., & Cimino, F. (2019). An interdisciplinary, multi-institution telehealth course for third-year medical students. *Academic Medicine, 94*(6), 833–837. doi:10.1097/ACM.0000000000002701 PMID:30870152

Jones, S., Rudin, R., Perry, T., & Shekelle, P. (2014). Health information technology: An updated systematic review with a focus on meaningful use. *Annals of Internal Medicine, 160*(1), 48–54. doi:10.7326/M13-1531 PMID:24573664

Judd, T., & Kennedy, G. (2011). Expediency-based practice? Medical students' reliance on Google and Wikipedia for biomedical inquiries. *British Journal of Educational Technology, 42*(2), 351–360. doi:10.1111/j.1467-8535.2009.01019.x

Kegan, E., & Lahey, L. L. (2009). *Immunity to change: How to overcome it and unlock the potential in yourself and your organization (leadership for the common good).* Boston, MA: Harvard Business School Publishing.

Knowles, M. (1970). *The modern practice of adult education.* New York, NY: Association Press.

Kwan, B., Bui, G., Jain, P., Shah, N., & Juang, D. (2017). Exploring simulation in the internal medicine clerkship. *The Clinical Teacher, 14*(5), 349–355. doi:10.1111/tct.12577 PMID:27885821

Law, M., Veinot, P., Campbell, J., Craig, M., & Mylopoulos, M. (2019). Computing for medicine: Can we prepare medical students for the future? *Academic Medicine, 94*(3), 353–357. doi:10.1097/ACM.0000000000002521 PMID:30431453

Liaison Committee on Medical Education (LCME). (2020). *Functions and structure of a medical school: Standards for accreditation of medical education programs leading to the MD degree.* Washington, DC: Author.

Lovell, K., & Vignare, K. (2009). MSU medical colleges blended learning for first year science courses: Uniting pedagogy to maximize experience and real world limitations. *Journal of Asynchronous Learning Networks, 13*(1), 55–63.

McLean, S. (2016). Case-based learning and its application in medical and health-care fields: A review of worldwide literature. *Journal of Medical Education and Curricular Development, 3*, 39–49. doi:10.4137/JMECD.S20377 PMID:29349306

McNulty, J., Hoyt, A., Chandrasekhar, A., Espiritu, B., Gruener, G., Price, R., & Naheedy, R. (2011). A three-year study of lecture multimedia utilization in the medical curriculum: Associations with performances in the basic sciences. *Medical Science Educator, 21*(1), 29–36. doi:10.1007/BF03341591

Mesko, B., Győrffy, Z., & Kollár, J. (2015). Digital literacy in the medical curriculum: A course with social media tools and gamification. *JMIR Medical Education, 1*(2), e6. doi:10.2196/mededu.4411 PMID:27731856

Miflin, B. (2004). Adult learning, self-directed learning and problem-based learning: Deconstructing the connections. *Teaching in Higher Education, 9*(1), 43–53. doi:10.1080/1356251032000155821

Miles, C., Lee, C., Foggett, K., & Nair, B. (2017). Reinventing medical teaching and learning for the 21st century: Blended and flipped strategies. *Archives of Medicine and Health Sciences, 5*, 97–102.

Misak, J. (2018). A (virtual) bridge not too far: Teaching narrative sense of space with virtual reality. *Computers and Composition, 50*, 39–52. doi:10.1016/j.compcom.2018.07.007

Mogali, S., Yeong, W., Tan, H. K. J., Tan, G. J. S., Abrahams, P. H., Zary, N., ... Ferenczi, M. A. (2017). Evaluation by medical students of the educational value of multi-material, multi-colored three-dimensional printed models of the upper limb for anatomical education. *Anatomical Sciences Education, 11*(1), 54–64. doi:10.1002/ase.1703 PMID:28544582

Moore, G. (1998). Cramming more components onto integrated circuits. *Proceedings of the IEEE, 86*(1), 82-85.

National Institutes of Health (NIH). (2017). *NIH 3D Print Exchange*. Bethesda, MD: U.S. Department of Health and Human Services. Retrieved from https://3dprint.nih. gov/

Office of the National Coordinator for Health Information Technology. (2017a). *Non-federal acute care hospital electronic health record adoption*. Retrieved from https://dashboard.healthit.gov/quickstats/pages/FIG-Hospital-EHR-Adoption.php

Office of the National Coordinator for Health Information Technology. (2017b). *Individuals use of technology to track health care charges and costs*. Retrieved from https://dashboard.healthit.gov/quickstats/pages/consumers-health-care-charges-costs-online.php

Orr, D., Weller, M., & Farrow, R. (2018). *Models for online, open, flexible and technology enhanced higher education across the globe: A comparative analysis*. Oslo, Norway: International Council for Open and Distance Education.

Phares, L., & Guglielmino, L. (2010). The role of self-directed learning in the work of community leaders. *International Journal of Self-directed Learning, 7*(2), 35–53.

Prunuske, A., Henn, L., Brearley, A., & Prunuske, J. (2016). A randomized crossover design to access learning impact and student preference for active and passive online learning modules. *Medical Science Educator, 26*(1), 135–141. doi:10.100740670-015-0224-5 PMID:27076992

Rideout, V., Foehr, U., & Roberts, D. (2010). *Generation M2: Media in the lives of 8- to 18-year-olds*. San Francisco, CA: Kaiser Family Foundation; Retrieved from http://www.kff.org/entmedia/mh012010pkg.cfm

Roberts, D., Newman, L., & Schwartzstein, R. (2012). Twelve tips for facilitating Millennials' learning. *Medical Teacher, 34*(4), 274–278. doi:10.3109/0142159X.2011.613498 PMID:22288944

Robinson, R. (2018). *Insights from a massive open online course (MOOC) for medical education (2014-2018)*. Retrieved from https://www.researchgate.net/ publication/326610346

Rossini, M. (2018). Healthcare IT spending trends: Where hospitals plan to invest. *Journal of the Academy of Chiropractic Orthopedists*. Retrieved from https://www.jacoinc.com/blog/healthcare-it-spending-trends-where-hospitals-plan-to-invest/

Skochelak, S. E., & Stack, S. J. (2017). Creating the medical schools of the future. *Academic Medicine*, *92*(1), 16–19. doi:10.1097/ACM.0000000000001160 PMID:27008357

Smiar, K., & Mendez, J. (2016). Creating and using interactive, 3D-printed models to improve student comprehension of Bohr model of the atom, bond polarity, and hybridization. *Journal of Chemical Education*, *93*(9), 1591–1594. doi:10.1021/acs.jchemed.6b00297

Smith, A., & Anderson, M. (2018). *Social media use in 2018*. Washington, DC: Pew Research Center; Retrieved from https://www.pewinternet.org/2018/03/01/social-media-use-in-2018/

Smith, M., & Jones, J. (2018). Dual-extrusion 3D printing of anatomical models for education. *Anatomical Sciences Education*, *11*(1), 65–72. doi:10.1002/ase.1730 PMID:28906599

Srinivasan, M., Wilkes, M., Stevenson, F., Nguyen, T., & Slavin, S. (2007). Comparing problem-based learning with cased based learning: Effects of a major curricular shift at two institutions. *Academic Medicine*, *82*(1), 74–82. doi:10.1097/01.ACM.0000249963.93776.aa PMID:17198294

Stead, W., Searle, J., Fessler, H., Smith, J., & Shortliffe, E. (2011). Biomedical informatics: Changing what physicians need to know and how they learn. *Academic Medicine*, *86*(4), 429–434. doi:10.1097/ACM.0b013e3181f41e8c PMID:20711055

Steakley, L. (2013). *A conversation about digital literacy in medical education*. Retrieved from https://scopeblog.stanford.edu/2013/05/09/a-conversation-about-digital-literacy-in-medical-education/

Stephens, M. B., Corcoran, T. S., & Motsinger, C. (2011). Clinical documentation in electronic medical records: The student perspective. *The Journal of the International Association of Medical Science Educators: JIAMSE*, *1*(1), 3–6. doi:10.1007/BF03341587

Sullivan, T. (2018). Gartner, IDC and HIMSS analytics say hospitals will invest the most in 2018. *Healthcare IT News*. Retrieved from https://www.healthcareitnews.com/news/follow-money-where-gartner-idc-and-himss-analytics-say-hospitals-will-invest-most-2018/

Talbot, T., Sagae, K., John, B., & Rizzo, A. (2012). Sorting out the virtual patient: How to exploit artificial intelligence, game technology and sound educational practices to create engaging role-playing simulations. *International Journal of Gaming and Computer-Mediated Simulations*, *4*(3), 1–19. doi:10.4018/jgcms.2012070101

Torbert, W., & ... (2004). *Action inquiry: The secret of timely and transforming leadership*. San Francisco, CA: Berrett-Koehler.

Tough, A. (1971). *The adult's learning projects*. Toronto, Canada: Ontario Institute for Studies in Education.

Triola, M., Friedman, E., Cimino, C., Geyer, E., Wiederhorn, J., & Mainiero, C. (2010). Health information technology and the medical school curriculum. *American Journal of Managed Care, 16*(12 Suppl. HIT), 54-56.

Tummons, J., Fournier, C., Kits, O., & MacLeod, A. (2018). Using technology to accomplish comparability of provision in distributed medical education in Canada: An actor-network theory ethnography. *Studies in Higher Education*, *43*(11), 1912–1922. doi:10.1080/03075079.2017.1290063

University of Louisville (UL). (n.d.). *Undergraduate medical education: Curriculum overview.* Retrieved from https://louisville.edu/medicine/ume/curriculum/curriculum-overview

U.S. Department of Education. (2019). *Use of technology in teaching and learning.* Retrieved from https://www.ed.gov/oii-news/use-technology-teaching-and-learning

Waite, G., Orndorff, B., Hughes, E., Saxon, D., White, G., Becker, S., & Duong, T. (2014). Distance education in medical education: Is there "value added"? *Medical Science Educator*, *24*(1), 135–142. doi:10.100740670-014-0020-7

Wald, H. S., George, P., Reis, S. P., & Taylor, J. S. (2014). Electronic health record training in undergraduate medical education: Bridging theory to practice with curricula for empowering patient- and relationship-centered care in the computerized setting. *Academic Medicine*, *89*(3), 380–386. doi:10.1097/ACM.0000000000000131 PMID:24448045

Welcher, C. M., Hersh, W., Takesue, B., Elliott, V., & Hawkins, R. E. (2018). Barriers to medical students' electronic health record access can impede their preparedness for practice. *Academic Medicine*, *93*(1), 48–53. doi:10.1097/ACM.0000000000001829 PMID:28746069

White, J., Anthony, D., WinklerPrins, V., & Roskos, S. (2017). Electronic medical records, medical students, and ambulatory family physicians: A multi-institution study. *Academic Medicine*, *92*(10), 1485–1490. doi:10.1097/ACM.0000000000001673 PMID:28379934

White, L. (2018). *MOOCs for medical education: Lesson learned from the Medical Neuroscience experience – Exploring the boundaries of online learning and what it means for higher education.* Paper presented at the Treasury Symposium, Savannah, GA.

Wish-Baratz, S., Gubatina, A., Enterline, R., & Griswold, M. (2019). A new supplement to gross anatomy dissection: Holoanatomy. *Medical Education*, *53*(5), 522–523. doi:10.1111/medu.13845 PMID:30891831

Wood, S. (2018). Framing wearing: Genre, embodiment, and exploring wearable technology in the composition classroom. *Computers and Composition*, *50*, 66–77. doi:10.1016/j.compcom.2018.07.004

World Health Organization (WHO). (2010). *Medical devices, managing the mismatch: An outcome of the Priority Medical Devices Project.* Geneva, Switzerland: Author.

Yazdani, S., Relan, A., Wilkerson, L., & Chung, P. J. (2017). Third-year medical students' perceptions and use of electronic diagnostic reasoning tools. *Medical Science Educator*, *27*(1), 97–103. doi:10.100740670-017-0373-9

Chapter 21
Digital Health

Cole A. Zanetti
ⓘ https://orcid.org/0000-0002-0443-0409
Rocky Vista University College of Osteopathic Medicine, USA

Aaron George
Meritus Health, USA

Regan A. Stiegmann
Rocky Vista University College of Osteopathic Medicine, USA

Douglas Phelan
Dartmouth Hitchcock Medical Center, USA

ABSTRACT

This chapter presents an assessment of the rapidly evolving state of health-related technology and its developing impact on health care, medical education, patient care, and care delivery. This is collectively referred to as the digital health movement in medicine. This chapter provides a broader understanding of how digital health is changing not only the practice of medicine, but the consumer market that pertains to health care and medicine at large. The authors discuss the current state of digital health in medicine, the challenges of conventionally assessing digital health-related competencies, and the relative difficulty of adapting contemporary medical education to include digital health modalities into traditional undergraduate medical education. This chapter also showcases three unique case studies of early-adopting medical institutions that have created digital health learning opportunities for their undergraduate medical student population.

INTRODUCTION

The field of digital health has seen rapid innovation and evolution over the last decade and shows no indication of slowing down in the future. Digital health empowers patients to take an active role in their health care through facilitated technologic changes. Likewise, it empowers physicians and other health care team members to transform care delivery with innovative tools and technology. Such transforma-

DOI: 10.4018/978-1-7998-1468-9.ch021

tion requires new and unique skill sets, and the willingness of academic centers to adapt curriculum and redesign training to support these needs. This chapter aims to discuss the transformational impact of digital health in medicine and the concurrent need for response in undergraduate medical education. Additionally, the chapter will address specific objectives pertaining to the current background of digital health, the growth and future of digital health, as well as integrated contemporary case studies that highlight successful undergraduate medical student curricular initiatives in digital health.

BACKGROUND

In its most simple form, digital health is the application of any digital technology to the practice or delivery of healthcare. In 2019, digital health refers to the use of any hardware or software solution which aids healthcare professionals and patients in the promotion of health and wellness, or in the optimization of disease management. Digital health is not a new concept, however with its constant evolution, it is a highly formative factor that contributes to shaping how healthcare is sought and delivered. The advent of the internet, the electronic health record, digital imaging, and countless other innovations have transformed not only patient care but medicine as a whole. Digital health is vast and encompasses a variety of subsections that include clinical informatics, telehealth, telemedicine, genomics, mobile apps, wearable technology, data analytics, behavioral change technologies, artificial intelligence, and much more.

One of the most ubiquitous digital health products is seen with patient portals. Typically accessed by patients in the comfort of their own home on either a computer or a mobile device, patient portals offer a secured digital link for patients to access their personal medical records, diagnoses, laboratory results, as well as the ability to contact their health care practitioners with questions or medication refill requests. Based on a recent data brief by the Office of the National Coordinator, 52% of patients have access to their medical records through an electronic portal either from their health system or insurer (Patel & Johnson, 2018). This represents 28% of individuals nationwide currently using a patient portal, with one third of these individuals using an electronic device for monitoring their health which is connected to their portal. More frequently seen are digital health-based interfaces that include apps and programs that allow patients the opportunity for home-monitoring of chronic conditions such as continuous blood glucose monitoring for diabetes mellitus or constant blood pressure monitoring for hypertension.

Digital health holds the potential to supplement and enhance the delivery and management of traditional health care, such as through expansion of telehealth and telemedicine. For example, the Veterans Health Administration administered over 2.3 million telehealth encounters across the country in 2018 alone; 45% of those Veterans Health Administration telemedicine encounters in 2018 were performed for veterans in rural areas or for veterans with transportation difficulties (U.S. Department of Veterans Affairs, 2019). Despite these kinds of digital health modalities being widely used in similarly innovative ways in many health systems, there persists a significant lack of healthcare professionals with the training, competency, and experience necessary to utilize and advance digital health. This is in addition to those challenges that are all too frequently faced by modern healthcare providers, with an overwhelming amount of physician burnout as well as skyrocketing numbers of underserved and unreached patient populations. Digital health interfaces exist at the forefront of innovation to confront these issues and hold the potential to improve medicine by making physician independence and physician access more feasible, promoting patient involvement and autonomy, enriching the patient-provider experience, and lowering the cost of healthcare.

Current State of Undergraduate Medical Education

The fast-paced rate of change as well as the increasing level of complexity in the world of medicine has accelerated over recent decades. These shifts have created a challenge for the already time-limited undergraduate medical education curriculum to keep pace. The overarching goal of any undergraduate medical education institution is to prepare the student physician for future practice. Rapid technological progression across society and within clinical practice has strained the medical school environment to reflect even present-day practice. Despite the staggering evolution in modern technology, the structure of most medical schools in the United States remains rooted in traditional models (Cooke et al., 2010). Where technology and digital health training have been adopted, the integration is typically only as a piece-meal supplement to the traditional curricular structure. However, there is hope for transformation, as some medical schools and institutions have engaged in purposeful integration of digital health and others are in the process.

Undergraduate medical education continues to focus very heavily on test performance both at the institutional level and at the national level. As has been the tradition for centuries, student performance, comparison, and ranking has typically been measured by grades in basic science and clinical rotations. These evaluation modalities lack the ability to assess students' readiness to help navigate patients through the growing digital health-centric complexity of healthcare. Beyond traditional clinical curriculum, sciences and physical exam skills, students must be prepared to respond to expanding medical data collection including data gathered from electronic medical records, population health data, mobile apps, and wearable technologies. Counseling patients requires an understanding of genetic testing and sequencing, including direct to consumer products such as 23andme. Online forums and community platforms disperse clinical knowledge in unique ways which often require careful guidance from skilled physicians. In other areas of higher education, harnessing technology has stimulated transformation by providing educational content to expanded audiences and the global e-learning market, which is projected to reach nearly $400 billion by 2026 (Statistics Market Research Consulting, 2018). Yet, undergraduate medical schools continue to cultivate local, customary, and duplicative content.

Implementation of ultrasound is one such example of slow adoption of technology within the undergraduate medical school experience. For more than 50 years, established diagnostic ultrasonography has been recognized as a key method for evaluating the heart, abdomen, and vasculature. Further, ultrasound has become a valuable tool in graduate medical training as well as in specialty practice. Recent peer reviewed studies have even shown that diagnostic ultrasonography can be superior to the physical exam (Kobal et al, 2005, and Mouratev et al, 2013). There is even data to suggest that premedical students are making their medical school choices based around the presence of ultrasound training (Hoppmann et al, 2015). Despite this, no accepted standard ultrasound curriculum is recognized in undergraduate medical education within the United States. Rather, most undergraduate medical students have been offered limited or episodic exposure to the technology. Where ultrasound has been added, the coursework that has been applied has most often been designed for practicing specialist clinicians well beyond the scope of the medical student (Stone-McLean et al., 2017). While more than half of medical schools in the United States offer some exposure to ultrasound, this is most often primarily a component of the clinical rotation experience and is not inherent within the foundational curricula. Further, when questioned in 2014, less than 20% of medical schools found ultrasound training to be of a priority (Bahner, Goldman, Way, Royall, & Liu 2014) It is possible that bedside ultrasound will replace the stethoscope within one to two decades. Given this, the lack of formal, longitudinal, and purposeful adaptive integration within medical school curriculum is demonstrative of the unfocused approach of medical schools to technology and digital health (Wittenberg, 2014).

Forward thinking medical schools can streamline and updated their curriculum content review process for curricular committees and expend financial resources to meaningfully integrate technology into the learning environment. Uncertainty as to the direction of the future of medicine as well as the increasing burden of debt to medical students challenges these efforts. Unfortunately, with regard to integration of digital health, there remains a lack of uniformity and consistency across the undergraduate academic medical education spectrum throughout the country, with varying levels of implementation.

Changes in Medical Education

The talents and skill sets of the modern matriculating medical student are much different than those of medical students even one or two decades ago. Medical schools today are catering to an audience of applicants who, even prior to matriculating into formal undergraduate medical education, have extensively diverse backgrounds, multiple degrees, and an increased facility with modern technology. Long gone are the days of medical students entering the medical school pipeline, assuming that they begin and end at definable career points and with uniform skill sets. Rather, medical schools must increasingly look to leverage training towards providing individual and tailored experiences. This requires meaningful integration of technology within and throughout the undergraduate medical education experience and beyond. One example of technologic adaptation that is becoming more commonplace in undergraduate medical education is the utilization of tablets and electronic devices. (Patel & Burke-Gaffney, 2018). These digital health tools are increasing student participation, elevating student interest, and have also been shown to accelerate the learning process. Medical schools have responded accordingly with increased exposure to different electronic health record platforms and educational optimization of documentation skills training. Leading medical schools provide meaningful electronic health record training in a longitudinal fashion as a complement to integration of technology as an inherent component of the clinical decision-making and care process.

In 2016, the American Medical Association invested 15 million dollars in digital health research (Siwicki, 2016). Since then, Stanford University, Rocky Vista University, and Johns Hopkins University, along with a small number of other medical schools in the United States, have integrated digital health programs into the curriculum they offer their medical students (Center for Digital Health at Stanford, 2019 and Henry, 2018 and Johns Hopkins, 2019). The goal in medical education is no longer solely to expose a student to medical experiences and clinical knowledge. Rather medical graduates need be trained to be "undifferentiated graduates". This concept of undifferentiation amongst graduates facilitates an adaptability to impact health outcomes in a contemporary fashion, as well as respond to changes in technology, medical evidence, and clinical care models.

Innovative Models

One example of digital health technology innovation has been the integration of cognitive simulations, such as virtual patients, within the undergraduate medical education experience. To date, the majority of such digital models have focused on surgical and procedural simulations. However, virtually simulated patient encounters and cognitive task trainers expand the accessibility of medical students to practice clinical episodes of care at any time, and to do so in a safe and cost-effective way. Rather than be constrained to the schedule of an in person standardized patient, students have round-the-clock access to practice and learn from limitless possible clinical scenarios. For example, first year medical students at the University of California San Francisco are given virtual reality goggles for anatomy training (Baker, 2017). Meanwhile University of California, Irvine has integrated a computer application that superimposes a hologram of a patient over a manikin to produce a more lifelike and responsive simulation for medical student education (Breining, 2018). Research now shows that virtual patients can be associated with improved learning outcomes (Cook, Erwin, & Triola, 2010). Similar practices have emerged over recent years in terms of teaching the coursework of basic anatomy. Many schools, pressured by difficulty in obtaining cadavers, rising costs of storage, and decreased anatomy faculty, have eliminated formal and traditional cadaver coursework altogether. Tablets and virtual reality headsets have replaced physical cadaver labs, and have allowed students to explore anatomy in individualized and easily accessible ways.

Though these health technologies have become incredibly useful for simulation based training, the fundamental goal of advancing digital health within undergraduate medical training is to adequately prepare the graduating medical student to address the demands of modern health care. This necessitates the understanding of care delivery through and within technology. Electronic medical record user interfaces impact the direct ability of medical providers to provide such care to their patients. Medical schools must not only teach students to interact with electronic health records, but also to inspire flexibility within them to adapt to different electronic medical record environments and future updates and upgrades. The modern medical resident performs duties in a multitude of clinical environments and must be facile with multiple possible electronic medical record models throughout the duration of their training.

SOLUTIONS AND RECOMMENDATIONS

Case Studies on How Curriculum can be Developed for Undergraduate Medical Education and Current Examples

There are many medical schools attempting to scratch the surface of digital health through various means of digital health training. According to AAMC data from 2017 and 2018, approximately 60% of medical schools provide either required or elective undergraduate medical education training in telemedicine (AAMC, 2018). However, there are some undergraduate medical education training centers that are taking a more robust approach to digital health. Showcased in this section are select case studies of current undergraduate medical education curriculum that exist in the field of digital health today. This list is not exhaustive of all programs, but provides a glimpse into the current landscape of digital health training in undergraduate medical education in the United States. Outlined in each case study is an overview of the program, the length of the course, and objectives of digital health training. In addition to this, strengths and weaknesses of each program based on current curriculum and content are provided.

Case Study:

Rocky Vista University College of Osteopathic Medicine Digital Health Track (RVUCOM-Colorado Campus, RVUCOM-Southern Utah Campus), Parker, CO:

Overview: The Digital Health Track at Rocky Vista University College of Osteopathic Medicine (RVUCOM) serves as the most extensive digital health training program identified to date. This training program is organized as an elective track that occurs throughout the duration of all four years of undergraduate medical education at RVUCOM. The training starts in the first year of medical school with one semester dedicated to 30 credit hours introducing the broad field of digital health. The second year of undergraduate medical education is also accompanied by one semester of 30 credit hours of digital health, diving more in depth and developing personal and professional skills necessary for the evolution of digital health expertise. During the third and fourth years at RVUCOM which focus more so on clinical application, there are rotation opportunities within local and national digital health startup organizations that provide medical students with the opportunity to practice the digital health skills they have learned while having an expert in digital health serve as a coach throughout the experiential process. The program at RVUCOM is also designed to work within current course curriculum to identify ways to enbed digital health training in all facets of the core required curriculum. (Rocky Vista University College of Osteopathic Medicine, 2019)

Curriculum Length: 4 years of undergraduate medical education

Requirement or Elective: Elective Track

Course Objectives:

At the end of this course the student should be able to:

- Have a firm understanding of digital health and its application across the medical field
- Discuss the ethical dilemmas within the field of digital health
- Identify how digital health can be applied in different health ecosystems
- Discuss the limitations of digital health through current technology and ethics
- Understand the costs and training associated with digital health use
- Have awareness of current digital health policy and law
- Realize the payment models associated with digital health
- Realize the application of artificial intelligence and predictive analytics and their application in care delivery.
- Have awareness of genetic medicine and nanotechnology and how they apply to personalized medicine
- Have exposure and training in telemedicine, understand its use, limitations, and care benefits
- Have a clear understanding of physician entrepreneurship in digital health
- Understand basic concepts of consulting within digital health
- Have experience in how social media and public health marketing can be used for prevention
- Comprehend the inherent biases of technology and STEM components within sociocultural contexts
- Have personal experience in remote monitoring from the perspective of patient as well as the data analysis from the healthcare team
- Apply digital health educational experiences to patient populations and clinical careers

Strengths: The RVUCOM digital health track is the only longitudinal digital health training program that provides the opportunity to span all 4 years of undergraduate medical education. It provides both content and experiential learning opportunities. RVUCOM also facilitates efforts to enable digital health training into required core curriculum. RVUCOM offers honors distinction and recognition for track participation at graduation for students who meet the requirements for the Digital Health track.

Weaknesses: The RVUCOM digital health track is not a required course. It is currently limited to only 24 students a year, 12 on each campus, but has potential for growth. The current core required curriculum at RVUCOM does not have dedicated digital health components at this time.

Case Study: Stanford School of Medicine Elective Digital Health Class, Stanford, CA

Overview: Stanford school of medicine, given a location proximal to many digital health startups, has a prime opportunity for digital health development. Currently Stanford School of Medicine offers a two-week elective course in digital health open to all medical students. The course description describes providing medical students with an opportunity to understand career trajectory for digital health from industry and academic leaders. In this two-week course, students learn how to design and develop a viable novel digital health related product or service idea in the context of a challenging dynamic market, legislative, and regulatory environment.

(Center for Digital Health, 2019)
Curriculum Length: 2 weeks
Requirement or Elective: Elective
Course Topics:

- Need criteria and filtering
- Leadership in Healthcare and Quality
- Office of technology licensing
- Radiology informatics
- Innovation
- Biomedical informatics
- Starting your own company
- Analytics
- Digital Health clinical trials
- Day in the life of a CMIO
- Market analysis
- Healthcare value and the changing economic landscape
- Case examples of current professions using digital health
- Clinical informatics regulatory influences and structure
- Inefficiencies in healthcare
- Bio-design
- Employer drive healthcare economy

  Strengths: The course provides access to in depth local expertise throughout the fields of digital health, startups, and medical technology. This elective provides a broad scope of exposure in digital health.

  Weaknesses: The Stanford School of Medicine Digital Health elective is limited to a 2-week training window. There currently is no longitudinal curriculum provided, and there is no specification of experiential learning opportunities. Currently, there is no core curriculum inclusion of digital health.

Case Study: Johns Hopkins School of Medicine Clinical Informatics Course

Overview: Johns Hopkins medical school offers a 4-day course (16 credit hours) of training in clinical informatics for its first-year medical students. This is a required course that according to the Johns

Hopkins website, "Introduces students to clinical informatics, an interdisciplinary field that explores effective uses of clinical data, information and knowledge in order to improve health. During the course, students hear both from Hopkins faculty who conduct research in the field of informatics as well as those with applied experiences in designing clinical decision support tools or deploying telemedicine. Students learn from a combination of online engaging lectures (that can be viewed remotely), in-person lectures, hands-on time in the Epic playground, demonstrations of MyChart from a patient perspective, a live telemedicine demo, and small group activities. In this course, students gain insight into the physician's evolving roles and responsibilities during this transformative time in healthcare." (Johns Hopkins Medicine, 2019)

Curriculum Length: 4 days (16 credit hours)
Required or Elective: Required
Course Objectives:

- Distinguish between the utility of different forms of clinical decision support embedded into electronic medical records.
- Critically evaluate the quality of electronic medical resources such as health-related websites and mobile health applications.
- Describe at least 3 clinical scenarios in which telemedicine can be used for healthcare delivery.
- Recognize the role of patient portals and personal health records in the doctor-patient-family relationship.
- Articulate the challenges to patient care posed by a lack of interoperability and the role of Health Information Exchanges (i.e. CRISP) in addressing these problems.

   Strengths: This course is required core curriculum training for all medical students during their first year. It provides all medical students with consistent exposure to at least some aspects of digital health like telemedicine, electronic health records, and clinical decision support.

   Weaknesses: The course has a very limited scope of digital health training. It does not provide a robust experiential learning program. The course also only occurs during the first year of training and does not span across all years of the medical school experience.

Assessment of Digital Health Competency

As the scope of digital health modalities continue to expand within undergraduate medical education, the importance of reliably measuring knowledge and assessing competence cannot be overlooked. Whether incorporating wearable devices into health monitoring or discussing telehealth and telemedicine, modalities of traditional assessment become less applicable and less conventionally measurable within this field. Digital health content and interfaces typically require the synthesis of effective integration for specific technology parameters to augment health care delivery. For example, in undergraduate medical education, most institutions teach a multi-disciplinary module on a medical topic such as hypertension. There are many models for this, one of which can be evidenced broadly from the University of Southern California Keck School of Medicine (Keck, 2019). Schools have different curricula that can blend a topic like pharmacology into a disease module like hypertension, or cover all pharmacology in a "block" style curriculum. The overarching theme of the pre-clinical education years is that of imparting and assessing basic science and system-based precepts necessary for clinical education to succeed and build upon.

Traditional competency assessments also include problem-based learning structures as well. In problem-based learning, students utilize case-study to integrate fields of knowledge they have previously experienced. Digital health competencies exist outside of these traditional realms, however, encompassing them. An example of this is the benefit of utilization of electronic medical record data to evaluate the health of a population (Kruse, Stein, Thomas, & Kaur, 2018). A more appropriate mental model for digital health to be considered in a curriculum is that of the longitudinal practice skill. To grind telehealth learning and assessment into this immediately post-Flexnerian model would be to miss an opportunity to bring new assessment to a new skill.

Digital health should be assessed similarly to clinical competencies, the delivery of patient care, and longitudinal population health and epidemiology. Consider a clinical skill such as suturing. While there are components of learning suturing that are suitable to a written test (e.g. identifying the suture techniques by image or what material is best for a specific purpose or anatomical area), the actual skill of suturing is developed in a workshop environment where competency is developed, not immediately passed or failed. Underperformance, in this mental model, is less valuable to assessment than ultimate competency after hours of practice and integration with other domains of learning.

Many institutions also teach population health management and epidemiologic evaluation in the traditionally didactic portions of undergraduate medical education. Two examples that are commonly referenced are an introduction to biostatistics course and a clinical epidemiology course within Harvard Medical School's core curriculum (Harvard Medical School, 2019). This further exemplifies, as with the suturing example, that while there are traditional and important written examinations that quantify medical knowledge comprehension throughout undergraduate medical education, methods for testing core material differ. An example includes contingency table comprehension in basic epidemiology, which is the means by which medical professionals mathematically evaluate prevalence, relative risk, and odds ratios. While critical to perform traditional test-based assessment for the underlying skills of utilizing that table, the actual use of those tables is in the handling of population data, which comes from digital health sources. This practical skill requires practice of combing through electronic medical record reports, gleaning pertinent statistics, performing the requisite statistical functions, and then wielding the resultant data to impact disease management. For these reasons, and in an effort to prepare trainees appropriately for their graduate medical education experience, we recommend an American College of Graduate Medical Education Milestones-type approach to assessment of digital health skills at the undergraduate medical education level. In order to fully assess a learner's ability to perform the executive function of applying their core knowledge through care delivery tools present in the field of digital health, they will progress stepwise through a series of predetermined competencies, which are present at other levels of medical education.

A Practical Milestones-Based Approach to Digital Health Assessment in Undergraduate Medical Education: Lessons Learned and Borrowed from the American College of Graduate Medical Education Milestones

The analysis below provides an in-depth examination of two sets of American College of Graduate Medical Education Milestone rubrics, those of preventive medicine residency programs and family medicine residency programs. Within these pre-existing structures, there are many competency segments which can accurately reflect benchmarks that can also apply to undergraduate medical education. While the American College of Graduate Medical Education evaluates graduate-level medical education, the earlier stages of these milestone evaluations are often expected upon arrival to residency programs. In addition, these tasks of digital health have previously fallen to the graduate medical education realm because undergraduate medical education had not adopted a curriculum for digital health. With this adoption, these skills garner practice and require assessment at the undergraduate medical education level. These milestone levels do not require the clinical sophistication of a medical resident, but rather longitudinal practical application that could be easily transferable from undergraduate medical education.

Current ACGME Preventive Medicine Milestones

This domain, as depicted in Figure 1, assesses preventive medicine resident's ability to monitor, diagnose, and investigate community health problems. Electronic medical record report interpretation is a useful digital health skill for inpatient and outpatient care alike. Insight into a community's health in this way not only has inherent value in this domain, but also allows for a narrative exploration of health equity tailored to a trainee's population. Digital health manifests throughout this competency by virtue of providing tools - in the medical record, report generation, wearable technology, telehealth, and other modalities - by which to perform the monitoring and investigatory functions of this competency.

This domain, as depicted in Figure 2, explores a preventive medical resident's ability to inform and educate populations regarding risk factors for their health. Currently, many telehealth and telemedicine platforms utilize text and e-mail information and reminders for risk-based preventive testing (Steffen et al., 2015). This also creates a communication method inclined toward notification of immediate important information, such as clinic or hospital-centric identification of highly contagious disease exposure (e.g. tuberculosis, measles) that a traditional mailer cannot provide, which is instructional for learners who

Figure 1. Patient care 2 (PC-2)
Source: (ACGME Preventive Medicine Milestone Project, 2015)

Figure 2. Patient care 3 (PC-3)
Source: (ACGME Preventive Medicine Milestone Project, 2015)

may choose a job in occupational health after completion of training. This ability to evaluate disease outbreak is also referenced more explicitly in the Patient Care 8 (PC-8) milestone.

This domain, as depicted in Figure 3, explores the ability to develop a policy or plan to support both individual and community health efforts. The data generated and housed in digital health platforms is imperative for local resource allocation, where more broad data (such as state or even county-based figures) may not provide the best insight. One potential application meeting milestones in this domain is the gleaning of population information in the development of hospital community health needs assessments (CHNAs) (Alberti, 2014). In a learner's capacity, shadowing a population health official or working in tandem with them on the needs assessment team longitudinally, a medical student can easily garner these skills for application both in medical school and, later, the graduate medical education realm.

This domain, as depicted in Figure 4, covers the ability to characterize the health of a community through descriptive epidemiology. This chapter references earlier the ability to develop facility with incidence, prevalence, and mortality via digital health tools. If only for these more basic skills, then, digital health can be incorporated into this competency.

Family Medicine Milestones

(ACGME Family Medicine Milestone Project, 2015)

Figure 3. Patient care 4 (PC-4)
Source: (ACGME Preventive Medicine Milestone Project, 2015)

Policies and Plans: Develop policies and plans to support individual and community health efforts — Patient Care 4				
Level 1	Level 2	Level 3	Level 4	Level 5
• Diagnoses disease and develops an individualized treatment plan	• Links individuals to needed personal health services including appropriate referrals and follow-ups	• Applies primary, secondary, and tertiary preventive approaches to disease prevention and health promotion for individuals or communities, with minimal supervision	• Applies primary, secondary, and tertiary preventive approaches to disease prevention and health promotion for the individuals and community	• Contributes to the development and/or implementation of a policy to improve community health efforts

Comments: Not yet rotated ☐

Figure 4. Patient care 6 (PC-6)
Source: (ACGME Preventive Medicine Milestone Project, 2015)

Descriptive Epidemiology: Able to characterize the health of a community — Patient Care 6				
Level 1	Level 2	Level 3	Level 4	Level 5
• Identifies and recognizes basic measures of disease frequency (incidence, prevalence, mortality) and risk (risk ratios, odds ratios)	• Knows methods for calculating basic measures of disease frequency and risk	• For a defined population, uses data to calculate measures of disease frequency and one or more risk factors for a specified disease or condition	• Uses data to characterize the health of a local population, compares it with that of other populations, identifies localities or groups with poorer health, and identifies and assesses the importance of different risk factors, for at least one disease or condition	• Uses data to fully characterize the health of a population, compares it with that of other populations, identifies localities or groups with poorer health, and identifies and assesses the importance of different risk factors, for a range of diseases and conditions

Comments: Not yet rotated ☐

The rubric for addressing cost-conscious, high-value medical care falls to this competency. Using telehealth and telemedicine services to extend the reach of outpatient care in addressing patient needs, in some cases without an office visit, can fall into all levels of this competency. There are many digital health domains which a medical student could gain experience with regard to cost in healthcare delivery, including but not limited to the comparison of telehealth services to face-to-face encounters, and the perusal of electronic medical record reports on care cost to inform them of the financial impact of physician orders.

This competency evaluates advocacy for individual and community health, which is incorporative of a community needs assessment. These assessments should be present in every health system, and easy to access for medical schools and their curriculum developers. The data developed through digital health platforms plays a critical role in the development and interpretation of the assessments.

This domain functions, for the purpose of this analysis, as a cognate to preventive medicine PC-6 domain. The value of digital health education also links well within family medicine to PBLI-3, identifying care gaps. Once again, as with other domains, this competency looks at epidemiology which can be taught with digital health tools, and in the evaluation of point-of-care resources (Level 2), learners may be exposed to digitally transmittable patient education tools (such as Mayo Clinic Online) as well as physician digital informational tools, such as UpToDate and MedCalc.

For digital health related competencies, C-4 is perhaps the most discrete and outright of associations. C-4 tracks a family medicine resident's ability to utilize technology to optimize communication. All levels of this competency are woven through the electronic medical record, as well as patient and

Figure 5. Systems based practice 1 (SBP-1)
Source: *(ACGME Family Medicine Milestone Project, 2015)*

SBP-1 Provides cost-conscious medical care					
Has not achieved Level 1	Level 1	Level 2	Level 3	Level 4	Level 5
	Understands that health care resources and costs impact patients and the health care system	Knows and considers costs and risks/benefits of different treatment options in common situations	Coordinates individual patient care in a way that is sensitive to resource use, efficiency, and effectiveness	Partners with patients to consistently use resources efficiently and cost effectively in even the most complex and challenging cases	Role models and promotes efficient and cost-effective use of resources in the care of patients in all settings
Comments:					

Figure 6. Systems based practice 3 (SBP-3)
Source: *(ACGME Family Medicine Milestone Project, 2015)*

SBP-3 Advocates for individual and community health					
Has not achieved Level 1	Level 1	Level 2	Level 3	Level 4	Level 5
	Recognizes social context and environment, and how a community's public policy decisions affect individual and community health	Recognizes that family physicians can impact community health. Lists ways in which community characteristics and resources affect the health of patients and communities	Identifies specific community characteristics that impact specific patients' health. Understands the process of conducting a community strengths and needs assessment	Collaborates with other practices, public health, and community-based organizations to educate the public, guide policies, and implement and evaluate community initiatives. Seeks to improve the health care systems in which he or she practices	Role-models active involvement in community education and policy change to improve the health of patients and communities
Comments:					

Figure 7. Practice-based learning and improvement 1 (PBLI-1)
Source: (ACGME Family Medicine Milestone Project, 2015)

PBLI -1 Locates, appraises, and assimilates evidence from scientific studies related to the patients' health problems					
Has not achieved Level 1	Level 1	Level 2	Level 3	Level 4	Level 5
	Describes basic concepts in clinical epidemiology, biostatistics, and clinical reasoning Categorizes the design of a research study	Identifies pros and cons of various study designs, associated types of bias, and patient-centered outcomes Formulates a searchable question from a clinical question Evaluates evidence-based point-of-care resources	Applies a set of critical appraisal criteria to different types of research, including synopses of original research findings, systematic reviews and meta-analyses, and clinical practice guidelines Critically evaluates information from others, including colleagues, experts, and pharmaceutical representatives, as well as patient-delivered information	Incorporates principles of evidence-based care and information mastery into clinical practice	Independently teaches and assesses evidence-based medicine and information mastery techniques
Comments:					

physician health informational tools, telehealth video, remote patient monitoring, and store-and-forward technologies (Chiron Health, 2019).

The authors are confident that an assimilation of even just these two American College of Graduate Medical Education Milestones frameworks into a new undergraduate medical education milestones rubric for digital health can provide a clear and stepwise progressive curriculum that remains broad and flexible enough to allow various institutions to work with the resources in their area.

Opportunities in Current Clerkship Training

As medical students complete their classroom-based didactic educational years and transition into their clinical years, the chance to partner with clinical experts expands. The training institution which engages in digital health education in the clinical years of medical school training may wish to seek the valuable partnership of a clinical informaticist, particularly one who is board certified. Currently only the American College of Preventive Medicine and American Board of Pathology provide board certification in clinical informatics. Furthermore, this pathway through the American College of Preventive Medicine is open to those who have practiced clinical informatics and who seek board certification later, or who undergo a two-year preventive medicine program with a focus in clinical informatics (American Board of Clinical Informatics, 2019). Residents trained in these programs can serve as board-certified subject matter

Figure 8. Communication 4 (C-4)
Source: (ACGME Family Medicine Milestone Project, 2015)

C-4 Utilizes technology to optimize communication					
Has not achieved Level 1	Level 1	Level 2	Level 3	Level 4	Level 5
	Recognizes effects of technology on information exchange and the physician/patient relationship Recognizes the ethical and legal implications of using technology to communicate in health care	Ensures that clinical and administrative documentation is timely, complete, and accurate Maintains key patient-specific databases, such as problem lists, medications, health maintenance, chronic disease registries Uses technology in a manner which enhances communication and does not interfere with the appropriate interaction with the patient	Ensures transitions of care are accurately documented, and optimizes communication across systems and continuums of care	Effectively and ethically uses all forms of communication, such as face-to-face, telephonic, electronic, and social media Uses technology to optimize continuity care of patients and transitions of care	Stays current with technology and adapts systems to improve communication with patients, other providers, and systems
Comments:					

experts, facilitating the on-site education of individuals who are less familiar with the finer workings of electronic medical records and telehealth. It is important to note that physicians who are board certified in clinical informatics are not typically found in every community. Therefore, a working relationship with the existing clinical technology department at an institution serves as an adjuvant to that specialist, and also more frequency, in lieu of them as well.

Prudent to the discussion surrounding the complexities of digital health, a common expression in this very subspecialized and diverse field is, "If you have seen one telehealth-electronic health record interface, you have seen one telehealth-electronic health record interface." As we approach 2020, dozens of telehealth platforms currently exist on the market, with more in the production pipeline. In combining those telehealth platforms with any number of electronic medical records, you have permutations in the hundreds to thousands. With these kinds of permutations in mind, it is imperative that medical educational institutions focus on preparing trainees for the basic functions of the most common telehealth platforms. It is also essential that medical students are prepared to be facile with the platform-electronic health record interface on-site and through the user interface. Finally, preparing medical students to have a basic understanding of preferentially selecting an electronic health record platform in the future will need to be captured through exposure and experience. These cross-comparisons will offer a more meaningful understanding of the characteristics of these varying platforms.

FUTURE RESEARCH DIRECTIONS

The advent of the *quantified self* movement, which currently exists on a worldwide scale has created a new age of doctor-patient interactions (Quantified Self, 2019). Patients now have the opportunity to bring vast amounts of medical grade data to an office visit for detailed conversations with their medical provider. This new advent in health technology requires providers to be able to explain, interpret, and converge monitored data with current medical evidence. One contemporary example of monitored data that currently exists is through the Apple Watch Series 4 which provides a two-lead electrocardiogram that has been FDA approved (Comstock, 2018). However, frequently physicians find themselves overwhelmed trying to address novel advents within medical technology and digital health parameters as well as the actual applicability to patient care and the standard of care. Despite these facts, widespread growth of health technology has created a new experience for both physicians and patients alike, learning to interact and communicate in new ways while providing clinical expertise that is up to date with clinical practice guidelines.

The field of digital health has become so pervasive that the FDA has created a digital health innovation action plan to address the revolution and rapid evolution of mobile applications, wearable monitoring systems, and other digital health-based interventions (Food and Drug Administration, 2018). This action plan details and tracks consumer-based health monitoring devices and applications. This is an effort by the FDA to create more modern policies to expedite safe digital health applications and oversight. The creation of this strategy is an indicator that medical schools should follow suit by addressing the need to educate medical students with a digital health related core curriculum of training expectations. A practical example of an immediate training need is conceptual understanding of 24-hour continuous or home-based blood pressure monitoring and the associated evidence-based guidelines. For example, blood pressure guidelines for office visits generally suggest that if a patient has two separate readings at or above 140/90 the patient should be started on a plan to modify current lifestyle practices, with the consideration for adding a blood pressure medication. With the advent of home monitoring, hypertension is no longer solely defined by two isolated measurements, but rather a mean measurement over time. Thus, repeated day time home blood pressure readings that average at or above 135/85 are now diagnostic for hypertension (Williams et al., 2018). There is reliable data to support that home-based monitoring is able to better predict end organ damage and cardiovascular risk than office-based blood pressure readings (Myers, 2010). This higher level of accuracy creates a demand for medical students to be trained in how to become more comfortable and effective at deploying 24-hour continuous monitoring programs. This training can easily exist both in classroom settings and in clinical settings. Educating on guidelines for remote monitoring and understanding when to activate remote monitoring for accuracy is key.

Many medical schools also have local partnerships with the Veterans Health Administration. These partnerships are a critical example of the opportunity for growth and ultimate adoption of digital health, to include exposure to telehealth, remote monitoring, smart-phone applications, and artificial intelligence research. The Veterans Health Administration, having a well-established home blood pressure monitoring program, provides in-the-field experience to medical students across the country. Capitalizing on partnerships with medical schools for first hand experiences in digital health would be a reasonable first step for medicals schools to immediately incorporate into their curriculum. There is a need for sufficient understanding of what very quickly becomes the new normal in patient care and traditional health care settings versus antiquated and typically outdated convention. This is a necessary tectonic shift for medicine and medical education alike in order to keep up with the change of technology-based care delivery models of the future.

Population health is a mainstay for value-based care models that have been evolving over the past decade in medicine (Porter & Tiesberg, 2005). The value-based care movement is attempting to improve the quality of care for a population at reduced costs. This is in stark contrast to the commonplace fee-for-service model which is predominately based on productivity of seeing more patients and performing more procedures. In order for value-based care to be successfully achieved, medical students need a strong foundational understanding of artificial intelligence, big data, natural language processing, business, and their applications in healthcare delivery on a population level.

Artificial Intelligence

An example that exemplifies the importance of artificial intelligence within the field of general medicine would be the machine learning applications within the field of radiology. The journal of the American College of Radiology expressed how artificial intelligence will improve not only the value and satisfaction of the field of radiology, but patient outcomes at the individual and population level as well (Recht & Bryan, 2017). Artificial intelligence has already proven to be exceptionally effective, accurate, and low cost at narrow scope efforts such as identifying cancerous lung nodules within chest x-rays (Hwang et al., 2018). Given these data, medical students will need to be trained in how to work with artificial intelligence algorithms to improve quality of care for the individual which has the potential to directly affect similar health outcomes for the population as well. Medical students need to learn when to identify opportunities where algorithms can be used to improve efficiency or quality of care within healthcare systems. This can be achieved by developing training experiences that offer artificial intelligence support for more accurate diagnoses once a differential has been established.

The area of artificial intelligence called natural language processing helps computers understand and interpret human language, and is currently being used to address the issue of rapidly reading, documenting, and structuring medical records. Natural language processing is being deployed to help with improved documentation within the healthcare system which is necessary for more accurate data (Bharadwaj, 2019). Accurate billing can be a long mundane process that is commonly fraught with errors in medicine. Artificial intelligence has been used to help improve accurate documentation which serves a critical role in how value-based healthcare functions. Without appropriately assessing risk, reimbursement of care for a population may be dramatically underestimated. Of importance to note, medical schools rarely train students in appropriate documentation of medical diagnoses. There is a great opportunity to utilize natural language processing to train medical students on how to appropriately document and use natural language processing as a feature to help mitigate patient safety risks that can occur during transitions of care. Transitions of care, when a patient changes care teams, are known areas where medical errors occur. Natural language processing can be used to rapidly summarize past medical records and to identify areas of necessary follow up in order to reduce missed opportunities and medical errors. Medical schools can partner with currently existing companies to deploy this technology within their institution to ensure a sufficient training environment for medical students.

Ethics in Artificial Intelligence

In addition to applications within healthcare, there are ethical dilemmas that also arise with the use of machine learning. Collectively, as a health profession we need to agree upon a structured ethical approach to identify when these technologies should be applied and when they might do harm by amplifying human biases. There has been a national effort through the AI Now Institute at New York University to look at the ethical implications of artificial intelligence in society and medicine (AI Now, 2019). An example of ethical implications being discussed is how data from the famous Framingham study can inaccurately predict risk of cardiovascular disease in non-white populations due to the limits and constraints of the study data (Char, Shar, & Magnus, 2018). Thus, when applying artificial intelligence to create better population and individual risk prediction, understanding the ethics and limitations of data and artificial intelligence technology are critical. These kinds of data-centric implications will be the next evolution of ethics in medicine that needs to be addressed with the medical students of today. As society works toward researching, innovating, and spreading these novel technologies, case studies should be designed in tandem with ethics classes to demonstrate the potential implications as well as potential pitfalls of these technologies.

As time progresses, artificial intelligence continues to establish its utility in medicine. More recently artificial intelligence has been used to assist with better risk predictions for 30 day hospital readmission for heart failure patients as well as length of stay predictions (Golas et al,. 2018, and Turgeman, May, & Sciulli, 2017). In these risk prediction models, artificial intelligence takes live data from the electronic health records and compares this data with correlative data points related to 30-day readmissions that occurred in the past. Specifically, selected data points, such as frequent changes in home address, are identified and weighted as stratified risk factors. These particular stratifications are then combined with other risk-based data points to produce a cumulative real time risk calculation. Both of these risk predictions can help improve medical team-based coordination of care and reduce costs of care for patients with the greatest need. Medical students need opportunities to practice how to best utilize these prediction models to coordinate and create the most effective team-based care in the future. Medical students also need training in how to serve as subject matter experts to enhance the data visualization of these solutions in order to optimize their utility in real world scenarios. The training necessary to accomplish this should be implemented through formal medical education that includes design thinking, human factor engineering, and end user experience. These elements are critical to ensure that novel technologies do not create waste in new ways, or create a new generation of distracted physicians (Kreimer, 2017). Currently, there exists a need for physicians to learn how to better collaborate with patients in co-creating these kinds of technology solutions and experiences.

Co-production of Digital Health Platforms

There will always be a difference between how healthcare professionals and medical teams experience a particular technology compared to how patients and their families experience the same technology (Batalden et al., 2016). These kinds of collaborative experiences could be achieved by ensuring that medical schools have a center for innovation or a health technology incubator as a part of their institution. Medical schools could require the establishment of partnerships with local healthcare startups to better train medical students on consulting techniques that consider ethical implications and co-production. Many such centers already exist in various collegiate university settings, though most are not directly partnered with medical schools over longitudinal educational endeavors. Currently, many institutions host "hackathons" which are intended to bring multi-disciplinary groups of computer scientists, patients, healthcare workers, and public health professionals to the table in short spurts to target a specific problem (Bhandari & Hayward, 2014 and Swiss Digital Health, 2019). Although these are great demonstrations of intellectual potential, a more longitudinal learning experience that applies these principles could easily be generated in a medical school setting. This would provide experiential learning while at the same time, work to solve serious healthcare quandaries.

Physician as Entrepreneur

Healthcare costs in the United States are crippling to the economy. The United States currently spends 3.5 trillion dollars annually in healthcare expenditures which constitutes 17.9% of our gross domestic product. Seventy five percent of this spending is on chronic, largely preventable disease (CMS, 2018). In order to better deploy value-based healthcare, medical students need to have foundational educational training in the business of medicine. Strategic and financial management of health systems enables physicians to help better guide the delivery of health care to a more sustainable path. Accounting methodologies such as time driven activity-based costing, which deploys an accounting system that attempts to use time-based cost and actual cost of goods to better identify true cost for care are essential for students to better quantify the delivery of care through a value-based lens. (Kaplan & Anderson, 2004). The expansion for telehealth and telemedicine services is growing rapidly, and in a highly variable manner. While being very entrepreneurial can be helpful for content generation and iterative technologic improvement, it poses many challenges for education surrounding telehealth and telemedicine. Currently, content experts for telehealth and telemedicine are not commonly found in bigger health systems given a general reluctance for larger networks to adopt telehealth modalities which are not reimbursed well (such as store-and-forward and remote patient monitoring). As of April 2019, Medicare has signaled a significant shift toward value-based care. Inherently, it is necessary to understand how telehealth and telemedicine can optimally fit into that framework. If early adopters of telehealth and telemedicine, through well-designed studies, are able to demonstrate improved efficiency, and better value of care delivered, telehealth and telemedicine will continue in the world of value-based compensation. As a result, education in how to manage a patient panel electronically will become critical to not only patient care, but the business or hospital management side of healthcare as well.

The advent of the physician as an entrepreneur is also an alluring business opportunity for medical students to pursue. Most medical schools also have partnerships with business schools, and could offer the opportunity to help medical students develop basic skills in accounting and strategic and financial management as an integrated professional learning experience. This would also be easily achievable and implementable at medical institutions that currently lack an educational business school partnership. A medical student should not be required to earn a Master's degree in business administration to function as a knowledgeable physician in today's healthcare environment. Medical students need to be trained in return on investment and the various funding opportunities that exist for initiatives within healthcare. Training in how to create a business or digital health company to help address the complex needs of healthcare today should be an educational training milestone of medical schools of the future. Though there is ample evidence that economic status impacts patients' outcomes, having transparency and awareness of cost of care or treatment for care is essential. In the United States, the state of Colorado has moved forward with the "Transparency in Healthcare Prices Act" which attempts to provide the public with transparent data showcasing the cost of services that hospitals and health care agencies in the state provide (Col. 2017). Caring for individual people and patient populations does not occur in a cost vacuum yet most medical education today does not include sufficient training in the cost component of healthcare.

CONCLUSION

Without question, the digital health revolution is changing not only the face of modern medicine, but also the pace of modern medicine. As medical education continues to adapt to this change there will be challenges and opportunities. The authors have outlined examples of modern, evidence based, digital health applications as well as demonstrated current curricular programs and the opportunities and struggles associated with the assessment of such programs. It is time to develop digital health as an integrated part of all divisions of undergraduate medical education throughout the entirety of the training experience. This is now a fundamental aspect of care and care delivery demonstrated by current research, the FDA, and health insurance investment. (LaRock, 2019, and Food and Drug Administration, 2018). The blueprint of how undergraduate medical education can attempt to successfully approach implementation of digital health training is now at your fingertips.

REFERENCES

ACGME Family Medicine Milestone Project. (2015). Retrieved June. 2, 2019 from https://www.acgme.org/Portals/0/PDFs/Milestones/FamilyMedicineMilestones.pdf

ACGME Preventive Medicine Milestone Project. (2015). Public Health and General Preventive Medicine, Retrieved June 2, 2019 from https://www.acgme.org/Portals/0/PDFs/Milestones/PreventiveMedicineMilestones-PublicHealthandGeneralPreventiveMedicine.pdf

AI Now Institute. (2019). Retrieved on June 1, 2019 from https://ainowinstitute.org/

Alberti, P. (2014). Community health needs assessments: Filling data gaps for population health research and management. *The Journal for Electronic Health Data and Methods*, 2(4), 1174. PMID:25848631

American Board of Clinical Informatics. (2019). Clinical informatics, Retrieved June 2, 2019 from https://www.theabpm.org/become-certified/subspecialties/clinical-informatic

Association of American Medical Colleges. (2018). Curriculum Reports, Retrieved June 2, 2019 from https://www.aamc.org/initiatives/cir/curriculumreports/

Bahner, D. P., Goldman, E., Way, D., Royall, N. A., & Liu, Y. T. (2014). The stae of ultrasound education in U.S. medical schools: Results of a national survey. *Academic Medicine*, 89(12), 1681–1686. doi:10.1097/ACM.0000000000000414 PMID:25099238

Baker, M. (2017). How vr is revolutionizing the way future doctors are learning about our bodies. Retrieved June 1, 2019 from https://www.ucsf.edu/news/2017/09/408301/how-vr-revolutionizing-way-future-doctors-are-learning-about-our-bodies

Batalden, M., Batalden, P., Margolis, P., Seid, M., Armstrong, G., Opipari-Arrigan, L., & Hartung, H. (2016). Coproduction of health care service. *BMJ Quality & Safety*, 25(7), 509–517. doi:10.1136/bmjqs-2015-004315 PMID:26376674

Bhandari, A., & Hayward, M. (2014). The rise of the healthcare hackathon: 6 insights from over 100 hackathons from around the world. Retrieved June 2, 2019 from http://hackingmedicine.mit.edu/health-hackathon-database/

Bharadwaj, R. (2019). Artificial intelligence for medical billing and coding. Emerj Artificial Intelligence Research, Retrieved June 2, 2019 from https://emerj.com/ai-sector-overviews/artificial-intelligence-medical-billing-coding/

Breining, G. (2018). Future or fad? Virtual reality in medical education. AAMC News, Retrieved June 1, 2019 from https://news.aamc.org/medical-education/article/future-or-fad-virtual-reality-medical-education/

Center for Digital Health. (2019). 2018 Pathway of distinction: Innovation, biodesign, and informatics elective course. Stanford Education, Retrieved June 2, 2019 from http://med.stanford.edu/cdh/Education.html

Center for Digital Health at Stanford. (2019) Shaping the future of digital health, together. Retrieved June 1, 2019, from http://med.stanford.edu/cdh.html

Center for Medicare and Medicaid Services. (2018). National Health Expenditures 2017, Retrieved June 2, 2019 from https://www.cms.gov/Research-Statistics-Data-and-Systems/Statistics-Trends-and-Reports/NationalHealthExpendData/Downloads/highlights.pdf

Char, D. S., Shah, N. H., & Magnus, D. (2018). Implementing Machine Learning in Health Care - Addressing Ethical Challenges. *The New England Journal of Medicine*, 378(11), 981–983. doi:10.1056/NEJMp1714229 PMID:29539284

Chiron Health. (2019). Definitive guide to telemedicine. Retrieved June 2, 2019 from https://chironhealth.com/definitive-guide-to-telemedicine/about-telemedicine/types-of-telemedicine/

Colorado General Assembly. (2017). SB17-065: Transparency in direct pay health care prices. Retrieved June 2, 2019 from https://leg.colorado.gov/bills/sb17-065

Comstock, J. (2018). Apple unveils watch series 4 with fda-approved ecg. Retrieved June 1, 2019 from https://www.healthcareitnews.com/news/apple-unveils-watch-series-4-fda-approved-ecg

Cook, D., Erwin, P. J., & Triola, M. M. (2010). Computerized virtual patients in health professions education: A systematic review and meta-analysis. *Academic Medicine*, *85*(10), 1589–1602. doi:10.1097/ACM.0b013e3181edfe13 PMID:20703150

Cooke, M., Irby, D. M., & O'Brien, B. C. (2010). Educating Physicians: A Call for Reform of Medical School and Residency. San Francisco, CA: Jossey-Bass.

Food and Drug Administration. (2018) Digital health action plan. Retrieved June 1, 2019 from https://www.fda.gov/media/106331/download

Golas, S. B., Shibahara, T., Agboola, S., Otaki, H., Sato, J., Nakae, T., & Jethwani, K. (2018). A machine learning model to predict the risk of 30-day readmissions in patients with heart failure: A retrospective analysis of electronic medical records data. *BMC Medical Informatics and Decision Making*, *18*(1), 44. doi:10.118612911-018-0620-z PMID:29929496

Harvard Medical School. (2019). Course catalog 2019-2020. Retrieved June 2, 2019 from http://www.medcatalog.harvard.edu/courselist.aspx?dep=200

Henry, T. A. (2018). How ai is driving new medical frontier for physician training. Retrieved June 1, 2019 from https://www.ama-assn.org/education/accelerating-change-medical-education/how-ai-driving-new-medical-frontier-physician

Hoppmann, R. A., Rao, V. V., Bell, F., Poston, M. B., Howe, D. B., Riffle, S., ... Catalana, P. V. (2015). The evolution of an integrated ultrasound curriculum (iUSC) for medical students: 9-year experience. *Critical Ultrasound Journal*, *7*(1), 18. doi:10.118613089-015-0035-3 PMID:26589313

Hwang, E. J., Park, S., Jin, K. N., Kim, J. I., Choi, S. Y., & Lee, J. H. (2018). Development and validation of a deep learning-based automatic detection algorithm for active pulmonary tuberculosis on chest radiographs. *Clinical Infectious Diseases*, ciy967. PMID:30418527

Johns Hopkins Medicine. (2019). Genes to society: a curriculum for the Johns Hopkins University School of Medicine. Retrieved June 1, 2019 from https://www.hopkinsmedicine.org/som/curriculum/genes_to_society/curriculum/year_one/time_clinical_informatics.html

Kaplan, R. S., & Anderson, R. (2004). Time-driven activity-based costing. *Harvard Business Review*, *82*(11), 131–138. PMID:15559451

Keck School or Medicine of USC. (2019). Medical student curriculum – years I and II. Retrieved June 2, 2019 from https://keck.usc.edu/pathology/training-education/medical-student-curriculum/

Kobal, S. L., Trento, L., Baharami, S., Tolstrup, K., Naqvi, T. Z., Cercek, B., ... Siegel, R. J. (2005). Comparison of effectiveness of hand-carried ultrasound to bedside cardiovascular physical examination. *The American Journal of Cardiology*, *96*(7), 1002–1006. doi:10.1016/j.amjcard.2005.05.060 PMID:16188532

Kreimer, S. (2017). Distracted doctor? Don't let computer come before patient during exam. American Association for Physician Leadership. Retrieved June 2, 2019 from https://www.physicianleaders.org/news/distracted-doctoring-dont-let-computer-come-before-patient-during-exam

Kruse, C. S., Stein, A., Thomas, H., & Kaur, H. (2018). The use of electronic health records to support population health: A systematic review of the literature. *Journal of Medical Systems*, *42*(11), 214. doi:10.100710916-018-1075-6 PMID:30269237

Mouratev, G., Howe, D., Hoppmann, R., Poston, M. B., Reid, R., Varnadoe, J., ... DeMarco, P. (2013). Teaching medical students ultrasound to measure liver size: Comparison with experienced clinicians using physical exam alone. *Teaching and Learning in Medicine*, *25*(1), 84–88. doi:10.1080/10401334.2012.741535 PMID:23330900

Myers, M. G. (2010). A proposed algorithm for diagnosing hypertension using automated office blood pressure measurement. *Journal of Hypertension*, *28*(4), 703–708. doi:10.1097/HJH.0b013e328335d091 PMID:20150823

Patel, S., & Burke-Gaffney, A. (2018). The value of mobile tablet computers (iPads) in the undergraduate medical curriculum. *Advances in Medical Education and Practice*, *9*, 567–570. doi:10.2147/AMEP.S163623 PMID:30127652

Patel, V., & Johnson, C. (2018, April). *Individuals' use of online medical records and technology for health needs*. ONC Data Brief, no. 40. Office of the National Coordinator for Health Information Technology: Retrieved May 22nd, 2019, from https://www.healthit.gov/sites/default/files/page/2018-03/HINTS-2017-Consumer-Data-Brief-3.21.18.pdf

Porter, M. E., & Tiesberg, E. (2005). *Redefining Healthcare*. Boston, MA: Harvard Business School.

Quantified Self. (2019) What is Quantified Self? Retrieved June 1, 2019 from https://quantifiedself.com/about/what-is-quantified-self/

Recht, M., & Bryan, R. N. (2017). Artificial intelligence: Threat or boon to radiologists. *Journal of the American College of Radiology*, *14*(11), 1475–1480. doi:10.1016/j.jacr.2017.07.007 PMID:28826960

Rocky Vista University College of Osteopathic Medicine. (2019). RVU Announces Pioneering Digital Health Track. Retrieved December 11, 2019 from http://www.rvu.edu/news/rvu-announces-pioneering-digital-health-track/

Siwicki, B. (2016). AMA invests $15 million to launch Silicon Valley Innovation Hub Health2047. Retrieved June 1, 2019 from https://www.healthcareitnews.com/news/ama-invests-15-million-launch-silicon-valley-innovation-hub-health2047

Statistics Market Research Consulting. *Report on e-learning - global market outlook (2017-2026)*. (2018). Retrieved May 22nd, 2019 from https://www.researchandmarkets.com/research/mjp4w2/global_elearning?w=4/

Steffen, L. E., Boucher, K. M., Damron, B. H., Pappas, L. M., Walters, S. T., Flores, K. G., ... Kinney, A. Y. (2015). Efficacy of a telehealth intervention on colonoscopy uptake when cost is a barrier: The family care cluster randomized controlled trial. *Cancer Epidemiology, Biomarkers & Prevention, 24*(9), 1311–1318. doi:10.1158/1055-9965.EPI-15-0150 PMID:26101306

Stone-McLean, J., Metcalfe, B., Sheppard, G., Murphy, J., Black, H., & McCarthy, H. (2017). Developing an undergraduate ultrasound curriculum: A needs assessment. *Cureus, 9*(9), e1720. PMID:29188164

Swiss Digital Health. (2019). Hackathons. Retrieved June 2, 2019 from https://swissdigitalhealth.com/ideate/hackathons/

Turgeman, L., May, J. H., & Sciulli, R. (2017). Insights from a machine learning model for predicting the hospital length of stay (LOS) at the time of admission. *Expert Systems with Applications, 78*, 376–385. doi:10.1016/j.eswa.2017.02.023

U.S. Department of Veterans Affairs. (2019). *Budget in brief 2020.* Retrieved May 22nd, 2019 from https://www.va.gov/budget/docs/summary/fy2020VAbudgetInBrief.pdf

Williams, B., Mancia, G., Spiering, W., Rosei, E. A., Azizi, M., & Burnier, M. (2018). 2018 ESC/ESH Guidelines for the management of arterial hypertension. *European Heart Journal, 39*(33), 3021–3104. doi:10.1093/eurheartj/ehy339 PMID:30165516

Wittenberg, M. (2014). Will ultrasound scanners replace the stethoscope? *British Medical Journal, 348*(May), g3463. doi:10.1136/bmj.g3463 PMID:24875141

ADDITIONAL READING

Christensen, C. M., Grossman, J. H., & Hwang, J. (2009). *The innovators prescription: A disruptive solution for health care.* New York: McGraw-Hill.

Meskó, B. (2017). *The guide to the future of medicine: Technology and the human touch.* USA: Webicina Kft.

Porter, M. E., & Teisberg, E. O. (2006). *Redefining health care: Creating value-based competition on results.* Boston, MA: Harvard Business School Press.

Siegel, E. (2016). *Predictive analytics: The power to predict who will click, buy, lie, or die.* Hoboken, NJ: Wiley.

Topol, E. J. (2013). *The creative destruction of medicine: How the digital revolution will create better health care.* New York: Basic Books.

Topol, E. J. (2016). *The patient will see you now: The future of medicine is in your hands.* New York: Basic Books.

Topol, E. J. (2019). *Deep medicine: How artificial intelligence can make healthcare human again.* New York: Basic Books.

Wachter, R. M. (2015). *The digital doctor: Hope, hype, and harm at the dawn of medicines computer age*. New York: McGraw-Hill Education.

KEY TERMS AND DEFINITIONS

Digital Health: The application of any digital technology to the practice or delivery of healthcare.

Digital Health Startup: Typically, a newly founded company that aims to provide some sort of technological product or resource to the medical market, typically targeting medical practitioners, patients, insurance providers, or corporate roundtables.

Digital Health Track: An elective educational opportunity at an undergraduate medical institution that provides the opportunity for medical students to augment their traditional medical education curriculum with digital health content.

Patient Portal: A patient-facing technological interface that allows patients to access various kinds of personal medical information such as laboratory results, imaging interpretation, diagnoses, and follow up care.

Telehealth: Larger in scope than telemedicine, it is the general collection health care services that are remotely practiced, not limited to clinical medical practices.

Telemedicine: Smaller in scope than telehealth, telemedicine more commonly refers to clinical medical practices that are engaged in and executed remotely.

Virtual Patient: Traditionally a computer-based simulated patient model that provides on-demand educational experience and exposure to various types of clinical presentations and different potential medical diagnoses.

Chapter 22
Expect What You Inspect:
A Worked Example of Dashboards That Support Continuous Quality Improvement in Medical Education

Daniel Alexander Novak

Keck School of Medicine, University of Southern California, USA

Ronan Hallowell

Keck School of Medicine, University of Southern California, USA

Donna Elliott

Keck School of Medicine, University of Southern California, USA

ABSTRACT

The Liaison Committee on Medical Education (LCME) requires that medical schools track compliance and continuous quality improvement (CQI) efforts across a broad range of LCME standards. However, LCME does not state what form these tracking efforts should take, or how medical schools should represent this information to the Committee or internally. This chapter provides an overview of the Keck School of Medicine of the University of Southern California's (KSOM) new approach to CQI tracking using an online dashboard. The project resulted in an online platform that represents the CQI project progress across a range of elements, maintains visual consistency across a range of data sources and file types, and is easily accessible by relevant stakeholders. This innovation from KSOM illustrates how a web-based platform supports CQI efforts, and how this design can be translated to other contexts. The design presented in this chapter provides guidelines for the development and innovation of CQI tracking initiatives at other schools.

DOI: 10.4018/978-1-7998-1468-9.ch022

INTRODUCTION

The Liaison Committee on Medical Education (LCME) requires that medical schools in the United States and Canada track compliance and continuous quality improvement (CQI) efforts across a broad range of LCME standards, as specified in Element 1.1 of the standards (LCME, 2017). However, the LCME does not specifically state what form these tracking efforts should take, or how medical schools should represent this information to the Committee or internally. The Keck School of Medicine of the University of Southern California (KSOM) has designed a new CQI tracking tool to address LCME's directive. Built in a commonly available online platform, the KSOM tracking platform serves as a starting template for use and adaptation by other schools and institutions who strive to monitor their ongoing efforts. This worked example provides an overview of the system developed at KSOM, the rationale and theoretical framework for the design, and lessons learned from the development of the system in KSOM's local context. This chapter presents the results of the development of the CQI tracking platform that began in October of 2017 and concluded in November of 2017, when administrators presented the dashboard during the LCME accreditation visit. Participants in the design and development processes included the Vice Dean for Medical Education, the Director of Educational Technology, two learning scientists, the CQI accreditation administrator, and the support of a medical illustrator. Total development time amounted to approximately 50 hours for all parties over the course of that month.

The platform described in this case was developed to serve as a central location for the multiple activities and parties that surround compliance and CQI tracking. KSOM's Vice Dean for Medical Education initiated the request for better CQI tracking tools during the school's Fall 2017 LCME accreditation cycle. As the Vice Dean noted in interviews following the accreditation process:

Our formal tracking of CQI initiatives began with the LCME process. Prior to that, there was not a central mechanism to track [improvement initiatives] from the various areas across the medical school. We maintained this data, but it was in the form of program evaluation data, and it was located in various offices. The information was brought together from those various sources and reviewed it at the appropriate meetings and gatherings, so it was not centralized. And as we learned going through the LCME process, we needed to capture all the relevant information and bring it together in one location. (2018)

For this reason, many schools of medicine have turned to the use of 'data dashboards' or data display systems to represent their CQI efforts in easy-to-consume formats. While information and analytics representation systems have existed for decades in business and information technology, recent advances in computer and network technologies have made it easier than ever to implement these systems in the context of academic medicine.

In developing this CQI tracking platform, the authors observed that few resources exist to guide the design of compliance and CQI tracking systems for LCME standards and elements. Searches in peer-reviewed literature found few contemporary studies that provide administrators with details about how to create tracking systems that conform to LCME's compliance and CQI tracking expectations. This constitutes a problem with severe consequences, as-without consistent guidelines to produce tools to serve that purpose, medical schools may fail to develop these systems and fail to fulfill the expectations of the LCME standards and suffer consequences such as probation (e.g., Miller, Dzowonek, McGuffin & Shapiro, 2014). Further, a disparity may emerge between large and well-resourced institutions that can invest resources in developing CQI tracking tools and smaller schools of medicine that cannot invest human resource time in the prolonged development of such a system. Finally, these systems can also support the tracking of CQI initiatives beyond the requirements of LCME, thus improving outcomes for endeavors beyond accreditation. KSOM would like to share its response to the challenge of creating CQI tracking systems to help other institutions avoid the pitfalls associated with this issue, along with a theory-driven approach to dashboard development. The components presented in this chapter may help to speed other schools' advances in CQI tracking and promote an ongoing dialog about how best to achieve the creation of a standardized yet flexible approach to developing these platforms.

This chapter presents a worked example of a process that medical schools can use to construct functional CQI dashboards in their own contexts. As described by James Gee (2010), worked examples provide readers with a deeper understanding of the learning potential of digital media through the analysis of media artifacts from both theoretical and technological lenses. As such, this chapter includes both the theoretical underpinnings and a practical process for developing a high-quality dashboard. The worked example is organized into two sections: 1) *Background on LCME Accreditation, CQI Tracking, and Data Dashboards*, and 2) *an Activity Theory Approach to the Development of CQI Data Dashboards*. In the first section, the chapter provides a review of research and theoretical frameworks from two key areas that inform the development of CQI initiatives and the dashboard technology to track them according to accreditation bodies' directives. In the second section, the authors draw on Cultural-Historical Activity Theory (Vygotsky, 1978; Leontiev, 1978; Luria, 1976; Engeström, 2000, 2001) to describe five steps that dashboard developers at other institutions can follow to develop a CQI data dashboard and support the development of new technological innovations. With both theoretical and practical frameworks at their disposal, the authors hope that readers will be able to adapt the design presented here to the needs of their local context in ways that draw from the best of current knowledge in CQI dashboard development.

BACKGROUND ON LCME ACCREDITATION, CQI TRACKING, AND DATA DASHBOARDS

While the emergence of new data display technologies has made the creation of online dashboards easier than ever, the creation of dashboards that effectively scaffold the work of CQI administrators and accreditation specialists requires some background in two key areas of research. To help provide context for KSOM's approach to the development of a CQI dashboard, this worked example briefly reviews the current research on LCME accreditation standards and CQI tracking practices. Second, it will examine current thinking on the role of data dashboards as powerful information technologies and as a CQI tool in medical education. These areas of research provide a sound knowledge base for administrators and developers who wish to adopt, localize, or innovate the design presented later in the chapter.

LCME Accreditation and CQI Tracking

Researchers in medical education have described the role of continuous quality improvement initiatives since the mid-1990s (Buchanan, 1995). Despite this long-term interest in CQI in medical education, the LCME only adopted standards that require medical schools to track their CQI efforts in 2015 (Barzansky et al., 2015). As of 2019, the LCME accreditation Standard 1, Element 1, contains key mandates related to the implementation of CQI processes in each medical school:

A medical school engages in ongoing strategic planning and continuous quality improvement processes that establish its short and long-term programmatic goals, result in the achievement of measurable outcomes that are used to improve educational program quality, and ensure effective monitoring of the medical education program's compliance with accreditation standards.

(LCME, 2017, p.1)

To explain the emergence of this new standard in 2015, Stratton (2019) notes that the growth of the importance of CQI efforts in medical schools has closely paralleled medical education's goals of rendering the activities of medical school 'rationalized,' or measurable, operational, and transparent to the various stakeholders who are invested in school performance.

While the LCME's CQI standard covers a broad range of accreditation expectations related to CQI processes, it does not provide guidance as to how medical schools should enact the standard in their local context. For this reason, schools have been left to their own devices to develop these processes and negotiate the implementation on their own. This lack of specificity has created opportunities for schools to develop innovative processes for CQI tracking but has also left schools to manage challenges with little guidance. Further, without consistent guidelines that produce tools to facilitate CQI tracking, it is possible that smaller medical schools with fewer financial and human resources may fail to develop these systems and maybe unable to fulfill all of the expectations of the LCME standards. For example, Barzansky et al. (2015), identified the labor-intensive nature of managing the data produced for periodic reviews among the challenges faced by schools that implement CQI processes, as well as the difficulty of developing solutions to these data management challenges.

Since the adoption of Standard 1.1, scholars such as Blouin, Tekian, Kamin, & Harris (2018) have begun new research on the role of accreditation standards and CQI initiatives in creating institutional change through the allocation of resources, engagement of multiple stakeholders in institutional self-assessment, and changes in the business processes of the school. Blouin & Tekian (2018) also note that accreditation processes may play a reciprocal role in causing these changes, as accreditation pressures reinforce the importance of CQI initiatives between cycles of LCME evaluation. In their review of 10 U.S. medical schools' approaches to CQI processes, Hedrick et al. (2019) provided further evidence for the role of the LCME CQI standard in facilitating a range of changes in schools' business processes. This included the creation of officers and committees to manage CQI projects, the promotion of accountability for initiatives, and shifts in culture that reframed accreditation as a process that must be maintained through constant improvement and accountability.

CQI Tracking and Data Dashboards

To ensure compliance with Standard 1.1, schools across North America have begun to investigate the development of new kinds of data dashboard technologies to support their CQI tracking processes. In the context of this chapter, the term 'data dashboard' describes digital technologies that facilitate the visual representation and summary of quantitative and qualitative data in centralized systems. More specifically, Few (2006, p.12) notes that visualization technologies qualify as data dashboards when they provide "a visual display of the most important information needed to achieve one or more objectives consolidated on a single screen so it can be monitored and understood at a glance." Similar technologies have existed for many years in business contexts and have emerged in response to personnel and time pressures faced by organizations in the private sector (Gemignani, Gemignani, Galentino, & Schuermann 2014; Rossett & Schaffer, 2012).

Power (2008) extends the definition of data dashboards by describing the function of a broad category of 'data-driven decision support systems' that exist in multiple business domains. This class of technologies support basic functions that include: 1) Ad-hoc data filtering and retrieval, 2) software-initiated alerts and triggers, 3) the capacity to create predefined data displays, 4) back-end software to support data aggregation and summarization for the visualization, and 5) the ability to interact with data warehousing and statistical analysis software. Evergreen & Metzner (2013) also identify several specific visual properties that make these systems effective, including the use of color, line weight, motion, and text and arrows. Evergreen & Metzner indicate that these graphic properties of information display play an important role in users' ability to make sense of data, particularly when these data are used to inform evaluation or call attention to important information represented by the data.

While Power's features of decision-support systems describe the technological aspects of the software and Evergreen & Metzner describe the relevant graphic properties, Smith (2013) identifies three main kinds of dashboards as defined by their purpose. These include data visualization tools that support humans in strategic, analytic, and operational domains. These dashboard types differ in how they combine system functions, graphics, and crucially, their role in the decision-support process. In this view, the purpose of the dashboard influences its form in ways that are unaccounted for in the technical and graphic properties examined in the research. Ongoing research on data dashboards in fields such as learning analytics (Verbert, Duval, Klerkx, Govaerts, & Santos, 2013) indicate that these dashboards can be designed in ways that support the effective use of data by educational leaders without imposing additional time burdens (Tyler, 2013; Wayman & Cho, 2008).

Due to the relative novelty of these dashboards in educational fields, current studies include only general guidelines for the designs of data visualization systems. For example, some researchers have suggested that practitioners may benefit from bringing together multiple forms of data from schools into units that facilitate analysis (Hernandez-Garcia & Conde, 2014; Knigge & Cope, 2006; Wayman, Stringfield, & Yakimowski, 2004). However, the design of dashboards that are useful in a particular setting may depend on various factors such as the kinds of data available in the system, the kinds of graphical representations available, and the kinds of analysis supported by the data system software (Verhaeghe, Schildkamp, Luyten, & Valcke, 2015). For this reason, medical education requires the application of a theory-grounded, generalizable approach to the development of medical education dashboards that specifically target the needs of CQI officers and data personnel in medical schools.

While the communications features of data dashboards have become clearer over time, the broad availability of data created by the automated collection of information via computer systems has simultaneously created an 'attention economy,' further complicating strategies for the tracking of CQI initiatives. Attention economies place pressure on humans to devote more of their cognitive resources to data analysis as human-machine systems routinely produce more data than they are able to consume and use (Simon, 1971). That is, even when medical schools develop the capacity to generate and access the right kinds of data, they are often unable to manage or make sense of this information because of a lack of available time for analysis.

Echoing the challenges faced by the abundance of data, Hedrick et al. (2019) found in their review of ten medical schools in the United States that the schools used a range of qualitative and quantitative data to provide the LCME with evidence of their CQI work. In describing the technological strategies used by these institutions, Hedrick et al. note that some institutions felt constrained by the limited spreadsheet technologies that were available to track their CQI projects. While the use of spreadsheets to manage and analyze CQI efforts may seem to be a trivial issue, broader research on data dashboards in educational environments indicates that the choice of display technology can have a substantive impact on how these data are used to inform decisions about improvements to student outcomes and performance (Wayman, Stringfield, & Yakimowski, 2004). For this reason, Hedrick et al. note that while eight of their ten schools used standard spreadsheet software to manage their CQI data, "others noted that standard spreadsheet software was not specific to the CQI process, is not customizable, is not searchable, requires many sheets, and needs better dashboarding" (2019, p. 289). For this reason, many schools have turned to the use of data dashboards as a means of tracking and supporting their CQI projects.

Within medical education, Shroyer, Lu, & Chandran (2016) have provided the beginnings of a data dashboard development process that specifically focuses on the LCME CQI standards. In their "drivers of dashboard development (3D)" process, administrators at the Stony Brook University Renaissance School of Medicine developed a methodology for developing CQI dashboards by identifying and tracking Key Performance Indicators (KPIs) that relate to LCME standards, creating dashboard-based reports based on these indicators and metrics, and creating successive rounds of feedback to improve the utility of these visualizations. While this approach to dashboard development provides a solid starting point for the development of dashboards for medical education, it does not provide further guidance on the development of dashboards that specifically track CQI efforts across multiple kinds of data and support users' decision-making processes.

Emerging Technologies and Strategies

While few institutions have published peer-reviewed articles about how they have approached the development of CQI tracking technologies, this issue has not gone unaddressed in the broader medical education community. While some large institutions use their existing accreditation management software to track their CQI initiatives, many report developing their own custom dashboards and tools using off-the-shelf technologies. For example, at the American Association of Medical College's Western Group on Educational Affairs (AAMC-WGEA) meeting in 2019, several large institutions such as Stanford University, the University of California at Irvine, and the University of Washington presented their approaches to tracking student performance and LCME standard performance using data dashboards that they have designed in-house. These approaches commonly featured a number of key innovations and limitations that provide some insight into how medical schools generally are working to adapt technologies to meet their CQI needs.

On the innovations front, several institutions have begun to move beyond Excel spreadsheets to integrate real-time data analysis tools such as Tableau into their data dashboard strategies. Tableau is a data display and dashboard platform produced by a Seattle-based company that uses a front-end interface to extract data from a data warehouse and present it as a visualization (colloquially called a 'viz'). These visualizations provide a high degree of flexibility for dashboard developers, as the software can reformat the same data into a range of formats such as timelines, bar graphs, or category charts. These visualizations can also be embedded into websites or presented as 'stories' that help users to make sense of the relationships between trends illustrated in multiple visualizations. Tableau also supports role-dependent views of dashboards, a feature that allows developers to restrict user access to data that they are not entitled to see due to HIPPA or FERPA compliance issues. For example, it is possible to create dashboards that present instructors with data related to their teaching performance, but to conceal data that relates to the performance of other instructors. Tableau also has an active user community that is continually innovating their practice and sharing new lessons at an annual meeting.

However, the innovations presented by these schools also come with limitations of three types. First, the implementation and installation of Tableau visualizations requires some support from information technology experts during setup (especially when importing or storing data in a data warehouse). Second, Tableau and similar technologies are usable by staff who have a moderate level of technological skill, but there is a learning curve associated with adopting the technology and implementing it in a medical education context. While sites such as Lynda.com and YouTube provide video tutorials on Tableau, schools may have to invest funds in sending their dashboard development staff to Tableau workshops or hiring developers to jump-start their dashboard. Third, the successful creation of a Tableau dashboard requires that developers approach the technology from a user-centered perspective. A user-centered dashboard focuses on promoting users' ability to derive meaning from the data in order to make decisions about the direction of their CQI projects and report its progress. However, creating user-centered dashboards requires more than just the right technology; developers must also communicate closely with accreditation and CQI administrators and staff in order to produce tools that serve their needs. The next section of the chapter provides a detailed view of a methodology for achieving a user-centered dashboard for CQI tracking.

An Activity Theory Approach to the Development of CQI Data Dashboards

Every medical school in the LCME jurisdiction exhibits a different profile of available resources and needs. Some schools are attached to Carnegie Research 1 universities, a feature that affords them with greater access to research laboratories or cutting-edge medical facilities and teaching hospitals. Other schools are part of a broader network of medical institutions that are only tangentially connected to local universities. The variance in available human and technological resources requires a flexible strategy for developing CQI dashboards that helps staff and administrators to make the best use of their materials. This part of the chapter provides a detailed worked example of one strategy for deploying resources in an effective and theory-oriented way.

Expanding on the work of Shroyer, Lu & Chandran, the authors have developed an approach to the data dashboard design process that other schools can adapt to their context. This section of the chapter contains a description of 1) the conceptual framework known as Cultural-Historical Activity Theory and how it relates to CQI dashboards, 2) the process used to design the CQI data dashboard at the Keck School of Medicine, and 3) the dashboard design itself. The worked example that results from this discussion will provide data dashboard designers with a stable process for developing their technology. Theoretical frameworks are crucial tools that enable scholars and practitioners to adapt research done in one context to the needs and demands of another context. Describing the KSOM dashboard in terms of Activity Theory will help scholars at other schools to manage the complex and interrelated decisions that lead to a successful implementation in their own context.

Theoretical Framework: Activity Theory

In selecting an appropriate framework for describing the dashboard design process in a generalizable way, this section of the chapter is grounded in Cultural-Historical Activity Theory (Vygotsky, 1978;

Leontiev, 1978; Luria, 1976; Engeström, 2001). Activity Theory focuses on the tensions that arise between key features of work in complex professional environments (Larsen, Nimmon, & Varpio, 2019). Among these crucial tensions are the ways that 'instruments' (such as physical or digital tools) influence the processes, practices, and outcomes of community efforts. These tools play central roles in how individuals communicate and make meaning in and from their work (Kaptelinin & Nardi, 2009; Engeström, 2000; Engeström, 2001; Cole & Hatano, 2007), continually co-evolving with the abilities and needs of their community. Additionally, theorists like Kaptelinin & Nardi (2006) assert that Activity Theory can also inform the design of technologies that scaffold and facilitate work. Recent developments in Human-Centered Design Engineering (HCDE), posit that digital tools and platforms play a similar co-evolutionary role, where users' approach to practical activity can change through interactions with technology (Broberg, Andersen, & Seim, 2011; Kaptelinin & Nardi, 2006). These tools play a crucial role in sensemaking and cognition during the use of data in practice. Recent research in Activity Theory elaborates features of technology design that can support users in accessing and making sense of data in ways that can improve their practice. (Arias-Hernandez, Green, & Fisher, 2012; Broberg, Andersen, & Seim, 2011; Farrell, 2014; Kaptelinin & Nardi, 2006; Kirk, 2012).

Using Activity Theory to plan these new systems can also help to coordinate the design of these CQI platforms with the functions of existing teams within a medical school. To help others understand the activity system and design process that produced our CQI dashboard, the authors diagramed the system using a schematic developed by Engeström (2000) to visualize the components involved in KSOM's longitudinal CQI initiative (Larsen, Nimmon, & Varpio, 2019). For example, the emergence of these platforms as mediating technological tools can connect stakeholders through the development of better business processes. Additionally, new roles, rules, lines of reporting, and tools may need to be developed as a result of the introduction of a CQI tool. Activity Theory provides technology designers with a means of identifying the systemic aspects that shape medical schools' data dashboards needs, and keeps designers focused on the ultimate goal of these data dashboard tools: to make the work of using data easier for accreditation teams and administrators. Figure 1 illustrates the CQI activity system; this diagram can be reused or adapted to other medical school contexts.

Activity Theory provides a powerful means of understanding how parties who are responsible for monitoring and enacting CQI initiatives use communications platforms to achieve their goals. However, in developing an Activity Theory approach to the design of CQI tracking systems, the authors recognize that this framework may pose challenges to designers due to a lack of expertise in Activity Theory within North American medical education. To help simplify this framework and make it easier to implement,

Figure 1. CQI activity system

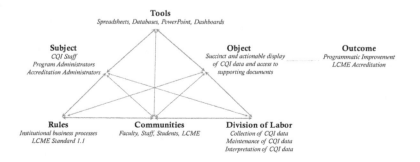

the CQI data dashboard process has been divided into five steps that correspond with important features of Activity Theory networks. These include:

Step 1:   Define Success for Your Dashboard (*Outcomes*)

In Activity Theory, the ultimate outcome of the activity system is the achievement of an outcome goal; however, these outcomes refer to the goals of the entire activity system (e.g. LCME accreditation or improved student performance), not the instrumental goals of a particular project (e.g. creating a data dashboard). Beginning with these outcome goals in mind will help designers to set reasonable definitions for success for the dashboard that actively support the broader strategic goals of the medical school. In the case of most medical schools and their CQI efforts, this goal is to achieve programmatic improvements that benefit students as well as to ensure LCME accreditation and compliance with LCME Standard 1.1.

Step 2:   Organize Your Data Heuristically (*Subjects*)

In Activity Theory and Human-Centered Design Engineering (Broberg, Andersen, & Seim, 2011; Kaptelinin & Nardi, 2006), the subjects in the system play central roles in conceptualizing and enacting their work, and in using their available tools to achieve the system's desired outcomes. For that reason, it is essential to develop technologies that map to the work of the subjects through their theories of action (Argyris & Schon, 1978). In their work on Action Science, Argyris, Putnam, & Smith (1985) define theories of action as complex, related propositions about the relationships between situations, actions, and consequences. Data dashboard designers who carefully map the theories of action of subjects in the activity system can create a through-line that links stakeholders, goals, data, and data-driven decision-making to produce effective tools for scaffolding decision making about CQI initiatives (illustrated in Figure 2). When this is accomplished, data dashboard designers can tailor the technologies to the work demands of the subjects. Technological developments that fail to balance the goals of the of the subjects, the needs of partners outside the activity system, and the available information and accountability pathways can reduce the utility of the technology and hamstring work within the activity system. In short, in order to help stake-holders use the dashboard to support their thinking, the dashboard must be structured with their thinking in mind. Figure 2 illustrates in generic terms how theory of action development can be applied in readers' home context.

Step 3:   Select Your Dashboard Platform (*Tools*)

Scholars in Human-Centered Design Engineering often describe the ability of technologies to improve work outcomes in terms of affordances and constraints (Norman, 2013). An affordance is any property of a technology that improves its utility for the end user in achieving their goals. However, a constraint is any physical, cultural, semantic, or logical component of a technology that frustrates the user's ability to accomplish their objective. Constraints can also arise in technological systems as a result of disconnects between how designers anticipate users' behavior and the actual behaviors of the user.

Figure 2. Illustration of the heuristic development process

Activity Theory extends these concepts into deeper socio-cultural dimensions of work, as the process of building technological tools can benefit work processes by revealing gaps in the larger work flow and supporting the planning of rigorous, data driven improvement efforts and coordinating the attention of various stakeholders (Engeström & Cole, 1997, Engeström, 2000, 2001, 2007; Kaptelinin & Nardi, 2006). In this part of the dashboard design process, developers must consider both the constraints and affordances of technologically-mediated tools, as well as the impact that these tools have on work itself.

Step 4:   Develop Dashboard and Element Views (*Rules, Communities, and Division of Labor*)

A crucial component of Activity Theory is its focus on the cultural and historical dimensions of the social reality of work (Nardi, 1995). In the work of Engeström and others (e.g. Engeström, 2000), culture and history are understood to be real forces that shape how subjects within an activity system understand their place in the work environment, how communities within the system form and interact, and how the organization divides rights and responsibilities amongst its members. Extending this concept to dashboard design, dashboard developers must consider how their technologies reinforce the expectations of the organization (rules), standardize communications between institutions and accreditors (communities), and support the work of a range of stakeholders (divisions of labor).

In addition to selecting technologies that accurately report information throughout the activity system, designers in other contexts should consider a visual layout that uses principles drawn from cognitive science (i.e. Clark & Mayer, 2016). Previous research on effective dashboards by the designers has identified several principles of data usage that should be integrated into dashboard designs. In interviews conducted by one of the authors at a large educational institution in Washington state, expert designers articulated five key attributes of well-designed dashboards:

- **Data consolidation:** Great dashboards bring together relevant data from different parts of the organization into one warehouse and dashboard and provides flexible disaggregation of data.
- **Data integration:** Great dashboards integrate relevant data sources into a parsimonious representation in one place.
- **Data interpretation:** Great data dashboards facilitate users' interpretation of data by grouping visualizations logically, managing users' cognitive load, and include text captions that explain the relevance of the data to decision making.
- **Data triangulation:** Great data dashboards facilitate users' ability to support their decisions using several sources of data.
- **Signaling:** Great dashboards use visual markers to help users quickly make sense of important data and information on a dashboard.

Dashboard developers should review their designs against these attributes before proceeding to user testing phases of the development process.

Step 5:   Test the Dashboard with Users (*Object*)

The development of a data dashboard is an iterative process that requires periodic reviews of the products of design processes. At the end of each cycle of design, dashboard designers should work with their stakeholders to determine whether the dashboard fits their needs and how it can be refactored around their work. Developers can use a variety of techniques to track how well their dashboards are performing with their end users. These can include quantitative evaluation methods such as page analytics that track the frequency and patterns of use by CQI administrators, as well as qualitative methods such as interviews and focus groups.

Following these five steps, and engaging in periodic cycles of redesign, will provide dashboard designers in medical education with a theoretically and practically achievable approach to the development of their tools that touches on the major Activity Theory framework constructs and ensures adherence to good design processes.

The Keck School of Medicine Data Dashboard Design Process

In applying the logic of the design process from the perspective of the designers and administrators, readers will be better prepared to create their own dashboards in their local context. This section of the chapter will proceed through each of these steps by providing details about the process that resulted in a successful dashboard implementation in the KSOM context.

Step 1:   Define Success for Your Dashboard (*Outcomes*)

In order to understand the desired outcomes of the CQI tracking process, KSOM's dashboard designers interviewed a few central CQI team members, and worked with the key administrative stakeholders to identify three parameters that would define success in the final project and reflect the priorities of the stakeholders at the strategic level. Following these discussions, the designers summarized that the resulting data dashboard design would:

- Address all relevant LCME standards and elements that might conceivably require a CQI initiative, and expand to encompass future elements that may be introduced later;
- Look aesthetically pleasing, maintain visual consistency across elements of the standards, accommodate a range of data sources, and communicate important information quickly using visual cues; and
- Be easy to access, use, and maintain by the staff of the school, as they are the ones who must ultimately do the work of tracking CQI initiatives.

Defining these priorities in ways that support the overall outcomes of the activity system and the demands of the key stakeholders provided the dashboard designers with a clear sense of the purposes that the dashboard would serve in the work of the CQI administrators, as well as a means of assessing the project at its conclusion.

Step 2:   Organize Your Data Heuristically (*Subjects*)

After mapping the initial round of school goals, administrators and partners, and accountability pathways, the dashboard design team worked with CQI project leaders to create Key Performance Indicators (KPIs), or measures of key constructs of the most proximate measures of success for a specific CQI initiative. The selection and organization of KPIs is particularly crucial, as it simplifies the process of selecting visualizations and graphic views later in the design process. In the context of this project, designers were able to adapt many KPIs from the existing Excel sheets used by CQI administrators, as they had already been through successive rounds of review by the other stakeholders in the CQI process. They also took careful note of the individuals responsible for these KPIs, and any partners (e.g. offices, individuals) associated with completing the CQI projects.

Working with the project leaders, the designers again reviewed the KPIs and developed a heuristic approach to organizing the information. Heuristics are understood to represent metacognitive mental shortcuts to information processing (Mark & Wong, 2001). These shortcuts can reduce the cognitive load associated with decision-making by organizing information into meaningful questions that can be answered with the data presented. In addition to creating a narrative around the KPIs that linked the proximate measures to their goals, heuristic questions can help to guide the thinking of the user. As an added benefit, organizing the KPIs into heuristic categories enabled the designers to easily transpose the design across multiple technologies during the prototyping phase.

Figure 3 represents the reorganization of KSOM's KPIs into a simple structure that facilitates the kinds of decision-making processes that users expected to use in their tracking of the progress of CQI initiatives. These heuristics are likely to vary by an institution's KPIs, but the organization of KPIs into heuristics should be an iterative and integral part of the dashboard design process. Each row in Figure 3 is designed to represent a question that scaffolds the thinking of the user, with each cell representing a piece of data that is necessary to answer that question. In the final phase of this iteration of KSOM's design definition, the rows answer the following questions:

- **Row 1:** Who is responsible and how much progress have we made?
- **Row 2:** What key data will help me to demonstrate that progress?
- **Row 3:** What are we doing and when do we need to return to this LCME element?
- **Row 4:** What LCME-related steps are necessary for follow-up?

The heuristic organization of these key pieces of information allow users to quickly make sense of the answers to these key questions. Other schools may wish to create similar organizational schema to reduce the cognitive load associated with interpreting and relating KPIs.

Step 3:   Select Your Dashboard Platform *(Tools)*

As a first step in development of the platform, designers examined existing practices of the staff and administrators in charge of tracking CQI initiatives across the school, and briefly interviewed some of the participants. Prior to the development of the CQI platform, the administrators in charge of CQI kept track of their progress using Excel spreadsheets, a common practice in LCME CQI tracking efforts. As a CQI administrator noted during our interviews:

I believe a lot of schools, when they're initially embarking on their CQI process for LCME, start with an Excel spreadsheet. I feel like it's a clunky mechanism to use because you're not able to put in a lot of detail, a lot of narrative, any kind of documentation or tables or data. It all has to be very text based....

Figure 3. Responsibilities, information, and KPIs for the LCME CQI dashboard template page, organized heuristically to facilitate user analysis of data

Responsible Administrator	Point of Contact	Status
Metric	Data Sources	Data and Evidence Files
Notes	Review Interval	Review History
Follow-Up		

That's when we recognized the need, that our Excel spreadsheet technology was not optimal to do all that we wanted to do regarding tracking CQI. And so [the Excel document] just became kind of a mass and it was difficult to share with people with, especially with having to supply documentation for backup or if there's multiple people or multiple dates, it all just becomes a little bit difficult to track in Excel. (CQI Administrator, June 2018)

As the administrator described in development discussions (echoing Hedrick et al., 2019), Excel spreadsheets have several significant limitations. First, Excel files can become unwieldy quickly and require significant scrolling and movement both horizontally and vertically, increasing the perceived visual distance between key pieces of information. Second, Excel sheets are difficult to use for tracking as they are text-oriented, row and column constrained, and based on the information organization logic of cells. This reduces the user's ability to flexibly control the layout of the information for visual communications. Third, Excel files do not allow users to easily access and view PDFs, real-time visualizations, or other files during the course of their compliance reviews. These intrinsic limitations in tool functionality produced serious limitations for the decision-making potential of the CQI tracking process. For example, the additional extrinsic cognitive load of interacting with CQI data in a cellular format would be expected to put pressure on the user's finite working memory resources (Clark & Mayer, 2016). These usability limitations were identified as issues that designers must overcome during development.

The designers identified four questions to guide the selection of an appropriate technology to house the CQI tracking tool:

- How might the tool support access, updates, and decision-making by multiple users?
- How might the tool best support multiple kinds of media, including web-based links, videos, PDFs, Microsoft Office documents, and data visualizations?
- How might the selected technologies support the continuous improvement of the CQI dashboard and more cohesive improvement activities?
- How does the technology enable visual signaling of important data, as well as the triangulation of data sources that will be used in heuristic decision-making?

These questions enabled the designers to evaluate available technological platforms in advance of the prototyping phase. For example, the designers recognized that the CQI tracking tool would need to be web-based in order to provide real-time access to multiple stakeholders. This decision, based on the idea that the CQI data should not become sequestered in a single individual's computer, helped to rule out several offline technological platforms such as Microsoft PowerPoint, Word, Excel, or other database tools like Filemaker Pro or Access (which do not easily sync the work of multiple users across the sources of data).

Ultimately, the ease of access to Microsoft's SharePoint through the Microsoft 365 platform made it a compelling option, as it supports the integration of multiple file types into a widely available online platform. The additional communications features available in SharePoint (such as Outlook integration, which automatically provided up-to-date contact information for responsible administrators in CQI efforts), as well as its ease of use and wide availability to members of the medical school, made it the final choice for the delivery of the dashboard. The SharePoint platform's affordances opened the project to a range of new possibilities for the collection and display of non-quantitative CQI data such as policy documents, committee reports, and videos. Further, the platform's pages could be archived, saved, and cloned as often as the users deemed necessary, creating a continuous record that can be referenced for other accreditation and reporting activities in the future.

Step 4: Develop Dashboard and Element Views (*Rules, Communities, and Division of Labor*)

To create a tool that supported the work of the CQI groups, designers at KSOM assembled the existing CQI information from our administrators' Excel files into an online platform that provided both a dashboard-level view of the status of the organization's CQI initiatives (Figure 4), as well as views of the heuristically-sorted responsibilities, information, and key performance indicators (Figure 5). In the main dashboard view in Figure 4, the current status of each project element is signaled to the user with a red 'X' icon, a yellow exclamation point icon (not shown), or a green checkmark icon. Standards with active CQI projects also feature a unique 'CQI' symbol that visually flags the element for review. This color coding provides higher-level administrators with an at-a-glance view of CQI project progress and is suitable for presentations at status meetings.

In addition to a dashboard-style interface, we designed the final iteration of the site to include integrated secure data and evidence storage locations, workflow automations, and other communications tools. Figure 5 provides an overview of the individual element page for each LCME standard. Each page follows the same pattern defined in the KPI and heuristic development phase, and includes:

- **Standard Text:** The full text of the LCME element standard, so that users are clear about what the included data describe.
- **Responsible Administrator:** The name of the individual or committee responsible for the project.
- **Point of Contact:** Displays the name of the person responsible for the information. In this system, the field is tied into the university's Outlook database of users, providing current email and telephone contact information for the individual.
- **Metrics:** A reference field for goals and related expectations.
- **Data Sources:** A listing of the available sources of data that address the element.
- **Data and Evidence Files:** Links to key web pages that provide supporting documentation. The site also includes access to a Microsoft OneDrive file management system to store and sort documents within the site.
- **Data Visualizations:** Built-in histograms of key data sources, with support for future integrations from Tableau or Microsoft PowerBI services.
- **Notes:** A text field for reminders, caveats, and other information about this version of the review.
- **Review Interval:** A text field that identifies the frequency of review events in the Review History.
- **Review History:** This field uses built-in Outlook calendaring functionality to add review event reminders to a user's work calendar and track past review deadlines.
- **Follow-Up:** An editable text field that includes notes on next steps and reminders for future activity
- **Comments:** Additional time-stamped comments from users.

Step 5: Test the Dashboard with Users *(Object)*

In the final step of the Activity Theory-derived development process, dashboard designers returned to the CQI administrators and allowed them to test a functional prototype of the final 'object' produced by the process. This type of user testing can play an important role in validating the assumptions of the designers and developers. In review meetings, the CQI Dashboard was evaluated against the initial design parameters produced in Step 1. In our discussion, administrators found that the final design was capable of addressing the LCME standards and elements at varying levels of granularity and could

Figure 4. Dashboard view of LCME CQI projects; CQI projects are signaled with a special symbol, as in element 1.1a, 2.2, 2.4, 3.3, and 3.6.

expand to accommodate future developments in the LCME standards or other CQI initiatives. Second, the administrators were asked if the individual pages of the dashboard maintained visual consistency across the site, were judged aesthetically pleasing, and integrated several data sources and file types, and communicated the information in a parsimonious way. Finally, we asked our administrators if they were able to easily access and manipulate the dashboard overview and element pages. Usage statistics from the SharePoint platform indicate that the site was accessed more than 1800 times by administrators during an 18-month period.

Figure 5. An example of the CQI Dashboard's LCME element pages, based on Key Performance Indicators and heuristic organization.

Another positive sign for the user acceptance of the dashboard came as end-users began to create their own approaches to their ongoing tracking strategies. For example, when the platform's built-in graphing functions were not able to produce trendline and stacked histograms within the dashboard software, the users began to include screenshots of their existing graphs from PowerPoint presentations and other sources. The users' ability to innovate within the platform to fit their own needs indicates that the dashboard platform provided a suitable base for future developments in CQI tracking. Further, the autonomous use and continued improvement of the platform by non-technical staff indicates that the platform is well suited to adaptation to other contexts.

FUTURE DEVELOPMENT

As data visualization tools become more broadly available, administrators and accreditation supervisors will be able to take advantage a range of new functionalities for their CQI data dashboards. These technologies provide high quality data visualization tools right out of the box at an affordable price. However, CQI dashboard developers will need to consider three new sets of challenges and opportunities as these tools become commonplace. Future research in CQI data dashboard development will need to work to better anticipate the consequences of the integration of 1) data warehouse technologies, 2) real time data representations, and 3) AI technologies into CQI tracking efforts in order to provide administrators with the best possible tracking technologies. We will briefly outline each of these challenges.

First, as data dashboard tools such as Tableau and Microsoft's PowerBI become more affordable, administrators are likely to request that developers create and integrate visualizations that track historical and long-term trends in medical school performance and map the current performance of the school against these trends as they relate to LCME standards. This will require the development of data warehouses capable of ingesting, organizing and presenting this information in flexible ways. The arrangement of the historical and current data in these warehouses can require careful deliberation in order to render these data usable in visualizations. Further, the hierarchy and arrangement of these data in warehouses can affect how dashboard software interprets these data

Second, CQI-specific dashboards will make greater use of real-time visualizations to allow administrators to make important decisions based on the most recent available data. However, these real-time dashboards must be designed to also present historical data in ways that make the context of the present situation clear. For example, a particular KPI might appear to have increased by 30% this year, but this statistic is misleading if not compared to overall historical declines evinced by the historical data set. This could lead to additional errors in interpretation by the LCME during its accreditation reviews. Therefore, designers must carefully consider the ways that real time visualizations can confound decision-making processes, and design around those pitfalls.

Third, the emergence of Artificial Intelligence (AI) and Big Data cloud services will create new opportunities in predictive analysis that will help administrators to anticipate changes or needs associated with specific CQI initiatives. AI is a generic term that describes a range of technologies that employ algorithms to make decisions about data based on calculations performed on large quantities of existing data (Zimmerman, 2018). While AI presents new opportunities for quality monitoring and improvement, ultimately humans must make decisions based on the analytic outputs of the algorithms that govern these systems (Williamson, 2016). Dashboard designers and CQI administrators must understand how these AI systems arrive at their conclusions in order to avoid the pitfalls of poor data interpretation.

The successful navigation of these issues has the potential to produce more useful decision-support systems for LCME and CQI accreditation administrators in the future. The ability to access historical data, compare it to real time data, and use AI to support interpretation presents real opportunities for improving the capacity of administrators to improve the work of their staff and student learning.

CONCLUSION

The goal of the CQI process is the improvement of medical education and to meet accreditation standards. A properly designed CQI dashboard has the capacity to facilitate the work of continuous quality improvement and track that work. In describing an Activity Theory-derived process for developing dashboards, the authors hope that readers will be able to use this technique to support their own CQI and accreditation activities.

The authors look forward to seeing the kinds of tools that other institutions develop based on the initial version of our tool described in this worked example. Further, this chapter will ideally support additional opportunities to help other schools to develop their own versions of the CQI dashboard through future presentations and publications.

ACKNOWLEDGEMENTS

The authors would like to thank Dr. Frank Sinatra, Dr. Patrick Crispen, Dr. Anne Vo, Amanda Frataccia, and Georgianna Newell for their contributions to the development of the online platform and chapter.

REFERENCES

Argryis, C., Putnam, R., & Smith, D. (1985). *Action science: Concepts, methods, and skills for research and intervention.* San Francisco, CA: Jossey-Bass.

Argyris, C., & Schön, D. A. (1978). *Organizational learning. A theory of action perspective.* Reading, MA: Addison-Wesley.

Arias-Hernandez, R., Green, T. M., & Fisher, B. (2012). From cognitive amplifiers to cognitive prostheses: Understandings of the material basis of cognition in visual analytics. *Interdisciplinary Science Reviews, 37*(1), 4–18. doi:10.1179/0308018812Z.0000000001

Barzansky, B., Hunt, D., Moineau, G., Ahn, D., Lai, C. W., Humphrey, H., & Peterson, L. (2015). Continuous quality improvement in an accreditation system for undergraduate medical education: Benefits and challenges. *Medical Teacher, 37*(11), 1032–1038. doi:10.3109/0142159X.2015.1031735 PMID:25897708

Blouin, D., & Tekian, A. (2018). Accreditation of medical education programs: Moving from student outcomes to continuous quality improvement measures. *Academic Medicine, 93*(3), 377–383. doi:10.1097/ACM.0000000000001835 PMID:28746072

Blouin, D., Tekian, A., Kamin, C., & Harris, I. B. (2018). The impact of accreditation on medical schools' processes. *Medical Education, 52*(2), 182–191. doi:10.1111/medu.13461 PMID:29044652

Broberg, O., Andersen, V., & Seim, R. (2011). Participatory ergonomics in design processes: The role of boundary objects. *Applied Ergonomics, 42*(3), 464–472. doi:10.1016/j.apergo.2010.09.006 PMID:20947061

Buchanan, H. S. (1995). The quality movement in higher education in the United States. *Health Libraries Review, 12*(3), 141–146. doi:10.1046/j.1365-2532.1995.1230141.x PMID:10159232

Clark, R., & Mayer, R. (2016). eLearning and the science of instruction, 4th Edition. Brentwood, CA: Wiley.

Cole, M., & Hatano, G. (2007). Cultural-historical activity theory: Integrating phylogeny, cultural history, and ontogenesis in cultural psychology. In S. Kitayama, & D. Cohen (Eds.), *Handbook of cultural psychology* (pp. 109–135). New York: Guilford Press.

Dinsmore, D. L., Alexander, P. A., & Loughlin, S. M. (2008). Focusing the conceptual lens on metacognition, self-regulation, and self-regulated learning. *Educational Psychology Review, 20*(4), 391–409. doi:10.100710648-008-9083-6

Engeström, Y. (2000). Activity theory as a framework for analyzing and redesigning work. *Ergonomics, 43*(7), 960–974. doi:10.1080/001401300409143 PMID:10929830

Engeström, Y. (2001). Expansive learning at work: Toward an activity theoretical reconceptualization. *Journal of Education and Work, 14*(1), 133–156. doi:10.1080/13639080020028747

Engeström, Y. (2007). Enriching the theory of expansive learning: Lessons from journeys toward coconfiguration. *Mind, Culture, and Activity, 14*(1-2), 23–39. doi:10.1080/10749030701307689

Engeström, Y., & Cole, M. (1997). Situated cognition in search of an agenda. In D. Kirshner, & J. A. Whitson (Eds.), *Situated cognition: Social, semiotic, and psychological perspectives* (pp. 301–309). Mahwah, NJ: Erlbaum.

Evergreen, S., & Metzner, C. (2013). Design principles for data visualization in evaluation. In T. Azzam, & S. Evergreen (Eds.), Data visualization for evaluation, part 2. New Directions for Evaluation, 140, 5–20. doi:10.1002/ev.20071

Farrell, C. C. (2014). Designing school systems to encourage data use and instructional improvement: A comparison of school districts and charter management organizations. *Educational Administration Quarterly, 51*(3), 438–471. doi:10.1177/0013161X14539806

Few, S. (2006). *Information dashboard design: The effective visual communication of data.* New York: O'Reilly.

Gee, J. P. (2010). *New digital media and learning as an emerging area and "worked examples" as one way forward.* Cambridge, MA: MIT Press.

Gemignani, Z., Gemignani, C., Galentino, R., & Schuermann, P. (2014). *Data fluency: Empowering your organization with effective data communication.* San Francisco, CA: John Wiley & Sons.

Hedrick, J. S., Cottrell, S., Stark, D., Brownfield, E., Stoddard, H. A., Angle, S. M., ... Park, V. (2019). A review of continuous quality improvement processes at ten medical schools. *Medical Science Educator, 29*(1), 285–290. doi:10.100740670-019-00694-5

Hernández-García, Á., & Conde, M. Á. (2014). Dealing with complexity: educational data and tools for learning analytics. In *Proceedings of the Second International Conference on Technological Ecosystems for Enhancing Multiculturality* (pp. 263-268). ACM. 10.1145/2669711.2669909

Kaptelinin, V., & Nardi, B. A. (2009). *Acting with technology: Activity theory and interaction design.* Cambridge, MA: MIT Press.

Kirk, D. E. (2012). *Optimal control theory: An introduction.* Mineola, NY: Dover Publications.

Knigge, L., & Cope, M. (2006). Grounded visualization: Integrating the analysis of qualitative and quantitative data through grounded theory and visualization. *Environment & Planning A, 38*(11), 2021–2037. doi:10.1068/a37327

Larsen, D. P., Nimmon, L., & Varpio, L. (2019). Cultural-historical activity theory: The role of tools and tensions in medical education. *Academic Medicine, 94*(8), 1255; Advance online publication. doi:10.1097/ACM.0000000000002736 PMID:30973361

Leontiev, A. N. (1978). *Activity, consciousness, and personality*. Englewood Cliffs, NJ: Prentice-Hall.

Liaison Committee on Medical Education. (2017). *Functions and structure of a medical school: Standards for accreditation of medical education programs leading to the MD degree*. Retrieved from http://lcme.org/wp-content/uploads/filebase/standards/2018-19_Functions-and-Structure_2017-08-02.docx. Accessed October 10, 2017.

Lowyck, J. (2014). Bridging learning theories and technology-enhanced environments: A critical appraisal of its history. In J. M. Spector, M. D. Merrill, J. Elen, & M. J. Bishop (Eds.), *Handbook of research on educational communications and technology* (pp. 3–20). New York: Springer. doi:10.1007/978-1-4614-3185-5_1

Luria, A. R. (1976). *The cognitive development: Its cultural and social foundations*. Cambridge, MA: Harvard University Press.

Mark, D. B., & Wong, J. B. (2001). Decision making in clinical medicine. In E. Braunwald (Ed.), *Harrison's Principles of Internal Medicine* (15th ed., pp. 8–14). New York: The McGraw-Hill Companies.

Miller, B., Dzwonek, B., McGuffin, A., & Shapiro, J. I. (2014). From LCME probation to compliance: The Marshall University Joan C. Edwards School of Medicine experience. *Advances in Medical Education and Practice*, 377–382. PMID:25337003

Nardi, B. (1995). *Context and consciousness: Activity theory and human-computer interaction*. Cambridge, MA: MIT Press. doi:10.7551/mitpress/2137.001.0001

Norman, D. (2013). *The design of everyday things: Revised and expanded edition*. New York: Basic Books.

Power, D. J. (2008). Understanding data-driven decision support systems. *Information Systems Management, 25*(2), 149–154. doi:10.1080/10580530801941124

Rossett, A., & Schaffer, L. (2012). *Job aids and performance support: Moving from knowledge in the classroom to knowledge everywhere*. San Francisco, CA: John Wiley & Sons.

Shroyer, A. L., Lu, W. H., & Chandran, L. (2016). Drivers of dashboard development (3-D): A curricular continuous quality improvement approach. *Academic Medicine, 91*(4), 517–521. doi:10.1097/ACM.0000000000001078 PMID:26796088

Simon, H. A. (1971). Designing organizations for an information-rich world. *Computers, Communication, and the Public Interest, 37*, 40-41.

Smith, V. S. (2013). Data dashboard as evaluation and research communication tool. *New Directions for Evaluation, 140*(140), 21–45. doi:10.1002/ev.20072

Stratton, T. D. (2019). Legitimizing continuous quality improvement (CQI): Navigating rationality in undergraduate medical education. *Journal of General Internal Medicine, 34*(5), 758–761. doi:10.100711606-019-04875-1 PMID:30788765

Tyler, J. H. (2013). If you build it will they come? Teachers' online use of student performance data. *Education Finance and Policy, 8*(2), 168–207. doi:10.1162/EDFP_a_00089 PMID:25593564

Verbert, K., Duval, E., Klerkx, J., Govaerts, S., & Santos, J. L. (2013). Learning analytics dashboard applications. *The American Behavioral Scientist, 57*(10), 1500–1509. doi:10.1177/0002764213479363

Verhaeghe, G., Schildkamp, K., Luyten, H., & Valcke, M. (2015). Diversity in school performance feedback systems. *School Effectiveness and School Improvement, 26*(4), 612–638. doi:10.1080/09243 453.2015.1017506

Von Hippel, E. (2005). *Democratizing innovation*. Cambridge, MA: MIT Press. doi:10.7551/mit-press/2333.001.0001

Vygtosky, L. S. (1978). *Mind in society: The development of higher psychological processes*. Cambridge, MA: Harvard University Press.

Wayman, J. C., & Cho, V. (2008). Preparing educators to effectively use student data systems. In T. J. Kowalski, & T. J. Lasley (Eds.), *Handbook on data-based decision-making in education* (pp. 89–104). Hoboken, NJ: Taylor & Francis.

Wayman, J. C., Stringfield, S., & Yakimowski, M. (2004). *Software enabling school improvement through analysis of student data*. Baltimore, MD: Center for Research of Students Placed at Risk, Johns Hopkins University.

Williamson, B. (2016). Digital education governance: Data visualization, predictive analytics, and 'real-time' policy instruments. *Journal of Education Policy, 31*(2), 123–141. doi:10.1080/02680939.2 015.1035758

Zimmerman, M. (2018). *Teaching AI: Exploring new frontiers for learning*. Washington, DC: International Society for Technology in Education.

ADDITIONAL READING

Boudett, K. P., City, E. A., & Murnane, R. J. (2013). *Data wise: A step-by-step guide to using assessment results to improve teaching and learning*. Cambridge, MA: Harvard Education Press.

Clark, R. C., & Lyons, C. (2010). *Graphics for learning: Proven guidelines for planning, designing, and evaluating visuals in training materials*. San Francisco, CA: Pfeifer.

Knaflic, C. N. (2015). *Storytelling with Data: A data visualization guide for business professionals*. Hoboken, NJ: Wiley. doi:10.1002/9781119055259

Piety, P. J., & Linn, M. C. (2013). *Assessing the educational data movement*. New York: Teachers College Press.

Tufte, E. (2006). *Beautiful evidence*. Cheshire, CT: Graphics Press.

Wexler, S., Shaffer, J., & Cotgreave, A. (2017). *The big book of dashboards: Visualizing your data using real-world business scenarios*. Hoboken, NJ: Wiley. doi:10.1002/9781119283089

Yau, N. (2013). *Data points: Visualizations that mean something*. Hoboken, NJ: Wiley.

KEY TERMS AND DEFINITIONS

Artificial Intelligence (AI): In the context of this chapter, a term for analytic tools that use advanced algorithms to analyze large data sets and augment human analysis of data.

Big Data: A term used to describe large-scale data sets that include multiple kinds of demographic, behavioral, or performance data. Sometimes used to describe the unique kinds of data analysis that can be performed on these data sets.

Continuous Quality Improvement (CQI): A business process philosophy that promotes goalsetting, data collection, and program evaluation towards the end of providing students with better experiences and outcomes.

Data Dashboard: A grouping of related data visualizations that provides users with information about the state of a system.

Data Visualization: A visual representation of data that uses a range of graphic forms to help the user make sense of a particular set of data.

Data Warehouse: A data system that ingests, stores, and retrieves data for use in other systems.

Key Performance Indicator (KPI): Proximate measures of performance that are used to identify how well a given program or system is operating based on predefined goals.

Liaison Committee on Medical Education (LCME): A joint body of the American Association of Medical Colleges (AAMC) and the American Medical Association (AMA) and other groups that evaluates and accredits physician training facilities in the United States and Canada.

Chapter 23
Alice in Simulation–Land:
Surgical Simulation in Medical Education

Vanessa Bazan
University of Kentucky, USA

Michael D. Jax
University of Kentucky, USA

Joseph B. Zwischenberger
University of Kentucky, USA

ABSTRACT

Surgical education has been compressed by integrated residency programs and restrictions on the number of hours surgical residents are allowed to work. Instilling basic technical skills as early as the first year of medical school can help maximize preparedness for surgical rotation and residency. This overview includes a detailed description of low, medium, and high-fidelity simulation-based training techniques and recommends introduction of surgical simulation early in the medical school curriculum. A personal vignette highlights this recommendation.

INTRODUCTION

For decades, surgical education was modeled after Halsted who felt residents should live in the hospital and care for patients in a longitudinal manner to understand the natural history of disease with and without surgery (Polavarapu, Kulaylat, Sun, & Hamed, 2013). Unfortunately, this approach resulted in a workload which usually totaled 100-120 hours per week or more (Hutter, Kellogg, Ferguson, Abbott, & Warshaw, 2006). The Accreditation Council for Graduate Medical Education Residency Review Committee (ACGME RRC) determined that an 80-hour work week is more conducive to learning and a healthy lifestyle (Philibert, Friedmann, Williams, & ACGME Work Group on Resident Duty Hours, 2002). All surgical residents are now restricted to "duty hour" regulation renamed "clinical work hours" in 2017 (Table 1). Despite efforts to achieve improved life balance and patient safety, the 80-hour cap

DOI: 10.4018/978-1-7998-1468-9.ch023

on resident work is estimated to decrease caseload by 28% in year one and 36% in year two of residency (Kamine, Gondek, & Kent, 2014). The influential paper "Why Johnny cannot operate" asked 114 residency program directors what operations graduating general surgery residents should be able to competently perform. The 121 procedures deemed essential by residency program directors were ranked by frequency performed and revealed an exponential decrease with nearly one-quarter of procedures never performed by graduating chief residents (Bell, 2009). Likewise, more than 20% of general surgery residents lack confidence in their surgical skills (Coleman, Esposito, Rozycki, & Feliciano, 2013). Trends toward integrated residencies compressing traditional general surgery (5-6 years) plus fellowships (1-3 years) into 6-year comprehensive programs has compounded the problem of potential gaps in resident experience and progression (Grant, Dixon, Glass, & Sakran, 2013). Many have observed that surgeons are less practice-ready and have achieved less graduated responsibility following completion of residency. Widespread concern for preparedness of general surgery residents to enter private practice or fellowship is shared by both fellowship directors and surgery residents (Matter et al., 2013).

Achieving surgical competency in this environment is possible but requires additional focus on the part of educators and participatory learning on the part of students and residents (Bell, 2009). Participatory learning can occur safely in the operating room when trainee autonomy is granted gradually, and competency is documented. The Zwisch scale is a new metric to evaluate the level of autonomy granted in the operating room based on faculty assessment and trust in the learner's ability (least to most trainee autonomy). The graduated scale entitled: Show and Tell, Active Help, Passive Help, or Supervision Only, captures the trainee's level of independence delegated during the majority of the key portion of a procedure. Each level is defined by specific behaviors, for example, Show and Tell has an attending surgeon perform a procedure that is carefully observed by a trainee. Active help has the attending surgeon lead the case and direct the tasks although the trainee may actually perform the case. Passive help allows the trainee to conduct and perform the procedure while the attending surgeon acts as an occasional advisory assistant. Supervision Only describes a procedure performed by a trainee with minimal unsolicited advice from the attending (George et al., 2014). After a procedure, the educator and trainee are prompted by a smartphone app such as "Zwisch Surgery" to rank operating room autonomy while the procedure is still fresh in their mind. The SIMPL app (System for Improving and Measuring Procedural Learning) tracks resident autonomy and readiness using the Zwisch scale and the validated SIMPL performance scale which labels trainee competency as Unprepared/Critical Deficiency, Unfamiliar with Procedure, Intermediate Performance, Practice Ready, and Exceptional Performance. The largest study of general surgery resident readiness (14 general surgery programs, 444 attendings, 536 residents, and 10,130 procedures), found approximately 80% of general surgery residents reached meaningful autonomy and competency in core procedures in the final 6 months of residency, using the Zwisch and SIMPL scores, respectively (George et al., 2017). The 20% considered deficient confirm concerns regarding surgical resident preparedness.

Increased use of simulation early in a surgeon's career is one possible way to improve surgeon readiness before they begin 3rd year medical school rotations or residency. Simulation training for surgery residents has been driven by the success of aviation and the military where young learners achieve a high level of proficiency and responsibility in a compressed educational process (de Montbrun & Macrae, 2012). Simulation based training helps medical students acquire basic technical skills needed during surgical rotations which function as auditions for highly competitive residency programs. Once a medical student matches to a surgical residency, additional burden to acquire surgical skills is immediate. Some institutions have introduced surgical skill boot camps to help incoming residents achieve a consistent level of surgical skills at the beginning of residency (Neylan et al., 2017). We propose instilling the availability of progressively sophisticated technical skills and simulated operating room scenarios as early as the first year of medical school instead of later years (or immediately upon residency) to maximize preparedness for surgical rotations during medical school, thoughtful choice of specialty, and residency readiness. The Zwisch and SIMPL scales can be used by medical students for self-assessment during simulation training to guide thoughtful practice and help students meet individual goals. Technical skills training is currently not emphasized in medical school curriculum and students have reported dissatisfaction with the level of basic surgical skills training provided (Preece et al., 2015). Although over 60% of surgery residents decide to become surgeons before beginning medical school (Hochberg et al., 2014) all students will benefit from additional exposure. Through acquisition of basic surgical skills by early simulation, all students can choose whether to enrich their medical school experience with more advanced surgical skills acquisition, mentored research and surgical career counselling. All surgical or procedural based specialties would benefit from these programs. This chapter summarizes low, medium, and high-fidelity approaches to simulation, discusses the costs, risks and benefits associated with simulation-based training, and describes the experience of a first-year medical student learning through low and medium fidelity simulation experiences.

LOW FIDELITY SIMULATION

Low fidelity simulation replicates a single component of a procedure or single skill and is focused on honing basic surgical technique through repetition (table 2). Task trainers are not necessarily designed for anatomic accuracy and can be fashioned from household items. Students can easily practice simple low fidelity exercises 10 minutes per day during study breaks or while watching television. A pair of reading glasses and a basic headlamp provide sufficient magnification and lighting for exercises.

Shoelaces are commonly used to demonstrate square knots. Tape marks one end of the shoelace indicating the position of a needle on suture. After the student can produce a basic knot on the shoelace, a soda can is a useful tool for learning how to manage knot tension. The goal is to tie knots in the tab without lifting or jerking the can. Difficulty is increased by gradually emptying the can. Students should learn to tie into both the dominant and non-dominant hands.

Surgical instruments are introduced beginning with forceps and 10-25 kernels of rice or un-popped corn. Students use forceps to transfer the kernels from a table top into a cup. This exercise is repeated three times, first using the shoulder as a fulcrum, then the elbow, and finally the wrist. Finally, it is repeated with the non-dominant hand. Muscles in the hands and forearm are easily fatigued in beginners and a stress ball can be used to build strength. Practicing this exercise blindfolded helps students develop spatial orientation and awareness as well as the subtle 'feel' of instrument handling.

Suturing can be introduced with a wide variety of materials. Suturing around the rim of a Styrofoam cup while keeping the cup still teaches a student about suture placement and how to handle a needle. Suturing a small incision on a grape without tearing the skin gives students feedback on appropriate suture tension. Expired suture is ideal, but a curved needle and polypropylene yarn used in fly-fishing can be substituted if there are no other options. Instrument ties and hand-knot tying practice are incorporated into suture training.

Other basic skills can also be addressed at this level. Posture at the operating room table and importance of supportive stockings and shoes, comfortable non-restrictive clothing (scrubs), to name a few.

Likewise, standardization of command and response including standardized nomenclature of instruments can greatly enhance the conduct of the surgery. How to pass and receive instruments also contributes to focus upon the actual complexities of the case.

The University of Kentucky College of Medicine Center for Advanced Training and Simulation (CATS) lab provides low fidelity simulation training including knot tying, suturing, and elementary laparoscopic technique (Figure 1) (Jax, 2019). This resource is made available to all medical students Monday-Friday 8:30am-5:30pm. Special events are organized in conjunction with residency directors and product vendors to teach trainees advanced skills. The 'Simulation Olympics' is a convivial tournament of timed simulation events where trainees compete for glory.

As part of the mandatory medical school curriculum, third year medical students complete simplified surgery resident skills during their surgery clerkship. Skills include hand knot tying, suturing, and laparoscopic skills including peg board exercises (illustrated in figure 1), 30-degree scope drills, and traction/counter-traction drills. All equipment that is provided for residents is also available for use by medical students. To prepare students for this curriculum, the CATS lab provides training sessions introduced by the surgery faculty, including the department chairman. In addition, a minimally invasive surgery elective is offered to first and second year medical students. These students undertake the same curriculum as 3rd year students and complete required shadowing (Figure 2) (Jax, 2019). These low-fidelity simulations aim to prepare students for clerkship as well as guide professional choices, mentorship and residency.

The minimally invasive surgery task trainer is designed to familiarize students with surgical instruments. The pegboard exercise requires students to transfer pegs from the pegboard to a tray and back to the pegboard in less than four minutes.

MEDIUM FIDELITY SIMULATION

Medium fidelity surgical simulation focuses on the critical elements of a more complex surgical procedure. This level focuses on a procedural component which must be mastered to conduct a specific operative procedure. Medium fidelity exercises include practicing procedures such as cosmetic skin closure using artificial skin, vascular anastomosis (connection) using synthetic blood vessels, bowel anastomosis using synthetic tubing, tracheal anastomosis using discarded animal or simulated tissue, and ultrasound guided central line insertion using synthetic tissue or animal tissue. Timing the simulation or adding a metronome adds to the intraoperative experience of pressure to move faster and more accurately.

Evidence suggests that skill improvements achieved during medium-fidelity simulation transfer to the operating room. A randomized control trial of 18 surgical residents at 2 academic institutions in Toronto compared performance of residents who practiced fascial closure on a synthetic model once

Figure 1. Pegboard minimally invasive surgery simulator

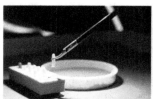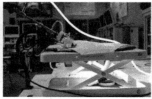

Figure 2. Elective skills curriculum

Elective Skills

Name: (Please Print)   Date:

Please enter your time for each skill attempt

#	Skills	Performance Standard		Time	Time	Time	Time	Time	Time	Time	Time	Time	Time	Time	Time	Time	Time
1	Cannulation	40 seconds each way	Dominant														
			Nondominant														
2	Peg Board	4 minutes for each part	Dominant														
			Nondominant														
3	Peg Pass	4 minutes for each part	Dominant														
			Nondominant														
4	Rope Pass	2 minutes each way	to R														
			to L														
5	Curve of the Needle	6 passes in 4 minutes															
6	Appropriate Bite	Completion in 4 minutes															
7	Suturing	4 stitches in 10 minutes															
8	Circle of Fire	Circuit both ways in 4 minutes															
9	Enclosed Suturing	4 stitches in 8 min															
10	30 degree scope drill	5 targets in 70 seconds															
11	Pegboard Level 2	10 pegs in 4 minutes	Dominant														
			Nondominant														
12	Reverse Camera	5 pegs in 10 minutes															
13	Cutting & Extraction	4 minutes & no errors															

(control group) to those who practiced on the model until technical proficiency was achieved (intervention group). Residents randomized to the intervention group had better technical performance in the operating room and better cognitive retention than their peers who did not train on the synthetic model (Palter, Grantcharov, Harvey, & Macrae, 2011).

Medium fidelity simulators can be progressively costly, but alternatives to commercial products can be engineered cheaply. The CATS lab at The University of Kentucky uses an in- house recipe to make artificial skin using readily available ingredients. Likewise, Hauglum et. al used chicken breasts purchased at a grocery store to create a model for ultrasound guided central line catheter insertion. The total cost for each animal was $15.66 versus $1,500-$27,000 commercial models (Hauglum, Crenshaw, Gattamorta, & Mitzova-Vladinov, 2018). Likewise, several 5-10 minute do it yourself videos are freely available on YouTube. Examples include Harvard's Center for Medical Simulation "Mad Simulationist's Lab" series intended to teach institutions how to make models such as bleeding wounds, retroperitoneal hemorrhages, chest skin with utricaria, and more. Other student resource videos demonstrate how to make simplified models of a variety of simulators including artificial skin https://youtu.be/645i6tO_An4 and artificial vessels https://youtu.be/hXYUo3-qh5I.

HIGH FIDELITY SIMULATION

High fidelity simulates a clinical scenario and correct anatomy in a realistic manner. High fidelity simulation can be computer driven simulations in which live perfusionists and anesthesiologists generate clinical scenarios that are complex, and the student must decide how to proceed. In these simulations, the anatomy is realistic, and the student is faced with making high pressure decisions. Computer programs can generate monitor readings, vital signs, laboratory values and abnormal physiology typical of a clinical scenario. Algorithms can be programed to respond in a physiologically predictable manner to reveal better or worse choices. Surprise findings or responses can also be created that increase stress levels and uncertainly, similar to real clinical situations. Actors, avatars, or holograms can substitute for real clinicians in some situations. Likewise, cadavers, prosections or manikins can be used for specific procedures.

High fidelity simulation was first introduced for basic cardiac life support (BCLS) and advanced cardiac life support (ACLS) training. Specialty, high fidelity simulation was popularized for anesthesia with the Comprehensive Anesthesia Simulation Environment (CASE) manikins developed to train and assess physician skill in anesthesia management and critical care. Manikins have since evolved to wireless, physiologically precise simulators that can react to treatment, give birth, and act as surgical patients (Maran & Glavin, 2003). Manikins are mobile and can be taken to the operating room for enhanced realism and surgery rehearsals (Satava, 2008). Computer driven virtual reality (VR) systems provide realistic, consistent, measurable training scenarios that combine actual instruments with computer generated images of the appropriate anatomy.

VR systems can range widely in sophistication. The simplest form of VR developed in the 1990s consists of a screen and a haptics unit, to stimulate the senses of touch and motion, for insertion of catheters, wires, balloons, and stents (Van Herzeele et al., 2008). VR systems can create a three-dimensional virtual world based on the multiplayer videogame experience. The most sophisticated VR simulators are immersive with head mounted displays or cave automatic virtual environments (CAVE) to place the trainee completely in a simulated world, much like the famous holodeck of Star Trek. These VR simulators are used to expose an individual to the emergency department, operating room, and disaster response training. Although the simulation experience may be very high fidelity, the stakes are low, thus allowing detailed review or repeated practice. Likewise, neither patients nor animals are harmed. There are over 50 institutions providing formal simulation training in the United States including the well-known Center for Medical Simulation in Boston, Massachusetts, where trainees from all over the country assemble in an operating room and work through simulated VR cases with manikins. The SIMPeds program at Boston Children's hospital uses patient specific imaging data to make three-dimensional replicas to rehearse a surgical procedure. This strategy is especially useful for high-stakes, low-volume procedures such as surgical treatment of hydrocephalus or complex congenital heart surgery.

Vascular surgery was also an early adopter of VR simulators and simulation remains an important component of training required by the Food and Drug Administration before granting privileges to perform procedures. VR and surgical rehearsal are likewise used across surgical disciplines. The validated EyeSi VR simulator replicates the operating room set-up for intraocular surgery complete with model head and surgical scenarios that vary in difficulty (Staropoli et al., 2018). A retrospective review of 17,831 cataract surgeries performed by 265 first- and second-year surgery residents reported in the Royal College of Ophthalmologists' National Ophthalmology Database showed a 38% reduction in complication rates corresponding to the introduction of the virtual reality (VR) simulator EyeSi (Ferris et al., 2019). Likewise, a single center review of 955 3rd year surgical residents found EyeSi simulator trained residents had a statistically significant reduction in complications compared to simulator naïve residents (Staropoli et al., 2018).

Introducing simulation early in the medical school curriculum carries associated costs, risks, and benefits. The cost of low fidelity simulation-based training is limited to the cost of supplies and space overhead and time, whereas high fidelity simulation centers found in major academic centers cost millions of dollars to purchase and staff. The benefits of simulation-based training are less time in the OR, fewer complications, less risk to patients, and enhanced skills and efficiencies (Asche et al., 2018). The risk of introducing simulation-based learning is failure to achieve competency. Some students may find this discouraging and avoid procedure-based specialties either due to lack of skills or lack of adequate training (Gillan et al., 2016). While simulation-based techniques are shown to transfer to the operating room, additional research is needed to establish best practices in simulation-based training (Stefanidis et al., 2015).

SIMULATION BASED TRAINING AS A FIRST-YEAR MEDICAL STUDENT

I (VB) began trying to learn square knots during the first month of medical school. I went to the CATS lab and received video instruction and suture. After months of daily 1-hour practice sessions, I advanced through other skills such as one-handed knot tying, and horizontal mattress suture placement while concurrently learning laparoscopic basics starting with peg-board skills and moving through suturing. This anecdote serves to emphasize the importance of learning basic skills early, so that time required for acquisition of basic skills isn't required during third and fourth year and even residency. Basic surgical skills should become muscle memory by the time a student or resident needs to be learning about intraoperative decision making.

I have performed weekly as first assistant to a resident during medium fidelity simulation of vascular graft anastomosis. Listening to his instruction as well as observing what I need to do to help the resident, has exposed me to the type of thinking that goes into managing the flow of operative procedure. I am able to get a feel for the need to strengthen my non-dominant hand before I need it in the operating room. I have started to use my left hand in my daily routine for personal hygiene (such as brushing my teeth and combing my hair), chopping vegetables, and controlling the computer mouse. Until recently, my non-dominant hand was never required to perform complex technical tasks. My personal observation is that even in simulation scenarios, males exhibit more confidence than females, even regarding such basic skills as knot tying. This impression aligns with finding of Meyerson, Sternbach, Zwischenberger, & Bender (2017) who reported that at the beginning of surgical residency male residents are relatively overconfident and women are relatively underconfident. These findings beg for an observational study using the Zwisch and SIMPL scales in simulation-based training, beginning early in medical school.

I also regularly participate in the monthly cardio-thoracic surgery wet-labs hosted by the CATS lab where I am able to practice medium fidelity exercises using ex-vivo animal models. The faculty has been receptive and encouraging, providing community and motivating me to continually practice.

Funding Statement: This research received no specific grant from any funding agency in the public, commercial, or not-for-profit sectors.

REFERENCES

Asche, C. V., Kim, M., Brown, A., Golden, A., Laack, T. A., Rosario, J., ... Okuda, Y. (2018). Communicating Value in Simulation: Cost-Benefit Analysis and Return on Investment. *Academic Emergency Medicine*, 25(2), 230–237. doi:10.1111/acem.13327 PMID:28965366

Bell, R. H. Jr. (2009). Why Johnny cannot operate. *Surgery.*, *146*(4), 533–542. doi:10.1016/j. surg.2009.06.044 PMID:19789010

Coleman, J. J., Esposito, T. J., Rozycki, G. S., & Feliciano, D. V. (2013). Early subspecialization and perceived competence in surgical training: Are residents ready? *Journal of the American College of Surgeons*, *216*(4), 764–771. doi:10.1016/j.jamcollsurg.2012.12.045 PMID:23521960

de Montbrun, S. L., & Macrae, H. (2012). Simulation in surgical education. *Clinics in Colon and Rectal Surgery*, *25*(3), 156–165. doi:10.1055-0032-1322553 PMID:23997671

Ferris, J. D., Donachie, P. H., Johnston, R. L., Barnes, B., Olaitan, M., & Sparrow, J. M. (2019). Royal College of Ophthalmologists' National Ophthalmology Database study of cataract surgery: Report 6. The impact of EyeSi virtual reality training on complications rates of cataract surgery performed by first- and second-year trainees. *The British Journal of Ophthalmology*, bjophthalmol-2018-313817; Epub ahead of print. doi:10.1136/bjophthalmol-2018-313817 PMID:31142463

George, B. C., Bohnen, J. D., Williams, R. G., Meyerson, S. L., Schuller, M. C., Clark, M. J., ... Fryer, J. P. (2017). Readiness of US General Surgery Residents for Independent Practice. *Annals of Surgery*, *266*(4), 582–594. doi:10.1097/SLA.0000000000002414 PMID:28742711

George, B. C., Teitelbaum, E. N., Meyerson, S. L., Schuller, M. C., DaRosa, D. A., Petrusa, E. R., ... Fryer, J. P. (2014). Reliability, validity, and feasibility of the Zwisch scale for the assessment of intraoperative performance. *Journal of Surgical Education*, *71*(6), e90–e96. doi:10.1016/j.jsurg.2014.06.018 PMID:25192794

Gillan, S. N., Okhravi, N., O'Sullivan, F., Sullivan, P., Viswanathan, A., & Saleh, G. M. (2016). Influence of medical student career aims on ophthalmic surgical simulator performance (part of the international forum for ophthalmic simulation studies). *The British Journal of Ophthalmology*, *100*(3), 411–414. doi:10.1136/bjophthalmol-2015-307127 PMID:26246344

Grant, S. B., Dixon, J. L., Glass, N. E., & Sakran, J. V. (2013). Early surgical subspecialization: A new paradigm? Part I. *Bulletin of the American College of Surgeons*, *98*(8), 38–42. PMID:24205574

Hauglum, S. D., Crenshaw, N. A., Gattamorta, K. A., & Mitzova-Vladinov, G. (2018). Evaluation of a low-cost, high-fidelity animal model to train graduate advanced practice nursing students in the performance of ultrasound-guided central line catheter insertion. *Simulation in Healthcare*, *13*(5), 341–347. doi:10.1097/SIH.0000000000000337 PMID:30286028

Hochberg, M. S., Billig, J., Berman, R. S., Kalet, A. L., Zabar, S. R., Fox, J. R., & Pachter, H. L. (2014). When surgeons decide to become surgeons: New opportunities for surgical education. *American Journal of Surgery*, *207*(2), 194–200. doi:10.1016/j.amjsurg.2013.10.010 PMID:24468025

Hutter, M. M., Kellogg, K. C., Ferguson, C. M., Abbott, W. M., & Warshaw, A. L. (2006). The impact of the 80-hour resident workweek on surgical residents and attending surgeons. *Annals of Surgery*, *243*(6), 864–875. doi:10.1097/01.sla.0000220042.48310.66 PMID:16772790

Jax, M. (2019). *Center for Advanced Training and Simulation (CATS)*. Retrieved from https://surgery.med.uky.edu/surgery-center-advanced-training-and-simulation-cats

Kamine, T. H., Gondek, S., & Kent, T. S. (2014). Decrease in junior resident case volume after 2011 ACGME work hours. *Journal of Surgical Education*, *71*(6), e59–e63. doi:10.1016/j.jsurg.2014.07.001 PMID:25241704

Maran, N. J., & Glavin, R. J. (2003). Low- to high-fidelity simulation - a continuum of medical education? *Medical Education, 37*(s1Suppl 1), 22–28. doi:10.1046/j.1365-2923.37.s1.9.x PMID:14641635

Mattar, S. G., Alseidi, A. A., Jones, D. B., Jeyarajah, D. R., Swanstrom, L. L., Aye, R. W., ... Minter, R. M. (2013). General surgery residency inadequately prepares trainees for fellowship: Results of a survey of fellowship program directors. *Annals of Surgery, 258*(3), 440–449. doi:10.1097/SLA.0b013e3182a191ca PMID:24022436

Meyerson, S. L., Sternbach, J. M., Zwischenberger, J. B., & Bender, E. M. (2017). The effect of gender on resident autonomy in the operating room. *Journal of Surgical Education, 74*(6), e111–e118. doi:10.1016/j.jsurg.2017.06.014 PMID:28669788

Neylan, C. J., Nelson, E. F., Dumon, K. R., Morris, J. B., Williams, N. N., Dempsey, D. T., ... Allen, S. R. (2017). Medical School Surgical Boot Camps: A Systematic Review. *Journal of Surgical Education, 74*(3), 384–389. doi:10.1016/j.jsurg.2016.10.014 PMID:27939818

Palter, V. N., Grantcharov, T., Harvey, A., & Macrae, H. M. (2011). Ex vivo technical skills training transfers to the operating room and enhances cognitive learning: A randomized controlled trial. *Annals of Surgery, 253*(5), 886–889. doi:10.1097/SLA.0b013e31821263ec PMID:21394017

Philibert, I., Friedmann, P., & Williams, W. T.ACGME Work Group on Resident Duty Hours. (2002). Accreditation Council for Graduate Medical Education. New requirements for resident duty hours. *Journal of the American Medical Association, 288*(9), 1112–1114. doi:10.1001/jama.288.9.1112 PMID:12204081

Polavarapu, H. V., Kulaylat, A. N., Sun, S., & Hamed, O. H. (2013). 100 years of surgical education: The past, present, and future. *Bulletin of the American College of Surgeons, 98*(7), 22–27. PMID:24010218

Preece, R., Dickinson, E. C., Sherif, M., Ibrahim, Y., Ninan, A. S., Aildasani, L., ... Smith, P. (2015). Peer-assisted teaching of basic surgical skills. *Medical Education Online, 20*(1), 27579. doi:10.3402/meo.v20.27579 PMID:26044400

Satava, R. M. (2008). Historical review of surgical simulation--a personal perspective. *World Journal of Surgery, 32*(2), 141–148. doi:10.100700268-007-9374-y PMID:18097716

Staropoli, P. C., Gregori, N. Z., Junk, A. K., Galor, A., Goldhardt, R., Goldhagen, B. E., ... Feuer, W. (2018). Surgical Simulation Training Reduces Intraoperative Cataract Surgery Complications Among Residents. *Simulation in Healthcare, 13*(1), 11–15. PMID:29023268

Stefanidis, D., Sevdalis, N., Paige, J., Zevin, B., Aggarwal, R., Grantcharov, T., & Jones, D. B. (2015). Simulation in surgery: What's needed next? *Annals of Surgery, 261*(5), 846–583. doi:10.1097/SLA.0000000000000826 PMID:25243562

Van Herzeele, I., Aggarwal, R., Neequaye, S., Darzi, A., Vermassen, F., & Cheshire, N. J. (2008). Cognitive training improves clinically relevant outcomes during simulated endovascular procedures. *Journal of Vascular Surgery. 48*(5), 1223-30, 1230.e1. doi:. doi:10.1016/j.jvs.2008.06.034

APPENDIX

Modified from Accreditation Council for Graduate Medical Education. Resident Duty Hours in the Learning and Working Environment. http://www.acgme.org/acgmeweb/Portals/0/PDFs/dh-ComparisonTable2003v2011.pdf. Accessed May 10, 2019.

Table 1. Modified from resident duty hours in the learning and working environment

	2003 revision	2011 and 2017 revisions
Maximum hours per week	80 hours per week including at-home call and **international moonlighting**	80 hours per week weeks including at-home call and **all moonlighting**
Maximum work period	Continuous clinical work period cannot exceed 24 hours including call, but an additional **6 hours** may be granted for patient safety, education, and effective transitions	Continuous clinical work period cannot exceed 24 hours including call, but an additional **4 hours** may be granted for patient safety, education, and effective transitions
Call	In-house call cannot exceed once every 3rd night Time spent in hospital during at-home call is counted toward 80 hours	In-house call cannot exceed once every 3rd night Time spent in hospital during at-home call is counted toward 80 hours
Mandatory free time	1 day off in a 7-day period including call and should have a 10-hour free period between shifts	1 day off in a 7-day period including call and should have a 10-hour free period between shifts (**mandatory 8 hours free**) with **14 hours free after a 24-hour shift**
Exceptions	A review committee may grant a program's request to increase hours to a maximum of 88 hours per week (10%)	A review committee may grant a program's request to increase hours to a maximum of 88 hours per week (10%)

Table 2. Comparison of low, medium, and high-fidelity simulation

Simulation Level	Simulators	Anatomy Representation	Cost	Example
Low fidelity	Knot tying, Basic needle and sewing techniques, Laparoscopic peg boards	Illustrations, line-drawings, photos	low	knot tying
Medium fidelity	Artificial skin, Synthetic model aorta, Animal model (ex vivo or live)	3-dimensional color-coded models	Low-medium	artificial skin
High fidelity	Animal or human cadaver, Team manikin procedures, Virtual reality, Avatar systems	Videos, Computer modeling, Virtual reality, Avatars	Medium-high	animal heart

Section 6
Student Voices

460

Chapter 24
You're a Med Student, so Now What?

Briana Christophers
https://orcid.org/0000-0001-5248-069X
Weill Cornell Medicine, USA

ABSTRACT

This reflection chapter is from the perspective of the first-year medical student: teetering the line between the naïveté of embarking into an ambiguous future and the wisdom developing in the midst of self discovery. From the early moments of dissecting in the anatomy lab to making decisions about which content to study further during spare time, the first year of medical school sets the stage for collecting signs and symptoms into a diagnosis and a plan. This lens extends into steps for self-reflection: outline values and current needs (akin to taking your own history); reflect on interests and skills (identifying signs); consider the roles of a physician in society (coming up with a differential for who you might become); identify opportunities for the future (crafting an action plan); seek out connections with other students, trainees, and physicians (assembling a team). In this way, students can be encouraged to take a moment to center themselves in the way they will for the patients under their care to make sense of it all.

The cadaver donors for medical school anatomy courses are often described as the medical student's "first patient," since, as students, we spend countless hours learning deeply (both figuratively and literally) from them about the human body. It is a rite of passage to go through dissecting the body while in turn assembling a personal mental map from these parts, appreciating commonalities and recognizing variations.

Medical school teaches you to start thinking in pieces: it is necessary to break complex physiologic processes and diseases into the details to understand fully, as we do during anatomy dissection. As a first-year student I found it inevitable to start applying this way of thinking to the rest of my life; each experience seems like a symptom of the bigger picture of what comes next. Starting medical school is a point of transition where we are opened up to a range of possibilities as physicians-in-training, which is different than other decisions we have had to make before. Students are thrust into an environment of innumerable opportunities and constantly changing information where there is no set roadmap for

DOI: 10.4018/978-1-7998-1468-9.ch024

the future. Applying the skills that we learn within the first few months of medical school to our own experiences can be used as a coping strategy where we dissect ourselves down while remaining whole through and after the process.

It can be tempting as a first-year student to get swept up in the novelty of the experience, the anxious energy of classmates, and the internal pressure to perform well. Amongst the endless content with which we are presented—flashcards, lecture slides, reference values, gene names, drug names and mechanisms—students may forget to take a step back, reflect and self-direct their learning. Preserving one's sense of authenticity can be challenging when faced with the uncertainty of which path to choose while in the current context of many curricular demands. In these first few months I have found myself coming back numerous times to my own personal mission, both as a future physician and a person. This reflective process has become crucial when I find myself getting lost in the minutiae, wondering how gene names and staging criteria fits into a future that is in so many ways uncertain. It has been comforting to recognize that the skills that we are gaining to serve our future patients—question, examine, and make a plan—are not separate from how we can approach our own lives.

It is critical for first year students to be encouraged to find time to reflect (and be given dedicated time for reflection) because it allows us to actively integrate being future physicians into our definition of self as we are getting more clarity about what this path entails. By having time to create a framework against which to compare and adapt, students are building a personal process of self-reflection that will mature throughout their training. Considering practicalities, first year of medical school is when students have the most unstructured time and are not constantly undergoing the emotionally- and physically-taxing work that is expected of them during clerkship training and beyond. It has been empowering to spend time this year to take a moment and center myself in the way that we are taught to methodically examine our patients.

My own strategy for self-reflection during this year has gone as follows:

Step 1:   Taking your own history

When we interview our patients, we start with the chief complaint or reason for visit. What do you want to consider at this moment? What matters right now? This reason is short and specific to what you are trying to figure out at this point in your life. Perhaps it is figuring out a research direction or project, narrowing down a list of specialties of interest, identifying new mentors for the direction on which you have settled. The information gathered during a history comes directly from the patient, and so, in this way, the information you gather during your own "history" will be very personal and may be things only you know about yourself.

Then we move onto the history of the present illness: symptoms of the current or recent moment. Notice what you have been feeling lately about your "chief complaint." Have you had any experiences that change how you have been feeling about your future? Write out your thoughts by starting a mind-map or journaling about a recent encounter.

The social history is an opportunity to think about how your lifestyle impacts what you do today and tomorrow. What are the things, moments or people you need around you in order to remain not only happy but also satisfied with how you spend your time? Consider where you hope to be, what continuing your education looks like, and how you will be spending the hours in the day.

The review of systems reminds us to take inventory of component parts to get a broader picture. Identify your own "systems:" the various roles you have in your life that fulfill you. How do you fit these into the present moment and the future? Do some of them relate to what you hope to do in your career? Some of my roles are scientist, advocate, photographer, mentor, which helps me choose opportunities and direct my learning accordingly. Some remain part of my personal interests while others are very much key to what I hope to pursue in the future. These roles evolve at each step but keep us connected to where we fit within communities and what our values are.

Step 2:   Identifying the signs

On a physical exam we look more closely at the outward-facing signs of why the patients are presenting to us in this way. Similarly, we can take a look at how we are changing throughout medical school. We can take a look at our interests and skills as manifestations of what we are able to do, what we have to contribute, and where we can grow. These can be important factors in our point of view and how we like to approach situations. Identify how you enjoy spending your time in medical school: is it thinking through the details of lab values and other test results? Or working on perfecting your techniques during hands-on activities like suturing or anatomy dissection or ultrasound?

These qualities may not only be identifiable by you, so ask the people you trust—friends, family, mentors—about what they would describe as your skills or interests from their perspective.

Step 3:   Differential diagnosis for who you are and who you might become

There is a broad range of possibilities for physicians throughout their careers, within clinical practice and beyond. Throughout our training we have to continue making choices about the kind of clinicians we want to become, often becoming more and more specialized as years go on based on what we have identified for ourselves in the steps mentioned above. For example, someone interested in pediatrics, may eventually discover that pediatric cardiology contains the cases that they would like to see in their careers. They may go on to become an expert in managing the cases of children with valve pathologies, even doing research on the best strategies for management as their patients become adolescents.

Physicians also play many other roles in society, including research, development of new translational applications, hospital administration, public or community health initiatives, health justice and advocacy work, and health policy at many levels. In the clinic we use the notes that we have assembled during our history-taking and physical exam to narrow down what seem to be the appropriate options to undertake. Similarly, the "diagnoses" we come up with for our own future can remain general categories of interest and then we can continue changing the primary list as we continue along our path.

Step 4:   Assessment

This is the step where we bring it all together, threading past, present, and possible future. Transition from thinking about recent events to how they might relate to your past, similar to a past medical history. Can you identify any trends in your life so far? How has your past shaped who you are, and what does this mean for your future? Think through how you have done things in the past since it may play into whether you would like to do things similarly or differently moving forward.

I have found it helpful to take a moment to draft a concrete summary into a sort of personal mission statement. Personal mission statements give an overall sense of what it is that makes you who you are and therefore provide a guiding framework to weigh future choices against each other as it reminds you of what your priorities and values are. The statement can be as expansive or as granular as you decide it to be, as long as you recognize that it will change but this is what you have recognized in the moment as your truth.

Step 5:   Crafting an action plan

In medical care the action plan pinpoints the crucial next steps for a patient's care, be it more tests or imaging, prescribing a new medication, or discharge with follow-up for a certain period of time. The action plan determines the direction that you will take next given the personal mission statement and differential diagnosis that you have determined for yourself. Go out and identify opportunities within or outside your institution that will help you grow in the areas that are of interest to you. In this way, you will explore new knowledge or skills with a concrete goal in line with your vision. Conferences, clubs, and activities can all be sources of opportunity for you to get involved. Get creative and combine skills and interests in a way that you had not considered before, so that you can create something that only you can. Remember to schedule in follow-ups for yourself and monitor how you are changing and adapt accordingly in the same way you would check in with a patient in your care.

Step 6:   Assembling a team

Connections to others keep you moving in a direction that is consistent with what you have come up with in your assessment and plan. Your team can include peers, mentors (both old and new), and colleagues. Work with peers who have similar interests to find ways to get involved together. Find and reconnect with mentors who might help you see new directions that you did not know were possible, but make sure they are clear on your goals and values. Touch base with your family and friends outside of medical school to keep them updated about your growth and also to keep yourself grounded in who you are. Some of these folks will be there with you every step of the way, while others you will consult as needed in the same way you do in a medical case. Seek out new teammates to get you to the points that you outlined in your action plan. These people are your sounding board and launching pad, so choose them wisely and ask for help.

As we dive into an ocean of endless information, many times with little guidance, the first year of medical school can feel daunting and exciting. Taking the time as a first year to go through a process of self-discovery—and being advised to do so by mentors and teachers—helps in developing a compass that makes navigating next steps more intentional. You begin to define your own metrics, which keep you grounded during a time when you are being taught to become a generalist but will ultimately have to choose something in which to become an expert. I definitely do not have all the answers, but regularly checking in with myself and defining my own expectations is helping me create my own personal map of who I am and who I am becoming. My own reflections on this year have emphasized that taking the time to develop a consistent practice of not only self-reflection but also self-care has improved my satisfaction in my training, and I hope that the medical education community will create more opportunities for students to reflect.

Chapter 25
My Mentors in Medicine

Anthony J. Finch
Weill Cornell Medicine, USA

ABSTRACT

The author describes his journey of learning in medicine from childhood through graduation from medical school. The author describes how each of his mentors played a specific role at crucial points in his development. His parents and a high school professor inspired him to pursue medicine as a career. Academic, clinical, and research mentors assisted in the author's preparation for medical school. Finally, medical school faculty and staff at Weill Cornell Medicine enriched his medical school experience, guided his choice of psychiatry as a specialty, and encouraged him to think about the structure of his future career. The author gratefully emphasizes the importance of all of his mentors' efforts and resolves to serve a similar mentorship role for the next generation of physicians.

INTRODUCTION

The path one takes on his or her journey towards becoming a physician can be as beautifully complex as is the field of medicine itself. One must first develop an interest in the field, then cultivate the necessary skills, perspective, and work ethic to prepare for medical school, and then, finally, make informed decisions regarding specialty selection and clinical focus. Mentors play key roles in guiding the individual along the way. This chapter demonstrates the importance of mentors in the life of one recent medical school graduate as told in his own words.

MAIN FOCUS OF THE CHAPTER

Last week, countless days and nights of hard work and studying culminated in my graduation from medical school. My commencement ceremony was a joyous occasion, the implications of which I have still not been able to fully wrap my mind around. I have completed a journey I set out on almost 30 years ago, and now stand on the precipice of yet another, longer journey, which will be completed only when my life's work as a physician has concluded. This moment is fitting to reflect on my path and to appreciate

DOI: 10.4018/978-1-7998-1468-9.ch025

the roles of all of the individuals who have served as mentors and guided me towards my destiny. These supporters have been family members, educators, clinicians, and researchers; they have been diverse in every imaginable way. However, each has played his or her own role in my story, and each has earned my deepest gratitude. I hope through this text to do them justice and to demonstrate for the reader how many different kinds of mentors are necessary in the development of a physician.

My fascination with medicine stretches back as far as I can remember. My mother is a physician, so I grew up around the hospital amazed by all the people in white coats who knew unimaginable things about the human body, science, and the world. Medicine permeated all aspects of my life from an early age: my favorite movies, television shows, and books as a child were all related in some way to medicine; my favorite classes in school were the science classes that taught me about how the body worked; my conversations with friends and family regularly revolved around some element of human physiology about which I had just learned and was curious.

My parents became my first mentors as they nurtured my budding curiosity and encouraged me to dream of one day becoming a doctor too. My mother taught me about the sacrifice and the fulfillment that those in the medical field experience. I remember her always coming to kiss my forehead good morning when I was a young child as she would leave the apartment at what was, at the time, an unthinkably early hour of the day. She would then come home in the evening tired but beaming and overflowing with stories, both joyous and sorrowful, from an eventful day at the hospital. "If I'm going to be tired, I'm going to be tired doing something worthwhile, helping those in need" I remember her saying. Through her example and encouragement, she pushed me to reach for my potential and to do so in the service of others. My father, a middle school teacher, drove this message home through countless hours spent helping me to improve my mind and to develop a strong set of service-oriented values. Every day he would supplement my schoolwork with a few extra assignments of his own – these ranged from extra math problems to reading passages and writing essays. The extra work never grew to be overwhelming and he always made it clear to me that I was loved and respected by him regardless of what I achieved. However, he frequently referenced duty and honor and instilled in me from the start a powerful motivation to be the best I could be and to cultivate and earn the gifts I have been given. True to form, he encouraged me to become involved in various service initiatives in and around my community, including many at our local church. He often said "the self is too small an object to interest a wise person for very long," and in so doing reminded me that the intellect he was helping me develop was neither solely nor primarily for my benefit – it was rather ultimately a mechanism to make the world around me a better place. My parents instilled in me a drive to learn, a motivation to grow, and a commitment to service from a very young age; in so doing, these two exemplary mentors first set me on my path towards medicine.

In high school I found another mentor in my freshman biology teacher—a man who poured his passion for his field into his teaching. He and I developed a close relationship, and it was in his class one day, during a lecture on skeletal anatomy, that I first determined irrevocably that I would become a physician. I found myself fascinated by the way he explained the body as a machine – intricate and beautiful – which somehow gives rise to human consciousness and experience. His love for his subject was inspiring, and he was always there for me, before school, between classes, and after school, to discuss the subject matter and nurture my interest. His impact on me was so formative that I would, one day, invite him to my medical school graduation. In the context of such amazing mentorship both at home and at school, my love of medicine developed, and I slowly began to understand the true nobility underpinning this field. Here, the brightest scientific knowledge is applied to address the darkest human pain. Here, people endeavor daily to lift up humanity in a compelling pursuit of knowledge and a fulfilling service to the suffering. As I watched, my fascination with medicine blossomed into a passion. During my undergraduate college years, this passion was further fueled by a new group of mentors. In school, I completed three separate biology classes with one professor who made it his stated mission to prepare his students for medical school. His classes were extremely challenging, and he pushed us sometimes harder than seemed reasonable. However, he was fair in his grading and was always willing to give extra help when needed. Through him I received my first glimpse of what the academic crucible of medical school might look like. His preparation and guidance were truly invaluable; later, in medical school, I often found myself revisiting my notes from his class to clarify a confusing concept.

Outside of school, I spent significant time volunteering in the Emergency Department at New York Methodist Hospital and performing laboratory research at Hospital for Special Surgery (HSS). The Emergency Department staff at Methodist became my first clinical mentors as they opened my eyes to the magnitude of the opportunity physicians have to serve others. I watched as my clinical preceptors worked to save lives, preserve futures, and keep families united right before my eyes, and my motivation to do the same grew. Simultaneously, my primary investigator at HSS introduced me to a different, but just as important, brand of service: in the laboratory, I found myself working to advance science and enhance the care of future generations. I was privileged to work with an experienced biomedical engineer who taught me the basics of laboratory research and fueled my fascination with the scientific pursuit. He mentored me in the design and execution of basic scientific research, the consolidation of findings, and the structure and logistics of manuscript submission to peer-reviewed journals. As a result of these experiences and strong mentorship in both environments, I knew even before I started medical school that I wanted to have both a clinical and a research dimension to my career.

When I entered medical school at Weill Cornell, I found, unsurprisingly, that I was captivated by every subject module and every clinical rotation I experienced: I found exploring all aspects of medical science elegant and applying knowledge in the service of humanity beautiful. Weill Cornell maximized my experience that first year by surrounding me with first-class mentors right from the start who welcomed me into the field of medicine and supported me as I began my journey. My didactic professors guided me in the development of a strong basic scientific foundation through clear, comprehensive lectures and small group sessions. My clinical preceptors introduced me to the art of clinical medicine by welcoming me into their schedules and skillfully giving me just enough responsibility to feel a little uncomfortable but never overwhelmed. The summer after that first year, I became involved in research by working to lay the foundation for my Area of Concentration (AOC) project. All students at Cornell complete six months of dedicated research time in third and fourth year through the AOC program, and I wanted to take full advantage of this opportunity by getting started early. At that point I had not yet decided on a medical specialty, but I followed my passion by seeking out research that would benefit underserved medical populations within the United States. I learned about the work Dr. Monika Safford's team was doing with rural, poor, chronically hypertensive African Americans in a part of southeastern United States known as the "Black Belt" (for the dark color of its rich soil) in a project named The Southeastern Collaboration to Improve Blood Pressure Control—or the SEC—and I reached out.

Dr. Safford was incredibly warm and welcoming right from the start. That first summer she encouraged me to become involved with content development for her web-based information portal, which aimed to enhance medical literacy in the Black Belt. She gave me the autonomy to collaborate with experts in the field of hypertension to modify a blood pressure management algorithm based upon my own research. She also created an opportunity for me to go down to Alabama that first summer to work firsthand in a medical clinic at the University of Alabama at Birmingham and to visit the homes of participants in her study throughout the region. This experience was transformative—I found it was one thing to read about underserved populations and another thing entirely to actually witness their struggle firsthand. Almost all of the patients I visited in Alabama lived in rural areas with minimal access to the basic necessities of life, and a majority lived over an hour's drive from the nearest hospital. I recall one patient in particular—a middle-aged man suffering from uncontrolled hypertension—who lived in a collapsing house with fire ants crawling up the walls. Also on those walls, right next to the fire ants, were his medal collection, which included the Silver Star and the Purple Heart he had been awarded in Vietnam 50 years ago. I left that day sickened at how the very society he had fought to defend had abandoned him and so many others like him. It became clear to me that something had to change, and I owe this perspective to Dr. Safford. By allowing me to work directly with her study participants on the ground in Alabama, she went above and beyond in her role as a mentor. Instead of confining herself to the typical mentorship responsibilities requested of AOC mentors (namely guiding students on research design and implementation—an area in which she also offered exemplary, comprehensive guidance), she found a way to teach me more about the world around me and the realities of the medical landscape physicians must contend with in the 21st century. In this way, her mentorship became truly priceless.

Third year (the clerkship year) of medical school was transformative for me in that I was offered the opportunity to engage with countless clinicians in their environments and to experience a small piece of each environment for myself. As I began, I resolved to maintain an open mind and experience each specialty clerkship for what it was, with no preconceived notions or biases. As I carried this mindset, every attending physician and resident with whom I worked became a mentor each in his or her own way, introducing me to and educating me on the specifics of each medical specialty. During my psychiatry clerkship, I developed an especially deep fascination and respect for a field I found at once beautiful, vital, intricate, and mystifying. In the hands of the psychiatric staff at Weill Cornell, my passion for psychiatry blossomed in much the same way my passion for medicine had years earlier: here I found an exciting field which offered an unparalleled opportunity to serve, as well as a uniquely compelling academic quest. Nothing in the human experience, I decided, was more fascinating—and more relevant to every person at every stage of his or her life—than the complexity of the human mind. As this interest grew, so did my already strong commitment to the Black Belt population. I realized that all of the challenges facing this group in terms of acquiring medical care were amplified in the mental health arena. I began to understand that everywhere in the healthcare system where there is stratification of access to healthcare, there is even more pronounced stratification of access to *mental* healthcare. With this in mind I approached Dr. Safford about the possibility of modifying my AOC project to study the same population but to focus primarily on mental health. She expressed her commitment to helping me succeed, and she guided me as I redefined the parameters of my project to evaluate depressive symptoms as a potential factor in the poor cardiovascular outcomes that define healthcare in the Black Belt. This modification required a few iterations; however, Dr. Safford and the wonderful team she surrounded me with were vital guides every step of the way. We ultimately completed a profoundly rewarding and academically fascinating project describing the interplay of mental health, social functioning, and cardiovascular outcomes in the Black Belt. I am now preparing this manuscript for publication and considering future avenues for research based upon additional questions this study uncovered. All of this was possible because Dr. Safford provided me with the perfect balance of direction and autonomy and was always willing to apply her impressive understanding of medicine, research design, and study implementation to guide me through every stage of the research process.

I have now graduated from medical school and ensured that medicine will be my future, just as it has defined my past and present. I have found the pursuit of knowledge just as compelling and treatment of the unwell just as fulfilling as I dreamed it would be as a child growing up around the hospital. The incredible mentorship and guidance that has been my privilege to experience on my journey so far, however, has been beyond what I could have dreamed. My parents encouraged me to be curious as a child and to deeply value service; my professors taught me the basic science behind some of medicine's greatest mysteries; my skilled preceptors educated me in the clinical art of medicine; and my outstanding research mentors trained me in a rigorous scientific method that has positioned me to contribute to science for years to come. These inspiring individuals have supported me as I learned about medicine, psychiatry, service, research, the world, and myself. As I stand on the threshold of becoming a practicing physician, it is now a new dream of mine to pay forward the gifts I have been given and to become the most valuable mentor possible to the generation of physicians who will come after me.

CONCLUSION

No medical degree is ever earned without decades of assistance and guidance from mentors of many different backgrounds and specialties. In my case, I have derived immeasurable benefit from my mentors at home, at school, in clinical settings, and in research environments. Each played a role in inspiring me to pursue a career in medicine, helping me achieve that goal, and, ultimately, guiding me in the selection of my specialty. I hope my experience demonstrates that there are many ways to mentor an aspiring physician because young medical professionals need guidance in a broad array of areas. I now look forward to meeting new mentors in my young career and, ultimately, to becoming an effective mentor in medicine myself.

Chapter 26
Training to Be an MD/PhD:
An Exercise in Futility/Humility

Salvatore Aiello
ⓘ https://orcid.org/0000-0002-2324-8768
Rosalind Franklin University of Medicine and Science, USA

ABSTRACT

The most influential assignment of the author's career was the first assignment in his first undergraduate class: take a picture and describe it in a thousand words. From there, the author found a way to spend each semester of college writing about the photo essays by Robert Frank and Brassai, exploring surrealistic works by Jorge Luis Borges and Federico Garcia Lorca, or pursing artistic musings. Given the author's enthusiasm for creative pursuits, his standing as an MD/PhD student may come as a surprise. However, creative courses served as outlets from his medical school prerequisite-heavy course load. The author craved their self-guided and exploratory approach. This craving grew to incorporate an interest in research. What follows is the tortuous route that led the author to join an MD/PhD program.

Fall of Freshman Year – Undergraduate

Mostly chaos.

February of Freshman Year – Undergraduate

Scheduling conflicts land me in a physics discussion section for honors students. I am not an honors student. Our first assignment is to write a one-page review of a scientific article. I have never read a scientific article. I must now share the review with the other members of the discussion section.

How does the assignment go? Imagine being told to make a meal from scratch using instructions from a cookbook. Then imagine you have no understanding of how ingredients and kitchen appliances interact. My review is an inedible mash of scientific jargon.

DOI: 10.4018/978-1-7998-1468-9.ch026

End of Freshman Year – Undergraduate

Despite my previous foray into scientific literature, I'm pre-med so I decide to join a research lab.

Summer After Freshman Year – Undergraduate

I join a lab that uses pig and sheep disease models. The technician that hired me jokingly defines two types of students in the lab: those smart enough to contribute academically to further the study and those strong enough to contribute physically to move the animals. As a 6'2'' corn-fed midwestern boy, I know how I'll be contributing.

Sophomore Year – Undergraduate

Still, mostly chaos.

Sophomore Year – Undergraduate

I am studying abroad in Bilbao, a northern Spanish city. It is commonly referred to as the Pittsburgh of Spain. Early during my studies, I need a haircut. Having to do everything in Spanish, I am terrified I will end up with a sheared head. The experience ends up being as mundane as any haircut. I make an appointment with the stylist. I show up on time the next day and make menial small talk. Navigating foreign territory suddenly seems quite manageable.

Junior Year – Undergraduate

"I think you should consider an alternate career path," Dr. B, my pre-med advisor, says to me as he turns away from the computer screen displaying my less-than-stellar undergraduate transcript. My MCAT and my GPA are not in the realm of a competitive applicant. I want to resent him and feel compelled to say some smug words of defiance to him. Instead, I sigh and resign myself to the hallway. I never visit his office again.

End of Senior Year – Undergraduate

Advising be damned, I am applying to medical school. Senior year has been a good year academically and I feel some momentum. There are some poster presentations and a publication with my name on them, and I think I've got a legitimate shot.

   The lies we tell ourselves to feel better.

Fall Gap Year

That physical contribution in the lab has paid off. I am a full-time tech contributing in academic ways. They still use me to lift the animals onto the table.

Winter of Gap Year

Unsurprisingly, I have not yet been offered an interview. Perhaps a different approach to get into medical school will be necessary.

Spring of Gap Year

The final school updates my status: denied.

I am dizzy with rejection. I want to throw blame around to steady myself, but I need help as I look for a way forward. The lab manager sits me down and says, "More research will not help you. You need to get out of here." There is no option but a new approach.

End of Gap Year

I leave my beloved college town and head home to live with my parents. I enroll in a post-baccalaureate program to demonstrate academic growth and I am guaranteed an interview at their medical school.

Start of Post-Baccalaureate

It turns out that my GPA is low even for this program. They place me on academic probation, which does wonders for my confidence. The classes are taught for medical students, and us Masters students are privileged guests. I have a preemptive case of imposter syndrome.

October of Post-Baccalaureate

There is no room for chaos. Waking up, working out, and studying slides is the extent of my daily activity. With each passing week, it is easier to spend another hour in the library, take another practice exam, or finish another lecture.

Winter of Post-Baccalaureate

I go to my childhood best friend's house for a dinner. Sitting at the table, I complain to his family about the rigors of the program. I mention something about how I am different now after growing up during undergrad. His mom looks at me and says, "You didn't grow up until you started this Masters."

Medical School Interview Day

Taking a tour of the school I currently attend creates a strange power dynamic with the other interviewing students in my group. In one interview, my molecular biology professor sits across the table from me and I crack a joke about one of his exam questions. He does not smile. After the interview, I swap my suit for jeans and a t-shirt then head over to the library.

March of Post-Baccalaureate

There are cheers of excitement in the library and students pacing the halls on their phones. The admissions committee has released their first wave of decisions. I am on the waitlist. The snow outside is gray, my food tastes gray, and I commit to spending more time within the gray walls of the library.

Lecture on Cardiopulmonary Resuscitation (CPR)

I don't expect much because I think the content will include instructions on how to do chest compressions to the pace of stayin' alive or that CPR on TV is not realistic. Instead, the professor focuses most of the lecture on his research. Turns out his research involves cardiac arrest in large animal models. After the lecture I ask him if his lab has any availability and tell him, "If nothing else, I know that I can help get the pig on the table."

He raises one eyebrow and says, "How convenient. I need a pig-guy for a new project."

That may prove to be one of the most pivotal conversations of my life.

April of Post-Baccalaureate

When I am on question five of the reproductive unit problem set, my inbox lights up and there is an e-mail with the subject, "Medical School Admissions Decision."

I stare at the notification with my hand hovering over my mouse. There is initial wave of excitement that is immediately replaced with fear. My friend's voice, unaware and still reading through the answer choices, turns into a numb buzzing. I click on the e-mail.

"Congratulations. We are plea—"

I jump up and tackle my friend off his chair. He tells me to stop over-reacting whenever I get a question wrong. A minute passes before I can properly explain myself.

May of Post-Baccalaureate

I meet with the CPR lecturer for a more formal interview process. Most of the meeting is spent discussing how difficult it is to intubate a pig and ends with my name on the experiment protocol. When talking with my friends, I stop referring to him as "that CPR professor" and switch to "my principal investigator."

End of Post-Baccalaureate

The admissions committee waits until my final grades are entered to finalize the acceptance. My transcript is a healthy split of A's and B's. I am accepted to medical school.

Start of Summer Before Medical School

Work on the large animal model has commenced. There is much to learn and high expectations to meet. The whole experiment should take about six hours. The first experiment day lasts twelve hours. The next day only lasts ten hours. This summer is one of my favorites on record.

End of Summer Before Medical School

In my previous lab, I mostly followed direction from the more senior personnel. I rarely made decisions that required actual thought. Now, armed with knowledge from my single physiology course, I discuss mechanistic effects of the experiment and troubleshoot with confidence. The principal investigator regularly sits with me and we discuss the experiment in the larger context of the field. I tell my friends about cardiac physiology and my research until they draw the line at pressure-volume loops and tell me to stop talking. Experiments fail in frustrating and spectacular ways. The quotes on work ethic in the principal investigator's e-mail signature are occasionally highlighted (he is trying to get across the point that I need to be more detailed oriented). My summer fellowship in the lab ends, but I decide to stay on the project and in the lab. I tell myself that I'll stay for at least the first year of medical school and then reassess next summer.

Beginning of Medical School

I do not have to retake the courses that were covered in the post-baccalaureate program. There is no denying that the incoming first-year medical students are bitter with us former post-baccalaureate students. I don't blame them. We have half as much coursework to do as them. I hope that my tutoring efforts mitigate some of their bitterness. Mostly though, I find myself working in the lab.

Fall of Medical School – Year 1

Every time I meet with the principal investigator, he asks me if I have considered the MD-PhD route. I am still overcoming having been preemptively placed on academic probation for a post-baccalaureate program designed for those with poor grades.

November of Medical School – Year 1

Our school is in a Chicago suburb. I have been a Chicago Cubs fan my whole life. For the first time in over 100 years, the Chicago Cubs win the World Series. The final game is during an exam week. The celebration parade is in the middle of our exam. It is the best of times. It is the worst of times.

December of Medical School – Year 1

Experiments are over. I have been listening to an hour-long podcast during my data-analysis sessions. Episode 48 of the podcast comes and goes. I pause the player and stare at the number 48. I have pressed the same three buttons, in the same seat, at the same computer, for two entire days. Pushing my chair from my desk, I get up and get a drink of water before promptly sitting down. I push play to start another episode and open the next experiment file.

January of Medical School – Year 1

We are in an anatomy practical; a cadaver's pacemaker starts to beep. The echo bounces off the steel tanks. The jaws of the living slacken. We are allowed an extra minute on our exam for "the inconvenience."

February of Medical School – Year 1

Data are analyzed, and manuscript preparation is over. Within a week, we have our first rejection letter.

March of Medical School – Year 1

I must perform a head to toe exam on a standardized patient to fulfill first year requirements. After introducing myself to the patient, I am so nervous that I miss the stool when I try to sit down. Later in the exam, I don't know if the undergarments the patient is wearing are considered underwear or pantyhose, so I ask her to lower the top of "those things." I relay this incident to my female classmate, and she tells me I should just refer to them as "bottoms."

May of Medical School – Year 1

The principal investigator invites me out to a fancy dinner with a guest lecturer that is also an MD-PhD in the cardiac arrest field. I attend his grand rounds presentation the next day. He introduces a clinical case and deconstructs how treatment decisions that saved the patient's life were made based off his lab's bench top and clinical research.

The next time I meet with the principal investigator, he asks me if I have considered the MD-PhD route. I tell him that I have already started the application.

Summer Between Year 1 And 2 Of Medical School

I am one of twenty privileged students selected to shadow at a hospital in Taizhou, China. One of the doctors I shadow has learned his English by watching YouTube and streaming episodes of "How I Met Your Mother." He is a vascular surgeon and describes the different categories of varicose veins to me. Later that day, I look up the textbook definitions of the categories. He had been, from memory, word for word reciting the guidelines.

Week One of China Trip

Our manuscript has been accepted for publication. I cannot submit my signed waivers to claim authorship because the journal site locked me out of their system. My activity from a new computer in China was flagged as suspicious.

Week Two of China Trip

I cannot lie down. I cannot sit down. I am in pain. I am shadowing a doctor and tell him this much. He brings me up to a floor with an empty examination room. Together with another doctor they examine me and speak to each other briefly. They confirm that a reoccurring infection on my lower back is most likely causing the pain. We go out to the pharmacy and they hand me a box. I use Google Translate to read the Chinese characters on the label. The inquiry returns "CAUSTIC AGENT." The doctors reassure me.

End of China Trip

It rains 29 out of the 30 days we are in Taizhou. I am sad when we are leaving because the street food no longer makes me violently ill.

Start of Medical School – Year 2

My life is lived in three-week intervals. On Monday of week 1, a new unit starts. I study until Friday of week 3 and then take an exam. I buy the newest edition of First-Aid and Pathoma, a year-long subscription to SketchyMedical, and noise-cancelling headphones.

October of Medical School – Year 2

My dog dies in the same week that I pay my registration fee for United States Medical Licensing Examination STEP 1.

Winter of Medical School – Year 2

STEP schedules are the topic of everyone's conversation. I find an online service that will provide daily schedules to tell me what subjects to study. Mostly, it tells me what I did not finish from the day before. When I come down with a cold, nobody sits at my table in the library. This is an unexpected perk of having sweater pockets full of tissues.

Graduate School Interview Day

For the second time, I find myself interviewing at a school I already attend. The tour group dynamics are still strange. My biochemistry professor interviews me in his office. I crack a joke about the Post-it note on his monitor that has a Hitchhiker's Guide to the Galaxy reference written on it. He smiles and says, "Okay. I'll give you points for knowing that one." After the interview, I trade out my suit for jeans and t-shirt then head over to the library.

February of Medical School – Year 2

A fourth-year medical student studying for STEP 2 tells me that studying for board exams is, "an exercise in futility."

March of Medical School – Year 2

I am watching Netflix during a lunch break when an e-mail notification pops up on my phone. I pause the show and navigate to my inbox. The e-mail is from the graduate school. I have been accepted into the MD-PhD program. I forward the e-mail to my parents, finish my lunch, and start a new block of practice STEP 1 questions.

Spring of Medical School – Year 2

I am barely passing the practice exams for STEP 1. I open my web browser and search for the average STEP scores of residencies at academic institutions. This is ill-advised. Remnants of the dizziness and rejection from the gap year start to return.

One Week Before USMLE STEP 1

I am pleasantly surprised with my final practice test score. Maybe this exam will not be a train wreck.

The Night Before USMLE STEP 1

I struggle falling asleep. Every time I look at the clock, I calculate how much sleep I can get if I fall asleep at that exact moment. I sleep for two hours.

The Morning of USMLE STEP 1

The Starbucks barista tilts her head and makes a sympathetic face when I step up to the counter. I order a very large coffee. I go to the bathroom to wash my hands and I look in the mirror. My eyes are bloodshot, and tufts of my hair are spiked in different directions.

During USMLE STEP 1

Chaos.

The Night of USMLE STEP 1

I walk out and call my friend who took the exam at the same time. I ask him if he also had a lot of questions about cervical dilation. We hang up and I am grateful to be alone on my drive home.

The Month After USMLE STEP 1

I drive to the Canadian Rocky Mountain Range and live out of a van for 30 days.

July of Medical School – Year 2

I complete paperwork to officially take a leave of absence from the medical school and enter the graduate school.

Start of Graduate School – Year 1

There are four students in my cohort. We are required to attend the all-school orientation. It is my third orientation at this university.

August of Graduate School – Year 1

I start forming my graduate committee. One of the members tells me that getting a PhD is, "an exercise in humility."

September of Graduate School – Year 1

I am living with third-year medical students that have been, until a month ago, my classmates since the post-baccalaureate program. They have interesting patient stories and tales of their own ineptitude in the clinic. I am hit with pangs of regret and envy as I return to my work on a literature review.

October of Graduate School – Year 1

There is plenty of funding in the lab, but I want to continue my previous project—for which there is no funding. A foundation is accepting grant proposals in the project field, but the deadline is rapidly approaching. My principal investigator is calling me at 11 pm to make changes to the application. The deadline is midnight.

Winter of Graduate School – Year 1

At a conference, a presenter says the average age of someone obtaining their first RO1 grant is 42 years old. I do some math and estimate that I've got practically another life to live until I get there. This same person tells us that the age to reach emeritus status, if we should be so lucky, has been raised to 78 years old.

February of Graduate School – Year 1

The polar vortex drops the wind chill in Chicago to $50°$ F below zero. My roommates and I get the week off from school. We play board games for two days straight and order an ice cream cake from Baskin Robbins. The deliveryman asks, "What is wrong with you guys?" It is $40°$ F above zero by the end of the week.

March of Graduate School – Year 1

At a party with my friends from medical school, I describe medical school as analogous to being stuck in a rip tide current. I swim as hard as I can and try to keep my head above water as waves crash on top of me.

I describe graduate school as analogous to being stuck on a raft in the middle of an ocean. I'm paddling at my own pace, but I might be headed in the wrong direction and I won't know for a couple of months. Also, I will later find out I am using the wrong type of paddle.

May of Graduate School – Year 1

I am describing my project to a friend from undergrad. I'm talking so rapidly that I'm stumbling over my words. I apologize for the haphazard delivery and tell him that I am excited about the topic but I don't want to leave anything out. He responds, "I think that is a good sign."

Chapter 27
Finding Meaning and Purpose as a Physician

Tenzing T. Lama
University of Washington, USA

ABSTRACT

Finding meaning in this age of the burnout epidemic has become the latest obsession in clinical medicine. Many choose introspection, mindfulness, or mental health treatments to refuel their moral reserves, but research may also help to serve that goal. In this chapter, the author writes about his journey as an immigrant to the United States at 16, navigating the educational system to eventually attend Oxford and Harvard on full scholarships, and finding meaning through research.

Early in medical school, I heard of residents who left medicine to join McKinsey or Morgan Stanley, respected attendings who left tenured positions for pharmaceutical companies, and fellow medical students who chose to forego residencies entirely to pursue non-medical ventures, including one who went on to join a dance company. I attributed this to the eccentricities of Harvard, where nontraditional paths are often celebrated. I felt encouraged by them following their own "*veritas*" not clearly understanding why after the arduous journey that is modern medical education, they would choose to retreat. There were whispers of a brewing epidemic of "burnout", which has since crescendoed more recently to become the latest obsession and rightly so, a chief concern among healthcare providers.

I had no innate talent for numbers or any life-sustaining hobbies, so I promised myself that I would work hard and ease past the "10, 000 hours rule" to become the best physician I could be. But personal tenacity is only one factor; I did not account for the intricacies of the hospital ecosystem awaiting me. Students matriculating in medical school have similar mental well-being profiles as age-matched college graduates but burnout rates go on to double in medicine compared to other fields even after adjusting for confounding factors such as age, sex, education level, and weekly hours worked (Drazeau et al., 2014; Shanafelt et al., 2015). "Death by a thousand clicks" was how one senior emergency physician described burnout to me. But the term was coined long before electronic health records became common. It is a concept attributed to Herbert Freudenberger, a New York psychologist, who described this phenomenon

DOI: 10.4018/978-1-7998-1468-9.ch027

among providers working in free clinics in the 1970s treating substance use disorders (Freudenberger, 1974).

Since then, burnout has become further recognized to mean a syndrome of emotional exhaustion, depersonalization, and diminished sense of personal achievement (Maslach & Leiter, 2016). There are recent estimates of billions of dollars in terms of the financial toll on the healthcare system from physician burnout. Equally grave are the individual human costs to both the patient and physician in the forms of medical errors, substance use, and suicides. There are numerous proposed solutions from fixing the electronic medical records system to using group reflections, mindfulness meditations, and wellness programs. The cognitive and behavioral approaches are designed to address not the inherent bureaucracies of modern healthcare system but instead to refuel one's moral reserves and reinvigorate a physician's sense of purpose. Might research also serve a role in repurposing one's life as it has with mine in providing meaning? In a way, my path to becoming an academic anesthesiologist has always been guided by the understanding that while a physician can serve one patient one at a time, the academic physician- through the impact of his or her research- might serve more, even populations at a time. The following chapter is about my journey in academic medicine from a Tibetan immigrant to the United States at sixteen to eventually attend Oxford and Harvard. But it is also a narrative about the purpose I find in research and how I have refashioned it to try inoculate myself against the drudgery of healthcare bureaucracy.

At the end of my third year clinical clerkship rotations in medical school, I decided to postpone graduation along with about half my class to take an additional year towards pursuing another degree such as an MBA or scientific research. As a premedical student, I had been accepted to several combined MD/PhD programs but decided ultimately to pursue a lone medical degree because my research interests had shifted drastically from basic sciences to interest in clinical trials research and my mentors recommended against the long, combined degrees. I compromised and decided to take that fifth year for research.

I also took that time to think and process. I do not believe that I was burned out but noticed changes to my own personhood and how I reacted to certain things that I found alarming. How I deal with a patient's death, for instance. On my first day, I was assigned to take care of Mrs. A., a patient on novel experimental immunotherapy for a recrudescent terminal cancer. All preparations had been afoot to ensure transition her to home hospice the next week when she suddenly passed away the night before I arrived for my third morning rounds. I had never experienced death before and did not know how to proceed. So, I went to see her family whom I had gotten to know over the previous two days and offered my condolences and asked if they needed anything. As the group of students, residents, and attending formed this semicircle to round on our other patients, an usher drove a stainless, sterile box carrying Mrs. A. through our group creating a silence that sounded more like an exasperated inconvenience. Then, the team promptly proceeded as if nothing had occurred. This response shocked me deeply so much so that I wrote about this experience and spoke to hospital leadership to process my emotions further. Soon I was caught in the deluge of board examinations, clinical tests, and rotations that I forgot about this experience until I landed in the intensive care unit ten months later. Just in my first week, three of my patients passed away in succession that made death appear more like a banality. I realized how different my response in just less than a year had been and this saddened me immensely. I wanted to use my year off away from boards and rotations to better realign my own moral axis so that I could be the best physician to my patients. And I felt research offered that perfect respite and opportunity for regrowth.

So, one late Boston summer, I found myself in the laboratory of Warren Zapol, a pioneer in the field of anesthesiology and critical care who was leading the charge to create innovations to help one of the sickest group of patients in the hospital, those undergoing cardiac surgeries. The laboratory was a curious mix of attending cardiologists, anesthesiologists, chemists, geneticists, engineers, rheumatologists and visiting Italian intensivists. Despite never having designed a clinical trial before, here was a mentor who trusted you with helping design a major trial translating years of laboratory work into improved care for the critically ill. In brief, we knew that nitric oxide binds hemoglobin that is released after a red blood cell is broken. In cardiac surgeries, where red blood cells are broken or hemolyzed to a great degree, we hypothesized that replenishing these patients with nitric oxide may help reverse the adverse effects of vasoconstriction and tissue damage associated with depleted nitric oxide. Phase II trial results suggest that nitric oxide may be the first pharmacologic agent that could prevent acute kidney injury in cardiac surgical patients. A phase III trial is currently underway.

This was different from the learning in the classroom and the wards. For example, if you wanted to know why patients with elevated bilirubin became jaundiced, that was time away from learning about the clinically relevant and often tested differential for elevated bilirubin; or why in taking a patient's history all are asked about "any fevers, night sweats or chills" but why nights? And that list continues but it pays in medical school to be less curious lest you should fall behind. If medical education is all about learning the "whats", "hows" and mnemonics as it is in our first years, it becomes more tedious, further removed, and not sustainable for a lifetime of learning. But it was exactly to satisfy my curiosity and rediscover my passion of medicine, that I took my research year.

In medicine, the phrase from the "bench to bedside" is a common trope used to explain the aspirations of future physician-scientists but that had always been an elusive task for me when I was working in labs before. And then to find myself involved in that exact task of translating innovations from the "bench to bedside" was exhilarating and the single most valuable lesson in medical school.

I was honestly more interested in becoming a writer than a doctor/researcher growing up. As a child, I looked forward to nights when my my *amagèn* or grandmother in Tibetan was in town. They meant only one thing: storytime. Be they Tibetan fables, supernatural tales or a *re*-re-telling of her harrowing escape across the Himalayas from Tibet into Nepal, I was truly spellbound. Those nights were precious indeed, especially as I set out to attend an English boarding school at the age of nine. Boarding school was like learning how to swim in the deep end of a pool. To stay afloat meant to seek others' help and empathize with newcomers. It taught me concentration and tenacity to succeed in school. The absence of my parents fostered independent thinking refined by years of learning from consequences. Meanwhile, I rediscovered my passion for stories this time through books.

As my interest bloomed from Blyton to Bunyan, I moved with my family to California at sixteen. At Vacaville High School, I skipped the 10th grade and eventually won a full scholarship to attend Bowdoin. And it was there that I serendipitously discovered biology. Not only was biology a world of mysteries and stories akin to the one I had grown accustomed to but it also offered me fulfillment not found in books. As I explored Darwin's selection theories or the confluence of genes and environment in certain personality traits, I realized that biology and literature were both studies of what makes us humans. Whereas one exposes the external mysteries of human behavior, the other reveals the underlying causes that contribute to such behavior. Biology, however, was no longer a mere abstraction but a real-life adaptation where I could participate and contribute to the "story"; perks that are denied in storybooks.

Such a realization drove me to seek research opportunities. The summer after my freshman year, I participated in a program organized by the Weill Cornell/Rockefeller/Sloan-Kettering MD-PhD Program that allowed me to characterize a family of proteins considered to be candidate subunits for a malaria vaccine. To have taken only Bio101 and then be immersed in state-of-the-art research was frustrating yet enlightening. Whether it was repeating my diagnostic gels seven times or having my cultures crash, I realized that failure is an inevitable part of research and that to succeed one must return the next day, reevaluate the process and patiently redo it. It was an important early lesson in research.

This awareness drove me to seek opportunities in laboratories and hospitals all around the world. As someone who grew up as a Tibetan refugee, I supported and empathized with the need to address issues and diseases affecting the poor, the neglected, and the disenfranchised. For several years, I worked on parasites that cause malaria and the African sleeping sickness with the objective to eventually develop drugs against these diseases.

To continue my fascination with malaria parasites from the previous year, I participated in a program funded by the NIH as the only undergraduate at the Université de Bamako in Mali the summer after my sophomore year. There I met my very first patient. His story was sadly no different from the children around him: a bloated stomach telling of starvation, frail bony arms and legs, and worst of all, a burning fever that often portends malaria in these places. The baby and his mother had arrived one evening having walked 15 kilometers from their village. As everyone had expected, testing confirmed it was malaria.

And the rainy season had not even begun. That summer, I realized just how little I knew of malaria. Even though I knew details of the architecture of certain proteins in the malaria parasite or how to make hypotheses based on surveys of the parasite's genome database, I knew little of the medical, social and economic burdens of this disease. Little of the helplessness, strife, or agony that the baby and his mother must have felt. In addition to helping me place faces and stories to my research, such experiences in the clinic inspired me to see the bigger picture and ask how my research can lead to the urgent relief that people need.

After graduating from Bowdoin, I enrolled at Oxford on a national scholarship, after a short malaria internship in Switzerland. At Oxford, I extended myself into another neglected tropical disease called the African sleeping sickness where I helped to characterize two essential proteins of the causative parasite in order to develop drugs that would inhibit their functions based on a rational structural understanding. However, prior to matriculating in medical school, my experiences made me realize that I cherished the human aspects of research more and decided to subsequently do clinical research instead of basic sciences.

As I approach the end of my first year of residency, I have seen firsthand the realities of burnout and unfortunately, there are systemic issues that will take time to fix. But what do you do when in the ICU, critically ill patients die day and night that you sometimes become numb, so emotionally exhausted that you realize you are not feeling as much empathy as the patient's story blurs into a disease entity. Instead of Mr. D., it becomes the idiopathic pulmonary fibrosis patient. Everyone has their own technique to combat this. I take a moment and set aside the charting. I speak to the patient's family and listen. But sometimes, I think back to my first patient and try to remember my own emotions and response to her death. I think of the medical innovations made such as those by my mentors and those still needed. And this prodigious task is ultimately what keeps me going.

REFERENCES

Drazeau, C. M., Shanafelt, T., Durning, S. J., Massie, F. S., Moutier, C., Satele, D. V., ... Dyrbye, L. N. (2014). Distress among matriculating medical students relative to the general population. *Academic Medicine*, *89*(11), 1520–1525. doi:10.1097/ACM.0000000000000482 PMID:25250752

Freudenberger, H. J. (1974). Staff burn-out. *The Journal of Social Issues*, *30*(1), 159–165. doi:10.1111/j.1540-4560.1974.tb00706.x

Maslach, C., & Leiter, M. P. (2016). Understanding the burnout experience: Recent research and its implications for psychiatry. *World Psychiatry; Official Journal of the World Psychiatric Association (WPA)*, *15*(2), 103–111. doi:10.1002/wps.20311 PMID:27265691

Shanafelt, T. D., Hasan, O., Dyrbye, L. N., Sinsky, C., Satele, D., Sloan, J., & West, C. P. (2015). Changes in Burnout and Satisfaction With Work-Life Balance in Physicians and the General US Working Population Between 2011 and 2014. *Mayo Clinic Proceedings*, *90*(12), 1600–1613. doi:10.1016/j.mayocp.2015.08.023 PMID:26653297

Compilation of References

AACOMAS Applicant and Matriculant Profile Summary Report . (2018). Retrieved from https://www.aacom.org/docs/default-source/data-and-trends/2018-aacomas-applicant-matriculant-profile-summary-report.pdf?sfvrsn=28753a97_12

AAMC Faculty Diversity in U.S. Medical Schools. Progress and Gaps Coexist (2019) Retrieved from https://www.aamc.org/data/aib/474174/december2016facultydiversityinu.s.medicalschoolsprogressandgaps.html

AAMC. (n.d.) AAMC Diversity Facts and Figures. Retrieved from http://www.aamcdiversityfactsandfigures2016.org/report-section/section-2

Abela, J. C. (2009). Adult learning theories and medical education: A review. *Malta Medical Journal*, *21*(1), 11–18.

Abiddin, N. Z. (2007). Mentoring and coaching the roles and practices. *J Human Res Adult Learn.*, 107–116.

AboutA. A. M. C. (2019). Retrieved from https://www.aamc.org/about/

Abrahams, F. (2015, July). Understanding Generation Z learning styles in order to deliver quality learning experiences. Retrieved May 8, 2019, from www.precisionindustries.com.au

Academy of Royal Medical Colleges. Ten Principles for CPD. 1999. Available from http://www.rcgp.org.uk/revalidation-and-cpd/~/media/Files/Revalidation-and-CPD/ACADEMY-GUIDANCE-CPD-HEADINGS.ashx

Accreditation Council for Graduate Medical Education. (2019). Retrieved from https://www.acgme.org/Residents-and-Fellows/Welcome

ACGME Clinical Learning Environment Review (CLER). (2019). Retrieved from https://www.acgme.org/What-We-Do/Initiatives/Clinical-Learning-Environment-Review-CLER

ACGME Family Medicine Milestone Project. (2015). Retrieved June. 2, 2019 from https://www.acgme.org/Portals/0/PDFs/Milestones/FamilyMedicineMilestones.pdf

ACGME Preventive Medicine Milestone Project. (2015). Public Health and General Preventive Medicine, Retrieved June 2, 2019 from https://www.acgme.org/Portals/0/PDFs/Milestones/PreventiveMedicineMilestones-PublicHealthand-GeneralPreventiveMedicine.pdf

Achenjang, J. N., & Elam, C. L. (2016). Recruitment of underrepresented minorities in medical school through a student-led initiative. *Journal of the National Medical Association*, *108*(3), 147–151. doi:10.1016/j.jnma.2016.05.003 PMID:27692354

Ackerly, D. C., Sangvai, D. G., Udayakumar, K., Shah, B. R., Kalman, N. S., Cho, A. H., ... Dzau, V. J. (2011). Training the next generation of physician–executives: An innovative residency pathway in management and leadership. *Academic Medicine*, *86*(5), 575–579. doi:10.1097/ACM.0b013e318212e51b PMID:21436663

Acosta, D., & Olsen, P. (2006). Meeting the needs of regional minority groups: The University of Washington's programs to increase the American Indian and Alaskan Native physician workforce. *Academic Medicine, 81*(10), 863–870. doi:10.1097/01.ACM.0000238047.48977.05 PMID:16985341

Adams, F. (1939). *The Genuine Works of Hippocrates*. Baltimore, MD: The Williams & Wilkins Company.

Adamson, R., Goodman, R. B., Kritek, P., Luks, A. M., Tonelli, M. R., & Benditt, J. Clinician-Educator Track of the University of Washington Pulmonary and Critical Care Medicine Fellowship Program. (2015). Training the teachers: The clinician-educator track of the University of Washington pulmonary and critical care medicine fellowship program. *Annals of the American Thoracic Society, 12*(1), 480–485. doi:10.1513/AnnalsATS.201501-032OT PMID:25763811

Addams, A. N., Bletzinger, R. B., Sondheimer, H. M., White, S. E., & Johnson, L. M. (2010). *Roadmap to diversity: Integrating holistic review practices into medical school admission processes*. Washington, DC: Association of American Medical Colleges.

Agency for Healthcare Research and Quality. (n.d.). *Teamstepps*. Retrieved May 1, 2019 from https://www.ahrq.gov/teamstepps/index.html

Ahmed, N., Devitt, K. S., Keshet, I., Spicer, J., Imrie, K., Feldman, L., ... Rutka, J. (2014). A systematic review of the effects of resident duty hour restrictions in surgery: Impact on resident wellness, training and patient outcomes. *Annals of Surgery, 259*(6), 1041–1053. doi:10.1097/SLA.0000000000000595 PMID:24662409

Ahn, J., Martin, S. K., Farnan, J. M., & Fromme, B. (2018). The graduate medical education scholars track: Developing residents as clinician-educators during clinical training via a longitudinal, multimodal, and multidisciplinary track. *Academic Medicine, 93*(2), 214–219. doi:10.1097/ACM.0000000000001815 PMID:28678096

AI Now Institute. (2019). Retrieved on June 1, 2019 from https://ainowinstitute.org/

Albanese, M. A., Snow, M. H., Skochelak, S. E., Huggett, K. N., & Farrell, P. M. (2003). Assessing personal qualities in medical school admissions. *Academic Medicine, 78*(3), 313–321. doi:10.1097/00001888-200303000-00016 PMID:12634215

Alberti, P. (2014). Community health needs assessments: Filling data gaps for population health research and management. *The Journal for Electronic Health Data and Methods, 2*(4), 1174. PMID:25848631

Allchin, D. (2013). Problem- and Case-Based Learning in Science: An Introduction to Distinctions, Values, and Outcomes. *CBE Life Sciences Education, 12*(3), 364–372. doi:10.1187/cbe.12-11-0190 PMID:24006385

Allen, M. J., & Yen, W. M. (2001). *Introduction to Measurement Theory*. Waveland Press.

Alpern, R. J., Belitsky, R., & Long, S. (2011). Competencies in premedical and medical education: The AAMC-HHMI report. *Perspectives in Biology and Medicine, 54*(1), 30–35. doi:10.1353/pbm.2011.0001 PMID:21399381

AMA Single accreditation system for graduate medical education: What to know (2016). Retrieved from https://www.ama-assn.org/residents-students/match/single-accreditation-system-graduate-medical-education-what-know

American Association of Colleges of Osteopathic Medicine. (2018). *AACOMAS Applicant Pool Profile Entering Class 2018*. Retrieved from https://www.aacom.org/reports-programs-initiatives/aacom-reports/applicants

American Association of Colleges of Osteopathic Medicine. (2019). *2019-2020 student guide to osteopathic medical colleges*. Bethesda, MD: American Association of Colleges of Osteopathic Medicine.

American Association of Colleges of Osteopathic Medicine. (2019, May). 2018-2019 First-Year Enrollment by Gender Race-Ethnicity and Osteopathic Medical College. Retrieved May 8, 2019, from https://www.aacom.org/reports-programs-initiatives/aacom-reports/student-enrollment

American Association of Medical Colleges. (2018). Matriculants to U.S. medical schools by race, selected combinations of race/ethnicity and sex, 2015-2016 through 2018-2019. Retrieved from https://www.aamc.org/download/321474/data/factstablea9.pdf

American Association of Physician Leadership. (n.d.). *Fundamentals of Physician Leadership.* Retrieved June 3, 2019, from https://www.physicianleaders.org

American Board of Clinical Informatics. (2019). Clinical informatics, Retrieved June 2, 2019 from https://www.theabpm.org/become-certified/subspecialties/clinical-informatic

American Board of Medical Specialties. (n.d.). *Board Certification.* Retrieved May 15, 2019 from https://www.abms.org/board-certification/steps-toward-initial-certification-and-moc/

American Board of Surgery. *Training and Recertification.* Retrieved May 10, 2019 from http://www.absurgery.org/default.jsp?exam-moc)

American Hospital Association and American Medical Association. (n.d.). *Integrated Leadership for Hospitals and Health Systems: Principles for Success.* Retrieved June 3, 2019, from https://www.ama-assn.org/sites/ama-assn.org/files/corp/media-browser/public/about-ama/ama-aha-integrated-leadership-principles_0.pdf

American Medical Association (AMA). (2015). *AMA president outlines physician leadership plan for digital health* [Press release]. Retrieved from https://www.ama-assn.org/press-center/press-releases/ama-president-outlines-physician-leadership-plan-digital-health/

American Medical Association (AMA). (2016). *AMA encourages telemedicine training for medical students, residents.* [Press release]. Retrieved from https://www.ama-assn.org/press-center/press-releases/ama-encourages-telemedicine-training-medical-students-residents

American Medical Association (AMA). (2019a). *AMA expansion of national effort creating medical school of the future* [Press release]. Retrieved from https://www.ama-assn.org/press-center/press-releases/ama-expansion-national-effort-creating-medical-school-future/

American Medical Association (AMA). (2019b). *AMA adopt policy, integrate augmented intelligence in physician training* [Press release]. Retrieved from https://www.ama-assn.org/press-center/press-releases/ama-adopt-policy-integrate-augmented-intelligence-physician-training

American Medical Association. (2017). *Creating a community of innovation.* Retrieved June 9, 2019, from https://www.ama-assn.org/sites/ama-assn.org/files/corp/media-browser/public/about-ama/ace-monograph-interactive_0.pdf

American Medical Association. (2019). *Code of medical ethics: professional self-regulation.* Retrieved June 9, 2019, from https://www.ama-assn.org/delivering-care/ethics/code-medical-ethics-professional-self-regulation

American Osteopathic Association. (2019). Osteopathic medical schools. Retrieved from https://osteopathic.org/about/affiliated-organizations/osteopathic-medical-schools/

Analysis in Brief - Data and Analysis - AAMC. Retrieved from https://www.aamc.org/data/aib/474174/december2016 facultydiversityinu.s.medicalschoolsprogressandgaps.html

Anand, T. (2014). *Team learning to narrow the gap between healthcare knowledge and practice* [Doctoral dissertation]. Retrieved from ProQuest.

Andarvazh, M., Afshar, L., & Yazdani, S. (2017). Hidden curriculum and analytical definition. *Journal of Medical Education, 16*(4), 198–207.

Anderson, M. (1996). *Imposters in the Temple: A Blueprint for Improving Higher Education in America.* Palo Alto, CA: Hoover Institution Press.

Andre, C., Deerin, J., & Leykum, L. (2017). Students helping students: Vertical peer mentoring to enhance the medical school experience. *BMC Research Notes, 10*(1), 176. doi:10.118613104-017-2498-8 PMID:28464902

Andriole, D. A., & Jeffe, D. B. (2011). Characteristics of medical school matriculants who participated in postbaccalaureate premedical programs. *Academic Medicine, 86*(2), 201–210. doi:10.1097/ACM.0b013e3182045076 PMID:21169786

Andriole, D. A., & Jeffe, D. B. (2012). A national cohort study of U.S. medical school students who initially failed Step 1 of the United States Licensing Examination. *Academic Medicine, 87*(4), 529–536. doi:10.1097/ACM.0b013e318248dd9c PMID:22361789

Andriole, D., & Jeffe, D. (2010). Pre-matriculation variables associated with suboptimal outcomes for the 1994–1999 cohort of US medical school matriculants. *Journal of the American Medical Association, 304*(11), 1212–1219. doi:10.1001/jama.2010.1321 PMID:20841535

Angood, P., & Birk, S. K. (2014). The value of physician leadership. *Physician Executive, 40*(3), 6–20. PMID:24964545

Antunes, J. (2019). Microsoft's HoloLens 2 mixed-reality headset: better specs, comfort, enterprise features. *Spar3D.* Retrieved from https://www.spar3d.com/news/ hardware/microsofts-hololens-2-mixed-reality-headset-better-specs-comfort-enterprise-features/

AOA The American Osteopathic Association Supports Revised ACGME Common Program Requirements. Retrieved from https://osteopathic.org/2017/03/10/the-american-osteopathic-association-supports-revised-acgme-common-program-requirements/

Applying to Medical School: 2018 AMCAS Medical School Applications by the Numbers. (2019). Retrieved from https://aamc-orange.global.ssl.fastly.net/production/media/filer_public/43/1b/431bc986-9e69-424f-8066-5fc95eba4a44/aamc-2018-amcas-medical-school-applications-by-the-numbers-infographic.pdf

Argryis, C., Putnam, R., & Smith, D. (1985). *Action science: Concepts, methods, and skills for research and intervention.* San Francisco, CA: Jossey-Bass.

Argyris, C., & Schön, D. A. (1978). *Organizational learning. A theory of action perspective.* Reading, MA: Addison-Wesley.

Arias-Hernandez, R., Green, T. M., & Fisher, B. (2012). From cognitive amplifiers to cognitive prostheses: Understandings of the material basis of cognition in visual analytics. *Interdisciplinary Science Reviews, 37*(1), 4–18. doi:10.1179/0308018812Z.0000000001

Ariely, D., & Lanier, W. L. *Disturbing trends in physician burnout and satisfaction with work-life balance: Dealing with malady among the nation's healers.* doi:// doi:10.1016/j.mayocp.2015.10.004

Arnold, L., Shue, C. K., Kalishman, S., Prislin, M., Pohl, C., Pohl, H., & Stern, D. T. (2007). Can There Be a Single System for Peer Assessment of Professionalism among Medical Students? A Multi-Institutional Study. *Academic Medicine, 82*(6), 578–586. doi:10.1097/ACM.0b013e3180555d4e PMID:17525545

Aronson, L. (2014). *The fundamentals of medical training: Every second counts.* Arnold P. Gold Foundation website, accessed July 19, 2019.

Artino, A. R. Jr, Gilliland, W. R., Waechter, D. M., Cruess, D., Calloway, M., & Durning, S. J. (2012). Does self-reported clinical experience predict performance in medical school and internship? *Medical Education*, *46*(2), 172–178. doi:10.1111/j.1365-2923.2011.04080.x PMID:22239331

Asche, C. V., Kim, M., Brown, A., Golden, A., Laack, T. A., Rosario, J., ... Okuda, Y. (2018). Communicating Value in Simulation: Cost-Benefit Analysis and Return on Investment. *Academic Emergency Medicine*, *25*(2), 230–237. doi:10.1111/acem.13327 PMID:28965366

Ash, S. L., & Clayton, P. H. (2009). Generating, deepening, and documenting learning: The power of critical reflection in applied learning. *Journal of Applied Learning in Higher Education*, *1*(1), 25–48.

Association of American Medical Colleges (AAMC). (2014). *Core entrustable professional activities for entering residency: Curriculum developer's guide*. Washington, DC: Author. Retrieved from https://store.aamc.org/downloadable/download/sample/sample_id/63/

Association of American Medical Colleges (AAMC). (2017). *Core entrustable professional activities for entering residency*. Washington, DC: Author. Retrieved from https://www.aamc.org/download/484778/data/epa13toolkit.pdf

Association of American Medical Colleges (AAMC). (n.d.). *Medical schools reporting regional campus information*. Retrieved from https://www.aamc.org/initiatives/ cir/406434/13a.html

Association of American Medical Colleges. (2013). Curriculum Changes in US Medical Schools: Types of Change in 2012-2013. Retrieved from https://www.aamc.org/initiatives/cir/427196/27.html

Association of American Medical Colleges. (2013). *Roadmap to excellence: Key concepts for evaluating the impact of medical school holistic admissions*. Retrieved from https://members.aamc.org/eweb/upload/Holistic%20Review%202013.pdf

Association of American Medical Colleges. (2016). *Diversity in medical education: Facts and figures 2016*. Retrieved from http://www.aamcdiversityfactsandfigures2016.org/

Association of American Medical Colleges. (2016). Medical Students, Selected Years, 1965-2015. Retrieved May 8, 2019, from https://www.aamc.org/download/481178/data/2015table1.pdf

Association of American Medical Colleges. (2017, December). *More women than men enrolled in U. S. Medical Schools in 2017*. Retrieved May 8, 2019, from https://news.aamc.org/press-releases/article/applicant-enrollment-2017/)

Association of American Medical Colleges. (2018). [Chart] Curriculum Changes in US Medical Schools: Types of Change in 2017-2018. Retrieved from https://www.aamc.org/initiatives/cir/427196/27.html

Association of American Medical Colleges. (2018). Curriculum Reports, Retrieved June 2, 2019 from https://www.aamc.org/initiatives/cir/curriculumreports/

Association of American Medical Colleges. (2018a). *AAMC data snapshot*. Washington, DC: Association of American Medical Colleges.

Association of American Medical Colleges. (2018a). *Table A-3: Applicants to U.S. Medical Schools by State of Legal Residence, 2009-2010 through 2018-2019*. Retrieved from https://www.aamc.org/download/321460/data/factstablea3.pdf

Association of American Medical Colleges. (2018b). *Matriculating student questionnaire 2018. All schools summary report*. Washington, DC: Association of American Medical Colleges.

Association of American Medical Colleges. (2018b). *Table A-4: Matriculants to U.S. Medical Schools by State of Legal Residence, 2009-2010 through 2018-2019*. Retrieved from https://www.aamc.org/download/321462/data/factstablea4.pdf

Association of American Medical Colleges. (2019). *Applying to Dual-Degree Programs.* Retrieved June 3, 2019, from https://students-residents.aamc.org/applying-medical-school/article/directory-md-mph-educational-opportunities

Association of American Medical Colleges. (2019). *Postbaccalaureate premedical programs.* Washington, DC: Association of American Medical Colleges.

Association of American Medical Colleges. (2019). U.S. Medical School Applications and Matriculants by School, State of Legal Residence, and Sex, 2018-2019. Retrieved from https://www.aamc.org/data/facts/applicantmatriculant/

Association of American Medical Colleges. (2019a). Core competencies for entering medical students. Retrieved from https://www.aamc.org/admissions/dataandresearch/477182/corecompetencies.html

Association of American Medical Colleges. (2019b). *Using MCAT Data in 2020 Medical Student Selection.* Retrieved from https://www.aamc.org/download/498250/data/usingmcatdatain2020medstudentselection.pdf

Atherley, A. E., Hambleton, I. R., Unwin, N., George, C., Lashley, P. M., & Taylor, C. G. (2016). Exploring the transition of undergraduate medical students into a clinical clerkship using organizational socialization theory. *Perspectives on Medical Education, 5*(2), 78–87. doi:10.100740037-015-0241-5 PMID:26951164

Author name. (n.d.). Personal financial literacy among US medical students. Retrieved from www.mededpublish.org/manuscripts/847 Not cited in text.

Autin, F., & Croizet, J. (2012). Reframing Metacognitive Interpretation of Difficulty of Anagram Task. *Journal of Experimental Psychology*, 610–618. doi:10.1037/a0027478 PMID:22390266

Bahner, D. P., Goldman, E., Way, D., Royall, N. A., & Liu, Y. T. (2014). The stae of ultrasound education in U.S. medical schools: Results of a national survey. *Academic Medicine, 89*(12), 1681–1686. doi:10.1097/ACM.0000000000000414 PMID:25099238

Bailey, J. A., & Willies-Jacobo, L. J. (2012). Are disadvantaged and underrepresented minority applicants more likely to apply to the Program in Medical Education-Health Equity? *Academic Medicine, 87*(11), 1535–1539. doi:10.1097/ACM.0b013e31826d6220 PMID:23018330

Baker, M. (2017). How vr is revolutionizing the way future doctors are learning about our bodies. Retrieved June 1, 2019 from https://www.ucsf.edu/news/2017/09/408301/how-vr-revolutionizing-way-future-doctors-are-learning-about-our-bodies

Baker, F. B. (2001). *The Basics of Item Response Theory* (2nd ed.)., Retrieved from https://eric.ed.gov/?id=ED458219

Baker, S., & Daginawala, N. (2011). Leadership training for radiologists: A survey of opportunities and participants in MBA and MPH programs by medical students, residents, and current chairpersons. *Journal of the American College of Radiology, 8*(8), 563–567. doi:10.1016/j.jacr.2011.02.013 PMID:21807350

Baldwin, D. C. Jr, & Daugherty, S. R. (2004). Sleep deprivation and fatigue in residency training: Results of a national survey of first- and second-year residents. *Sleep, 27*(2), 217–223. doi:10.1093leep/27.2.217 PMID:15124713

Ballejos, M. P., Olsen, P., Price-Johnson, T., Garcia, C., Parker, T., Sapién, R. E., & Romero-Leggott, V. (2018). Recruiting American Indian/Alaska Native students to medical school: A multi-institutional alliance in the U.S. Southwest. *Academic Medicine, 93*(1), 71–75. doi:10.1097/ACM.0000000000001952 PMID:29045274

Ballejos, M. P., Rhyne, R. L., & Parkes, J. (2015). Increasing the relative weight of noncognitive admission criteria improves underrepresented minority admission rates to medical school. *Teaching and Learning in Medicine, 27*(2), 155–162. doi:10.1080/10401334.2015.1011649 PMID:25893937

Bandura, A. (1977). Self-efficacy: Toward a unifying theory of behavioral change. *Psychological Review, 84*(2), 191–215. doi:10.1037/0033-295X.84.2.191 PMID:847061

Bannister, S. L., Wickenheiser, H. M., Kin, B., & Keegan, D. A. (2014). Key elements of highly effective teams. *Pediatrics, 133*(2), 184–186. doi:10.1542/peds.2013-3734 PMID:24446450

Barchi, R., & Lowery, B. (2000). Scholarship in the medical faculty from the university perspective: Retaining academic values. *Academic Medicine, 75*(9), 899–905. doi:10.1097/00001888-200009000-00011 PMID:10995611

Barnes, E., & Souza, T. (2019). Intercultural dialogue partners: Creating space for difference and dialogue. Retrieved from https://www.facultyfocus.com/articles/teaching-and-learning/intercultural-dialogue-partners-creating-space-for-difference-and-dialogue/

Bar-On, R. (2006). The Bar-On model of emotional-social intelligence (ESI). *Psicothema, 18*(Suppl), 13–25. PMID:17295953

Barr, D. A., Gonzalez, M. E., & Wanat, S. F. (2008). The leaky pipeline: Factors associated with early decline in interest in premedical studies among underrepresented minority undergraduate students. *Academic Medicine, 83*(5), 503–511. doi:10.1097/ACM.0b013e31816bda16 PMID:18448909

Barrows, H. (1986). A taxonomy of problem-based learning methods. *Medical Education, 20*(6), 481–486. doi:10.1111/j.1365-2923.1986.tb01386.x PMID:3796328

Barrows, H. (1994). *Practice-based learning*. Springfield, IL: Southern Illinois University School of Medicine.

Barrows, H. S., & Kelson, A. C. (1995). Problem-based learning in secondary education and the problem-based learning institute. *Springfield, IL. Problem-Based Learning Institute, 1*(1), 1–5.

Barzansky, B. (2019, May 8). Survey Prep Workshop to prepare schools for their upcoming full survey visit. Presented at the 2019 annual LCME Secretariat Workshop, Washington, DC.

Barzansky, B., & Etzel, S. I. (2011). Medical schools in the United States. *Journal of the American Medical Association, 306*, 1007–1014. PMID:21900145

Barzansky, B., Hunt, D., Moineau, G., Ahn, D., Lai, C.-W., Humphrey, H., & Peterson, L. (2015). Continuous quality improvement in an accreditation system for undergraduate medical education: Benefits and challenges. *Medical Teacher, 37*(11), 1032–1038. doi:10.3109/0142159X.2015.1031735 PMID:25897708

Basco, W. T. Jr, Gilbert, G. E., Chessman, A. W., & Blue, A. V. (2000). The ability of a medical school admission process to predict clinical performance and patient's satisfaction. *Academic Medicine, 75*(7), 743–747. doi:10.1097/00001888-200007000-00021 PMID:10926028

Basha, M. E., Bauer, L. J., Modrakowski, M. C., & Baker, H. H. (2018). Women in osteopathic and allopathic medical schools: An analysis of applicants, matriculants, enrollment, and chief academic officers. *The Journal of the American Osteopathic Association, 118*(5), 331–336. doi:10.7556/jaoa.2018.064 PMID:29710355

Batalden, M., Batalden, P., Margolis, P., Seid, M., Armstrong, G., Opipari-Arrigan, L., & Hartung, H. (2016). Coproduction of health care service. *BMJ Quality & Safety, 25*(7), 509–517. doi:10.1136/bmjqs-2015-004315 PMID:26376674

Batistatou, A., Doulis, E. A., Tiniakos, D., Anogiannaki, A., & Charalabopoulos, K. (2010). The introduction of medical humanities in the undergraduate curriculum of Greek medical schools: Challenge and necessity. *Hippokratia, 14*(4), 241–243. PMID:21311630

Bauer, T., & Erdogran, B. (2011). Organizational socialization: The effective on boarding of new employees. In S. Zedeck (Ed.), *Maintaining, expanding, and contracting the organization* (pp. 51–64). Washington, DC: American Psychological Association. doi:10.1037/12171-002

Belling, C. (2010). Commentary: Sharper instruments: On defending the humanities in undergraduate medical education. *Academic Medicine, 85*(6), 938-940. DOI:10.1097/ACM. Obo13e 318dc 1820

Bell, R. H. Jr. (2009). Why Johnny cannot operate. *Surgery., 146*(4), 533–542. doi:10.1016/j.surg.2009.06.044 PMID:19789010

Benbassat, J. (2012). Undesirable features of the medical learning environment: A narrative review of the literature. *Advances in Health Sciences Education: Theory and Practice, 18*(3), 527–536. doi:10.100710459-012-9389-5 PMID:22760724

Benditz, A., Pulido, L., Renkawitz, T., Schwarz, T., Grifka J., & Weber, M. (2018). Are there gender-dependent study habits of medical students in times of the World Wide Web? *Biomed Research International,* Dec. 6, 3196869.

Benson, N. M., Stickle, T. R., & Raszka, W. V. Jr. (2015). Going "Fourth" From Medical School: Fourth-Year Medical Students' Perspectives on the Fourth Year of Medical School. *Academic Medicine, 94*(3), 348–342. PMID:27002891

Berg, D. N., & Huot, S. J. (2007). Middle manager role of the chief medical resident: An organizational psychologist's perspective. *Journal of General Internal Medicine, 22*(12), 1771–1774. doi:10.100711606-007-0425-8 PMID:17940827

Berk, R. (2009). Teaching strategies for the Net Generation. *Teaching and Learning Journal, 3*(2), 1–24.

Bertman, S. H., & Marks, S. C. Jr. (1985). Humanities in medical education: Rationale and resources for the dissection laboratory. *Medical Education, 19*(5), 374–381. doi:10.1111/j.1365-2923.1985.tb01340.x PMID:4058336

Betancourt, J. R., Corbett, J., & Bondaryk, M. R. (2014). Addressing disparities and achieving equity: Cultural competence, ethics, and health-care transformation. *Chest, 145*(1), 143–148. doi:10.1378/chest.13-0634 PMID:24394825

Bhandari, A., & Hayward, M. (2014). The rise of the healthcare hackathon: 6 insights from over 100 hackathons from around the world. Retrieved June 2, 2019 from http://hackingmedicine.mit.edu/health-hackathon-database/

Bharadwaj, R. (2019). Artificial intelligence for medical billing and coding. Emerj Artificial Intelligence Research, Retrieved June 2, 2019 from https://emerj.com/ai-sector-overviews/artificial-intelligence-medical-billing-coding/

Bhawuk, D., & Bruslin, R. (1992). The measurement of intercultural sensitivity using the concepts of individualism and collectivism. *International Journal of Intercultural Relations, 16*(4), 413–436. doi:10.1016/0147-1767(92)90031-O

Biese, K., Leacock, B. W., Osmond, C. R., & Hobgood, C. D. (2011). Engaging senior residents as leaders: A novel structure for multiple chief role. *Journal of Graduate Medical Education, 3*(2), 236–238. doi:10.4300/JGME-D-10-00045.1 PMID:22655148

Bjork, R. A., & Bjork, E. L. (1992). A new theory of disuse and an old theory of stimulus fluctuation. In A. F. Healy, S. M. Kosslyn, & R. M. Shiffrin (Eds.), *From learning processes to cognitive processes: Essays in honor of William E. Estes* (Vol. 2, pp. 35–67). Hillsdale, NJ: Erlbaum.

Bjork, R. A., Bjork, E. L., & Pomerantz, J. R. (2009). Making things hard on yourself, but in a good way: Creating desirable difficulties to enhance learning. In M. A. Gernsbacher, R. W. Pew, & L. M. Hough (Eds.), *Psychology and the real world: Essays illustrating fundamental contributions to society* (pp. 56–64). New York, NY: Worth.

Blakely, A. W., & Broussard, L. G. (2003). Blueprint for establishing an effective postbaccalaureate medical school pre-entry program for educationally disadvantaged students. *Academic Medicine: Journal of the Association of American Medical Colleges, 78*(5), 437–447. doi:10.1097/00001888-200305000-00004 PMID:12742777

Bleakley, A. (2015). *How the medical humanities can shape better doctors*. London, UK: Routledge. doi:10.4324/9781315771724

Blease, C. (2015). In defense of utility: The medical humanities and medical education. *Medical Humanities*, *42*(2), 103–108. doi:10.1136/medhum-2015-010827 PMID:26842744

Bloch, R., & Norman, G. (2012). Generalizability theory for the perplexed: A practical introduction and guide: AMEE Guide No. 68. *Medical Teacher*, *34*(11), 960–992. doi:10.3109/0142159X.2012.703791 PMID:23140303

Blohm, M., Krautter, M., Lauter, J., Huber, J., Weyrich, P., Herzog, W., ... Nikendei, C. (2014). Voluntary undergraduate technical skills training course to prepare students for clerkship assignment: Tutees' and tutors' perspectives. *BMC Medical Education*, *14*(1), 71. doi:10.1186/1472-6920-14-71 PMID:24708782

Bloom, B. S. (1956). *Taxonomy of Educational Objectives, Handbook I: The Cognitive Domain*. New York: David McKay Co.

Blouin, D., & Tekian, A. (2018). Accreditation of medical education programs: Moving from student outcomes to continuous quality improvement measures. *Academic Medicine*, *93*(3), 377–383. doi:10.1097/ACM.0000000000001835 PMID:28746072

Blouin, D., Tekian, A., Kamin, C., & Harris, I. B. (2017). The impact of accreditation on medical schools' processes. *Medical Education*, *52*(2), 182–191. doi:10.1111/medu.13461 PMID:29044652

Blumenstyk, G. (2019). Do your academic programs actually develop 'Employability'? There's an assessment for that. Retrieved from https://www.chronicle.com/article/Do-Your-Academic-Programs/246120

Boatright, D. H., Samuels, E. A., Cramer, L., Cross, J., Desai, M., Latimore, D., & Gross, C. P. (2018). Association Between the Liaison Committee on Medical Education's Diversity Standards and Changes in Percentage of Medical Student Sex, Race, and Ethnicity. *Journal of the American Medical Association*, *320*(21), 2267. doi:10.1001/jama.2018.13705 PMID:30512090

Bollinger, L. C. (2003). The Need for Diversity in Higher Education. *Academic Medicine*, *78*(5), 431–436. doi:10.1097/00001888-200305000-00002 PMID:12742776

Bond, T., & Fox, C. M. (2015). *Applying the Rasch Model: Fundamental Measurement in the Human Sciences* (3rd ed.). Routledge. doi:10.4324/9781315814698

Bonwell, C. C., & Eison, J. A. (1991). ASHE-ERIC Higher Education Report: Vol. 1. *Active learning: creating excitement in the classroom*. Washington, DC: The George Washington University School of Education and Human Development.

Borges, N. J., Navarro, A. M., Grover, A., & Hoban, J. D. (2010). How, when, and why do physicians choose careers in academic medicine? A literature review. *Academic Medicine*, *85*(4), 680–686. doi:10.1097/ACM.0b013e3181d29cb9 PMID:20354389

Boulet, J. R., & Durning, S. J. (2019). What we measure… and what we should measure in medical education. *Medical Education*, *53*(1), 86–94. doi:10.1111/medu.13652 PMID:30216508

Branch, W. T., Kroenke, K., & Levinson, W. (1997). The clinician- educator --- present and future roles. *Journal of General Internal Medicine*, *12*(S2supplement 2), S1–S3. doi:10.1046/j.1525-1497.12.s2.16.x PMID:9127237

Bray, A., Webb, J., Enquobahrie, A., Vicory, J., Heneghan, J., Hubal, R., ... Clipp, R. (2019). Pulse physiology engine: An open-source software platform for computational modeling of human medical simulation. *SN Comprehensive Clinical Medicine*, *1*(5), 362–377. doi:10.100742399-019-00053-w

Brazeau, C. M., Shanafelt, T., Durning, S. J., Massie, F. S., Eacker, A., Moutier, C., ... Dyrbye, L. N. (2014). Distress among matriculating medical students relative to the general population. *Academic Medicine, 89*(11), 1520–1525. doi:10.1097/ACM.0000000000000482 PMID:25250752

Breining, G. (2016, Sept. 29). 3D printers are revolutionizing medicine. *AAMCNews.*

Breining, G. (2018). Future or fad? Virtual reality in medical education. AAMC News, Retrieved June 1, 2019 from https://news.aamc.org/medical-education/article/future-or-fad-virtual-reality-medical-education/

Brendan, M. (2017). *4 phases to making goal of lifelong physician learner a reality.* Retrieved June 9, 2019, from https://www.ama-assn.org/education/accelerating-change-medical-education/4-phases-making-goal-lifelong-physician-learner

Brennan, N., Cole, L., & Campea, M. (2014) *Allopathic and osteopathic medical communities commit to a single graduate medical education accreditation system.* Retrieved from http://www.acgme.org/portals/0/pdfs/nasca-community/singleaccreditationrelease2-26.pdf

Brennan, R. L. (2010). Generalizability Theory and Classical Test Theory. *Applied Measurement in Education, 24*(1), 1–21. doi:10.1080/08957347.2011.532417

Broberg, O., Andersen, V., & Seim, R. (2011). Participatory ergonomics in design processes: The role of boundary objects. *Applied Ergonomics, 42*(3), 464–472. doi:10.1016/j.apergo.2010.09.006 PMID:20947061

Brockett, R., & Hiemstra, R. (1991). *Self-direction in adult learning: Perspectives on theory, research and practice.* London, UK: Routledge.

Brosnan, C., Southgate, E., Outram, S., Lempp, H., Wright, S., Saxby, T., ... Kelly, B. (2016). Experiences of students who are first in family to attend university. *Medical Education, 50*(8), 842–851. doi:10.1111/medu.12995 PMID:27402044

Brown, P. C. (2014). *Make It Stick: The Science of Successful Learning.* Cambridge, MA: The Belknap Press of Harvard University Press. doi:10.4159/9780674419377

Buchanan, H. S. (1995). The quality movement in higher education in the United States. *Health Libraries Review, 12*(3), 141–146. doi:10.1046/j.1365-2532.1995.1230141.x PMID:10159232

Bullock, A., Fox, F., Barnes, R., Doran, N., Hardyman, W., Moss, D., & Stacey, M. (2013). Transitions in medicine: Trainee doctor stress and support mechanisms. *Journal of Workplace Learning, 25*(6), 368–382. doi:10.1108/JWL-Jul-2012-0052

Buntin, M., Burke, M., Hoaglin, M., & Blumenthal, D. (2011). The benefits of health information technology: A review of the recent literature shows predominantly positive results. *Health Affairs, 30*(3), 464–471. doi:10.1377/hlthaff.2011.0178 PMID:21383365

Burgess, A. W., McGregor, D. M., & Mellis, C. M. (2015). Applying established guidelines to team-based learning programs in medical schools: A systematic review. *Academic Medicine, 89*(4), 678–688. doi:10.1097/ACM.0000000000000162 PMID:24556770

Burgess, A., Dornan, T., Clarke, A. J., Menezes, A., & Mellis, C. (2016). Peer tutoring in a medical school: Perceptions of tutors and tutees. *BMC Medical Education, 16*(1), 85. doi:10.118612909-016-0589-1 PMID:26956642

Burgess, A., & Nestel, D. (2014). Facilitating the development of professional identity through peer assisted learning in medical education. *Advances in Medical Education and Practice, 5*, 403–406. doi:10.2147/AMEP.S72653 PMID:25378965

Burg, F. D., Croll, S. R., Ruff, G. E., & Stemmler, E. J. (1988). Competency requirements. A new approach to medical school admissions. *Journal of the American Medical Association, 259*(3), 389–391. doi:10.1001/jama.1988.03720030049032 PMID:3336163

Burg, G., & French, L. (2012). The age of Gutenberg is over: A consideration of medical education – past, present and future. *Der Hautarzt, 63*(S1Supplement 1), 38–44. doi:10.100700105-011-2301-z PMID:22543945

Burk-Rafel, J., Santen, S. A., & Purkiss, J. (2017). Study behaviors and USMLE Step 1 performance: Implications of a student self-directed parallel curriculum. *Academic Medicine, 92*(11S), S67–S74. doi:10.1097/ACM.0000000000001916 PMID:29065026

Buser, B. R., Swartwout, J. E., Biszewski, M., & Lischka, T. (2018). Single accreditation system update: A year of progress. *The Journal of the American Osteopathic Association, 118*(4), 264–268. doi:10.7556/jaoa.2018.051 PMID:29582061

Butrymowciz, S. (2017). Most colleges enroll many students who are not prepared for higher education. In *The Hechinger Report*. Retrieved from https://hechingerreport.org/colleges-enroll-students-arent-prepared-higher-education/

Byerley, J., & Tilly, A. (2018). A Simple Pyramid Model for Career Guidance. *Journal of Graduate Medical Education, 10*(5), 497–499. doi:10.4300/JGME-D-18-00028.1 PMID:30386473

Callaway, P., Melhado, T., Walling, A., & Groskurth, J. (2017). Financial and Time Burdens for Medical Students Interviewing for Residency. *Family Medicine, 49*(2), 137–140. PMID:28218940

Cameron, E. A., & Pagnattaro, M. A. (2017). Beyond millennials: Engaging generation z in business law classes. *Journal of Legal Studies Education, 34*(2), 317–324. doi:10.1111/jlse.12064

Campbell-Sills, L., Cohan, S. L., & Stein, M. B. (2006). Relationship of resilience to personality, coping, and psychiatric symptoms in young adults. *Behaviour Research and Therapy, 44*(4), 585–599. doi:10.1016/j.brat.2005.05.001 PMID:15998508

Canavan, M. M., Saavedra, R., & Russell, A. Y. (1993). A health science center's pre-matriculation retreat. *Academic Medicine, 68*(5), 358–359. doi:10.1097/00001888-199305000-00017 PMID:8484847

Candy, P. (1991). *Self-direction for lifelong learning: A comprehensive guide to theory and practice.* San Francisco, CA: Jossey-Bass.

Cantillon, P., & Sargeant, J. (2008). Giving feedback in clinical settings. *BMJ (Clinical Research Ed.), 337*(nov10 2), a1961. doi:10.1136/bmj.a1961 PMID:19001006

Cao, L., & Nietfeld, J. L. (2007). College students' metacognitive awareness of difficulties in learning the class content does not automatically lead to adjustment of study strategies. *Australian Journal of Educational Developmental Psychology, 7*, 31–46.

Capers, Q. I. V. IV, Clinchot, D., McDougle, L., & Greenwald, A. G. (2017). Implicit bias in medical school admissions. *Academic Medicine, 92*(3), 365–369. doi:10.1097/ACM.0000000000001388 PMID:27680316

Careers in Medicine (CiM), Association of American Medical Colleges (AAMC). (2013). *Clinical rotation evaluation.* Retrieved June 9, 2019 from https://www.aamc.org/cim/download/382812/data/clinicalrotationevaluation.pdf

Careers in Medicine (CiM), Association of American Medical Colleges (AAMC). (2019). *About self-assessment.* Retrieved June 9, 2019 from https://www.aamc.org/cim/specialty/understandyourself/472322/aboutself-assessment.html

Careers in Medicine (CiM), Association of American Medical Colleges (AAMC). (2019). *Apply smart: new data to consider.* Retrieved June 9, 2019 from https://www.aamc.org/cim/480276/applysmartnewdatatoconsider.html

Careers in Medicine (CiM), Association of American Medical Colleges (AAMC). (2019). *Residency preference exercise.* Retrieved June 9, 2019 from https://www.aamc.org/cim/residency/programs/residencypreferenceexercise/

Carle Illinois College of Medicine (UIUC). (n.d.). *The Illinois model for medical education.* Retrieved from https://medicine.illinois.edu/education/paradigm-shifting-curriculum

Carrero, E., Gomar, C., Penzo, W., Fábregas, N., Valero, R., & Sánchez-Etayo, G. (2009). Teaching basic life support algorithms by either multimedia presentations or case based discussion equally improves the level of cognitive skills of undergraduate medical students. *Medical Teacher, 31*(5), e189–e195. doi:10.1080/01421590802512896 PMID:19241215

Casazza, M. (2018). Accreditation: A value-added proposition. *NADE Digest, 9*(2), 3–7.

Castiglioni, A., Aagaard, E., Spencer, A., Nicholson, L., Karani, R., Bates, C. K., ... Chheda, S. G. (2012). Succeeding as a clinician educator: Useful tips and resources. *Journal of General Internal Medicine, 28*(1), 136–140. doi:10.100711606-012-2156-8 PMID:22836953

Castillo-Page, L. (2016). *Diversity in medical education: Facts & figures 2016.* Washington, DC: Association of American Medical Colleges.

Cataldi, E., Bennett, C., & Chen, X. (2018). First-generation students: College access, persistence and post-bachelor's outcomes. U.S. Department of Education, NCES.

Cathcart-Rake, W., Robinson, M., & Paolo, A. (2017). From infancy to adolescence: Kansas University School of Medicine- Salina: A rural medical campus story. *Academic Medicine, 92*(5), 622–627. doi:10.1097/ACM.0000000000001455 PMID:27805948

Center for Digital Health at Stanford. (2019) Shaping the future of digital health, together. Retrieved June 1, 2019, from http://med.stanford.edu/cdh.html

Center for Digital Health. (2019). 2018 Pathway of distinction: Innovation, biodesign, and informatics elective course. Stanford Education, Retrieved June 2, 2019 from http://med.stanford.edu/cdh/Education.html

Center for Medicare and Medicaid Services. (2018). National Health Expenditures 2017, Retrieved June 2, 2019 from https://www.cms.gov/Research-Statistics-Data-and-Systems/Statistics-Trends-and-Reports/NationalHealthExpendData/Downloads/highlights.pdf

Center for Teaching Excellence, University of Waterloo. *Active Learning Activities.* (2019). Retrieved May 8, 2019, from https://uwaterloo.ca

Centers for Medicare and Medicaid Services (CMS). (n.d.). *National health expenditures by type of service and source of funds, CY 1960-2017.* Retrieved from https://www.cms.gov/research-statistics-data-and-systems/statistics-trends-and-reports/nationalhealthexpenddata/nationalhealthaccountshistorical.html

Cepeda, N. J., Pashler, H., Vul, E., Wixted, J. T., & Rohrer, D. (2006). Distributed practice in verbal recall tasks: A review and quantitative synthesis. *Psychological Bulletin, 132*(3), 354–380. doi:10.1037/0033-2909.132.3.354 PMID:16719566

Chang, C. W. D., & Erhardt, B. F. (2015). Rising Residency Applications. *Otolaryngology - Head and Neck Surgery, 153*(5), 702–705. doi:10.1177/0194599815597216 PMID:26243024

Char, D. S., Shah, N. H., & Magnus, D. (2018). Implementing Machine Learning in Health Care - Addressing Ethical Challenges. *The New England Journal of Medicine, 378*(11), 981–983. doi:10.1056/NEJMp1714229 PMID:29539284

Chatelain, M. (2018). We must help first-generation students master academe's "hidden curriculum." *The Chronicle of Higher Education.* Retrieved from https://www.chronicle.com/article/We-Must-Help-First-Generation/244830

Chattopadhyay, S. (2007). Religion, spirituality, health and medicine: Why should Indian physicians care. *Journal of Postgraduate Medicine, 53*(4), 262–266. doi:10.4103/0022-3859.33967 PMID:18097118

Chaudhry, B., Wang, J., Wu, S., Maglione, M., Mojica, W., Roth, E., ... Shekelle, P. G. (2006). Systematic review: Impact of health information technology on quality, efficiency, and costs of medical care. *Annals of Internal Medicine*, *144*(10), 742–752. doi:10.7326/0003-4819-144-10-200605160-00125 PMID:16702590

Chen, D. C., Miloslavsky, E. M., Winn, A. S., & McSparron, J. I. (2018). Fellow as Clinical Teacher (FACT) curriculum: Improving fellows' teaching skills during inpatient consultation. *MedEdPORTAL*, *14*(10), 1–6. PMID:30800928

Chene, A. (1983). The concept of autonomy in adult education: A philosophical discussion. *Adult Education Quarterly*, *1*(1), 38–47. doi:10.1177/0001848183034001004

Chen, H. C., Wamsley, M. A., Azzam, A., Julian, K., Irby, D. M., & O'Sullivan, P. S. (2017). The health professions education pathway: Preparing students, residents, and fellows to become future educators. *Teaching and Learning in Medicine*, *29*(2), 216–227. doi:10.1080/10401334.2016.1230500 PMID:27813688

Chen, P., & Scanlon, M. (2018). Teaching radiology trainees from the perspective of a Millennial. *Academic Radiology*, *25*(6), 794–800. doi:10.1016/j.acra.2018.02.008 PMID:29573938

Chiron Health. (2019). Definitive guide to telemedicine. Retrieved June 2, 2019 from https://chironhealth.com/definitive-guide-to-telemedicine/about-telemedicine/types-of-telemedicine/

Chittenden, E. H., Henry, D., Saxena, V., Loeser, H., & O'Sullivan, P. S. (2009). Transitional clerkship: An experiential course based on workplace learning theory. *Academic Medicine*, *84*(7), 872–876. doi:10.1097/ACM.0b013e3181a815e9 PMID:19550179

Choi-Lundberg, D., Low, T., Patman, P., Turner, P., & Sinha, S. (2016). Medical student preferences for self-directed study resources in gross anatomy. *Anatomical Sciences Education*, *9*(2), 150–160. doi:10.1002/ase.1549 PMID:26033851

Chumley, H., Olney, C., Usatine, R., & Dobbie, A. (2005). A short transitional course can help medical students prepare for clinical learning. *Family Medicine*, *37*(7), 496–501. https://www.ncbi.nlm.nih.gov/pubmed/15988643 PMID:15988643

Cizek, G. J. (2012). *Setting Performance Standards: Foundations, Methods, and Innovations*. Routledge. doi:10.4324/9780203848203

Clark, R., & Mayer, R. (2016). eLearning and the science of instruction, 4th Edition. Brentwood, CA: Wiley.

Clarke, A. J., Burgess, A., Menezes, A., & Mellis, C. (2015). Senior students' experience as tutors of their junior peers in the hospital setting. *BMC Research Notes*, *8*(1), 743. doi:10.118613104-015-1729-0 PMID:26631241

Classic, D. I. S. C. 2.0 Profile. (2019). John Wiley & Sons. Retrieved June 3, 2019, from https://www.everythingdisc.com/Home.aspx

Clauser, J., Clauser, B., & Hambleton, R. (2014). Increasing the Validity of Angoff Standards Through Analysis of Judge-Level Internal Consistency. *Applied Measurement in Education*, *27*(1), 19–30. doi:10.1080/08957347.2013.853071

Cleland, J., Leggett, H., Sandars, J., Costa, M., Patel, R., & Moffat, M. (2013). The remediation challenge: Theoretical and methodological insights from a systematic review. *Medical Education*, *47*(3), 242–251. doi:10.1111/medu.12052 PMID:23398010

Coates, W. C., Hobgood, C. D., Birnbaum, A., & Birnbaum, A. (2008). Faculty development: Academic opportunities for emergency medicine faculty on education career tracks. *Academic Emergency Medicine*, *10*(10), 1113–1117. doi:10.1197/S1069-6563(03)00369-5 PMID:14525747

Coates, W. C., Lin, M., Clarke, S., Jordan, J., Guth, T., Santen, S. A., & Yarris, L. M. (2012). Defining a core curriculum for education scholarship fellowships in emergency medicine. *Academic Emergency Medicine*, *19*(12), 1411–1418. doi:10.1111/acem.12036 PMID:23279248

Cohan, D. (2019). Racist like me - A call to self-reflection and action for white physicians. [doi]. *The New England Journal of Medicine*, *380*(9), 805–807. doi:10.1056/NEJMp1814269 PMID:30811907

Cohen, J. J. (2006). Professionalism in medical education, an American perspective: From evidence to accountability. *Medical Education*, *40*(7), 607–617. doi:10.1111/j.1365-2929.2006.02512.x PMID:16836532

Cohen, J. J. (2013). Will Changes in the MCAT and USMLE Ensure That Future Physicians Have What It Takes? *Journal of the American Medical Association*, *310*(21), 2253. doi:10.1001/jama.2013.283389 PMID:24302085

Colbert, C. Y., Myers, J. D., Cable, C. T., Ogden, P. E., Mirkes, C., McNeal, T., & Skeen, S. (2012). An alternative practice model: Residents transform continuity clinic and become systems thinkers. *Journal of Graduate Medical Education*, *3*(2), 232–236. doi:10.4300/JGME-D-11-00133.1 PMID:23730447

Colby, S. L., & Ortman, J. M. (2014). The baby boom cohort in the United States: 2012 to 2060. The US Census Bureau, 1-6.

Cole, M., & Hatano, G. (2007). Cultural-historical activity theory: Integrating phylogeny, cultural history, and ontogenesis in cultural psychology. In S. Kitayama, & D. Cohen (Eds.), *Handbook of cultural psychology* (pp. 109–135). New York: Guilford Press.

Coleman, J. J., Esposito, T. J., Rozycki, G. S., & Feliciano, D. V. (2013). Early subspecialization and perceived competence in surgical training: Are residents ready? *Journal of the American College of Surgeons*, *216*(4), 764–771. doi:10.1016/j.jamcollsurg.2012.12.045 PMID:23521960

Coleman, M. C., Blatt, B., & Greenberg, L. (2012). Preparing students to be academicians: A national student-led summer program in teaching, leadership, scholarship, and academic medical career-building. *Academic Medicine*, *87*(12), 1734–1741. doi:10.1097/ACM.0b013e318271cfd6 PMID:23095923

Colliver, J. A., Conlee, M. J., & Verhulst, S. J. (2012). From test validity to construct validity … and back? *Medical Education*, *46*(4), 366–371. doi:10.1111/j.1365-2923.2011.04194.x PMID:22429172

Colorado General Assembly. (2017). SB17-065: Transparency in direct pay health care prices. Retrieved June 2, 2019 from https://leg.colorado.gov/bills/sb17-065

Columbia University. (2019, n.d.). At a glance. Retrieved from https://gs.columbia.edu/postbac/postbac-at-a-glance

Commission on Osteopathic College Accreditation Handbook. (2018). Retrieved from https://osteopathic.org/wp-content/uploads/2018/02/coca-handbook.pdf

Commission on osteopathic college accreditation of colleges of osteopathic medicine: COM accreditation standards and procedures. (2019). Retrieved from https://osteopathic.org/wp-content/uploads/2018/02/com-continuing-accreditation-standards.pdf

Commission on Osteopathic College Accreditation. (2019). *Accreditation of Colleges of Osteopathic Medicine: COM Continuing Accreditation Standards*. Chicago, IL: American Osteopathic Association.

Comstock, J. (2018). Apple unveils watch series 4 with fda-approved ecg. Retrieved June 1, 2019 from https://www.healthcareitnews.com/news/apple-unveils-watch-series-4-fda-approved-ecg

Cook, A. F., Arora, V. M., Rasinski, K. A., Curlin, F. A., & Yoon, J. D. (2014). The prevalence of medical student mistreatment and its association with burnout. *Academic Medicine*, *89*(5), 740–754. doi:10.1097/ACM.0000000000000204 PMID:24667503

Cook, C. J., Cook, C. E., & Hilton, T. N. (2016). Does emotional intelligence influence success during medical school admissions and program matriculation? A systematic review. *Journal of Educational Evaluation for Health Professions*, *13*, 40. doi:10.3352/jeehp.2016.13.40 PMID:27838916

Cook, D. A., & Artino, A. R. Jr. (2016). Motivation to learn: An overview of contemporary theories. *Medical Education*, *50*(10), 997–1014.

Cook, D. A., Castillo, R. M., Gas, B., & Artino, A. R. Jr. (2017). Measuring achievement goal motivation, mindsets, and cognitive load: Validation of three instruments' scores. *Medical Education*, *51*(10), 1061–1074. doi:10.1111/medu.13405 PMID:28901645

Cook, D., Erwin, P. J., & Triola, M. M. (2010). Computerized virtual patients in health professions education: A systematic review and meta-analysis. *Academic Medicine*, *85*(10), 1589–1602. doi:10.1097/ACM.0b013e3181edfe13 PMID:20703150

Cook, D., & Triola, M. (2009). Virtual patients: A critical literature review and proposed next steps. *Medical Education*, *43*(4), 303–311. doi:10.1111/j.1365-2923.2008.03286.x PMID:19335571

Cooke, M., Irby, D. M., & O'Brien, B. C. (2010). *Educating Physicians: A Call for Reform of Medical School and Residency*. San Francisco, CA: Jossey-Bass.

Cooke, M., Irby, D., Sullilvan, W. & Ludmerer, K.M. (2006). American medical education100 years after the Flexner report. *New England Journal of Medicine, 355, 1339-1344. DOI: 055445.* doi:10.056/NEJMra

Cooke, M., Irby, D. M., & O'Brien, C. S. (2010). *Educating Physicians: A Call for Reform of Medical School and Residency*. San Francisco, CA: Jossey-Bass.

Cooke, M., Irby, D. M., Sullivan, W., & Ludmerer, K. M. (2006). American Medical Education 100 Years after the Flexner Report. *The New England Journal of Medicine*, *355*(13), 1339–1344. doi:10.1056/NEJMra055445 PMID:17005951

Core Competencies for Entering Medical Students. (2019). Retrieved from https://www.aamc.org/admissions/dataandresearch/477182/corecompetencies.html

Coumarbatch, J., Robinson, L., Thomas, R., & Bridge, P. (2010). Strategies for identifying students at risk for USMLE Step 1 failure. *Family Medicine*, *42*(2), 105–110. PMID:20135567

Cox, M., Cuff, P., Brandt, B., Reeves, S., & Zierler, B. (2016). Measuring the impact of interprofessional education on collaborative practice and patient outcomes.

Cronbach, L. J., Gleser, G. C., Nanda, H., & Rajaratnam, N. (1972). *The Dependability of Behavioral Measurements: Theory of Generalizability for Scores and Profiles*. New York: John Wiley & Sons.

Cronbach, L. J., & Meehl, P. E. (1955). Construct validity in psychological tests. *Psychological Bulletin*, *52*(4), 281–302. doi:10.1037/h0040957 PMID:13245896

Crossley, J., Humphris, G., & Jolly, B. (2002). Assessing health professionals. *Medical Education*, *36*(9), 800–804. doi:10.1046/j.1365-2923.2002.01294.x PMID:12354241

Cruess, R. L., Cruess, S. R., Boudreau, J. D., Snell, L., & Steinert, Y. (2015). A schematic representation of the professional identity formation and socialization of medical students and residents: A guide for medical educators. *Academic Medicine*, *90*(6), 718–725. doi:10.1097/ACM.0000000000000700 PMID:25785682

Cruess, R., & Creus, S. (2014). Reframing medical education to support professional identity formation. *Academic Medicine, 89*(11), 1446–14451. doi:10.1097/ACM.0000000000000427 PMID:25054423

Crumly, C., Dietz, P., & DAngelo, S. (2014). *Pedagogies for student-centered learning: Online and on-ground.* Minneapolis, MN: Fortress Press.

Crump, C., Ned, J., & Winkleby, M. A. (2015). The Stanford Medical Youth Science Program: Educational and science-related outcomes. *Advances in Health Sciences Education: Theory and Practice, 20*(2), 457–466. doi:10.100710459-014-9540-6 PMID:25096792

Crump, W., & Fricker, R. (2015). A medical school prematriculation program for rural students: Staying connected with place, cultivating a special connection with people. *Teaching and Learning in Medicine, 27*(4), 422–430. doi:10.1080/10401334.2015.1077709 PMID:26508001

Current Trends in Medical Education. Retrieved from http://www.aamcdiversityfactsandfigures2016.org/report-section/section-3/

Cutrer, W. B., Miller, B., Pusic, M. V., Mejicano, G., Mangrulkar, R. S., Gruppen, L. D., ... Moore, D. E. Jr. (2017). Fostering the development of master adaptive learners: A conceptual model to guide skill acquisition in medical education. Academic Medicine [PubMed]. *Journal. Association of American Medical Colleges, 92*(1), 70–75.

Dahlstrom, J., Dorei-Rag, A., McGill, D., Owen, C., Tymms, K., & Watson, D. A. (2005). What motivates senior clinicians to teach medical students? *BMC Medical Education, 5*(1), 27–37. doi:10.1186/1472-6920-5-27 PMID:16022738

DallaPiazza, M., Padilla-Register, M., Dwarakanath, M., Obamedo, E., Hill, J., Soto-Greene, M. L. (2018). Exploring racism and health: an intensive interactive session for medical students. *MedEdPORTAL, 14*, 10783.

Dalley, B., Podawiltz, A., Castro, R., Fallon, K., Kott, M., Rabek, J., ... Smith, Q. (2009). The Joint Admission Medical Program: A Statewide Approach to Expanding Medical Education and Career Opportunities for Disadvantaged Students. *Academic Medicine, 84*(10), 1373–1382. doi:10.1097/ACM.0b013e3181b6c76b PMID:19881424

Danek, J., & Borrayo, E. (2012). *Urban universities: Developing a health workforce that meets community needs.* Washington DC: Urban Universities for Health. Retrieved from http://urbanuniversitiesforhealth.org/media/documents/Urban_Health_Workforce_Final_Report.pdf

Danner, O. K., Lokko, C., Mobley, F., Dansby, M., Maze, M., Bradley, B., ... Childs, E. (2017). Hospital-based, multidisciplinary, youth mentoring, and medical exposure program positively influences and reinforces health care career choice: "The Reach One Each One Program early Experience. *American Journal of Surgery, 213*(4), 611–616. doi:10.1016/j.amjsurg.2016.12.002 PMID:28040097

Data Reports in Osteopathic Medical Education . (2017). Retrieved from https://www.aacom.org/docs/default-source/data-and-trends/gme-special-report-2017.pdf?sfvrsn=dfb22c97_6

Davies, J. (2005). Expressions of gender: An analysis of pupil's gendered discourse styles in small group classroom discussions. *Discourse & Society, 14*(2), 115–132. doi:10.1177/0957926503014002853

Davis, D. (2018). The medical school without walls: Reflections on the future of medical education. *Medical Teacher Volume, 40*(10), 1004–1009. doi:10.1080/0142159X.2018.1507263 PMID:30259766

Davis, D. A., Prescott, J., Fordis, C. M. Jr, Greenberg, S. B., Dewey, C. M., Brigham, T., ... Tenner, T. E. Jr. (2011). Rethinking CME: An imperative for academic medicine and faculty development (2011). *Academic Medicine: Journal of the Association of American Medical Colleges, 86*(4), 468–473. doi:10.1097/ACM.0b013e31820dfacf PMID:21346497

Davis, D. A., Rayburn, W. F., & Smith, G. A. (2017). Continuing professional development for faculty: An elephant in the house of academic medicine or the key to future success? *Academic Medicine: Journal of the Association of American Medical Colleges, 92*(8), 1078–1081. doi:10.1097/ACM.0000000000001777 PMID:28562453

Day, L., & Benner, P. (2014). The hidden curriculum in nursing education. In F. W. Hafferty, & J. F. O'Donnell (Eds.), The Hidden Curriculum in Health Professional Education (140-149). Hanover, NH: Dartmouth College Press.

de Ayala, R. J. (2013). *The Theory and Practice of Item Response Theory*. Guilford Publications.

De Champlain, A. F. (2010). A primer on classical test theory and item response theory for assessments in medical education. *Medical Education, 44*(1), 109–117. doi:10.1111/j.1365-2923.2009.03425.x PMID:20078762

De Menezes, S., & Premnath, D. (2016). Near-peer education: A novel teaching program. *International Journal of Medical Education, 7*, 160–167. doi:10.5116/ijme.5738.3c28 PMID:27239951

de Montbrun, S. L., & Macrae, H. (2012). Simulation in surgical education. *Clinics in Colon and Rectal Surgery, 25*(3), 156–165. doi:10.1055-0032-1322553 PMID:23997671

Deane, K., & Ringdahl, E. (2012). The family medicine chief resident: A national survey of leadership development. *Family Medicine, 44*(2), 117–120. PMID:22328478

DeAngelis, C. D. (2015). Medical professionalism. *Journal of the American Medical Association, 313*(18), 1837–1838. doi:10.1001/jama.2015.3597

DeBard, R. (2004). Millennials coming to college. *New Directions for Student Services, 106*(106), 33–45. doi:10.1002s.123

Deci, E. L., & Ryan, R. M. (1991). A motivational approach to self: Integration in personality. In R. Dienstbier (Ed.), *Nebraska Symposium on Motivation:* Vol. 38. *Perspectives on Motivation* (pp. 237–288). Lincoln, NE: University of Nebraska Press.

Dedy, N. J., Zevin, B., Bonrath, E. M., & Grantcharov, T. P. (2013). Current concepts of team training in surgical residency: A survey of North American program directors. *Journal of Surgical Education, 7*(5), 578–584. doi:10.1016/j.jsurg.2013.04.011 PMID:24016367

Defoe, D. M., Power, M. L., Holzman, G. B., Carpentieri, A., & Schulkin, J. (2001). Long hours and little sleep: Work schedules of residents in obstetrics and gynecology. *Obstetrics and Gynecology, 97*(6), 1015–1018. PMID:11384712

DeIorio, N., Carney, P., Kahl, L., Bonura, E., & Miller Juve, A. (2016). Coaching: A new model for academic and career achievement. *Medical Education Online, 21*(1). doi:10.3402/meo.v21.33480 PMID:27914193

DeMaria, A. N. (2013). Here come the millennials. *Journal of the American College of Cardiology, 61*(15), 1654–1656. doi:10.1016/j.jacc.2013.03.009 PMID:23524049

Deming-the-man. (2019). Retrieved from https://deming.org/deming/deming-the-man The W. Edwards Deming Institute

Deming, W. E. (1986). *Out of the crisis*. Cambridge, MA: Massachusetts Institute of Technology, Center for Advanced Engineering Study.

Desy, J. R., Reed, D. A., & Wolanskyj, A. P. (2017). Milestones and millennials: A perfect pairing – competency-based medical education and the learning preferences of generation Y. *Mayo Clinic Proceedings, 92*(2), 243–250. doi:10.1016/j.mayocp.2016.10.026 PMID:28160874

Dewey, J. (1900). *The child and the curriculum; The school and society*. Chicago, IL: University of Chicago Press.

Diemers, A. D., Dolmans, D. H., Santen, M. V., Luijk, S. J., Janssen-Noordman, A. M., & Scherpbier, A. J. (2007). Students' perceptions of early patient encounters in a PBL curriculum: A first evaluation of the Maastricht experience. *Medical Teacher*, 29(2–3), 135–142. doi:10.1080/01421590601177990 PMID:17701623

Diemers, A. D., Dolmans, D. H., Verwijnen, M. G., Heineman, E., & Scherpbier, A. J. (2007). Students' opinions about the effects of preclinical patient contacts on their learning. *Advances in Health Sciences Education: Theory and Practice*, 13(5), 633–647. doi:10.100710459-007-9070-6 PMID:17629786

Dinsmore, D. L., Alexander, P. A., & Loughlin, S. M. (2008). Focusing the conceptual lens on metacognition, self-regulation, and self-regulated learning. *Educational Psychology Review*, 20(4), 391–409. doi:10.100710648-008-9083-6

Distlehorst, L. H., Dawson, E., Robbs, R. S., & Barrows, H. S. (2005). Problem-Based Learning Outcomes: The Glass Half-Full. *Academic Medicine*, 80(3), 294–299. doi:10.1097/00001888-200503000-00020 PMID:15734816

Docs, A. (n.d.). *Dealing with application anxiety*. Retrieved from https://students-residents. aamc.org/applying-medical-school/article/dealing-application-anxiety

Dolmans, D. H. J. M., Loyens, S. M. M., Marcq, H., & Gijbels, D. (2016). Deep and surface learning in problem-based learning: A review of the literature. *Advances in Health Sciences Education: Theory and Practice*, 21(5), 1087–1112. doi:10.100710459-015-9645-6 PMID:26563722

Dolmans, D. H., Grave, W. D., Wolfhagen, I. H., & Cees, P. (2005). Problem-based learning: Future challenges for educational practice and research. *Medical Education*, 39(7), 732–741. doi:10.1111/j.1365-2929.2005.02205.x PMID:15960794

Dolmans, D., Michaelsen, L., Van Merrienboer, J. V., & Van der Vleuten, C. (2015). Should we choose between problem-based learning and team-based learning? No, combine the best of both worlds! *Medical Teacher*, 37(4), 354–359. doi:10.3109/0142159X.2014.948828 PMID:25154342

Dornan, T., Boshuizen, H., King, N., & Scherpbier, A. (2007). Experience-based learning: A model linking the processes and outcomes of medical students' workplace learning. *Medical Education*, 41(1), 84–91. doi:10.1111/j.1365-2929.2006.02652.x PMID:17209896

Dos Santos Boni, R. A., Paiva, C. E., de Oliveira, M. A., Lucchetti, G., Fregnani, J. H. T. G., & Paiva, B. S. R. (2018). Burnout among medical students during the first years of undergraduate school: Prevalence and associated factors. *PLoS One*, 13(3). doi:10.1371/journal.pone.0191746 PMID:29513668

Doty, J., & Taylor, D. (2019). Developing physician leaders. *Current Sports Medicine Reports*, 18(2), 45. doi:10.1249/JSR.0000000000000561 PMID:30730339

Doukas, D. J., McCullough, L. B. & Wear, S. (2012). Perspective: Medical education in medical ethics and humanities as the foundation for developing medical professionalism. *Academic Medicine,* 87(3), 334-341. DOI:. 0b013e318244728c. doi:10.1097/ACM

Dow, A., & Thibault, G. (2017). Interprofessional Education-A Foundation for a New Approach to Health Care. *The New England Journal of Medicine*, 377(9), 803–805. doi:10.1056/NEJMp1705665 PMID:28854090

Downing, S. M. (2003). Validity: On meaningful interpretation of assessment data. *Medical Education*, 37(9), 830–837. doi:10.1046/j.1365-2923.2003.01594.x PMID:14506816

Dreyfus, S. E. (2004). The five-stage model of adult skill acquisition. *Bulletin of Science, Technology & Society*, 24(3), 177–181. Retrieved from https://moleseyhill.com/2009-08-27-dreyfus-model.html

Dreyfus, S. (2004). The Five-Stage Model of Adult Skill Acquisition. *Bulletin of Science, Technology & Society*, 24(3), 177–181. doi:10.1177/0270467604264992

Dubin, B. (2016). Innovative Curriculum Prepares Medical Students for a Lifetime of Learning and Patient Care. *Missouri Medicine*, *113*(3), 170–173. PMID:27443039

Duffy, T. P. (2011). The Flexner Report – 100 years later. *The Yale Journal of Biology and Medicine*, *84*(3), 269–276. PMID:21966046

Dunleavy D. M. & Whittaker, K. M. (2011). The Evolving Medical School Admissions Interview. *Analysis in Brief, 11*(7).

Dunleavy, D., Sondheimer, H., Castillo-Page, L., & Beer Bletzinger, R. (2011). *Medical school admissions: More than grades and test scores*. Retrieved from https://www.aamc.org/download/261106/data/

Dunleavy, D. M., Kroopnick, M. H., Dowd, K. W., Searcy, C. A., & Zhao, X. (2013). The predictive validity of the MCAT exam in relation to academic performance through medical school: A national cohort study of 2001-2004 matriculants. *Academic Medicine*, *88*(5), 666–671. doi:10.1097/ACM.0b013e3182864299 PMID:23478635

Dunleavy, D., Sondheimer, H., Bletzinger, R., & Castillo-Page, L. (2011). Medical school admissions: More than grades and test scores. *Analysis in Brief*, *11*(6), 1–2.

Dunn, T. J., Baguley, T., & Brunsden, V. (2014). From alpha to omega: a practical solution to the pervasive problem of internal consistency estimation. *British Journal of Psychology (London, England: 1953)*, *105*(3), 399–412. doi:10.1111/bjop.12046

Durning, S. J., Dong, T., Hemmer, P. A., Gilliland, W. R., Cruess, D. F., Boulet, J. R., & Pangarao, L. N. (2015). Are commonly used premedical school or medical school measures associated with board certification? *Military Medicine*, *180*(4), 18–23. doi:10.7205/MILMED-D-14-00569 PMID:25850122

Durning, S., Cleary, T., Sandars, J., Hemmer, P. A., Kokotailo, P., & Artino, A. R. (2011). Perspective: Viewing "strugglers" through a different lens: How a self-regulated learning perspective can help medical educators with assessment and remediation. *Academic Medicine*, *86*(4), 488–495. doi:10.1097/ACM.0b013e31820dc384 PMID:21346503

Dweck, C. S. (2006). *Mindset: The new psychology of success*. New York: Random House.

Dweck, C. S. (2013). *Self-theories: Their role in motivation, personality, and development*. New York: Psychology Press. doi:10.4324/9781315783048

Dwivedi, Y., Wastell, D., Laumer, S., Henriksen, H., Myers, M., Bunker, D., ... Srivastava, S. C. (2014). Research on information systems failures and successes: Status update and future directions. *Information Systems Frontiers*, *17*(1), 143–157. doi:10.100710796-014-9500-y

Dyrbye, L. N., Thomas, M. R., Eacker, A., Harper, W., Massie, F. S., Power, D. V., ... Shanafelt, T. D. (2007). Race, ethnicity, and medical student well-being in the United States. [Not cited in text]. *Archives of Internal Medicine*, *167*(19), 2103–2109. doi:10.1001/archinte.167.19.2103 PMID:17954805

Dyrbye, L. N., Thomas, M. R., Massie, F. S., Power, D. V., Eacker, A., Harper, W., ... Shanafelt, T. D. (2008). Burnout and suicidal ideation among U.S. medical students. *Annals of Internal Medicine*, *149*(5), 334–341. doi:10.7326/0003-4819-149-5-200809020-00008 PMID:18765703

Dyrbye, L. N., Thomas, M. R., Power, D. V., Durning, S., Moutier, C., Massie, F. S. Jr, ... Sloan, J. A. (2010). Burnout and serious thoughts of dropping out of medical school: A multi-institutional study. *Academic Medicine*, *85*(1), 94–102. doi:10.1097/ACM.0b013e3181c46aad PMID:20042833

Dyrbye, L. N., Thomas, M. R., & Shanafelt, T. D. (2006). Systematic review of depression, anxiety, and other indicators of psychological distress among U.S. and Canadian medical students. *Academic Medicine*, *81*(4), 354–373. doi:10.1097/00001888-200604000-00009 PMID:16565188

Dyrbye, L., & Shanafelt, T. (2012). Nurturing resiliency in medical trainees. *Medical Education*, *46*(4), 343. doi:10.1111/j.1365-2923.2011.04206.x PMID:22429167

Eaglen, R. H. (2017). *Academic quality and public accountability in academic medicine: the 75-year history of the Lcme.* Washington, DC: Association of American Medical Colleges.

Eaton, J. S. (2015). *An overview of U.S. accreditation.* Washington, DC: CHEA.

Eckleberry-Hunt, J., & Tucciarone, J. (2011). The challenges and opportunities of teaching "Generation Y". *Journal of Graduate Medical Education*, *3*(4), 458–461. doi:10.4300/JGME-03-04-15 PMID:23205190

Edler, A., Adamshick, M., Fanning, R., & Piro, N. (2010). Leadership lessons from military education for postgraduate medical curricular improvement. *The Clinical Teacher*, *7*(1), 26–31. doi:10.1111/j.1743-498X.2009.00336.x PMID:21134139

Edmondson, A. (2012). *Teaming: How organizations learn, innovate and compete in the knowledge economy.* San Francisco, CA: Jossey-Bass.

Edwards, J. C., Johnson, E. K., & Molidor, J. B. (1990). The interview in the admission process. *Academic Medicine*, *65*(3), 167–177. doi:10.1097/00001888-199003000-00008 PMID:2407259

Elks, M. L., Herbert-Carter, J., Smith, M., Klement, B., Knight, B. B., & Anachebe, N. F. (2018). Shifting the curve. Fostering academic success in a diverse student body. *Academic Medicine*, *93*(1), 66–70. doi:10.1097/ACM.0000000000001783 PMID:28678099

Ellaway, R. H., Cooper, G., Al-Idrissi, T., Dube, T., & Graves, L. (2014). Discourses of student orientation to medical education programs. *Medical Education Online*, *19*(23714). PMID:24646440

Elliot, D., Baumfield, V., Reic, K., & Makara, K. (2016). Hidden treasure: Successful international doctoral students who found and harnessed the hidden curriculum. *Oxford Review of Education*, *42*(6), 733–748. doi:10.1080/03054985.2016.1229664

Ely, S., LaConte, L., Fogel, S., & Vari, R. (2015). *Student perception of patient-centered problem-based learning in one medical school curriculum varies with stage of training; a mid-study report.* Poster presented at the 19th Annual Meeting of the International Association of Medical Science Educators, San Diego, CA.

Embretson, S. E., & Reise, S. P. (2000). *Item Response Theory for Psychologists.* L. Erlbaum Associates.

Engeström, Y. (2000). Activity theory as a framework for analyzing and redesigning work. *Ergonomics*, *43*(7), 960–974. doi:10.1080/001401300409143 PMID:10929830

Engeström, Y. (2001). Expansive learning at work: Toward an activity theoretical reconceptualization. *Journal of Education and Work*, *14*(1), 133–156. doi:10.1080/13639080020028747

Engeström, Y. (2007). Enriching the theory of expansive learning: Lessons from journeys toward coconfiguration. *Mind, Culture, and Activity*, *14*(1-2), 23–39. doi:10.1080/10749030701307689

Engeström, Y., & Cole, M. (1997). Situated cognition in search of an agenda. In D. Kirshner, & J. A. Whitson (Eds.), *Situated cognition: Social, semiotic, and psychological perspectives* (pp. 301–309). Mahwah, NJ: Erlbaum.

Epps, A. C. (2015). The strategic impact of a post baccalaureate pre-medicine intervention program on medical school academic performance. *Journal of Health Care for the Poor and Underserved*, *26*(1), 8–20. doi:10.1353/hpu.2015.0008 PMID:25702723

Epstein, R. M. (2007). Assessment in medical education. *The New England Journal of Medicine*, *356*(4), 387–396. doi:10.1056/NEJMra054784 PMID:17251535

Epstein, R. M., & Hundert, E. M. (2002). Defining and assessing professional competence. *Journal of the American Medical Association, 287*(2), 226–235. doi:10.1001/jama.287.2.226 PMID:11779266

Epstein, R. M., & Krasner, M. S. (2013). Physician resilience: What it means, why it matters, and how to promote it. *Academic Medicine, 88*(3), 301–303. doi:10.1097/ACM.0b013e318280cff0 PMID:23442430

Ericsson, K. A. (2004). Deliberate practice and the acquisition and maintenance of expert performance in medicine and related domains. *Academic Medicine: Journal of the Association of American Medical Colleges, 79*(10Suppl), 70–81. doi:10.1097/00001888-200410001-00022 PMID:15383395

Esposito, J. (2011, November). Negotiating the gaze and learning the hidden curriculum: A critical race analysis of the embodiment of female students of color at predominantly white institutions. *The Journal for Critical Education Policy Studies, 9*, 143–164.

Eubank, D., Geffken, D., Orzano, J., & Ricci, R. (2012). Teaching adaptive leadership to family medicine residents: What? Why? How? *Families Systems & Health, 30*(3), 241–252. doi:10.1111/j.1743-498X.2009.00336.x 10.1037/a0029689

Eva, K. W., & Regehr, G. (2008). I'll never play professional football and other fallacies of self assessment. *The Journal of Continuing Education in the Health Professions, 28*(1), 14–19. doi:10.1002/chp.150 PMID:18366120

Eva, K. W., Reiter, H. I., Trinh, K., Wasi, P., Rosenfeld, J., & Norman, G. R. (2009). Predictive validity of multiple mini-interview for selecting medical trainees. *Medical Education, 43*(8), 767–775. doi:10.1111/j.1365-2923.2009.03407.x PMID:19659490

Eva, K. W., Rosenfeld, J., Reiter, H. I., & Norman, G. R. (2004). An admissions OSCE: The multiple mini-interview. *Medical Education, 38*(3), 314–326. doi:10.1046/j.1365-2923.2004.01776.x PMID:14996341

Evans, H. M., & Greaves, D. A. (2010). Ten years of medical humanities: A decade in the life of a journal and discipline. *Medical Humanities, 36*(2), 66-68. DOI:. 2010.005603 doi:10.1136/jmh

Evergreen, S., & Metzner, C. (2013). Design principles for data visualization in evaluation. In T. Azzam, & S. Evergreen (Eds.), Data visualization for evaluation, part 2. New Directions for Evaluation, 140, 5–20. doi:10.1002/ev.20071

Ewell, P. T. (2009, November). Assessment, accountability, and improvement: Revisiting the tension (NILOA Occasional Paper No. 1). Urbana, IL: University of Illinois and Indiana University, National Institute of Learning Outcomes Assessment. Retrieved from http://www.learningoutcomeassessment.org/documents/PeterEwell_005.pdfGarun

FACTS: Applicants, Matriculants, Enrollment, Graduates, MD-PhD, and Residency Applicants Data Table A-6 . (2017). Retrieved from https://www.aamc.org/download/321468/data/factstablea6.pdf

FACTS: Applicants, Matriculants, Enrollment, Graduates, MD-PhD, and Residency Applicants Data. (2018). Retrieved from https://www.aamc.org/data/facts/

Fang, Z. (1996). A review of research on teacher beliefs and practices. *Educational Research, 38*(1), 47–65. doi:10.1080/0013188960380104

Farrell, C. C. (2014). Designing school systems to encourage data use and instructional improvement: A comparison of school districts and charter management organizations. *Educational Administration Quarterly, 51*(3), 438–471. doi:10.1177/0013161X14539806

Favia, A., Frank, L., Gligorov, N., Birnbaum, S., Cummins, P., Fallar, R., Ferguson, K.... Rhodes, R. (2013). A model for the assessment of medical students' competency in medical ethics. *AJOB Primary Research, 4*(4), 68-83. DOI:. doi:10.1080/21507716.2013.768308

Federation of State Medical Boards. (2018). *U.S. Medical Regulatory Trends and Actions 2018*. Retrieved May 10 from https://www.fsmb.org/siteassets/advocacy/publications/us-medical-regulatory-trends-actions.pdf

Feinberg, R. N., & Koltz, E. F. (2015). Getting started as a medical teacher in times of change. *Medical Science Educator, 25*(1), 69–74. doi:10.100740670-014-0098-y

Ferris, J. D., Donachie, P. H., Johnston, R. L., Barnes, B., Olaitan, M., & Sparrow, J. M. (2019). Royal College of Ophthalmologists' National Ophthalmology Database study of cataract surgery: Report 6. The impact of EyeSi virtual reality training on complications rates of cataract surgery performed by first- and second-year trainees. *The British Journal of Ophthalmology*, bjophthalmol-2018-313817; Epub ahead of print. doi:10.1136/bjophthalmol-2018-313817 PMID:31142463

Few, S. (2006). *Information dashboard design: The effective visual communication of data*. New York: O'Reilly.

Filipe, H. P., Golnik, K. C., & Mack, H. G. (2018). Professional development? What happened to CME? CME and beyond. *Medical Teacher, 40*(9), 914–916. doi:10.1080/0142159X.2018.1471200 PMID:29793386

Filipe, H. P., Silva, E. D., Stulting, A. A., & Golnik, K. C. (2014). Continuing professional development: Best practices. *Middle East African Journal of Ophthalmology, 21*(2), 134–141. doi:10.4103/0974-9233.129760 PMID:24791104

Finch, W. H., & French, B. F. (2018). *Educational and Psychological Measurement*. Routledge. doi:10.4324/9781315650951

Firth, J. (1986). Levels and sources of stress in medical students. *British Medical Journal, 292*(6529), 1177–1180. doi:10.1136/bmj.292.6529.1177 PMID:3085772

Flexner, A. (1910). *Medical Education in the United States and Canada. A Report to the Carnegie Foundation for the Advancement of Teaching*. Retrieved from http://archive.carnegiefoundation.org/pdfs/elibrary/Carnegie_Flexner_Report.pdf

Flexner, A. (1910). *Medical education in the United States and Canada*. Washington, DC: Science and Health Publications.

Food and Drug Administration. (2018) Digital health action plan. Retrieved June 1, 2019 from https://www.fda.gov/media/106331/download

Fornari, A., & Poznanski, A. (2015). *How-to guide for active learning*. Huntington, WV: International Association of Medical Science Educators.

Fralick, M., & Flegel, K. (2014). Physician burnout: Who will protect us from ourselves? *Canadian Medical Association Journal, 186*(10), 731. doi:10.1503/cmaj.140588 PMID:24890102

Frankl, S., Newman, L., Burgin, S., Atasoylu, A., Fishman, L., Gooding, H., ... Schwartzstein, R. (2017). The case-based collaborative learning peer observation worksheet and compendium: An evaluation of tool for flipped classroom facilitators. *MedEdPORTAL, 13*, 10583. doi:10.15766/mep_2374-8265.10583 PMID:30800785

Frayha, N., Raczek, J., Lo, J., Martinez, J., & Parker, D. (2019). An Electronic Interview Tracking Tool to Guide Medical Students Through the Match; Improvements in Advising and Match Outcomes. *Academic Medicine, 94*(3), 348–352. doi:10.1097/ACM.0000000000002522 PMID:30431454

Freeman, B. K., Trevino, R., Grande, D., Shea, J. A., & Shea, J. A. (2016). Understanding the leaky pipeline: Perceived barriers to pursuing a career in medicine or dentistry among underrepresented-in-medicine undergraduate students. *Academic Medicine, 91*(7), 987–993. doi:10.1097/ACM.0000000000001020 PMID:26650673

Freeman, D. (2004). *Trends in educational equity of girls and women*. Washington, DC: United States Department of Education, National Center for Educational Statistics.

Freeman, S., Eddy, S. L., McDonough, M., Smith, M. K., Okoroafor, N., Jordt, H., & Wenderoth, M. P. (2014). Active learning increases student performance in science, engineering and mathematics. [PNAS]. *Proceedings of the National Academy of Sciences of the United States of America*, *111*(23), 8410–8415. doi:10.1073/pnas.1319030111 PMID:24821756

Frenk, J., Chen, L., Bhutta, Z. A., Crisp, N., Evans, T., Fineberg, T., ... Kistnasamy, B. (2010). Health professionals for a new century: Transforming education to strengthen health systems in an interdependent world. *Lancet*, *376*(9756), 1923–1958. doi:10.1016/S0140-6736(10)61854-5 PMID:21112623

Freudenberger, H. J. (1974). Staff burn-out. *The Journal of Social Issues*, *30*(1), 159–165. doi:10.1111/j.1540-4560.1974.tb00706.x

Frich, J. C., Brewster, A. L., Cherlin, E. J., & Bradley, E. H. (2015). Leadership development programs for physicians: A systematic review. *Journal of General Internal Medicine*, *30*(5), 656–674. doi:10.100711606-014-3141-1 PMID:25527339

Frosch, E., & Goldstein, M. (2019). Relationship-Centered Advising in a Medical School Learning Community. *Journal of medical education and curricular development*, 6. doi:10.1177/2382120519827895

Fry, E., & Schulte, F. (2019, March 18). Death by a thousand clicks: Where electronic health records went wrong. *Fortune*.

Functions and structure of a medical school – LCME Standards . (2018). Retrieved from http://lcme.org/publications/

Gagnon, M.-C. J., Durand-Bush, N., & Young, B. W. (2016). Self-regulation capacity is linked to wellbeing and burnout in physicians and medical students: Implications for nurturing self-help skills. *International Journal of Wellbeing*, *6*(1), 101–116. doi:10.5502/ijw.v6i1.425

Gallagher, S. A. (1997). Problem-based learning: Where did it come from, what does it do, and where is it going? *Journal for the Education of the Gifted*, *20*(4), 332–362. doi:10.1177/016235329702000402

Gauer, J. L., & Jackson, J. B. (2018). Relationships of demographic variables to USMLE physician licensing exam scores: A statistical analysis on five years of medical student data. *Advances in Medical Education and Practice*, *9*, 39–44. doi:10.2147/AMEP.S152684 PMID:29391841

Gauer, J. L., Wolff, J. M., & Jackson, J. B. (2016). Do MCAT scores predict USMLE scores? An analysis on 5 years of medical student data. *Medical Education Online*, *21*(1). doi:10.3402/meo.v21.31795 PMID:27702431

Gawande, A. (2011). Personal best. *The New Yorker*. Oct. 3. Retrieved May 15, 2019 from http://www.newyorker. com/magazine/2011/10/03/personal-best

Gee, J. P. (2010). *New digital media and learning as an emerging area and "worked examples" as one way forward*. Cambridge, MA: MIT Press.

Gemignani, Z., Gemignani, C., Galentino, R., & Schuermann, P. (2014). *Data fluency: Empowering your organization with effective data communication*. San Francisco, CA: John Wiley & Sons.

George, B. C., Bohnen, J. D., Williams, R. G., Meyerson, S. L., Schuller, M. C., Clark, M. J., ... Fryer, J. P. (2017). Readiness of US General Surgery Residents for Independent Practice. *Annals of Surgery*, *266*(4), 582–594. doi:10.1097/SLA.0000000000002414 PMID:28742711

George, B. C., Teitelbaum, E. N., Meyerson, S. L., Schuller, M. C., DaRosa, D. A., Petrusa, E. R., ... Fryer, J. P. (2014). Reliability, validity, and feasibility of the Zwisch scale for the assessment of intraoperative performance. *Journal of Surgical Education*, *71*(6), e90–e96. doi:10.1016/j.jsurg.2014.06.018 PMID:25192794

George, P., Macnamara, M. M., Gainor, J., & Taylor, J. S. (2013). An integrated virtual family curriculum to introduce specialty-specific clinical skills to rising third-year medical students. *Teaching and Learning in Medicine, 25*(4), 342–347. doi:10.1080/10401334.2013.827977 PMID:24112204

Geraci, S. A., & Thigpen, S. C. (2017). A review of mentoring in academic medicine. *The American Journal of the Medical Sciences, 353*(2), 151–157. doi:10.1016/j.amjms.2016.12.002 PMID:28183416

Gerhardt, M. W. (2016). The importance of being...social? Instructor credibility and the millennials. *Studies in Higher Education, 41*(9), 1533–1547. doi:10.1080/03075079.2014.981516

Gevitz, N. (2019). *The DOs: osteopathic medicine in America.* Baltimore, MD: Johns Hopkins University Press.

Ghazi, A., Stone, J., Candela, B., Richards, M., & Joseph, J. (2015). Simulated inanimate model for physical learning experience (SIMPLE) for robotic partial nephrectomy using a 3-D printed kidney model. *The Journal of Urology, 193*(4SSupplement), e778. doi:10.1016/j.juro.2015.02.2285

Gibson, K. E., & Silverberg, M. (2000). A two-year experience teaching computer literacy to first-year medical students using skill-based cohorts. *Bulletin of the Medical Library Association, 88*(2), 157–164. PMID:10783971

Giger, J., Davidhizar, R. E., Purnell, L., Harden, J. T., Phillips, J., & Strickland, O. (●●●). American academy of nursing expert panel report: Developing cultural competence to eliminate health disparities in ethnic minorities and other vulnerable populations. *Journal of Transcultural Nursing, 18*(2), 95–102. doi:10.1177/1043659606298618

Gijselaers, W. H., & Schmidt, H. G. (1990). Development and evaluation of a causal model of PBL. *Innovation in Medical Education. An Evaluation of Its Present Status.*,95-113.

Gillan, S. N., Okhravi, N., O'Sullivan, F., Sullivan, P., Viswanathan, A., & Saleh, G. M. (2016). Influence of medical student career aims on ophthalmic surgical simulator performance (part of the international forum for ophthalmic simulation studies). *The British Journal of Ophthalmology, 100*(3), 411–414. doi:10.1136/bjophthalmol-2015-307127 PMID:26246344

Girdano, D., Everly, G. S., & Dusek, D. E. (1996). *Controlling stress and tension: A holistic approach.* Needham Heights, MA: Allyn & Bacon.

Godefrooij, M. B., Diemers, A. D., & Scherpbier, A. J. (2010). Students' perceptions about the transition to the clinical phase of a medical curriculum with preclinical patient contacts; a focus group study. *BMC Medical Education, 10*(1), 28. doi:10.1186/1472-6920-10-28 PMID:20367885

Gohara, S., Shapiro, J., Jacob, A., Khuder, S., Gandy, R., Metting, P., & Kleshinski, J. (2011). Joining the conversation: Predictors of success on the United States Medical Licensing Examinations (USMLE). *Learning Assistance Review, 16*(1), 11–20.

Golas, S. B., Shibahara, T., Agboola, S., Otaki, H., Sato, J., Nakae, T., & Jethwani, K. (2018). A machine learning model to predict the risk of 30-day readmissions in patients with heart failure: A retrospective analysis of electronic medical records data. *BMC Medical Informatics and Decision Making, 18*(1), 44. doi:10.118612911-018-0620-z PMID:29929496

Goldzweig, C., Towfigh, A., Maglione, M., & Shekelle, P. (2009). Costs and benefits of health information technology: New trends from the literature. *Health Affairs, 28*(Supplement 2), w282–w293. doi:10.1377/hlthaff.28.2.w282 PMID:19174390

Goleman, D., Boyatzis, R. E., & Mckee, A. (2004). *Primal leadership: Learning to lead with emotional intelligence.* Boston, MA: Harvard Business School Press.

Goncalves, S. A., & Trunk, D. (2014). Obstacles to success for the nontraditional student in higher education. *Psi Chi Journal of Psychological Research*, *19*(4), 164–172. doi:10.24839/2164-8204.JN19.4.164

Gonnella, J. S., Erdmann, J. B., & Hojat, M. (2004). An empirical study of the predictive validity of number grades in medical school using 3 decades of longitudinal data: Implications for a grading system. *Medical Education*, *38*(4), 425–434. doi:10.1111/j.1365-2923.2004.01774.x PMID:15025644

Goodchild, T., & Speed, E. (2018). Technology enhanced learning as transformative innovation: A note on the enduring myth of TEL. *Teaching in Higher Education*. doi:10.1080/13562517.2018.1518900

Goodman, R. (2010). Healthcare technology and medical education: Putting physical diagnosis in its proper place. *Academic Medicine*, *85*(6), 945–946. doi:10.1097/ACM.0b013e3181dbb55b PMID:20505391

Gordon, J. (2005). Medical humanities: To cure sometimes, to relieve often, to comfort always. *The Medical Journal of Australia*, *182*(1), 5–8. doi:10.5694/j.1326-5377.2005.tb06543.x PMID:15651937

Gordon, J. S. (2014). Mind-body skills groups for medical students: Reducing stress, enhancing commitment, and promoting patient-centered care. *BMC Medical Education*, *14*(1), 198. doi:10.1186/1472-6920-14-198 PMID:25245341

Grabowski, C. J. (2018). Impact of holistic review on student interview pool diversity. *Advances in Health Sciences Education: Theory and Practice*, *23*(3), 487–498. doi:10.100710459-017-9807-9 PMID:29288323

Graduate QuestionnaireA. A. M. C. (GQ) Retrieved from https://www.aamc.org/data/gq/

Grady, C. M., & Hinings, C. R. (2018). *Turning the Titanic: Physicians as both leaders and managers in healthcare reform. Leadership in Health Services*. Retrieved from 1108/LHS-09-2017-0058

Graffam, B. (2007). Active learning in medical education: Strategies for beginning implementation. *Medical Teacher*, *29*(1), 38–42. doi:10.1080/01421590601176398 PMID:17538832

Granovskiy, B. (2018). *Science, Technology, Engineering, and Mathematics (STEM) Education: An Overview*. Retrieved from https://fas.org/sgp/crs/misc/R45223.pdf

Grant, G. B. (2017). Exploring the possibility of peak individualism, humanity's existential crisis, and an emerging age of purpose. *Frontiers in Psychology*, *8*, 1478. doi:10.3389/fpsyg.2017.01478 PMID:28928689

Grant, S. B., Dixon, J. L., Glass, N. E., & Sakran, J. V. (2013). Early surgical subspecialization: A new paradigm? Part I. *Bulletin of the American College of Surgeons*, *98*(8), 38–42. PMID:24205574

Grbic, D., Morrison, E., Sondheimer, H. M., Conrad, S. S., & Milem, J. F. (2019). The association between a holistic review in admissions workshop and the diversity of accepted applicants and students matriculating to medical school. *Academic Medicine*, *94*(3), 396–403. doi:10.1097/ACM.0000000000002446 PMID:30188373

Greenberg, L., & Blatt, B. (2010). Perspective: Successfully negotiating the clerkship years of medical school: a guide for medical students, implications for residents and faculty. *Academic Medicine*, *85*(4), 706–709. doi:10.1097/ACM.0b013e3181d2aaf2 PMID:20354392

Greer, T., Kost, A., Evans, D. V., Norris, T., Erickson, J., McCarthy, J., & Allen, S. (2016). The WWAMI Targeted Rural Underserved Track (TRUST) Program: An innovative response to rural physician workforce shortages. *Academic Medicine*, *91*(1), 65–69. doi:10.1097/ACM.0000000000000807 PMID:26200575

Griffith, C. H., Wilson, J. F., Haist, S. A., & Ramsbottom-Lucier, M. (1998). Do students who work with better housestaff in their medicine clerkships learn more? *Academic Medicine*, *73*, S57–S59. doi:10.1097/00001888-199810000-00045 PMID:9795652

Griffith, K., de Cataldo, R., & Fogarty, K. (2016). Do-it-yourself: 3D models of hydrogenic orbitals through 3D printing. *Journal of Chemical Education*, *93*(9), 1586–1590. doi:10.1021/acs.jchemed.6b00293

Gross, M., & Masters, C. (2017). Virtual dissection: Using active learning with the Anatomage Table to enhance student learning. The *FASEB (Federation of American Societies for Experimental Biology) Journal*, *31*(1)-Supplement.

Gross, D. A., Mattox, L. C., & Winkleman, N. (2016). Priming the physician pipeline: A regional AHEC's use of in-state medical school data to guide its health careers programming. *Journal of Health Care for the Poor and Underserved*, *27*(4A), 8–18. doi:10.1353/hpu.2016.0194 PMID:27818409

Grover, S., Sood, N., & Chaudhary, A. (2019). Reforming pathology teaching in medical college by peer-assisted learning and student-oriented interest building activities: A pilot study. *Education for Health*, *30*(2), 126–132. doi:10.4103/efh.EfH_267_16 PMID:28928342

Guglielmino, L. (1978). Development of the Self-Directed Learning Readiness Scale. *Dissertation Abstracts International*, *38*, 6476A.

Guide to the Planning Self-study for Preliminary Accreditation. LCME. (2019, May). Retrieved August 16, 2019, from https://lcme.org/publications/

Guidelines for Premedical and Medical Students Providing Patient Care During Clinical Experiences Abroad. (2011). Retrieved from https://www.aamc.org/download/181690/data/guidelinesforstudentsprovidingpatientcare.pdf

Guidelines for Writing a Letter of Evaluation for a Medical School Applicant. (2019) Retrieved from https://www.aamc.org/download/349990/data/lettersguidelinesbrochure.pdf

Guilford, J. P. (1936). The determination of item difficulty when chance success is a factor. *Psychometrika*, *1*(4), 259–264. doi:10.1007/BF02287877

Gullo, C., Ha, T., & Cook, S. (2015). Twelve tips for facilitating team-based learning. *Medical Teacher*, *37*(9), 819–824. doi:10.3109/0142159X.2014.1001729 PMID:25665624

Gunderman, R., & Kanter, S. L. (2009). Perspective: Educating physicians to lead hospitals. *Academic Medicine: Journal of the Association of American Medical Colleges*, *84*(1348–1351).

Gupta, R., Singh, S., & Kotru, M. (2011). Reaching people through medical humanities: An initiative. *Journal of Educational Evaluation for Health Professions*, *8*, 5. doi:10.3352/jeehp.2011.8.5 PMID:21716596

Hafferty, F., & O'Donnell, J. (Eds.). (2014). *Hidden curriculum in health professions education.* Hanover, NH: Dartmouth College Press.

Haglund, M. E., aan het Rot, M., Cooper, N. S., Nestadt, P. S., Muller, D., Southwick, S. M., & Charney, D. S. (2009). Resilience in the third year of medical school: A prospective study of the associations between stressful events occurring during clinical rotations and student well-being. *Academic Medicine*, *84*(2), 258–268. doi:10.1097/ACM.0b013e31819381b1 PMID:19174682

Haidet, P., Kubitz, K., & McCormack, W. T. (2014). Analysis of the Team-Based Learning Literature: TBL Comes of Age. *Journal on Excellence in College Teaching*, *25*(3-4), 303–333.

Haidet, P., Levine, R. E., Parmelee, D. X., Crow, S., Kennedy, F., Kelly, A., ... Richards, B. F. (2012). Perspective: Guidelines for reporting team-based learning activities in the medical and health sciences education literature. *Academic Medicine*, *87*(3), 292–299. doi:10.1097/ACM.0b013e318244759e PMID:22373620

Haist, S. A., Katsufrakis, P. J., & Dillon, G. F. (2013). The Evolution of the United States Medical Licensing Examination (USMLE). *Journal of the American Medical Association, 310*(21), 2245. doi:10.1001/jama.2013.282328 PMID:24302081

Ha, J. F., Anat, D. S., & Longnecker, N. (2010). Doctor-patient communication: A review. *The Ochsner Journal, 10*, 38–43. PMID:21603354

Hall, J. N., Woods, N., & Hanson, M. D. (2014). Is Social Sciences and Humanities (SSH) Premedical Education Marginalized in the Medical School Admission Process? A Review and Contextualization of the Literature. *Academic Medicine, 89*(7), 1075–1086. doi:10.1097/ACM.0000000000000284 PMID:24826852

Halperin, E. C. (2010). Preserving the humanities in medical education. *Medical Teacher, 32*(1), 76–79. doi:10.3109/01421590903390585 PMID:20095779

Hammer, M. R. (2011). Additional cross-cultural validity testing of the Intercultural Development Inventory. *International Journal of Intercultural Relations, 35*(4), 474–487. doi:10.1016/j.ijintrel.2011.02.014

Handelsman, M. M., Briggs, W. L., Sullivan, N., & Towler, A. (2005). A measure of college student course engagement. *The Journal of Educational Research, 98*(3), 184–192. doi:10.3200/JOER.98.3.184-192

Hanna, W. C., Mulder, D. S., Fried, G. M., Elhilali, M., & Khwaja, K. A. (2012). Training future surgeons for management roles: The resident-surgeon-manager conference. *Archives of Surgery, 147*(10), 940–944. doi:10.1001/archsurg.2012.992 PMID:23117834

Harcleroad, F. F., & Eaton, J. S. (2005). The hidden hand: External constituencies and their impact. In P. G. Altbach, R. O. Berdahl, & P. J. Gumport (Eds.), *American higher education in the twenty-first century: social, political, and economic challenges* (p. 263). Baltimore, Md.: JHU Press.

Harden, R. M. (2007). Learning outcomes as a tool to assess progression. *Medical Teacher, 29*(7), 678–682. doi:10.1080/01421590701729955 PMID:18236255

Harris, D. L., Krause, K. C., Parish, D. C., & Smith, M. U. (2007). Academic competencies for medical faculty. *Family Medicine, 39*(5), 343–350. PMID:17476608

Harrison, L. E., White, B. A., & Sanker, R. (2017). Exposing premedical students to the full continuum and practice of a physician for informed decisions: Innovative partnership between an undergraduate program and a medical school. *The Advisor,* 9-13.

Harrison, L. E. (2019). Using holistic review to form a diverse interview pool for selection to medical school. *Baylor University Medical Center Proceedings, 32*(2), 218–221. doi:10.1080/08998280.2019.1576575 PMID:31191132

Hartling, L., Spooner, C., Tjosvold, L., & Oswald, A. (2010). Problem-based learning in pre-clinical medical education: 22 years of outcome research. *Medical Teacher, 32*(1), 28–35. doi:10.3109/01421590903200789 PMID:20095771

Harvard Medical School. (2019). Course catalog 2019-2020. Retrieved June 2, 2019 from http://www.medcatalog.harvard.edu/courselist.aspx?dep=200

Hauer, K. E., Ciccone, A., Henzel, T. R., Katsufrakis, P., Miller, S. H., Norcross, W. A., ... Irby, D. M. (2009). Remediation of the deficiencies of physicians across the continuum from medical school to practice: A thematic review of the literature. *Academic Medicine, 84*(12), 1822–1832. doi:10.1097/ACM.0b013e3181bf3170 PMID:19940595

Hauglum, S. D., Crenshaw, N. A., Gattamorta, K. A., & Mitzova-Vladinov, G. (2018). Evaluation of a low-cost, high-fidelity animal model to train graduate advanced practice nursing students in the performance of ultrasound-guided central line catheter insertion. *Simulation in Healthcare, 13*(5), 341–347. doi:10.1097/SIH.0000000000000337 PMID:30286028

Hawkins, D. (2014). Creating a team-based learning pedagogical culture. In D. Hawkins (Ed.), *A team-based learning guide for faculty in the health professions* (pp. 89–95). Bloomington, IN: AuthorHouse LLC.

Hayes, T. (2015). Are electronic medical records worth the costs of implementation? *American Action Forum.* Retrieved from https://www.americanactionforum.org/research/are-electronic-medical-records-worth-the-costs-of-implementation/

Health, U. S. F. (2018). *Medical Science Skills Development Program.* Retrieved from https://health.usf.edu/medicine/mdprogram/diversity/prematriculationprogram

Health, U. S. F. (2018). *The SELECT Experience.* Retrieved from https://health.usf.edu/medicine/mdprogram/select/experience

Health, U. S. F. (2019). *Institutional Core Values.* Retrieved from https://health.usf.edu/care/hr/Culture

Heath, S. (2019). Hospitals need targeted plan for social determinants of health. Retrieved from https://patientengagementhit.com/news/hospitals-need-targeted-plan-for-social-determinants-of-health

Heck, A. (2014). Students' activities in a pre-matriculation course as a predictor of initial academic performance in medical school. *Medical Science Educator, 24*(3), 239–243. doi:10.100740670-014-0050-1

Heck, A. J., Gibbons, L., Ketter, S. J., Furlano, A., & Prest, L. (2017). A survey of the design of pre-matriculation courses at us medical schools. *Medical Science Educator, 27*(2), 229–236. doi:10.100740670-017-0379-3

Heck, A. J., & Underwood, T. (2016). A pre-matriculation course that focuses on a metacognitive approach to learning. *Medical Science Educator, 26*(4), 515–516. doi:10.100740670-016-0320-1

Hedrick, J. S., Cottrell, S., Stark, D., Brownfield, E., Stoddard, H. A., Angle, S. M., ... Park, V. (2019). A review of continuous quality improvement processes at ten medical schools. *Medical Science Educator, 29*(1), 285–290. doi:10.100740670-019-00694-5

Heeneman, S., & Driessen, E. W. (2017). The use of a portfolio in postgraduate medical education–reflect, assess and account, one for each or all in one? *GMS Journal for Medical Education, 34*(5). PMID:29226225

Hegji, A. (2017). *An overview of accreditation of higher education in the United States.* Congressional Research Report (CRS) Report R43826, Washington, DC.

He, J., Baxter, S. L., Xu, J., Xu, J., Zhou, X., & Zhang, K. (2019). The practical implementation of artificial intelligence technologies in medicine. *Nature Medicine, 25*(1), 30–36. doi:10.103841591-018-0307-0 PMID:30617336

Helfin, M. T., Pinheiro, S., Kaminetzky, C. P., & McNeill, D. (2009). So you want to be a clinician-educator: Designing a clinician-educator curriculum for internal medicine residents. *Medical Teacher, 31*(6), e233–e240. doi:10.1080/01421590802516772 PMID:19296370

Heller, C. A., Rua, S. H., Mazumdar, M., Moon, J. E., Bardes, C., & Gotto, A. M. Jr. (2014). Diversity efforts, admissions, and national rankings: Can we align priorities? *Teaching and Learning in Medicine, 26*(3), 304–311. doi:10.1080/10401334.2014.910465 PMID:25010244

Hendler, J., & Golbeck, J. (2008). Metcalfe's Law, Web 2.0, and the Semantic Web. *Journal of Web Semantics, 6*(1), 14–20. doi:10.1016/j.websem.2007.11.008

Henry, T. A. (2018). How ai is driving new medical frontier for physician training. Retrieved June 1, 2019 from https://www.ama-assn.org/education/accelerating-change-medical-education/how-ai-driving-new-medical-frontier-physician

Hernández-García, Á., & Conde, M. Á. (2014). Dealing with complexity: educational data and tools for learning analytics. In *Proceedings of the Second International Conference on Technological Ecosystems for Enhancing Multiculturality* (pp. 263-268). ACM. 10.1145/2669711.2669909

Hesser, A., & Lewis, L. (1992). Evaluation of a summer prematriculation program for black and other nontraditional students. *Academic Medicine, 67*(4), 270–272. doi:10.1097/00001888-199204000-00016 PMID:1558602

Hesser, A., & Lewis, L. (1992). Prematriculation program grades as predictors of black and other nontraditional students' first-year academic performances. *Academic Medicine, 67*(9), 605–607. doi:10.1097/00001888-199209000-00015 PMID:1520422

HistoryA. M. A. (2019). Retrieved from https://www.ama-assn.org/about/ama-history/ama-history

Hitch, D., & Nicola-Richmond, K. (2017). Instructional practices for evidence-based practice with pre-registration allied health students: A review of recent research and developments. *Advances in Health Sciences Education: Theory and Practice, 22*(4), 1031–1045. doi:10.100710459-016-9702-9 PMID:27469244

Hochberg, M. S., Billig, J., Berman, R. S., Kalet, A. L., Zabar, S. R., Fox, J. R., & Pachter, H. L. (2014). When surgeons decide to become surgeons: New opportunities for surgical education. *American Journal of Surgery, 207*(2), 194–200. doi:10.1016/j.amjsurg.2013.10.010 PMID:24468025

Hojat, M., Gonnella, J. S., Mangione, S., Nasca, T. J., Veloski, J. J., Erdman, J. B. … Magee, M. (2002). Empathy in medical students as related to academic performance, clinical competence, and gender. *Medical Education, 36*(6), 533-527. DOI: . 1365-2923.2002.01234.x. doi:10.1046/j

Holden, L., Berger, W., Zingarelli, R., & Siegel, E. (2015). After-school program for urban youth: Evaluation of a health careers course in New York City high schools. *Information Services & Use, 35*(1-2), 141–160. doi:10.3233/ISU-150773 PMID:26316659

Holistic Review in Medical School Admissions. (n.d.). In *Choosing a Medical Career*. AAMC. Retrieved from https://students-residents.aamc.org/choosing-medical-career/article/holistic-review-medical-school-admissions

Holland, C. (2016). Critical review: Medical students' motivation after failure. *Advances in Health Sciences Education: Theory and Practice, 21*(3), 695–710. doi:10.100710459-015-9643-8 PMID:26443085

Hollands, F., & Tirthali, D. (2014). Why do institutions offer MOOCs? *Online Learning, 18*(3).

Hopkins, L., Hampton, B. S., Abbott, J. F., Buery-Joyner, S. D., Craig, L. B., Dalrymple, J. L., … Page-Ramsey, S. M. (2018). To the point: Medical education, technology and the millennial learner. *American Journal of Obstetrics and Gynecology, 218*(2), 188–192. doi:10.1016/j.ajog.2017.06.001 PMID:28599897

Hoppmann, R. A., Rao, V. V., Bell, F., Poston, M. B., Howe, D. B., Riffle, S., … Catalana, P. V. (2015). The evolution of an integrated ultrasound curriculum (iUSC) for medical students: 9-year experience. *Critical Ultrasound Journal, 7*(1), 18. doi:10.118613089-015-0035-3 PMID:26589313

Horton, M. E. K. (2019). The orphan child: Humanities in modern medical education. *Philosophy, Ethics, and Humanities in Medicine. 14*(1), 1. DOI:130-018-0067-y. doi:10.1186

Horton, J. (2017). A content analysis of 3D printing policies at academic libraries. *Journal of Library Administration, 57*(3), 267–281. doi:10.1080/01930826.2016.1258876

Howard, S. (2013). Risk-aversion: Understanding teachers' resistance to technology integration. *Technology, Pedagogy, and Education.* Retrieved from https://www.academia.edu/2042088/Risk-aversion_Understanding_teachers_resistance_to_technology_integration/

Howse, K., Harris, J., & Dalgarno, N. (2017). Canadian National Guidelines and Recommendations for Integrating Career Advising into Medical School Curricula. *Academic Medicine, 92*(11), 1543–1548. doi:10.1097/ACM.0000000000001720 PMID:28445219

Huber, S. (2003). The white coat ceremony: A contemporary medical ritual. *Journal of Medical Ethics, 29*(6), 364–366. doi:10.1136/jme.29.6.364 PMID:14662817

Huff, L., & Fang, L. (1999). When are students most at risk of encountering academic difficulty? A study of the 1992 matriculants to U.S. medical schools. *Academic Medicine, 74*(4), 454–460. doi:10.1097/00001888-199904000-00047 PMID:10219232

Human Resources for Health Global Resource Center. (2019). *Why is teamwork in health care important?* Retrieved June 9, 2019, from https://www.hrhresourcecenter.org/HRH_Info_Teamwork.html

Hunt, D., Migdal, M., Waechter, D. M., Barzansky, B., & Sabalis, R. F. (2016). The Variables That Lead to Severe Action Decisions by the Liaison Committee on Medical Education. *Academic Medicine, 91*(1), 87–93. doi:10.1097/ACM.0000000000000874 PMID:26287918

Hunt, D., Migdal, M., Waechter, D., & Barzansky, B. (2015). *Expanding the LCME Severe Action Decisions Analysis to Gauge the Effect of the 2002 Accreditation Standards Reformatting. Expanding the LCME Severe Action Decisions Analysis to Gauge the Effect of the 2002 Accreditation Standards Reformatting.* Washington, DC: AAMC.

Hunter, K. M., Charon, R., & Conlehan, J. L. (1995). The study of literature in medical education. *Academic Medicine, 70*, 787–794. PMID:7669155

Hutter, M. M., Kellogg, K. C., Ferguson, C. M., Abbott, W. M., & Warshaw, A. L. (2006). The impact of the 80-hour resident workweek on surgical residents and attending surgeons. *Annals of Surgery, 243*(6), 864–875. doi:10.1097/01.sla.0000220042.48310.66 PMID:16772790

Hwang, E. J., Park, S., Jin, K. N., Kim, J. I., Choi, S. Y., & Lee, J. H. (2018). Development and validation of a deep learning-based automatic detection algorithm for active pulmonary tuberculosis on chest radiographs. *Clinical Infectious Diseases*, ciy967. PMID:30418527

Innova. (2015, April). *How effective are these five teaching styles?* Retrieved May 8, 2019, from https://www.innova-designgroup.co.uk/news/how-effective-are-these-five-teaching-styles/

Institute for Healthcare Improvement Multimedia Team. (2017). How to reduce implicit bias. Retrieved from http://www.ihi.org/communities/blogs/how-to-reduce-implicit-bias

Institute for the Future. (2011). Future working skills 2020. Retrieved from http://www.iftf.org/futureworkskills/

Institute of Medicine. (2004). *Academic health centers: Leading change in the 21st century.* Washington, DC: National Academy Press.

Intercultural Development Inventory®. (2019). IDI general information: external, prestigious reviews of the IDI. Retrieved from https://idiinventory.com/generalinformation/external-prestigious-reviews-of-the-idi/

Jackson, E. R., Shanafelt, T. D., Hasan, O., Satele, D. V., & Dyrbye, L. N. (2016). Burnout and alcohol abuse/dependence among U.S. medical Students. *Academic Medicine, 91*(9), 1251–1256. doi:10.1097/ACM.0000000000001138 PMID:26934693

Jackson, N., Jamieson, A., & Khan, A. (2007). *Assessment in Medical Education and Training: A Practical Guide.* Radcliffe Publishing.

Jackson, R. E. (1972). The effectiveness of a special program for minority group students. *Journal of Medical Education, 47*(8), 620–624. PMID:5057182

Jackson, T. N., Pearcy, C. P., Khorgami, Z., Agrawal, V., Taubman, K. E., & Truitt, M. S. (2018). The physician attrition crisis: A cross-sectional survey of the risk factors for reduced job satisfaction among US surgeons. *World Journal of Surgery, 42*(5), 1285–1292. doi:10.100700268-017-4286-y PMID:29067517

Jacobs, J. C., Bolhuis, S., Bulte, J. A., Laan, R., & Holdrinet, R. S. (2005). Starting learning in medical practice: An evaluation of a new introductory clerkship. *Medical Teacher, 27*(5), 408–414. doi:10.1080/01421590500087001 PMID:16147793

Jacobson, K., Fisher, D. L., Hoffman, K., & Tsoulas, K. D. (2010). Integrated cases section: A course designed to promote clinical reasoning in Year 2 medical students. *Teaching and Learning in Medicine, 22*(4), 312–316. doi:10.1080/10401334.2010.512835 PMID:20936581

Jacoby, L. L. (1978). On interpreting the effects of repetition: Solving a problem versus remembering a solution. *Journal of Verbal Learning and Verbal Behavior, 17*(6), 649–667. doi:10.1016/S0022-5371(78)90393-6

Jacoby, L. L., Wahlheim, C. N., & Coane, J. H. (2010). Test-enhanced learning of natural concepts: Effects on recognition memory, classification, and metacognition. *Journal of Experimental Psychology. Learning, Memory, and Cognition, 36*(6), 1441–1451. doi:10.1037/a0020636 PMID:20804279

Jardine, D., Correa, R., Schultz, H., Nobis, A., Lanser, B. J., Ahmad, I., ... Hinds, B. (2015). The need for a leadership curriculum for residents. *Journal of Graduate Medical Education, 7*(2), 307–309. doi:10.4300/JGME-07-02-31 PMID:26221472

Jax, M. (2019). *Center for Advanced Training and Simulation (CATS)*. Retrieved from https://surgery.med.uky.edu/surgery-center-advanced-training-and-simulation-cats

Jenkins, D. M., & Allen, S. J. (2017). Aligning instructional strategies with learning outcomes and leadership competencies. *New Directions for Student Leadership, 156*(156), 43–58. doi:10.1002/yd.20270 PMID:29156115

Jeong, D., Presseau, J., ElChamaa, R., Naumann, D. N., Mascaro, C., Luconi, F., ... Kitto, S. C. (2018). Barriers and facilitators to self-directed learning in continuing professional development for physicians in Canada: A scoping review. *Academic Medicine: Journal of the Association of American Medical Colleges, 93*(8), 1245–1254. doi:10.1097/ACM.0000000000002237 PMID:29642101

Jerant, A., Fancher, T., Fenton, J. J., Fiscella, K., Sousa, F., Franks, P., & Henderson, M. (2015). How medical school applicant race, ethnicity, and socioeconomic status relate to multiple mini-interview based admissions outcomes: Findings from one medical school. *Academic Medicine, 90*(12), 1667–1674. doi:10.1097/ACM.0000000000000766 PMID:26017355

Jerant, A., Griffin, E., Rainwater, J., Henderson, M., Sousa, F., Bertakis, K. D., ... Franks, P. (2012). Does applicant personality influence multiple mini-interview performance and medical school acceptance offers? *Academic Medicine, 87*(9), 1250–1259. doi:10.1097/ACM.0b013e31826102ad PMID:22836836

Jernigan, V. B., Hearod, J. B., Tran, K., Norris, K. C., & Buchwald, D. (2016). An examination of cultural competence training in US medical education guided by the tool for assessing cultural competence training. *Journal of Health Disparities Research and Practice, 9*(3), 150–167. PMID:27818848

Jhala, M., & Mathur, J. (2019). The association between deep learning approach and case-based learning. *BMC Medical Education, 19*(1), 106. doi:10.118612909-019-1516-z PMID:30975134

Jibson, M., Hilty, D., Arlinghaus, K., Ball, V., McCarthy, T., Seritan, A., & Servis, M. (2010). Clinician-educator tracks for residents: Three pilot programs. *Academic Psychiatry, 34*(4), 269–276. doi:10.1176/appi.ap.34.4.269 PMID:20576984

Johns Hopkins Medicine. (2019). Genes to society: a curriculum for the Johns Hopkins University School of Medicine. Retrieved June 1, 2019 from https://www.hopkinsmedicine.org/som/curriculum/genes_to_society/curriculum/year_one/time_clinical_informatics.html

Johnson, T., Wisniewski, M., Kuhlemeyer, G., Issacs, G., & Krzykowski, J. (2012). Technology adaptation in higher education: Overcoming anxiety through faculty bootcamp. *Journal of Asynchronous Learning Networks*, *16*(2), 63–72.

Jonas, C. E., Durning, S. J., Zebrowski, C., & Cimino, F. (2019). An interdisciplinary, multi-institution telehealth course for third-year medical students. *Academic Medicine*, *94*(6), 833–837. doi:10.1097/ACM.0000000000002701 PMID:30870152

Jones, D. S. (2014). A complete medical education includes the arts and humanities. *AMA Journal of Ethics*, *16*(8), 636–641. doi:10.1001/virtualmentor.2014.16.8.msoc1-1408 PMID:25140687

Jones, M. D. Jr, Rosenberg, A. A., Gilhooly, J. T., & Carraccio, C. L. (2011). Perspective: Competencies, outcomes, and controversy --- Linking professional activities to competencies to improve resident education and practice. *Academic Medicine*, *86*(2), 161–165. doi:10.1097/ACM.0b013e31820442e9 PMID:21169788

Jones, S., Rudin, R., Perry, T., & Shekelle, P. (2014). Health information technology: An updated systematic review with a focus on meaningful use. *Annals of Internal Medicine*, *160*(1), 48–54. doi:10.7326/M13-1531 PMID:24573664

Judd, T., & Kennedy, G. (2011). Expediency-based practice? Medical students' reliance on Google and Wikipedia for biomedical inquiries. *British Journal of Educational Technology*, *42*(2), 351–360. doi:10.1111/j.1467-8535.2009.01019.x

Ju, H., Choi, I., & Yoon, B. Y. (2017). Do medical students generate sound arguments during small group discussions in problem-based learning? An analysis of preclinical medical students' argumentation according to a framework of hypothetico-deductive reasoning. *Korean Journal of Medical Education*, *29*(2), 101–109. doi:10.3946/kjme.2017.57 PMID:28597873

Kalet, A., & Chou, C. (2014). Preface. In A. Kalet, & C. Chou (Eds.), *Remediation in Medical Education. (xvii-xxi)*. New York, NY: Springer. doi:10.1007/978-1-4614-9025-8

Kalet, A., Guerrasio, J., & Chou, C. (2016). Twelve tips for developing and maintaining a remediation program in medical education. *Medical Teacher*, *38*(8), 787–792. doi:10.3109/0142159X.2016.1150983 PMID:27049798

Kalkhurst, D. (2018, March). *Engaging Gen Z students and learners*. Retrieved May 8, 2019, from https://www.pearsoned.com/engaging-gen-z-students/

Kamei, R. K., Cook, S., Puthucheary, J., & Starmer, C. F. (2012). 21st Century learning in medicine: Traditional teaching versus team-based learning. *Medical Science Educator*, *22*(2), 57–64. doi:10.1007/BF03341758

Kamine, T. H., Gondek, S., & Kent, T. S. (2014). Decrease in junior resident case volume after 2011 ACGME work hours. *Journal of Surgical Education*, *71*(6), e59–e63. doi:10.1016/j.jsurg.2014.07.001 PMID:25241704

Kaplan, R. S., & Anderson, R. (2004). Time-driven activity-based costing. *Harvard Business Review*, *82*(11), 131–138. PMID:15559451

Kaptelinin, V., & Nardi, B. A. (2009). *Acting with technology: Activity theory and interaction design*. Cambridge, MA: MIT Press.

Karnieli-Miller, O., Frankel, R. M., & Inui, T. S. (2013). Cloak of compassion, or evidence of elitism? An empirical analysis of white coat ceremonies. *Medical Education*, *47*(1), 97–108. doi:10.1111/j.1365-2923.2012.04324.x PMID:23278829

Kassebaum, D. G., & Szenas, P. L. (1994). Factors influencing the specialty choices of 1993 medical school graduates. *Academic Medicine*, *69*(2), 163–170. doi:10.1097/00001888-199402000-00027 PMID:8311892

Kassebaum, D. K. (1992). Origin of the LCME, the AAMC– AMA partnership for accreditation. *Academic Medicine, 67*(2), 85–87. doi:10.1097/00001888-199202000-00005 PMID:1547000

Kassirer, J. P. (2010). Teaching Clinical Reasoning: Case-Based and Coached. *Academic Medicine, 85*(7), 1118–1124. doi:10.1097/ACM.0b013e3181d5dd0d PMID:20603909

Kaufmann, D. M. (2003). ABC of learning and teaching in medicine: Applying educational theory to practice. *British Medical Journal, 326*(7382), 213–216. doi:10.1136/bmj.326.7382.213 PMID:12543841

Kaufman, P., & Bradbury, D. (1992). *Characteristics of at-risk students in NELS: 88. National education longitudinal study of 1988. Statistical analysis report. Contractor report. NCES 92-042. (0160380111).* Jessup [ED Pubs]. *MD Medical Newsmagazine,* 20794–21398.

Kebaetse, M. B., Kebaetse, M., Mokone, G., Nkomazana, O., Mogodi, M., Wright, J., ... Park, P. (2018). Learning support interventions for Year 1 medical students: A review of the literature. *Medical Education, 52*(3), 263–273. doi:10.1111/medu.13465 PMID:29058332

Keck School or Medicine of USC. (2019). Medical student curriculum – years I and II. Retrieved June 2, 2019 from https://keck.usc.edu/pathology/training-education/medical-student-curriculum/

Kegan, E., & Lahey, L. L. (2009). *Immunity to change: How to overcome it and unlock the potential in yourself and your organization (leadership for the common good).* Boston, MA: Harvard Business School Publishing.

Kelchen, R. (September, 2017). Higher education accreditation and the federal government. Elevate the Debate. Washington, D.C.: Urban Institute.

Kelley, T. L. (1939). The selection of upper and lower groups for the validation of test items. *Journal of Educational Psychology, 30*(1), 17–24. doi:10.1037/h0057123

Kelley, T., Ebel, R., & Linacre, M. (2002). Item discrimination indices. *Rasch Measurement Transactions, 16*(3), 883–884.

Kentli, F. (2009). Comparison of hidden curriculum theories. *European Journal of Education Studies, 1*(2), 83–88.

Kern, D. E. (1998). *Curriculum Development for Medical Education: A Six Step Approach.* Baltimore, MD: Johns Hopkins University Press.

Khalil, M. K., & Kibble, J. D. (2014). Faculty reflections on the process of building an integrated preclerkship curriculum: A new school perspective. *Advances in Physiology Education, 38*(3), 199–209. doi:10.1152/advan.00055.2014 PMID:25179608

Kidd, M. G., & Connor, J. H. (2008). Striving to do good things: Teaching humanities in Canadian medical schools. *The Journal of Medical Humanities, 29*(1), 45–54. doi:10.100710912-007-9049-6 PMID:18058208

Kilminster, S., Zukas, M., Quinton, N., & Roberts, T. (2011). Preparedness is not enough: Understanding transitions as critically intensive learning periods. *Medical Education, 45*(10), 1006–1015. doi:10.1111/j.1365-2923.2011.04048.x PMID:21916940

Kinkade, S. (2005). A snapshot of the status of problem-based learning in U.S. medical schools, 2003-04. *Academic Medicine, 80*(3), 300–301. doi:10.1097/00001888-200503000-00021 PMID:15734817

Kirch, D. G. (2007). *Culture and the Courage to Change.* AAMC President's Address 2007 Annual Meeting. Retrieved June 9, 2019, from https://www.aamc.org/download/169722/data/kirchspeech2007.pdf

Kirch, D. G., Mitchell, K., & Ast, C. (2013). The new 2015 MCAT: Testing competencies. *Journal of the American Medical Association, 310*(21), 2243–2244. doi:10.1001/jama.2013.282093 PMID:24302080

Kirk, D. E. (2012). *Optimal control theory: An introduction.* Mineola, NY: Dover Publications.

Kirkpatrick, D. L. (1994). *Evaluating Training Programs.* San Francisco, CA: Berrett-Koehler Publishers.

Kitto, S., Price, D., Jeong, D., Campbell, C., & Reeves, S. (2018). Continuing professional development. *Understanding Medical Education: Evidence. Theory into Practice*, 263–274.

Klamen, D. L., & Williams, R. G. (2011). The efficacy of a targeted remediation process for students who fail standardized patient examinations. *Teaching and Learning in Medicine*, *23*(1), 3–11. doi:10.1080/10401334.2010.536749 PMID:21240775

Klapheke, M., Cubero, M., & Johnson, T. (2017). Assessing entrustable professional activities during the psychiatry clerkship. *Academic Psychology*, *41*(3), 345–349. doi:10.100740596-017-0665-9

Kline, P. (2014). *The New Psychometrics: Science, Psychology and Measurement.* Routledge. doi:10.4324/9781315787817

Knigge, L., & Cope, M. (2006). Grounded visualization: Integrating the analysis of qualitative and quantitative data through grounded theory and visualization. *Environment & Planning A*, *38*(11), 2021–2037. doi:10.1068/a37327

Knight, C. L., Windish, D. M., Haist, S. A., Karani, R., Chheda, S., Rosenblum, M., ... Aagaard, E. M. (2017). The SGIM TEACH program: A curriculum for teachers of clinical medicine. *Journal of General Internal Medicine*, *32*(8), 948–952. doi:10.100711606-017-4053-7 PMID:28409434

Knobloch, A., Ledford, C., Wilkes, S., & Saperstein, A. (2018). The Impact of near-peer teaching on medical students' transition to clerkships. *Family Medicine*, *50*(1), 58–62. doi:10.22454/FamMed.2018.745428 PMID:29346691

Knowles, M. (1970). *The modern practice of adult education.* New York, NY: Association Press.

Knowles, M. S. (1950). *Informal adult education.* New York, NY: Association Press.

Knowles, M. S. (1975). *Self-directed learning: A guide for learners and teachers.* New York: New York Association Press.

Knowles, M. S. (1980). *The modern practice of adult education: From pedagogy to andragogy.* Wilton, CN: Association Press.

Knowles, M. S. (1985). Application in continuing education for the health professions: Chapter five of "Andragogy in action". *Mobius*, *5*(2), 80–100. doi:10.1002/chp.4760050212 PMID:10271191

Kobal, S. L., Trento, L., Baharami, S., Tolstrup, K., Naqvi, T. Z., Cercek, B., ... Siegel, R. J. (2005). Comparison of effectiveness of hand-carried ultrasound to bedside cardiovascular physical examination. *The American Journal of Cardiology*, *96*(7), 1002–1006. doi:10.1016/j.amjcard.2005.05.060 PMID:16188532

Koenig, T. W., Parrish, S. K., Terregino, C. A., Williams, J. P., Dunleavy, D. M., & Volsch, J. M. (2013). Core personal competencies important to entering students' success in medical school: What are they and how could they be assessed early in the admission process? *Academic Medicine*, *88*(5), 603–613. doi:10.1097/ACM.0b013e31828b3389 PMID:23524928

Koh, G. C. H., Khoo, H. E., Wong, M. L., & Koh, D. (2008). The effects of problem-based learning during medical school on physician competency: A systematic review. *Canadian Medical Association Journal*, *178*(1), 34–41. doi:10.1503/cmaj.070565 PMID:18166729

Koles, P., Stolfi, A., Borges, N., Nelson, S., & Parmelee, D. X. (2010). The impact of team-based learning on medical students' academic performance. *Academic Medicine*, *85*(11), 1739–1745. doi:10.1097/ACM.0b013e3181f52bed PMID:20881827

Komenda, M., Víta, M., Vaitsis, C., Schwarz, D., Pokorná, A., Zary, N., & Dušek, L. (2015). Curriculum Mapping with Academic Analytics in Medical and Healthcare Education. *PLoS One, 10*(12). doi:10.1371/journal.pone.0143748 PMID:26624281

Konerman, M. C., Alpert, C. M., & Sinha, S. S. (2016). Learning to be a clinician-educator: A fellow-driven curricular reform. *Journal of the American College of Cardiology, 67*(3), 338–342. doi:10.1016/j.jacc.2015.11.032 PMID:26796400

Kopachek, J., Bardales, C., Lash, A., Walker, C. Jr, Pfeil, S., & Ledford, C. (2017). Coaching the Coach: A Program for Development of Faculty Portfolio Coaches. *Teaching and Learning in Medicine, 29*(3), 326–336. doi:10.1080/104013 34.2016.1273781 PMID:28632014

Kornell, N., & Bjork, R. A. (2008a). Learning Concepts and Categories. *Psychological Science, 19*(6), 585–592. doi:10.1111/j.1467-9280.2008.02127.x PMID:18578849

Kornell, N., & Bjork, R. A. (2008b). Optimising self-regulated study: The benefits—and costs—of dropping flashcards. *Memory (Hove, England), 16*(2), 125–136. doi:10.1080/09658210701763899 PMID:18286417

Kornitzer, B., Ronan, E., & Rifkin, M. R. (2005). Improving the adjustment of educationally disadvantaged students to medical school: The summer enrichment program. *The Mount Sinai Journal of Medicine, New York, 72*(5), 317–321. PMID:16184295

Kosobuski, A. W., Whitney, A., Skildum, A., & Prunuske, A. (2017). Development of an interdisciplinary pre-matriculation program designed to promote medical students' self efficacy. *Medical Education Online, 22*(1), 1272835. doi:10.1080/ 10872981.2017.1272835 PMID:28178916

Kozinsky, S. (2017, July). *How Generation Z is Shaping the Change in Education.* Retrieved May 8, 2019, from https://www.forbes.com/sites/sievakozinsky/2017/07/24/how-generation-z-is-shaping-the-change-in-education/#57e1ad716520

Kreimer, S. (2017). Distracted doctor? Don't let computer come before patient during exam. American Association for Physician Leadership. Retrieved June 2, 2019 from https://www.physicianleaders.org/news/distracted-doctoring-dont-let-computer-come-before-patient-during-exam

Kreiter, C. D., & Kreiter, Y. (2007). A validity generalization perspective on the ability of undergraduate GPA and the medical college admission test to predict important outcomes. *Teaching and Learning in Medicine, 19*(2), 95–100. doi:10.1080/10401330701332094 PMID:17564535

Krupat, E., Pelletier, S. R., & Dienstag, J. L. (2017). Academic performance on first-year medical school exams: How well does it predict later performance on knowledge-based and clinical assessments? *Teaching and Learning in Medicine, 29*(2), 181–187. doi:10.1080/10401334.2016.1259109 PMID:28098483

Kruse, C. S., Stein, A., Thomas, H., & Kaur, H. (2018). The use of electronic health records to support population health: A systematic review of the literature. *Journal of Medical Systems, 42*(11), 214. doi:10.100710916-018-1075-6 PMID:30269237

Kubiak, N. T., Guidot, D. M., Trimm, R. F., Kamen, D. L., & Roman, J. (2012). Recruitment and retention in academic medicine: What junior faculty and trainees want department chairs to know. *The American Journal of the Medical Sciences, 344*(1), 24–27. doi:10.1016/S0002-9629(15)30914-9 PMID:22744375

Kuhn, T., Gordon, V. N., & Webber, J. (2006). The Advising and Counseling Continuum: Triggers for Referral. *NACADA Journal, 26*(1), 24–31. doi:10.12930/0271-9517-26.1.24

Kumar, L. R., & Chacko, T. V. (2010). Using appreciative inquiry on learning styles to facilitate student learning. *Medical Education, 44*(11), 1121–1122. doi:10.1111/j.1365-2923.2010.03842.x PMID:20946485

Kumwenda, B., Cleland, J. A., Walker, K., Lee, A. J., & Greatrix, R. (2017). The relationship between school type and academic performance at medical school: A national, multi-cohort study. *BMJ Open*, *7*(8). doi:10.1136/bmjopen-2017-016291 PMID:28860227

Kuo, A. K., Thyne, S. M., Chen, H. C., West, D. C., & Kamei, R. K. (2010). An innovative residency program designed to develop leaders to improve the health of children. *Academic Medicine*, *85*(10), 1603–1608. doi:10.1097/ACM.0b013e3181eb60f6 PMID:20703151

Kwan, B., Bui, G., Jain, P., Shah, N., & Juang, D. (2017). Exploring simulation in the internal medicine clerkship. *The Clinical Teacher*, *14*(5), 349–355. doi:10.1111/tct.12577 PMID:27885821

Lamb, E. G., Berry, S. L., & Jones, T. (2019). *Health Humanities Baccalaureate Programs in the United States*. Retrieved from https://www.hiram.edu/wp-content/uploads/2019/03/Health-Humanities-Program_2019_final.pdf

Larsen, D. P., Nimmon, L., & Varpio, L. (2019). Cultural-historical activity theory: The role of tools and tensions in medical education. *Academic Medicine*, *94*(8), 1255; Advance online publication. doi:10.1097/ACM.0000000000002736 PMID:30973361

Laurencin, C. T., & Murray, M. (2017). An American crisis: The lack of black men in medicine. *Journal of Racial and Ethnic Health Disparities*, *4*(3), 317–321. doi:10.100740615-017-0380-y PMID:28534304

Law, M., Veinot, P., Campbell, J., Craig, M., & Mylopoulos, M. (2019). Computing for medicine: Can we prepare medical students for the future? *Academic Medicine*, *94*(3), 353–357. doi:10.1097/ACM.0000000000002521 PMID:30431453

LCME DCI for Full Accreditation Surveys. (2019). Retrieved from https://lcme.org/publications/

LCME Functions and Structures of a Medical School. (2019). Retrieved from http://lcme.org/publications/

LCME Renewal of Recognition by the U.S. Department of Education (LCME). (2019). Retrieved from http://lcme.org/doe-renewal-recognition/

LCME Renewal of Recognition by the U.S. Department of Education Timeline (LCME). (2019). Retrieved from http://lcme.org/accreditation-preparation/schools/2020-21-academic-year/2020-21-full-survey-visit-preparation/#Timeline

Learning Communities Institute Members. (n.d.). In Learning Communities Institute Website. Retrieved from http://www.learningcommunitiesinstitute.org/content/schools

Lehman, L. S., Kasoff, W. S., Koch, P., & Federman, D. D. (2014). A survey of medical ethics education at US and Canadian medical schools. *Academic Medicine*, *79*(7), 682–689. doi:10.1097/00001888-200407000-00015

Leontiev, A. N. (1978). *Activity, consciousness, and personality*. Englewood Cliffs, NJ: Prentice-Hall.

Leung, J. M., Mohit Bhutani, M., Leigh, R., Pelletier, D., Good, C., & Sin, D. D. (2015). Empowering family physicians to impart proper inhaler teaching to patients with chronic obstructive pulmonary disease and asthma. *Canadian Respiratory Journal*, *22*(5), pp. 266-270. doi:10.1155/2015/731357

Levine, W. N., & Spang, R. C. III. (2014). ACGME duty hour requirements: Perceptions and impact on resident training and patient care. *The Journal of the American Academy of Orthopaedic Surgeons*, *22*(9), 535–544. doi:10.5435/JAAOS-22-09-535 PMID:25157035

Levinsohn, E., Weisenthal, K., Wang, P., Shahu, A., Meizlish, M., Robledo-Gil, T., ... Berk-Krauss, J. (2017). No time for silence: An urgent need for political activism among the medical community. *Academic Medicine: Journal of the Association of American Medical Colleges*, *92*(9), 1231–1233. doi:10.1097/ACM.0000000000001724 PMID:28422815

Levinson, W., & Rubenstein, A. (2000). Integrating clinician-educators into academic medical centers: Challenges and potential solutions. *Academic Medicine*, *75*(9), 906–912. doi:10.1097/00001888-200009000-00012 PMID:10995612

Lewis, J. S. D., Dubosh, N., & Ullman, E. (2017). Participation in an emergency medicine bootcamp increases self-confidence at the start of residency. *Western Journal of Emergency Medicine: Integrating Emergency Care with Population Health*, *18*(5), s22.

Lewis, K. O., & Baker, R. C. (2007). The development of an electronic educational portfolio: An outline for medical education professionals. *Teaching and Learning in Medicine*, *19*(2), 139–147. doi:10.1080/10401330701332219 PMID:17564541

Liaison Committee on Medical Education (LCME). (2019). *Function and structure of a medical school, standards for accreditation of medical education programs leading to the MD degree.* Washington, DC: Association of American Medical Colleges and American Medical Association.

Liaison Committee on Medical Education (LCME). (2019). Retrieved from http://lcme.org/accreditation-preparation/schools/2020-21-academic-year/2020-21-full-survey-visit-preparation/

Liaison Committee on Medical Education (LCME). (2019). Retrieved from https://www.aamc.org/members/osr/committees/48814/reports_lcme.html

Liaison Committee on Medical Education (LCME). (2020). *Functions and structure of a medical school: Standards for accreditation of medical education programs leading to the MD degree.* Washington, DC: Author.

Liaison Committee on Medical Education. (2017). *Functions and structure of a medical school: Standards for accreditation of medical education programs leading to the MD degree.* Retrieved from http://lcme.org/wp-content/uploads/filebase/standards/2018-19_Functions-and-Structure_2017-08-02.docx. Accessed October 10, 2017.

Liaison Committee on Medical Education. (2019). Accredited MD programs in the United States. Retrieved from http://lcme.org/directory/accredited-u-s-programs/

Liaison Committee on Medical Education. (2019). *Functions and structure of a medical school: standards for accreditation of medical education programs leading to the MD degree.* Retrieved June 9, 2019, from http://lcme.org/publications/

Liang, M., Curtin, L. S., Signer, M. M., & Savoia, M. C. (2017). Unmatched U.S. Allopathic Seniors in the 2015 Main Residency Match: A Study of Applicant Behavior, Interview Selection, and Match Outcome. *Academic Medicine*, *92*(7), 991–997. doi:10.1097/ACM.0000000000001501 PMID:28657556

Lievens, F. (2013). Adjusting medical school admission: Assessing interpersonal skills using situational judgement tests. *Medical Education*, *47*(2), 182–189. doi:10.1111/medu.12089 PMID:23323657

Lindner, I., Sacks, D., Sheakley, M., Seidel, C., Wahlig, B. C., Rojas, J. D., & Coleman, M. T. (2013). A pre-matriculation learning program that enables medical students with low prerequisite scores to succeed. *Medical Teacher*, *35*(10), 872–873. doi:10.3109/0142159X.2013.786812 PMID:24050196

Lin, K. Y., Parnami, S., Fuhrel-Forbis, A., Anspach, R. R., Crawford, B., & De Vries, R. G. (2013). The undergraduate premedical experience in the united states: A critical review. *International Journal of Medical Education*, *4*, 26–37. doi:10.5116/ijme.5103.a8d3 PMID:23951400

Lin, S., Sattler, A., Yu, G. C., Basaviah, P., & Schillinger, E. (2016). Training future clinician-educators: A track for family medicine residents. *Family Medicine*, *48*(3), 212–216. PMID:26950910

Lipscomb, W. D., Mavis, B., Fowler, L. V., Green, W. D., & Brooks, G. L. (2009). The effectiveness of a postbaccalaureate program for students from disadvantaged backgrounds. *Academic Medicine*, *84*(10Suppl), S42–S45. doi:10.1097/ACM.0b013e3181b37bd0 PMID:19907383

Lobas, J. G. (2006). Leadership in academic medicine: Capabilities and conditions for organizational success. *The American Journal of Medicine*, *119*(7), 617–621. doi:10.1016/j.amjmed.2006.04.005 PMID:16828636

Lord, F. M. (1952). The relation of the reliability of multiple-choice tests to the distribution of item difficulties. *Psychometrika*, *17*(2), 181–194. doi:10.1007/BF02288781

Lord, F. M. (1980). *Applications of Item Response Theory to Practical Testing Problems*. Routledge.

Lord, F. M., & Novick, M. R. (2008). *Statistical Theories of Mental Test Scores*. Information Age Pub.

Lovell, B. (2018). What do we know about coaching in medical education? A literature review. *Medical Education*, *52*(4), 376–390. doi:10.1111/medu.13482 PMID:29226349

Lovell, K., & Vignare, K. (2009). MSU medical colleges blended learning for first year science courses: Uniting pedagogy to maximize experience and real world limitations. *Journal of Asynchronous Learning Networks*, *13*(1), 55–63.

Lowyck, J. (2014). Bridging learning theories and technology-enhanced environments: A critical appraisal of its history. In J. M. Spector, M. D. Merrill, J. Elen, & M. J. Bishop (Eds.), *Handbook of research on educational communications and technology* (pp. 3–20). New York: Springer. doi:10.1007/978-1-4614-3185-5_1

Loyens, S. M., Magda, J., & Rikers, R. M. (2008). Self-Directed Learning in Problem-Based Learning and its Relationships with Self-Regulated Learning. *Educational Psychology Review*, *20*(4), 411–427. doi:10.100710648-008-9082-7

Lu, D. W., Dresden, S., McCloskey, C., Branzetti, J., & Gisondi, M. A. (2015). Impact of burnout on self-reported patient care among emergency physicians. *The Western Journal of Emergency Medicine*, *16*(7), 996–1001. doi:10.5811/westjem.2015.9.27945 PMID:26759643

Ludmerer, K. M. (1996). *Learning to heal: The development of American medical education Paperback*. Baltimore, MD: Johns Hopkins University Press.

Luria, A. R. (1976). *The cognitive development: Its cultural and social foundations*. Cambridge, MA: Harvard University Press.

Lyasere, C. A., Baggett, M., Romano, J., Jena, A., Mills, G., & Hunt, D. P. (2016). Beyond continuing medical education: Clinical coaching as a tool for on-going professional development. *Academic Medicine: Journal of the Association of American Medical Colleges*, *91*(12), 1647–1650. doi:10.1097/ACM.0000000000001131 PMID:26910898

MacDowell, M., Glasser, M., & Hunsaker, M. (2013). A decade of rural physician workforce outcomes for the Rockford Rural Medical Education (RMED) Program, University of Illinois. *Academic Medicine*, *88*(12), 1941–1947. doi:10.1097/ACM.0000000000000031 PMID:24128632

Maclaughlin, B. W., Wang, D., Noone, A. M., Liu, N., Harazduk, N., Lumpkin, M., ... Amri, H. (2011). Stress biomarkers in medical students participating in a mind body medicine skills program. *Evidence-Based Complementary and Alternative Medicine*, *2011*, 950461. doi:10.1093/ecam/neq039 PMID:21799696

MacNaughton, J. (2000). The humanities in medical education: Context, outcome, structure. *Medical Humanities*, *26*(1), 23–30. doi:10.1136/mh.26.1.23 PMID:12484317

MacPherson, A., & Kimmelman, J. (2019). Ethical development of stem-cell-based-interventions. *Nature Medicine*, *25*(7), 1037–1044. doi:10.103841591-019-0511-6 PMID:31270501

Maiers, M. (2017). Our future in the hands of millennials. *Journal of the Canadian Chiropractic Association, 61*(3), 212–217. PMID:29430050

Mains, T. E., Wilcox, M. V., & Wright, S. M. (2016). Medical education resources initiative for teens program in Baltimore: A model pipeline program built on four pillars. *Education for Health, 29*(1), 47–50. doi:10.4103/1357-6283.178935 PMID:26996799

Malloy, E., Butt, S., & Sorter, M. (2010). Physician leadership and quality improvement in the acute child and adolescent psychiatric care setting. *Child and Adolescent Psychiatric Clinics of North America, 19*(1), 1–19. doi:10.1016/j.chc.2009.08.008 PMID:19951803

Malloy, E., Butt, S., & Sorter, M. (2010a). Physician leadership in residential treatment for children and adolescents. *Child and Adolescent Psychiatric Clinics of North America, 19*(1), 21–30. doi:10.1016/j.chc.2009.08.001 PMID:19951804

Maniar, K. P., Arva, N., Blanco, L. Z. Jr, Mao, Q., Morency, E. G., Rodriguez, R., ... Nayar, R. (2019). Accreditation Council for Graduate Medical Education (ACGME) Self-Study for Pathology: One Institutions Experience and Lessons Learned. *Archives of Pathology & Laboratory Medicine, 143*(10), 1271–1277. doi:10.5858/arpa.2018-0467-RA PMID:31017451

Manning, S. (2018). Quality assurance and quality improvement. In *Accreditation on the Edge: Challenging quality assurance in higher* (pp. 13–30). Baltimore, MD: JOHNS HOPKINS UNIV Press.

Maran, N. J., & Glavin, R. J. (2003). Low- to high-fidelity simulation - a continuum of medical education? *Medical Education, 37*(s1Suppl 1), 22–28. doi:10.1046/j.1365-2923.37.s1.9.x PMID:14641635

Margolis, E., Soldatenko, M., Acker, S., & Gair, M. M. (2001). Peekabo hiding and outing the curriculum. In E. Margolis (Ed.), The Hidden Curriculum in Higher Education (1-20). New York, NY: Routledge.

Mark, D. B., & Wong, J. B. (2001). Decision making in clinical medicine. In E. Braunwald (Ed.), *Harrison's Principles of Internal Medicine* (15th ed., pp. 8–14). New York: The McGraw-Hill Companies.

Martins, H. M. G. (2010). Why management and leadership education for internists? *European Journal of Internal Medicine, 21*(5), 374–376. doi:10.1016/j.ejim.2010.04.014 PMID:20816587

Maslach, C., & Leiter, M. P. (2016). Understanding the burnout experience: Recent research and its implications for psychiatry. *World Psychiatry; Official Journal of the World Psychiatric Association (WPA), 15*(2), 103–111. doi:10.1002/wps.20311 PMID:27265691

Maslow, A. H. (1943). A theory of human motivation. *Psychological Review, 50*(4), 370–396. doi:10.1037/h0054346

Masters, D. E., O'Brien, B. C., & Chou, C. L. (2013). The third-year medical student "grapevine.". *Academic Medicine, 88*(10), 1534–1538. doi:10.1097/acm.0b013e3182a36c26

Mattar, S. G., Alseidi, A. A., Jones, D. B., Jeyarajah, D. R., Swanstrom, L. L., Aye, R. W., ... Minter, R. M. (2013). General surgery residency inadequately prepares trainees for fellowship: Results of a survey of fellowship program directors. *Annals of Surgery, 258*(3), 440–449. doi:10.1097/SLA.0b013e3182a191ca PMID:24022436

Mavani, P. S. (2007). Restructuring medical education. *Indian Journal of Medical Ethics, 4*, 62–63. PMID:18630222

Mayer, J. D., & Salovey, P. (1993). The intelligence of emotional intelligence. *Intelligence, 17*(4), 443–442. doi:10.1016/0160-2896(93)90010-3

Mazur, E. (2009, Nov. 12). Confessions of a Converted Lecturer: Eric Mazur. Retrieved from https://www.youtube.com/watch?v=WwslBPj8GgI

MCAT and GPAs for Applicants and Matriculants to U.S. Medical Schools by Primary Undergraduate Major, 2018-2019. (2018). Retrieved from https://www.aamc.org/download/321496/data/factstablea17.pdf

McCann, D. P., & Blossom, H. J. (1990). The physician as a patient educator. From theory to practice. *The Western Journal of Medicine, 153*(1), 44–49. PMID:2202158

McConnell, M. M., & Eva, K. W. (2012). The role of emotion in the learning and transfer of clinical skills and knowledge. *Academic Medicine, 87*(10), 1316–1322. doi:10.1097/ACM.0b013e3182675af2 PMID:22914515

McCoy, K. L., & Carty, S. E. (2012). There is no "i" in "team": Comment on "a surgical simulation curriculum for senior medical students based on TeamSTEPPS.". *Archives of Surgery, 147*(8), 766–767. doi:10.1001/archsurg.2012.1573 PMID:22911076

McCullough, B., Marton, G. E., & Ramnanan, C. J. (2015). How can clinician-educator training programs be optimized to match clinician motivations and concerns? *Advances in Medical Education and Practice, 6*(1), 45–54. doi:10.2147/AMEP.S70139 PMID:25653570

McDonald, R. P. (1999). *Test Theory: A Unified Treatment.* Taylor & Francis.

McDougle, L., Way, D. P., Lee, W. K., Morfin, J. A., Mavis, B. E., Matthews, D. A., ... Clinchot, D. M. (2015). A national long-term outcomes evaluation of U.S. premedical postbaccalaureate programs designed to promote health care access and workforce diversity. *Journal of Health Care for the Poor and Underserved, 26*(3), 631–647. doi:10.1353/hpu.2015.0088 PMID:26320900

McDougle, L., Way, D. P., & Rucker, Y. L. (2010). Survey of care for the underserved: A control group study of practicing physicians who were graduates of The Ohio State University College of Medicine premedical postbaccalaureate training program. *Academic Medicine, 85*(1), 36–40. doi:10.1097/ACM.0b013e3181c46f35 PMID:20042818

McDougle, L., Way, D. P., & Yash, C. (2008). Effectiveness of a premedical postbaccalaureate program in improving medical college admission test scores of underrepresented minority and disadvantaged students. *Journal of the National Medical Association, 100*(9), 1021–1024. doi:10.1016/S0027-9684(15)31438-3 PMID:18807429

McGaghie, W. C. (2002). Assessing readiness for medical education: Evolution of the Medical College Admission Test. *Journal of the American Medical Association, 288*(9), 1085–1090. doi:10.1001/jama.288.9.1085 PMID:12204076

McGrath, J., Bischof, J., Greenberger, S., Bachmann, D., Way, D., Gorgas, D., & Kman, N. (2016). 'Speed advising' for medical students applying to residency programs: An efficient supplement to traditional advising. *Medical Education Online, 21*(1), 31336. doi:10.3402/meo.v21.31336 PMID:27056564

McLean, S. (2016). Case-based learning and its application in medical and health-care fields: A review of worldwide literature. *Journal of Medical Education and Curricular Development, 3*, 39–49. doi:10.4137/JMECD.S20377 PMID:29349306

McMahon, G. T. (2016). What do I need to learn today?: The evolution of CME. *The New England Journal of Medicine, 374*(15), 1403–1406. doi:10.1056/NEJMp1515202 PMID:27074064

McMahon, T. (2005). Teaching medicine and allied disciplines in the 21st century; lessons from Ireland on the continuing need for reform. *Radiography, 11*(1), 61–65. doi:10.1016/j.radi.2004.05.005

McManus, I. C. (1995). Humanity and the medical humanities. *Lancet, 346*(8983), 1143–1145. doi:10.1016/S0140-6736(95)91806-X PMID:7475609

McNulty, J., Hoyt, A., Chandrasekhar, A., Espiritu, B., Gruener, G., Price, R., & Naheedy, R. (2011). A three-year study of lecture multimedia utilization in the medical curriculum: Associations with performances in the basic sciences. *Medical Science Educator, 21*(1), 29–36. doi:10.1007/BF03341591

Medical School Admission Requirements^{TM}. (2019). Retrieved from https://students-residents.aamc.org/applying-medical-school/applying-medical-school-process/medical-school-admission-requirements/

Medina, M. S., Castleberry, A. N., & Persky, A. M. (2017). Strategies for improving learner metacognition in health professional education. *American Journal of Pharmaceutical Education*, *81*(4), 78. PMID:28630519

Meier, A. H., Boehler, M. L., McDowell, C. M., Schwind, C., Markwell, S., Roberts, N. K., & Sanfey, H. (2012). A surgical simulation curriculum for senior medical students based on TeamSTEPPS. *Archives of Surgery*, *147*(8), 761–766. doi:10.1001/archsurg.2012.1340 PMID:22911075

Meng, K. (2007). Teaching medical humanities in Korean medical schools: Tasks and prospects. *Korean Journal of Medical Education*, *19*(1), 5-11. DOI:. 2007.19.1.5. doi:10.3946/KJME

Mercuri, M., Sherbino, J., Sedran, R. J., Frank, J. R., Gafni, A., & Norman, G. (2015). When guidelines don't guide: The effect of patient context on management decisions based on clinical practice guidelines. *Academic Medicine*, *90*(2), 191–196. doi:10.1097/ACM.0000000000000542 PMID:25354075

Merriam, S. B., & Bierema, L. L. (2013). *Adult Learning: Linking Theory and Practice*. San Francisco, CA: Jossey-Bass.

Mesko, B., Győrffy, Z., & Kollár, J. (2015). Digital literacy in the medical curriculum: A course with social media tools and gamification. *JMIR Medical Education*, *1*(2), e6. doi:10.2196/mededu.4411 PMID:27731856

Messick, S. (1994). Validity of Psychological Assessment: Validation of Inferences from Persons' Responses and Performances as Scientific Inquiry into Score Meaning. *ETS Research Report Series*, *1994*(2), i–28. doi:10.1002/j.2333-8504.1994.tb01618.x

Metz, A. M. (2017). Medical school outcomes, primary care specialty choice, and practice in medically underserved areas by physician alumni of MEDPREP, a postbaccalaureate premedical program for underrepresented and disadvantaged students. *Teaching and Learning in Medicine*, *29*(3), 351–359. doi:10.1080/10401334.2016.1275970 PMID:28632012

Metzel, J. M., Petty, J., & Olowojoba, O. V. (2018). Using a structural competency framework to teach structural racism in pre-health education. *Social Science & Medicine*, *199*, 189–201. doi:10.1016/j.socscimed.2017.06.029 PMID:28689630

Meurling, L., Hedman, L., Felländer-Tsai, L., & Wallin, C. J. (2013). Leaders' and followers' individual experiences during the early phase of simulation-based team training: An exploratory study. *BMJ Quality & Safety*, *22*(6), 459–467. doi:10.1136/bmjqs-2012-000949 PMID:23293119

Meyerson, S. L., Sternbach, J. M., Zwischenberger, J. B., & Bender, E. M. (2017). The effect of gender on resident autonomy in the operating room. *Journal of Surgical Education*, *74*(6), e111–e118. doi:10.1016/j.jsurg.2017.06.014 PMID:28669788

Mgbako, O. (2019). The unicorn. *Journal of the American Medical Association*, *321*(2), 149–150. doi:10.1001/jama.2018.21048 PMID:30644986

Michaelson, L., & Richards, B. (2005). Drawing conclusions from the team-learning literature in health-sciences education. *Teaching and Learning in Medicine*, *17*(1), 85–88. doi:10.120715328015tlm1701_15 PMID:15691820

Miflin, B. (2004). Adult learning, self-directed learning and problem-based learning: Deconstructing the connections. *Teaching in Higher Education*, *9*(1), 43–53. doi:10.1080/1356251032000155821

Mileder, L., Wegscheider, T. & Dimai, H. P. (2014). Teaching first-year medical students in basic clinical and procedural skills – A novel course concept at a medical school in Austria. *GMS Zeitschrift fuer Medizinische Ausbildung*, *31*(1): Doc6.Doi:10.3205/zma000898

Miles, C., Lee, C., Foggett, K., & Nair, B. (2017). Reinventing medical teaching and learning for the 21st century: Blended and flipped strategies. *Archives of Medicine and Health Sciences*, 5, 97–102.

Miller, B., Dzwonek, B., McGuffin, A., & Shapiro, J. I. (2014). From LCME probation to compliance: The Marshall University Joan C. Edwards School of Medicine experience. *Advances in Medical Education and Practice*, 377–382. PMID:25337003

Miller, C. (2014). Implementation of study skills programs for entering at risk medical students. *Advances in Physiology Education*, *38*(3), 229–234. doi:10.1152/advan.00022.2014 PMID:25179612

Miller, G. E. (1990). The assessment of clinical skills/competence/performance. *Academic Medicine*, *65*(9), S63–S67. doi:10.1097/00001888-199009000-00045 PMID:2400509

Miller, S., Shipper, E., Hasty, B., Merrell, S. B., Lee, E. L., Lin, D., & Lau, J. N. (2018). Introductory surgical skills course: Technical training and preparation for the surgical environment. *MedEdPORTAL*, *14*(10775). doi:10.15766/mep_2374-8265.10775 PMID:30800975

Miloslavsky, E. M., Boyer, D., Winn, A. S., Stafford, D. E. J., & McSparron, J. I. (2016). Fellows as teachers: Raising the educational bar. *Annals of the American Thoracic Society*, *13*(4), 465–468. PMID:26835749

Misak, J. (2018). A (virtual) bridge not too far: Teaching narrative sense of space with virtual reality. *Computers and Composition*, *50*, 39–52. doi:10.1016/j.compcom.2018.07.007

Mitchall, A., & Jaeger, A. (2018). Parental influences on low-income, first generation students' motivation on the path to college. *The Journal of Higher Education*, *89*(4), 582–606. doi:10.1080/00221546.2018.1437664

Mogali, S., Yeong, W., Tan, H. K. J., Tan, G. J. S., Abrahams, P. H., Zary, N., ... Ferenczi, M. A. (2017). Evaluation by medical students of the educational value of multi-material, multi-colored three-dimensional printed models of the upper limb for anatomical education. *Anatomical Sciences Education*, *11*(1), 54–64. doi:10.1002/ase.1703 PMID:28544582

Monroe, A., Quinn, E., Samuelson, W., Dunleavy, D. M., & Dowd, K. W. (2013). An overview of the medical school admission process and use of applicant data in decision making: What has changed since the 1980s? *Academic Medicine*, *88*(5), 672–681. doi:10.1097/ACM.0b013e31828bf252 PMID:23524917

Moore, D. E. Jr, Green, J. S., & Gallis, H. A. (2009). Achieving desired results and improved outcomes: Integrating planning and assessment throughout learning activities. *The Journal of Continuing Education in the Health Professions*, *29*(1), 1–14. doi:10.1002/chp.20001 PMID:19288562

Moore, G. (1998). Cramming more components onto integrated circuits. *Proceedings of the IEEE*, *86*(1), 82-85.

Morgan, H. K., Haggins, A., Lypson, M. L., & Ross, P. (2016). The Importance of the Premedical Experience in Diversifying the Health Care Workforce. *Academic Medicine*, *91*(11), 1488–1491. doi:10.1097/ACM.0000000000001404 PMID:27603037

Morgan, K. M., Northey, E. E., & Khalil, M. K. (2017). The effect of near-peer tutoring on medical students' performance in anatomical and physiological sciences. *Clinical Anatomy (New York, N.Y.)*, *30*(7), 922–928. doi:10.1002/ca.22954 PMID:28726243

Morris, N. P. (2016, May 12). It's time to retire premed. Retrieved from https://blogs.scientificamerican.com/guest-blog/it-s-time-to-retire-premed/?redirect=1

Mouratev, G., Howe, D., Hoppmann, R., Poston, M. B., Reid, R., Varnadoe, J., ... DeMarco, P. (2013). Teaching medical students ultrasound to measure liver size: Comparison with experienced clinicians using physical exam alone. *Teaching and Learning in Medicine*, *25*(1), 84–88. doi:10.1080/10401334.2012.741535 PMID:23330900

Murray, T. S., Clermont, Y., & Binkley, M. (2005). *Measuring adult literacy and life skills: New frameworks for assessment*. Ottawa, Canada: Statistics Canada.

Myers, M. G. (2010). A proposed algorithm for diagnosing hypertension using automated office blood pressure measurement. *Journal of Hypertension*, 28(4), 703–708. doi:10.1097/HJH.0b013e328335d091 PMID:20150823

Mylopoulos, M., & Regehr, G. (2009). How student models of expertise and innovation impact the development of adaptive expertise in medicine. *Medical Education*, 43(2), 127–132. doi:10.1111/j.1365-2923.2008.03254.x PMID:19161482

Nardi, B. (1995). *Context and consciousness: Activity theory and human-computer interaction*. Cambridge, MA: MIT Press. doi:10.7551/mitpress/2137.001.0001

Nasca, T. J., Philibert, I., Brigham, T., & Flynn, T. C. (2012). The Next GME Accreditation System— Rationale and Benefits. *The New England Journal of Medicine*, 366(11), 1051–1056. doi:10.1056/NEJMsr1200117 PMID:22356262

National Academies of Sciences, Engineering, and Medicine. (2018). *Graduate medical education outcomes and metrics: Proceedings of a workshop*. Washington, DC: The National Academies Press. doi:10.17226/25003

National Center for Education Statistics. (2017). *Bachelor's, master's, and doctor's degrees conferred by postsecondary institutions, by sex of student and discipline division: 2015-16*. Retrieved June 3, 2019, from https://nces.ed.gov/programs/digest/d17/tables/dt17_318.30.asp

National Institutes of Health (NIH). (2017). *NIH 3D Print Exchange*. Bethesda, MD: U.S. Department of Health and Human Services. Retrieved from https://3dprint.nih. gov/

National Resident Matching Program. (2018). *Results of the 2018 NRMP Program Director Survey*. Retrieved July 26, 2019, from https://mk0nrmp3oyqui6wqfm.kinstacdn.com/wp-content/uploads/2018/07/NRMP-2018-Program-Director-Survey-for-WWW.pdf

Nendaz, M. R., & Tekian, A. (1999). Assessment in problem-based learning medical schools: A literature review. *Teaching and Learning in Medicine*, 11(4), 232–243. doi:10.1207/S15328015TLM110408

Neylan, C. J., Nelson, E. F., Dumon, K. R., Morris, J. B., Williams, N. N., Dempsey, D. T., ... Allen, S. R. (2017). Medical School Surgical Boot Camps: A Systematic Review. *Journal of Surgical Education*, 74(3), 384–389. doi:10.1016/j.jsurg.2016.10.014 PMID:27939818

NHS Institute for Innovation and Improvement and Academy of Medical Royal Colleges. (2010). Medical leadership competency framework: enhancing engagement in medical leadership. 3rd ed. Retrieved June 9, 2019, from https://www.leadershipacademy.nhs.uk/wp-content/uploads/2012/11/NHSLeadership-Leadership-Framework-Medical-Leadership-Competency-Framework-3rd-ed.pdf

Nickens, H. W., Ready, T. P., & Petersdorf, R. G. (1994). Project 3000 by 2000. Racial and ethnic diversity in U.S. medical schools. *The New England Journal of Medicine*, 331(7), 472–476. doi:10.1056/NEJM199408183310712 PMID:8035847

Ning, G. D., & Lamdan, R. M. (2009). The chief resident for education: Description of a novel academic teaching position. *Academic Psychiatry*, 33(2), 163–165. doi:10.1176/appi.ap.33.2.163 PMID:19398635

Nivet, M. A. (2010). Minorities in academic medicine: Review of the literature. *Journal of Vascular Surgery*, 51(4), S53–S58. doi:10.1016/j.jvs.2009.09.064 PMID:20036099

Norcini, J. J., & McKinley, D. W. (2007). Assessment methods in medical education. *Teaching and Teacher Education*, 23(3), 239–250. doi:10.1016/j.tate.2006.12.021

Norman, D. (2013). *The design of everyday things: Revised and expanded edition*. New York: Basic Books.

Norman, G. (2012). Medical education: Past, present and future. *Perspectives on Medical Education*, *1*(1), 6–14. doi:10.100740037-012-0002-7 PMID:23316454

Norman, G. (2016). Is psychometrics science? *Advances in Health Sciences Education: Theory and Practice*, *21*(4), 731–734. doi:10.100710459-016-9705-6 PMID:27501689

Norman, G. R., & Schmidt, H. G. (1992). The psychological basis of problem-based learning: A review of the evidence. *Academic Medicine*, *67*(9), 557–565. doi:10.1097/00001888-199209000-00002 PMID:1520409

Nothnagle, M., Anandarajah, G., Goldman, R. E., & Reis, S. (2011). Struggling to be self-directed: Residents' paradoxical beliefs about learning. *Academic Medicine: Journal of the Association of American Medical Colleges*, *86*(12), 1539–1544. doi:10.1097/ACM.0b013e3182359476 PMID:22030764

Nyland, R. L., Sawarynski, K. E. (2017). Setting students up for success: A short interactive workshop designed to increase effective study habits. *MedEdPORTAL*, *13*(10610).

O'Brien, B. C., & Poncelet, A. N. (2010). Transition to clerkship courses: Preparing students to enter the workplace. *Academic Medicine*, *85*(12), 1862–1869. doi:10.1097/ACM.0b013e3181fa2353 PMID:20978432

O'Brien, B., Cooke, M., & Irby, D. M. (2007). Perceptions and attributions of third-year student struggles in clerkships: Do students and clerkship directors agree? *Academic Medicine*, *82*(10), 970–978. doi:10.1097/ACM.0b013e31814a4fd5 PMID:17895662

O'Brien, S. E., Simpkin, A. L., & Spector, N. D. (2017). Promoting resilience in academic medicine: Fertile ground for future work. *The Journal of Pediatrics*, *182*, 6–7. doi:10.1016/j.jpeds.2016.11.056 PMID:28007471

O'Donnell, J. (2014). Introduction: The hidden curriculum: A focus on learning and closing the gap. In F. W. Hafferty & J. F. O'Donnell (Eds.), *The Hidden Curriculum in Health Professional Education* (pp. 1–20). Hanover, NH: Dartmouth College Press.

O'Neill, L. D., Wallstedt, B., Eika, B., & Hartvigsen, J. (2011). Factors associated with dropout in medical education: A literature review. *Medical Education*, *45*(5), 440–454. doi:10.1111/j.1365-2923.2010.03898.x PMID:21426375

O'Sullivan, P. S., & Irby, D. M. (2011). Reframing research on faculty development. *Academic Medicine: Journal of the Association of American Medical Colleges*, *86*(4), 421–428. doi:10.1097/ACM.0b013e31820dc058 PMID:21346505

Oettingen, G. (2000). Expectancy effects on behavior depend on self-regulatory thought. *Social Cognition*, *18*(2), 101–129. doi:10.1521oco.2000.18.2.101

Office of Disease Prevention and Health Promotion. (2019). Social determinants of health. Retrieved from https://www.healthypeople.gov/2020/topics-objectives/topic/social-determinants-of-health

Office of the National Coordinator for Health Information Technology. (2017a). *Non-federal acute care hospital electronic health record adoption*. Retrieved from https://dashboard.healthit.gov/quickstats/pages/FIG-Hospital-EHR-Adoption.php

Office of the National Coordinator for Health Information Technology. (2017b). *Individuals use of technology to track health care charges and costs*. Retrieved from https://dashboard.healthit.gov/quickstats/pages/consumers-health-care-charges-costs-online.php

Oliveira, A. C. P., Machado, A. P. G., & Aranha, R. N. (2017). Identification of factors associated with resilience in medical students through a cross-sectional census. *BMJ Open*, *7*(11). doi:10.1136/bmjopen-2017-017189 PMID:29133319

Olson, L. E. (2014). Articulating a Role for Program Evaluation in Responsible Conduct of Research Programs. *Accountability in Research*, *21*(1), 26–33. doi:10.1080/08989621.2013.822265 PMID:24073605

Ono, S. J. (2016, April 1). Holistic admissions: What you need to know. *The Association of Governing Boards - Trusteeship, 24*. Retrieved from https://agb.org/trusteeship-article/holistic-admissions-what-you-need-to-know/

Orr, C., & Sonnandara, R. (2019). Coaching by design: Exploring a new approach to faculty development in a competency-based medical education curriculum. *Advances in Medical Education and Practice, 10*, 229–244. doi:10.2147/AMEP.S191470 PMID:31118862

Orr, D., Weller, M., & Farrow, R. (2018). *Models for online, open, flexible and technology enhanced higher education across the globe: A comparative analysis.* Oslo, Norway: International Council for Open and Distance Education.

Orsmond, P., & Merry, S. (2017). Tutors' assessment practices and students' situated learning in higher education: Chalk and cheese. *Assessment & Evaluation in Higher Education, 42*(2), 289–303. doi:10.1080/02602938.2015.1103366

Ousager, J., & Johannessen H. (2010). Humanities in undergraduate medical education: A literature review. *Academic Medicine, 85*(6), 988-998, DOl:. doi:10.1097/ACM.Ob013e3181dd226b

Oyewole, S. (2001). Sustaining minorities in pre-health advising programs: Challenges and strategies for success. In B. Smedley, A. Sith, L. Colburn, & C. Evans (Eds.), *The Right Thing to Do: Enhancing Diversity in the Health Professions: Summary of the Symposium in Honor of Herbert N. Nickens M. D.* Washington DC: National Academies Press. Retrieved from https://www.ncbi. nlm.nih.gov/books/NBK223624

Pacifici, L. B., & Thomson, N. (2011). Undergraduate science research: A comparison of influences and experiences between premed and non-premed students. *CBE Life Sciences Education, 10*(2), 199–208. doi:10.1187/cbe.11-01-0005 PMID:21633068

Paller, M. S., Becker, T., Cantor, B., & Freeman, S. L. (2000). Introducing residents to a career in management: The physician management pathway. *Academic Medicine, 75*(7), 761–764. doi:10.1097/00001888-200007000-00025 PMID:10926031

Palmer, J. S. (2015). The millennials are coming: Improving self-efficacy in law students through universal design in learning. *Cleveland State Law Review, 63*, 675–706.

Palter, V. N., Grantcharov, T., Harvey, A., & Macrae, H. M. (2011). Ex vivo technical skills training transfers to the operating room and enhances cognitive learning: A randomized controlled trial. *Annals of Surgery, 253*(5), 886–889. doi:10.1097/SLA.0b013e31821263ec PMID:21394017

Papa, F. J., & Harasym, P. H. (1999). Medical curriculum reform in North America, 1765 to the present. *Academic Medicine, 74*(2), 154–164. doi:10.1097/00001888-199902000-00015 PMID:10065057

Parmelee, D., DeStephen, D., & Borges, N. (2009). Medical students' attitudes about team-based learning in a pre-clinical curriculum. *Medical Education Online, 14*(1), 4503. doi:10.3402/meo.v14i.4503 PMID:20165515

Patel, V., & Johnson, C. (2018, April). *Individuals' use of online medical records and technology for health needs.* ONC Data Brief, no. 40. Office of the National Coordinator for Health Information Technology: Retrieved May 22nd, 2019, from https://www.healthit.gov/sites/default/files/page/2018-03/HINTS-2017-Consumer-Data-Brief-3.21.18.pdf

Patel, M. S., Arora, V., Patel, M. S., Kinney, J. M., Pauly, M. V., & Asch, D. A. (2014). The role of MD and MBA training in the professional development of a physician: A survey of 30 years of graduates from the Wharton Health Care Management Program. *Academic Medicine, 89*(9), 1282–1286. doi:10.1097/ACM.0000000000000366 PMID:24979286

Patel, S., & Burke-Gaffney, A. (2018). The value of mobile tablet computers (iPads) in the undergraduate medical curriculum. *Advances in Medical Education and Practice, 9*, 567–570. doi:10.2147/AMEP.S163623 PMID:30127652

Patil, S. Y., Gosavi, M., Bannur, H. B., & Ratnakar, A. (2015). Blueprinting in assessment: A tool to increase the validity of undergraduate written examinations in pathology. *International Journal of Applied & Basic Medical Research*, *5*(4Suppl 1), S76–S79. doi:10.4103/2229-516X.162286 PMID:26380218

Patterson, F., Ashworth, V., Zibarras, L., Coan, P., Kerrin, M., & O'Neill, P. (2012). Evaluation of situational judgement tests to assess non-academic attributes in selection. *Medical Education*, *46*(9), 850–868. doi:10.1111/j.1365-2923.2012.04336.x PMID:22891906

Patterson, F., Knight, A., Dowell, J., Nicholson, S., Cousans, F., & Cleland, J. (2016). How effective are selection methods in medical education? A systematic review. *Medical Education*, *50*(1), 36–60. doi:10.1111/medu.12817 PMID:26695465

Pau, A., Jeevaratnam, K., Chen, Y., Fall, A., Khoo, C., & Nadarajah, V. (2013). The Multiple Mini-Interview (MMI) for student selection in health professions training – A systematic review. *Medical Teacher*, *35*(12), 1027–1041. doi:10.31 09/0142159X.2013.829912 PMID:24050709

Paul, R., & Elder, L. (2008). Critical thinking: The art of Socratic questioning, part III. *Journal of Developmental Education*, *31*(3), 34–35.

Pekrun, R., Goetz, T., Titz, W., & Perry, R. P. (2002). Academic Emotions in Students Self-Regulated Learning and Achievement: A Program of Qualitative and Quantitative Research. *Educational Psychologist*, *37*(2), 91–105. doi:10.1207/S15326985EP3702_4

Pell, G., Fuller, R., Homer, M. S., & Roberts, T. (2013). Advancing the OSCE: Sequential testing in theory and practice. *Medical Education*, *47*, 569–577. doi:10.1111/medu.12136 PMID:23662874

Pell, G., Fuller, R., Homer, M., & Roberts, T. (2010). How to measure the quality of the OSCE: A review of metrics - AMEE guide no. 49. *Medical Teacher*, *32*(10), 802–811. doi:10.3109/0142159X.2010.507716 PMID:20854155

Peña, A. (2010). The Dreyfus model of clinical problem-solving skills acquisition: A critical perspective. *Medical Education Online*, *15*(6). doi:10.3402/meo.v15i0.4846 PMID:20563279

Perry, W. G. (1999). *Forms of Ethical and Intellectual Development in the College Years*. San Francisco, CA: Jossey-Bass Publishers.

Peteet, J. B., Montgomery, L., Jerren, C., & Weekes, J. C. (2015). Predictors of imposter phenomenon among talented ethnic minority undergraduate students. *The Journal of Negro Education*, *84*(2), 175–186. doi:10.7709/jnegroeducation.84.2.0175

Peter, D., Robinson, P., Jordan, M., Lawrence, S., Casey, K., & Salas-Lopez, D. (2015). Reducing readmissions using teach-back: Enhancing patient and family education. *J Nurs Adm.*, *45*(1), 35–42. Epub 2014/12/06. pmid:25479173.

Phares, L., & Guglielmino, L. (2010). The role of self-directed learning in the work of community leaders. *International Journal of Self-directed Learning*, *7*(2), 35–53.

Philibert, I., Friedmann, P., & Williams, W. T.ACGME Work Group on Resident Duty Hours. (2002). Accreditation Council for Graduate Medical Education. New requirements for resident duty hours. *Journal of the American Medical Association*, *288*(9), 1112–1114. doi:10.1001/jama.288.9.1112 PMID:12204081

Phillips, S., & Clarke, M. (2012). More than an education: The hidden curriculum, professional attitudes and career choice. *Medical Education*, *46*(9), 887–893. doi:10.1111/j.1365-2923.2012.04316.x PMID:22891909

Phipps-Taylor, T. M., & Shortell, S. M. (2016). More than money: Motivating physician behavior change in accountable care organizations. *The Milbank Quarterly*, *94*(4), 832–861. doi:10.1111/1468-0009.12230 PMID:27995705

Pluta, W. J., Richards, B. F., & Mutnick, A. (2013). PBL and beyond: Trends in collaborative learning. *Teaching and Learning in Medicine, 25*(1), S9–S16. doi:10.1080/10401334.2013.842917 PMID:24246112

Pock, A. R., Durning, S. J., Gilliland, W. R., & Pangaro, L. N. (2019). Post-Carnegie II Curricular Reform: A North American Survey of Emerging Trends & Challenges. *BMC Medical Education, 19*(1), 260. doi:10.118612909-019-1680-1 PMID:31299948

Pock, A., Daniel, M., Santen, S., Swan Sein, A., Fleming, A., & Harnik, V. (2019). Challenges Associated With Moving the United States Medical Licensing Examination (USMLE) Step 1 to After the Core Clerkships and How to Approach Them. *Academic Medicine, 94*(6), 775–780. doi:10.1097/ACM.0000000000002651 PMID:30768466

Polavarapu, H. V., Kulaylat, A. N., Sun, S., & Hamed, O. H. (2013). 100 years of surgical education: The past, present, and future. *Bulletin of the American College of Surgeons, 98*(7), 22–27. PMID:24010218

Pololi, L. H., Evans, A. T., Civian, J. T., Vasiliou, V., Coplit, L. D., Gillum, L. H., ... Brennan, R. T. (2015). Mentoring faculty: A US national survey of its adequacy and linkage to culture in academic health centers. *The Journal of Continuing Education in the Health Professions, 35*(3), 176–184. doi:10.1002/chp.21294 PMID:26378423

Poncelet, A., & O'Brien, B. (2008). Preparing medical students for clerkships: A descriptive analysis of transition courses. *Academic Medicine, 83*(5), 444–451. doi:10.1097/ACM.0b013e31816be675 PMID:18448897

Porter, M. E., & Tiesberg, E. (2005). *Redefining Healthcare*. Boston, MA: Harvard Business School.

Power, D. J. (2008). Understanding data-driven decision support systems. *Information Systems Management, 25*(2), 149–154. doi:10.1080/10580530801941124

Poyet, M., Groussin, M., Avila-Pacheco, J., Jiang, X., Kearny, S. M., ... Alm, E. J. (2019). A library of human gut bacterial isolates paired with longitudinal multiomics data enables mechanistic microbiome research. *Nature Medicine, 25*(9), 1442–1452. doi:10.103841591-019-0559-3 PMID:31477907

Practice. (2009). In *Merriam-Webster.com*. Retrieved January 22, 2019, from https://www.merriam-webster.com/dictionary/practice

Preece, R., Dickinson, E. C., Sherif, M., Ibrahim, Y., Ninan, A. S., Aildasani, L., ... Smith, P. (2015). Peer-assisted teaching of basic surgical skills. *Medical Education Online, 20*(1), 27579. doi:10.3402/meo.v20.27579 PMID:26044400

Price, M. (2019, Feb. 7). How do you say 'Culturally competent care' in Korean? Retrieved from https://medium.com/@mirissaprice/how-do-you-say-culturally-competent-care-in-korean-3cadf7a5eac6

Price, L. R. (2016). *Psychometric Methods: Theory Into Practice*. Guilford Publications.

Prince, K. J., Boshuizen, H. P., van der Vleuten, C. P., & Scherpbier, A. J. (2005). Students' opinions about their preparation for clinical practice. *Medical Education, 39*(7), 704–712. doi:10.1111/j.1365-2929.2005.02207.x PMID:15960791

Prober, C. G., & Khan, S. (2013). Medical education reimagined: A call to action. *Academic Medicine, 88*(10), 1407–1410. doi:10.1097/ACM.0b013e3182a368bd PMID:23969367

Prunuske, A., Henn, L., Brearley, A., & Prunuske, J. (2016). A randomized crossover design to access learning impact and student preference for active and passive online learning modules. *Medical Science Educator, 26*(1), 135–141. doi:10.100740670-015-0224-5 PMID:27076992

Quantified Self. (2019) What is Quantified Self? Retrieved June 1, 2019 from https://quantifiedself.com/about/what-is-quantified-self/

Quinn, J., & White, B. (2019). Cultivating Leadership in Medicine. Dendall Hunt Publishers. 155-164.

Rabinowitz, H. K. (2011). AM last page: Truths about the rural physician supply. *Academic Medicine*, *86*(2), 272. doi:10.1097/ACM.0b013e31820add6c PMID:21270556

Rabow, M. W. (2014) Becoming a doctor: Learning from the hidden curriculum in medical education. In F. W. Hafferty & J. F. O'Donnell (Eds.), The Hidden Curriculum in Health Professional Education (130-139). Hanover, NH: Dartmouth College Press.

Radcliffe, C., & Lester, H. (2003). Perceived stress during undergraduate medical training: A qualitative study. *Medical Education*, *37*(1), 32–38. doi:10.1046/j.1365-2923.2003.01405.x PMID:12535113

Ragins, B. R., & Kram, K. E. (2007). *The handbook of mentoring at work: Theory, research, and practice*. Thousand Oaks, CA: Sage.

Rakel, D. P., & Hedgecock, J. (2008). Healing the healer: A tool to encourage student reflection towards health. *Medical Teacher*, *30*(6), 633–635. doi:10.1080/01421590802206754 PMID:18677663

Ramani, S. (2006). Twelve tips to promote excellence in medical teaching. *Medical Teacher*, *28*(1), 19–23. doi:10.1080/01421590500441786 PMID:16627316

Ramani, S., Mann, S., Taylor, D., & Thampy, H. (2016). Residents as teachers: Near peer learning in clinical work settings. *Medical Teacher*, *38*(7), 642–655. doi:10.3109/0142159X.2016.1147540 PMID:27071739

Raymond, M. R., Mee, J., King, A., Haist, S. A., & Winward, M. L. (2011). What New Residents Do During Their Initial Months of Training. *Academic Medicine*, *86*, S59–S62. doi:10.1097/ACM.0b013e31822a70ff PMID:21955771

Razack, S., Hodges, B., Steinert, Y., & Maguire, M. (2015). Seeking inclusion in an exclusive process: Discourses of medical school student selection. *Medical Education*, *49*(1), 36–47. doi:10.1111/medu.12547 PMID:25545572

Recht, M., & Bryan, R. N. (2017). Artificial intelligence: Threat or boon to radiologists. *Journal of the American College of Radiology*, *14*(11), 1475–1480. doi:10.1016/j.jacr.2017.07.007 PMID:28826960

Reddy, M. S. (2009). Humanities in medical education. *Indian Journal of Psychologic Medicine, 31*(2), 57. DOI:. doi:10.4103/0253-7176.63573

Reede, J. Y. (2003). A recurring theme: The need for minority physicians. *Health Affairs*, *22*(4), 91–93. doi:10.1377/hlthaff.22.4.91 PMID:12889755

Reeves, R. E., Vishwanatha, J. K., Yorio, T., Budd, M., & Sheedlo, H. J. (2008). The post-baccalaureate premedical certification program at the University of North Texas Health Science Center strengthens admission qualifications for entrance into medical school. *Academic Medicine*, *83*(1), 45–51. doi:10.1097/ACM.0b013e31815c641c PMID:18162749

Related. 2019. In *Merriam-Webster.com*. Retrieved May 11, 2019, from https://www.merriam-webster.com/dictionary/practice

Reynolds, R. C., & Carson, R. A. (1976). Editorial: The place of humanities in medical education. *Journal of Medical Education*, *51*, 142–143. PMID:1249830

Richardson, T., Mulvihill, T., & Latz, A. O. (2014). Bound and Determined: Perceptions of Pre-Med Seniors Regarding Their Persistence in Preparing for Medical School. *Journal of Ethnographic and Qualitative Research*, *8*(4), 222–238.

Rideout, V., Foehr, U., & Roberts, D. (2010). *Generation M2: Media in the lives of 8- to 18-year-olds*. San Francisco, CA: Kaiser Family Foundation; Retrieved from http://www.kff.org/entmedia/mh012010pkg.cfm

Rifkin, M. R., Smith, K. D., Stimmel, B. D., Stagnaro-Green, A., & Kase, N. G. (2000). The Mount Sinai humanities and medicine program: An alternative pathway to medical school. *Academic Medicine*, *75*(10Supplement), S124–S126. doi:10.1097/00001888-200010001-00040 PMID:11031196

Riley, B. (2018). Using the flipped classroom with simulation-based medical education to engage millennial osteopathic medical students. *The Journal of the American Osteopathic Association*, *118*(10), 673–678. doi:10.7556/jaoa.2018.147 PMID:30264142

Roberts, D. H., Schwartzstein, R. M., & Weinberger, S. E. (2014). Career development for the clinician-educator: Optimizing impact and maximizing success. *Annals of the American Thoracic Society*, *11*(2), 254–259. doi:10.1513/AnnalsATS.201309-322OT PMID:24575995

Roberts, D., Newman, L., & Schwartzstein, R. (2012). Twelve tips for facilitating Millennials' learning. *Medical Teacher*, *34*(4), 274–278. doi:10.3109/0142159X.2011.613498 PMID:22288944

Robinson, R. (2018). *Insights from a massive open online course (MOOC) for medical education (2014-2018)*. Retrieved from https://www.researchgate.net/ publication/326610346

Robinson, M., Macneily, A., Afshar, K., McInnes, C., Lennox, P., Carr, N., ... Arneja, J. (2013). Leadership in Canadian urology: What is the right stuff? *Journal of Surgical Education*, *70*(5), 606–612. doi:10.1016/j.jsurg.2013.04.013 PMID:24016371

Rocky Vista University College of Osteopathic Medicine. (2019). RVU Announces Pioneering Digital Health Track. Retrieved December 11, 2019 from http://www.rvu.edu/news/rvu-announces-pioneering-digital-health-track/

Romanello, M. (2005). Generational diversity: Teaching and learning approaches. *Nurse Educator*, *30*(5), 212–216. doi:10.1097/00006223-200509000-00009 PMID:16170263

Rosen, M. A., DiazGranados, D., Dietz, A. S., Benishek, L. E., Thompson, D., Pronovost, P. J., & Weaver, S. J. (2018). Teamwork in healthcare: Key discoveries enabling safer, high-quality care. *The American Psychologist*, *73*(4), 433–450. doi:10.1037/amp0000298 PMID:29792459

Rosenzweig, S., Reibel, D. K., Greeson, J. M., Brainard, G. C., & Hojat, M. (2003). Mindfulness-based stress reduction lowers psychological distress in medical students. *Teaching and Learning in Medicine*, *15*(2), 88–92. doi:10.1207/S15328015TLM1502_03 PMID:12708065

Rose, S. M. S. F., Contrepios, K., Moneghetti, K. J., Zhou, W., Mishra, T., Mataraso, S., ... Snyder, M. P. (2019). A longitudinal big data approach for precision health. *Nature Medicine*, *25*(5), 792–804. doi:10.103841591-019-0414-6 PMID:31068711

Rossett, A., & Schaffer, L. (2012). *Job aids and performance support: Moving from knowledge in the classroom to knowledge everywhere*. San Francisco, CA: John Wiley & Sons.

Rossini, M. (2018). Healthcare IT spending trends: Where hospitals plan to invest. *Journal of the Academy of Chiropractic Orthopedists*. Retrieved from https://www.jacoinc.com/blog/healthcare-it-spending-trends-where-hospitals-plan-to-invest/

Rules of procedure LCME. (2018). Retrieved from http://lcme.org/publications/

Russell, P. C. (2002). The White Coat Ceremony: Turning Trust Into Entitlement. *Teaching and Learning in Medicine*, *14*(1), 56–59. doi:10.1207/S15328015TLM1401_13 PMID:11865752

Ryan, M. S., Levine, L. J., Colbertz-Getz, J. M., Spector, N. D., & Fromme, H. B. (2015). Advising Medical Students for the Match: A National Survey of Pediatric Clerkship Directors. *Academic Pediatrics*, *15*(4), 374–379. doi:10.1016/j.acap.2015.03.009 PMID:25922334

Ryan, M. S., Lockeman, K. S., Feldman, M., & Dow, A. (2016). The gap between current and ideal approaches to the core EPAs: A mixed methods study of recent medical school graduates. *Medical Science Educator, 26*(3), 463–473. doi:10.100740670-016-0235-x

Ryan, R. M., & Deci, E. L. (2000). Self-determination theory and the facilitation of intrinsic motivation, social development, and well-being. *The American Psychologist, 55*(1), 68–78. doi:10.1037/0003-066X.55.1.68 PMID:11392867

Saddawi-Konefka, D., Baker, K., Guarino, A., Burns, S. A., Oettingen, G., Gollwitzer, P. M., & Charnin, J. E. (2017). Changing resident physician studying behaviors: A randomized, comparative effectiveness trial of goal-setting versus use of WOOP. *Journal of Graduate Medical Education, 9*(4), 451–457. doi:10.4300/JGME-D-16-00703.1 PMID:28824757

Saguil, A., & Kellermann, A. L. (2014). The community college pathway to medical school: A road less traveled. *Academic Medicine, 89*(12), 1589–1592. doi:10.1097/ACM.0000000000000439 PMID:25076201

Sakai, D. H., Fong, S. F., Shimamoto, R. T., Omori, J. S., & Tam, L. M. (2012). Medical school hotline: Transition to clerkship week at the John A. Burns School of Medicine. *Hawai'i Journal of Medicine & Public Health: A Journal of Asia Pacific Medicine & Public Health, 71*(3), 81–83. PMID:22454819

Samarakoon, L., Fernando, T., Rodrigo, C., & Rajapakse, S. (2013). Learning styles and approaches to learning among medical undergraduates and postgraduates. *BMC Medical Education, 13*(1), 42. doi:10.1186/1472-6920-13-42 PMID:23521845

Sánchez, J. P., Poll-Hunter, N., Stern, N., Garcia, A. N., & Brewster, C. (2016). Balancing Two Cultures: American Indian/Alaska Native Medical Students' Perceptions of Academic Medicine Careers. *Journal of Community Health, 41*(4), 871–880. doi:10.100710900-016-0166-x PMID:26896055

Sánchez, N. F., Rankin, S., Callahan, E., Ng, H., Holaday, L., Mcintosh, K., ... Sánchez, J. P. (2015). LGBT Trainee and Health Professional Perspectives on Academic Careers—Facilitators and Challenges. *LGBT Health, 2*(4), 346–356. doi:10.1089/lgbt.2015.0024 PMID:26788776

Sandars, J., & Homer, M. (2012). Pause 2 Learn: A "learning to learn" course to help undergraduate medical students to become more effective self-regulated learners. *Education for Primary Care, 23*(6), 437–439. PMID:23232136

Sandars, J., Patel, R., Steele, H., & McAreavey, M. (2014). Developmental student support in undergraduate medical education: AMEE Guide No. 92. *Medical Teacher, 36*(12), 1015–1026. doi:10.3109/0142159X.2014.917166 PMID:25072412

Sanfey, H., Boehler, M., DaRosa, D., & Dunnington, G. L. (2012a). Career Resources Career development resource: Educational leadership in a department of surgery: Vice chairs for education. *American Journal of Surgery, 204*, 121–125. doi:10.1016/j.amjsurg.2012.04.003 PMID:22704712

Sanfey, H., Boehler, M., DaRosa, D., & Dunnington, G. L. (2012b). Career development needs of vice chairs for education in departments of surgery. *Journal of Surgical Education, 69*(2), 156–161. doi:10.1016/j.jsurg.2011.08.002 PMID:22365859

Sargeant, J., Wong, B. M., & Campbell, C. M. (2018). Professional development of the future: A partnership between quality improvement and competency-based education. *Medical Education, 52*(1), 125–135. doi:10.1111/medu.13407 PMID:28984354

Satava, R. M. (2008). Historical review of surgical simulation--a personal perspective. *World Journal of Surgery, 32*(2), 141–148. doi:10.100700268-007-9374-y PMID:18097716

Saunders, P. A., Tractenberg, R. E., Chaterji, R., Amri, H., Harazduk, N., Gordon, J. S., ... Haramati, A. (2007). Promoting self-awareness and reflection through an experiential mind-body skills course for first year medical students. *Medical Teacher, 29*(8), 778–784. doi:10.1080/01421590701509647 PMID:17852720

Scheinman, S. J., Fleming, P., & Niotis, K. (2018). Oath taking at U.S. and Canadian medical school ceremonies: Historical perspectives, current practices, and future considerations. *Academic Medicine, 93*(9), 1301–1306. doi:10.1097/ACM.0000000000002097 PMID:29239902

Schmidt, H. (2000). Assumptions underlying self-directed learning may be false. *Medical Education, 34*(4), 243–245. doi:10.1046/j.1365-2923.2000.0656a.x PMID:10733717

Schnapp, B. H., Fant, A. L., & Gisondi, M. A. (2017). A ten-year program evaluation of an emergency medicine scholarly track in education using a qualitative approach. *Society for Academic Emergency Medicine, 1*, 215–220. PMID:30051037

Schneid, S., Apperson, A., Laiken, N., Mandel, J., Kelly, C., & Brandl, K. (2018). A summer prematriculation program to help students succeed in medical school. *Advances in Health Sciences Education: Theory and Practice, 23*(3), 499–511. doi:10.100710459-017-9808-8 PMID:29340892

Schwartz, A. W., Abramson, J. S., Wojnowich, I., Accordino, R., Ronan, E. J., & Rifkin, M. R. (2009). Evaluating the impact of the humanities in medical education. *Mount Sinai Journal of Medicine, 76*(4), 372-380. DOl:. doi:10.1002/msj.20126

Schwartzstein, R. M., Rosenfeld, G. C., Hilborn, R., Oyewole, S. H., & Mitchell, K. (2013). Redesigning the MCAT Exam: Balancing Multiple Perspectives. *Academic Medicine, 88*(5), 560–567. doi:10.1097/ACM.0b013e31828c4ae0 PMID:23524933

Scott, L. D., & Zerwic, J. (2015). Holistic review in admissions: A strategy to diversify the nursing workforce. *Nursing Outlook, 63*(4), 488–495. doi:10.1016/j.outlook.2015.01.001 PMID:26187088

Seabrook, M. A. (2004). Clinical students initial reports of the educational climate in a single medical school. *Medical Education, 38*(6), 659–669. doi:10.1111/j.1365-2929.2004.01823.x PMID:15189263

Seifert, K., & Sutton, R. (2009). *Educational Psychology.* Retrieved May 8, 2019, from https://courses.lumenlearning.com/suny-educationalpsychology/chapter/gender-differences-in-the-classroom/

Selden, W. K. (1962). The history and role of accrediting in higher education. *Journal of the American Medical Association, 181*(7), 613–615. doi:10.1001/jama.1962.03050330043009 PMID:13910406

Shacklady, J., Holmes, E., Mason, G., Davies, I., & Dornan, T. (2009). Maturity and medical students' ease of transition into the clinical environment. *Medical Teacher, 31*(7), 621–626. doi:10.1080/01421590802203496 PMID:19811146

Shahid, R. J., Stirling, J., & Adams, W. (2018). Promoting wellness and stress management in residents through emotional intelligence training. *Advances in Medical Education and Practice, 9*, 681–686. doi:10.2147/AMEP.S175299 PMID:30310341

Shanafelt, T. D., Hasan, O., Dyrbye, L. N., Sinsky, C., Satele, D., Sloan, J., & West, C. P. (2015). Changes in Burnout and Satisfaction With Work-Life Balance in Physicians and the General US Working Population Between 2011 and 2014. *Mayo Clinic Proceedings, 90*(12), 1600–1613. doi:10.1016/j.mayocp.2015.08.023 PMID:26653297

Shankar, P. R. (2014). Designing and conducting a two day orientation program for first semester undergraduate medical students. *Journal of Educational Evaluation for Health Professions, 11*(31). PMID:25417865

Shapiro, J., & Rucker, L. (2003). Can poetry make better doctors? Teaching the humanities and arts to medical students and residents at the University of California, Irvine, College of Medicine. *Academic Medicine, 78*(10), 953–957. doi:10.1097/00001888-200310000-00002 PMID:14534086

Sharpless, J. M., Oxman, A. D., Mahtani, K. R., Chalmers, I., Oliver, S., Collins, K., … Hoffman, T. (2017). Critical thinking in healthcare and education. BM J2017, 357, j2234 doi:10.1136bmj.j2234.

Shavelson, R. J., & Webb, N. M. (1991). Generalizability Theory: A Primer. *Sage (Atlanta, Ga.).*

Sherbino, J., Frank, J. R., & Snell, L. (2014). Defining the key roles and competencies of the clinician-educator of the 21st century: A national mixed-methods study. *Academic Medicine, 89*(5), 783–789. doi:10.1097/ACM.0000000000000217 PMID:24667507

Sheri, K., Too, J. Y. J., Chuah, S. E. L., Toh, Y. P., Mason, S., & Radha Krishna, L. K. (2019). A scoping review of mentor training programs in medicine between 1990 and 2017. *Medical Education Online, 24*(1), 1555435. doi:10.108 0/10872981.2018.1555435 PMID:31671284

Shields, P. (1994). A survey and analysis of student academic support programs in medical schools focus: Underrepresented minority students. *Journal of the National Medical Association, 86*(5), 373–377. PMID:8046766

Shochet, R. B., Colbert-Getz, J. M., Levine, R. B., & Wright, S. M. (2013). Gauging events that influence students' perceptions of the medical school learning environment: Findings from one institution. *Academic Medicine, 88*(2), 246–252. doi:10.1097/ACM.0b013e31827bfa14 PMID:23269291

Shroyer, A. L., Lu, W. H., & Chandran, L. (2016). Drivers of dashboard development (3-D): A curricular continuous quality improvement approach. *Academic Medicine, 91*(4), 517–521. doi:10.1097/ACM.0000000000001078 PMID:26796088

SibleyJ.SpirdinoffS. (n.d.). What is PBL? Retrieved from http://www.teambasedlearning.org/

Sijtsma, K. (2009). On the Use, the Misuse, and the Very Limited Usefulness of Cronbach's Alpha. *Psychometrika, 74*(1), 107–120. doi:10.100711336-008-9101-0 PMID:20037639

Silver, I., & Leslie, K. (2017). Comparing and contrasting faculty development and continuing professional development 2003-2019. In D. A. Davis, & K. Wolters, *W. F. Rayburn, & M. G. Turco*, Continuing Professional Development in Medicine and Health Care (1st ed.).

Silverman, M., Murray, T. J., & Bryan, C. S. (Eds.). (2007). *The Quotable Osler.* Philadelphia, PA: American College of Physicians.

Simon, H. A. (1971). Designing organizations for an information-rich world. *Computers, Communication, and the Public Interest, 37,* 40-41.

Simon, F. A., & Aschenbrener, C. A. (2005). Undergraduate medical education accreditation as a driver of lifelong learning. *The Journal of Continuing Education in the Health Professions, 25*(3), 157–161. doi:10.1002/chp.23 PMID:16173065

Simpson, M., Buckman, R., Stewart, M., Maguire, P., Lipkin, M., Novack, D., & Till, J. (1991). Doctor-patient communication: The Toronto Consensus Statement. *British Medical Journal, 303*(6814), 1385–1387. doi:10.1136/ bmj.303.6814.1385 PMID:1760608

Singh Ospina, N., Phillips, K. A., Rodriguez-Gutierrez, R., Castaneda-Guarderas, A., Gionfriddo, M. R., Branda, M. E., & Montori, V. M. (2019). Eliciting the patient's agenda- secondary analysis of recorded clinical encounters. *Journal of General Internal Medicine, 34*(1), 36–40. doi:10.100711606-018-4540-5 PMID:29968051

Siwicki, B. (2016). AMA invests $15 million to launch Silicon Valley Innovation Hub Health2047. Retrieved June 1, 2019 from https://www.healthcareitnews.com/news/ama-invests-15-million-launch-silicon-valley-innovation-hub-health2047

Skarupski, K. A., Welch, C., Dandar, V., Mylona, E., Chatterjee, A., & Singh, M. (2019). Late-career expectations: a survey of full-time faculty members who are 55 or older at 15 U. S. medical schools. *Academic Medicine,* epub ahead of print.

Skochelak, S. E., & Stack, S. J. (2017). Creating the medical schools of the future. *Academic Medicine, 92*(1), 16–19. doi:10.1097/ACM.0000000000001160 PMID:27008357

Slamecka, N. J., & Graf, P. (1978). The generation effect: Delineation of a phenomenon. *Journal of Experimental Psychology. Human Learning and Memory*, *4*(6), 592–604. doi:10.1037/0278-7393.4.6.592

Slater, C. E., & Cusick, A. (2017). Factors related to self-directed learning readiness of students in health professional programs: A scoping review. *Nurse Education Today*, *52*, 28–33. doi:10.1016/j.nedt.2017.02.011 PMID:28229917

Small, R. M., Soriano, R. P., Chietero, M., Quintana, J., Parkas, V., & Koestler, J. (2008). Easing the transition: Medical students' perceptions of critical skills required for the clerkships. *Education for Health*, *20*, 1–9. PMID:19967639

Smiar, K., & Mendez, J. (2016). Creating and using interactive, 3D-printed models to improve student comprehension of Bohr model of the atom, bond polarity, and hybridization. *Journal of Chemical Education*, *93*(9), 1591–1594. doi:10.1021/acs.jchemed.6b00297

Smith, M. C., Rose, A. D., Smith, T. J., & Ross-Gordon, J. M. (2015). Adults' readiness to learn and skill acquisition and use: An analysis of PIAAC. *Adult Education Research Conference*. Retrieved from http://newprairiepress.org/aerc/2015/papers/50

Smith, A., & Anderson, M. (2018). *Social media use in 2018*. Washington, DC: Pew Research Center; Retrieved from https://www.pewinternet.org/2018/03/01/social-media-use-in-2018/

Smith, B. (2013). *Mentoring at risk students through the hidden curriculum of higher education*. Lanham, MD: Lexington Book.

Smith, C. C., McCormick, I., & Huang, G. C. (2014). The clinician-educator track: Training internal residents as clinician-educators. *Academic Medicine*, *89*(6), 888–891. doi:10.1097/ACM.0000000000000242 PMID:24871239

Smith, C. C., Newman, L. R., & Huang, G. C. (2018). Those who teach, can do: Characterizing the relationship between teaching and clinical skills in a residency program. *Journal of Graduate Medical Education*, *10*(4), 459–463. doi:10.4300/JGME-D-18-00039.1 PMID:30154980

Smith, G. A., Stark, A. M., Rayburn, W., Davis, D., & Turco, M. (2017). Enhancing continuing professional development with insights from implementation science. In *Continuing Professional Development in Medicine and Healthcare: Better Education, Improved Outcomes, Best Care*. Philadelphia, PA: Wolters Kluwer.

Smith, M. M., Rose, S. H., Schroeder, D. R., & Long, T. R. (2015). Diversity of United States medical students by region compared to US census data. *Advances in Medical Education and Practice*, *6*, 367–372. PMID:26028982

Smith, M., & Jones, J. (2018). Dual-extrusion 3D printing of anatomical models for education. *Anatomical Sciences Education*, *11*(1), 65–72. doi:10.1002/ase.1730 PMID:28906599

Smith, S. D., Dunham, L., Dekhtyar, M., Dinh, A., Lanken, P. N., Moynahan, K. F., ... Skochelak, S. E. (2016). Medical student perceptions of the learning environment: Learning communities are associated with a more positive learning environment in a multi-institutional medical school study. *Academic Medicine*, *91*(9), 1263–1269. doi:10.1097/ACM.0000000000001214 PMID:27119332

Smith, V. S. (2013). Data dashboard as evaluation and research communication tool. *New Directions for Evaluation*, *140*(140), 21–45. doi:10.1002/ev.20072

Sobocan, M., Turk, N., Dinevski, D., Holj, R., & Balon, B. P. (2016). Problem-based learning in internal medicine: Virtual patients or paper-based problems? *Internal Medicine Journal*, *47*(1), 99–103. doi:10.1111/imj.13304 PMID:27800653

Soemantri, D., Mccoll, G., & Dodds, A. (2018). Measuring medical students' reflection on their learning: Modification and validation of the motivated strategies for learning questionnaire (MSLQ). *BMC Medical Education*, *18*(1), 274. doi:10.118612909-018-1384-y PMID:30466427

Soliman, M., & Al-Shaikh, G. (2015). Readiness for self-directed learning among first year Saudi medical students: A descriptive study. *Pakistan Journal of Medical Sciences*, *31*(4), 799–802. PMID:26430406

Solomon, H. F. (2016, June). Pre-professional health advising in the eighties. *The Advisor*, *36*(2), 15–17.

Soo, J., Brett-Maclean, P., Cave, M., & Oswald, A. (2015). At the precipice: A prospective exploration of medical students' expectations of the pre-clerkship to clerkship transition. *Advances in Health Sciences Education: Theory and Practice*, *21*(1), 141–162. doi:10.100710459-015-9620-2 PMID:26164285

Soto-Greene, M., Wright, L., Gona, O. D., & Feldman, L. A. (1999). Minority enrichment programs at the New Jersey Medical School: 26 years in review. *Academic Medicine*, *74*(4), 386–389. doi:10.1097/00001888-199904000-00032 PMID:10219218

Spura, A., Werwick, K., Feissel, A., Gottschalk, M., Winkler-Stuck, K., Bernt-Peter, R., ... Stieger, P. (2016). Preparation courses for medical clerkships and the final clinical internship in medical education – The Magdeburg Curriculum for Healthcare Competence. *GMS Journal for Medical Education*, *33*(3), 2366–5017. PMID:27275505

Srinivasan, M., Li, S. T., Meyers, F. J., Pratt, D. D., Collins, J. B., Braddock, C., ... Hilty, D. M. (2011). Teaching as a competency: Competencies for medical educators. *Academic Medicine*, *86*(10), 1211–1220. doi:10.1097/ACM.0b013e31822c5b9a PMID:21869655

Srinivasan, M., Wilkes, M., Stevenson, F., Nguyen, T., & Slavin, S. (2007). Comparing Problem-Based Learning with Case-Based Learning: Effects of a Major Curricular Shift at Two Institutions. *Academic Medicine*, *82*(1), 74–82. doi:10.1097/01.ACM.0000249963.93776.aa PMID:17198294

Staats, C., Capatosto, K., Wright, R. A., & Contractor, D. (2015). *State of the Science Implicit bias review 2015*. Retrieved June 9, 2019, from http://kirwaninstitute.osu.edu/wp-content/uploads/2015/05/2015-kirwan-implicit-bias.pdf

StaffA. O. A. (2018). *The DO*. Retrieved from https://thedo.osteopathic.org/2018/08/coca-receives-usde-renewal-as-recognized-accrediting-agency

Stahn, B., & Harendza, S. (2014). Role models - major determinant of specialty choice and training program. *GMS Zeitschrift für Medizinische Ausbildung*, *31*(4), 1–15. PMID:25489345

Standards for accreditation and requirements of affiliation MSCHE . (2019). Retrieved from https://www.msche.org/standards/

Standards, Publications, & Notification Forms: LCME. (n.d.). Retrieved from https://lcme.org/publications/

Staropoli, P. C., Gregori, N. Z., Junk, A. K., Galor, A., Goldhardt, R., Goldhagen, B. E., ... Feuer, W. (2018). Surgical Simulation Training Reduces Intraoperative Cataract Surgery Complications Among Residents. *Simulation in Healthcare*, *13*(1), 11–15. PMID:29023268

Statistics Market Research Consulting. *Report on e-learning - global market outlook (2017-2026)*. (2018). Retrieved May 22nd, 2019 from https://www.researchandmarkets.com/research/mjp4w2/global_elearning?w=4/

Status, D. (2020). *n.p* (p. 25). AMCAS Application Guide; Retrieved from https://apps.aamc.org/amcas/guide/2020_AMCAS_applicant_guide.pdf

Stead, W., Searle, J., Fessler, H., Smith, J., & Shortliffe, E. (2011). Biomedical informatics: Changing what physicians need to know and how they learn. *Academic Medicine*, *86*(4), 429–434. doi:10.1097/ACM.0b013e3181f41e8c PMID:20711055

Steakley, L. (2013). *A conversation about digital literacy in medical education*. Retrieved from https://scopeblog.stanford.edu/2013/05/09/a-conversation-about-digital-literacy-in-medical-education/

Steele, M. M., Fisman, S., & Davidson, B. (2013). Mentoring and role models in recruitment and retention: A study of junior medical faculty perceptions. *Medical Teacher*, *35*(5), e1130–e1138. doi:10.3109/0142159X.2012.735382 PMID:23137243

Stefanidis, D., Sevdalis, N., Paige, J., Zevin, B., Aggarwal, R., Grantcharov, T., & Jones, D. B. (2015). Simulation in surgery: What's needed next? *Annals of Surgery*, *261*(5), 846–583. doi:10.1097/SLA.0000000000000826 PMID:25243562

Steffen, L. E., Boucher, K. M., Damron, B. H., Pappas, L. M., Walters, S. T., Flores, K. G., ... Kinney, A. Y. (2015). Efficacy of a telehealth intervention on colonoscopy uptake when cost is a barrier: The family care cluster randomized controlled trial. *Cancer Epidemiology, Biomarkers & Prevention*, *24*(9), 1311–1318. doi:10.1158/1055-9965.EPI-15-0150 PMID:26101306

Stempsey, W. E. (1999). The quarantine of philosophy in medical education: Why teaching the humanities may not produce humane physicians. *Medicine, Health Care, and Philosophy*, *2*(1), 3–9. doi:10.1023/A:1009936630946 PMID:11080973

Stephens, M. B., Corcoran, T. S., & Motsinger, C. (2011). Clinical documentation in electronic medical records: The student perspective. *The Journal of the International Association of Medical Science Educators: JIAMSE*, *1*(1), 3–6. doi:10.1007/BF03341587

Stewart, S., Betson, C., Marshall, I., Wong, C., Lee, P., & Lam, T. (1995). Stress and vulnerability in medical students. *Medical Education*, *29*(2), 119–127. doi:10.1111/j.1365-2923.1995.tb02814.x PMID:7623698

Stillwell, N. A., Wallick, M. M., Thal, S. E., & Burleson, J. A. (2000). Myers-Briggs Type and Medical Specialty Choice: A New Look at an Old Question. *Teaching and Learning in Medicine*, *12*(1), 14–20. doi:10.1207/S15328015TLM1201_3 PMID:11228862

Stoller, J. K., Taylor, C. A., & Farver, C. E. (2013). Emotional intelligence competencies provide a developmental curriculum for medical training. *Medical Teacher*, *35*(3), 243–247. doi:10.3109/0142159X.2012.737964 PMID:23360483

Stone-McLean, J., Metcalfe, B., Sheppard, G., Murphy, J., Black, H., & McCarthy, H. (2017). Developing an undergraduate ultrasound curriculum: A needs assessment. *Cureus*, *9*(9), e1720. PMID:29188164

Storey, V. A. (2019). Advancing healthcare leadership: Physicians as agents of change. In *Preparing Physicians to Lead in the 21st Century* (pp. 1–25). Hershey, PA: IGI Global.

Stratton, T. D. (2019). Legitimizing Continuous Quality Improvement (CQI): Navigating Rationality in Undergraduate Medical Education. *Journal of General Internal Medicine*, *34*(5), 758–761. doi:10.100711606-019-04875-1 PMID:30788765

Stringfellow, T. D., Rohrer, R. M., Lowenthal, L., Gorrard-Smith, C., Sheriff, I. H. N., Armit, K., ... Spurgeon, P. C. (2015). Defining the structure of undergraduate medical leadership and management teaching and assessment in the UK. *Medical Teacher*, *37*(8), 747–754. doi:10.3109/0142159X.2014.971723 PMID:25301039

Student Guide to Osteopathic Medical Colleges . (2019). Retrieved from https://www.aacom.org/student-guide

Student ParticipationL. C. M. E. in Accreditation. (2019). Retrieved from http://lcme.org/accreditation-preparation/students/#Student-Participation-in-Accreditation

Sukhera, J., & Watling, C. (2018). A framework for integrating implicit bias recognition into health professions education. *Academic Medicine: Journal of the Association of American Medical Colleges*, *93*(1), 35–40. doi:10.1097/ACM.0000000000001819 PMID:28658015

Sullivan, T. (2018). Gartner, IDC and HIMSS analytics say hospitals will invest the most in 2018. *Healthcare IT News*. Retrieved from https://www.healthcareitnews. com/news/follow-money-where-gartner-idc-and-himss-analytics-say-hospitals-will-invest-most-2018/

Sundberg, K., Josephson, A., Reeves, S., & Nordquist, J. (2017). Power and resistance: Leading change in medical education. *Studies in Higher Education*, *42*(3), 445–462. doi:10.1080/03075079.2015.1052735

Surmon, L., Bialocerkowski, A., & Hu, W. (2016). Perceptions of preparedness for the first medical clerkship: A systematic review and synthesis. *BMC Medical Education*, *16*(1), 89. doi:10.118612909-016-0615-3 PMID:26968816

Swanwick, T. (2014). Understanding medical education. In T. Swanwick (Ed.), *Understanding Medical education: Evidence, theory and practice* (2nd ed.). Medford, MA: John Wiley & Sons.

Swanwick, T., Forrest, K., & O'Brien, B. C. (2019). *Understanding Medical Education: Evidence, Theory, and Practice*. John Wiley & Sons.

Swiss Digital Health. (2019). Hackathons. Retrieved June 2, 2019 from https://swissdigitalhealth.com/ideate/hackathons/

Talamantes, E., Henderson, M. C., Fancher, T. L., & Mullan, F. (2019). Closing the gap: Making medical school admissions more equitable. *The New England Journal of Medicine*, *380*(9), 803–805. doi:10.1056/NEJMp1808582 PMID:30811906

Talamantes, E., Jerant, A., Henderson, M. C., Giffin, E., Fancher, T., Grbic, D., ... Franks, P. (2018). Community college pathways to medical school and family medicine residency training. *Annals of Family Medicine*, *16*(4), 302–307. doi:10.1370/afm.2270 PMID:29987077

Talamantes, E., Mangione, C. M., Gonzalez, K., Jimenez, A., Gonzalez, F., & Moreno, G. (2014). Community college pathways: Improving the U.S. physician workforce pipeline. *Academic Medicine*, *89*(12), 1649–1656. doi:10.1097/ACM.0000000000000438 PMID:25076199

Talbot, T., Sagae, K., John, B., & Rizzo, A. (2012). Sorting out the virtual patient: How to exploit artificial intelligence, game technology and sound educational practices to create engaging role-playing simulations. *International Journal of Gaming and Computer-Mediated Simulations*, *4*(3), 1–19. doi:10.4018/jgcms.2012070101

Tavakol, M., & Dennick, R. (2011a). Making sense of Cronbach's alpha. *International Journal of Medical Education*, *2*, 53–55. doi:10.5116/ijme.4dfb.8dfd PMID:28029643

Tavakol, M., & Dennick, R. (2011c). Post-examination analysis of objective tests. *Medical Teacher*, *33*(6), 447–458. doi:10.3109/0142159X.2011.564682 PMID:21609174

Taylor, J., & Wendland, C. (2014). The hidden curriculum in medicine's "culture of no culture": Health professional education. In F. W. Hafferty, & J. F. O'Donnell (Eds.), The Hidden Curriculum in Health Professional Education (53-62). Hanover, NH: Dartmouth College Press.

Taylor, D., & Miflin, B.Taylor & Miflin. (2008). Problem-based learning: Where are we now? *Medical Teacher*, *30*(8), 742–763. doi:10.1080/01421590802217199 PMID:18946818

Taylor, J. S., George, P. F., MacNamara, M. M., Zink, D., Patel, N. K., Gainor, J., & Dollase, R. H. (2014). A new clinical skills clerkship for medical students. *Family Medicine*, *46*(6), 433–439. https://fammedarchives.blob.core.windows.net/imagesandpdfs/pdfs/FamilyMedicineVol46Issue6Taylor433.pdf PMID:24911298

ten Cate, O. (2013). Nuts and bolts of entrustable professional activities. *Journal of Graduate Medical Education*, *5*(1), 157–158. doi:10.4300/JGME-D-12-00380.1 PMID:24404246

ten Cate, O. (2014). What is a 21st-century doctor? Rethinking the significance of the medical degree. *Academic Medicine*, *89*(7), 966–969. doi:10.1097/ACM.0000000000000280 PMID:24979164

Tenhouse, A. (n.d.) College extracurricular activities impacts on students: Types of extracurricular activities. *8 Minute Reads*. Retrieved from https://education.stateuniversity.com/pages/1855/ College-Extracurricular-Activities.html

Tervalon, M., & Murray-Garcia, J. (1998). Cultural humility versus cultural competence: A critical distinction in defining physician training outcomes in multicultural education. *Journal of Health Care for the Poor and Underserved, 9*(2), 117–125. doi:10.1353/hpu.2010.0233 PMID:10073197

Teunissen, P. W., & Westerman, M. (2011). Opportunity or threat: The ambiguity of the consequences of transitions in medical education. *Medical Education, 45*(1), 51–59. doi:10.1111/j.1365-2923.2010.03755.x PMID:21155868

The Core Competencies for Entering Medical Students. (n.d.) In *Applying to Medical School, AAMC.* Retrieved from https://students-residents.aamc.org/applying-medical-school/article/core-competencies

The History and Application of the LCME's Diversity Standards. Retrieved from https://www.aamc.org/download/279018/data/brazanskyslides.pdf

The University of Texas Southwestern Medical Center. (2019). *Texas STAR.* Retrieved July 26, 2019, from https://www.utsouthwestern.edu/education/medical-school/about-the-school/student-affairs/texas-star.html

Theeboom, T., Beersma, B., & van Vianen, A. (2014). Does coaching work? A meta-analysis on the effects of coaching on individual level outcomes in an organizational context. *The Journal of Positive Psychology, 9*(1), 1–18. doi:10.1080/17439760.2013.837499 PMID:26640507

Thelin, J. R. (2011). *A history of American higher education.* Baltimore, MD: Johns Hopkins University Press.

Thistlethwaite, J. E., Davies, D., Ekeocha, S., Kidd, J. M., Macdougall, C., Matthews, P., ... Clay, D. (2012). The effectiveness of case-based learning in health professional education. A BEME systematic review: BEME Guide No. 23. *Medical Teacher, 34*(6), e421–e444. doi:10.3109/0142159X.2012.680939 PMID:22578051

Thistlewaite, J. (2014). Hidden among us: The language of inter- and outer-professional identity and collaboration. In F. W. Hafferty, & J. F. O'Donnell (Eds.), The Hidden Curriculum in Health Professional Education (158-168). Hanover, NH: Dartmouth College Press.

Thomas, B. R., & Dockter, N. (2019). Affirmative action and holistic review in medical school admissions: Where we have been and where we are going. *Academic Medicine, 94*(4), 473–476. doi:10.1097/ACM.0000000000002482 PMID:30277960

Thomas, P. A., Kern, D. E., Hughes, M. T., & Chen, B. Y. (2016). *Curriculum Development: A Six-Step Approach for Medical Education* (3rd ed.). Baltimore, MD: Johns Hopkins University Press.

Thompson, B. M., Schneider, V. F., Haidet, P., Perkowski, L. C., & Richards, B. F. (2007). Factors Influencing Implementation of Team-Based Learning in Health Sciences Education. *Academic Medicine, 82*(Suppl), S53–S56. doi:10.1097/ACM.0b013e3181405f15 PMID:17895691

Titus, S., & Ballou, J. (2013). Faculty members' perceptions of advising versus mentoring: Does the name matter? *Science and Engineering Ethics, 19*(3), 1267–1281. doi:10.100711948-012-9366-7 PMID:22660987

Topol, E. J. (2013). *The Creative Destruction of Medicine: How the Digital Revolution Will Create Better Health Care.* New York, NY: Basic Books.

Topol, E. J., Steinhubl, S. R., & Torkamani, A. (2015). Digital medical tools and sensors. *Journal of the American Medical Association, 313*(4), 353–354. doi:10.1001/jama.2014.17125 PMID:25626031

Torbert, W., & ... (2004). *Action inquiry: The secret of timely and transforming leadership.* San Francisco, CA: Berrett-Koehler.

Tough, A. (1971). *The adult's learning projects.* Toronto, Canada: Ontario Institute for Studies in Education.

Triola, M., Friedman, E., Cimino, C., Geyer, E., Wiederhorn, J., & Mainiero, C. (2010). Health information technology and the medical school curriculum. *American Journal of Managed Care, 16*(12 Suppl. HIT), 54-56.

Trizano-Hermosilla, I., & Alvarado, J. M. (2016). Best Alternatives to Cronbach's Alpha Reliability in Realistic Conditions: Congeneric and Asymmetrical Measurements. *Frontiers in Psychology, 7*. doi:10.3389/fpsyg.2016.00769 PMID:27303333

Tulving, E. (1966). Subjective organization and effects of repetition in multi-trial free-recall learning. *Journal of Verbal Learning and Verbal Behavior, 5*(2), 193–197. doi:10.1016/S0022-5371(66)80016-6

Tummons, J., Fournier, C., Kits, O., & MacLeod, A. (2018). Using technology to accomplish comparability of provision in distributed medical education in Canada: An actor-network theory ethnography. *Studies in Higher Education, 43*(11), 1912–1922. doi:10.1080/03075079.2017.1290063

Turgeman, L., May, J. H., & Sciulli, R. (2017). Insights from a machine learning model for predicting the hospital length of stay (LOS) at the time of admission. *Expert Systems with Applications, 78*, 376–385. doi:10.1016/j.eswa.2017.02.023

Turner, S. R., White, J., Poth, C., & Rogers, W. (2012). Preparing students for clerkship. *Academic Medicine, 87*(9), 1288–1291. doi:10.1097/ACM.0b013e3182623143 PMID:22836844

Tyler, J. H. (2013). If you build it will they come? Teachers' online use of student performance data. *Education Finance and Policy, 8*(2), 168–207. doi:10.1162/EDFP_a_00089 PMID:25593564

Tyler, R. W. (1949). *Basic Principles of Curriculum and Instruction*. University of Chicago Press.

U.S. Department of Education. (2019). *Accreditation in the United States*. Retrieved from http://www2.ed.gov/admins/finaid/accred/accreditation.html#Overview

U.S. Department of Education. (2019). *Use of technology in teaching and learning*. Retrieved from https://www.ed.gov/oii-news/use-technology-teaching-and-learning

U.S. Department of Health and Human Services. (n.d.). Agency for Healthcare Research and Quality Team Strategies and Tools to Enhance Performance and Patient Safety (TeamStepps). Retrieved July 15, 2019, from https://www.ahrq.gov/teamstepps/index.html

U.S. Department of Veterans Affairs. (2019). *Budget in brief 2020*. Retrieved May 22nd, 2019 from https://www.va.gov/budget/docs/summary/fy2020VAbudgetInBrief.pdf

U.S. Medical Regulatory Trends and Actions. (2018). *Federation of State Medical Boards*. Accessed May 1, 2019 from https://www.fsmb.org/siteassets/advocacy/publications/us-medical-regulatory-trends-actions.professional development

Ugbolue, A., Whitley, P. N., & Stevens, P. J. (1987). Evaluation of a preentrance enrichment program for minority students admitted to medical school. *Journal of Medical Education, 62*(1), 8–16. PMID:3795249

United States Census Bureau. (2016). Retrieved from https://www.census.gov/newsroom/press-releases/2016/cb16-210.html

University of Cincinnati's Office of Equity and Inclusion. (2018). Diversity datapoints. Retrieved from https://www.uc.edu/inclusion/latest/diversitydata.html

University of Cincinnati's Office of Institutional Research. (2018). Student diversity & internationalization. Retrieved from https://www.uc.edu/provost/about-us/peopleandoffices/institutional_research/institutional-dashboards/student-data/student-diversity.html

University of Louisville (UL). (n.d.). *Undergraduate medical education: Curriculum overview*. Retrieved from https://louisville.edu/medicine/ume/curriculum/curriculum-overview

Urban Universities for HEALTH. (2014). *Holistic admissions in the health professions. Findings from a national survey.* Retrieved from http://urbanuniversitiesforhealth.org/media/documents/holisticadmissionsinthehealthprofessions.pdf

Van Gessel, E., Nendaz, M. R., Vermeulen, B., Junod, A., & Vu, N. V. (2003). Development of clinical reasoning from the basic sciences to the clerkships: A longitudinal assessment of medical students' needs and self-perception after a transitional learning unit. *Medical Education, 37*(11), 966–974. doi:10.1046/j.1365-2923.2003.01672.x PMID:14629409

Van Hell, E. A., Kuks, J. B., Schonrock-Adema, J., van Lohuizen, M. T., & Cohen-Schotanus, J. (2008). Transition to clinical training: Influence of pre-clinical knowledge and skills, and consequences for clinical performance. *Medical Education, 42*(8), 830–837. doi:10.1111/j.1365-2923.2008.03106.x PMID:18564098

Van Herzeele, I., Aggarwal, R., Neequaye, S., Darzi, A., Vermassen, F., & Cheshire, N. J. (2008). Cognitive training improves clinically relevant outcomes during simulated endovascular procedures. *Journal of Vascular Surgery. 48*(5), 1223-30, 1230.e1. doi:. doi:10.1016/j.jvs.2008.06.034

Vanderbilt University. (2015). *The Cost of Federal Regulatory Compliance in Higher Education: A Multi-Institutional Study.* Nashville, TN: Vanderbilt University.

Vandergrift, J. L., Gray, B. M., & Weng, W. (2018). Do state continuing medical education requirements for physicians improve clinical knowledge? *Health Services Research, 53*(3), 1682–1701. doi:10.1111/1475-6773.12697 PMID:28419451

Veloski, J. J., Callahan, C. A., Xu, G., Hojat, M., & Nash, D. B. (2000). Prediction of students' performances on licensing examinations using age, race, sex, undergraduate GPAs, and MCAT scores. *Academic Medicine, 75*(10Suppl), S28–S30. doi:10.1097/00001888-200010001-00009 PMID:11031165

Verbert, K., Duval, E., Klerkx, J., Govaerts, S., & Santos, J. L. (2013). Learning analytics dashboard applications. *The American Behavioral Scientist, 57*(10), 1500–1509. doi:10.1177/0002764213479363

Verdonk, P., & Janczukowicz, J. (2018). Editorial: Diversity in Medical Education. *MedEdPublish, 7*(1). doi:10.15694/mep.2018.000001.1

Verghese, A. (2003, Sept. 14). A season in hell. *The New York Times*, pp. 7007011. Retrieved from https://www.nytimes.com/2003/09/14/books/a-season-in-hell.html

Verhaeghe, G., Schildkamp, K., Luyten, H., & Valcke, M. (2015). Diversity in school performance feedback systems. *School Effectiveness and School Improvement, 26*(4), 612–638. doi:10.1080/09243453.2015.1017506

Verschelden, C. (2017). *Bandwidth recovery helping students reclaim cognitive resources lost to poverty, racism and social marginalization.* Sterling, VA: Stylus Publishing.

Von Hippel, E. (2005). *Democratizing innovation.* Cambridge, MA: MIT Press. doi:10.7551/mitpress/2333.001.0001

Vygotsky, L. S. (1987). Thinking and speech. In R. W. Rieber, & A. S. Carton (Eds.), The collected works of L. S. Vygotsky, Volume 1: Problems of general psychology (pp. 39–285). New York: Plenum Press. (Original work published 1934.)

Vygtosky, L. S. (1978). *Mind in society: The development of higher psychological processes.* Cambridge, MA: Harvard University Press.

Wabash College. (2019). Using the intercultural development inventory to assess liberal arts outcomes. Retrieved from https://www.wabash.edu/news/displaystory.cfm?news_ID=2646

Wagner, R., Patow, C., Newton, R., Casey, B. R., Koh, N. J., & Weiss, K. B. (2016). The Overview of the CLER Program: CLER National Report of Findings 2016. *Journal of Graduate Medical Education, 8*(2Suppl 1), 11–13. doi:10.4300/1949-8349.8.2s1.11 PMID:27252798

Wagoner, N. E. (2006). Admission to medical school: Selecting applicants with the potential for professionalism. In D. T. Stern (Ed.), *Measuring Medical Professionalism* (pp. 235–263). New York: Oxford University Press.

Waite, G., Orndorff, B., Hughes, E., Saxon, D., White, G., Becker, S., & Duong, T. (2014). Distance education in medical education: Is there "value added"? *Medical Science Educator, 24*(1), 135–142. doi:10.100740670-014-0020-7

Wald, H. S., George, P., Reis, S. P., & Taylor, J. S. (2014). Electronic health record training in undergraduate medical education: Bridging theory to practice with curricula for empowering patient- and relationship-centered care in the computerized setting. *Academic Medicine, 89*(3), 380–386. doi:10.1097/ACM.0000000000000131 PMID:24448045

Waliany, S., Caceres, W., Merrell, S. B., Thadaney, S., Johnstone, N., & Osterberg, L. (2019). Preclinical curriculum of prospective case-based teaching with faculty- and student-blinded approach. *BMC Medical Education, 29*(1), 31. doi:10.118612909-019-1453-x PMID:30674302

Waljee, J. F., Chopra, V., & Saint, S. (2018). Mentoring millennials. *Journal of the American Medical Association, 319*(15), 1547–1548. doi:10.1001/jama.2018.3804 PMID:29677306

Walsh, K. (2013). *Oxford Textbook of Medical Education.* OUP Oxford. doi:10.1093/med/9780199652679.001.0001

Ward, M., Gruppen, L., & Regehr, G. (2002). Measuring self-assessment: Current state of the art. *Advances in Health Sciences Education: Theory and Practice, 7*(1), 63–80. doi:10.1023/A:1014585522084 PMID:11912336

Warren, K. S. (1984). The humanities in medical education. *Annals of Internal Medicine, 101*(5), 697-701. DOI:. 4819-101-5-697. doi:10.7326/0003

Warren, L. (2012). *Generational Learning Differences: Myth of Reality?* Retrieved May 8, 2019, from https://www.microassist.com/learning-dispatch/arelearning-differences-between-generations-a-myth/)

Watanabe-Crockett, L. (2019, July). 10 Innovative Formative Assessment Examples for Teachers to Know. Retrieved May 8, 2019, from https://www.wabisabilearning.com/blog/formative-assessment-examples

Watkins, K. D. (2016). Faculty development to support interprofessional education in healthcare professions: A realist synthesis. *Journal of Interprofessional Care, 30*(6), 695–701. doi:10.1080/13561820.2016.1209466 PMID:27459591

Wayman, J. C., & Cho, V. (2008). Preparing educators to effectively use student data systems. In T. J. Kowalski, & T. J. Lasley (Eds.), *Handbook on data-based decision-making in education* (pp. 89–104). Hoboken, NJ: Taylor & Francis.

Wayman, J. C., Stringfield, S., & Yakimowski, M. (2004). *Software enabling school improvement through analysis of student data.* Baltimore, MD: Center for Research of Students Placed at Risk, Johns Hopkins University.

Wear, D., Zarconi, J., & Garden, R. (2014). Disorderly conduct: Calling out of the hidden curriculum(s) of professionalism. In F. W. Hafferty, & J. F. O'Donnell (Eds.), The Hidden Curriculum in Health Professional Education (63-75). Hanover, NH: Dartmouth College Press.

Wear, D., Zarconi, J., Aultman, J. M., Chyatte, M. R., & Kumagai, A. K. (2017). Remembering freddie gray: Medical education for social justice. *Academic Medicine: Journal of the Association of American Medical Colleges, 92*(3), 312–317. doi:10.1097/ACM.0000000000001355 PMID:27580436

Webb, A. M. B., Tsipis, N. E., McClellan, T. R., McNeil, M. J., Xu, M. M., Doty, J. P., & Taylor, D. C. (2014). A first step toward understanding best practices in leadership training in undergraduate medical education: A systematic review. *Academic Medicine, 89*(11), 1563–1570. doi:10.1097/ACM.0000000000000502 PMID:25250751

Weinstein, C., & Mayer, R. (1986). The teaching of learning strategies. In M. C. Wittrock (Ed.), *Handbook of research on teaching* ((3rd ed., pp. 315–327). New York, NY: Macmillan.

Weiss, R. L., Hassell, L. A., & Parks, E. R. (2014). Progress toward improved leadership and management training in pathology. *Archives of Pathology & Laboratory Medicine*, *138*(4), 492–497. doi:10.5858/arpa.2013-0288-RA PMID:24678679

Welcher, C. M., Hersh, W., Takesue, B., Elliott, V., & Hawkins, R. E. (2018). Barriers to medical students' electronic health record access can impede their preparedness for practice. *Academic Medicine*, *93*(1), 48–53. doi:10.1097/ACM.0000000000001829 PMID:28746069

Welfare, L., Nolan, M., & Vari, R. (2016). Patient-centered learning curricula: Evaluating the impact of the Friday wrap-up on student conceptualization of patient psychosocial characteristics. *Medical Science Educator*, *26*(4), 543–546. doi:10.100740670-016-0315-y

Wendling, A. L., Phillips, J., Short, W., Fahey, C., & Mavis, B. (2016). Thirty years training rural physicians: Outcomes from the Michigan State University College of Human Medicine Rural Physician Program. *Academic Medicine*, *91*(1), 113–119. doi:10.1097/ACM.0000000000000885 PMID:26332428

Wenger, E. (1998). Communities of practice: Learning as a social system. *The Systems Thinker*, *9*(5), 2–3.

Wenrich, M., Jackson, M. B., Scherpbier, A. J., Wolfhagen, I. H., Ramsey, P. G., & Goldstein, E. A. (2010). Ready or not? Expectations of faculty and medical students for clinical skills preparation for clerkships. *Medical Education Online*, *15*(5295). doi:10.3402/meo.v15i0.5295 PMID:20711483

West, C. P., Dyrbye, L. N., Rabatin, J. T., Call, T. G., Davidson, J. H., Multari, A., & Shanafelt, T. D. (2014). Intervention to promote physician well-being, job satisfaction, and professionalism: A randomized clinical trial. *JAMA Internal Medicine*, *174*(4), 527–533. doi:10.1001/jamainternmed.2013.14387 PMID:24515493

White, J., & Lowenthal, P. (2019). Academic Discourse and the Formation of an Academic Identity: Minority College Students and the Hidden Curriculum. Academic Press.

White, L. (2018). *MOOCs for medical education: Lesson learned from the Medical Neuroscience experience – Exploring the boundaries of online learning and what it means for higher education.* Paper presented at the Treasury Symposium, Savannah, GA.

White, C. B., Dey, E. L., & Fantone, J. C. (2009). Analysis of factors that predict clinical performance in medical school. *Advances in Health Sciences Education: Theory and Practice*, *14*(4), 455–464. doi:10.100710459-007-9088-9 PMID:18030590

White, C. B., Ross, P. T., & Gruppen, L. D. (2009). Remediating students' failed OSCE performances at one school: The effects of self-assessment, reflection, and feedback. *Academic Medicine*, *84*(5), 651–654. doi:10.1097/ACM.0b013e31819fb9de PMID:19704203

White, J., Anthony, D., WinklerPrins, V., & Roskos, S. (2017). Electronic medical records, medical students, and ambulatory family physicians: A multi-institution study. *Academic Medicine*, *92*(10), 1485–1490. doi:10.1097/ACM.0000000000001673 PMID:28379934

Wiggins, G., & McTighe, J. (2005). *Understanding by design.* Alexandria, VA: ASCD.

Williams, B., Mancia, G., Spiering, W., Rosei, E. A., Azizi, M., & Burnier, M. (2018). 2018 ESC/ESH Guidelines for the management of arterial hypertension. *European Heart Journal*, *39*(33), 3021–3104. doi:10.1093/eurheartj/ehy339 PMID:30165516

Williamson, B. (2016). Digital education governance: Data visualization, predictive analytics, and 'real-time' policy instruments. *Journal of Education Policy*, *31*(2), 123–141. doi:10.1080/02680939.2015.1035758

Wilson, W., Henry, M., Ewing, G., Rehmann, J., Canby, C., Gray, J., & Finnerty, E. (2011). A prematriculation intervention to improve the adjustment of students to medical school. *Teaching and Learning in Medicine*, 23(3), 256–262. doi:10.1080/10401334.2011.586923 PMID:21745061

Windish, D. M., Paulman, P. M., Goroll, A. H., & Bass, E. B. (2004). Do clerkship directors think medical students are prepared for the clerkship years? *Academic Medicine*, 79(1), 56–61. doi:10.1097/00001888-200401000-00013 PMID:14690998

Winkleby, M. A. (2007). The Stanford Medical Youth Science Program: 18 years of a biomedical program for low-income high school students. *Academic Medicine*, 82(2), 139–145. doi:10.1097/ACM.0b013e31802d8de6 PMID:17264691

Winkleby, M. A., Hed, J., & Crump, C. (2015). Tapping underserved students to reshape the biomedical workforce. *Journal of Community Medicine & Health Education*, 5(2), 340. doi:10.4172/2161-0711.1000340 PMID:26120496

Winston, K. A., van der Vleuten, C. P. M., & Scherpbier, A. J. (2010). An investigation into the design and effectiveness of a mandatory cognitive skills programme for at-risk medical students. *Medical Teacher*, 32(3), 236–243. doi:10.3109/01421590903197035 PMID:20218839

Winston, K. A., van der Vleuten, C. P. M., & Scherpbier, A. J. (2014). Prediction and prevention of failure: An early intervention to assist at-risk medical students. *Medical Teacher*, 36(1), 25–31. doi:10.3109/0142159X.2013.836270 PMID:24083365

Wish-Baratz, S., Gubatina, A., Enterline, R., & Griswold, M. (2019). A new supplement to gross anatomy dissection: Holoanatomy. *Medical Education*, 53(5), 522–523. doi:10.1111/medu.13845 PMID:30891831

Wittenberg, M. (2014). Will ultrasound scanners replace the stethoscope? *British Medical Journal*, 348(May), g3463. doi:10.1136/bmj.g3463 PMID:24875141

Witteveen, D., & Attwell, P. (2017). The college completion puzzle: A hidden Markov model approach. *Research in Higher Education*, 58(4), 449–467. doi:10.100711162-016-9430-2

Wong, J. G. (2019). *The real questions behind three challenging interview questions and how to answer them.* Careers in Medicine (CiM), Association of Medical Colleges. Retrieved June 9, 2019, from https://www.aamc.org/cim/residency/application/interviewing/338086/interviewquestions.html

Wood, S. (2018). Framing wearing: Genre, embodiment, and exploring wearable technology in the composition classroom. *Computers and Composition*, 50, 66–77. doi:10.1016/j.compcom.2018.07.004

World Federation for Medical Education (WFME). (2003). Continuing professional development of medical doctors: WFME global standards for quality improvement. Available at https://wfme.org/standards/cpd/

World Health Organization (WHO). (2010). *Medical devices, managing the mismatch: An outcome of the Priority Medical Devices Project.* Geneva, Switzerland: Author.

World Health Organization. (2010). Regional Guidelines for Continuing Medical Education (CME)/Continuing Professional Development (CPD) Activities. Available at https://www.wbginvestmentclimate.org/toolkits/health-in-africa-policy-toolkit/upload/WHO-CME-Requirements.pdf

Worthen, M. (2018). The misguided drive to measure 'learning outcomes.' The New York Times Sunday Review. Retrieved from https://www.nytimes.com/2018/02/23/opinion/sunday/colleges-measure-learning- outcomes.htm

Wright-Peterson, V., & Bender, C. (2014). Making the invisible visible: Uncovering the hidden curriculum in allied health education. In F. W. Hafferty, & J. F. O'Donnell (Eds.), The Hidden Curriculum in Health Professional Education (140-147). Hanover, NH: Dartmouth College Press.

Wright, S., Wong, A., & Newill, C. (1997). The impact of role models on medical students. *Journal of General Internal Medicine*, *12*(1), 53–56. doi:10.100711606-006-0007-1 PMID:9034946

Yarris, L. M., & Coates, W. C. (2012). Creating educational leaders: Experiences with two education fellowships in emergency medicine. *Academic Emergency Medicine*, *19*(12), 1481–1485. doi:10.1111/acem.12042 PMID:23240922

Yazdani, S., Relan, A., Wilkerson, L., & Chung, P. J. (2017). Third-year medical students' perceptions and use of electronic diagnostic reasoning tools. *Medical Science Educator*, *27*(1), 97–103. doi:10.100740670-017-0373-9

Yew, E., & Goh, K. (2016). Problem-based learning: An overview of its process and impact on learning. *Health Profession Education*, *2*(2), 75–79. doi:10.1016/j.hpe.2016.01.004

Yoon, M., Burns, C., & Michaelsen, V. (2014). Team-based learning in different classroom settings. *Medical Science Educator*, *24*(2), 157–160. doi:10.100740670-014-0024-3

Young, A., Chaudhry, H. J., Pei, X., Arnhart, K., Dugan, M., & Snyder, G. B. (2017). A census of actively licensed physicians in the United States. *Journal of Medical Regulation*, *103*(2), 7–21. doi:10.30770/2572-1852-103.2.7

Yu, P. T., Parsa, P. V., Hassanein, O., Rogers, S. O., & Chang, D. C. (2013). Minorities struggle to advance in academic medicine: A 12-y review of diversity at the highest levels of Americas teaching institutions. *The Journal of Surgical Research*, *182*(2), 212–218. doi:10.1016/j.jss.2012.06.049 PMID:23582226

Zanten, M. V., Boulet, J. R., & Greaves, I. (2012). The importance of medical education accreditation standards. *Medical Teacher*, *34*(2), 136–145. doi:10.3109/0142159X.2012.643261 PMID:22288991

Zimmerman, B. J. (2002). Becoming a self-regulated learner: An overview. *Theory into Practice*, *41*(2), 64–70. doi:10.120715430421tip4102_2

Zimmerman, B. J., & Schunk, D. H. (Eds.). (2001). *Self-regulated learning and academic achievement: Theoretical perspectives* (2nd ed.). Mahwah, NJ: Lawrence Erlbaum Associates Publishers.

Zimmerman, M. (2018). *Teaching AI: Exploring new frontiers for learning*. Washington, DC: International Society for Technology in Education.

Zinbarg, R. E., Yovel, I., Revelle, W., & McDonald, R. P. (2006). Estimating Generalizability to a Latent Variable Common to All of a Scale's Indicators: A Comparison of Estimators for ωh. *Applied Psychological Measurement*, *30*(2), 121–144. doi:10.1177/0146621605278814

Zonia, S. C., LaBaere, J. R. II, Stommel, M., & Tomaszewski, D. D. (2005). Resident attitudes regarding the impact of the 80-duty-hours work standards. *The Journal of the American Osteopathic Association*, *105*(7), 307–313. PMID:16157519

About the Contributors

Ruth Gotian is the inaugural Assistant Dean of Mentoring and Executive Director of the newly launched Mentoring Academy at Weill Cornell Medicine. She is also the Chief Learning Officer in Anesthesiology and Assistant Professor of Education in Anesthesiology. Dr. Gotian received her doctorate in Adult Learning and Leadership from Teachers College Columbia University. Her B.S. and M.S.are in Business Management from the University at Stony Brook in New York. She also obtained certificates in Executive Leadership and Managing for Execution from Cornell University.

Joseph E. Safdieh is currently the Lewis and Rachel Rudin foundation Education Scholar, Assistant Dean – Clinical Curriculum, Vice Chairman for Education and Associate Professor of Neurology at Weill Cornell Medicine. He received his bachelor degree in neuroscience, summa cum laude, from the College of Arts and Science of New York University. He received his medical degree (MD) from the New York University School of Medicine, where he received the Alpha Omega Alpha Award for graduating first in his class. He completed his neurology residency training at the Weill Cornell Campus of New York Presbyterian Hospital, where he also served as Chief Resident in the Department of Neurology. Dr. Safdieh is a member of Phi Beta Kappa and Alpha Omega Alpha, the medical honors society. Dr. Safdieh is the director of the medical student Neurology Clerkship for the Weill Cornell Medical College, and has been in this role since 2007. He previously served as medical director of the Neurology Clinic at New York-Presbyterian Hospital and also served as Director of Outpatient Training for the Neurology Residency Program As assistant dean, he is responsible for overseeing the clinical curriculum at Weill Cornell. He is well respected as an innovative medical educator, and has developed numerous curricula for the teaching of neurology to both medical students and other physicians. He has been recognized for his excellence in medical student education locally, nationally and internationally. Dr. Safdieh currently serves on the education committee of the American Academy of Neurology, as well as the publications committee and the Undergraduate Education Subcommittee. He recently completed a 2-year term as chair of the Consortium of Neurology Clerkship Directors of the AAN. He is currently editor-in-chief of Neurology Today, the official news source of the American Academy of Neurology.

* * *

Salvatore Aiello is an MD/PhD student at Rosalind Franklin University.

Leila Amiri is the Assistant Dean for Admissions and Recruitment at the University of Illinois College of Medicine. Prior to transitioning to medical school admissions she worked as an undergraduate prehealth advisor and instructor. She has worked at four US medical schools since 2009 and has served in the areas of admissions, recruitment, combined BA/MD programs and financial aid. She has held leadership roles regionally and nationally through the Association of American Medical Colleges (AAMC) including serving as a Holistic Review Facilitator for five years and serving as the southerns representative to the Committee on Admissions.

Shohreh Anand has a doctorate from Teachers College, Columbia University in adult and organizational learning and degrees in Computer Science. Her research interests are at the intersection of health, illness and technology. Her dissertation research was on learning of patients with chronic condition and the management of their illness within the healthcare system. Previously, she contributed breakthrough research in medical imaging, in particular digital mammography. She is the director of Center on Patient Engagement and Learning at LearnLong Institute and is an educator who promotes technology literacy by teaching college computer science courses.

Tej Anand is an award-winning business-technology strategist, advisor, innovator, educator and practitioner with a passion for conceiving and successfully implementing transformative data-driven strategic initiatives. As an electrical engineer and computer scientist who specialized in artificial intelligence (AI) research in the late 1980's, he pioneered commercial data mining, now known as data science. After spending three decades teaching computers how to learn and creating meaning from data for business professionals, Tej embarked on a doctorate program in adult learning and organizational leadership at Teachers College, Columbia University that he completed in 2014. His passion is helping businesses find their edge at the intersection of business, data and technology with a central focus on people. Tej spent the first 10 years of his career working for technology companies – NCR/Teradata, A. C. Nielsen and Philips Research Laboratories – where his work led to several patents and profitable revenue producing products. After spending 5 years honing his skills as a technology executive and management consultant, Tej moved over to healthcare where for the past 15 years, as a senior business-technology executive at Medco and CareCentrix he implemented data-driven technology-enabled business models and processes to lower healthcare costs and improve clinical outcomes. His work led to several patents. In June 2018, Tej redirected his focus to education. He currently is a Professor of Practice at the University of Texas in Austin and a visiting faculty at Columbia University. He teaches graduate and undergraduate courses in leadership, disruptive change, digital technologies, AI, machine learning, cybersecurity and Blockchain. He is advising early stage start-ups on using Blockchain and AI to disrupt healthcare.

Andrea Anderson is the Associate Chief of the Division of Family Medicine and an Associate Clinical Professor at the GW School of Medicine and Health Sciences. She earned her Bachelor of Arts in Human Biology and African American Studies cum laude and her Medical Degree in the combined BA/MD Program in Liberal Medical Education at Brown University. She is the course director for the Transitions to Residency fourth year capstone course as well as a faculty member for the Practice of Medicine: Professional Development and Clinical Skills and Reasoning longitudinal components of the medical school curriculum. Her research interests include professional identity development, professionalism, mentoring, advocacy by physicians, and primary care workforce development.

Vanessa Bazan is a medical student at The University of Kentucky College of Medicine.

David Brawn is an associate director in an academic advising center for the liberal arts college at a large mid-western public university. He supervises a staff including four full time pre-health advisors, who provide direct pre-health advising and programming for a student population of over 17,000, including more than 6000 self-identified as having interest in health professions careers. His academic training includes a PhD in Cultural Anthropology with subsequent research done in the area of Medical Anthropology.

Aaron Burshtein is a Medical Student at the Donald and Barbara Zucker School of Medicine at Hofstra/Northwell.

Joshua Burshtein is a Medical Student at the Donald and Barbara Zucker School of Medicine at Hofstra/Northwell.

Sophia Chen is an assistant professor of Pediatrics at Rutgers New Jersey Medical School in Newark, NJ. As the assistant dean for preclerkship education, she oversees Years 1 and 2 of the medical school curriculum.

Stephanie Chervin is an academic advisor and premedical advisor in the LSA Honors Program at the University of Michigan. An experienced education professional with a PhD in chemistry, she has expertise in higher education administration, student advising, undergraduate admissions, curriculum support, teaching and research.

Briana Christophers is an MD-PhD student at the Tri-Institutional MD-PhD Program at Weill Cornell/Memorial Sloan Kettering/Rockefeller University with interests in developmental biology, health justice and advocacy, and mentoring the next generation of diverse physicians. She recently co-authored the e-book "The Free Guide to Medical School Admission." She graduated from Princeton University with a degree in Molecular Biology. You can follow her reflections on being a Latina woman growing into the role of physician-scientist on Twitter (@BriChristophers) where she is also the co-leader of @LatinasInMed and @MedStudentChat.

Courtney E. Cross is an assistant professor of Genetics at the TCU and UNTHSC School of Medicine in Fort Worth, Texas. She completed her PhD in the Department of Preventive Medicine and her postdoctoral research in Maternal Fetal Medicine with a focus on genetic toxicology at UTMB Galveston. Her educational research focus is predicting student success using pre-matriculation data. Dr. Cross is a member of the Association of Professors of Human and Medical Genetics, the International Association of Medical Science Educators, and a former board member of the Joubert Syndrome and Related Disorders Foundation.

Deborah DeWaay is an associate professor and Associate Dean of Undergraduate Medical Education, Department of Medical Education, University of South Florida, Morsani College of Medicine. She is a board certified physician of Internal Medicine.

Dawn Dillman is Professor, and Vice-Chair for Education in the Department of Anesthesiology & Perioperative Medicine at Oregon Health & Science University.

David Elkowitz is the Associate Dean and Director of the Academy of Medical Educators and Director of Undergraduate Medical Education for the Department of Pathology and Laboratory Medicine as well as Co-Director for the Structure Lab and Associate Director of the PEARLS program (case-based curriculum) at the Zucker School of Medicine at Hofstra/Northwell. Dr. Elkowitz has a dual appointment as an Associate Professor in the Departments of Science Education and Pathology/Laboratory Medicine and is a full-time facilitator in the case-based component of the curriculum (PEARLS), lecturer, and lab preceptor. Previously, Dr. Elkowitz directed the problem-based learning curriculum and the Office of Academic Medicine Fellowship at the New York College of Osteopathic Medicine in Old Westbury, NY. He served on the Dean's council, admissions committee, and curriculum committee, as well as the academic senate, serving as president in 2003-2004. Dr. Elkowitz has published over 40 articles, book chapters, and abstracts and has been an invited speaker at schools and meetings across the country talking about medical education topics including curricular reform, content integration, and the student centered approach. Dr. Elkowitz was awarded Mentor of the Year at the New York College of Osteopathic Medicine in 2004 and was a finalist for American Osteopathic Association Educator of the Year in 2004. Dr. Elkowitz received many teaching awards including Professor of the Year in 2006, and 2008, NYCOM's Standard of Excellence Award in 2006 and Distinguished Teacher of the Year Award in 2013 and 2019 at the Zucker School of Medicine at Hofstra/Northwell. He was inducted as an inaugural member in the Academy of Medical Educators at the Zucker School of Medicine at Hofstra/Northwell in 2017. Dr. Elkowitz received his Doctor of Osteopathic Medicine degree from the New York College of Osteopathic Medicine in 1997.

Donna Elliott is Vice Dean of Medical Education and Chair of the Department of Medical Education in the Keck School of Medicine of the University of Southern California.

Susan Ely is Professor and Assistant Dean for Student Affairs and Enrollment at the California Health Sciences University College of Osteopathic Medicine. She was previously Professor of Biomedical Science at Virginia Tech Carilion School of Medicine prior to becoming Professor of Molecular Biology, Immunology and Microbiology, and Director of Clinical Case-Based Learning at California Northstate University College of Medicine.

Anthony J. Finch was born and raised in New York, NY, USA. His mother is a physician and his father is a schoolteacher. He attended Polytechnic Institute of New York University for his undergraduate education from 2009-2013 and earned a BS in Chemical and Biomolecular Engineering. He then spent two years working as a research assistant in the Tissue Engineering, Regeneration, and Repair Laboratory at Hospital for Special Surgery where he conducted multiple projects studying cartilage repair and investigating the relationship between osteoarthritis and tumor metastasis. He began medical school at Weill Cornell Medicine in 2015 and graduated with his MD in 2019. He is preparing to begin a psychiatry residency at New York-Presbyterian Hospital Weill Cornell Medical Center.

Emanuele Fino is PhD in Psychology of Social Representations, MSc in Psychology, PG Cert in Medical Education and Fellow of the Higher Education Academy. Psychologist with expertise in assessment and psychometrics, he is currently leading on the development and implementation of evidence-informed assessment and psychometric service at Aston Medical School. His main interests are research methods and psychometrics in several domains, including medical education.

Arthur L. Frank received his MD degree from the Mount Sinai School of Medicine in 1972 and his PhD in biomedical sciences from the City University of New York in 1977. He taught at Mount Sinai from 1977 to 1983, then headed the Department of Preventive Medicine and Environmental Health at the University at the University of Kentucky from 1983 to 1994. Next, he taught and headed medical education at the University of Texas Health Sciences Center in Tyler from 1994 to 2002. Since 2002 he has been a professor of medicine and professor of public health at Drexel University in Philadelphia. He has consulted on education matters in China, India, Colombia, Mongolia, and elsewhere. He was the Topperman Professor of Medical Education in Texas, the first recipient of the Educator of the Year Award of the Association of Teachers of Preventive Medicine, and a recipient of the Ramazzini Award from the Collegium Ramazzini in Italy.

Aaron George is currently designing a telemedicine-driven family medicine residency curriculum, and has contributed to the journals of Academic Medicine and Medical Education. He regularly writes for Medical Economics and previously investigated implementation of wearable technology for patients while at Duke University Medical Center.

Peter Gold is an Orthopaedic Surgeon Northwell Health, Executive Director Strong City Inc.

Christina Grabowski is the Associate Dean for Admissions and Enrollment Management and Assistant Professor of Medical Education at the University of Alabama at Birmingham (UAB) School of Medicine. Prior to joining UAB, she served as the founding admissions dean at the Oakland University William Beaumont School of Medicine. She has held national and regional positions through the Association of American Medical Colleges (AAMC) including serving as a Holistic Review Workshop Facilitator for five years and serving on the Committee on Admissions. Dr. Grabowski current serves as the Vice Chair for the Southern Group on Student Affairs (SGSA).

Bonnie Granat is the Associate Dean, Director of Assessment, SUNY Downstate, College of Medicine.

Joanne Greenawald is the Director of Problem-Based Learning and a faculty member in the Department of Basic Science Education at Virginia Tech Carilion School of Medicine.

Ronan Hallowell is an Assistant Professor of Clinical Medical Education in the Department of Medical Education at the Keck School of Medicine of the University of Southern California.

Bishoy Hanna-Khalil is a Clinical Teaching Fellow at Aston Medical School in the UK. He has experience working in the National Health System (UK) as a doctor, and international experience in the medical field.

Leila Harrison is the Interim Senior Associate Dean for Student Affairs, Admissions, and Recruitment and Clinical Assistant Professor at the WSU Elson S. Floyd College of Medicine. She has worked for three US medical schools since 2002 (WSU ESFCOM, Texas A&M College of Medicine, and University of North Texas Health Science Center Texas College of Osteopathic Medicine) and has served in the areas of admissions, recruitment, pathways, inclusion, and student affairs. She has held leadership roles regionally and nationally through the Association of American Medical Colleges (AAMC) including serving as a Holistic Review Facilitator for four years and serving on the Committee on Admission.

Sonya Hayes is an Assistant Professor in the Department of Educational Leadership and Policy Studies at the University of Tennessee in Knoxville. She received her PhD in Educational Administration from Texas A&M University in 2016 and held a faculty position at LSU in Baton Rouge for two years. Prior to entering the professoriate, Dr. Hayes served in public education as a teacher and principal for 23 years. Her research interests include leadership development and support for both pre and post service school principals, principal preparation, and leadership for learning. Specifically, she is interested in how principals are prepared and supported for the complex and demanding role of improving teaching and learning. She has publications in both national and international journals as well as several book chapters. Dr. Hayes is the 2017 recipient of the Kottcamp award for dissertation of the year.

Yolanda Haywood was born and raised in Washington, D.C. She completed her early education in the D.C. public school system and earned her Bachelor of Science degree in Biology from Howard University. She earned a second Bachelor of Science degree from The George Washington University School of Medicine and Health Sciences as a graduate of the Physician Assistant Program and had a brief career as a Physician Assistant before matriculating to the Howard University School of Medicine where she graduated with honors in 1986. Dr. Haywood did her residency training in Emergency Medicine at the George Washington University Medical Center in Washington D.C. and joined the faculty of the George Washington University Medical Center Department of Emergency Medicine in 1990. Her tenure in the Department of Emergency Medicine included serving as the clerkship director, the Associate Program Director and Program Director. In 2000, she transitioned to the dean's office as Assistant Dean for Student and Curricular Affairs and subsequently as Associate Dean for Student Affairs. In 2013 she was appointed the inaugural Associate Dean for Diversity and Inclusion. Her work in Diversity and Inclusion is highlighted by her interest in unconscious bias. She completed training as a facilitator in the area of unconscious bias in conjunction with the American Association of Medical Colleges and Cook-Ross, Inc. In 2017 Dr. Haywood was promoted to Senior Associate Dean for Diversity and Inclusion overseeing the schools strategic efforts to train a diverse health care work force and to help eliminate health disparities. Dr. Haywood has three children and seven grandchildren.

Amber J. Heck is an Associate Professor of Physiology at the TCU and UNTHSC School of Medicine and earned her Ph.D. in Biomedical Sciences at UNTHSC. Previously, she has overseen the design and implementation of a prematriculation course and orientation program that promote metacognitive practice. Her current academic interests focus on postmatriculation interventions that promote academic preparation. She is involved in research and mentoring nationally and internationally and was a 2016 International Association of Medical Science Educators (IAMSE) Fellow. She currently serves as Chair of the IAMSE Educational Scholarship Committee and a member of the IAMSE Board of Directors.

Grace E. Henry is a college administrator and adjunct faculty member at The George Washington University in Washington, DC. Her research focuses on institutional diversity and inclusion, and promoting access and success in higher education.

Alexis Huckleberry graduated from the University of Cincinnati College of Allied Health Sciences with a Bachelor of Science in Physiological Health Sciences and a Pre-Med certificate. She is continuing her education at Vanderbilt University to pursue a Master of Science in Nursing.

Michael D. Jax runs the Center for Advanced Training and Simulation(CATS) an MIS training lab, and has for over 3 years and has spent over 10 years in academic technology and support.

Vinita C. Kiluk received her MD from the Medical College of Virginia and completed her Pediatrics internship at the University of Florida. She completed her Pediatrics residency at the Medical College of Georgia. She is an associate professor at the University of South Florida Morsani College of Medicine Pediatrics Department. During the last six years, Vinita been teaching transition courses, she has been the Course Director for the Introduction to Clerkship course as well as the Course Director for the Return to Clerkship Course. Her courses have successfully transitioned hundreds of medical students to the next phase of their medical career.

Tenzing T. Lama is a resident physician in the department of Anesthesiology and Pain Medicine at the University of Washington and a Fellow at the Ethics and Transformative Values Center at the Massachusetts Institute of Technology. He graduated from Harvard Medical School and Oxford.

Sangeeta Lamba is a Professor of Emergency Medicine and the Associate Dean of Education at Rutgers New Jersey Medical School.

Michael Leitman is a graduate of the Boston University School of Medicine having been a Commonwealth Foundation scholar. He received his general surgical training at the New York Presbyterian-Weill Cornell Medical Center and completed a fellowship in surgical critical care at North Shore University Hospital. He is certified by the American Board of Surgery in Surgery and in Surgical Critical Care. He has been a career medical and surgical educator. As a member of the faculty at North Shore University Hospital, he was appointed Director of Surgical Endoscopy, Physician-in-charge of Surgical Education, Program Director and Chief of Surgical Critical Care in 1995. In 1997, Dr. Leitman moved to Lenox Hill Hospital in New York City where he became the Program Director of the Surgical Residency. He joined the Department of Surgery at Mount Sinai Beth Israel in 2005 where he is presently Program Director of the General Surgery Residency. In 2007, he was appointed Associate Chief Medical Officer and in 2010 Chief of Graduate Medical Education. He is Professor of Surgery and Professor of Medical Education at the Icahn School of Medicine at Mount Sinai where he is also Dean for Graduate Medical Education. In 2008, Dr. Leitman was the recipient of the Murry G. Fischer Distinguished Educator Award. He is a Fellow of the American College of Surgeons, Society of Surgical Oncology and the author of more than 130 published articles, abstracts and book chapters. He is on the editorial board of 20 surgical journals and is on the Continuing Education Committee of the American Society of Colon and Rectal Surgery and the Society for Surgery of the Alimentary Tract.

Juliet Lee, MD, MA, FACS is a board-certified general surgeon, a fellow of the American College of Surgeons, and currently an Assistant Professor of Surgery at The George Washington University (GWU) School of Medicine. She is the director of many courses across the entire medical school curriculum. Dr. Lee earned her medical degree from the Icahn School of Medicine at Mount Sinai and completed her residency at GWU. She received a Masters degree in Education and Human Development from GWU. Dr. Lee has won many teaching awards, recognized by the surgical house staff and the medical students. GWU awarded Dr. Lee the Bender Teaching Award in 2015, one of four recipients for that year from over 400 nominees. Dr. Lee's research interests include surgical education and innovations, surgery outcomes, and patient safety and quality improvement. She has been recognized by peers as a Washingtonian magazine "Top Doctor" continuously since 2012.

Mariella Mecozzi is senior assistant director of pre-professional services at the University Career Center at the University of Michigan. She is an active member of the Central and National Association of Advisors for the Health Professions, has served on numerous national boards, committees and task forces, including multiple terms on the American Medical College Application Service (AMCAS) Advisory Committee and the National Association of Advisors for the Health Professions Board of Directors.

Alisa Nagler is the Assistant Director for Accreditation, Validation and Credentialing with the American College of Surgeons, in Chicago, IL and holds an adjunct faculty appointment as Associate Professor of the Practice of Medical Education at Duke University School of Medicine. Within the ACS Division of Education, Dr. Nagler is responsible for oversight and advancement of several major initiatives. The Continuous Professional Development Accreditation Program approves internal and external educational activities for CME Credit, utilizing best practices in process and promoting innovation in education and evaluation. The Program for Educational Validation and Credentialing offers individuals personalized tracking and guidance for lifelong learning needs through MyCME and identifies opportunities for research and project implementation related to the evaluation and validation of knowledge and skills for surgeons across their careers. Lastly, just launched in 2018, Dr. Nagler provides oversight of the ACS Academy of Master Surgeon Educators, intended to advance the science and practice of education across all surgical specialties through innovation and promotion of the highest achievements in lifelong learning. Before the American College of Surgeons, Dr. Nagler was the Assistant Dean for Graduate Medical Education at Duke University School of Medicine. There she helped build a GME faculty development infrastructure, developed institution-wide educational programs for residents and fellows, and was instrumental in moving medical education research and scholarship at Duke forward. Dr. Nagler has served as a leader for numerous national organizations. She is currently the Co-Chair of the Academies Collaborative. She has been an active member of the AAMC GEA for the last 10 years, currently serving as the CGEA-CPD Chair-Elect. She has been engaged in Continuous Professional Development (CPD) for the last 5 years and in addition to work with the GEA, is an active member of the Society for CME (SACME), Illinois Alliance for CME (IACME), and the Council for Medical Specialty Societies - CPD Component Group. Dr. Nagler is passionate about medical and surgical education scholarship and has been involved in numerous research collaborations across institutions. She has more than 30 peer-reviewed publications and has presented on medical education topics across the country.

Radha Nandagopal is a pediatric endocrinologist and Clinical Associate Professor overseeing the clinical skills, communication, professionalism, and ethics education for WSU medical students. At the inception of the WSU medical school, she led the admissions-related accreditation effort, and has held the role of Admissions Committee Chair for the past several years.

Brian J. Nickerson has over 20 years of multi-faceted experience in academic institutions, including 15 years in senior management positions ranging from Director, Department Chair, Academic Dean, to Senior Vice President. Dr. Nickerson has launched over 20 successful programs or institutes in his career, many of which were "first-of-its kind". He currently serves as the Senior Associate Dean for Master's Programs in the Graduate School of Biomedical Sciences, Director for the Health Care Delivery Leadership Program, and Professor in the Department of Population Health Science & Policy. He is responsible for related academic program development and management, digital learning, and academic partnerships. Professor Nickerson has earned his PhD from the Rockefeller College of the State University of New York at Albany, a Juris Doctor and an MPA from Pace University, and his BA from Iona College.

Daniel Novak is an Assistant Professor of Clinical Medical Education in the Department of Medical Education in the Keck School of Medicine of the University of Southern California.

Doug Phelan completed his family medicine residency at the New Hampshire Dartmouth Family Medicine Residency in Concord, NH. He then trained in the Dartmouth-Hitchcock Leadership Preventive Medicine Residency in Lebanon, NH. He earned his MPH from The Dartmouth Institute and has done extensive work in medical education and telemedicine policy.

Renee Prater is Professor of Immunology and Associate Dean for Curriculum, Assessment, and Medical Education at the Edward Via College of Osteopathic Medicine Virginia Campus. Dr. Prater earned her Doctor of Veterinary Medicine, completed a residency in clinical pathology, and then earned a PhD in immunotoxicology from the Virginia-Maryland College of Veterinary Medicine in Blacksburg, VA prior joining VCOM in 2002. In addition to teaching immunology at both VCOM and Bluefield College, Dr. Prater maintains an active role in research and scholarly activity, and coordinates the preclinical curriculum at the VCOM Virginia Campus.

Claudia Ranniger is an Emergency Physician and a Medical Director of the George Washington University School of Medicine and Health Sciences' Clinical Learning and Simulation Skills (CLASS) Center.

Jan Reichard-Brown earned her PhD from the University of Cincinnati in 1982. She teaches and mentors undergraduate students as an Associate Professor of Biology and Health Care Studies at Susquehanna University and serves as the current president, (2018-2020), of the Northeast Association of the Advisors of the Health Professions (NEAAHP). In 2004 she became the Pre-Health Professions Advisor in addition to her faculty duties, which triggered her interests in the barriers that disadvantaged students face when pursuingcareers as health professionals. She has presented many times on these topics at conferences and written articles for the professional journal, The Advisor.

Richard Sanker is the Senior Director for the Offices of Prehealth Studies, Undergraduate Research and the Science and Health Living and Learning Center at Baylor University. He also serves as an adjunct professor in Baylor's Honors Programs. Before joining the academic community at Baylor, he served as the assistant director of Prehealth Programs and as a counselor in the Academic Success Center and Office of Undergraduate Admissions at Saint Louis University. He also served for 6 years as a national officer of Alpha Epsilon Delta, a prehealth honor society. He has been involved in areas of undergraduate research, prehealth programs, academic advising and undergraduate enrollment management during his professional career.

Barbara A. Schindler is Vice Dean Emerita, Educational and Academic Affairs, Professor of Psychiatry and Pediatrics at Drexel University College of Medicine and the Medical Director/Founder of the Caring Together addiction treatment program for women. As Vice Dean from 1996-2014, Dr. Schindler was responsible for the admission and medical education of over 1050 medical students per year on multiple clinical campuses and for Continuing Medical Education for the medical school. She is an elected professional member of the Liaison Committee on Medical Education (LCME) and has served as a regular site visitor for the LCME since 2002.

Dawn M. Schocken is the Director of the Center for Experiential Learning and Simulation (ELS) at USF Health Morsani College of Medicine in Tampa, Florida. ELS hosts all of the students' hands on learning over the course of the four years of medical students. She has developed several life-long courses for students including a novel hands-on quality improvement course taught as an interprofessional educational session. Her Capstone TIPS helps medical students begin their residencies documenting they have met their EPA competencies prior to graduation. She serves on several national committees to broaden the scope of education in simulation and healthcare.

Robin Selzer is an Associate Professor of Experience-Based Learning and Career Education with the Pre-Health Internship Program at the University of Cincinnati. She is a Gallup Certified CliftonStrengths Coach and Qualified Administrator of the Intercultural Development Inventory (IDI). Her research and presentations center on social justice education and women's leadership.

Maria Soto-Greene is a professor of medicine, Director of Hispanic Center of Excellence and the Executive Vice Dean at Rutgers New Jersey Medical School.

Antoinette C. Spoto-Cannons is an Associate Professor of Pediatrics in the Division of General Pediatrics at the University of South Florida Morsani College of Medicine. Her clinical responsibilities include caring for pediatric patients in the acute care setting while supervising residents and medical students. She is the Co-Director of the third-year medical student Primary Care Clerkship and serves as a mentor, educator, adviser and coach to medical students across all 4 years.

Rohan Srivstava graduated from the University of Cincinnati with his Bachelor of Science in Medical Sciences and a certificate in Spanish in Social Work and Healthcare Services. He attends the University of Cincinnati College of Medicine as a medical student.

Regan A. Stiegmann currently serves as Director of the Digital Health Track at Rocky Vista University College of Osteopathic Medicine's Southern Utah Campus, and also serves as an Active Duty Flight Surgeon with the United States Air Force in Colorado Springs, CO. She received her Masters in Public Health at the Uniformed Services University of the Health Sciences and her medical degree from Rocky Vista University College of Osteopathic Medicine. She is a double board-certified physician who completed her residency training in Preventive Medicine at the Uniformed Services University of the Health Sciences with a subspecialization in Lifestyle Medicine. Dr. Stiegmann is passionate about human performance optimization, positive psychology, and health promotion. Over the past decade, Dr. Stiegmann has proudly served in many leadership roles in a variety of nationally and internationally recognized medical platforms, medical colleges, universities, and health care mediums. She currently practices Lifestyle and Performance Medicine in Colorado.

Michael W. Stumpf is an assistant professor of clinical medicine in the department of internal medicine at Louisiana State University Health Sciences Center. He earned a B.S. in Electrical Engineering from LSU in 1999 and worked at the Lockheed Martin Corporation before entering medical school. He earned his M.D. from the LSU School of Medicine in New Orleans in 2008 and completed his Internal Medicine residency at LSU's Earl K. Long Hospital in Baton Rouge. He remained with the internal medicine department as a chief resident then transitioned into his current role of assistant professor. Professional interests include community health and medical education and he is a member of the American College of Physicians and the Alpha Omega Alpha honor society. He currently resides in Baton Rouge and enjoys spending time with his wife and four kids.

Veronica Y. Tatum is an assistant professor of Pathology at the TCU and UNTHSC School of Medicine in Fort Worth, Texas. She received her M.D. from UT Southwestern Medical Center in Dallas and completed her Anatomic and Clinical Pathology Residency at Baylor College of Medicine in Houston. She completed her Cytopathology Fellowship at UC San Francisco and practiced in both private and academic settings prior to transitioning to full-time medical education. Dr. Tatum is a member of the College of American Pathologists and the International Association of Medical Science Educators.

Christin Traba is an assistant professor of Pediatrics at Rutgers New Jersey Medical School in Newark, NJ. As the assistant dean for clerkship education, she oversees Years 3 and 4 of the medical school curriculum.

Richard Vari is the Senior Dean for Academic Affairs at the Virginia Tech Carilion School of Medicine. He was appointed in 2008 as the Founding Associate Dean for Medical Education at the Virginia Tech Carilion School of Medicine in Roanoke, VA. He led the development of the medical curriculum at this new school which includes a PBL-Hybrid basic science approach, integration of clinical science and skills beginning in Year 1, an intensive research requirement, and a longitudinal interprofessionalism domain. Prior to moving to Roanoke, Dr. Vari was Associate Dean for Medical Education and Professor of Physiology at the University of North Dakota School of Medicine & Health Sciences for sixteen years. Dr. Vari has received numerous awards from students for teaching in both lecture and PBL-small group settings, and has been recognized for contributions to both educational program and faculty development. He was awarded the AAMC/AMA/AOA Robert J. Glaser Distinguished Teacher Award in 2017. He has served on several national and international education committees including the American Physiological Society Education Committee, the NBME Step 1 Physiology Committee, and the IAMSE Board of Directors (2 terms) and Chair of the IAMSE Web- Seminar Committee for five years. He now serves as president of IAMSE.

Ellen Watts has been in admissions and pre-health advising for over 25 years, serving at Director of Admissions at Columbia College of Dental Medicine, and Assistant Dean of Students in the Columbia University Postbaccalaureate Premedical Program. She is currently the Assistant Dean for Prehealth

Professions Advising at Fordham University. Ellen has presented both nationally and regionally on issues related to both traditional and non-traditional applicant pathways, and has been recognized by the United State Air Force and the NYS College Science Technology Entrance Program (CSTEP) for her dedication and service to pre-professional student advising. Ellen earned her BA degree from Le Moyne College.

Shari Whicker is Assistant Dean for Faculty Development and Associate Professor in the Departments of Pediatrics and Interprofessionalism for Virginia Tech Carilion School of Medicine as well as Senior Director of the Offices of Continuing Professional Development and TEACH (Teaching Excellence Academy for Collaborative Healthcare) at Carilion Clinic. Dr. Whicker's career in adult learning began in 1994 and her focus shifted to medical education in 1999. Over the past 20 years, she has fostered a passion for medical education teaching, learning, and education research in educator and educational leadership roles in the Wake Forest, Duke University, and Virginia Tech Carilion School of Medicine and Carilion Clinic Health System. Her roles in medical education have spanned the continuum of medical education to include medical students, trainees, and physician faculty as well as staff and learners from affiliated health professions. Within these roles, her primary focus has been and continues to be on the development of faculty/health care professionals and trainees as lifelong learners, teachers, and medical education researchers. Dr. Whicker completed her undergraduate degree at the University of North Carolina (Greensboro), her Master's Degree in Education (MEd) in 2005 and her Doctorate in Adult Learning (EdD) in 2012, both at North Carolina State University.

Lolita Wood-Hill has been a pre-health advisor for over 25 years, currently the Executive Director of Pre-Professional Advising at Yeshiva College. Lolita has received national and local recognition for her work with disadvantaged students, receiving service awards from the Association of American Medical Colleges, The National Association of Medical Minority Educators, and the Associated Medical Schools of NY. She has written many blogs, for Go Dental, Kaplan, and others, and presents workshops for students and advisors hoping to widen the pipeline to medicine for disadvantaged students.Lolita earned her MS degree in Urban Affairs at Hunter College of CUNY in 2010.

Cole Zanetti currently serves as the Director of the Digital Health Track at Rocky Vista University College of Osteopathic Medicine's Colorado Campus, and also serves as a Primary Care Section Chief at the Veteran Affairs Eastern Colorado Healthcare System. Dr. Zanetti was selected as a national library of medicine's biomedical informatics course fellow, the 2019 National Emerging Leader Award by the American Osteopathic Foundation, the Primary Care Innovation Award from the American College of Physicians in 2014, has served as a consultant for Kensci, a healthcare predictive analytics company, was appointed by the Mayor of the City of Denver to serve on the Board of Public Health & Environment for Denver Colorado, currently serves on the board of directors for the American Osteopathic Information Association and served as a Member of the Blue Ribbon Commission for Transformation of Osteopathic Medical Education. Dr. Zanetti has also worked with the Dartmouth Center for Health Care Delivery Science on innovative mobile health initiatives in Haiti and was selected by the Robert Wood Johnson Foundation as a Thought Leader for their symposium on Health and Health Care in 2032. Dr. Zanetti and Dr. Stiegmann developed the Digital Health Track at Rocky Vista University College of Osteopathic Medicine in Colorado and Utah. Dr. Zanetti is a double board-certified physician who completed his Family Medicine and Preventive Medicine residency at Dartmouth. He received his Masters in Public Health at the Dartmouth Institute and his medical degree from the University of North Texas, Texas College of Osteopathic Medicine, he also earned his BA in Psychology from the University at Buffalo and a Certificate in Leadership, Organizing and Action from Harvard University, John F. Kennedy School of Government, Executive Education.

Shoshana Zeisman-Pereyo has nearly 20 years of experience supporting students in post-secondary educational settings with over 5 years in medical education. She completed her Doctorate of Education at Portland State University in 2012. Through her work in medical education, she has helped launch a pipeline program for Alaska Native/American Indians for entrance into medical school, as well as worked tirelessly to ensure that all students have the resources, skills and academic support necessary to meet their educational goals. This has been done through serving on key leadership committees, training faculty on topics related to student success, and always keeping the student at the heart of her work.

Alina Zhu is a medical student at the Morsani College of Medicine in Tampa, Florida. She grew up in the California Bay Area and pursued her undergraduate education in biochemistry and philosophy at the University of California, San Diego, where she also found fascination in medical ethics and co-captained the archery team. In the following years, she served as an Emergency Medical Technician in San Diego County, then went on to work as an EMT teaching assistant, medical scribe, and research assistant. She has a great love for being in nature and exploring new crafts.

Index

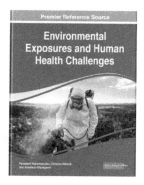

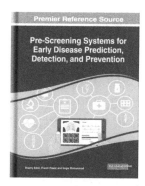

Ensure Quality Research is Introduced to the Academic Community

Become an IGI Global Reviewer for Authored Book Projects

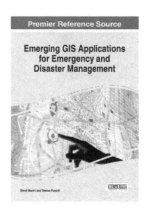
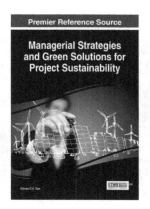

The overall success of an authored book project is dependent on quality and timely reviews.

In this competitive age of scholarly publishing, constructive and timely feedback significantly expedites the turnaround time of manuscripts from submission to acceptance, allowing the publication and discovery of forward-thinking research at a much more expeditious rate. Several IGI Global authored book projects are currently seeking highly-qualified experts in the field to fill vacancies on their respective editorial review boards:

Applications and Inquiries may be sent to:
development@igi-global.com

Applicants must have a doctorate (or an equivalent degree) as well as publishing and reviewing experience. Reviewers are asked to complete the open-ended evaluation questions with as much detail as possible in a timely, collegial, and constructive manner. All reviewers' tenures run for one-year terms on the editorial review boards and are expected to complete at least three reviews per term. Upon successful completion of this term, reviewers can be considered for an additional term.

If you have a colleague that may be interested in this opportunity,
we encourage you to share this information with them.

IGI Global Proudly Partners With eContent Pro International

Receive a 25% Discount on all Editorial Services

Editorial Services

IGI Global expects all final manuscripts submitted for publication to be in their final form. This means they must be reviewed, revised, and professionally copy edited prior to their final submission. Not only does this support with accelerating the publication process, but it also ensures that the highest quality scholarly work can be disseminated.

English Language Copy Editing

Let eContent Pro International's expert copy editors perform edits on your manuscript to resolve spelling, punctuaion, grammar, syntax, flow, formatting issues and more.

Scientific and Scholarly Editing

Allow colleagues in your research area to examine the content of your manuscript and provide you with valuable feedback and suggestions before submission.

Figure, Table, Chart & Equation Conversions

Do you have poor quality figures? Do you need visual elements in your manuscript created or converted? A design expert can help!

Translation

Need your documjent translated into English? eContent Pro International's expert translators are fluent in English and more than 40 different languages.

Email: customerservice@econtentpro.com   **www.igi-global.com/editorial-service-partners**

www.igi-global.com

Publisher of Peer-Reviewed, Timely, and
Innovative Academic Research Since 1988

IGI Global's Transformative Open Access (OA) Model:
How to Turn Your University Library's Database Acquisitions Into a Source of OA Funding

In response to the OA movement and well in advance of Plan S, IGI Global, early last year, unveiled their OA Fee Waiver (Offset Model) Initiative.

Under this initiative, librarians who invest in IGI Global's InfoSci-Books (5,300+ reference books) and/or InfoSci-Journals (185+ scholarly journals) databases will be able to subsidize their patron's OA article processing charges (APC) when their work is submitted and accepted (after the peer review process) into an IGI Global journal.*

How Does it Work?

1. When a library subscribes or perpetually purchases IGI Global's InfoSci-Databases including InfoSci-Books (5,300+ e-books), InfoSci-Journals (185+ e-journals), and/or their discipline/subject-focused subsets, IGI Global will match the library's investment with a fund of equal value to go toward subsidizing the OA article processing charges (APCs) for their patrons.

   Researchers: Be sure to recommend the InfoSci-Books and InfoSci-Journals to take advantage of this initiative.

2. When a student, faculty, or staff member submits a paper and it is accepted (following the peer review) into one of IGI Global's 185+ scholarly journals, the author will have the option to have their paper published under a traditional publishing model or as OA.

3. When the author chooses to have their paper published under OA, IGI Global will notify them of the OA Fee Waiver (Offset Model) Initiative. If the author decides they would like to take advantage of this initiative, IGI Global will deduct the US$ 1,500 APC from the created fund.

4. This fund will be offered on an annual basis and will renew as the subscription is renewed for each year thereafter. IGI Global will manage the fund and award the APC waivers unless the librarian has a preference as to how the funds should be managed.

Hear From the Experts on This Initiative:

"I'm very happy to have been able to make one of my recent research contributions, 'Visualizing the Social Media Conversations of a National Information Technology Professional Association' featured in the *International Journal of Human Capital and Information Technology Professionals*, freely available along with having access to the valuable resources found within IGI Global's InfoSci-Journals database."

– Prof. Stuart Palmer,
Deakin University, Australia

For More Information, Visit: www.igi-global.com/publish/contributor-resources/open-access or contact IGI Global's Database Team at eresources@igi-global.com.

CPSIA information can be obtained
at www.ICGtesting.com
Printed in the USA
BVHW090016310120
571013BV00001B/1